THE LEFT IN IRAN
1941-1957

Revolutionary History Volume 10, No 3
Socialist Platform Ltd
MERLIN PRESS

Revolutionary History

Founding Editor: Al Richardson (1941-2003)

Edition Editor: Cosroe Chaqueri

Editorial Coordinating Team: Ted Crawford, Paul Flewers, Esther Leslie, John Plant

Reviews and Obituaries Editor: John Plant

Website Coordinator: Alun Morgan

Editorial Board: Toby Abse, Ian Birchall, Tony Borton, David Broder, Barry Buitekant, Clarence Chrysostom, Mildred Gordon, Chris Gray, Dave Renton, Mike Jones, Stuart King, Richard Kirkwood, George Leslie, Sheila Leslie, Ben Lewis, Mike Pearn, Jim Ring, Alejandra Rios

Foreign Advisory Board: Andy Durgan, Fritz Keller, Rick Kuhn, Steffan Lindhe, Jean Jacques Marie, Einde O'Callaghan, Tom O'Lincoln, Reiner Torsstorff

ISBN 9780850366563

Copyright © 2011

Web site: www.revolutionaryhistory.co.uk

tcrawford@revhist.datanet.co.uk (editorial)

barry.buitekant@hotmail.com (business)

trusscott.foundation@blueyonder.co.uk (text processing)

Socialist Platform Ltd, BCM 7646, London WC1N 3XX

Merlin Press
6 Crane Street Chambers, Crane Street, Pontypool NP4 6ND
www.merlinpress.co.uk

Printed in the UK by Lightning Source

Contents

Editorial   9

The Left in Iran, 1941-1957

Cosroe Chaqueri, The Left in Iran: A Critical Review: 1941-1957   11

1: First Period: The Tudeh Party of Iran from its Inception to its First Proscription

I: The Foundation of the Tudeh Party and its Early Programme and Activities   13

II: The Tudeh Party's First Conference   15

III: The Tudeh Party's Trade Unions and the Growth of the Organisation   16

IV: The Difficult Task of Organising the Peasantry   24

V: The Tudeh Party's First Congress   25

VI: The Tudeh Party and the Soviet Demand for Iranian Oil   29

VII: Increasing Attacks on the Tudeh Party   34

VIII: The Azerbaijan Crisis   37

IX: Moscow's Plan for 'Sovietising' Iran   39

X: The Soviet Politbureau's Directives on Action in Northern Iran   42

XI: The Creation of the Democratic Party of Azerbaijan and the Autonomous Government of Azerbaijan   45

XII: The Demise of the Soviet-sponsored Autonomous Government of Azerbaijan   51

XIII: Premier Qavam's 'Democratic Party'   54

XIV: The First Split in the Tudeh Party and the Second Congress   60

XV: The Second Party Congress   69

2: Second Period: The Proscription of the Tudeh Party

I: The Royal Plot Against the Tudeh Party   75

II: The Tudeh Military Organisation and the Reorganisation of the Party   78

III: The Revival of the Tudeh Party During the Resurgence of the National-Democratic Movement   81

IV: Opposition to the Patriotic-Democratic Movement under Mosaddeq, First Phase	83
V: The Tudeh Leadership's Knowledge of Theory and History	89
VI: The Tudeh Party's Charges Against the Nationalisation Movement	91
VII: Continued Opposition to Mosaddeq after the July 1952 Popular Uprising, Second Phase	99
VIII: The Tudeh Party's Controversial Incapacity vis-à-vis the 1953 Anglo-American Putsch	107
IX: The Tudeh Party's Reaction on the Morrow of the Putsch (August 1953–August 1954)	118
X: Dismantling the TMO, the TPI's Protective Umbrella	120
XI: The TMO's Failure to Confront the Coup	127
XII: The TPI's Department of Information Dismantled	135
XIII: The 1957 Plenum and its Appraisal of Party Life since its Foundation	141
XIV: A Few Tentative Remarks	157
Cosroe Chaqueri, Moscow and the Tudeh Party: Did the Soviets Play a Role in Founding the Tudeh Party in Iran?	195
Cosroe Chaqueri, The Iranian Left in the Twentieth Century: A Critical Appraisal of its Historiography	231
Introduction	233
I: General Consideration of the Problematic of Sources in the Historiography of the Iranian Left	235
II: Social Democracy	240
III: Historiography of the Communist Party	244
IV: The Allied Occupation of Iran and the Historiography of the Iranian Left	248
V: The Arani Circles of 1926-32 and 1934-35	249
VI: The Founding of the Tudeh Party	253
VII: The Azerbaijan Crisis of 1945-46	257
VIII: Proscription of the Tudeh or the Shah's First Coup in 1949	259
IX: The 1953 Coup and the 1957 Fourth Plenum of the Tudeh	260
X: The Soviet Government and the Iranian National Movement	265
XI: The Leftist Organisations After the Coup d'État	267
XII: Infiltration of Leftist Organisations and Leaks to the Political Police	270

XIII: Conclusion	283
Postscript	
I: The Pahlavi-Stalinist Mental Merger Leading to a New Breed	300
II: The Tudeh Party and the 1953 Putsch	312
Peyman Vahabzadeh, SAKA: Iran's Grassroots Revolutionary Workers' Organisation	348
Peyman Vahabzadeh, Mostafa Sho'a'iyan: An Iranian Leftist Political Thinker Unlike His Peers	360
Documents:	
Letter by the Chief of the Information Section of the Tudeh Party Organ (October 1942)	376
British Ambassador's Directives to British Consular Offices Regarding the Tudeh Party (1943)	376
UK Foreign Office: Sir Reader Bullard's Instructions to British Consulates (1943)	378
US State Department: Résumé of Tudeh Party's Programme (November 1943)	379
UK Foreign Office: Proceedings of the First General Conference of the Tudeh Party (August 1944)	380
Soviet Embassy Report on the Tudeh Party's First Congress (October 1944)	386
CPSU: Measures to Organise a Separatist Movement in Southern Azerbaijan and Other Provinces of Northern Iran (July 1945)	397
Secret Soviet Instructions for a Separatist Movement in Northern Iran (July 1945)	399
US State Department: Report on the Tudeh Party (Extract, August 1945)	402
US State Department: Tudeh Party Programme	404
UK Foreign Office: Tudeh Views Expressed to the British (1945)	407
UK Foreign Office: Tudeh's Private Hint to the British (1945)	411
Declaration of the CC of the Tudeh Party on the Eve of the Coalition with Premier Qavam (June 1946)	412
Pravda: The Tudeh, Premier Qavam and the British (June 1946)	418
US State Department: Foreign Policy of Tudeh Party (August 1947)	419
The Tudeh Socialist Party (January-February 1948)	420
UK Foreign Office: Concern About Tudeh (March-April 1948)	430

A Tudeh Memorandum (August 1948)	434
US State Department: Memorandum of the US Embassy on the Project to Proscribe the Tudeh Party (November 1948)	435
Iranian Government: The Decree Suppressing the Tudeh Party (1949)	436
Tudeh CC Against its Proscription and Oppression (July 1949)	437
Declaration of the Tudeh Party CC in its Own Defence (1949)	439
The Tudeh Party, the Soviet Government and the Pro-Imperialist Government of General Razmara (1950-51)	445
Tudeh: Concerning the Liberal Bourgeois Movement (June 1950)	448
Tudeh: The Martyrdom of [Imam] Ali (July 1950)	449
Tudeh CC Statement Sent to the American, British, and French Embassies (July 1950)	449
US State Department: Escape of Ten Tudeh Party Leaders from Qasr Prison, Tehran (December 1950)	450
Statement by the CC of the Tudeh Party of Persia on the Anniversary of 4 February 1949 (February 1951)	455
Tudeh Party's CC New Year Greeting (March 1951)	457
Tudeh: Dr Mosaddeq's Government (May 1951)	458
An Open Letter by the Tudeh CC to Dr Mosaddeq (May 1951)	459
Tudeh: Dr Mosaddeq and the Oil Problem (May 1951)	461
The Tudeh Against Mosaddeq (July 1951)	463
Declaration of the Tudeh Party CC on the Elections for the Seventeenth Legislature (December 1951)	463
US State Department: The Tudeh Against Mosaddeq (December 1951)	468
The Tudeh Party on 'Mosaddeq's Terrorism' (April 1952)	470
Letter of the National Society Combating Colonialism (August 1952)	471
US State Department: List of Known Tudeh Newspapers in Iran During the Mosaddeq Premiership (October 1952)	472
Daily Worker: People's Party Leaders Show Britain the Struggle in Persia (March 1953)	476
Resolution Passed by Pro-Tudeh Demonstrators on the First Anniversary of 1952 Uprising (July 1953)	479
An Open Letter to Dr Mosaddeq by the CC of the Tudeh Party (July 1953)	481

Declaration of the Tudeh Party CC on the Morrow of the 1953 Putsch
    (August 1953)   484

US State Department: Recent Tudeh Activities
    and the Zahedi Government (October 1953)   488

US State Department: Request for Anti-Communist Material (1954)   491

US State Department: Memorandum Concerning
    a Splinter Communist Party in Iran (April 1954)   492

US State Department: Tudeh Party's
    English-Language Publications Reports of Iran (1954)   496

Isolated Support for Fatemi and Tudeh Officers
    upon Condemnation to Death (1954-55)   504

UK Foreign Office: Tudeh Party Leaders Arrested (April 1956)   510

UK Foreign Office: Tudeh Military Leader Khosrow Rouzbeh
    in the Military Tribunal (1958)   514

Other Material

Work in Progress   517

Letters   518

For

Dr Catherine Voyer Professor Daniel Thomas

In gratitude

C. Chaqueri

Editorial

This issue of *Revolutionary History* is the second instalment of the history of the left in Iran assembled for us by Dr Cosroe Chaqueri, and covers the period from the founding of the Tudeh Party of Iran in 1941 until the party's Fourth Plenum in 1957, at which the party's leadership, in that brief moment of openness in the Stalinist world afforded by Khrushchev's 'Secret Speech' in 1956, discussed the various blunders and failures that had dogged the party over the years and had led to its almost total destruction after the Anglo-American *coup d'état* against Mohammad Mosaddeq's government in 1953 and the installation of the Shah's repressive regime.

As the Tudeh Party was the only substantial left-wing organisation in Iran during the 1940s and 1950s, the main article in this issue of *Revolutionary History* is focused very largely upon this party's activities, investigating its relationship with the labour movement in Iran and the mass movement demanding the nationalisation of the Anglo-Iranian Oil Company, its attitudes towards the various governments of the country, its relationship with the Soviet Union and in particular its dealing with Moscow's attempt to establish a pro-Soviet autonomous government in Iranian Azerbaijan in 1945, its construction of a powerful clandestine organisation within the Iranian armed forces, and its failure to use this asset in opposing the coup against Mosaddeq.

One of the less edifying aspects of left-wing historiography is that the influence of Stalinism extends rather further than those historians who are directly under its spell. The history of the Iranian left is no exception to this trend, and Dr Chaqueri has provided a lengthy critique of several historians of the Iranian left whose explicit or implicit acceptance of many of the Tudeh Party's assumptions have, in his opinion, resulted in their producing a distorted historical account. Should any author criticised in this piece wish to provide a response, we will provide suitable space in a future issue of our journal.

We also present two essays by Professor Peyman Vahabzadeh. The first investigates SAKA, a current that was unusual on the Iranian left in that it attempted to base itself upon workers' committees. The second looks at Mostafa Shoʻaʻiyan, who attempted to develop a Marxist approach that could counter the orthodoxies presented by the dominant pro-Moscow and pro-Beijing currents on the Iranian left.

Dr Chaqueri has produced a number of pioneering studies on Iran and its left-wing movements, in particular the sole major work on the ill-fated soviet republic on the Caspian coast of Iran, *The Soviet Socialist Republic of Iran, 1920-1921: Birth of the Trauma* (Pittsburgh University Press, 1995). He is currently preparing two major studies on the Iran communist movement of the interwar period. He has also compiled over 30 volumes of documents from the labour and left-wing movements of Iran, thus enabling students of Iranian history to read material which might otherwise be forgotten and which, in some cases, its authors would prefer people to forget. Professor Vahabzadeh has recently produced a substantial study, *A Guerrilla Odyssey: Modernization, Secularism, Democracy, and the Fadai Period of National Liberation in Iran, 1971-1979* (Syracuse University Press, 2010), which we hope to review in a future issue.

Because of the depth and breadth of Dr Chaqueri's study and the number of documents he has presented, we have been obliged to halt the narrative in this issue in the late 1950s. We will in a future issue cover the history of the left in Iran from that date until its physical annihilation by the Islamic Republic of Iran in the mid-1980s, with essays by Dr Chaqueri and Professor Vahabzadeh and a selection of documents produced by left groups and from official archives. Reasons of space have also forced us to place some of the documents for the period covered by the current issue on our website. For the same reason, we are unable to feature our normal reviews and obituaries sections, and these have been held over to our next issue. This issue will be investigating the solidarity work in support of the Algerian War of 1954-62, and we hope it will appear in good time for the fiftieth anniversary of Algerian independence.

Editorial Board
Revolutionary History

Cosroe Chaqueri
The Left in Iran
A Critical Review: 1941-1957

Introduction

This introduction is not meant to offer a history of the Tudeh Party of Iran (TPI), nor of the postwar Iranian Left. It is simply a critical review of the path the TPI and its offshoots, and other independent leftist organisations, took after the outbreak of the Second World War. Accounting for the history of this period is an enormous task and needs to be written yet by a team of researchers, particularly because historians have access neither to the TPI's own archives in exile — which, on the eve of the fall of the Berlin Wall, were removed from Leipzig to the USSR[1] — nor to its documents seized by the Iranian authorities during the reigns of repression inside the country — although some of them have been published drop by drop when politically convenient. The case of other postwar leftist organisations is even more difficult, for much of their internal discussion, perhaps for reasons of security, was oral, and what was not oral either has not survived or has not been made available to historians.

Lack of space also impedes us from taking this review to the mid-1980s when the Iranian Left, for all practical purposes, was extinguished.[2] We have, therefore, chosen to bring this critical review of the TPI to the morrow of the *coup d'état* against Dr Mohammad Mosaddeq's government in August 1953 and the Tudeh's 'self-criticism' at its Fourth Plenum in 1957, hoping that the period beginning with the TPI's revival of practical activities in exile after its suppression inside the country will be published in a later issue of this journal.

Also, in view of the lack of space, we have to be brief. The introduction for the remaining period, between 1958 and mid-1980s, dealing with the TPI's activities, concentrated mainly in the field of propaganda — the regular publication of a party organ and what the party called a 'theoretical review' as well as a nightly radio programme, transmitted first from East Berlin and then Sofia — will also be published in a later issue of *Revolutionary History*. The study of the TPI's two offshoots, the Maoist 'Tudeh Party's Revolutionary Organisation' and 'Toufan', as well as some other minor groups, will also have to wait for another issue, as will several contributions by Professor Vahabzadeh on the guerrilla groups that were formed after the failure of the TPI and the Patriotic Front to carry on an effective struggle against the regime in the early 1960s, at a time when both the economic-political crisis in the country and the international climate lent themselves to more advanced methods of fighting the military dictatorship of the shah. We do, however, include in this volume short studies by Professor Vahabzadeh of two rather unparalleled phenomena: a workers' red cells organisation known as SAKA and the life and works of the maverick theorist and militant Mostafa Sho'a'iyan.

A good number of exemplary documents of the TPI and about that party, mainly by the UK and US Embassies, are included in this issue in order to familiarise the interested reader with the actual thinking of the Iranian Left and how its opponents evaluated it.

Soviet internal documents on the TPI are scarcely available, and it is thus difficult for observers to see how the Communist Party of the Soviet Union assessed the effectiveness of the party in advancing its objectives. Some interesting documents of the East German Socialist Unity Party and Soviet journalistic estimates have been found in the STASI archives, to which reference will be made in this and the next issue of this journal, but, except for a couple, they are too trivial to be reproduced in their entirety here.

The reader will notice that in this introduction there is less discussion of the TPI's theory and programme than of its activities and internal strife. The reason is simple: this is a reflection of that party's actual life. The early programmatic issues are represented in the documentary section of this issue.

As for the period of the TPI's life in exile, we will deal in a subsequent issue of this journal with its attempt to draft a programme that would be both Marxist-Leninist and 'democratic', an attempt that ultimately led to its alignment with Khomeini's 'anti-imperialist programme', one that is again represented in the documents for the period of the 1979 revolution and thereafter.

Because we do not cover the entire period from 1941 to 1985 in this issue, no definitive conclusion can be attempted in this part of the introduction. Instead, as regards the period under review in this introduction, we will attempt to provide the reader with a few tentative remarks we think necessary.

1: First Period: The Tudeh Party of Iran from its Inception to its First Proscription

I: The Foundation of the Tudeh Party and its Early Programme and Activities

The legacy of the Arani Group — the 'Group of Fifty-Three' — and the survival of its members (except its leader Dr Taqi Arani, who was killed in prison in 1940) led to the creation of the Tudeh Party of Iran in November 1941, that is, some three months after the forced abdication of Reza Shah under the Allied occupation of Iran, and not in September as the Tudeh myth has it. There is now little doubt that the creation of the TPI as a 'democratic front', with a group of Communist cadres as its nucleus, was a plan proposed by the Comintern, and effected by the Political Department of the Soviet Army occupying northern Iran. Although some Tudeh founders in exile strove to downplay, or even to deny outright, this aspect of the party's birth, there is enough evidence from the Comintern archives to make such a statement a highly credible one.[3]

The TPI, created principally by the exigencies of Soviet foreign policy during an intense moment of the Second World War, when Nazi influence in the Middle East was on the rise, was increasingly instrumentalised by Soviet foreign policy without much opposition developing within it, at least not on theoretical or political grounds, and not until a couple of years after the end of the Second World War.

The first impression of the British authorities watching Iran after its occupation shows that they suspected the existence of a pro-Soviet tendency in the TPI. A report on newly-founded Iranian political parties, listing the TPI first, depicts it as 'Socialist and anti-Fascist... popularly supposed to be Communist, which certainly shows a movement towards the Left'. It adds that the:

> ... controllers of the party deny that they are Communists, but it is hardly possible to doubt that the party, and its organ the newspaper *Siyasat*, is supported and subsidised by the Soviet Embassy... Its members fall roughly into two groups, firstly rather theoretical pseudo-Communists and a few Social Democrats, and secondly a number of place-hunters. The party cultivates a Democratic outlook and supports the Tripartite Treaty generally, though its public utterances are very cautious.

The report concludes by pointing to the TPI's specificity: 'It is almost the only party with any semblance of local organisation in the country, mostly in the north, though the organisation is believed to be very sketchy.'[4]

However, despite this democratic semblance, the instrumentalisation of the Iranian Communist movement by the Comintern was intended to eradicate the influences of Western Marxism, first introduced into Iran by another current in Iranian Social Democracy (namely, the Social-Democratic Group of Tabriz, discussed in the previous issue of this journal), and later by Arani. To consolidate the roots of Russian 'Marxism', first disseminated in Iran through Iranian workers whose political formation was mainly influenced by their experience in their Caucasian emigration, the Stalinist apparatus even liquidated the rare elements, such as Avetis Sultanzade, who, within the Iranian Communist Party, went beyond Russian dogmas and found theoretical inspiration in Western Marxism.

Unlike the ICP (and its forerunner 'Adalat), the TPI turned out to be a mass organisation whose membership, after a very slow start with only several hundred old Communists and some careerist elements, extended, notably after the Soviet victory at Stalingrad, into a wide range of non-labouring social strata. Also in contrast to the ICP, the TPI began as a legal organisation (its legality lasting until 5 February 1949). Under these conditions, it thus managed, by drawing on overt Soviet support and its gradually rising membership, to send several deputies from the northern regions of the country under occupation to the Fourteenth Legislature (1943-45). Again, in contradistinction to the ICP, the Tudeh leadership had hardly any significant membership with a working-class background. The social background of its leadership was mainly aristocratic, clerical and bureaucratic, and their knowledge of Marxism was meagre and superficial.[5]

The programme of the TPI was drafted on the basis of the resolutions and recommendations of the Seventh Comintern Congress. It was checked and amended by the Soviets concerning its demands for land reform and the purging from the police of repressive elements who had been working during the interwar dictatorial period, and it was finally approved by the Kremlin.[6] It thus restricted itself to limited democratic demands. Consequently, the party, despite its own will, because it was pressed by the Soviet party, sought collaboration and coalition not only with 'democratic' forces, including such powerful landlords as Premier Qavam during the Azerbaijan crisis in the summer of 1946, but also with pro-British circles during the war when it formed the 'Liberty Front' against the repression of the press. These policies, and its overt support for Soviet economic concessions in Iran, seriously undermined the TPI's commitment to Iran's national interest and increasingly isolated it from the mainstream democratic movement in the country.

II: The Tudeh Party's First Conference

Initially, the TPI was led by the 15 individuals who constituted themselves as the provisional leading organ of the party, the 'Provisional Committee'. This body set itself several basic aims:[7]

1. To mobilise and organise workers, peasants and progressive elements in the rest of society.
2. To put forth a progressive programme.
3. To promote an anti-fascist and anti-imperialist policy.
4. To improve the lot of the working class by organising the workers in labour unions, and to advance their rights by legislation.[8]

These aims had been heavily qualified at Soviet insistence. Demands concerning agrarian reforms were deleted, and, contrary to the claim by the Tudeh leader Iraj Eskandari, they were not included in the party's programme.[9] Even the demands that did appear in the programme were undermined by wartime exigencies. Anti-British and anti-American positions were shelved for the duration of the war. The party could not defend, for instance, higher wages for workers in the north of Iran, as they worked for factories that supplied the Soviet army; nor could it do so in other regions of the country as this would have 'harmed' the anti-Fascist alliance. The workers and peasants had, therefore, to carry the burden of the war, with no benefits after it ended.

One of the first steps of the party was to publish newspapers. The first of these was *Siyasat*[10] whose license was held by one of the 15 members of the committee, Abbas Eskandari, an opportunist politician close to reactionary circles, who later either left the party or was expelled. The second newspaper was *Mardom*, published under a licence for a typesetter named Safar No'i that was obtained by Mostafa Fateh, the only Iranian director of the Anglo-Iranian Oil Company (AIOC), who a year later founded a rival 'socialist' party named *Hamrahan*, literally 'Fellow-Travellers'. These two newspapers greatly helped to disseminate the party's message to a population released from military dictatorship but caught in the hardships of the war. As the party's fortunes improved, it published a series of newspapers in Tehran and the provinces; it had various organs: *Rahbar*, of the Central Committee; *Razm*, of the Tudeh Youth Organisation; *Razm-e mahaneh*, the political publication of the Tudeh; *Besouye-Ayandeh*, an unofficial organ of the party published legally during Dr Mosaddeq's premiership, after the ban of the party in 1949; *Zafar*, the organ of the Tudeh labour unions, and over 100 other newspapers and reviews in various cities at various times.[11]

By the time it organised its first provincial conference in Tehran, the TPI had grown beyond the meagre membership with which it had started. The first gathering of the TPI, the Tehran Provincial Conference,[12] a milestone in the party's history, was held in June 1942 and, according to Iraj Eskandari, some 120 of its activists, or 'delegates', took part in it. The participants came from various social strata: the educated professionals (physicians, lawyers, etc), government employees, students and factory workers.[13] Once again the membership was far less imposing than what Eskandari claims for propaganda purposes.[14]

During the conference the provisional statutes of the party were adopted, emphasising Leninist 'democratic centralism' as the organisational character of the party. The following major demands were also put forth:

* A struggle for the formation of a democratic government, representing vast strata of the people.
* The full execution of the articles of the 1906-07 Constitution regarding political liberties and human rights; the abolition of the anti-socialist law of 1931 adopted under Reza Shah;[15] the reform of the electoral law and the granting of voting rights to women.
* The distribution of state agricultural lands as well as the properties of Reza Shah among peasants; the expropriation of big landed properties for the benefit of peasants, with compensation by the state to former owners.
* The adoption of labour legislation, official recognition of labour unions, the establishment of an eight-hour work-day, and the right to strike.[16]

The conference also insisted on dealing with the 'problem of the ideological and practical education of cadres', preparing them for contact with the masses, as well as 'the vulgarisation of the fundamental principles of the Tudeh Party', that is, a disguised form of Marxism-Leninism. Given the meagre Marxist knowledge of the Tudeh leaders and the insistence on the 'ideological education' of members along 'Marxist-Leninist', that is, Stalinist, lines, it is not surprising that the TPI sealed its own fate from the outset.

III: The Tudeh Party's Trade Unions and the Growth of the Organisation

One of the essential tasks before the TPI's Provisional Committee was the organisation of the working masses, especially those who had moved to the cities in the 1930s and had had almost no background in a professional organisation. The weak and small trade unions the ICP had created within the framework of the Central Council of Trade Unions had disintegrated under the military dictatorship of the first Pahlavi king. The central mistake that the Central Council had made, as stated by one of its delegates to the Fourth Profintern Congress, was the 'politicisation' of the organisation, that is, its direct linking with the ICP, whereby it went down with the party under the repression. Now, the TPI was making the same mistake, and it later reaped the same results.

The TPI was facing an enormous task. It had to struggle against the political backwardness of first-generation workers in the urban areas, as well as against the reactionary forces that did not wish to see the rebirth of trade unions. Aside from the labour unions created by the TPI's agents in various factories, especially in the Soviet-occupied north during the war, small independent unions were formed by activists who distanced themselves from the Soviet Union. These activists were not reactionary. In accordance with its Stalinist schooling, however, the TPI adopted the motto 'take them or kill them'. In Azerbaijan, a general union was created by a member of Arani's 'Group of Fifty-Three', Khalil Enqelab. The union began organising strikes in factories in order to demand wage raises. As this action interfered with the work of industrialists working with the Soviet army, the union's action came under fire from the TPI and it was systematically defamed until its leader accepted to be integrated into the new Central Council of United Trade Unions (CCUTU) that the TPI had established and which was led by Reza Rousta, a KUTV-trained[17] cadre and Comintern agent who was known in party circles as an 'illiterate' man. Once the Azerbaijani union was integrated into the Central Council, the leader — who had been 'cleared of all charges' — was defamed again and thrown out.[18]

Another, and more important, case is the creation of the oil workers' union by the Communist leader of the 1929 strike in Abadan, Yusef Eftekhari,[19] who had, by the way, also been trained at the KUTV and worked in the Soviet Union before going to Abadan as a worker. The 1929 strike had paralysed the huge British refinery, at the time the biggest in the world. The British government had mobilised the police of the shah and warships to intimidate the workers. Eftekhari was arrested and spent nearly 12 years in prison where he, because of his critical views of the USSR, was accused by Stalinist prisoners of being a 'Trotskyist'. He had, through personal experience, discovered that the Stalinist state was not socialist. Once freed from jail, he and his few comrades founded a new oil workers' union, which soon came under constant attack from the Tudeh union, and they were defamed as agents of the AIOC.[20]

Given the strong support and financial resources that the TPI received from the Soviet Union for its professional cadres, it also won the battle against Eftekhari's union. Surely, the TPI organised the majority of industrial workers in Abadan, Isfahan, Shahi, Tehran, Behshahr and Tabriz, and even non-industrial workers. It organised government employees from top to bottom of the hierarchy. The most important unions were, however, the oil workers in Khuzistan and Kermanshah. Finally in 1943 the CCUTU was formally established and was recognised by the World Federation of Trade Unions, where the pro-Soviet trade unions enjoyed hegemony.[21] Efforts by British and American 'Labour Attachés' to help pro-government or anti-communist trade unions did not succeed for two simple reasons. Their leaders were not truly labour leaders and they were lured to the positions they came to hold by the attraction of leadership privileges and the salaries they received; such unions were seen as being pro-Western, pro-government organisations, and they were denounced by the TPI as such.[22]

Eskandari claims that, while 'autonomous' labour unions — that is, the Tudeh unions — were being 'spontaneously' formed in various industrial centres, 'on the initiative of the TPI's Provisional Committee' labour leaders freed from prison and workers' representatives laid the first bases of a new labour union centre called the CCUTU.[23] How could these unions have been autonomous and independent of political parties, if the 'initiative' came from the TPI?

Various figures have been advanced as regards the membership of the TPI and its organised workers.[24] But they are exaggerated and do not stand the scrutiny of verification. In his *Histoire du Parti Toudeh* in the French Communist Party's review *Moyen-Orient*, Eskandari also paints a rosy picture of the 'brilliant' results of his party's activities among workers as early as 1942-43 and attributes the success of some sporadic strikes by workers in Isfahan, Tehran, Shahi and Tabriz to his party. He claims that 'within the first days of its foundation, the Tudeh Party had brilliant successes among workers and intellectuals [sic: educated strata]. Within a few months in Tehran, the membership was above the 10 000 mark.'[25] In fact, according to a secret report sent to the Comintern, during the first year of its existence the TPI had no more than 2000 members in the whole country. This kind of claims fits in well with Stalinist propaganda, but not historiography![26]

In his *Histoire*, Eskandari also paints a glorious picture of the membership of both the TPI and the CCUTU. Yet the facts we know do not confirm his claims. He writes that during May Day 1946 in 'Tehran as in all the big cities peasants, artisans, government employees, students and intellectuals', and, naturally, also workers, who demonstrated amounted to 700 000 people; the implication is that all these people were supporters and members of the TPI.[27] Other fantastic claims were made by the TPI.

* On 17 October 1943, barely two years after its foundation, it held a demonstration in Tehran with '40 000 party members',[28] the great majority of whom must have been workers.
* On May Day 1945, the TPI and the CCUTU held their joint demonstration with — so they claimed — 80 000 participants in Tehran and 25 000 in the provinces[29]
* On 12 May 1945, the TPI and the CCUTU together organised a procession celebrating the defeat of Nazi Germany, with 40 000 participants.[30]

* On May Day 1946 (during the premiership of Qavam, a reactionary grand landlord notorious for his corrupt practices in and out of office, and who tried to placate the Soviets) some 10 000 oil workers in Aghajari went on strike for a rise in wages, a minimum of health care, drinking water and ice, and it lasted 14 days, succeeding in its aim.[31]
* On 14 July 1946, a week before the formation of the Tudeh–Qavam coalition cabinet, 80 000 workers in the oil region went on strike, demanding the removal of the governor of Khuzistan, the dissolution of the political office of the AIOC, and the satisfaction of the economic demands of the workers, in retaliation to which AIOC incited the Arab tribes against the workers and in their attacks 47 workers lost their lives and 170 were injured; the strike went on until the government intervened and the workers' economic demands were satisfied;[32] it was settled by the joint intervention of Qavam's deputy Firouz and Tudeh leader Reza Radmanesh.
* On 20 March 1951, the day when the call for the nationalisation of oil was adopted by the Senate, 8000 oil workers in Bandar Ma'shour went on strike to prevent the reduction of their wages by the AIOC — certainly a provocation by the AIOC against nationalisation.
* On 28 May 1951, the Tudeh workers' trade union organised a demonstration against the AIOC with 100 000 participants.[33]

Aside from the fact that the workers' participation was occasionally massive, but not to the exaggerated extent the TPI has claimed, for their own economic demands, one cannot accept the above contradictory numbers as true figures of Tudeh members and/or participants in Tudeh-organised demonstrations or processions. How could one have a 50 per cent reduction in the number of demonstrators between May Day and 12 May of the same year? Besides, if the TPI had had so many adherents, it could easily have won more votes in Tehran's relatively free election than its leader had managed in 1944, that is, a mere 5000. As for the demonstration on 28 May 1951 in Khuzistan, it is sheer propaganda, for the AIOC had no more than between 40 000 and 45 000 workers in the whole country. These falsifications show how the TPI tries to make up for its disastrous political record by demonstrative 'facts'.

As for the claim of 700 000 demonstrators, it is utterly false, given that at that time the majority of Iranians were living in the countryside and very small townships. Tehran and the big cities with some industry put together had barely a population that large, including women and children. Such propagandistic exaggerations, in addition to being dishonest, had the effect of frightening the reactionary forces that seized upon every possible occasion to seek help from the Anglo-American coalition for the suppression of democratic liberties.

The same kind of exaggeration, typical of Stalinist statistics, about the growth of the TPI after its second Tehran Provincial Conference in August 1945 is made by Abdul-Samad Kambakhsh. Quoting the party organ *Rahbar* after that conference, he states that at that time, that is, only a year after the first congress, '200 000 prominent workers, intellectuals [that is, a term in Iran referring to the educated strata], artisans and peasants' had joined the party. In Tehran and Tabriz, respectively, '40 000 and 50 000' people participated in demonstrations![34] Obviously, the exaggeration had much to do with painting a picture of the strength of the party, at a time when the Democratic Party of Azerbaijan (see Section I:XI) was being created, so as to frighten the reactionary government in Tehran. A detailed report by the American Military Attaché states that the TPI had at most a total of 69 000 members, of whom 45 000 were to be found in the Russian-controlled zone of northern Iran — Azerbaijan: 30 000; the Caspian provinces; 9000; and Khorasan: 6000.[35] One of the reasons that the party inflated its membership is that it counted the total number of Iranian workers in every industry — not all of whom were, by the way, syndicated in Tudeh trade unions — including the traditional labourers who had little consciousness of their interests.

The figures that the Secretary of the TPI's Executive Committee gives in his 1956 report to the Central Committee in Moscow clears up the picture. He explains that in the period of Mosaddeq's premiership (1951-53) the figures were at their apex. He also adds that the majority of syndicated workers were party members.[36]

These figures, showing that only 1.8 per cent of workers were syndicated in Tudeh unions, demonstrate that the claims by the TPI were much ado about little.

During these manifestations, while the workers' slogans were demands for a labour law, recognition of their democratic rights, increase of wages in order to synchronise them with the rate of inflation, and serious measures for combating unemployment and lay-offs, the small minority of peasants under Tudeh influence chanted slogans such as 'land to the peasants' and 'the harvest belongs to those who cultivate the land'; and others chanted 'Iran for the Iranians', 'power to the people', and 'cancel the British oil concession [of 1933], the source of the misery of the people', and 'long live the Tudeh Party, the leader of the Iranian people', and demanding 'independence and democracy'. Eskandari states that this huge demonstration of '700 000' people had a 'considerable political impact', for it had not only united the working masses behind its programme, but also mobilised a great part of the anti-imperialist forces belonging to other social classes.[37]

Total Number of Workers and Syndicated Workers in Various Localities, 1951-53[38]			
	Locality	Union Members	Approx no of workers in each locality	Comment
1	Tehran	7 000	120 000 to 150 000	
2	Khuzistan	1 500	80 000	Oil workers only, not including railway workers, etc
3	Gilan	350	30 000	Seasonal workers not included
4	Isfahan	1 000	60 000	
5	Kashan/Yazd/Kerman	300	60 000	
6	Azerbaijan	500	110 000	Number must be greater
7	Mazandaran	400	20 000	Number of workers on files; reports were false
8	Khorasan	100	40 000	Number must be greater
9	Fars	100	15 000	Number must be greater
10	Semnan	200	5 000	Number must be greater
11	Hamadan	50	5 000	Number must be greater
12	Kermanshah	250	10 000	
13	Qom	50	5 000	Number must be greater
14	Qazvin	150	5 000	Number must be greater
	Total	10 920	Ca 600 000	

It is amazing that, writing four years after the event, Eskandari did not see the tactical move by Premier Qavam (see Section I:XIII), for shortly after the departure of Soviet forces, reactionary forces driven by Qavam and the Royal Court not only did not live up to the promises made in respect of the workers' and peasants' demands, but also attacked the TPI's local organisations and launched repressive measures against all progressive forces. Apparently, for Eskandari and his party the TPI's propaganda was more important than a serious analysis of recent history.

Eskandari writes that, despite all the difficulties created by the reactionary forces and in spite of the unjust electoral system, the TPI obtained 200 000 votes for its candidates standing for the Fourteenth Legislature (1323-

1325/1944-46), and those elected had obtained a total of 120 000 votes cast in their constituencies.[39] If the figures given by the party organ at the time are any indication, Eskandari has inflated the total by one-fourth.[40] It is true that the system was unjust, but not only for the TPI, but for all the democratic forces. There were also various kinds of manipulation of votes by the government, the Court, the army and the powerful landlords. But Eskandari fails to mention the factors that helped the Tudeh candidates to be elected. Firstly, the Soviet military occupation of the northern part of the country enabled Soviet consuls to point out to local potentates that they wished to see Tudeh leaders elected.[41] A good example is the letter that former Premier Qavam wrote to his assistant Ali Amini (the future signatory of the infamous post-1953 *coup d'état* oil consortium agreement and future Prime Minister) stating that he was ready to help Tudeh leader Radmanesh be elected in Lahijan, his own fief on the Caspian littoral, provided it remained a secret.[42] And the Tudeh leader was duly elected to the Fourteenth Legislature. It is true that Eskandari cites the case of Dr Freydoun Keshavarz, whom he states was elected in Anzali by means of a 'deal' with the Amini landlord family and the Soviets, whereas he won his seat unaided, although his mentioning of this one example is most probably due to his sense of revenge upon a former comrade who had critically turned against the party.[43] Secondly, during the same elections, Reader Bullard, the British Ambassador in Tehran, advised his consuls in Iran:

> It is true that we are opposed to the Tudeh because it is pro-Russian or, more precisely, because it is much under Russian influence as to constitute at least a potential danger to Persia's independence... But it is not true that we are opposed to the Tudeh on the grounds of its published programme of far-reaching social reforms; and it is often assumed that we, as representatives of the classical example of a capitalist power, must be opposed to the Tudeh on these grounds also.
>
> It is essential to correct this impression. You should point out [to Iranians] that 'capitalist' Britain possesses in fact so advanced a social legislation that there is in fact no reason why the British should sympathise with an extremely backward and socially inadequate regime... In short, even if our mutual sympathies were with the extreme conservatism, we should be opposed to it in Persia as unstable and hence a menace to our Imperial interests.
>
> The published programme of the Tudeh contains nothing revolutionary. Other political parties have published almost equally advanced programmes; but, although these anti-Tudeh parties have a large majority in the Majles, they have done nothing whatsoever to better the state of

the country... In these circumstances it is inevitable that the oppressed classes of the population — that is, the great majority — should listen to the Tudeh and believe them more sincere than their opponents in the matter of social reform, as indeed they probably are.[44]

... the British disapprove of the resort to violent and illegal methods against the Tudeh... Members of the Tudeh Party and other groups of the left, provided they are not irresponsible, may in many cases be serving the best interest of their country and be far preferable to the present reactionary and obstructive elements in the Majles, and it is not in our interest that such candidates should be prevented from standing at the elections simply because they hold left views.[45]

This instruction must have had, at least in the north, the effect of preventing the usual reactionary candidates from standing or manipulating electoral results. Yet no TPI candidate was elected in the capital — where Eskandari claims the party had 10 000 members — and where elections were least manipulated during periods of relative freedom, a fact that means that the TPI did not enjoy the support it claimed it had. In fact, it is not clear why in the capital the TPI is claimed to have 10 000 members, while one of its Central Committee members who was a member of the Arani Group, according to the party organ *Rahbar*, received only '5000 votes', half the number of the membership![46] What is more, the book published by one of the leading officers of the Office of the Military Government, later the SAVAK, claims that the total number of TPI members in the summer of 1952 — under Mosaddeq when it enjoyed its freest period of its activity — was no more than 7000, including 4500 members of the Youth Organisation, which embraced students and high-school teenagers. It had also managed to mobilise some 8000 workers of a total of approximately 80 000, mostly non-industrial, toilers in the Tehran area.[47]

At any rate, the TPI managed to have eight deputies elected in the first legislature after the abdication of Reza Shah. One among the eight, Taqi Fadakar, was elected from a region not under Russian occupation, Isfahan. He was a lawyer and labour leader, and he later broke with the TPI. The election of Tudeh leaders to the parliament boosted its prestige and enlarged its audience in a population that had emerged exhausted, starved and disillusioned by the false promises the Allied leaders had made to Iran when the occupation began, as the former watched a handful of hoarders and speculators enriching themselves by collaborating with the occupiers.

However, another candidate, the veteran Communist Mir Ja'far Pishevari, close to the Soviets, and one of the surviving ICP leaders, who had spent some 12 years in jail under Reza Shah, could not enter the parliament, though elected legally as others were in the same elections from Azerbaijan or its provincial capital city of Tabriz. Elected from Tabriz, he saw his credentials rejected by the Majles on the false grounds that he had been elected by manipulating the votes cast. The fact that this rejection was politically motivated was quite clear even then, for the credentials of other candidates elected along with him were approved. The votes for and against him were equal, 50 against 50.[48] The speaker of the Majles, who usually did not vote, cast a vote against him; Dr Mosaddeq opposed this procedure, not simply because it was unjust, but because he knew the refusal of his credential would have serious political repercussions.

It is not clear, however, who, apart from the die-hard reactionaries, had not voted for him. It has been suggested orally by some that Kambakhsh, a Tudeh leader known for his particular connections with the Stalinist apparatus, voted against him so as to impede his entering the parliament where he would be engaged in legal struggle. One cannot know;[49] but if Kambakhsh did vote against him, his negative or abstention vote prepared the grounds for Pishevari — who had, since the abdication of Reza Shah, accepted to play the parliamentary game — to join the Soviet project for the unification of Iranian Azerbaijan with Soviet Azerbaijan — a project that triggered off the Cold War right after the end of the World War in 1945. (The story of this crisis and its repercussions on Iran's political scene for decades to come requires a separate article, although we shall discuss it briefly below, Sections I:VIII, I:XI and I:XII.)

Given the prevailing conditions, the TPI's fortunes soared after the legislative elections, particularly when the party was seen to be in tune with the veteran Constitutionalist democrat Dr Mosaddeq, who had been the only parliamentarian with the courage in the mid-1920s to oppose in the parliament the rising military dictatorship of Reza Shah, and who had spent the subsequent years of his life in semi-banishment or banishment outright. However, when the Soviets, with thinly disguised threats, demanded an oil concession in northern Iran, the majority of Iranians, who had already suffered some 40 years under the yoke of the AIOC, could not bow to the Soviet demand. The TPI's attempt to defend the Soviet demand spoiled its recently-won successes, a problem we turn to further below (Section I:VI).

IV: The Difficult Task of Organising the Peasantry

While the initial programme of the TPI was not to have, on Soviet 'recommendation', any reference to land distribution, the Tudeh leadership decided that, if it was to mobilise the majority of the population of Iran — the peasantry — it had to deal with this complex problem which both the ICP and the Jangali movement had unsuccessfully tackled.

As Eskandari admits, faced with enormous practical difficulties, the TPI was unable to find a solution to the problem of organising the rural masses. The reactionary forces of Iran, mainly composed of big landowners, would not tolerate any intrusion into their domains under the slogan of 'land to the peasants'. Defeats suffered by the peasants in the past had made them sceptical of any chances of success, while the landowners were supported by the government and its gendarmerie. It took the TPI two years to create an organisation for the peasantry, which followed the advent of the first unions in Mazandaran. It was only after the party congress in 1944 that the TPI managed to put the organisation of the peasantry on a serious basis. The party, in spite of a certain number of enclaves, could never turn the peasants' isolated moves into a movement across the country. It was only during the Azerbaijan crisis that peasant organisations were formed by the Autonomous Government of Azerbaijan — organisations that melted away on the morrow of the demise of that Soviet-made 'government'. One of the reasons for this fiasco was that the distribution of lands was limited to those belonging to the state and to private-property owners who had fled the province, not of those landlords who had made their peace with the new 'regime' and sat in its 'national assembly'.

It is interesting to recall, however, that as soon as the old shah had abdicated on the morrow of Iran's occupation by the Allies and the state officials had fled from the north-western provinces to the capital, peasants of the region had spontaneously formed their own *anjomans* — councils — initiatives which the British attributed to the Soviets, and the latter to German machinations.[50] They were destroyed with the creation of official organisations under the AGA.

By the time the TPI's First Congress took place in the summer of 1944, the victories of the Soviet armies at Stalingrad had left a great impact on Iran and many members of the educated élite (wrongly referred to 'intellectuals') had shaken off their Nazi sympathies and opted for the Tudeh. Such individuals, who eventually rose to leadership positions in the party, have been known as the 'Stalingrad Generation'. One such element was Noureddin Kianouri, who was 'elected',[51] under direct Soviet pressure, as a member of the Central Committee of the party, and later was to become First-Secretary in January 1979, on the eve of the fall of the shah.

V: The Tudeh Party's First Congress

By the time the TPI was preparing its First Congress in August 1944, its growing strength had naturally been frightening the reactionary forces, and it had come under greater pressure from those forces that the British Ambassador Bullard referred to as opposed to even small reforms benefiting the oppressed masses. Nevertheless, at this time, the TPI was confident and hopeful of a brighter future.

The congress was inaugurated by the oldest delegate, an old democrat, Razban, comrade-in-arms of the late chairman of the organisation committee (of the provisional Central Committee) of the party, Solayman Mirza Eskandari. One hundred and sixty-eight delegates took part in the congress, most of whom were reported to be workers, but the 'intellectuals' were 'numerous' and these elements, who mainly came from well-to-do families, dominated the congress. Only a few prominent delegates came from modest origins. This was the very opposite of the leadership of the ICP.

The congress had to deal with a number of problems and leave behind the 'provisional' state in which the party had lived for two and half years. It finally adopted its statutes and the programme of the self-appointed leadership with a number of revisions, and elected its Central Committee, thus giving its leadership organ the necessary legitimacy.[52] The congress also adopted various resolutions on issues relating to the party, the internal affairs of the country, and foreign relations.[53]

According to a secret report by the Soviet Embassy in Tehran, on the eve of the TPI congress and during in the sessions:

> ... serious differences emerged among the delegates. A considerable group of delegates, comparatively young members of the party, including a member of the provisional Central Committee, Artashes [Ovanesian], took up a sharply negative attitude towards the provisional Central Committee.

They labelled the provisional Central Committee 'opportunist', called its work 'politically incorrect and practically insignificant, and demanded a complete renewal of the CC's composition'.

The attacks on the Central Committee for its work in the Majles elections were 'especially sharp' in view of its having formed a bloc with former Prime Minister Qavam al-Saltaneh and others. This group, led by the KUTV-trained Artashes Ovanesian, demanded a change in the party's composition, 'purging' it of merchants, landlords and capitalists, regardless of their views, in order to 'make it a party of the working people'. Ovanesian and his colleagues, who at the time of the founding of the party were pressured by the Soviets to present a non-Communist face, now at the end of the war with Germany decided to radicalise the party by means of their proposed measures.[54]

According to Eskandari, Khalil Maleki, a member of Arani's 'Group of Fifty-Three', criticised the Tudeh leadership for its 'opportunistic' policy of participating in the national elections of the Fourteenth Legislature, which had 'an anti-democratic character' and could not but 'deceive' the people and 'weaken the revolutionary élan of the masses'. Maleki went so far as demanding that membership be limited only to individuals who, 'by their family origins, could give sufficient guarantee' to the revolutionary character of the party. This demand, according to Eskandari, meant that 'the sons of landowners and all those who had reactionary parents' would be eliminated from the party. Maleki accused the former Central Committee of 'a certain emulation' ('*suivisme*') (of the Soviet Union?). While admitting that the congress found Maleki's criticism of organisational shortcomings to be correct, Eskandari argues that the re-election of the majority of the leaders to the Central Committee and Political Bureau (Politbureau) showed that his criticism of the leadership was not 'well-founded' and proved to be a 'defeat' for Maleki, although he was, nevertheless, elected to the Control Commission.[55]

The congress was reportedly all prearranged, and those in charge of the proceedings were obliged to take into account the long-running factionalism in the party when carrying out their task of preselecting the future members of the Central Committee. At the Fourth Plenum held in 1957 the veteran Communist and NKVD liaison man Kambakhsh revealed that, *before the congress*, Rousta, also a Comintern liaison man, had told him:

> '... the arrangement is that you be the head of the Control Commission.' It was strange to me that they had already divided up positions and places, for a group had sat down and worked out the destiny [of the leaders] and knew in advance the results of the congress.[56]

The secret Soviet report on the congress referred to above adds that the 'differences became so acute that there was fear lest the mutual discrediting and calumniating of many leading members of both groups might result in *chance elements* getting into the party's leadership'. Here, the Soviet advisers of the party had to prevent such an eventuality, as the party had to be in 'safe hands'. The report states this point quite clearly: 'The [Soviet] comrades engaged in work with the Tudeh Party set about intervening in this affair', and, as a result, the congress was 'advised' that the 'differences' were to be 'eliminated'. Consequently, further work of the congress 'proceeded in a relatively normal fashion'. In the end, a mixed composition of 10 leaders agreeable to both sides was elected.[57]

It is interesting that, despite the fact that the TPI sought to hide its Soviet connections, it soon became clear that it was obedient to Soviet directives, as its very formation had been arranged between the Soviet Colonel Siliukov and Solayman Mirza.[58] No less interesting is that a left-wing British MP, Michael Foot, later the Labour Party leader, in one of his articles published after his visit to Iran in 1945, whilst appreciative, nevertheless underlined the dependence of the TPI on the Soviet party:

> Tudeh is the only organised party in Persia. It was founded early in 1941 in the last days [sic] of the old shah and there is little doubt that it was started as a genuine party of reform. Today it claims a million members and sympathisers; the figure is almost certainly a gross exaggeration, but Tudeh is a formidable force in Persian politics.[59]

Foot speaks well of Central Committee member Dr Keshavarz,[60] but another Tudeh leader:

> Mr Kambakhsh... was connected with the Royal family [the Qajars] which ruled from the end of the eighteenth century until Reza Shah's usurpation. His father was a wealthy landowner and he himself was trained as a pilot in Russia.

The TPI 'denies that it is Communist, but its newspaper echoes slavishly every line in the Russian press'. Foot's comment about the TPI's programme is revealing. He states that the programme of former premier Seyyed Zia, the political leader who, along with the Cossack strongman Reza Khan, carried out the pro-British *coup d'état* in 1921, was 'not very different from the Tudeh's, except that he sought also a revival in the traditions of Islam'.[61]

It should be recalled, however, that during the congress, while Soviet advisers were behind the scenes, the Tudeh leaders all denied its being a left-wing party. A few quotes from their speeches at the congress make this point very clear. Eskandari stated:

> [Firstly]... the Tudeh Party is nationalist in the sense that it has no international leanings and, secondly, its goal is to form a real nationalist state, that is, a state that is supported by the oppressed classes which form the majority of Iranian nation; thirdly, it struggles against the exploitation which is the result of imperialist capitalism.[62]

Even the more radical members of the leadership, who had wanted to establish a Communist Party in 1941, rejected the statements that made the TPI an opponent of capitalism: 'Is our party against capitalism? No; our programme is in accordance with the principles of [our] constitutional government. Therefore, what is said about us is nonsense.'[63] The congress resolution regarding the class nature of party stated: 'The Tudeh Party is the party of the working classes, that is, workers, peasants, artisans, and freedom-loving intellectuals.'[64] In other words, up until its proscription in February 1949, it played the role of a united front of various 'social classes'.

The Tudeh congress finally elected three of its founders, who had been in the 'Group of Fifty-Three', to its Secretariat — Iraj Eskandari, Noureddin Alamouti and Dr Mohammad Bahrami — who, along with the Central Committee, were, according to the new statutes, put in charge of the party leadership. The three, as will be seen, were removed at the end of 1946, after the demise of the Azerbaijan Autonomous Government and replaced by a Provisional Executive Committee (PEC), which excluded the leaders held responsible for the open support given to the Democratic Party of Azerbaijan/AGA and the ensuing crisis.[65] This decision, according to Eskandari, did not have 'very good results' and was modified, at the Second Congress in 1948,[66] by the election of only one Secretary-General, who turned out to be Radmanesh, a man who showed complete obedience to Soviet directives, and who held the post until he was removed in 1970, at a Soviet hint, by the Central Committee.

VI: The Tudeh Party and the Soviet Demand for Iranian Oil

Only a short while before the Soviets demanded an oil concession in the northern provinces of the country, the American companies' demand for an oil concession had been rejected by the Majles. During the short period between the two demands, Radmanesh, the Tudeh deputy in the parliament, took a firm patriotic position opposing *all* concession to foreigners. On 19 Mordad 1323/10 August 1944, he declared:

> My [Tudeh] comrades are, on the whole, opposed to granting concessions to foreign governments. I am convinced that, just as the Iranian nation could construct its own railway system, we can, with the help of the people and domestic capital, exploit all the riches of this country and perhaps put an end to the misery of the people of this country.[67]

Yet, soon thereafter, the TPI supported the Soviet demand and, under the protection of Soviet tanks in the streets, held demonstrations in favour of it. When the patriotic democrat Mosaddeq rose to speak against the granting of oil concessions to any foreign company or any foreign state while the country was occupied by the Allied armies — for he knew that thereafter the Americans and the British would, *quid pro quo*, ask for their share of concessions — the TPI, the party that had thus far praised him for his opposition to dictatorship and for his patriotism, slandered and portrayed him as a stooge of imperialism. In parliament as in party newspapers, Mosaddeq came under severe attacks from the TPI for his opposition to the concessions demanded by the USSR.

Mosaddeq argued that the granting of any concession to the Soviet Union during the war would encourage Western powers also to demand concessions in Iran, a situation that would further crush Iran under foreign exploitation. He reminded his opponents that he was not against the Soviet Union; as a neutralist, he declared that, in fact, he thought that the existence of the Soviet neighbour was much appreciated by Iranians as a counterforce against incursions by Western powers. He also stated that he had nothing against sharing Iran's wealth with other nations, provided this would be a reciprocal matter. The TPI would not tolerate such arguments, and indeed could not, as its founder Solayman Mirza Eskandari had been told by Colonel Siliukov, in October 1941, that the Soviet authorities wanted the party to serve their interests.

Three leaders of *Rahbar*, the party organ, denounced Mosaddeq as 'part and parcel' of the imperialist plot to exploit Iran. Strangely enough, these articles were penned by a German-educated member of Arani's 'Group of Fifty-Three', Khalil Maleki, the severe critic at the First Congress, who soon thereafter broke with the TPI and later, when ferociously anti-Tudeh, joined Mosaddeq during the campaign for the nationalisation of the oil industry in 1949-53.[68] Maleki had not written these articles purely on his own initiative. Another leader in *Rahbar*, discussing the failure of the Soviet mission for an oil concession, stated that the object of the Soviet government 'was not to obtain an imperialist concession, but, on the contrary, to prevent imperialist influence in Persia and it considered an oil concession as a means of achieving this'. As for the role Mosaddeq played in preventing foreign concessions under duress during the war, the Tudeh organ repeated the same accusation clearly:

> The reactionary government of Persia opposed with all its force the granting of an oil concession to the Soviet Union and welcomed with joy the bill of Dr Mosaddeq, which, like the orders of Reza Khan [for the British oil concession to the Majles in 1933], was ratified without discussion, lest any deviation from his one-sided policy as a result of the granting of this concession should occur.

The party organ added: 'Dr Mosaddeq and his followers had not resolved the problem [of oil]; they had merely removed its solution from the competence of the Persian government and handed it over to foreign [imperialist] circles.'[69]

Yet, according to Eskandari, the task of the TPI's parliamentary group had been 'to support the progressive minority' of the Majles, led by Mosaddeq — against the attempts of the reactionary pro-British majority led by Seyyed Zia al-Din Tabataba'i, the leader of the 1921 putsch — striving to bring to power this minority,[70] an ambition that, in retrospect, does not seem very realistic, if only because of the Tudeh leadership's opposition to attempts by Mosaddeq to bar the granting of concessions to foreigners during the wartime occupation.

Mosaddeq, who had a long record of opposition to local despotism and its twin sister, the imperialist domination of the country, had called for the abrogation of the special powers that the pro-Western governments in Tehran had granted to the pro-British, American financial adviser Dr Millspaugh, who had also been engaged in the mid-1920s, in order to put Iranian finances in order. In both periods, the measures taken by Dr Millspaugh had provoked inflation and caused the impoverishment of the Iranian masses. The TPI naturally had supported this move by Mosaddeq, whom Eskandari had named 'the leader of the progressive forces'.[71]

Yet, when it came to Mosaddeq's opposition to granting oil concessions to foreign companies (American, Soviet, and possibly the British in Baluchistan) during the war, the TPI turned against him, ruining any chance of a democratic front against internal reaction and foreign imperialists. The TPI tried to portray Mosaddeq as someone who wanted to block only the Soviet government from obtaining Iranian oil; on the contrary, Mosaddeq specifically proposed forming an Iranian company for mining Iranian oil in the north for the purpose of selling it at a fair price to the USSR[72] — a move that heralded the nationalisation of the AIOC some years later.

The TPI's position in favour of the Soviet demand for an oil concession and its attacks on Mosaddeq backfired and it suffered greatly in popularity, even within its own ranks, particularly because, as noted above, only a short while before, the Tudeh leader Radmanesh had taken the same stand as Mosaddeq on the question of granting exploitation rights to foreign firms or governments.[73] In his *Memoirs*, Eskandari claims that he had discussed Mosaddeq's draft of the law with the Soviet Ambassador; the latter had, in turn, asked Moscow's approval, but apparently no response was given; thus, the Tudeh deputies either abstained or voted against it. Eskandari denies that his party specifically supported the Soviet demand.[74] Yet the aforementioned articles by Maleki in the party organ tells the true story of the TPI's position. In addition, now, as opposed to months before when Radmanesh had made his statement in the Majles opposing foreign concessions, the Tudeh's 'theoretician' Ehsan Tabari defended the granting of an oil concession to the Soviet government. He went so far as stating that, just as the US sought political and economic influence through its companies in Iran, 'it is very natural that the northern neighbour [too] does the same for the advancement of its international interests'. He put it bluntly that the Soviet government had as much right to a 'zone of influence' as did the Western powers[75] — a situation that would have amounted to the division of Iran, as was the case in 1907 between tsarist Russia and Britain.

The more serious problem was the demonstrations that were held under the protection of the Soviet armed forces.[76]

Years later, some Tudeh leaders — but not Tabari — recognised their blunder, albeit in a disguised fashion — or admitted what some independently-minded Tudeh cadres had believed then — in regard to the Soviet oil demand and regretted their decision to back the Soviet demand when their demonstration, held on 27 October 1944, was supported by the Red Army in the streets of Tehran.[77]

While the American Embassy puts the number of demonstrators on that day at 12 000,[78] Keshavarz claims 150 000 people demonstrated against the Sa'ed government, demanding its resignation.[79] Eskandari, while admitting in the Persian version of his *Memoirs* that the Soviet demand had provoked the 'displeasure of the Iranian people',[80] in his *Histoire* he states that the 'hostile attitude' of the Sa'ed government and its 'secret bargaining with the Anglo-Americans provoked a storm of protests':

> Huge demonstrations were organised in Tehran and the provinces, demanding the resignation of the Sa'ed government... The government, frightened by the magnitude of the movement, decided to resort to armed force to put an end to the popular movement. But at a gigantic demonstration in Tehran, with the participation of around 100 000 demonstrators, the soldiers refused to carry out orders of their superiors to shoot at them while marching towards the Parliament. Sa'ed had to give in and a few days later resigned; this was a political victory of great importance for the masses.[81]

Eskandari argues that, according to the Irano-Soviet Friendship Treaty of 1921, Iran had agreed to grant priority to Soviet demands for any oil concessions in the north — a claim that is, of course, incorrect. Whatever the reason, because Soviet troops were present around the demonstration and created the impression that they were supporting it, the TPI went down in history as supporting the Soviet demand for a concession. As noted by Eskandari, similar demonstrations were held in Tabriz, Reza'iyeh (Urmia), Ardebil, Qazvin, Rasht, Bandar-e Shah, Pahlavi (Anzali), Mashhad, Arak and Isfahan.[82] According to the British Military Attaché, in Tabriz the crowd:

> ... tried to rush the police headquarters and was fired on, one man being killed and a few wounded. Russian troops intervened and allowed neither the police nor Persian military patrols to interfere with the mob; moreover, they prohibited the carrying of arms in the town by any member of the Persian forces, and officers carrying arms were prevented from leaving

their barracks... At Rasht also the Persian police were similarly prevented from taking any measures to restore order. In Isfahan and Sultanabad [Arak], where there are no Russian troops, the demonstrators were tame and a small crowd, who, when they were first collected, had no idea that they were to demonstrate in favour of an oil concession to the Russians, soon spread.[83]

Eskandari's justification is, however, not valid, for Tudeh publications of the time fully attest to the TPI's clear-cut support, as in the case of the articles by Maleki mentioned above. There are here two inexactitudes, not to say falsifications, in Eskandari's statement that must be stressed. Here, too, we can observe how another Tudeh leader exaggerates the number of participants in a city which had barely a total of 500 000 souls, families with more than five children included! In addition, Eskandari turns around the subject of a demonstration which, according to him years later in his Persian *Memoirs*, was being protected by the units of the Soviet army. The number of demonstrators is definitely exaggerated because, according to Eskandari himself, the party had, years later, about 10 000 members or followers. Besides, if the party had had so many members and followers in the capital at the time, it would have been able to send several deputies to the Majles from Tehran, where electoral manipulations were very rare and where Mosaddeq and his followers had been easily elected by votes of about 100 000, while Dr Yazdi of the TPI's Central Committee obtained no more than 5000. And, if the number of demonstrators had been so great, why would the TPI have accepted to demonstrate under the protection of the Soviet army in Tehran? Secondly, the demonstrations *were* in support of the Soviet mission, headed by one of Beria's men, M Kavtaradzé, Vice-Commissar for Foreign Trade, demanding an oil concession from Iran, and not merely against Premier Sa'ed.[84] These prevarications by Tudeh leaders demonstrate, on the one hand, their indisputable attachment to the Soviet Union and its wishes and, on the other, their Stalinist method of distorting historical facts, a method that was inculcated in the future leftist youth.

As opposed to the critical stand that he takes in his *Memoirs* in 1984,[85] in his articles of 1949-50 Eskandari attempts to justify the posture of the TPI towards the Soviet Union with regard to the oil concession, by claiming that the Soviets provided assistance to famine-stricken Iranians during the war by sending 'sugar, textiles, etc'. But this 'reasoning' is sheer propaganda, as we know that foodstuffs during the war, in addition to being hoarded for speculation, were confiscated, or bought forcefully by the Allies — a reason for the penury and famine in those years in Iran. Eskandari writes that the quasi-secret *pourparlers* of the Iranian government with Anglo-American oil companies would have 'caused a tempest of protestations' and would have been 'opposed' by the Iranian people.[86] Eskandari does not explain why the same would not have been true in the case of a similar demand by the Soviet Union.

Eskandari turns around the history of the Soviet demand and claims that the demonstrations were against the Anglo-American concessions, and not in favour of the Soviet one, and the subsequent resignation of Premier Sa'ed was 'a political victory of great importance'.[87] The question of oil concessions was, however, rather a defeat for the TPI, whose motto was that 'just as we recognise a sphere of influence for the Western powers, we recognise the same for the Soviet Union'.[88] As opposed to the position taken by Radmanesh in August 1944, the party now did not have any objections to concessions given to the imperialist powers for the exploitation of Iranian oil so long as the same was granted to the Soviet Union. This new position marked the beginning of the mistrust of the Iranian people towards the TPI, although for several more years many who had been ideologically galvanised by the party continued to think that what was good for the Soviet Union was also good for the whole world, including the oppressed masses of Iran. This was the first time the TPI was seen, not only by the general public, but by some of its own members, as a defender of a foreign power. The best proof of this were the remarks in the memoirs of its leaders and cadres. Be that as it may, this débâcle provided the reactionary forces in Iran, as elsewhere, the excuse to associate any socialist thought with service to the Soviet Union.

VII: Increasing Attacks on the Tudeh Party

At the same time as the TPI was preparing itself for the postwar period, the reactionary forces planned to oppose the growth of leftist influence in Iran, using the pretext of blocking Soviet influence. For this reason, after its congress, the TPI came under growing attacks from right-wing forces, including the military headed by the Chief of Staff, the hard-line, pro-British General Arfa. A wave of terror began against the TPI; its clubs and labour union offices were sacked. Tudeh organs were suppressed along with other progressive or pro-Tudeh newspapers. The assaults certainly meant to destroy the party or at least to impede it from making progress, now that it had lost some of its legitimacy in the light of its staunch pro-Soviet stand on the oil question and its open support for the Azerbaijan separatist move. Eskandari claims that the Council of Ministers, with the aid of the secret service (presumably the Second Bureau of the army and the police) had elaborated a plan to put an end to the party's activities[89] — a suggestion that does not seem unreasonable in the light of the plan put into effect in February 1949, which will be discussed below (see Section II:I).[90]

Apparently, by then the British Embassy had abandoned the above-mentioned instructions issued by Ambassador Bullard regarding the TPI, for it would have been impossible for the reactionaries to move against it either without that embassy's consent or its turning a blind eye to the repression. The war with Germany had been practically won and the Soviet control of Eastern Europe made it clear to the British government that the Iranian oil should not fall into the hands of the Soviets. The few Soviet documents that have recently come to light leave little doubt regarding Moscow's well-planned designs to take over Iran. The TPI was to be the instrument of this plan, but it turned out to be its victim.

A newly-found document in the STASI archives, written by one of the SED moles in the TPI, introduces a new element of explanation for the organised attacks on it. It runs as follows.

After explaining who Kambakhsh was — that he had been a member of the ICP, that he had betrayed the 'Group of Fifty-Three',[91] that he had been barred from membership of the TPI in 1941 on the grounds of 'several betrayals' and that he had been taken into membership a few years later after the intervention of the Soviet general-consul in Tehran[92] — the mole describes in detail the relations between Kambakhsh and his brother-in-law Kianouri along with his wife Maryam Firouz (Farmanfarma), with the members of the Qajar princely family, especially Mozaffar Firouz, who is said to have had close relations with the imperialist powers. Detailing the activities of the latter in connection with Seyyed Zia and Qavam's Democrat Party, the mole speaks at length about Kianouri's wife and her family connections with the reactionary princely élite Farmanfarma, including General Firouz and 'many other family members... who stood close to the British and American secret services'. He adds that the Farmanfarma (Firouz) family had been awarded the Queen Victoria decoration.[93] He recalls that Mozaffar Firouz supported the appointment of the pro-British American Millspaugh as Iran's economic boss. He quotes Kianouri, too, who, in 1944, had defended, in the party organ *Rahbar*, granting Millspaugh full authority over the Iranian economy.[94] He also cites Kianouri as having said that the 'main condition for the withdrawal' of the troops of the foreign powers occupying Iran during the war — that is, Britain, the USA and the USSR — was that 'their just interests be ensured'.[95]

The main point the mole stresses is that in 1945 Kianouri, Kambakhsh and Mozaffar Firouz 'organised a plot against the Tudeh Party and the USSR'. Recalling that after the founding of the TPI some Iranian officers had joined the party and that Kambakhsh was in charge of them, he states that a 'list of these officers' names was put at the disposal of the Second Bureau of the general staff of the Iranian army', whose chief decided 'to transfer the suspected officers', above all to garrisons in the southern provinces of the country with poor climatic conditions. According to the mole — recounting an episode that has been a matter of rumour in the TPI for years — Kambakhsh 'incited comrade officers' stationed in Khorasan to rebel against the government (see Section II:II). At the same time, Kambakhsh got in touch with the Soviet General Atakishiev, the political-military commissar of Soviet troops in the occupied territories in the north, informing him that there reigned disquiet among 'comrade officers' who 'intended' to rebel against the army. He then told the 'comrade officers' that 'high Soviet authorities favoured an armed uprising against the Iranian administration'. The STASI mole relates that Kambakhsh organised all this without informing the Tudeh Politbureau. He then sent the infantry officer B Danesh in the hope of obtaining approval for the uprising from Secretariat member Iraj Eskandari. The mole mistakenly adds that Danesh could not see Eskandari and hurriedly returned to Mashhad, where the revolt of 16 officers was launched on 15 August 1945. In his *Memoirs*, Eskandari recalls that he in fact saw Danesh and another officer named Colonel Azar, whom he took to a meeting with Central Committee members, who disagreed with the plan of the uprising.[96] What is more, Kambakhsh had then reported that it had been Eskandari who had authorised the officers to rise — an accusation similar to his act in 1937 against Arani; of course, those two officers denied any such accusation.

The revolt was quickly suppressed, as a result of which seven officers were killed, others escaped to the Soviet Union, a number of other officers were blacklisted as Tudeh sympathisers and arrested, Tudeh party and trade unions centres were sacked, Tudeh newspapers were shut down, and anti-communist propaganda was increased. Both the TPI and the Soviet authorities declared that they had known nothing of the plan for the revolt and denied the accusations of their preparing the revolt. The mole concludes that the revolt was harmful to the TPI and to relations between Tehran and Moscow. He then asks: why was such an 'arbitrary and treacherous' act planned by Kambakhsh?[97] His implicit answer is that Kambakhsh and his brother-in-law Kianouri were agents of non-communist secret services. He adds that the 'revolt' was discussed at the TPI's Enlarged Fourth Plenum held in the summer of 1957 (see Section II:XIII), and it was clearly stated that Kambakhsh and Kianouri had been informed of the opposition of the Central Committee to it. 'It was stated that Kambakhsh was a partner in the murder of the seven officers who had been killed by the Iranian Gendarmerie.' Withal, the mole underlines that a collection of Tudeh declarations and viewpoints published by Kianouri in 1981 censored a passage of the declaration of the revolting officers[98] — the compiler naturally remaining faithful to Stalinist traditions.

In an 'Inquiry' in 1942, a Comintern cadre noted that in 1926 Kambakhsh had reportedly been accused of entering the summer compounds of the British Legation in Qolhak, in northern Tehran. Kambakhsh had denied the accusation (of treachery?) stating that he had entered the compound only 'in order to wash his hands and face in the stream' there. The author of the inquiry adds that the accusation (of treachery?) against him was 'not proven',[99] although in the foothills of the Alborz mountain in northern Tehran there are plenty of streams. Vilkov adds that the cousin of his wife Akhtar and of his brother-in-law Kianouri was the chief of the Intelligence Department of the police.[100]

Another Comintern report states that Kambakhsh had been accused of 'treachery' with regard to his revelations to the police in 1937 when he helped the police arrest some 40 members of the 'Group of Fifty-Three'. While he had confessed to having made 'errors' in this regard, the Comintern report states: 'The question of the harm inflicted on the party by Kambakhsh's confession has not been elucidated.'[101] In addition, according to a report by the Comintern cadre Guliaev, dated 21 November 1941,[102] there was 'in his personal records material accusing Kambakhsh of *provocative work*', without specifying exactly what that was. There was, however, also in his Soviet records material describing him as 'an honest Communist and an able organiser in party work'. Due to a lack of data on Kambakhsh in the recent years (prior to 1941), Guliaev, nonetheless, thought that '*it is essential to check on him*'.[103]

Given all these points, one cannot but help maintain a certain suspicion about these two Tudeh leaders, whose questionable acts in later years — discussed below — also strengthen these suspicions.

VIII: The Azerbaijan Crisis

The reasons for the initial relative success of the Soviet attempt to create a separatist movement in Azerbaijan, provoking the first postwar international crisis between the USSR and the West, are manifold, but in the main are economic. As the American Ambassador in Tehran put it:

> [The Iranians]… still wear the same ragged clothing which breeds typhus-bearing lice in the winter. In the south of Tehran, people live like animals in cellars, hovels and chicken houses or sleep in the streets with the dogs. In the villages or in the country they continue to slave with bent back and careworn face for the rich landowners. In the factory, children toil for wages that will not buy even food, for the benefit of capitalists who are able to pay as much as $20 000 for a Buick automobile. These conditions, one may say, have always existed in Iran. That is true, but today there are numerous new elements. First and foremost, the Iranians in Tehran have suffered

this winter as seldom before. Bread, their only staple food and the only one their limited funds can buy, has been scarce and at present is almost not to be had. Due to Allied exploitation of the railways for aid to Russia, the vital commodity kerosene is so scarce that women and children wait in block-long queues for hours to get it and then are often disappointed.

This [happens] in a country which exports petroleum and in a world which talks of Atlantic Charters, a better world and a new order. Is it any wonder that the Iranians are being swayed by the promises of the teachers of socialism?[104]

Others observed the same in Iran. The Labour MP Michael Foot, in an article written after his visit to Iran, stated that:

Reza Shah did little or nothing for the health of his people; it is not only disease which he left untouched. He did not tamper with the social structure whereby a few thousands of landowners, merchants, shareholders and highly-placed government employees gorged themselves on the labour of a [poverty-]stricken peasantry and a small-town proletariat. A bare 100 000 Persian rule and profit; 300 000 government employees bribe and are bribed. A small middle-class chafes under the restraints of feudalism and begins to feel the impact of political ferment; ten millions or more, uncounted, unprotected and unheeded, fight a monotonous war for existence.[105]

In a subsequent article, Foot noted:

It is probably still easier for a camel to pass through the eye of a needle than for a poor uncorrupted, incorruptible spokesman of the people to enter the Persian parliament. In the main, those elected to the 1944 parliament represented almost exclusively the landowners and the rich men of Persia.[106]

As regards Azerbaijan itself, the American Consul, after describing the appalling conditions prevailing in the province, even on one of the main streets of Tabriz where the American Consulate and some American charitable organisations were located, noted that 'democracies do not need political observers in Azerbaijan so much as they need a corps of hard-fisted social workers armed with sufficient police powers, including probably some guns, to oust and keep ousted the self-seeking Iranian government officials who are rapidly completing their work of social and economic destruction of this province'. He, nevertheless, expressed 'doubts as to whether this country's social, political and moral structure [in both the centre and the province] will prove sufficiently sturdy to support such a very great and grave weight, and I devoutly hope that other and rather more suitable testing grounds will be found and used [for the Atlantic Charter].'[107]

Considering Azerbaijan to be the 'richest Iranian province', another American report stated that it owed its ills to its land system, for which reason the agitation by the pro-Soviet radicals continually adverted to the oppression of the agricultural worker by landlords and landed proprietors. The oppression was such that, in case of disagreement, the peasant was 'in no position to enforce his rights through judicial procedure... Even if the peasant could obtain a court degree in settlement of a dispute, he would be faced with eviction which entails certain economic penalties.'[108] The American Consul reported the views of a peasant who, upon the arrival of Soviet troops in 1941, 'believed that the power of the landlords was to be abolished and the land divided', for through the 'intimidation methods of administrative officials, the agricultural labourers had been reduced to their former positions'.[109] For this reason, landlords preferred 'an inefficient government' as favourable to 'the protection of their own interests'. The landlords also considered — the American consul added — the United States 'as a good friend who will assist' them 'in prevailing upon the Soviets to withdraw from Azerbaijan'. The merchants, too, were interested in a minimal government so as to increase their own profits, as opposed to the general welfare of the area. The American Consul explained that workers, agricultural workers and peasants feared that with the departure of Soviet forces Pahlavi repression would be resumed.[110]

IX: Moscow's Plan for 'Sovietising' Iran

The newly-available Soviet archival records reveal that, for the purpose of Soviet acquisition of Iranian oil, Lavrenti Beria had prepared an 'analytic' report for Stalin in which he proposed 'to set out vigorously to negotiate with the Iranian government with the goal of obtaining a [Soviet] concession in Northern Iran'. The aim was to ensure the success of the Soviet leaders in participating 'on a par' in the postwar competition with the great powers 'for the right to possess the new oilfields in the Middle East',[111] that is, the idea echoed by some Tudeh leaders. To ensure its success, he also proposed that the USSR insist on participation in the Anglo-American oil talks 'to defend Soviet interests in the sphere of international oil affairs'. With Kavtaradzé's mission having failed to obtain an oil concession in the northern provinces of Iran, the Soviet government launched a plan to separate those provinces from Iran as a first stage to take over Iran completely. As we have already noted, the TPI was to be one of the instruments to achieve this aim.

As can be seen from the statement of the Tudeh leaders, the USSR had to have its sphere of influence in Iran, just as the Western powers did. The Department of International Information (DII), which had replaced the Comintern at its dissolution, and its successor, the Department of Foreign Policy (DFP) of the CPSU, was to ensure that the Soviet plan would be put into effect. The DII and DFP had two 'well-concealed representatives' in Iran to control the TPI for precisely this purpose. After the failure of Kavtaradzé's mission, one of the secret agents of the CPSU proposed: 'Before we leave Iran, there is a possibility to gain a majority in the [forthcoming Fifteenth] Majles [elections] and then to use it to pursue the interests of our state as well as the interests of the democratic movement of the Iranian people.' The aim was to have all the 54 deputies of the northern region 'elected', by way of fraud or imposition, while those provinces were still under Soviet occupation. Through such elections, a pro-Soviet majority in the new legislature would be obtained.[112] The secret representative of the CPSU in Iran must have either been blinded by ideology, or not to have known Iran at all, or, worse yet, underestimated the power wielded by the Western powers in Iran. He also reported to Moscow that the law of December 1944, prohibiting any negotiation regarding concessions to foreign powers during Iran's occupation, proposed and secured in the Majles by Dr Mosaddeq, had been a 'British ploy',[113] as stated by the TPI, thus the change henceforth of the party's attitude towards Mosaddeq and its incessant attacks upon him until his overthrow in August 1953.

The Soviet demand for an oil concession having been frustrated by the Majles, the Soviets worked out a plan that was to create separatist governments in Iran's northern provinces. Such a plan was a continuum of the pre-Second World War Germano-Soviet Pact,[114] according to which Iran was to become a satellite of the USSR. Preparation for the secession of Iranian Azerbaijan had taken place in the late 1920s and early 1930s, when the historical leaders of the new Soviet Republic of Azerbaijan, such as Nariman Narimanov and his Hemmat Party colleagues, had been eliminated, one after the other, by the Stalinist apparatus and its Azeri henchman Ja'far Bagirov. In the mid-1930s some 60 000 Iranian residents, mostly miners and agricultural workers, in Soviet Azerbaijan and Central Asia, who were not prepared to renounce their Iranian citizenship and take up Soviet nationality, had been expelled from Soviet Azerbaijan and the Central Asian Soviet Republics and sent back to Iran. Among them were also sent by the NKVD a good number of well-trained agents for future tasks.[115] Bagirov's aim was not only to add the fertile lands of northern Iran to the republic he ruled; he also considered Qazvin and Tehran to be within the boundaries of the 'Azerbaijani motherland' as well. His appetite was so great that he declared Tehran to be 'truly an ancient Azeri city'! He was so ignorant that he did not know that Tehran had been founded only at the end of the eighteenth century.[116] The optimistic evaluation in Moscow was influenced through reports by Bagirov's men in Tabriz who, for instance, had reported that 'the course of historical development of Iran' was such that 'the people of Azerbaijan should be liberated from the Persian yoke, since the Iranian state is on the decline, on the eve of collapse, and its government is in no position to uphold the country's independence'.[117]

As noted above, the execution of this plan in northern Iran occupied by the Red Army was greatly facilitated by economic and other factors in Iran, particularly in Azerbaijan.

1. Firstly, the economic conditions prevailing in Azerbaijan, having worsened under Reza Shah during the 1920s and 1930s, were assessed as preconditions that had prepared the grounds for some sort of a social movement in that part of Iran: the upsurge of multi-ethnic *anjomans* in Azerbaijan as early as 1942. Important here was the deep-seated desire of the people to take hold of their destiny.

2. The decisive shift in American policy after the death of President Roosevelt, on the one hand, towards the Soviet Union, and on the other, *vis-à-vis* the reactionary ruling élites in neo-colonial and semi-colonial countries of the world, particularly those in the oil-rich Middle East such as in Iran, made the question of oil in the postwar period particularly important. The Anglo-American rivalry over the oil resources of the region must also be considered as an important factor in the Azerbaijan crisis.

3. The strong tendency of the young shah and the reactionary guard surrounding him, most of whom had been in the service of his father, towards re-establishing the dictatorship that had been dismantled by the Allies.

4. The desire of various anti-Pahlavi forces, in the particular case of the TPI with the support of the USSR, to prevent Iran from falling into the abyss of a right-wing royal dictatorship. In addition to the TPI, the patriotic-democratic forces, gradually clustering around Dr Mosaddeq, were also determined to forestall the return of a new dictatorship. Moreover, even right-wing strongmen of Iranian politics, such as Seyyed Zia and Qavam, who had been discarded by Reza Shah, also were initially opposed to the then shah's great desire to re-establish his father's dictatorship.

5. The internecine feuds within the ranks of the TPI were easily exploited by the internal reactionary forces as well as by foreign powers with great interests in Iran. Thus, Iran's political culture and the behaviour of Iranian politicians had also to be considered as a serious factor in the making of the Azerbaijan crisis and its long-term consequences.

6. The fact of rivalries and power struggles within the CPSU and amongst

the Soviet republics, which were juggling for a greater share of the Soviet pie, also played an important role in the development of that crisis. In this connection, the ambitious head of the Azerbaijan SSR, Bagirov, who certainly sought to improve his position in Moscow, should be considered more carefully than hitherto, particularly if other documents of the Soviet archives eventually become available.[118]

7. Soviet policy in Iran, aiming at greater influence, was to be assisted even through conservative and reactionary forces, namely, landowners and rich comprador merchants, such as Rafi'i from Tabriz, who had been leading figures in the Majles.

X: The Soviet Politbureau's Directives on Action in Northern Iran

On 6 July 1945 the CPSU Politbureau convoked Bagirov and handed him a 'secret' directive for the purpose of organising a 'separatist movement' in Azerbaijan and other northern provinces of Iran, namely Gilan, Mazandaran, Khorasan and Gorgan. The same directive allocated one million convertible roubles for the purpose of arming fighting groups, armed with non-Russian weapons, to support the project. The Democratic Party of Azerbaijan (DPA), yet to be created, was assigned the task of carrying out the plan.[119] The directive also included recommendations for 'appropriate work' among the Kurdish-speaking population of Iran for the same purpose.[120] Thereafter, the veteran Communist Ja'far Pishevari, whose parliamentary mandate had just been rejected, and Kambakhsh, widely known in Iran as a Soviet agent in the TPI, were called by Bagirov to Baku and assigned the task of carrying out the project. The plan was put into effect after the defeat of Japan.

It seems, however, that long before the decision by the Politbureau, other preparations had been made, at least by Bagirov's men in Iranian Azerbaijan. According to one British report, as early as December 1944 — that is to say, right after the failure of Kavtaradzé's mission — the Tudeh Provincial Committee had already been providing a 'foretaste of what is doubtless the Russian policy'.[121] This 'foretaste' was indicated in a Tudeh broadsheet published in Tehran, quoting demands of 'an alleged meeting of 50 000 people at Tabriz on 1 December' and 'other meetings in towns and villages of Azerbaijan. Oaths are said to have been taken on the blood of the martyrs of freedom for the Constitution [of 1906], and to put Fundamental Laws into operation.' The manifesto demanded: a) provincial councils; b) the trial of Premier Sa'ed and exile of Seyyed Zia; c) the abrogation of the Military Governorship in Tehran; d) the exclusion of agents of Reza Shah's dictatorship from power; e) the formation of a coalition government including 'lovers of freedom', that is, the TPI; f) a foreign policy based on a (positive) equilibrium, that is, concessions for both the Western powers and the USSR; g) good relations with the Soviet people; h) reforms in regard to workmen, peasants and social insurance. The manifesto concluded by stating that 'Azerbaijanis will take speedy steps to put [the demands of] the manifesto into operation. If the government agrees, so much the better; if they oppose, the duty of the people towards the government is clear.'[122] The threat was hardly veiled. It is not clear who, in the name of the TPI, issued this broadsheet, for no party leadership, especially centralised as the TPI's was, could allow a provincial committee to make threatening demands in the name of the national leadership. Either the significance of the matter escaped the attention of the Tudeh leaders who were not as yet fully committed to the USSR, or they must have intentionally ignored it until such time that they could investigate the problem. Maleki's mission, as a member of the Control Committee, to Azerbaijan may explain this initial disregard. Be that as it may, the Azerbaijani demands, although not illegal, did point to the demands later made by the DPA, especially regarding relations with the Soviet Union and the establishment of provincial councils, and the threat to carry them out. Who were these activists of the TPI Provincial Committee who made these demands? The very persons who less than a year later dissolved the Provincial Committee and joined the DPA, the same individuals who had created an 'Azeri' organisation as a rival to the TPI in late 1941, when the Soviet officer Siliukov was discussing with Solayman Mirza Eskandari the creation of the TPI,[123] which they later joined.

More or less the same demands appeared in the manifesto of the Freedom Front in Azerbaijan which the TPI created in the spring of 1945, on the eve of Germany's defeat. This time, with the victory of the USSR being practically assured and collaboration with the Allies no longer an exigency, the TPI, in addition to promoting 'firm friendship with the Soviet Union' and 'the formation of provincial councils', finally came out with the demand the Soviets had initially not allowed it to express in its draft programme, namely, 'agrarian reform', coupled with 'economic development'. As the British Consul in Tabriz pointed out to Ambassador Bullard, there was 'nothing in such a programme to alarm anyone', but it was 'customary for the conservative part of the population to see the published programme as a cloak for more sinister goings-on inspired by the Soviet Consul-General'[124] — an alarm that galvanised the reactionary forces against the progressive part of society.

This, however, was taking place at a time when the TPI was much weaker than in the previous spring, because of its stand on the Soviet oil concession and its demonstration in favour of it in October 1944. This was reflected in a report by Ambassador Bullard to the Foreign Secretary Anthony Eden stating that 'the general opinion' was that the TPI 'was not altogether a genuine Persian left-wing movement, but a political organisation largely under Soviet control'. It is, therefore, no surprise that when on 2 March the TPI announced a demonstration, and whereupon the Military Governor of Tehran 'showed a bold face', the demonstration in Tehran was cancelled and the local Tudeh leaders in Tabriz drew in their horns, 'trying to restrain the activities of their more unruly followers'. Yet it was also reported by the American Consul on 8 March that 3000 people marched in procession to the Municipal Building of that city with the usual slogans.[125] And a month before, also in Tabriz, the Freedom Front, the Tudeh front organisation led by pro-Soviet elements under Bagirov's men, celebrated the second anniversary of Stalingrad's victory on 2 February where they paraded effigies of the Nazi leaders. At the end, the organisers sent a telegram to Stalin on behalf of '70 000 liberals' in Tabriz, thanking him for the Stalingrad victory.[126]

The Soviet connection became obvious once again towards the end of March when Tudeh leaders addressed crowds in the streets of Tehran where Soviet tommy-gunners were patrolling.[127] Here, too, Tudeh leaders, emotionally attached to the Soviet Union, which was rapidly approaching victory at the end of the war, could not see the preparations for what was in store for them. Despite the decline in the TPI's fortunes in many parts of Iran, according to the American Consul in Tabriz the influence of the Tudeh Provincial Council there was already on the rise by the beginning of March. Factory owners were complaining that they were 'unable to earn satisfactory profits owing to the increasing demands of labour organised in the labour union and the Tudeh Party' — a phenomenon newly developing, for during the war the same unions prevented labourers from demanding higher wages, as factory owners supplied the Soviet Union and its forces in Iran. One rug factory owner named Javan closed down his carpet units because, he claimed, he was unable to earn 'satisfactory profits'. Anyone familiar with the carpet industry in Iran would know how miserable were the wages paid to carpet weavers; usually small children with fine fingers were paid piece-work wages, barely allowing them to eat, children who, after a few years, developed bodily deformations.[128] It is therefore hard to believe that the inability to earn 'satisfactory profits' was the real reason for their complaints and factory closures, as growing demands for the creation of local and provincial councils,[129] provided for in the Supplementary Laws of the Constitution, must have given them a 'foretaste' of a Soviet takeover. What confirmed the fears of a Soviet takeover was the article in *Pravda* dealing with the Iranian political situation that was broadcast over the Moscow Radio Persian Service. Its message was: 'The Tudeh Party is not unsupported.' The Persian translation of the whole article was published on 19 July in the organ of the Tudeh's Provincial Council, *Khavar-e no*.[130] Preceding it was a short note on the preparations for a Soviet plan that was to have a great decisive impact, not only on Iran's future political developments, but also on world politics.

XI: The Creation of the Democratic Party of Azerbaijan and the Autonomous Government of Azerbaijan

On 3 September 1945 the founding of the Democratic Party of Azerbaijan was announced. The TPI's Provincial Committee, as planned by the aforementioned directive, was dissolved into the DPA, provoking the private anger of the Tudeh leaders. At the same time, the leaders of the DPA and the subsequently formed Autonomous Government of Azerbaijan (AGA), in a letter addressed to Bagirov and Stalin, informed them of their own intentions. They said:

> In order to protect the rights of the Azeri people... we consider it necessary to found an independent republic of Azerbaijan. Therefore... we ask you to render us assistance and create the conditions to realise the treasured dream of our people, consisting of the unification of these two republics.[131]

It seems that, while the British government was, as in 1907, ready for an unofficial partition of Iran between the Soviet government and the two major Western powers, Stalin did not opt for such a choice, apparently because he wished to, and considered it likely that he could, control Iran entirely. As General Arfa was told by foreign diplomats, during the tripartite Moscow conference held after the surrender of Japan, Stalin refused the offer by Ernest Bevin, the new British Foreign Secretary, according to which the provisions of the Supplementary Laws of the Iranian Constitution were to be applied, as in other regions, in order to legalise the newly-founded AGA.[132] The idea was to create similar 'autonomous regions or governments' in other provinces, which would have been the prelude to the partition of Iran, or its complete takeover, but Stalin did not want the British to take part in this adventure.

The British Ambassador Sir Reader Bullard clearly understood the Soviet position. He later wrote: 'The Soviet-sponsored Tudeh Party in Azerbaijan thought it wise to change its name to "democrat" [sic: DPA] and in October the "democrats" demanded full provincial autonomy for Azerbaijan.'[133]

In fact, Bevin's proposal was received with alarm by patriotic forces in Iran. In a speech in the Majles, Dr Mosaddeq denounced the proposal as harmful to Iran's territorial integrity and independence.[134] He also made it clear that he did not agree with the 'one-sided federalism' announced by the AGA; if Iran were to adopt a federal system, a 'federated government', all Iranian people should take part in such a decision.[135]

The establishment of the DPA and then the AGA in the autumn of 1945 worried not only the ruling élites in Iran, and the whole of the anti-imperialist, patriotic and progressive forces, but also the TPI. Former Central Committee member Keshavarz relates the story of the Central Committee being surprised by the DPA's sudden creation. He recalls that on the eve of the establishment of the DPA an Azeri Tudeh member arrived from Tabriz at a meeting of the Central Committee, and simply announced that the next day the whole Tudeh organisation would break away from the party and join the DPA. He adds that of the 15 Central Committee members 'not even one agreed' with the creation of DPA,[136] 'although we know that Kambakhsh had been informed in advance by the Soviet Azeri leader Bagirov'.[137] Many years after Keshavarz, Eskandari writes in his *Memoirs* that the TPI Central Committee had no prior knowledge of the DPA's establishment and was surprised by this *'fait accompli'*.[138] The Tudeh leaders were simply shocked. Terrified by what was happening in Azerbaijan and its repercussions on their party, the Central Committee, after a long discussion, decided to write a *secret* letter to the Soviet party, 'making the Soviets understand that what they are doing is detrimental to the Tudeh as it is harmful to the Soviet Union'.[139] While Eskandari believes that the decision to write the secret letter was approved by a majority and vaguely recalls that a few of them, like Kambakhsh and perhaps Alamouti, opposed it,[140] Keshavarz firmly asserts that 'not even one opposed it, or did not dare oppose it'.[141] The *secret* letter to the Soviet party described the reasons for their opposition to the whole affair.

Yet, in retrospect, one can observe that, before the DPA was founded and its programme publicly announced, there had been hints that the Soviets were preparing the ground for it within public opinion, at least in the Soviet-occupied zones. For example, on 20 February 1945, the chief of the National Police reported that, 10 days previously, about a thousand people had gathered at a demonstration organised by the TPI's Qazvin committee. Artashes Ovanesian, the Armenian minority deputy from Northern Iran, spoke to the public present and demanded, *inter alia*, the creation of provincial councils according to the articles of the 1907 Supplement to the Constitution.[142] Sometime later in Ardebil, a speaker of the local Tudeh committee spoke about observance of the Constitution and the need to establish provincial and regional councils in order to undertake social reforms. He added that the patience of the people had run out and there would be 'dire consequences'. At the end of the demonstration a resolution was adopted demanding the full application of the Constitution, of which copies were sent to the Majles, Dr Mosaddeq and the press.[143] The same sort of demonstration was held in other cities. It is sufficiently clear that the reason why provincial and district councils had not been established immediately after the Constitutional Revolution was that the reactionary forces, who had seized power right after the ousting of Mohammad Ali Shah, were worried about its consequences, but the sudden desire now expressed for them by certain Tudeh provincial committees in the north meant that not all the Central Committee members who had voted for the aforementioned secret letter to the CPSU were sincere in their protestation, and that they were tuned in with the Soviet plan.

The same lack of sincerity is manifested by Eskandari when narrating these events in his *Histoire*, as he writes approvingly of what was taking place in Azerbaijan; he fails to mention that the TPI's Central Committee was quite alarmed by what had been happening in Azerbaijan, as a result of which not only had the DPA absorbed the TPI's Provincial Committee, but also reactionary forces had begun a campaign to suppress the TPI, which was perceived to have initiated the action in Azerbaijan. Attacks upon the TPI began soon after the Khorasan uprising; they were so alarming that the prominent leaders of the party who were Majles deputies addressed an open letter to the Speaker of the Parliament with copies sent to the US Secretary of State, the British Under-Secretary of State for Foreign Affairs and the Soviet Commissar for Foreign Affairs. In it, they referred to the campaign of repression during which party clubs were shut down, party newspapers confiscated wholesale, trade union offices occupied, party and union property destroyed, party members attacked with bayonets, party members tortured 'with unheard of brutality', and documents seized. On 16 September, the military even went so far as attacking and injuring the parliamentary deputy and university professor Keshavarz.

The signatories of the letter 'strongly protested against these abominable acts of this fascist government', informing 'the whole world that there exists not the faintest sign of freedom and democracy in Iran'. They stressed that 'in spite of suspicions and calumnies against us, our organisation has a legitimate social goal', indicating that the TPI had 'always supported the maintenance of peace and order, and to this end, has hitherto fiercely resisted with all its power any acts of a disorderly nature', and had demanded 'the full application of Constitutional Law and the principles of true democracy'. Alarmed by the pursuit of 'the exact policy of the fascist government of Reza Khan', by the 'present corrupt governing body of the country', Tudeh deputies, therefore, considered it the 'irrevocable duty of the great countries of the world to lend their energetic assistance in the establishment of democracy and the granting of freedom to the Persian people, who have helped with a sense of sacrifice in the furtherance of the cause of freedom-lovers during the war'.[144] No help came, not even from their 'brother party' to the north.

Thus, contrary to what Eskandari relates in his *Histoire*,[145] the Tudeh leadership had been against the formation of the DPA and initially believed that Pishevari had taken the initiative on his own, but later understood that 'comrades who had closer contacts' with the Soviets were of the opinion that the initiative was being supported by the Soviets.[146]

Eskandari states in his *Memoirs* that right after the formation of the DPA and the absorption of the TPI's Provincial Committee into it, the Tudeh leadership had secretly manifested its opposition to it, and he had been commissioned by the Central Committee to address a letter to the Soviet party, taking it to Moscow personally when *en route* to Paris to attend the congress of the International Federation of Labour Unions. The TPI has never published the letter that had been approved by the Central Committee and signed by Eskandari on its behalf.[147]

The salient points of the letter are as follows:

* In addition to a great number of workers, representatives of 'intellectual' (that is, the educated élite) circles, government employees, artisans, engineers employed in private or governmental enterprises, university professors and lecturers are TPI members.
* The TPI enjoys vast popularity.
* Workers and peasants look to the day when the TPI will free them from oppression.
* Iranian 'intellectuals' look to the TPI.
* Some progressive elements of the well-to-do and landowners do not view the TPI with a disapproving eye.
* The TPI suffers from the fact that in the northern regions of the country a large number of immigrants (of Iranian origin, with a particular mission)[148] from the Soviet Union have entered the party and constitute its active membership.
* In the provinces party organisations are not in a good condition and 'in fact the majority of them are very weak'.
* Relations between the TPI Central Committee and officials of 'our' — that is, Soviet — friends in Iran are not good and the Central Committee's efforts to improve them have yielded no results; some immigrants' personal profiteering from these relations have hurt the party.
* Because the party does not have 'enough meritorious cadres', DPA officials have no choice but to yield to immigrants in the party. (Eskandari did not realise that their being there had been planned long in advance!)
* Azerbaijan having particular problems — such as those caused by immigrants and incompetent individuals, such as Biriya, the illiterate leader of the labour unions — the TPI's efforts to overcome them have been frustrated by the Soviet 'friends' in charge; 'in short, the majority of these undesirable measures take place over the head of the Central Committee and without its knowledge'.

* The uprising of Tudeh army officers in the summer of 1945 in Khorasan (in which, it is now clear, the KGB-connected Central Committee member Kambakhsh had played a primordial role) took place in spite of the Central Committee's orders to the contrary.
* Not only was the DPA formed without the prior knowledge of the TPI's Central Committee, but also the latter's provincial section and the labour unions joined the DPA upon the recommendation of Soviet 'friends', that is, Soviet agents.
* Under the present conditions, 'all Iranians consider the formation of the DPA and its constitution as a first step towards the break-up of Iran'; in the general view of the nation and in the opinion of all freedom-seeking individuals, the DPA was created on the recommendation of Soviet representatives with a view of separating Azerbaijan from Iran.
* If the TPI had supported the DPA and accepted the absorption of its provincial section by that party, the former could no longer act as an active element on the Iranian political scene — thus the Tudeh foresaw the looming débâcle.
* With regard to the DPA, the TPI is in a cul-de-sac, as it can neither attack the DPA nor support it.
* Already one can see the manifestations of shame and ignominy which that party has provoked among freedom-seeking circles and even 'leftist elements'.
* In spite of Soviet declarations regarding the territorial integrity of Iran, the formation of the DPA and the policy it pursues have sullied the good intentions of the Soviet Union and caused it great damage.

Finally, the letter concluded:

> ... the policy that the [Soviet] friends have carried out has been threatening the vast popular movement, and has been to no advantage to the well-intentioned Soviet policy [in Iran]... We request with determination that the [Soviet] officials in charge here be recalled and at least two [Soviet] party officials be sent to Tehran so that they can rapidly appraise and revise the policy that has been carried out, thereby preventing a [further] strong battering to our [Soviet] friends and our common undertaking.[149]

This letter was, indeed, a devastating document, not only because it was a clear affront to the Soviet policy, but also, paradoxically, because it demonstrates, on the one hand, the direct Soviet intervention into the internal affairs of Iran and the policies of the TPI, and, on the other, the paralysis of the TPI as a result of its dependency upon the CPSU. It also shows to what extent the Tudeh leaders, whether or not aware of the deal between Solayman Mirza Eskandari and Colonel Siliukov in the autumn of 1941, were naïve and how much they misunderstood the nature of the much-proclaimed 'Russian internationalism'. Four decades later Eskandari relates in his *Memoirs*[150] that upon his return from Paris to Moscow, *en route* to Tehran, he was shunned by Soviet officials and not one of them, who had previously received him, would have anything to do with him, simply because, as the party Secretary who had signed and delivered that letter, he was held responsible for it.

Apparently, the TPI's Central Committee members did not content themselves with the letter Eskandari took to Moscow, and they also wrote a public declaration to announce their opposition to the DPA. It is reported to have been drafted by Khalil Maleki and was to be published by Kambakhsh, but it was not in the end published on the grounds that, reportedly, the latter had told them that their 'Soviet comrades' had 'opposed it'.[151]

More importantly, while Eskandari was still in Paris, the other two members of the TPI's Secretariat, Alamouti and Dr Bahrami, were summoned to the Soviet Embassy to meet the Ambassador and Ali Aliev, the Embassy Counsellor (that is, an official of the NKVD in the Tehran Embassy), who 'explained' to them the 'correctness' of the Soviet policy with regard to the Azerbaijan affair. They were told that they should not oppose the DPA. They also were asked whether the letter delivered by Eskandari had been approved by the Central Committee, and they lied and said 'no'; it must have then been understood as a personal initiative of Eskandari alone!derna[152] As a result, while Eskandari was still in Paris, the two party Secretaries, on behalf of the TPI's Central Committee, addressed another letter to the CPSU, declaring that the TPI would henceforth 'obey' the Soviet party — a letter about which the whole Tudeh leadership preferred to remain silent.[153]

We have already seen how, on the morrow of the Khorasan 'uprising', General Arfa sought to annihilate the TPI. In this connection, Eskandari states that at this time a plan had been worked out by General Arfa — the 'fascist' Army Chief of General Staff, 'favoured by the British Embassy' — and adopted by the Council of Ministers to 'dismantle the Tudeh Party and the labour unions by way of terror', a fact that, as noted above, is confirmed by Arfa himself.[154] Great amounts of arms had been distributed among tribes and armed bands in order to attack the TPI's headquarters, clubs and press. In Tehran, the seat of the CCUTU was occupied by the army and its organ *Zafar* was suppressed, as were the Tudeh's *Rahbar* and other progressive newspapers. These acts of violence against the TPI were certainly part of the damage the party's Central Committee had foreseen in its letter addressed to the CPSU. In response to these measures, the TPI organised large demonstrations of protest, and in the provinces of

Mazandaran and Gorgan its followers took over towns by organising 'workers' self-defence' committees and put themselves in charge of roads, railway stations and town security.[155]

Eskandari holds that the attitude of the government 'provoked general indignation amongst the Azerbaijanis and accelerated the course of events that led to the insurrection of November 1945' by the DPA, the creation of which had been announced in September 1945, and later the creation of the AGA. In his *Histoire*, contrary to the aforementioned letter of the TPI's Central Committee, that he himself had delivered to the Soviet party, he states that the appeal of the DPA had 'resounded among all the strata of the people. In less than two months, several thousand people joined the DPA, which, thus, acquired an incontestable political force.' He adds, *approvingly*:

> The provincial section of the Tudeh Party also decided to join the movement in order to unite all the democratic forces of the province and to bring about the realisation of the legitimate demands of the population of Azerbaijan.[156]

This, in spite of the above-mentioned letter in which he had denounced the forceful dissolution of the TPI's Provincial Committee in Azerbaijan and its integration into the newly-founded DPA!

In his *Histoire*, Eskandari goes on to describe the adoption of a 'constitution' for the AGA and the announcement of the 'creation of people's power', that is, the 'Kurdish Republic', 'presided over by the famous progressive Kurdish prelate Qazi Mohammad'.[157] The problem with this falsified 'history' of those events, written some five years later, is that Eskandari distorts his own record, who, as a party secretary, had delivered a letter of protest to the Russian party regarding the creation of the DPA and its absorption of the TPI's provincial section. In addition, documents that have recently come to light demonstrate beyond a shred of doubt that the whole DPA–AGA operation had been planned by the Soviets, and not by Pishevari and his collaborators.[158]

XII: The Demise of the Soviet-sponsored Autonomous Government of Azerbaijan

The Iranian governments tried to solve the problem of Azerbaijan by either negotiating with the Soviet Union or taking their complaint to the UN Security Council. The Soviet government systematically refused to negotiate with Tehran until such time that a government with a favourable attitude towards the USSR came into office, headed by Ahmad Qavam. Given London's lukewarm attitude and Washington's hesitations, Moscow was certain to get its way.

In his 1950 *Histoire* Eskandari boasts of the 'the advance of the popular movement' which the government led by Sadr could not suppress and, as a result, brought about his resignation. The fact is that the Soviets refused to deal with either him or his successor Hakimi, both of whom were long-standing Anglophiles. The Soviets wanted to deal with someone else who had secretly met Soviet envoys in Iran, as far back as the arrival of the Soviet oil delegation led by Deputy-Minister Kavtaradzé. In a secret meeting with the latter's aide N Baybakov, Qavam had promised, if he became premier with Soviet blessings, he would promote Soviet interests in Iran.[159]

It should be recalled that Qavam had first become Prime Minister in the summer of 1921 by the recommendation of Captain Grey — a British intelligence officer in Iran — to War Minister Reza Khan, who had wanted to rid himself of his co-putschist Premier Seyyed Zia.[160] Later Reza Khan got rid of Qavam too, and sent him into exile to France. Allowed to return to Iran in 1928, again with the recommendation of the British Embassy in Tehran,[161] he continued to live in internal exile on his lusciously profitable estates, whence, towards the end of the 1930s, he established secret contacts with both Nazi Germany and the Japanese government in connection with a plot to unseat Reza Shah. Yet, after the abdication of Reza Shah in 1941, he made every effort to become premier with the help of the British and the Americans. In spite of the initial opposition of British Ambassador Bullard, the British Embassy consented to his premiership in 1943, under the pressure of another British officer who had known him in the 1920s. When Bullard gave his consent, he wrote that Qavam would know 'where his bread is buttered'!'[162] His premiership came to an end soon thereafter as both the economic and political situation deteriorated. His attempts to return to office failed until after the start of the Azerbaijan crisis.

In his *Histoire*, Eskandari recalls that the TPI's Central Committee held that, given 'the national and international conditions..., the people's movement at the time did not as yet have the possibility to take and keep power. *It, therefore, decided to support Qavam's premiership.*'[163] He adds:

> ... the absence of other liberal political personalities with the possibility of having a majority in the Majles made Qavam the only possible premier in the delicate days at the end of 1945. [The Tudeh Party]... had to choose between Qavam, who promised to put into effect a relatively democratic programme and the risk of a military dictatorship, the spectre of which was already looming on the horizon.

Thus, the 'Central Committee of the Tudeh Party decided to support Qavam and to facilitate his premiership in order to gain time for the consolidation of the victories that the people had already won'.[164] The TPI's simple reason, apparently, was that Qavam's programme of government, which included a solution to the Azerbaijan issue, the question of an oil concession to the USSR, and the evacuation of the Red troops from Iran, seemed to be sufficiently reasonable.[165] Strangely enough, Eskandari explains that, when making this decision, the Central Committee, having been aware of Qavam's reactionary past and his attachment to the big landowning system, had no illusions about him![166]

Aside from the fact that the consequences of a military dictatorship under Qavam would not have been very different from what actually happened as a result of Qavam's premiership, thus demonstrating the mistaken policy of the Tudeh leadership, Eskandari falsifies his party's history, once again, in order to cover its 'obedience' to the Soviet party in collaborating with a reactionary latifundista who had promised to grant the USSR an oil concession. The historical fact that recent revelations of Soviet documents bring to light is that the TPI's Central Committee was strongly opposed to Qavam's premiership and it was forced by the Soviets to vote for him.[167]

Eskandari goes even further and declares that during the 'first phase' of Qavam's government 'the democratic movement made enormous strides in the labour and peasant unions'.[168] Yet he recalls the terrible conditions of workers and other working people who were beleaguered by inflation, miserable wages, terrible diseases,[169] illiteracy, all caused by various governments during the war, including — especially — Qavam's previous tenure in office.

At any rate, once voted in as premier by a majority of one vote, Qavam immediately left for Moscow to negotiate with the Soviet government. Despite his 'sufficiently reasonable' programme, his mission was a total failure, as he admitted both in his press communiqué and his report to the Majles. He could not get the Soviet government to agree to evacuate Iran of its forces that were scheduled to leave by 2 March 1946, six months after the end of the war. It seems, however, that he had — secretly — agreed to give Soviet Russia the oil concession she had wanted all along.[170] Upon his return, he received the new Soviet Ambassador with whom he — this time openly — signed an agreement on 4 April 1946 *at three o'clock in the morning* for the creation of a joint Irano-Soviet oil company to extract oil in the northern provinces of the country. In exchange, the Soviet government promised to evacuate its forces and declared that the AGA affair was an internal matter of Iran alone. Nevertheless, the Soviet Ambassador played the role of an intermediary between the Qavam government and the AGA in order to reintegrate Azerbaijan as a province with a certain amount of internal autonomy.

In the meantime, the Soviet forces left Iran, but not because, as Eskandari's and Qavam's supporters have put it, that Qavam had 'fooled' Stalin with an oil agreement. Eskandari overlooks how the agreement of 4 April between Qavam and the Soviet Ambassador in Tehran concerning Azerbaijan autonomy and a mixed (51 to 49 per cent) Irano-Soviet Oil Company was worked out, not by Qavam's 'impression' on the Soviet government, but by President Truman's threat that he would treat the Soviet Union in the same manner he had dealt with recent enemies, that is, Nazi Germany and Japan. Truman had appointed General Walter Bedell-Smith, a former Allied commander in Europe and the first CIA director, as his new Ambassador to the Kremlin, and he transmitted Truman's barely-veiled threatening message to Stalin.[171] His message was delivered only a few hours before the Soviet Ambassador convoked Premier Qavam in the middle of the night of 4 April 1946 to agree to the evacuation of Soviet forces from Iran.

In addition, it should be recalled that Truman had also summoned the Soviet Ambassador Gromyko in Washington DC to threaten Stalin with the menace of the nuclear bomb.[172] According to the memoirs of Bagirov's private secretary, in the middle of the same night Stalin telephoned Baku to tell the President of the Azerbaijan SSR — who had been executing Moscow's plan for the Sovietisation of northern Iran — to start withdrawing Soviet forces from the province of Azerbaijan. This was only a few hours after the meeting between Stalin and General Bedell-Smith in the Kremlin, during which Truman's threatening message had been delivered. When Bagirov tried to resist Stalin, the latter told him: 'This is an order.' And it was, indeed, an order obeyed.[173] Interestingly, Mirza Ebrahimov, an Iranian-born Azeri living in Soviet Azerbaijan and a member of the Azerbaijan Akademi Nauk, who played an important role in the DPA–AGA affair, wrote an article about the AGA in which he sought to justify the sudden retreat of the Soviet forces and the collapse of the AGA; this retreat took place within the context of the 'world balance of power' as a necessity to avoid the 'conspiratorial plans of world imperialism' against the Soviet Union, the 'great inspiration' for all the freedom-loving peoples of the world.[174] To put it briefly, the TPI was, thus, once more the victim of its own naïveté.

XIII: Premier Qavam's 'Democratic Party'

In July 1946, while negotiating with the AGA, Qavam created the Democratic Party of Iran (DPI). His aim was 'to compete' simultaneously with the DPA and the TPI. Its programme imitated that of the TPI; one could even think of it as ultra-democratic, as in part its demands went even further than those of the TPI. To make his programme more credible and to placate the Soviet government and the TPI, Qavam had a few pro-British politicians of his own ilk, such as Seyyed Zia and General Arfa, arrested and imprisoned without charge.[175] Already on 17 May 1946, the Qavam government, while negotiating with the Soviet government over the departure of their forces from Iran and the problem of the AGA, had proclaimed a labour law, elaborated a project according to which 15 per cent of land revenues would be allotted to peasants, and announced the division of state lands among the peasantry — a manoeuver that put the TPI in a still more difficult position.[176] It should have been obvious to all, including the TPI, that Qavam's party was no more than a façade on his part behind which all the reactionaries could be organised with the aim of confronting and disarming the TPI and other progressive forces in the country so as to establish his own dictatorship.[177] So much was perceived by Dr Mosaddeq at the time. The very composition of Qavam's party made this clear. It was composed of rich and powerful landlords and tribal leaders, big merchants linked to the import trade, 'the comprador bourgeoisie', reactionary journalists, and right-wing 'intellectuals'. What is more, its rank-and-file was filled with compulsorily enrolled government employees and small traders who depended on the government for various licences and authorisations, as well as roughnecks of the red light districts of major cities.[178] There could be little doubt that Qavam's DPI would not have succeeded in this competition on a political level with its sham programme and its hybrid membership composition.

In his *Histoire*, Eskandari defends Qavam's oil agreement with the Soviets by comparing it advantageously to the Anglo-Iranian Oil Co concession, which paid only 16 per cent of the profits to Iran. On the other hand, Eskandari denies any intentions by the Soviet government regarding Iranian territorial integrity. One can be sure that, given the letter he himself had delivered to the Soviet Central Committee — with specific reference to separatism — he must have known of the Soviet intentions during the crisis, but his Leninist discipline must have prevented him from giving a truthful account of the cause of the crisis and its solution.

Eskandari is either naïve or hypocritical when he defends Qavam as an 'old hand of Iranian politics', who not only 'fooled Stalin' in Moscow, but also, upon his return to Tehran, in August 1946 invited three Tudeh leaders to participate in his new cabinet. The fact that Qavam suggested Eskandari for Ministry of the Economy, Dr Yazdi for Health, and *the Soviet agent Kambakhsh for the sensitive Ministry of Communications* (PTT) should have told Eskandari something of the collusion of Qavam with the Soviet government. Interestingly, Eskandari opposed the appointment of Kambakhsh, no doubt on account of his past treachery, and naively proposed Dr Keshavarz instead. However, Keshavarz refused the PTT Ministry, despite the Soviet Ambassador's pressure, and asked for the Education portfolio, which was given to him in spite of the shah's opposition.[179]

A report published in *Pravda* nearly two months before the formation of the coalition government, whether true in substance or not, reveals the optimism with which Moscow viewed Qavam. The report, sent from Tbilisi to *Pravda*,[180] stated that 'a well-informed person' had declared:

> ... recently Mr Le Rougetel, the British Ambassador in Tehran, visited Qavam al-Saltaneh and endeavoured to bring pressure to bear on the Prime Minister. Mr Le Rougetel expressed particular dissatisfaction at the fact that the Prime Minister should have come to an understanding with the Tudeh Party and mentioned that it seemed that the officials of the government in Khuzistan were unable to take steps to prevent strikes occurring among the workpeople of the AIOC.

The ambassador is reported to have added that 'it seemed the government had not taken the necessary steps in regard to these strikes'. What is more, Le Rougetel 'opposed the inclusion in the cabinet of representatives of the Tudeh Party, although he was not asked for his views on this matter'. The British Ambassador also 'threatened' Qavam in respect of the results of the Fifteenth Majles, not expecting the deputies from Azerbaijan to be from the DPA. According to this 'secret report' published in *Pravda*, Qavam had:

> ... repulsed the attacks of the Ambassador, repeating that he desired good relations with Great Britain, but was unable to permit that the English should interfere in the internal affairs of Persia. The Prime Minister further reminded the Ambassador that the Persian government in future would vigorously defend the independence of the country.

It is clear that the Soviets wished to portray Qavam as an independently-minded premier, which is, of course, far from the truth. He never had the courage to stand up to the British Embassy or that of the US. He was more than subservient to the British and American governments.[181]

In its declaration justifying its participation in Qavam's coalition government, the TPI stated:

> In order to impede the plots of the elements who still undertake nefarious measures against the democratic movements and continue plundering and murdering the toilers, and also in order to make practical plans aiming at developing industrial and agricultural projects as well as the generalisation of education and health, and ensuring the supply of bread, employment, and judicial security, the Tudeh Party thought it necessary to take part in the cabinet and to contribute to the realisations of the ideals and aims of

the nation.[182]

In his 1950 *Histoire*, Eskandari attributes the attacks on Tudeh labour unions and workers' strikes to 'instigations of British imperialism', forgetting that Qavam as premier was responsible for the crushing blows by the reactionary forces, including tribal forces against workers, particularly in the oil industry. His interpretation of the events is as follows: 'Qavam, strongly impressed by the turn of events, was increasingly convinced by Iran's reactionary milieux that sought to use him to crush the popular movement and change the situation in their favour', thus absolving him from his own intentions. On the other hand — he adds — the American imperialists sought to reconcile the shah and Qavam in order to create a common front against the TPI.[183] It does not occur to him that Qavam, as a reactionary landlord, had every interest in crushing the democratic movement and did not need the advice of the British or American governments for the actions he took.

Thus, Qavam's coalition did not last very long, as he no longer needed the TPI. In addition, he came under pressure from the shah, the tribal leaders and the American Embassy to reshuffle his cabinet and throw out the Tudeh ministers, without informing them in advance. They read about their 'resignations' in the press![184] It was suggested at the time that, in fact, the tribal uprising against Qavam's coalition with the TPI had been instigated by Qavam himself, a point that cannot easily be dismissed, given his cunning and vile character.

In spite of all that Qavam did, particularly against the TPI, Eskandari defends the policies declared by Qavam as sincere intentions on his part to improve the lot of the underdog in Iran. The real reason for the defence by the Tudeh leader as an 'historian' of Qavam is to justify his party's short-lived coalition with him,[185] just as the TPI's Second Congress had done in 1948.

In 1950, Eskandari realises, quite belatedly, that Qavam's aim in creating the DPI was to crush the TPI's organisations:

> In fact, as of this period — before the coalition — collisions between Qavam and the democratic organisations became increasingly frequent. Arbitrary arrests of militants of the party and labour unions, pillaging of [their] offices, and armed attacks against democratic organisations repeatedly occurred. Qavam's 'Democrat' [Party] obviously took the place of [General] Arfa's and Seyyed Zia's reactionary organisations, however, with the difference that foreign support had changed hands [that is, the Americans had replaced the British].[186]

Yet Eskandari nonetheless justifies the coalition that the TPI entered into with

Qavam. In his *Histoire* he rationalises the coalition in the name of the 'still serious differences' existing between Qavam and the shah, on the one hand, and, on the other, the 'considerations of the imminent legislative elections', which, as we will see, were devastating for all progressive forces. He finally exculpates the coalition accord with Qavam, on the one hand, on the basis of the premier's wish to demonstrate his 'goodwill' towards the USSR, and, on the other, 'to defeat the intrigues by the [Royal] Court'.[187]

Given all this, one cannot but conclude that the Tudeh leadership was not a dupe, but was taking Soviet orders word for word, as Jamil Hasanli has demonstrated on the basis of Soviet archives. Instead of blaming his Soviet mentors and the party's 'obedience' to the Soviet party, Eskandari speaks of Qavam's 'volte-face',[188] as if Qavam had been sincere in his earlier protestations! As if the party had not known Qavam, Eskandari surprisingly accuses the prime minister of colluding with foreign imperialists instead of discussing matters of policy with his cabinet, and assuring London and Washington that his government would not take any damaging actions against the British oil company in Iran. Eskandari also speaks of an 'imperialist plot' to 'execute *en masse*' Tudeh and labour union leaders, against which Qavam did not put up any serious resistance.[189] As attacks upon the TPI and its various front organisations increased, Eskandari *claims*, the TPI Central Committee decided that their ministers would no longer participate in the Council of Ministers, after which Qavam submitted his resignation to the shah in order to form a new cabinet.[190] This is, of course, a face-saving statement. *In the light of all this, it is amazing to speak of Qavam's initial good intentions.*

While these attacks were being carried out, the TPI, still a partner in Qavam's cabinet, celebrated the fifth anniversary of its foundation on 2 October. It gave a luncheon party for foreign journalists and a reception attended by Premier Qavam, ministers, senior officers of the services, and the principal officials of various ministries. Two days later a mass 'orderly' demonstration of the TPI and its trade unions was held in the Baharestan Square in front of the parliament, in which its supporters took part. The party organ put out a special 10-page edition, of which it later claimed 120 000 copies had been sold[191] — an amazing figure for a party that claimed it had 10 000 members in the capital! Only a fortnight later the Tudeh ministers were dumped.

Aside from repressive actions to crush the TPI, the only other success of Qavam's party was his 'victory' in the elections of the Fifteenth Legislature, albeit temporary, held under anti-democratic conditions by way of manipulation and rigging that was legendary in Iran's constitutional history, so fraudulent that the TPI, despite its hopeful 'considerations' of 'imminent legislative elections', decided to boycott them. The Majles was packed with reactionary members of the DPI as 'deputies'. Even Dr Mosaddeq, the most popular statesman, who never had any problem getting elected in the capital when relatively free elections were held, was eliminated. In two letters, one public and the other private, that have now come to light, Mosaddeq had warned Qavam against his anti-constitutional electoral procedures which were to have long-lasting repercussions on the development of Iran's young democracy. The elections of the Fifteenth Legislature were yet another open political attack by Qavam and his reactionary allies upon the democratic forces. No candidate opposed to Qavam or the Royal Court was elected. Yet, not only was the oil agreement he had signed with the Soviet Ambassador rejected against his wishes by his hand-picked Majles, but the Court managed to have Qavam ejected by the very same deputies whom he had put on the Majles seats.[192] Soon thereafter, once the TPI had been seriously weakened and the Azerbaijan question 'settled', the DPI split and disintegrated.[193] The final results the TPI reaped in that period were, to a great extent, due to its policy of obedience to Moscow in forming a coalition with Qavam.

As for the Soviets and the TPI, a few quotations from various positions regarding their collaboration with Qavam may throw light on their disappointment with a miscalculated, time-serving policy.

The short *Pravda* article mentioned above, depicting Qavam as an 'independent' premier alongside the unbelievably rosy coalition programme that he presented to the shah when introducing his coalition cabinet — which, *inter alia*, promised 'execution of those persons embezzling and misappropriating public property and funds; prosecution of traitors; industrial and agricultural developments by means of national capital; providing work for the unemployed; protection of the complete independence and territorial integrity of Iran; and the prevention of foreigners from interfering in the internal affairs of Iran'[194] — could not but be described as a time-serving policy, which cost the TPI, particularly its membership, a great deal, including its very reputation, or whatever had remained of it.

Not surprisingly, then, after Qavam dropped the Tudeh leaders from the cabinet, without even informing them in advance, and taking repressive measures against their party, the prestigious Soviet publication *Literaturnaya Gazetta*[195] ran a severe article against Qavam, belatedly denouncing his younger days, at the time he had been in the service of the reactionary Minister Ayn al-Doleh, when a 'day on which no one had been executed was a wasted day for him'; his days as Minister of the Interior (December 1911–June 1912), when 'in company of the Russian hangman Colonel Liakhov, Qavam [had] drowned the Iranian revolution in blood';[196] his premiership in 1921-22, when he, just as when he returned to power in 1946, had been under the auspices of 'Anglo-American circles'; his land-grabbing practices; his collaboration with Nazi Germany; his collaboration with the Americans during the Second World War; and finally his 'ready-made plan' to serve the interests of the Anglo-American powers and the ruling élite of Iran. Yet Moscow, 'hospitable to friends of peace', had received him 'as the envoy of the Iranian people', chosen by a reactionary Majles! Then Qavam's 'ready-made plan', his 'promise' of an oil concession to the USSR and internal autonomy for Azerbaijan, his coalition government with the TPI, etc, are described as a 'mask', which was cast off when he no longer needed it. He suppressed Azerbaijan, packed the Majles with 'reactionary feudal' elements, used the services of 'American generals accustomed to lynching Negroes', such as General Schwarzkopf, whom he brought to Iran to train the Gendarmerie — who, by the way, later also became one of the pillars of the 1953 Anglo-American putsch.

All the charges against Qavam by *Literaturnaya Gazetta* were, of course, correct. However, one point had 'escaped' the attention of the Soviet journalist. Why did the Soviets help Qavam to become premier? Why did Stalin trust him and under whose pressure did he evacuate his forces from Iran? Were they hoping he would be strong enough to give them what they wanted? Although his 'murky past' had, admittedly, been known to the Soviets, they trusted his manoeuvrability that was sufficiently powerful, till it became clear that he had put his plan into effect under the pressure and with the help of Truman, the American Ambassador and their generals in Iran. The article also said 'Progressive opinion in Iran treated America's hireling with contempt and loathing… There is a feeling of revolt against him among the Iranian people.' The article expressed the Soviet's regret of a policy that cannot be considered as anything but time-serving: 'History knows no case of a corrupt flunkey being the saviour of his country. History is against Qavam, because the Iranian people are against him.' All this invective was, of course, to no avail. The damage had been done to the progressive forces in Iran and, more importantly, gone was the possibility of the development of a healthy Marxian school taking roots among a growing number of workers interested in organising themselves and an enthusiastic youth who were led astray by Soviet 'Marxism'.

XIV: The First Split in the Tudeh Party and the Second Congress

Discontent caused by repeated blunders by the Tudeh leadership ran deep amongst the party's cadres and members. The Azerbaijan crisis and the unfortunate coalition with Qavam — which Eskandari calls '*les prétendues erreurs*' — 'the so-called mistakes' — of the leadership[197] — brought the internal crisis to the fore and eventually led to a split.

Several days after the demise of the Autonomous Government of Azerbaijan, on 20 December 1946, a plenary session of the Tudeh leadership, an *ad hoc* council, was held, with the participation of members of the Central Committee, the Control Commission, and the Tehran Provincial Council Bureau. At the end of discussions about the 'so-called mistakes' committed by the Executive Committee and the Central Committee elected at the First Congress, a new leadership, called the Provisional Executive Committee (PEC), was chosen on 25 December 1946. The PEC excluded various former leaders, notably Eskandari, who was held responsible for the mistaken policies and the blunder of the coalition with Qavam, and took in 11 members, younger ones such as Maleki and Tabari, but also others such as Ahmad Qasemi, Gholam-Hussein Foroutan and Abdol-Hussein Noushin.[198] To be brief, the *ad hoc* plenary session also elected a new Central Committee for Tehran's Provincial Committee, in which Maleki's supporters had a majority — a majority that was disturbing to both the old guard and the pro-Soviet elements.

While the removal of the former Executive Committee members, notably Eskandari, was carried out in the name of the Qavam coalition fiasco, it cannot be excluded that the real reasons for this may have been a Soviet behind-the-scenes operation through Kambakhsh and his brother-in-law Kianouri, both widely known as Soviet 'agents'. These two were among the leading members of the so-called 'reformist group' which unseated the old guard, especially Eskandari, who had signed and delivered the Central Committee's letter of disapproval of the formation of the DPA. The principal mission of the PEC was to organise the party's Second Congress. One of the first decisions of the PEC was to dissolve the Tudeh Military Organisation (see Section II:II), apparently to avoid future adventures like that in Khorasan (although it was subsequently revived when the party was declared illegal in February 1949). In a declaration published on 15 Day 1325/5 January 1947, the PEC reaffirmed the TPI's commitment to the Constitution, the monarchy and a parliamentary path to a progressive democracy, as in the progressive states in the West.[199]

The party managed to reorganise itself and re-launch the publication of a new organ, *Mardom*, in lieu of *Rahbar*. The PEC, elected after the demise of the AGA, also published a manifesto in reply to the accusations of the reactionary forces. The question of Soviet influence or pressure in taking the erroneous decisions was obviously not raised; nor was any reference made to the letter to the Soviet party which Eskandari had prepared and which the Central Committee adopted. The election of the new leadership did not end the quarrels in the party; it only intensified them as personal rivalries also added fuel to the internal conflict. Although back on its feet within a year, the party could not recover all the support it had lost during the two years of deep crisis.[200]

Eskandari, instead of accepting the errors of the leadership during the crisis, as discussed at the *ad hoc* council referred to above, resorted to the Stalinist tactics of accusing the dissidents of not being 'alone', that is, of their being allied to hostile elements:

> ... for, in addition to the reactionary press, the different organs of government, which now pitied the fate of 'liberty' and the 'revolution', as if they were discredited in the eyes of the people by exaggerations and the 'errors of the Tudeh Party as well as those of the Democrats of Azerbaijan', have natural allies both inside and outside the party.

Some 'progressive intellectuals', while declaring to be in agreement with the TPI's fundamental principles — he writes — 'had remained outside the ranks of the party either by lack of courage or through conservatism, and sought to justify their political inaction by "paternalistic criticism" of the political line and tactics of the party'. Others were 'factionalists who had, after the party's First Congress, succeeded in developing, to some extent, their underground agitation among the intellectuals with the demagogic slogan of "reform" and "purging" of the party'.[201] Among the reformers he specifically names were Maleki and the young Assyro-Iranian Dr Es'haq Eprim, a former student of Arani and a graduate of the London School of Economics under the Marxist economist Joan Robinson, who, after his disappointment with the TPI left Iran, worked for the UN in collaboration with the radical economist Michael Kaleski, and ended up teaching economics at Oxford.[202]

Eprim's basic argument was that the TPI had been a party open to various social groups or classes. What was needed was to create a vanguard party of knowledgeable Marxists and a wide front in which progressive democrats could actively participate. The vanguard could lead the wide democratic front from within.[203]

Eskandari, himself coming from the Qajar aristocracy, accuses the critics of the party of being 'petty-bourgeois' who were 'incapable of analysing the situation calmly'.[204] His rancour against these 'factionalist' elements must be attributed to their success in removing the *troika* of the Executive Committee: that is, him, Alamouti and Bahrami. In a situation such as this, Eskandari speaks of the 'leniency' of the Central Committee because 'it did not take disciplinary measures against the reformists'. He derides the followers of the reformists as having witnessed 'their beautiful dreams of revolution' disappear through the party's setbacks.[205] The study of Eskandari's *Histoire*, especially in comparison with what he relates in his *Memoirs* some 35 years later, would reveal the Stalinist nature of the Tudeh leadership in its fabricating of 'facts' and 'truths'. He goes so far as accusing those who broke away from the party of being 'opportunists and careerists of every nature who abandoned the party, some of them going over to the camp of reaction, others in order to avoid the risk of persecution, imprisonment or unemployment as Tudeh members'.[206] The fact is that hardly anyone of the leading members of the opposition to the leadership joined the reaction or abandoned political struggle, although some of their activists did, just as some prominent Tudeh leaders, cadres and activists recanted and joined the Pahlavi regime, reaching even ministerial positions.[207]

Initially, those who split from the party belonged to the 'reformist' group, in which one could see not only Maleki, a member of the 'Group of Fifty-Three', a leader writer for the party organs and a member of the Control Commission, as well as his supporters, but also the most pro-Soviet elements, such figures as Kambakhsh, Kianouri and Tabari, the future 'theoretician' of the party — the latter figures being ignored by Eskandari in his 1950 writings, because they retreated from their dissident position. The latter's association with secessionists was later recalled as follows:

> After the Azerbaijan affair, Tabari told Maleki: 'Let us leave this infamous party, Tudeh, and leave it to the Rousta–Alamouti band!' Maleki told him: 'You are nuts; the Tudeh Party is a going concern, because it is known to the masses; we must remain and continue to be active in it.'[208]

This dialogue reveals the opportunistic attitude of both the one who preserved the name 'Tudeh' in the appellation of the new party, the Iran-Tudeh Socialist Party (ITSP); and the one who remained to the end in the old party and defended Soviet interests.

The split, which took place in February 1948, a little over a year after the fall of the AGA, had little to do with the Soviet domination of the TPI,[209] as one of Maleki's supporters relates. He states that after the declaration of the secession, the creation of the ITSP and the publication of its manifesto,[210] Maleki and some of his supporters listened to the Moscow Radio Persian Service, hoping that the creation of their new party would be approved by the Soviets. They were shocked to hear that they had been condemned as 'traitors' and 'enemies of socialism'.[211] According to one secessionist, Kashani, hardly anyone believed that the Soviets would not approve of their plan.[212] Only a few days after its foundation, the ITSP announced its dissolution, admitting that 'without the cooperation of the Tudeh Party, a left-wing movement is impossible'. The signatory was Maleki, who had come under attack from the Tudeh press as having engineered the split 'on behalf of British imperialism'.[213]

Al-e Ahmad, Maleki's closest collaborator, recalls: 'We did not have the courage to stand up to Stalinism.'[214] He admits they had created a 'party within the party' and when they heard the rumour that they were going to be expelled, hurriedly overnight wrote their manifesto, printed it, and distributed it early in the morning.[215] He writes that the dissidents' *'basic error was that we considered the Tudeh leaders as the fundamental sinners, not Stalin's policies'*. He adds that *they did not believe that 'Soviet Russia with all its greatness would support those who in our view had dishonoured the party'*.[216]

Indeed, at the beginning of the Azerbaijan crisis, Maleki, the editorialist of the party organ, when visiting Britain in the summer of 1945 along with a delegation of journalists from Iran, had defended the TPI against accusations of its following the Soviet line. In a conversation with Ernest Bevin, who had told him that 'We [in Britain] are not content to see elements working in the interests of foreign powers under the cloak of democracy', Maleki had replied:

> I deny completely that the Tudeh Party is working in the interests of foreign powers. The Tudeh Party's inclination towards Russia is actuated by international sympathy, sympathy which will be expressed towards all Labour governments established anywhere in the world. A government respecting Persian democracy will receive the friendship of the Tudeh Party.[217]

Either Maleki was naïve or he considered the Soviet party's influence within the TPI to be salutary.[218]

While Tabari, Kianouri, Noushin and Kambakhsh backed out just before the declaration of the split, some other dissidents who had left the party along with Maleki rejoined it after the hostile Soviet declarations. As a result of the atmosphere of intimidation, the number of dissidents dwindled and they were isolated, for the authority of the Soviet party was still widely prevalent.[219]

If close Soviet 'agents' such as Kambakhsh and Kianouri had merely collaborated with the reformists, with the aim of fanning the anti-Executive Committee sentiments in the party without wishing to split from it, they must have carried out a scheme initiated by their Soviet mentors to kill two birds with one stone; that is, on the one hand, to get rid of Eskandari and his close associates for their letter of protest to the CPSU and, on the other, to rid the party of reformists whose programmes and discontent with the party line did not fall within the orbit of the Soviet line.

The basic points of the ITSP's manifesto were:

1. Experience has shown during the last year that the achievement of any of the reforms supported by the majority of [Tudeh] Party members is impossible under the guidance of the present leaders.
2. The Provisional Executive Committee's decision concerning the party

congress shows clearly that the committee in question is afraid of facing the majority opinion within the party and that it intends to influence the structure of the congress in the course of time and under more suitable conditions. [That is, more suitable for defending its own narrow interests.]

3. The ITSP considers itself the continuator of the course originally adopted by the Tudeh Party of Iran and its more progressive aspects, and will follow the principles and aims originally laid down by that party; it will also refrain from committing the unnecessary and avoidable errors for which the Tudeh leaders are held responsible.
4. The ITSP takes the logic and philosophy of Scientific Socialism as its guide, in order to avoid all sorts of hesitation or tactical error. In the meantime, it should be noted that, according to the very principles of this Scientific Socialism, our programme cannot be similar to the Socialistic programmes of the progressive countries where social, economic and political conditions are more advanced than in our country. [Here it is not clear which countries were meant: Western or Soviet.]
5. *We will try to make Iran's progressive industrialists realise the fact that the extension of Iranian industries is in their own interests*, and can be achieved through the improvement of the workers' conditions and the struggle against imperialism.[220]

The first point of the secessionists' manifesto summed up their fundamental attitude towards the parent party: that its leaders were incapable of achieving the demands set out in the Tudeh programme.

Al-e Ahmad relates that their group did not last long and they had to abandon the project within two months for several reasons. Firstly, they had no party organ to publicise their views. Secondly, they did not express their views clearly. Thirdly, the whole weight of Soviet propaganda and Moscow Radio was behind the TPI. Fourthly, not having fully grasped the nature of Stalinism, they could not dare to stand up against it.[221] One could point to still another reason, that is, there was no charismatic or well-known leader among them, as had been the case with the foundation of the TPI in the person of the veteran Constitutionalist Solayman Mirza Eskandari or the recuperated 'heritage' of the 'martyr' Arani who had been identified with the Tudeh. Yet another, and perhaps the main reason is what Ahmad himself relates: they had expected Moscow to support them. This means they either had been Stalinists or had no notion of its actual nature. This is confirmed by the manner in which Eprim had left the party. He did not join any of the splinters, but gradually took his distance from the party and left for Britain. He could read Russian and had lived in the Stalinist state. He had a clear understanding of how Stalinism could destroy its critics.

What the secessionist reformers finally reaped was social excommunication, to the point that even their personal friends in the TPI labelled them 'traitors' with whom not even the slightest personal contact was permissible.[222] The Tudeh's Stalinist propaganda was so effective that the conservative British 'Iranologue' Peter Avery in his *Modern Iran*[223] considered that Maleki's socialist Third Force Party was a kind of a 'fascist' organisation.[224]

One of the individuals who broke along with Maleki from the TPI was Anvar Khameh'i, a youthful student and a member of Arani's 'Group of Fifty-Three' in the mid-1930s, when he had been arrested, undergone interrogation and shown weakness thereunder, and had been condemned in 1938 and released in 1941. Unlike many of the group, he had not joined the TPI formally till its First Congress, but had worked as a journalist for its organ. He had sympathised, however, with Ovanesian's 'communist faction'. Sometime after the split from the TPI, he also broke with Maleki's group and founded, apparently with a few other people, a group called *Jam'iyat-e raha'i-ye kar va andisheh* (Society for the Liberation of Labour and Thought), with no apparent effect on the leftist political scene. His Marxist-Leninist organisation published *Hajjar (The Stonecutter)*, which defended the Soviet Union under Stalin and the latter's 'brilliant' thesis on the 'national bourgeoisie' in the colonised countries.[225] He believed that 'the comprehensiveness of the views and the information of the world [Communist] movement leadership are undeniable'; yet he also thought this was no reason for 'blind obedience, for the axis of Marxism-Leninism is conscious discipline'.[226]

Stalin's theory of the national bourgeoisie was a classic example of doubletalk: whether a nationalist movement or nationalist regime was progressive and thus worthy of support was predicated upon its specific relationship with the Soviet Union. The independence towards Moscow shown by Mosaddeq and the national-democratic movement in Iran resulted in their being branded as irredeemably reactionary. In line with Stalin, Khameh'i stated that:

> In truth, even the national bourgeoisie [that is, Mosaddeq and his Patriotic Front], which according to the leaders of Marxism-Leninism must be taken into the anti-imperialist front, has often, in practice, shown itself not to be irreconcilably opposed to imperialism, and does not wish to side with socialism in the world struggle against imperialism.[227]

Continuing to follow at length the TPI's hysterical opposition to the nationaldemocratic movement fighting against British imperialism, he reiterates Stalin's line according to which 'during the general crisis of capitalism, the liberal national bourgeoisie in the dependent colonised countries compromises [with imperialism], and, therefore no value can be attributed to its anti-imperialist struggle'.[228] Quoting Stalin on the Kuomintang, he compares the Chinese nationalist movement with Mosaddeq's Patriotic Front;[229] ignoring the fact that, while the former had hunted down and crushed members of the Chinese Communist Party, Mosaddeq restored practically full liberties to the outlawed TPI. Scornfully stating that the Mosaddeq government and the Patriotic Front's policies 'in general, have demonstrated what is expected of the anti-imperialist national bourgeoisie',[230] he adds: 'The view of our organisation is that the Mosaddeq government does not have a strong position against imperialism, but shows a circumspective attitude towards the US and the ruling class.'[231]

Be that as it may, Khameh'i was not arrested after the 1953 coup, while prisons were being filled with all sorts of anti-imperialist militants. What is more, he was soon given a position on the Iran Radio to broadcast a programme on Persian literature for the youth.[232] Not surprisingly, considering his disruptive actions in left-wing organisations and his relentless attacks upon Mosaddeq and the national-democratic movement, and his subsequent career, suspicions have been raised about his true motives.

It is thus worth mentioning the testimony of a witness about him. According to Shirin Sami'i, the ex-wife of Mosaddeq's grandson, in the summer of 1955 she had seen Khameh'i visiting the house of her mother and her husband (Colonel Ghaffouri, Shirin's step-father). Once, the Colonel, who was a deputy of the Military Governor of Tehran General Bakhtiar, explained to her that their visitor 'A Khameh'i was collaborating with them [that is, the Office of the Military Governor and the Second Bureau of the army] in the suppression of the Tudeh. He also much praised Kahmeh'i for his collaboration [against the Tudeh].' Shocked by this collaboration, after dinner Shirin, who was no sympathiser of the Tudeh but of Mosaddeq, asked Khameh'i 'why he, with his background, was collaborating with the Second Bureau of the army'. He gave her 'much advice, stating that I was young, inexperienced, and should not be fooled by Tudeh members, for they were such and such'. She recalls having heard years later from Fereydoun Manou, a young lawyer arrested along with Arani's students in 1937, that he had been arrested because Khameh'i had informed the police that he had been, like him, reading Marx's *Capital* in the Majles Library. Manou had had no connection with Arani, but spent over four years in prison because of Khameh'i's service to the police — a service to which Arani referred in his tribunal speech.[233]

The split in the TPI provided the Stalinists in the party with a golden opportunity to attack the dissidents incessantly and to label them as enemies of the democratic movement in Iran, in the hope of galvanising the disgruntled members who were unhappy with past policies.[234] If Eskandari stops short of calling Maleki and his colleagues 'imperialist agents', and Kambakhsh, known for his close relations with the Soviet party and even the NKVD/KGB, in his 'history' of the Iranian Communist movement,[235] briefly mentions the 1948 split, calling Maleki and his colleagues by the softer labels taken from the Stalinist arsenal for suppressing the opposition — not 'agents of imperialism', but 'opportunists, defeatists and revisionists' — Bozorg Alavi, the party novelist, in his book written in the DDR seven years after the split and in the aftermath of the 1953 putsch, does not spare them. Alavi speaks of the former editorialist of party organs as:

> A teacher, a certain Maleki, who later revealed himself to be a *completely clever agent of the imperialists*, took a hostile position towards the Central Committee and used his partly correct criticism of organisational shortcomings as a pretext to create suspicion about Central Committee members in order to break the unity of the party.

He refers to Maleki's criticism as statements used 'in the reactionary attempts' — '*Versuche der Reaktion*' — to propagate anti-party propaganda.[236] Interestingly, another former reformist, who did not split with Maleki and who turned Maoist in 1964 in his DDR exile, called him all possible names except an 'imperialist agent'.[237] On the other hand, the American and British Embassies showed interest in the split, hoping that it would reduce the influence of the Soviet government in Iran's labour movement.[238] (We shall deal with Maleki's social-democratic endeavours in a subsequent issue of this journal.)

Interestingly, the tone of the declaration of the PEC[239] to the party's Second Congress on the split was much less aggressive than what we read in Eskandari's *Histoire*. The difference may be explained by Eskandari's personal animosity towards Maleki, who was a leading opponent of the *troika* — and in particular of Eskandari — which organ was elected as the Executive Committee by the First Congress. The Second Congress, however, made harsh attacks upon Maleki and Eprim and their comrades, and the congress resolution condemned the split as a 'prepared conspiracy' by a 'secret faction' related to the imperialists, and as 'treason' with the aim of 'destroying' the party from within.[240]

In fact, the reformists were not a coherent group. On the one hand, there were those who remained faithful to the Soviet line, such as Kambakhsh and his brother-in-law Kianouri. On the other, there was Maleki who turned social-democrat and during the oil nationalisation campaign supported the patriotic leader Mosaddeq and his government. There were still other individuals, such as Khameh'i, who remained an admirer of Stalin and behaved as such.

XV: The Second Party Congress

After the split, with the 'quiet' that now reigned in the TPI, the Tudeh leaders managed to 'cover up the errors', reorganise the party, and re-launch the publication of its organs. Back on its feet within a year, the party found the atmosphere in which to hold the Second Congress 'favourable';[241] yet it could not recover all the support it had lost during the Azerbaijan crisis.[242] Because one of the main reasons for the split was the PEC's intentional postponement of the Second Congress, the split, in turn, facilitated its organisation and its quiet progress.

The Second Congress, held in May 1948, nearly four years after the first one, was meant to lend a legitimate respectability to the party reorganisation after the crisis and the split. As opposed to the widely publicised debates of the First Congress, not much was published about what really went on within this congress. No part of its proceedings was widely published even during the TPI's long exile in Eastern Europe, although after the revolution of 1979 Kianouri published a number of its resolutions.[243] Even those party leaders who have written their memoirs have hardly talked about this congress. In one of the few articles about the congress, written by Tabari in 1948,[244] it is discreetly said that it took place under 'difficult conditions of social struggle'. He notes that that, given the 'sensitive and effective role of our party in Iranian history', and taking into account 'this truth that our party is the best organised democratic organisation in the country, and is the only organisation that struggles for the attainment of the welfare of the masses of our nation and the rescue of the country, one can easily understand that the second party congress is an important historical event worth of attention'. Referring to the imperialists' 'general assault', he repeats this self-congratulatory remark throughout the short article. For him, the PEC had planned the work of the congress in a precise manner so that it was, under the leadership of its presidium, brought to a successful conclusion. He does not make clear what this success actually was. He calls the congress a 'success', because it managed to carry out its 'duties', which are not specified. He admits that the PEC would have preferred to have held the congress under calm conditions, *without making any propaganda about it*. Speaking of the new 'unity' of the party, Tabari attacks the reactionaries and his former reformist colleagues who had broken from the party, stating that their hopes had been dashed. He proclaims that the delegates to the congress manifested a great deal of 'social consciousness, a sense of responsibility'.

As for what the congress achieved, Tabari notes that a new party constitution was approved, reinforcing 'democratic centralism', a better division of duties and a better sense of responsibility. The congress adopted political resolutions and judged the policies of the party without hypocrisy. In his view, the 'political document' of the congress is a 'precious document, which proves the growth, faith and the personality of the congress'. Other resolutions regarding organisational principles, education of party members, propaganda, finances, workers, peasants, youth, women, each had 'precise points, useful recommendations and appropriate criticism'. This discourse, of course, does not tell the reader anything about the content of what the congress actually decided upon.

The specific information published about the resolutions of the congress was that the split in the party had been condemned by a resolution 'which was approved in the midst of exciting applause' — as it had also condemned 'Krouzhokism'.[245] The congress struck a 'death blow' at the reformers who had taken the path of 'treachery'. Yet Tabari states that some of those who had broken with the party could return, if they were ready to 'confess' to, and make up for, their 'mistakes' and show their 'sincerity' to the party — the kind of lessons learnt from the Soviet party, as in the case of Bukharin, for example!

Kambakhsh also discusses the Second Congress and relates that, in addition to other reports, there was a 'special' one regarding the split in the party. The congress passed a resolution on the split, declaring it 'treason'.[246] According to Kambakhsh, an important point was that the government coalition with Qavam was 'on the whole correct', was intended to 'spread the influence of the Tudeh Party and reaped useful results', and took place 'far from opportunism' and without 'compromising' any principles. Any position to the contrary would have demonstrated opposition to the Soviet line, to which the TPI had committed itself to obey. However, Kambakhsh forgets to recall that he had, in fact, told the Soviet Azerbaijani leadership that the Central Committee had been opposed to such a coalition and had only done so under pressure from the Soviet party![247] Nevertheless, the congress concluded that in participating in the coalition government the leadership 'showed too much confidence in Qavam' and did not possess the 'necessary caution' and did not prepare itself for the coming crisis.

The congress also elected 19 members to the new Central Committee, some of them *in absentia* and who were well-known for their close ties with the Soviet apparatus — as they had already escaped to the USSR — and 15 alternates with consultative votes; the two groups would together constitute the plenum of the party, which was to meet every three months. This body met only twice between 1948 and 1957. For the first time in the history of Iranian Left, the TPI elected, on the Stalinist model, a Secretary-General: Dr Reza Radmanesh, one of the weakest characters among the Tudeh leaders, and who thus proved most obedient to Soviet wishes. In his aforementioned article, Tabari expresses the view that the election of the 'new leadership', not only proved the unity of the party, but was also 'effective in the suppression of the deviationists' — remember Stalin's Russia in the 1930s! It should be recalled that the very vicious attacks on the splinter group, much in the same manner as had been done with all dissidents after the first split in the Russian Social Democratic Workers Party, had begun months before the congress.[248]

Interestingly, the resolutions adopted by the Second Congress,[249] in brief, were:

* Firstly, it justified its 'agreement' with Qavam when he 'pretended to support the wishes of the people and took action in this direction', just as it followed a correct line opposing Qavam when he, 'following American imperialism and discarding his previous path, strove to violate the legitimate rights of people; each policy was sound in its time'.
* Regarding the origins of the DPA–AGA episode, the congress, once again, expressed its approval of its own policy of defending the 'popular movement of Azerbaijan', 'based on the power of the workers, peasants and artisans', aiming at the 'liberation of the toilers'. It rejected the 'accusations of secessionism' against the DPA, whose demands were 'in harmony with the spirit of the Constitution'.

As party records show, up until the Second Congress the TPI had zigzagged between its desire to be a working-class party of the Leninist type and a popular front, attending even to the eulogy of Shiite saints. A brief look at its programme and declarations makes this point very clear. The lip-service the TPI paid to Islam did not begin with the statement during the 1979 revolution that its founder SM Eskandari had gone on the Hajj trip to Mecca along with Ayatollah Khomeini — who at the time of the visit was, of course, neither an ayatollah nor a political personality. The Tudeh's reference to Islam is as old as its foundation. For instance, as early as the 1940s the TPI had spoken highly of the first Shiite Imam Ali.[250] In addition, party newspapers stressed that either they would not be published on the anniversaries of Shiite saints, or, by way of paying their respect, they would publish some statement for the occasion. Withal, as the Second World War was drawing to a close, the Qazvin Provincial Committee published a statement in which it severely attacked the former pro-British putschist Premier Zia for having accused Tudeh members of being 'lax in their religious beliefs' and 'in politics obedient to the northern neighbour', that is, the Soviet Union. Under the NKVD agent Kambakhsh, the committee denied the accusations, declaring the TPI to be 'the only freedom-loving' party that strove for the independence of the country, was not obedient to foreigners, and considered *'religion a God-sent responsibility which we respect dearly'*.[251]

As for class struggle, in a statement by the editorial board of the party organ *Rahbar*, while the TPI was still in the coalition government, it was said that one of its characteristics 'is persistence and courage in the class struggle',[252] while in another statement by the Central Committee we read that 'the Tudeh Party of Iran does not provoke the intensification of class differences'.[253] This is why reformists such as Eprim wished to distinguish between 'class demands' and 'democratic demands' of the party and to wage a struggle for them in two separate, but interrelated, organisations.

There are other aspects of time-serving policies which distanced the party from being a genuine workers' party with Marxian thoughts and methods. In one of its newspaper articles, the TPI had not only used religious arguments to advance its programme, but also paid lip-service to non-proletarian strata of society:

> Religion prohibits hoarding, theft, embezzlement and oppression; religion forbids that, while the vast majority of people die of hunger, a few know not what to do with their wealth, and the Tudeh Party of Iran, too, says the same, and struggles and fights against such injustices.
>
> The Tudeh Party, without wishing to take anything away from anyone, believes that through increasing public wealth and strengthening the financial power of the country the conditions of the incarcerated classes of workers and peasants will improve and everyone's welfare as well as public comfort will be assured; through the initiative of the Tudeh Party, the hand of the hoarder will be removed; that initiative will not degrade the conditions of artisans and honest, just merchants, but will protect them against the plunder of fraudulent agents, judicial anarchy, and economic disorder...
>
> The reactionaries have been frightened by the progress of the Tudeh Party and strive to organise the people of the bazaar [merchants and artisans] against our party. In order to succeed, they depict as the enemy of wealth as well as public security and welfare the very party which they formerly named the 'party of the capitalists'...
>
> In sum, the economic policy of the Tudeh Party is to remove the great divide of living standards through useful legislation and to strengthen national wealth. *This party is neither against commerce and merchants, nor the foe of capitalists. This is the plain and undisguised economic policy of the Tudeh Party of Iran...*[254]

After its Second Congress, when the TPI took a turn to the left, the careful attitude of the party towards security was not lost on governmental circles or the British Embassy in Tehran. In a report on the Second Congress, the British Oriental Secretary Lancelot Pyman noted that the situation regarding the TPI was a 'disturbing one', for it was said, after the Second Congress, to control 35 per cent[255] of the industrial population of the country. Although this was a:

> ... small proportion of the whole population (say a couple of hundred thousand in a population of 12 000 000 or 15 000 000)..., control of the industrial population would bring rewards out of all proportion to the numbers involved. Altogether, apart from the effect of Tudeh control over the labour of the Anglo-Iranian Oil Company (60 000), the Tudeh Party could seriously embarrass the central government through control of, for example, the railway workers and printers.

What was more, if it 'can control the printers, Tudeh would have the usual Communist hold over the rest of the press'. In the embassy's opinion: 'Perhaps the most disturbing feature... [is] that, so far as Persian workers and peasants are aware of any remedy for their needs, they look to the Soviet-controlled Tudeh movement for it.'[256] In this connection, the British Ambassador Sir John Le Rougetel asked whether there was 'nothing that we and the Americans can do to stimulate the formation of a Progressive Party not under Soviet control in order to fill this alarming vacuum'.[257] Pyman's exaggerated figures were given in order to provide an excuse for restrictive action against the TPI. On the other hand, any such suggestions from the British and US Embassies for reforms that would help the Iranian government to undermine the TPI came to nothing as these powers could not tolerate the programme of any progressive party, as this would inevitably come into conflict with their own interests and those of their client-élite in power in Iran.

Another unwritten result of the Second Congress was the strengthening of the position of elements directly linked to the Soviet Union, that is, the Kambakhsh–Kianouri faction. Central Committee member Hussein Jowdat writes that this faction, who had been elected to the Central Committee *in absentia*, had 'marched one big step forward', adding: 'While the congress was still in progress, you could see the cards that Kambakhsh's supporters were trying to hide up their sleeves.' Jowdat explains:

> While the name of Kianouri's wife Maryam Firouz was not among the candidates for the Central Committee, once the votes were read, she was elected an alternate member of the Central Committee. Of course, this would not have been possible but by factional fraud.

He underlines the role of this factionalism in the subsequent Fourth Plenum, which led to the faction's majority in the new Executive Committee.[258]

Three months after the congress, the Third Plenum of the party leadership was held, to which the new Secretary-General Radmanesh presented his report.[259] After a long section on the international situation along the lines presented by the Stalinist parties in the late 1940s, especially about the peaceful intentions of the USSR as opposed to Western aggressive imperialist designs, the report dealt with the internal situation in Iran.

It notes that the new government under Premier Hazhir, a marionette of the shah's sister Ashraf Pahlavi, was intent on serving both the British and American imperialists. The Third Plenum attacked the shah, especially for his trip to Britain — where he was given the special honour of being hosted at Buckingham Palace — for having discussed Anglo-Iranian relations with Labour Ministers Herbert Morrison and Ernest Bevin, without, however, giving the Iranian people any notion of the substance of the talks. The report accuses the new government of building new airfields in northern Iran, alluding to the preparation of the terrain for attacks on the USSR. It refers to the restrictions imposed on press freedom; British attempts to obtain better terms by revising the 1933 oil agreement; the dwindling share of Iran in the proceeds of the sale of oil by the AIOC; continued martial law in the oil-producing region in southern Iran in order to prevent workers' strikes for higher wages and better working conditions; and the dismissal and/or arrest of AIOC workers. It concludes that the Iranian government, as the instrument of imperialism, was unable to compel the AIOC to restore the rights it had withdrawn from its workers. Thus, this government wished to prevent Iranian workers, peasants, artisans, students and intellectuals from participating in the political affairs of the country.

Radmanesh reports that in the mid-summer of 1948 the TPI's Central Committee had handed its 12-point 'views on reforms' to the prime minister. The two Tudeh representatives had discussed in detail these points with Premier Hazhir, reminding him that the TPI, with full knowledge of the nature of Hazhir's government, had formulated and handed to him those 12 points on reform, in order both to inform public opinion of its views on necessary reforms in the country and to expose the reactionary nature of his government. The report concludes with the oft-repeated Tudeh claim that it was 'the only patriotic, nationally-organised party that could realise the wishes of the majority of the Iranian nation'.

It was certainly also a tactic to tell the public that the regime's propaganda about the TPI being a revolutionary party was false,[260] as in less than a year, after its proscription, it declared itself to be a 'Marxist-Leninist' party.

Given the conditions under which the Second Congress had been held and the leadership's careful conduct of party affairs thereafter, it seems that at that moment the TPI might have been aware that a plot was being prepared against it, without knowing its precise form. At the time that Radmanesh's report was being published, the Royal Court was preparing a plan designed both to outlaw the TPI and to drive out all other opponents and critics of Mohammad Reza Shah who were deemed obstacles to his intention of restoring the dismantled military dictatorship over which his father had presided, a restoration that was to see him become the new dictator.

2: Second Period: The Proscription of the Tudeh Party

I: The Royal Plot Against the Tudeh Party

In the autumn of 1948 two members of the reactionary ruling élite visited the American and British Embassies and also met officials at the State Department in Washington with a plan to outlaw the TPI in order to prepare the terrain for a 'constitutional reform' that was intended to grant the shah rights which he, as a ceremonial monarch and symbolic head of state, had not thus far enjoyed. It appears from the documents that, at least, the American diplomats consulted did not agree with the plan, and recommended serious reforms in order to undermine the influence of the TPI and the Soviet Union in Iran.[261] The plan, as presented to Western diplomats, was to have the parliament — the very same one that was elected under Premier Qavam — adopt a law proscribing the TPI.

In spite of the advice from Western diplomats, the plan that had been worked out by the new government under Premier Sa'ed was put into effect on 4 February 1949.

Every year on the anniversary of the founding of Tehran University, faculty members attended a ceremony on campus in the presence of the shah. Usually, the shah would alight from his automobile in front of faculty members who were lined up to be received. Journalists would also be present. On 4 February 1949, however, a man presenting himself as a journalist was allowed to approach the shah's automobile — and only this journalist, as faculty members were standing at some distance for the commencement of the ceremony. Nobody had ever approached the shah in this way in previous years. He was said to have fired a few shots at the shah as he alighted from his automobile. The shah was declared injured and taken immediately to the military hospital where he was said to have been treated by his private physicians. The 'assailant', Fakhr-Ara'i, who according to reports by the US Embassy in Tehran had been an employee of the Second Bureau of the army,[262] was shot on the spot, although he had, after 'firing the shot', immediately thrown down his gun and raised his arms in the air. When he noticed that he was being shot at on the spot, he cried out: 'But this was not part of the agreement.' The shah, although said to have been hit that afternoon by several bullets — reportedly one in the cheek whence the bullet had passed through his mouth and hit his upper jaw — gave a speech at seven in the evening on the national radio, without any change in his voice or any difficulty in diction, assuring the nation that his life had been saved by Allah's hand — a surprising fact insofar as it is impossible for someone hit in the mouth to be able to utter a normal speech. Research carried out by this author demonstrates that the whole affair had been stage-managed by the shah, his Court, the army and politicians very close to him.[263]

Having read the documents in the British and American archives, there is little doubt in this author's mind that this was a *coup d'état* by the shah and his Court in order to re-establish his father's military dictatorship. Upon examining the French archives, any remaining doubts dissipated. On the eve of 3 February 1948, at a banquet held at the shah's palace, the monarch's Swiss childhood friend Ernest Peron told the French military attaché about '*Le Projet de Coup d'État du Chahinchah*':

> On 3 February in the course of an intimate banquet at the Palace, the private adviser of the Shahanshah [Ernest Peron][264] confided to me the imminence of an important decision the sovereign wanted to take. In the light of parliamentary disorder and of corruption of the entire administrative system, which neutralises all social reforms and increasingly adds to the misery of the working classes, the Shahanshah has decided to put an end to it all. The Constitution does not give him any right to intervene in the parliament or even in political affairs. His father Reza Shah Pahlavi, an absolute dictator, did not consider it necessary to abolish the Constitution, which he trampled underfoot during his reign. The Shahanshah has thus the intention of amending the Constitution to grant himself the right to dismiss the parliament and to nominate the Prime Minister and his cabinet.[265]

Immediately after the 'assassination attempt', army and police units tracked down and arrested a good number of Tudeh leaders and upper cadres. The TPI's headquarters were attacked and documents were seized. Some Tudeh leaders managed to go underground and eventually escaped to the USSR. Some political non-Tudeh opponents of the shah were also arrested, including the pro-British former premier Seyyed Zia; the Machiavellian former premier Qavam al-Saltaneh, known for his past relations with all foreign embassies, including those of the UK, US, USSR and Nazi Germany; as well as Ayatollah Abul-Qasem Kashani, an opponent of the British, but a close friend of the Court and the former shah, for whom he had cast a 'yes' vote to mount the Peacock Throne in 1925. Dr Mosaddeq had already been confined, since the elections for the Fifteenth Legislature, to his private estate at some 115 kilometres from Tehran.

While Zia was released upon pressure by the UK Embassy, Qavam was exiled to France, and Kashani was sent into internal exile and finally to Lebanon. The next day the government promptly introduced a bill to the parliament and had it approved instantly to outlaw the TPI. The excuse for this attack and arrests was that there had been found on the dead assailant two press cards, an outdated one 'issued' to him by a Tudeh newspaper and another by a journal run by a mullah known for his close ties with the Court. Another 'proof' was subsequently said to have been the TPI's direct involvement through a Tudeh cadre who had been a childhood friend of the assailant Fakhr-Ara'i.

It was asserted that Fakhr-Ara'i's childhood friend, a man named Aragani, a member of the TPI and close to Kianouri, had been consulted by Fakhr-Ara'i. Aragani had, in turn, informed Kianouri about Fakhr-Ara'i's assassination plan.[266] The latter had presumably received the 'consent' of the Central Committee. In fact, it is reported that Kianouri had proposed to hold the annual anniversary of the death of Dr Arani on 4 February, instead of the 5th, so that it would coincide with the attempt by Fakhr-Ara'i. This fact came to light years later in exile when two Tudeh leaders arrested and imprisoned in 1949, having escaped from prison, reported to the party's Fourth Plenum that Aragani had told them in prison that he had received the consent of the leadership through Kianouri. This revelation led to the belief among many, including some Tudeh leaders, that Kianouri had conspired to have the party outlawed and its leaders arrested *en masse* at the cemetery.[267] Of course, in such matters there can never be proof either way. What matters is that Kianouri later admitted to have been in contact with Aragani, who, in turn, had been in touch with the 'assailant' regarding his 'personal' plan to kill the shah.

At a press conference held in 1949 in his Paris exile, Eskandari called the incident a '*coup d'état*'. Three weeks after the coup, Eskandari published a manifesto in Paris in the name of the TPI Central Committee, protesting against the dissolution of the party, and denouncing the repressive measures by the Tehran government. Recalling the Tudeh's fundamental principles that energetically rejected terrorism, the manifesto condemned the campaign of repression launched by the Iranian authorities in the wake of the 'attempt'. During the press conference, Eskandari stated that it was possible for him to prove that the 'attempt had been completely fabricated as a pretext for the dissolution of all democratic organisations of Iran'. He noted that the assailant had been killed on the spot, although he had thrown away his gun and raised his hands to give himself up. Eskandari attributed the plot to the actions of the government and Anglo-American oil interests.[268]

At any rate, the repercussions of the 'attempt on the life of the shah' for the TPI and the country were enormous. After having arrested a number of party leaders and cadres and condemned them to various prison terms running up to 10 years of solitary confinement,[269] the shah organised a rigged constituent assembly and, according to plans previously explained to the American, British and French Embassies, amended the Constitution so that he would have rights beyond those accorded to a constitutional monarch, notably the ability to dissolve the parliament, and to create a senate, half of whose members he would personally appoint.

The proscription of the TPI, on the other hand, drove the party underground, weakened it with the escape abroad of the most prominent leaders, frightened many members, and more importantly led to the ascendancy of the more 'radical' and pro-Soviet leaders — such as members of the faction run by the Soviet agent Kambakhsh, who, as we have seen, in 1937 had betrayed Dr Arani and his colleagues to the police, and his brother-in-law Kianouri, also known to have begun working for the Soviet secret service after Kambakhsh's departure for the USSR. The organisation became increasingly Stalinist, more prone to take orders, and less open to internal criticism. Leaders could thus silence any criticism in the name of the dangers that would ensue from the state's repressive apparatus.

The established role of Kianouri in the 'assassination affair' is the first of three historical moments when the party's fate was sealed by paralysis brought about though his direct intervention.

II: The Tudeh Military Organisation and the Reorganisation of the Party

We know very little about the military organisation created by the ICP. It is clear that its Second Congress in 1927 resolved to recruit members from among army officers and staff. Documents in the Comintern archives demonstrate that reports from the internal workings of the royal army reached the ECCI. On the other hand, in the early 1930s two officers of Iran's air force — the branch of the armed forces that had been organised by the Soviets — were, as mentioned above, arrested, tried and condemned to long prison terms for espionage on behalf of the USSR. Kambakhsh had also been arrested about the same time on the same charge, but released after a little less than a year, apparently absolved of the charge of espionage. He, who had, in the late 1920s, been sent on a scholarship to the USSR for aviation training, claims that the prosecutor found nothing to prove him of any wrongdoing.

It is also claimed that some of the officers who first joined the Tudeh Military Organisation (TMO) in the air force branch had also been recruited by the

ICP,[270] but one cannot be sure of such claims. Some like Major Eskandani, who headed the military uprising in the summer of 1945 in Khorasan, must have been influenced by his family background — particularly his father who had been a Constitutionalist and later an ICP leader.

We know that at least two army officers were recruited by Kambakhsh to join the 'revived ICP' under him, both of whom were among the founders of the TMO — Mohammad-Ali Mobasheri and Ezat-Allah Siamak.[271] In addition to them, another key man in this organisation, who joined the new pro-communist organisation of army officers, was Captain Khosrow Rouzbeh, famed for his talent as a mathematician and as a teacher of chess.

He and many others like him had come from extreme nationalist background, some even with Nazi tendencies in the past — tendencies that must have prevented them from acquiring truly democratic values and made them prone to being completely subservient to party orders. Few had come from a left-wing background. The reason for their adherence to the TMO must be sought, on the one hand, in their opposition to the colonial status of the country, and on the other, in the victories of the Soviet army after the battle of Stalingrad, as was the case for the rush to membership of the civilian members in 1943. Rouzbeh was certainly not of this latter category, and, with his military background, he considered himself to be above the Tudeh leadership.[272]

By 1944, the TMO had become so strong that the army intelligence was disturbed by the prospects of Soviet penetration into Iran. The reason for this disquiet can be attributed to the fact that those in charge of the TMO were rather careless in their mode of open operation and meeting in public cafés, etc[273] — a fact that has led to the suggestion that the regime had infiltrated it. What is more, during the presence of Tudeh deputies in the Fourteenth Legislature, deputy Kambakhsh — who had been taken into the party, under Soviet pressure and in spite of the Tudeh leaders' reticence,[274] and 'elected' from the Qazvin constituency in the Russian zone of occupation — in his speeches in the Majles occasionally revealed army secret reports about political and other types of abuse, thus revealing the existence of pro-Tudeh officers in the army. It is not clear why an old Communist with ties with the Soviet secret service should have behaved in such a slack manner, putting in danger the party and officers who had, because of their patriotic and progressive tendencies, joined the party and the TMO. One wonders whether here, too, he had the same motive as he had in the case of Dr Arani in 1937.

As alluded to above, on the evening of 24 Mordad 1324/15 August 1945, a group of Tudeh officers in the Eighth Army Division stationed in the province of Khorasan staged an uprising and issued a declaration according to which they had risen to begin the revolution. They had intended to create a *revolutionary bastion* in Gorgan, in northern Iran, where the Turkmen tribes lived, taking the path, they believed, of Mao and Tito. There are many contradictory reports about who in the Tudeh leadership had been informed in advance of this uprising, or whether in fact the TPI Central Committee had approved of this serious act of defiance of the central government. There are those, such as Eskandari, who state that Kambakhsh had planned it, and blame him for it.[275] Clearly, Kambakhsh would not have taken such an initiative without the approval of some Soviet authority, especially on the eve of the plan for the creation of the Autonomous Government of Azerbaijan. On the other hand, some surviving participants of the uprising do not believe this claim, and state that Kambakhsh had been opposed to it or did not know anything about it. Khosropanah, who has authored the only history of the TMO, concludes that Kambakhsh did not play any role in this affair and had been against it, especially because Soviet forces in the adjacent province of Gorgan did not help the insurgents when they were on the run, and because such an insurgency would have interfered with the AGA project. On the basis of a reported statement by Major Eskandani, who is portrayed as someone who had wished to risk an uprising in order to force the hand of the party leadership into adopting a revolutionary orientation, Khosropanah holds that Eskandani was the brains-trust of the uprising, not Kambakhsh and his Soviet mentors. It is probable that Eskandani, especially given his family background — his father having been a veteran Social Democrat and later one of the ICP leaders who had sent the aforementioned letter of protest to Lenin during the massacre of revolutionaries in northern Iran after the demise of the Soviet Socialist Republic of Iran with the complicity of Soviet Russia[276] — did not believe in the non-violent, parliamentary road to socialism in Iran. In addition, Eskandani and his close colleague, Colonel Azar, who together had received their military education in France and were acquainted with revolutionary literature, are on record as having argued along Mao's line to the effect that power comes from the barrel of a gun.[277] Yet the report by the STASI mole referred to above refutes such arguments and points to Kambakhsh's exploitation of the revolutionary fever of Colonel Azar and Major Eskandani, and Khosropanah's arguments are based on speculation rather than facts.

The timing of the uprising, coinciding with the creation of the DPA and the Soviet plan to create autonomous governments in occupied northern Iran, does, in fact, tell us more than Khosropanah knew when he wrote his study. As noted above, the creation of autonomous governments in northern Iran and Kambakhsh's involvement with that plan confirms the repeated statements by Eskandari, who insists on Kambakhsh's involvement in that adventure, taking advantage of the proclivities of restless, revolutionary officers who had joined the party.

Be that as it may, the uprising failed miserably for it was quickly nipped in the bud, provoking a serious problem for the party that had been peddling the parliamentary road to a constitutional order. The surviving insurgents fled to Soviet Turkmenistan, whence they were taken to Baku and then to Tabriz to serve in the newly-created AGA army.

The uprising intensified the existing crisis within the TPI for two reasons. Firstly, it provoked discontent among those in the party who felt unhappy about the leadership's 'inaction' in the face of the suppression of the insurgency. Secondly, the moderate members thought that such adventurism damaged the standing of the party in the eyes of the larger sympathising public.

Despite the repression of the TPI after the 'attempt on the shah's life', the TMO grew considerably during the national-democratic movement for the nationalisation of Iranian oil and the democratic conditions prevailing under Premier Mosaddeq. By the 1953 *coup d'état*, the TMO had recruited over 600 officers in all branches of the armed forces, as well as in the Gendarmerie and the National Police. What is more, some of the important officers in the Royal Guards, including the aide-de-camp and bodyguards of the shah and other high-ranking military leaders, including some in the army's Second Bureau, had become faithful members of the TMO. Given the TMO's growing strength, we shall return to it and discuss how it was dismantled after the 1953 putsch.

III: The Revival of the Tudeh Party During the Resurgence of the National-Democratic Movement

The story of the national-democratic movement for the nationalisation of Iranian oil has been discussed in many works and we need not deal with it here.[278] Suffice it to say that the rise of that movement and Mosaddeq's premiership, in the advent of which the clandestine TPI had played no role, offered the much weakened party a golden opportunity to rise again.

The clandestine TPI had also been helped by the TMO. In 1950, it helped the 10 imprisoned Tudeh leaders, who had been arrested and condemned for the fake attempt on the life of the shah, to escape from prison. According to a well-organised plan, during the cold night of 16 December 1950, at 8pm, they were rescued from prison[279] and were looked after in safe houses for more than three years. Most of them left to join their comrades in Moscow exile during the premiership of Mosaddeq or after the discovery of the TMO. Despite the declaration of the Chief of the Tehran Police to the contrary, the 'incident' was discovered just 14 hours after it had taken place. The government of General Razmara (June 1950–March 1951), which had just signed a commercial treaty with the Soviet government, was thought to have had a hand in this affair. Yet the American Embassy reported that the public appeared 'in general apathetic toward the incident and there are signs that the government was really endeavouring to recapture the escapees'.[280]

Deprived of legal activity and having lost some of its followers as a result, the TPI now became increasingly dependent on Soviet support. According to the American Embassy, the TPI in this period was receiving financial assistance from the Soviet government for 'propaganda, bribes, agitation, influence on the press, and the operation of the clandestine Azerbaijan radio', which was estimated to be between two million and two and a half million US dollars.[281] The escape of these leaders from prison, among whom figured Kianouri, in view of his later destructive behaviour — both during the time of the national-democratic movement and after the 1979 revolution — raises some questions, especially because the original plan was to free only Kianouri. This had been opposed by other Tudeh leaders, and, as a result, all 10 top leaders were taken out of prison.[282]

While in the early period of the national-democratic movement for oil nationalisation the TPI published two clandestine newspapers that were distributed with not inconsiderable difficulty, under the premiership of Mosaddeq it enjoyed full liberty of action, propaganda and organisation, although it still remained formally illegal.

Curiously, during this period, when the whole nation was struggling hard for the nationalisation of oil, the TPI raised its counter-slogan of 'Cancellation of the 1933 Agreement' signed between the AIOC and Reza Shah's government, a slogan that did not catch on and once more discredited the party, in addition to being from an international legal point indefensible (see Section II:IV). The remaining leaders of the TPI, who had now fallen under the inevitable control of the recently rescued Kianouri — who had taken the place of his brother-in-law Kambakhsh, both in contact with the Soviet Embassy 'advisors' and the TMO — instead of supporting the anti-imperialist national-democratic movement, adopted a hostile attitude towards it. The TPI attacked the Iranian Patriotic Front, formed on the French model of the Second World War period,[283] under Mosaddeq's leadership, as an agent and mouthpiece of American imperialism. The ostensible reason for the adoption of this line was, on the one hand, the initial rivalry between the American and British governments over Middle East oil in the postwar period, and on the other, the attempt by Mosaddeq and his collaborators to exploit that rivalry in order to break the British economic and political domination of Iran. However, the real reason, in this author's view, must be sought, not only in the hostile attitude of the Stalinist state towards Mosaddeq, who had prevented the granting of oil concessions to all foreign powers during the occupation of the country — a hostile attitude disguised in the 'theory' of the 'unreliability of the national bourgeoisie sold out to imperialism' — but also in the fear of the prospects of the development of a progressive, democratic, independent Iran, which would have left little room for the expansion of a Soviet–type political current — a thesis to which the former TMO leader Lieutenant-Colonel Azarnour subscribes. Be that as it may, the consequences of a forceful application of such a policy against the anti-imperialist national-democratic movement, as we will see, proved fatal for both the TPI and the country as a whole.

Moreover, since the TPI had been outlawed, it had removed its constitutional cloak and openly adopted a Marxist-Leninist dressing. Members now were recruited in the name of that ideology. This was a radical change in its outlook and increased its enemies' determination to combat it, especially the Anglo-American secret services that collaborated closely both with the Iranian police and the army's Second Bureau as well as the reactionary press financed by funds from the CIA and the British Embassy in Tehran.[284]

The newly-found freedom of action under Mosaddeq's government permitted the TPI to increase its propaganda and recruit new members among the country's educated strata, especially high-school and university students, and among the workers, leading to the revival of the workers' unions which had gone under after the attacks from Qavam's government, especially after the proscription of the TPI. With the advent of Mosaddeq's government, the party managed not only to act semi-legally through front organisations, such as the Society for Combating Colonialism and the National Peace Movement, but also to publish a great number of newspapers and weeklies, the main features of which were praise for the Soviet Union and hysterical attacks upon the national-democratic movement and its leader Mosaddeq. In the light of the TPI's support for the reactionary Qavam and its coalition with him, as 'recommended' by the Soviet party, the hostile position of the Soviet party and especially the TPI towards the national-democratic movement is most revealing.

We now turn to the TPI's specific policy during premiership of Mosaddeq.

IV: Opposition to the Patriotic-Democratic Movement under Mosaddeq, First Phase

In 1949, when the elections for the Sixteenth Legislature were held, vote rigging was general across the country. In Tehran, however, the democratic opposition was strong enough to exert pressure to hold fresh elections. Dr Mosaddeq and those who supported him at the time attempted a sit-in at the Royal Court and began popular agitation until the shah yielded and cancelled the rigged elections in the capital. During the fresh elections, the Patriotic Front, having been founded during the campaign in the capital against electoral rigging, managed to win the majority of the Tehran seats in the new parliament. The unexpected success of the Patriotic Front led by Mosaddeq frightened the clandestine TPI; it grew weary of the rising influence of the Front and its leader. In a demagogic broadsheet, the TPI ridiculed those who had resorted to a sit-in in order to arouse the population in Tehran and bring pressure to bear on the government to cancel the rigged elections in the capital. It stated that they had 'begged cap in hand before the bastion of despotism', that is to say, they petitioned the despot for justice.[285]

The TPI soon began, either through its clandestine organ *Mardom,* or in broadsheets distributed during the premiership of General Razmara (who wished to appease the USSR), to attack the Patriotic Front as an appendage of American imperialism. Since the Front had decided to direct its attacks against the dominant imperialist power in Iran — that is, the British government — the TPI systematically depicted it as an American instrument to drive out the British so that the US could replace it. Then, after Mosaddeq had taken office on 1 May 1951, it added that the negotiations that his government held with Britain over the settlement of the oil issue were against the interests of the people of Iran. When Mosaddeq reiterated that nationalisation was not expropriation and that the British company would be compensated for its refinery equipment on the same basis as the recent British nationalisations, he was violently pounced upon for a policy that 'compromised' the Iranian national interest.[286]

The success of the Patriotic Front, against tremendous odds, to push through the Majles the bill nationalising the Iranian oil industry by way of mobilising the masses could not have been imagined by the TPI, which had, since its proscription in the underground, grown 'radical', but lost any sense of reality. The success of the Front was so much more glaring in the eyes of the Tudeh leadership because the overwhelming majority of the deputies in the Sixteenth Legislature, who voted for the bill, were arch-reactionaries and linked to British interests. The TPI could not understand how a new loose coalition led by a veteran Constitutionalist could have mustered so much popular support as to force the arch-reactionary majority of the parliament to vote against its own wishes and interests. The British Foreign Office, on the other hand, explained it in terms of the 'Iranians' natural xenophobia', which could 'turn or… be turned against the nation whose interests are to the fore at any given moment. In 1944-1947 it turned against the USSR. Now it is turned against Britain.'[287]

A few months after Mosaddeq took office, the TPI issued a declaration on the occasion of its own tenth anniversary, which — ignorant of the history of the ICP — stressed it was the 'first' party to propagate 'the ideology of the working class', carrying out vast propaganda among the peasantry and taking into its fold the 'best individuals of the *democratic classes* who were nurtured with the *ideology of the working class*.[288] All this was naturally an attempt to portray itself as the saviour of the 'democratic classes'!

The TPI's hostility to Mosaddeq — which later, indeed, rather too late, it accepted was mistaken — was not in line with the formatted Stalinist theories of the 'national liberation movement', according to which the 'national bourgeoisie',[289] as opposed to the landed proprietors (called 'feudals'), was a natural ally of the working class, at least up to a certain stage of the development of the liberation movement, although in practice Stalin was often hostile to national movements that he could not control. Yet even in its 'self-criticism', either immediately after the 1953 putsch or at its Fourth Plenum in 1957, the TPI never explained why it had adopted such an extremely one-sided, exaggerated interpretation of not just the Stalinist theory but indeed the practice when Stalin himself was still alive. As noted above, one might suggest that the real reason for its opposition to the patriotic-democratic movement led by Mosaddeq was the latter's law of 1944, according to which no concession should be granted to foreign powers occupying the country during the Second World War, including the USSR, and of course the nationalisation of Iran's oil *throughout the country*, which also barred the Soviets from acquiring a concession.

Thus, when that nationalisation bill was about to be enacted, the TPI intensified its opposition to the Patriotic Front. On 16 March 1951, the Tudeh front organisation the 'National Organisation for Fighting Against the AIOC' organised a demonstration in opposition to the Front's drive for the nationalisation of the oil industry. As the American Ambassador saw it, the reasons for this opposition were: 1) to create confusion and further excitement after Razmara's assassination; 2) to place on record their objection to a law which might later be turned against Soviet interests in respect of Iranian oil concessions; 3) to attack the National [that is, Patriotic] Front and Dr Mosaddeq for 'stealing from the Communists the popular political slogan' of 'Drive Out British Influence'.[290] If we do not forget that the TPI had already suffered the loss of confidence of the Iranian people over two issues, namely, its support for the 1944 Soviet demand for an oil concession and the Azerbaijan fiasco in 1946, the third reason seems more reasonable.

Paradoxically, during this period, when the nation was struggling hard in defence of the nationalisation of oil, the TPI did all it could to discredit Mosaddeq by opposing the nationalisation bill through a legally impertinent and politically dangerous slogan demanding the annulment of the 1933 agreement with the British company under Reza Shah — once more discrediting the party, as the Fourth Plenum later testified, for Mosaddeq had explained the legal reasons for which Iran could not defend the annulment, but could win the legal battle for nationalisation through international law.[291] It is not clear who made that decision, although we know that three of the most dogmatic Tudeh leaders — Qasemi, Foroutan and Kianouri — were opposed to the Patriotic Front, its slogan and Mosaddeq's government, even to the end of their lives. Given the Soviet Union's hostility to Mosaddeq — demonstrated even after the 1953 coup by Soviet historians of Iran — what Tabari relates is very revealing. He recalls that the Tudeh leaders, when they were still in prison after their arrest in 1949, wrote a letter opposing the oil nationalisation across the country as a 'sly move against the Soviet Union, thereby preventing that country to achieve it final goal'. He adds that the Soviet Union 'must have inculcated them with this idea through one of its well-trained spies'.[292]

The leading TMO officer Azarnour evokes a number of actions and inactions of the Soviet Union *vis-à-vis* the Iranian national-democratic movement to demonstrate that such decisions were not mere accidents and reflected a policy aimed at defeating the movement. These included the absence of the Soviet judge at the International Court of Justice where Iran's case against Britain was to have a decisive impact on the struggle against imperialism by Iran and similar countries; the rejection by the Soviet government of the Iranian demand to pay its wartime debts to Iran (amounting to 15 million dollars in gold); and the refusal to buy Iranian oil, or to encourage other 'socialist governments' to purchase it, even when Mosaddeq reduced its price to half of the going rate on the international market, so that Iran could overcome the Anglo-American economic blockade.[293]

The reason for him was clear:

> In general, Soviet policy could in no way allow, in an adjacent country, the national movement to rise to a point where it would, in both the short and long run, by taking the affairs of state into its hands, achieve results such as true independence and progress as well as the establishment of social justice, for its influence and manifestations in the Central Asian and Caucasian republics, with all their historical attachments to Iran, would provoke nationalist sentiments. The goals and characteristics of the Iranian national movement under Mosaddeq's leadership did herald such a victory.[294]

As already noted, with the advent of the national-democratic movement for oil nationalisation and Mosaddeq's government, the TPI, in addition to holding quite frequent demonstrations, began publishing a number of legal newspapers in the name of its front organisations, their number eventually exceeding 100 newspapers and journals for propaganda and organisational activity, although the party still remained formally illegal. It is important to note that Mosaddeq, in spite of the hysterical attacks in the Tudeh press upon him and his colleagues, was intent on removing the unjust proscription of the party. In fact, contrary to the 'analysis' produced by the Tudeh leadership right after the 1953 *coup d'état*,[295] as soon as Mosaddeq took office, the Twelfth Criminal Court announced that seven important Tudeh prisoners, including the infamous Shoureshian who, in 1937, had helped the police 'discover' Arani's 'Group of Fifty-Three', and who now was a Tudeh labour activist and had been jailed after the fake attempt on the life of the shah, were released on bail. Thereafter, other criminal courts freed on bail some trade union activists, including the veteran Ali Omid, whom the US Embassy called 'communist agitators'. The US Ambassador Grady reported that, 'Although [the] Prime Minister [Mosaddeq] affirmed his anti-communist sentiments in conversation with me', he 'has opposed suppression as means of combating communism' in Iran. (This was, of course, Mosaddeq's way of stressing his democratic principle of freedom for everyone to an American Ambassador.) The latter also considered it 'noteworthy' that, after Mosaddeq took office, Tudeh cases were no longer placed before military tribunals, as had been the case since the 1949 proscription, but under the jurisdiction of civil courts 'who may grant bail to all, except convicted murderers... [The] National [Patriotic] Front has for [a] long time opposed incarceration [of] civilians tried by military tribunals.'[296] What is more, Mosaddeq, in an unprecedented move, 'instructed the Tehran police to permit communist [Tudeh] demonstrations so long as they remained orderly'.[297] Increasingly, he allowed greater freedom to the Tudeh front organisations. After the July 1952 uprising (see Section II:VII below), when the reactionary forces suffered a great defeat and he was brought back into office, Mosaddeq asked his Minister of Justice to have the case of the 1949 'attempt' on the life of the shah re-examined and to see whether the TPI had, in fact, had a hand in it or not. His suspicions were confirmed and the Tudeh leaders were absolved of the charges for which they had been condemned. Yet none of those in exile returned to Iran, no doubt due to Soviet opposition, as we will see why; nor did the aforementioned documents of 'self-criticism' ever acknowledge this change of their status. On the contrary, they kept accusing Mosaddeq of having kept the TPI under lock and key. The increasing liberty given by Mosaddeq to the TPI was such that in the spring of 1953 Mullah Kashani — formerly of the Patriotic Front — months after having taken an open stand against Mosaddeq, had his mouthpiece *Demokrat-e Islam* attack Mosaddeq for making a secret arrangement with Tudeh leaders. It declared that Mosaddeq's close collaborator, Foreign Minister Dr Hussein Fatemi, who had gone to Europe for an operation after having been seriously injured by a right-wing Islamic gunman close to the young Khomeini, had, in fact, travelled to Europe to arrange the return of the Tudeh leaders.[298]

Nevertheless, the Tudeh leaders who continued living in the underground inside the country and under the inevitable guidance of Soviet 'advisers', through Kianouri, persisted in their hostile attacks on Mosaddeq as a 'stooge' or 'agent' of American imperialism, thereby dividing the anti-imperialist forces and weakening the struggle of the nation for the nationalisation of Iranian oil and against the British government, which was doing all it could to overthrow Mosaddeq's government. The attempt by Mosaddeq and his collaborators to exploit that rivalry between the US and Britain in order to break the British economic and political domination of Iran and the ensuing blockade was portrayed by the TPI as an attempt by US oil companies to dominate the Iranian oil industry, supposedly with the consent of a patriotic veteran democrat of the Constitutional era who was known for his past and present opposition to concessions to foreign companies.

After the nationalisation of the oil industry, while the newly legally-authorised Tudeh press — through its front organisations — carried on its opposition to the national-democratic movement engaged in a life-and-death struggle resisting British political and economic pressure, vilifying Mosaddeq as an 'agent of American imperialism', the TPI Central Committee *published open letters addressed to him proposing demands that could not be satisfied in the circumstances*, for their entire fulfilment in the heat of the struggle would have immediately precipitated a *coup d'état*, as army commanders were under the control of the shah and his men.

These demands were: 1) that all political parties, that is, the TPI, be permitted to operate freely (legally); 2) the removal of every single trace of the imperialist British oil company, all its influence from the country, and take measures so that the sovereignty of Iran be assured over Bahrain; 3) to revoke the judicial and legislative measures passed after 'the attempted assassination of the shah'; 4) martial law be abolished in the oil-producing province of Khuzistan — where British agents could have instigated trouble; 5) all political prisoners be released immediately; voting privileges be given to all adults, without any literacy requirement — a provision that existed;[299] 6) devote the efforts of the government to maintaining world peace, avoid alliances with warmongers, and recognise the People's Government of China.[300] Of course, several of these measures had already been either taken or were being taken. Some, such as the open legalisation of the TPI, had to await better times.

As alluded to above, since it had been outlawed, the TPI was no longer inhibited by its own 'constitutional' cloak and had openly adopted a Marxist-Leninist line. Now it reinforced its activity of teaching its members the Soviet brand of 'Marxism'. Given the 1931 'Anti-Socialist Law', which could have only been repealed by the Majles, a parliament arch-reactionary in its majority and supported by the Anglo-American Embassies, it was hardly possible for Mosaddeq to engage openly on another front in the struggle against the reactionary forces and their foreign supporters. What he did prudently was a gradual easing of the situation as the mass movement gathered momentum, that is, what has been described above. The TPI wanted it all at one stroke, not because it thought it possible or prudent, but because it felt obliged to accuse the leader of the national-democratic movement of being in the service of reaction and imperialism, to besmirch him, and to weaken the struggle against the British oil company. We have already alluded to the reasons for the adoption of this policy, which ran against the Stalinist theory of the national bourgeoisie. Probably, however, there are other reasons to which we shall return below when we discuss the nefarious role Kianouri played all along in the life of the TPI, particularly in the light of a comparison of its attitude *vis-à-vis* Mosaddeq with the TPI's coalition with the arch-reactionary Qavam who, linked with the Anglo-American imperialists, suppressed the party.

V: The Tudeh Leadership's Knowledge of Theory and History

In order to explain the motivation of those who followed the Tudeh line, we must point to the social composition of the party. It is difficult to know what percentage of party members were workers and how great was the number of those from non-working-class strata. What is certain is that the great majority of workers were first-generation *déraciné* toilers, with immediate peasant or tribal backgrounds, and illiterate, who, for their political education, had to depend on party cadres coming from other social strata, mostly from the petty bourgeoisie. At the time, Iran's only industry worthy of the name, in addition to a few small textile factories, was the British oil enterprise, where the Iranians were labourers without any technical know-how; the technical jobs were occupied by Indians brought over from the subcontinent. As regards Iranian toilers, it is important to underline that they had no political education at all, aside from the propaganda sheets and brochures which party cadres read to them. Suffice it to take note of the publications of the TPI during the period of 1941-53. In addition to reprinting some short passages of Marxian works, such as Karl Marx's *Wage, Price and Profit*, which had already been published by the ICP, with a short biographical introduction on Marx, and a translation of *Socialism Utopian and Scientific* by Frederick Engels, three important handbooks used in the party were Stalin's *History of the Communist Party of the Soviet Union*, *The Constitution of the USSR*, and *Elementary Principles of Philosophy* written by the Franco-Hungarian Georges Pulitzer in France in the 1930s. There was also a republication of the ICP's translation of the *Communist Manifesto;* a reprint of the 12 issues of Arani's *Donya* (1932-34); a booklet by Kianouri called *Class*

Struggle, which was republished in November 1948 at a time when the party had already been preparing itself for an eventual attack, which came three months later when the party was outlawed; a book titled *Anti-Capital* by a certain Edgard de Vigan that was originally published in Paris in 1935; and *Scientific Socialism* by Gabriel Deville, a theoretician of Guesde's French Workers Party (POF) — a strange translation for a Leninist party.[301]

In addition to Lenin's *One Step Forwards, Two Steps Back*, Stalin's *On the Strategy and Tactic of Russian Communists* and *Economic Problems of Socialism in the USSR*, others by Stalin's close collaborators such as Zhdanov's *Socialist Realism in the Arts*, G Kazlov's *Stalin on Commodity Production and the Law of Value*, and works by A Kashkarov and the 'academician' TD Lysenko were translated for the 'Marxist education' of members and sympathisers. *Das Kapital* was at last translated (not very comprehensibly) by Eskandari and its first volume was published abroad only a couple of years before the 1979 revolution, on the eve of the party's demise, too late to educate the rank-and-file.

In fact, one of the members of the TPI Executive Committee in that period, Foroutan, admits that 'the young Tudeh leadership did not as yet have either a sufficient knowledge of the theory of struggle or long practical experience...', the assumption being that at the time the party was established in 1941, the leadership, a good number of whose members were university professors, should not have known any more about Marxism or history than ordinary citizens who joined the party. He rejects the idea that the Tudeh leadership knew about the theory of the 'national bourgeoisie'.

> As far as I remember [he retorts], a social category called the 'national bourgeoisie' was not known to the EC till 1952. Only in this period did a volume of Mao's works fell into someone's hand, but it was soon snatched away; when I wanted to study it for a few days my wish was not satisfied.[302]

(Even in the 1990s he did not know that this 'category' had existed as far back as the Second Congress of the Comintern.)

Given the TPI's shallow level of analysis and the overdependence of its leadership on Soviet writings, one could not but seriously question the familiarity of its top leaders with Marx's teachings. Dr Keshavarz writes that his colleagues in the Central Committee, Dr Bahrami and Dr Yazdi, both having finished their medical studies in Germany, were 'politically ignorant', but had been taken in because of their past friendship with Dr Arani.[303] Perhaps the only one among Arani's student-collaborators who knew anything of Marxism was Iraj Eskandari. The little attention paid to Marxist theory as well as to the history of the workers' movement around the world, including that of Iran,[304] explains the poverty of the TPI's policies from its very birth, and its total dependence, as an article of faith, on the Soviet party.

Turning to the specific policies of the TPI during the 28 months of the premiership of Mosaddeq, one could observe that its policies during that time were constantly hysterical and obstinately in opposition to the national-democratic movement and its leader Mosaddeq, always resorting to provocative actions (demonstrations involving fights with reactionary elements who sought to create an atmosphere of instability and fear with the aim of precipitating a putsch), undermining the national-democratic movement on the morrow of the Chinese revolution and during the Korean War, by way of creating, in the McCarthy era, an atmosphere of 'communist peril' looming on the horizon and the image of the immediate take-over of Iran by the Soviet Union. Thus were strengthened the hands of the internal and external enemies of the national-democratic movement. Given the repercussions of the Azerbaijan crisis, the propaganda issued by reactionary forces directed against the national-democratic movement, the propaganda funded by the CIA and SIS offices in Iran and their buying of the services of unscrupulous, anti-patriotic journalists as well as civil and military officials, the Royal Court and Majles deputies,[305] gradually became effective in demobilising a population living under dire economic conditions.

During this period, the TPI created or revived several front organisations which openly carried out its policies, with a propagandistic content. They were the Peasants Association, in the mid-1940s; the Tehran University Students Union, April 1950; the Society for the Struggle Against the Colonial Oil Company in the South (later the Society for the Struggle Against the Colonial AIOC), December 1950, renamed at its first congress in 1952 as the Society for the Struggle Against Colonialism, notably American, since the British had been chased out and one was not to bother about it! Others were the Association of the Democratic Youth (DY), April 1951, whose first festival took place in August 1952; the Organisation of Iranian Women, May 1951, whose first national congress was held in May 1953; the Iranian Society for the Defence of Children, March 1952; the National Peace Movement, whose congress was also held in 1952. Interestingly, despite a vast array of organisations, a multitude of possibilities, and especially the boastings of the TPI about how all Iranian 'intellectuals', the cream of the crop in Iranian society, had been attracted to and integrated into the party, there was hardly any Marxian study of Iranian history in the twentieth century. A couple of books on Iranian history by the party 'theoretician' Tabari are nothing but plagiarism of works by Stalinist 'Iranologues'.[306]

VI: The Tudeh Party's Charges Against the Nationalisation Movement

In the light of all these means — organisations, newspapers, weeklies, monthlies, demonstrations, congresses — it is difficult to see how the TPI could have claimed that Mosaddeq 'killed' democracy. A few examples of the kind of attacks in the leaders of Tudeh newspapers throw light on the gravity of the situation:

> Mosaddeq's government of murderers and the demagogic gang of the National Front must know that no trick or political manoeuvre can absolve them. The Iranian nation has no confidence in the murderous and villainous gang of imperialist agents and will not vote for them.[307]
>
> Mosaddeq's government[308] and the band of 'honourable people' have mobilised all their possible means to strip the 'National [Tudeh electoral] Coalition Commission' of their liberty and to stuff the ballot boxes to win the elections.[309]
>
> Shame on the government of Mosaddeq that kills freedom; the agents of imperialism will be buried along with their wish of dominating the Iranian nation.[310]
>
> Your viewpoint of shutting down the British consulates in Iran is the very viewpoint of the US imperialists who want to drive out their [British] rivals.[311]
>
> The elections in Tehran exposed the true nature of Mosaddeq's government more than ever before.[312]
>
> Mosaddeq's reign of repressive, fascist terror extends across the country. Crimes in the towns of Khuzestan against the toilers represent great treason against freedom and democracy.[313]
>
> The Iranian nation will continue its struggle against US imperialism and their agents who pretend to be Iranian; Mosaddeq's rogues imitate the style of American gangsters.[314]
>
> Every day, Mosaddeq's anti-national government commits new violations against the everyday freedoms and the rights of the nation. No pressure, no violation will disarm the nation.[315]
>
> Mosaddeq's government is steeped in the quagmire of murder and fascism.[316]
>
> The International Court of Justice has no validity in the eyes of the Iranian nation.[317] [Mosaddeq's intention was to prove at the Hague Court that it had no jurisdiction over the oil issue, and won the case against Britain in spite of great odds.]
>
> The rule of the dishonoured National Front nurtures fascist bands in its bosom, but the Iranian nation will not tolerate fascism.[318]
>
> Mosaddeq's counter-proposals [to the British] are rejected by the

Iranian nation.³¹⁹ [None of Mosaddeq's proposals or counter-proposals was acceptable to the British; thus the putsch.]

On the eve of his demand for plenipotentiary powers, Mosaddeq wants the parliament to yield completely. The [reactionary Seventeenth] Majles loses its last privileges [by granting, under popular pressure, plenipotentiary powers to Mosaddeq to carry out social reforms!].³²⁰

The unprecedented blood-shedding of Mosaddeq's agents has imposed fascist terror upon Azerbaijan.³²¹

The politics of hesitation and leniency [towards the imperialists] is treachery to the interest of the nation.³²²

Amazing as it may seem, the TPI had never brought such violent attacks against any of the reactionary governments before Mosaddeq, or even against the putschist Zahedi–Shah government afterwards. The impact of these attacks upon the unity of the progressive forces was devastating. This can hardly be explained by Stalin's 'theory of the national bourgeoisie'. The hysterical character of these attacks against a government fighting on all fronts against British imperialism can be seen more clearly when we recall that in no Western country then could any newspaper attack the head of a government in such insulting terms; not even today does any newspaper insult even Berlusconi in such terms. In the light of the freedom of the press that the TPI enjoyed, just as the reactionary papers did, in throwing unprecedented filth on the head of the government, the untruthful nature of accusations against the 'fascist' and 'freedom-killing' policies of the national-democratic government can be explained, not only by Stalin's personal opposition to Mosaddeq for his 1944 bill banning the granting of any concession to foreigners while the country was under occupation, but also by the infiltration of British (and/or American) agents into the top echelons of the Tudeh leadership, to which we shall turn below. (Both the British and the Americans were aware of Stalin's opposition to Mosaddeq; all they needed was to give it an hysterical touch.)

As for Mosaddeq's 'stripping' the TPI's electoral 'coalition' for the Seventeenth Legislature of its rights, it should be recalled that, according to a keen observer at the American Embassy,³²³ the TPI was 'bolder' than ever before during the campaign; its 'clandestine' papers were no longer clandestine and were openly distributed; Tudeh front organisations held electoral rallies, despite martial law instituted against a possible putsch, or in spite of the government's refusal to grant permission for rallies. They had so much freedom that Abbas Eskandari, Iraj's uncle and one of the 'founders' of the TPI who had either been expelled or left the party, in a meeting on 27 November 1951 with an envoy of the American Embassy, speaking on behalf of the former Premier Qavam, misinformed the

American envoy that Mosaddeq had reached an agreement with the TPI to permit 25 Tudeh candidates enter the Majles, adding that, due to Mosaddeq's 'weakness', 'bad' deputies would enter the Seventeenth Majles and Mosaddeq's opponents had the intention of asking the UN to send a control commission for the elections.

As for electoral frauds by the army and local potentates allied with the Royal Court, against which Mosaddeq had issued strict instructions to the Interior Ministry and provincial governors, it should be noted that, as the American Embassy reported, in at least two constituencies of Mashhad and Kurdistan, Tudeh front organisation candidates 'nearly won', victory being prevented by intervention by the shah's forces. The American report admits that the 'Communists are obviously stronger in this [Kurdish] district than the results indicate and undoubtedly would have won the election, had it been in any way "free"'.[324] Yet this was an exception, for according to official results, Tudeh candidates obtained between 1.8 and 13.1 per cent of the votes cast.[325] In Tehran, where, thanks to the vigilance of popular watchdog committees, elections were least interfered with by the shah's forces, while the Patriotic Front's winning candidates obtained over 100 000 votes, Tudeh coalition candidates received no more than several thousand, not surprisingly, since in 1943, when the TPI was legal and not known for its pro-Soviet inclinations, its top leader Dr Yazdi had received only 5000 votes, half the number that the last of 12 winners had obtained. Therefore, the TPI's accusations in this regard, too, were without foundation and were based on the fundamental line of the party against the national-democratic movement. The same perversion of the facts was shown in the allegation that Mosaddeq carried out a 'fascist murderous' policy against the TPI. Arrests were the work of the military and the police which were controlled by the shah and his men. It was Mosaddeq's government that had the task of obtaining their release.[326]

The first of the TPI's provocative actions was the organisation of a big demonstration in Tehran on the occasion of the arrival of Averill Harriman, President Truman's envoy, who had gone to Iran, followed by the British Lord Privy Seal Sir Richard Stokes, to negotiate a settlement of the oil nationalisation and eventually some compensation for the AIOC, such as the Abadan refinery. It is true that at the beginning Mosaddeq had refused to permit the British Ambassador Sir Francis Shepherd to meddle in the question of nationalisation — a question that, according to the Iranian government, was a domestic matter solely between the Iranian government and a private British company operating in Iran.[327] However, in order to be able quickly to settle the question before reactionary forces could conspire to overthrow the government, Mosaddeq decided to negotiate with the British government, the majority shareholder of the company, for he was well aware that not only the pro-British latifundistas, the comprador bourgeoisie and the Court headed by the shah were against the nationalisation[328] and the attempt to eradicate colonial influences in the country, but also American fears of the 'communist peril' in Iran, fanned by the British government, would unite the US with the British. The TPI's rowdy and unruly demonstration against Harriman's arrival, organised without authorisation by the Prime Minister or even his knowledge, was attacked by the police, whose chief had always been appointed by the shah. The ensuing bloodshed caused a scandal and Mosaddeq immediately had the chief of police fired and tried for his violent treatment of the demonstrators.[329]

The provocative character of the demonstration was obvious at the time, and was thought to be the result solely of a decision by the Tudeh leadership. On the eve of the 1979 revolution, however, it was revealed by Kermit Roosevelt,[330] the CIA operative who carried out the 1953 *coup d'état*, that, in fact, his agents, the Boscoe Brothers, had played a role in the provocations by means of 'fake' Tudeh crowds provoking violence, causing the incident in order to prove the existence of a 'communist peril' to the American public, and justifying united action by Britain and the US against the Iranian national-democratic movement. In spite of Mosaddeq's measures to punish the chief of police responsible for the violent treatment of the demonstrators, the occasion was seized upon by the TPI to denounce, in true Stalinist fashion, Mosaddeq as an 'imperialist agent', and to claim that his government had spilt the blood of patriotic demonstrators.[331]

Other provocative demonstrations continued to be held in the same manner in order to 'prove' that Mosaddeq was an agent of both the British and American imperialists.[332] The TPI's 'analysis' regarding the provocative demonstration against Harriman in Tehran concluded that the 'Bloody Incident' was an 'imperialist conspiracy executed under the supervision of Dr Mosaddeq's government, his official spokesman Dr Fatemi',[333] and his Interior Minister General Zahedi — he, having been removed by Mosaddeq, later turned against him and headed the coup, as was the case with Pinochet in Allende's government in Chile. It is to be recalled that the demonstration was carried out by the party's Youth Organisation, headed by the ambitious young Stalinist Shermini, who had created a cult of his own personality in the organisation. Interestingly, he was arrested shortly after the 1953 coup, and then recanted and disappeared into thin air.

All through the period, Tudeh journals continued to attack Mosaddeq unabatedly and violently in the Stalinist style. The Patriotic Front and one of its constituent parties, the Toilers, in whose socialist wing the head of the 1948 splinter group from the Tudeh, Khalil Maleki, played a prominent role, were labelled 'the hireling enemies of the toilers' of Iran. Mosaddeq was accused of imposing 'tragedies on the masses of the nation'. It was impressed on Tudeh members and sympathisers that 'the continuation of Mosaddeq's policy on the oil question [negotiations] will end up with a compromise in the interests of Anglo-American colonialism'.[334]

Just before the International Court of Justice handed down its judgement — the court where Premier Mosaddeq had defended the country's cause and the nation's right to nationalise her oil industry, discrediting and rejecting the British claim against Iran — the TPI held a demonstration, with the participation of 'tens of thousands of men and women, workers, intellectuals [meaning educated individuals!], artisans, peasants and businessmen' commemorating the 'Bloody Sunday Incident' of the previous year, denouncing the 'imperialist character' of the International Court whose judges were 'at the service of imperialism' and 'whose judgements had no value in the eyes of the Iranian people'. In fact, only a week later, the court's judgement was announced in favour of Mosaddeq's arguments and against the British claim. The additional disappointing aspect of it all for the TPI must have been that the Soviet judge had not attended the final session of the court, thus abstaining from voting by pretending to be 'ill', while the American judge voted against Iran. Surprisingly, the British judge voted against his own government and in favour of Iran.[335]

The TPI's venomous attacks against the national-democratic movement continued until after the end of February 1953, that is, the time of the 'dress rehearsal' of the August 1953 putsch. Yet the American government too accused Mosaddeq of leaning on the support of the TPI in respect of the failure of Qavam's ephemeral American-sponsored government in July 1952,[336] while, as early as 1951, the British government increasingly frightened the West by evoking the 'communist peril' looming on the Iranian horizon.[337] In an analysis of the Iranian situation, the British Foreign Office claimed that 'the tacit support of the Communists' for the Mosaddeq government was evident. It added that, while 'Moscow Radio does not abuse Mosaddeq', the 'Free Azerbaijan Demokrat Radio attacks him only for not being sufficiently extreme in the matter of the oil question'. The analysis also acknowledged Mosaddeq's relaxation of the anti-Tudeh laws and restrictions as proof therefor.[338]

In his 1984 *Memoirs*, Eskandari claims that he was the only TPI Central Committee member who opposed the anti-Mosaddeq policy of the Executive Committee in Tehran.[339] To do this, he says, he wrote an article for the journal of the World Federation of Trade Unions (WFTU) 'with a sort of dexterity', which, while 'not negating party policy directly', discussed the views that he still held in 1984, including those on Mosaddeq. 'There, I proposed that this issue [oil nationalisation] is the demand of the workers, of the whole people of Iran, and is supported by them, etc..., without showing any opposition to party policy and tactics.' He adds that a few days later he was informed by his British colleagues in the WFTU that the *Daily Worker* had run his article as its own leader. He further states that a British colleague in the WFTU told him that there was a debate in the Communist Party of Great Britain as to the 'character' of the Iranian nationalisation movement. One group, basing itself on the positions of the TPI, believed that Mosaddeq's was an 'American movement', therefore there was no need to support a 'policy that was against British interests and favoured those of the US'; hence, opposition to Mosaddeq! When Eskandari's article was published in the *World Trade Union Movement*, others discussed it in the CPGB's Central Committee, stating that Eskandari, a TPI Central Committee member, held different views on the question. As a result, the CPGB's Central Committee 'corrected its line and decided to publish the article as a leader' in the *Daily Worker*, which it did, in an abridged form, not as a leader but as a feature article in its issue for 26 June 1951.[340]

While Eskandari's claims in respect of the internal discussion within the CPGB's leadership remain to be verified, his articles we have studied in the *World Trade Union Movement*, reprinted in the collection on the conditions of the working class in Iran,[341] do not confirm his claim. True, one might expect that his articles, published in an international journal, could be devoid of the usual Tudeh-style hysterical slanders against Mosaddeq; yet the general line of his articles does not differ greatly from that of the TPI during this period in the *World Trade Union Movement*. Besides, the one relating to the question he discusses in his 1984 *Memoirs*, written before Mosaddeq took office, is mild in tone, but attacks the British, the Iranian ruling class 'tied body and soul to British interests', as well as American oil monopolies. It never mentions Mosaddeq or the Patriotic Front as the leaders of the movement that was to achieve the nationalisation; nor does it recall the TPI's opposition to that movement. All it does is to state that the 'miracle' of the nationalisation is 'the exclusive work of the Iranian people, who, by their determined action forced the reactionary Parliament to vote for a law which struck a serious blow at British interests' in Iran.[342] The article recalls a number of strikes by workers which had little to do with the nationalisation movement, and mentions the collection of signatures for the National Peace Movement, which ran in parallel, if not in competition, with the national-democratic movement. It also attacks 'American intrigues against the British [oil] monopoly', which insinuates that the Patriotic Front's deputies who led the nationalisation campaign peddled the American line. In sum, his article, in substance, is only different from the Tudeh line inside the country by its mild tone and silence on the national-democratic movement.[343] Thus, especially by not giving precise reference to his articles, he attempts to whitewash his own inaction or complicity with those Tudeh leaders who ran the anti-nationalisation campaign.

Of course, Eskandari is not the only Tudeh leader who claims that he differed in his views from the rest of his comrades who opposed the national-democratic movement. Foroutan, who belonged to the Kambakhsh–Kianouri faction in the Executive Committee in Tehran, states, just like Kianouri himself, that while they had been critical of Mosaddeq at the time on certain issues, they had, as members of the minority in the Executive Committee, disagreed with the majority which took hostile positions against Mosaddeq.[344] This is, of course, not true, as the decisions of the Executive Committee were taken unanimously. What is more, Kianouri was not only in charge of the press that poured all the dirt on the national-democratic movement, but was also the contact man with the 'Soviet friends', without whose directives no major decision could be taken by the TPI Executive Committee in Tehran.

As for the Tudeh leaders abroad, they were prevented from taking any action contrary to the line of the party inside the country. The majority of them living in Moscow did not even have the right to consult the newspapers published inside Iran, and thus were kept completely in the dark until the 1953 putsch.[345] It seems clear that the line followed in Tehran was dictated by the Soviet 'friends', either in the embassy or in one of the Soviet trade organisations in Iran, through Kianouri, because he had replaced his brother-in-law Kambakhsh as the liaison contact with Soviet 'advisers'; thus Executive Committee majority decisions had always to be reached in agreement with what Kianouri conveyed, hence the unanimity in the leadership!

Regarding the line followed by the CPGB, it should be noted that the frequent reports on Iran in the *Daily Worker* at the time of its running Eskandari's article in mid-1951 noted on many occasions Mosaddeq's stance on the question of oil nationalisation in a neutral or approving manner, and rarely mentioned the TPI.[346] There were, however, hints of a less approving attitude towards Mosaddeq. The party's theoretician Rajani Palme Dutt — who could always be relied upon to relay to his readers what Moscow wished them to read — in late 1951 mentioned the role of the US, 'which, under cover of profound expressions of sympathy [to Iran], proved itself not averse to assisting the discomfiture of British oil imperialism at the hands of Mosaddeq', which can be interpreted as considering Mosaddeq as a pawn of US designs in Iran.[347] The stance of the CPGB's daily was indeed to harden, and we can recall an interview by the *Daily Worker*'s correspondent in Moscow with prominent Tudeh leaders, notably Secretary-General Dr Radmanesh and his close colleagues Tabari and Qasemi, in the Soviet capital, which is very telling about what they continued to propagate against a democratic government that had, for two years, given them every opportunity to revive their organisation and disseminate their hostile ideas across the country. Only a few days after the aforementioned 'dress rehearsal' of the August 1953 coup, in February 1953, they said, *inter alia*, the following about a government whose overthrow was being energetically prepared by the SIS and CIA, particularly since the inauguration of the Eisenhower administration on 20 January 1953:

> The National Front, while conducting a limited struggle against British imperialism, in fact, helps the penetration of American influence into Persia. And it is hostile to the real national movement which is under the leadership of the Tudeh Party.[348]

It seems that Eskandari's assertion was correct: the CPGB's line *had* changed, but in this way: it had moved from the general Stalinist line of critical support for nationalist movements fighting against imperialism to the particular line in respect of Iran of outright hostility towards the national-democratic movement. This, however, does not provide an alibi for Eskandari, who, for a foreign audience, covered his own party's hostility to that movement with carefully-crafted diplomatic phrases in his articles in the *World Trade Union Movement* and the *Daily Worker*.[349]

Moreover, in this period the unfortunate and gloomy situation for Iran's national-democratic movement, striving for the political and economic independence of the country, was exacerbated by the lack of any kind of support from progressive forces in the West.[350] Western communist parties naturally supported or, in the British case, came to support the Soviet–Tudeh position and expressed hostility towards Mosaddeq's government, while independent progressive intellectuals, such as Bertrand Russell, astonishingly remained silent.[351] By contrast, in the 'Third World' — from India to the Middle East, North Africa and Latin America — great sympathies were expressed for the Iranian national-democratic movement — support, however, which could not bring any pressure to bear on governments that were preparing the putsch that was to take place in August 1953. The examples of the continued hostility of the TPI and its sister organisations in the West and even in the Middle East towards Iran's national-democratic movement are revealing about Soviet policy under Stalin.

VII: Continued Opposition to Mosaddeq after the July 1952 Popular Uprising, Second Phase

Thus, contrary to claims by Anglo-American propaganda, the TPI, as witnessed by the *Daily Worker* interview, not only refused to support or collaborate with the national-democratic movement, but remained hostile to it even after the July 1952 popular uprising that restored Mosaddeq to office.[352] He had resigned after the inauguration of the Seventeenth Legislature, as required by the Constitution. In dispute with the shah, he refused to be nominated premier again, for the shah would not let him choose the War Minister, as, contrary to the Constitution, he considered that ministry to be his own fiefdom. This refusal was also the result of secret machinations by the British and American Embassies which wanted to bring a subservient premier into office who would accept the British proposals on the oil issue — either the putschist former premier Seyyed Zia or the corrupt former premier Qavam. The shah would not accept the former for personal reasons related to Zia's opposition to the former shah, but would concede to the latter. Voted in by the reactionary majority of the Majles, Qavam immediately issued a strong, dictatorial warning to frighten and silence the people. It backfired and opposition to his government grew. On 18 July, 30 Majles deputies who had supported Mosaddeq issued a statement inviting the people to resist Qavam's government; they then called on all people to close down every enterprise on 21 July, in what amounted to a general strike.[353] As a result, immediately in every city and town people shut down, demonstrated in the streets, were fired upon, and many of them were killed. The killings provoked further opposition to the new premier. A huge number of petitions and telegrams were sent by the people in various parts of the country to Majles deputies in support of Mosaddeq.[354]

On the day Mosaddeq had resigned and refused the premiership unless he himself could appoint the War Minister, the Tudeh front organisations daily stated that domestically Mosaddeq 'depended on classes whose interests were in contradiction with those of the great majority of the Iranian people', while at the international level he 'leans on an international world-devouring imperialism'. It concluded that his government could not bring about any social reforms.[355] Two days later, another Tudeh journal declared that Mosaddeq and Qavam were two wings of the Iranian ruling class and neither could serve the interests of the Iranian people.

In the meantime, reportedly, the TPI Executive Committee made contact with Premier Qavam — the same Qavam of 1946 — to negotiate a deal, the conditions of which are unfortunately not known.[356] Apparently, Qavam refused the deal; therefore, finally, late in the evening of 20 July — on the eve of the day of strike called by the pro-Mosaddeq deputies — a Tudeh front organisation, the National Society for Combatting Colonialism (NSCC) issued its 'Appeal', proposing a 'united front' with the Patriotic Front.[357] Paradoxically, the 'Appeal', though mild in tone, was no less than a demagogic version of previous accusations, stating, for instance, that during the Seventeenth Legislature elections 'Mosaddeq wanted to seat American agents in the parliament, aiming at forming a parliament with an American majority'.[358] The declaration was written in such a way that members and militants of the party would be reinforced in their faith in the party line, and Patriotic Front supporters would continue to reject any collaboration with the TPI. Paradoxically, the former TPI Executive Committee member Foroutan derides his Executive Committee comrades for having called upon Mosaddeq in the summer of 1952 to form a united front, still labelling him an 'agent of imperialism'.[359]

As for participation in the announced day of strike and the demonstrations that followed, according to JAMI — that is, the group whose members had formerly been of the upper-echelon TPI cadres — it was only after the spontaneous rising wave of workers in a number of industries in Tehran voting to strike 'in support' of the aforementioned Tudeh 'Appeal', that the party leadership, trailing behind the popular movement, issued during the night of 20-21 July a 'half-hearted instruction' for participation in the proclaimed general strike. As a result, the party could not lead the uprising, but the most experienced cadres managed to lead scattered groups onto the scene of action.[360] Despite this claim, however, it must be pointed out that there is no evidence that the TPI ever issued a statement publicly inviting the people in Tehran and the provinces to take part in the strike or the demonstrations that followed.

Foroutan, one of the die-hard Stalinist leaders of the TPI at the time in Tehran, contests the JAMA version of the events and claims that the Tudeh leadership was in the forefront of the uprising and led the masses, while the Patriotic Front manifested cowardice. He quotes the same statement by Front deputies calling upon the people to demonstrate peacefully and avoid provocations by the army, one that he claims was read over the Tehran Radio, calling on people to stay at home and be peaceful. He concludes that, in fact, the Front yielded to the Qavam government.[361] This is, of course, a complete distortion of history, for the Front deputies issued the statement only when they realised that the people who were spontaneously demonstrating against Qavam were being shot at and that streets at sensitive points in the capital and every town were filled with Sherman tanks and truckloads of armed soldiers; they simply could not risk, on the day of a general strike, the massacre of the people, whom they called upon to remain calm and peaceful. Foroutan can make such a claim only *after the event*, because the people provoked by the nomination of Qavam in place of Mosaddeq could not restrain their anger and spontaneously manifested it in the streets against the Court, Qavam and their imperialist supporters, shouting, not Tudeh slogans, but 'Ya Marg ya Mosaddeq' ('Either death or Mosaddeq'). This is how many died by gunfire or by tanks.[362]

Moreover, in spite of all the claims by anti-Tudeh sources, from the American Embassy reports to domestic reactionary elements, as well as the Western press, the TPI as a party did not really participate in the July uprising, though some Tudeh militants may have done so of their own will. In fact, in a secret letter to the Central Committee in Moscow, Kianouri, one of the staunch Stalinist adversaries of the national-democratic movement in the party leadership, admits that:

> Perhaps, comrades [in Moscow] are aware that, in truth, during the events of 21 July, [our] party forces played a small role; firstly, they appeared too late on the scene; they moved only in Tehran and some [other] provinces; in Tehran in the heat of the struggle on 21 July a small number of our forces were on the scene, while we directly had a considerable force of organised elements in various organisations, amounting to about 25 000...'[363]

Thus, Kianouri's secret letter refutes the public claim by his erstwhile ally in the Tudeh leadership, Foroutan.[364] The report by Kianouri was also confirmed by Keshavarz in his platform presented at the Fourth Plenum in 1957.[365]

In spite of, or in harmony with, the aforementioned 'Appeal', thereafter the Tudeh press continued to lash at Mosaddeq's policies on a daily basis, especially regarding oil negotiations — on which point he did not yield an inch to the Anglo-American demands, for it would have been contrary to Iran's national sovereignty — carrying on an hysterical campaign to denounce his government as an 'anti-national' administration, one with which it nonetheless wished to form a 'united front' — a contradiction that may be due to the desire of the majority and the minority in the Executive Committee to reach unanimity.

The Tudeh press, abusing the freedom it said did not exist, also consistently ridiculed Mosaddeq in cartoons, curiously just as the imperialist and the reactionary domestic press did. Suffice it to recall a few aforementioned statements by the Tudeh press and declarations to demonstrate how the TPI sowed the seeds of discord and animosity among the masses, thereby weakening a democratic, anti-imperialist government that was increasingly coming under, on the one hand, great economic and financial pressure from the British colonialists, and, on the other, political pressure from its internal allies.

The British government was warning potential buyers not to purchase Iranian oil, threatening to confiscate the oil tankers on the high seas as 'stolen British property', as was the case with the Italian and Japanese purchases of Iranian oil. The British government also fanned imperialist propaganda around the world, and especially in Iran through a hired reactionary press, propagating the idea that Iran would soon become a Soviet satellite.

The Korean war and the TPI's sustained campaign added grist to the mill of McCarthyism in the US, eventually contributing, with the financial input of

Tudeh Newspaper Cartoon depicting Mosaddeq as supporter of the US Military

Mosaddeq depicted by Tudeh Journal as an American Stooge

major oil concerns, to the victory of the Republican presidential candidate in 1952, just as the hysterical propaganda against the nationalisation of Iranian oil in the press in Britain and on the BBC had helped the Conservative Party to return to power a year earlier. British propaganda, using the 'threat of communism', as exemplified by the TPI's provocations over oil negotiations with the US administration and UK government, was successful in convincing President Eisenhower that the answer to the Iranian 'problem' was a putsch. Anyone familiar with US-UK diplomatic negotiations over Iranian oil could easily see that.[366]

The British embargo and the confiscation of Iranian holdings in British banks, as well as the refusal of the Soviet government to return Iranian gold holdings in Moscow after the Second World War, helped to worsen the economic situation, especially for the working people, including some 50 000 oil workers who remained unemployed but were paid out of the government's meagre budget. The TPI worked hard to use this economic pressure to mobilise the working population against Mosaddeq's government, not always successfully, however. To finance some government expenses, especially to pay the unemployed oil workers, Mosaddeq expanded the money supply by printing a limited amount of official currency, which had only a slight inflationary effect, much less than what happened after the putsch when the new government had both foreign aid and the oil income. Studies of Mosaddeq's economic policies by Western scholars demonstrate that all the forecasts by Anglo-American services predicting the imminent fall of his government under economic pressure were erroneous — but they were errors that the TPI shared. In fact, Mosaddeq, by encouraging home industries, reducing luxury imports used by the rich and increasing taxes on the rich, managed both to strengthen the national economy and to stop the depletion of foreign reserves — those sequestered in London and Moscow notwithstanding. Mosaddeq's economic programme was not limited to encouraging and reinforcing domestic production and cutting down on non-essential imports, for which there was no foreign exchange available. He also authorised the foreign exchange rate to fluctuate so as to let the overvalued currency reach a level making non-essential imported goods, consumed by the rich, more expensive and highly taxed.

On the other hand, Mosaddeq, who had, during the first phase of his premiership before July 1952, avoided internal reforms in order not to open new fronts to complicate the struggle against British imperialism, once back in office with greater popularity and having weakened the reactionaries in the parliament, asked the Majles for plenipotentiary powers in order to enact *experimental* legal projects to be put into effect for a limited trial period with two purposes in mind; firstly, to familiarise the public with the need for social and political reforms; secondly, to examine the efficiency of the experimental projects in the midst of the struggle on the external front. The TPI, which had loudly cried for a 'united front' with Mosaddeq and his supporters, now continued, in unison with the most reactionary elements, to oppose Mosaddeq's reforms.

In spite of gloomy forecasts by the British and American Embassies that the blockade would disrupt the economy and increase discontent amongst the population, Mosaddeq managed to improve economic conditions and avoid the disaster that the British and American governments were preparing by their blockade and boycott of oil purchases. That is why, at long last, the option of the *coup d'état* proved to be the only one to which they could resort.[367]

Thus, on the morrow of the July uprising, Mosaddeq, both as Premier and Defence Minister, began to have the armed forces purged of reactionary, corrupt generals by means of elected officers' committees,[368] sending them into retirement. According to one source, some 136 senior officers, among whom were one marshal, four four-star generals, 10 three-star generals, and many colonels were retired. After the February 1953 attempt to lynch Mosaddeq at the Palace gates, Mosaddeq retired more high-ranking officers, notably the Chief of General Staff who had been appointed by the shah.[369] After these retirements, several military candidates manifested their readiness to the British and the Americans to work for the execution of the putsch. The Conservative government in Britain managed to convince the American administration, first the Democrats and later the Republicans, to collaborate fully with it and to carry out the coup, as there was no other way of bringing Mosaddeq's government to its knees. Yet, in spite of increasingly alarming rumours regarding a coup to prevent a 'communist take-over' of Iran and then the news that a *coup d'état* was being planned against Mosaddeq's government, the Tudeh leadership continued its policy of sowing dissension in the anti-imperialist movement. Its press persisted in its attacks against Mosaddeq, although in the autumn of 1952 Mosaddeq, more popular and stronger than before the July uprising, as alluded to above, asked his Minister of Justice, at the risk of being accused by the US and UK governments of strengthening communism, to review the circumstances of the 1949 'attempt on the life of the shah' and see whether the TPI had really been involved in it or not. The judicial review absolved the Tudeh leadership of the charges, thus declaring the leaders in Moscow exile free to return to Iran.

Another result of this judicial decision should have been serenity and less hostility on the part of the TPI against the national-democratic movement. Alas, it was not so, as Stalin's Russia could not tolerate a democratic regime which would provide the terrain for the growth of healthy socialist thinking in a society badly in need of it. This democratic development and Mosaddeq's social and political reform programmes, on the one hand, and his opposition to the illegal expectations of some of his erstwhile 'liberal' allies in the Patriotic Front, on the other[370] — those who had taken up pro-Anglo-American positions and opposed the reforms which would have eventually eradicated privileges and democratised the society — led such elements to break away from the Front and join the reactionary putschists. In the parliament and in the press they campaigned against Mosaddeq, working hand in hand with the Court, the latifundistas, reactionary retired army officers and the comprador bourgeoisie, for the overthrow of the national-democratic government headed by Mosaddeq.

The first attempt to get rid of Mosaddeq was to have him killed, or lynched, by a mob of roughnecks supporting the shah, when leaving the Royal Palace. To do this, the shah had informed Mosaddeq that he wished to leave the country for a period of rest. Mosaddeq had opposed the idea. Upon his insistence, Mosaddeq conceded, provided he left quietly, without any official announcements. Protocol required that Mosaddeq bid farewell to the monarch. The day he was to depart, Mosaddeq went to the Court. Suddenly, there appeared a big crowd of ruffians and roughnecks at the gate of the palace as Mosaddeq was to leave. They were shouting anti-Mosaddeq slogans. Mosaddeq's erstwhile ally Mullah Kashani, who had recently broken with him, had asked the parliament to prevent the shah from leaving the country, as if it had been Mosaddeq's plan to expel him; the well-known royalist Mullah Behbehani had also issued a declaration asking the 'people' not to let the shah leave the country. This is why the roughnecks and ruffians had been brought to the gate of the Palace in the name of the 'people'. As they were about to put their plan into effect when Mosaddeq was leaving the Court, an employee of the Court accompanying the Premier to the gate quickly realised the danger and led him through another gate on the north side of the palace. When the crowd discovered that Mosaddeq had left safely through another gate, they drove to his house in the vicinity and forced the iron gate of his residence in order to lynch him there. His residence being defended by loyal officers, the rowdy crowd was driven away.[371]

At this point, the supporters of the government began to stage demonstrations defending the premier. Demonstrations on both sides went on for several days. Again, contrary to the claims by the Anglo-American media,[372] the TPI entered the scene belatedly and had a lukewarm attitude in defending the national-democratic government. In a secret telegram to Foreign Secretary Anthony Eden on board RMS *Queen Elizabeth*, on 3 March 1953 the Foreign Office informed him that the TPI had also taken part in the demonstration taking place after the failure of the plan, but after a delay, adding that in this event the TPI was on Mosaddeq's side, but this did not necessarily mean that they were allies; and nor were Mosaddeq's supporters happy about the TPI's support.[373] As noted above, even after the Royal Palace incident, the Tudeh leaders in Moscow, in their interview with the *Daily Worker*, accused Mosaddeq of serving American interests.

The next blow was the kidnapping and murder of Mosaddeq's new chief of police, who was not a royalist. The news of his kidnap and murder obviously weakened the image of Mosaddeq's hold on power. Mosaddeq had the culprits arrested, except for his erstwhile ally Deputy Baqa'i, who enjoyed parliamentary immunity. The culprits, charged with kidnapping and murder, awaited trial, according to Mosaddeq's legalist procedure, instead of being court-martialed immediately as some, even among Mosaddeq's supporters, wished.

Having abolished the reactionary Senate by a vote of the parliament as demanded by the public, Mosaddeq now could also arrest General Zahedi, the prime candidate to lead the coup. Zahedi moved from his hide-out to the Majles and was given sanctuary by the parliament's new speaker Mullah Kashani, recently elected by the reactionary majority. Having received great publicity by the hired reactionary press while in the sanctuary of the Majles and at a publicised meeting with Kashani, he went back into hiding to prepare the coup under Kermit Roosevelt's guidance.[374]

In the meantime the TPI fanned its 'united front' proposition, without reducing its hostility and animosity towards the national-democratic movement. The insincerity of the TPI in this regard can be understood from the fact that only shortly before chanting the slogan of a 'united front' with the Patriotic Front, of which Maleki's socialist Third Force Party was a leading unit, it had published a booklet called *The Maleki Clique at the Service of Imperialism*. As for the radical wing of the Front, events showed clearly that the parties and personalities who remained loyal to Mosaddeq did not, or could not, galvanise the people and organise them into units that could resist the reactionary forces in case of a coup. The proposal by Mosaddeq's radical Foreign Minister and the editor of the widely-read daily *Bakhtar-e emrouz* to form a national guard for the defence of the movement and the government was not taken seriously by the Front's deputies. As will be discussed below, one of the main reasons for the Front's inability to organise itself in the face of the looming menace of the coup was the internecine rivalry of its leaders, something that was also the case with the Tudeh leaders, an historically deep-rooted characteristic of Iranian society.

VIII: The Tudeh Party's Controversial Incapacity *vis-à-vis* the 1953 Anglo-American Putsch

The 1953 coup and especially the TPI's actions — or rather inaction — in those days have been a very controversial issue, contested by every side involved, and is a question about which various versions have been related, often involving premeditated lies, particularly by the last Tudeh First-Secretary Kianouri. In spite of our limitation of space, it is necessary to deal in some detail with what took place in those few days, contrasting various versions in order to clarify the issue, trying to reconstruct a clear picture of what happened.

In the aftermath of the Royal Palace incident in February, a Tudeh front organisation asked Mosaddeq's government to be authorised to hold a rally on the occasion of Stalin's death on 5 March 1953. Permission granted, the TPI mustered all its forces for a show of force. On its part, the Anglo-American coalition used the demonstration as a proof of the growing 'communist menace' against the 'free world' in Iran. At the same time, Stalin's death intensified the rivalry in the Kremlin amongst his lieutenants, especially between Khrushchev and Beria. The Americans found the confused state of the leadership in Moscow most opportune to expedite the preparations for the coup, hoping that Moscow would not be in a position to react.[375] The confusion must have further encouraged the Americans when, on 26 June, the plot Khrushchev had planned against Beria was successfully hatched with the help of Malenkov, Bulganin and Molotov in the Presidium, where Beria was accused of being an 'enemy' and a 'traitor', arrested by officers loyal to Khrushchev, and done away with.[376]

At this time, Kermit Roosevelt, the CIA chief for Middle Eastern affairs, was secretly dispatched to Iran to establish contacts and make the coup preparations locally. Above all, he secretly visited the shah, who was in a state of desperation and unable to act. He was finally persuaded through assurances given by the British Premier Churchill — via a coded BBC message — and consented to issuing two *firmans* (decrees), one dismissing Mosaddeq and another appointing General Zahedi as Prime Minister — an act that was, in spite of continued claims to the contrary, unconstitutional.[377]

Army commanders deemed likely to sympathise with a coup were approached to collaborate with the scheme. Only one division commander, Colonel Bakhtiar in Kermanshah, who after the coup was appointed Military Governor of Tehran and later founded and became the first chief of the SAVAK, went over to the putschist camp, while most others, though certainly not royalist, remained uncommitted, awaiting the outcome of the uncertain situation. Rumours regarding an impending putsch were printed in the press, especially that of the TPI, on the occasion of an unexpected and unplanned short visit to Iran by the American General Schwarzkopf, who was to rally officers he had trained in the 1940s. During the war, he had been appointed by Premier Qavam to reorganise the Iranian Gendarmerie, where he had managed to make friends with a number of upper-echelon and middle-rank officers.[378] The American Office of Strategic Studies (OSS) and later the CIA had also established contacts in Iran for an operation codenamed BEDAMN,[379] which basically aimed at anti-communist propaganda, whose two Iranian operatives were codenamed Nerren and Cilley.[380]

As regards the role of other civilians who took part in the planned coup, both the American and the British Embassies had their hirelings, who, in the parliament as well as in the press, were disseminating disinformation against Mosaddeq and about the 'communist menace' looming on the horizon. (After the closure of the British Consulates and Embassy, the British agents were put in contact with the CIA office in Iran that had been carrying out the project BEDAMN, now also aimed against Mosaddeq.)

These agents worked especially among the clergy in order to incite the people through them against the 'communist menace' and Mosaddeq and his government. Majles deputies were won over by bribes so as to weaken the government and hopefully bring about the downfall of Mosaddeq through a vote of no-confidence. Aware of such plans, Mosaddeq first severed relations with Britain, in November 1952, in order to prevent contacts between the embassy and the reactionary forces, deputies, journalists, newspaper owners and army officers, as well as those who were in a position to organise the roughnecks and ruffian mobs. What he did not foresee was that the British agents would be linked to the US Embassy.

What is more, Iranian agents of the SIS, notably the Rashidian brothers, established contacts with Mullah Kashani and other 'liberals' who had left the Patriotic Front in order to win them over to the candidate who was to lead the coup, that is, General Zahedi. This was not a difficult task, as Kashani and Zahedi had collaborated in the past, that is, since their arrest as Nazi agents during the war. On the other hand, the British Embassy expert in religion, Robin Zaehner, working with MI6,[381] had worked on an understanding between the pro-British former Premier Seyyed Zia, known for his Islamic rigor, and the fanatic terrorist sect Fada'iyan-e Islam, in order to incite them to assassinate Mosaddeq's collaborators, and even the Premier himself. The first victim was Mosaddeq's radical and closest aide, government spokesman and Foreign Minister, Dr Fatemi, who survived the attempt, but was seriously injured and permanently disabled. (He was executed a year after the coup.)

In spite of all these schemes, Mosaddeq did not attempt to arrest and jail his active opponents arbitrarily. Even his attempt to put on trial those guilty of crimes was slow, even in the case of those responsible for kidnapping and assassinating, in the spring of 1953, the country's new Chief of Police, who was fully committed to Mosaddeq. Mosaddeq always acted within the framework of existing laws, although he wished to change or amend the ones he did not find democratic or just. He was a staunch legalist. He did not wish, unlike his reactionary rivals, to go down in history as someone who did not respect the

Constitution — a policy that, although highly admirable, did not ensure the safety of his government. He finally decided to organise a referendum — for which there was no Constitutional ground — to let the people choose between his government and the Majles, reactionary in its majority and in the pay of the Anglo-American secret services. The majority of the people participated in the referendum and voted overwhelmingly, never witnessed before in Iran, to dissolve the Majles; fresh elections were to be held under the new radicalised conditions. Had the *coup d'état* not occurred, some Tudeh candidates would have found their way into the Majles.

Naturally, the unprecedented collaboration of the TPI with the national referendum, which raised both the participation and the 'yes' votes, provided the reactionaries with the pretext to accuse Mosaddeq of both 'uniting with the communists' and rigging the ballots. When he was accused by the internal reaction as well as the Western media of acting illegally, he retorted that the 'will of the people' was above the law, especially at extraordinary times. For the first time, the TPI agreed with him. True, the referendum was not foreseen in the Iranian Constitution; neither was it in the French Constitution when General de Gaulle organised one in September 1958, nor when the shah did the same in 1963. No Western commentator ever accused the shah or de Gaulle of acting illegally!

Be that as it may, with the dissolution of the parliament, the pace of the coup was accelerated. In the aftermath of the referendum, the CIA operative Roosevelt managed to get the shah's signature for two unwritten *firmans*, the texts of which were later filled in. The plan simply was to have the *firman* to dismiss Mosaddeq delivered to him at midnight on 12 or 13 August by a loyal commanding officer of the Royal Guards, Colonel Nasiri. At the same time Mosaddeq and his closest colleagues were to be arrested, jailed and probably liquidated, while the sensitive points of the capital were to be taken over and telephone exchanges of Tehran occupied by the putschist forces. However, the execution of the plan was delayed for three days.[382] Kianouri claims that it was the announcement of an impending coup in one of the Tudeh's legal newspapers that made the putschists postpone the plan for 'one' day. There is no doubt that the TPI had been informed of the coup plan by its TMO officers in the Royal Guards and had accordingly revealed it in one of its newspapers, but the reason for the delay is not what Kianouri claims.[383] Kianouri's claim that he also informed Mosaddeq by telephone on 15 August has also been questioned by his opponents in the party.[384]

When it was decided once more to stage the coup, Colonel Nasiri managed to get hold of a few tanks and some arms and munitions that had been locked up, on Mosaddeq's orders, after the Royal Guards had been disarmed. It has not been revealed who was responsible for this disloyalty to the government, although it is now clear, as Mosaddeq stated during his trial, that his Army Chief of General Staff General Riahi had been slack in carrying out his duties with regard to disarming the Royal Guards and seizing their equipment.[385]

On 15 August, at around 7pm, before they could attempt to put the plot into action at midnight, someone, who did not identify himself, informed Mosaddeq by telephone that the coup was to take place in a few hours.[386] The Premier had previously learned of such a plot via other sources. At this time the Premier immediately convoked General Riahi to take precautionary actions.[387] Towards midnight, putschist elements of the armed forces occupied sensitive points in the capital; by surprise late in the evening, the radical Foreign Minister Fatemi was arrested by a platoon of 60 military men just as some other Mosaddeq collaborators were seized in their homes, while General Riahi, resting at his summer resort in northern Tehran, had already been called to duty by the Prime Minister, thus narrowly escaping arrest. What is more, the putschists managed to carry out some of their plans, including disabling the telephone lines to the headquarters of the Chief of General Staff of the armed forces as well as those of Tehran's commercial centre, the bazaar, which was one of Mosaddeq's staunch support centres. The Kermanshah division under Colonel Bakhtiar was directed by the putschists to Tehran to help the forces in the capital if necessary.[388]

When Nasiri and his forces reached Mosaddeq's residence, they were encircled and arrested by the loyal army units protecting his residence. While Fatemi and other Mosaddeq collaborators were released after Nasiri's arrest, other putschists elsewhere in the capital were taken into custody.

On 16 August, when Iranians woke up, they heard, at seven in the morning, the government's announcement that the expected coup had been nipped in the bud, but not all the putschists, including General Zahedi, had been arrested. The latter was 'at large', with a 100 000 rial prize for information leading to his arrest; the prize for his arrest did not tempt those who knew his whereabouts. Some said he was hiding in the US Embassy. It is now confirmed that, as Mosaddeq told Ambassador Henderson during their last encounter on 18 August, Zahedi and his collaborators were scheming in a US Embassy safe-house under the leadership of Roosevelt.[389] After the government's announcement of the failure of the coup and the flight of the shah in a private plane to Baghdad and then to Rome, huge demonstrations were immediately held all over Iran, especially in the capital, against the putschists and the shah who had collaborated with them.

In Tehran, two demonstrations were held, one by the Patriotic Front in the Parliament Square (Baharestan), where its deputies denounced the coup in moderate speeches; another was held in the adjacent avenue by the TPI, which, bolder than ever, launched the demand for the establishment of a 'people's republic' and a 'people's democracy'.[390] Notable is that also the Mosaddeqist Third Force Party, despite the views of its titular leader Maleki, demanded simply the establishment of a 'republic'. The crowds in Baharestan, too, chanted anti-shah slogans, demanding the establishment of a 'republic'.

It was later reported that the Patriotic Front leaders had tried to prevent Foreign Minister Fatemi from speaking on that occasion to avoid the radicalisation of the demonstration. Fatemi finally spoke as the huge crowds demanded that he address the demonstrators. His speech, much to the pleasure of the demonstrators, was radical, directly attacking the Pahlavi family as well as the shah himself.[391] Fatemi was later blamed by his colleagues for his 'unauthorised attacks' upon the Pahlavi family; in one of his secret notes later written from the underground to a leader of the National Resistance Movement, he explained that all he had said and written during those three fateful days had been cleared in advance with Premier Mosaddeq himself.[392] Mosaddeq never disclaimed his statement.

Be that as it may, the TPI's radical slogans and the radical anti-Pahlavi speech by Fatemi provided the pretext for the Western media, especially those fed by the secret services of the US and the UK, to publicise the impending creation of a 'people's democracy' subservient to the USSR in Iran.

As regards the two slogans of the TPI on that and the next two days — the demands for a 'people's republic' and a 'people's democracy' — it has been suggested that the CIA played a role in their adoption, perhaps inadvertently, by the TPI, as a means of scaring the non-communist patriotic forces and demobilising the people in general out of fear of a communist take-over, as well as to galvanise the royalists.[393] Whether they were launched in the name of the party by Roosevelt's agents within the upper ranks of the Tudeh leadership or in the street demonstrations cannot be known. As discussed below, Azarnour, a notable TMO officer and later also a TPI Central Committee member, is, on the basis of his investigations, of the strong opinion that at least one enemy agent had infiltrated the upper echelons of the party, most probably at the level of the Tehran Provincial Committee, while he does not exclude that Kianouri might have also been linked to the Western secret agencies.[394] To be added is that Azarnour had no access to the secret STASI reports quoted above.

At any rate, that atmosphere was in turn used by Roosevelt in Tehran to mobilise some of the hesitant military elements and clerical forces to move on to the scene and make a second attempt to overthrow Mosaddeq, in spite of instructions from Washington to him that he was to pack and leave Iran, with the US not being able for the time being to take any action, and had to 'snuggle with Mosaddeq, if we are going to save anything there'.[395]

It is important to recall that Mosaddeq's close collaborator and Minister of Finance, M Nariman, recollects that at the cabinet meeting on 16 August he proposed to court-marshal those who had been arrested for the attempted coup the night before and, and if found guilty and condemned — which was certain — they should be executed immediately. This would certainly have discouraged many officers who collaborated afterwards with the successful coup three days later. His proposal was not approved by the cabinet.[396]

In the meantime, Iranian agents of the CIA, for instance, pretending to be Tudeh militants, wrote threatening letters to prominent clerics in which they stated that their communist regime would soon hang them by their turbans.[397] This was intended to have them rally behind the second coup that Roosevelt was hatching. At the same time, a 'large crowd' was hired by CIA agents to march in central Tehran on 17 August 'shouting Tudeh slogans and carrying signs denouncing the shah'. This fake Tudeh crowd, which was hired for $50 000 by the CIA agents, was 'designed to provoke fears of a Tudeh takeover and thus rally support for Zahedi'. Reportedly, the crowd was soon joined by genuine Tudeh members, who 'were not aware that it was a CIA provocation'.[398] If so, it remains a mystery why the TPI's cadres did not prevent the provocation, as any participation in demonstrations was usually strictly organised and controlled by the party. It is likely that the foreign mole in the leadership performed his task well. Interestingly, one important TPI Executive Committee document confirms that the demonstration during which the anti-monarchy and pro-'Democratic Republic' slogan was chanted took place 'without previous preparations'.[399] Was it because a CIA agent had infiltrated the Tudeh leadership at the summit or at the very top of its Youth Organisation under the effective control of Shermini? These are questions that will be discussed below.

The issue of the 'unknown' individual who had informed Mosaddeq by telephone of the impending coup on the evening of 15 August has long been discussed and contested, and still remains a controversial question. Tudeh leaders have made much of the claim that either Kianouri or one of the TMO officers was the 'unknown' person. Kianouri, known for his remarkable talent at prevarication, has repeatedly claimed that he was the person who informed the Prime Minister by telephone of the forthcoming putsch. On the other hand, others in the TPI have argued that it was not Kianouri, but Colonel Mobasheri of the TMO Secretariat. Still others have stated that the 'unknown' man was Colonel Fouladvand, an officer in the Royal Guards faithful to Mosaddeq. In the military tribunal, Mosaddeq spoke of more than one person who had informed him of the impending coup. Fouladvand might have been his first source a few days before the coup, rather than the individual who telephoned him at about seven o'clock on the evening of 15 August. It is very probable that it had been on Fouladvand's tip that the premier had asked his Chief of Staff to disarm the Royal Guards and lock up their arms a few days before the attempted coup.

The problem with the Tudeh claim, however, is that it was made years after Mosaddeq's trial, during which he had spoken of the 'unknown' individual, who had not wished to identify himself. For this reason, as pointed out by some,[400] Kianouri's attempt to attribute this contribution to himself is dishonest. There are many contradictions in his claim. The most serious reason for refuting Kianouri's claim is that he had not made such a claim in his secret letter, written in the winter of 1332/1954, to his Central Committee comrades in Moscow,[401] where he could have boasted of his great contribution to nip the coup in the bud. Kianouri makes the same claim as regards the attempt to come to the rescue of Mosaddeq's government on the day of the second coup, 19 August. For that occasion, he asserts that he spoke to Premier Mosaddeq three times, at 11.00, 13.00 and 14.00, and that is why the Executive Committee did not take any action until it was too late at two o'clock in the afternoon. Yet, with regard to the TPI's lack of action against the putschists, the secret letter by the majority of three of the Executive Committee to the Central Committee in Moscow expressly states that:

> Kianouri, in opposition [to the suggestion by Executive Committee member Ollovi] to organise a general strike[402] in order to bring the people on to the streets, insisted that no action be taken before getting in touch with [Premier] Mosaddeq; thus, we could not decide [what to do] because no contact could be made with Mosaddeq before 12 o'clock. By the afternoon, when we had consultations with comrades of Tehran [Provincial Committee], Mosaddeq had been overthrown.[403]

The strangest thing is that the 'resolution' of the TPI's Enlarged Fourth Plenum held in Moscow in the summer of 1957 (see Section II:XIII), without the participation of two of the three members of the Tehran Executive Committee majority — that is, Ollovi, Bahrami and Yazdi[404] — ignored their aforementioned statement and adopted Kianouri's newly-coined version of the events, that is:

> After the beginning of the [second] *coup d'état* and the development of ambiguity as to the nature of the events of 19 August, lest any action be taken in contradiction to Mosaddeq's policy, the EC telephoned him and left it at that [!]; they were reassured by his statement that he was in control of the situation. With the further development of events and their dangerous aspects becoming evident, they telephoned Mosaddeq again. When they heard him say that 'I can do nothing; do whatever you can',

first they considered the situation to be out of his hands, and when at 3pm they wanted to do something, party communications had been disabled as a result of the second instruction [to party members] after the second[405] phone call to Mosaddeq on 19 August — a decision taken unanimously instructing party comrades to go home and destroy party documents and papers. At this time, the leadership could have taken various courses of action, but due to its lack of attention to the possibilities, no action was taken.[406]

Thus, taking advantage of the absence of his former Tehran Executive Committee comrades, who had, in the meantime, been arrested in Iran (in January 1956) and renounced their allegiance to the TPI and the USSR — under torture or not, no one knows — and the execution by the regime of the fifth member of the Executive Committee, Ollovi, Kianouri managed, with the complicity of Jowdat, the third member of the Executive Committee majority, to coin a falsified version of the history of that episode. Why the plenum took seriously such a resolution has not been explained.

The contradiction resides in the fact that in a letter dated 9 Farvardin 1333/30 March 1954 sent from Tehran to the Central Committee in Moscow, A-A Shandermani, Secretary[407] of the Executive Committee who was more on the side of Kianouri than of the majority, does not confirm the former's claim that the Executive Committee had been in contact with Mosaddeq by telephone,[408] but in a report written two years later, after Kianouri's arrival in Moscow, which he handed to First-Secretary Radmanesh, Shandermani repeats Kianouri's claim that the Executive Committee had decided — he does not say exactly when — to ask Mosaddeq by telephone whether or not to start demonstrations in the streets through a general strike, to which the premier had, so he claims, replied that the party should not do anything because he was in control of the situation! He adds that 'a few hours later' the Executive Committee decided again to 'discuss' the situation 'with Mosaddeq', by telephone, to encourage him to speak to the people on the radio, asking them for help, so that the party could instruct its members to suppress the roughnecks and members of the Royal Guards. Mosaddeq, so he claims again, asked him to phone back within 'an hour or two' because the Council of Ministers was in session. In a third telephone call to Mosaddeq, the latter reportedly told Kianouri that 'the situation is out of my hands; do whatever you consider to be your duty',[409] that is, repeating Kianouri's version. This is, of course, false, for there was no meeting of the Council of Ministers going on at Premier's residence, although some of his collaborators were with him; nor is the timing correct, for by noon his residence had been under fire by an armoured car of the putschist forces and no 'discussion' could have taken place over the phone with the leaders of a party that had opposed him over several years and in whom he had no trust. Besides, Mosaddeq is reported by a reliable source to have been in constant telephone contact with his Chief of General Staff for as long as it was possible.[410] The new version of events by Shandermani, which contradicts the aforementioned Executive Committee letter to the Central Committee in Moscow, must be a fabrication that Kianouri fed others from the moment he arrived in Moscow, particularly because the reports written previously inside the country never mentioned any actual contact with Mosaddeq on the phone. Besides, Mosaddeq's elder son writes in his memoirs that, having been worried about his father, he had tried all morning to reach him on the phone and had not been able to do so.[411]

Withal, in his letter of the winter of 1954 to the Central Committee in Moscow, Kianouri clearly states that:

> ... we really did not believe in the possibility of a [further] coup, its negative effects, and the repercussions of a defeat. We reached the conclusion that the imperialists no longer had the possibility for a coup; even after the coup of 16 August and its failure, when drafting the Central Committee declaration, in the section on the existence of putschist elements, the discussion was that there was no longer the possibility of a [further] putsch. They [the Central Committee majority] had even doubts as to the probability of a coup on 16 August.[412]

Yet Kianouri adds that his four Executive Committee comrades believed that, although the situation was such that 'we could not achieve any success..., it would have been correct to come out at any rate, and even if defeated, through our struggle we would have acquired prestige'. Kianouri personally believed that 'had we come out (by midday) even with the little means we had, the enemy would probably not have been victorious'.[413] If both these claims are honestly reported, then it is not clear why they did not do so and then related a false version of events.

As for the phone calls to Mosaddeq which Shandermani raises again, one should recall the reasoning by the prominent TMO member Azarnour who, on the basis of the letter of the three members of the Executive Committee, concludes that no contact with Mosaddeq took place on 19 August.[414] Central Committee member Dr Keshavarz, too, seriously questions Kianouri's claim that he had spoken to Mosaddeq on the telephone.[415] No less important is the statement by Colonel Zibayee, of the Office of the Military Governor, most probably based on confessions by arrested members of the TPI Tehran Provincial Committee who were present at that meeting, according to which, up until midday all efforts by the Tudeh leadership to speak to Mosaddeq on the phone proved useless, and when they managed to establish contact 'to ask him what to do', it was already too late, for the putschist forces were reaching the Tehran radio transmitter.[416]

What is more, in its brochure on the coup, *Darbareh-ye 28 Mordad (Concerning 19 August)*,[417] the Executive Committee also does not mention any telephone conversation with Mosaddeq, although it provides still another version: that the 'Military Governor' of Tehran 'refused any assistance by the democratic organisations', that is, the NSCC, adding that until midday Dr Mosaddeq claimed that he held sway over the situation, but a few hours later he had no hope for resistance. Only the [military] unit protecting his residence did not give up...' On the other hand, it has also been reported that a leader of the NSCC named Qodveh managed, in the morning of 19 August, to meet Mosaddeq's secretary and 'inform' him of what was going on in the city.[418] This claim was not confirmed by either Mosaddeq or anyone in his entourage.[419] All these contradictory claims prove one thing: that each Tudeh leader has invented his 'fact of contact with Mosaddeq' in order to justify his party's inaction on that fateful day.

Kianouri's prevarications are more extensive. For instance, he affirms that, because the TPI had informed Premier Mosaddeq in advance of the impending coup, its leadership had also instructed the TMO officers to come to the defence of Mosaddeq's government. One of the glaring examples of his illustrations, so he claims, is that Captain A-A Shoja'iyan, of the TMO and ostensibly:

> ... collaborating with the putschists, commanded the unit that was to suppress the Defence Guards of Mosaddeq's residence. We had instructed him to do his revolutionary work, and when the putschist Colonel Nasiri arrived at Mosaddeq's residence to engage in battle with Mosaddeq's guards and arrest Mosaddeq, Shoja'iyan joined Mosaddeq's Guards and thus Nasiri was arrested.

He and those who have systematically supported him have stated that Captain I Davarpanah and Captain M Fesharaki, officers in charge of Mosaddeq's Guards, 'confirmed' this claim after the revolution, citing them:

> The unit commanded by Captain Shoja'iyan, who was apparently collaborating with the putschists but in fact was a member of TMO, had the mission to destroy us, but Captain Shoja'iyan under instruction from his party, instead of killing us, encircled Nasiri and his men.[420]

The fact is that Shoja'iyan was a member of the Guards protecting Mosaddeq's residence[421] and needed no instructions from the party to oppose the putschists. Withal, he has never confirmed what Kianouri and others have claimed in his name. After the second coup, Shoja'iyan was one of the five officers accused by the putschist government of having 'killed and injured people on 19 August 1932', committed 'treason' against the monarchy and the 'nation's rights;'[422] he was No 32 on the list of officers and civilians prosecuted in military tribunals, along with Premier Mosaddeq, for crimes against the monarchy.[423]

IX: The Tudeh Party's Reaction on the Morrow of the Putsch (August 1953–August 1954)

While the Tudeh leadership, admittedly, made no timely and correct decisions on the fateful days of 16-19 August, apparently due to quarrels, on the morrow of the coup it took a number of precipitous decisions to confront the new power in place. One cannot be certain whether these decisions were genuinely meant or were merely meant to cool off the anger of the rank-and-file of the party and the TMO officers. At any rate, the party 'theoretician' Tabari states that while up to the putsch there were constant quarrels in the Executive Committee, suddenly thereafter there was unity among its members and everyone agreed with Kianouri in opposing the new regime, as a result of which a 'series of adventurist measures were taken, which the Fourth Plenum was to call "Blanquist"'.[424]

The first measure the Tudeh leadership took in a state of panic after the putschists had succeeded in establishing themselves was to tell cadres and members to go home, burn all compromising documents, and break all contacts with the party. Then a few hours later they issued a directive to re-establish contacts and be prepared for an armed uprising on 21 August on the streets against the regime; the party would provide the demonstrators with hand-grenades it had manufactured for use against the military forces that would want to crush the uprising. Captain Madani of the TMO, who was executed in 1954, in his interrogations states that TMO officers had on 20 August received instructions to be ready, preferably in small groups, to carry out orders aimed against the Zahedi regime the next day, but on 21 August orders were given to officers and cadres to return to their normal lives, for no uprising was to take place.[425]

The original intention was to inspire the ordinary people to take to the streets and begin a new round of struggle against the new government. In a declaration distributed on 20 August 1953, the TPI Central Committee twice spoke of a 'rising' against the putschist government: 'We must rise and use all our power to destroy the treacherous government of Reza Khan's son without any fear and fully confident of final victory.'

While not seriously determined to carry on with the abrupt resolution, the

Central Committee made a terrible *faux pas* by announcing:

> The seeds of resistance exist in the army. They must be encouraged to disobey the orders of their commanders and to join the ranks of the people. There is no doubt that, if the people start the resistance movement a considerable number of honourable army personnel, officers who respect the national prestige, will join hands with the masses.

It went on:

> Dear compatriots, anti-imperialist combatants, army elements are available for the victory of the people over the imperialists and their puppet government. We must utilise these elements to our best advantage. Resistance movements must be organised; a united front must be created. Do not fear the preliminary victories of the enemy.[426]

Yet on the next day the decision was reversed. No reason has been reported for calling off the uprising; this is why it may have been merely a deceptive plan responding to the disappointment of the cadres with the leadership. One such cadre, Lieutenant-Colonel Abdul-Aziz Rostami-Gouran recalls:

> Many opportunities were lost. The outcome of the struggle of the Iranian nation under the leadership of Dr Mosaddeq to take over its oil industry fell upon that evil day. In a word, the honour of the Tudeh Party was besmirched. Today, as I look back at that fateful period and remember the treacherous deeds of the likes of Kianouri and the unworthy individual leaders [of the party], I have a sense of abasement.[427]

Ostensibly, one plan was to launch partisan warfare in the north of the country. The TMO, whose leadership had been angry because of the TPI Executive Committee's indecision, were contacted. The TMO did some preliminary studies of such an undertaking. Kianouri boasts about this plan, but claims that it was not put into operation because of an initial blow to its execution.[428] No one else in the party has confirmed this claim by Kianouri, which is held to be nothing but a prevarication.[429] The rudimentary, unrealistic plan was soon abandoned, particularly when the TMO officer Rostami-Gouran, second in command of the Kermanshah Division which had been ordered to come the capital, was mysteriously arrested.[430]

Another decision taken by the TPI Executive Committee two to three months after the putsch was the plan to have interested cadres and members trained in the methods of warfare in groups of 20 to 25 trainees by TMO officers;

about 100 groups are said to have been formed.[431] This plan was intended to complement the other measures, for ostensibly no uprising could take place without individuals trained in military arts. As the other plans were abandoned, this, too, had to be discontinued.

Still other actions undertaken by the Executive Committee was to destroy military installations, apparently to boost the morale of the people. A more serious plan was to collaborate with the southern tribes of Qashqai, whose leaders had been pro-Mosaddeq. Three top Tudeh cadres, including Rouzbeh, were sent south to discuss a plan. The TPI blamed the Qashqais for the refusal to cooperate; one Qashqai leader has confirmed that the council of the tribe, having considered the proposal, decided that they did not have the means to engage in such an undertaking. Yet the question is whether the TPI would have been able to start guerrilla warfare with the help of the Qashqai tribes, for the Royal Court also had its supporters among the tribes not merely in the south, but also in the west and in Azerbaijan. This plan also seems to have been rather illusory.[432] Besides, it is now known that the Second Bureau of the army had a full report on the Tudeh–Qashqai negotiations, that is, according to Azarnour, someone in the Tudeh delegation worked for the Second Bureau and had tape-recorded all the discussions, for the chief of the Bureau had said he was in possession of the tapes. Azarnour thinks this agent must have been the same mole who had exposed Rostami-Gouran.[433] Thus, given the information the regime had on the mission, the Qashqai adventure, too, was doomed to failure from the very start.

X: Dismantling the TMO, the TPI's Protective Umbrella

Exactly a year after the putsch, on 21 Mordad 1333/12 August 1954, in the early morning, Abul-Hassan Abbasi, a former army captain who had been several years previously expelled from the army because of his Tudeh connections, was arrested on the corner of a small street in the poor southern district of Tehran. His revelations to the Office of the Military Governor were fatal for the TPI, for they first led to the discovery of the TMO, and later to the uncovering of the TPI's Intelligence Department, and finally to the arrest of a good number of Tudeh leaders, cadres and members, as well as the discovery of the party's printing press. As a result, by the end of 1956, the party was to have totally disintegrated. A number of leaders, along with some 40 TMO officers, managed to flee secretly abroad. The only leader of the TMO who managed, for four years, to evade persecution was Khosrow Rouzbeh.

Almost all the Tudeh leaders and cadres who could not, or did not wish to, escape abroad were caught, imprisoned, broke down in prison, and recanted. A few even collaborated with the authorities. Of the captured TMO officers, 27 top cadres and leaders of the organisation, with 600 members, were executed between 19 October 1953 and 17 August 1955, the rest receiving either life imprisonment or long sentences.[434] Most of these surviving officers were, after some years, 'pardoned' by the shah and released; only a few who reportedly refused to ask for a 'pardon' remained in prison till the fall of the monarchy. Most of those who were released found jobs within the governmental system or with the help of the government created businesses which made them successful entrepreneurs. A few ended up working with the SAVAK.[435] After the revolution in 1979, some of them returned to the party's fold, a few provided it with funds, and a couple of them were executed after the party's second proscription under the very Ayatollah Khomeini whom it had praised and supported.

The annihilation of the TMO devastated the TPI. There was total disenchantment, not only among the party's membership, but also within the political opposition circles of the country who had much regretted their arrests. What would have been the fate of the TPI had Abbasi not been arrested or had died under torture without revealing any secrets?

Several contradictory versions have been offered as to how Abbasi was arrested; how and why he revealed to the authorities what he knew, revelations which put in motion a process leading to an irreparable débâcle which completely destroyed the party. Unfortunately, no independent study of this débâcle has been made in Persian or any other language. We must, therefore, content ourselves with a general picture of it and its consequences by working our way through the contradictory details of the many variants of the story.

One major reason for the uncovering of the TMO, which acted as the protective umbrella for the TPI, as noted above, was that, from the outset, the TMO's military information was naively used, *inter alia*, for propagandistic purposes, as a result of which the military authorities realised that there was some kind of military organisation obedient to the TPI that procured sensitive information which was then published in the Tudeh press. The débâcle was not merely the result of Abbasi saving his own skin. It was, above all, due to the ineptitude of the Tudeh leaders in their running an organisation that they boasted of being 'the vanguard of the proletariat' and the 'proletarian party of the new type' in Iran. Deputy Kambakhsh would boast of the information he knew about what went on in the armed forces, no doubt prompting the authorities to investigate his party's links with military officers. The lack of discretion of Tudeh leaders with regard to the TMO can be witnessed, for example, from boastful statements such as one by a Tudeh speaker in Rasht. He said: 'Our Tudeh [Party] has grown so strong and taken root that we have infiltrated the army.' Then he read a few verses of a poem an army officer had composed, to the effect that 'we army officers are not colonialists, we want freedom, and we serve [in the army] to support you'.[436] The Tudeh leaders' intellectual incapacity and negligence were witnessed during the Azerbaijan crisis and in respect of the oil nationalisation movement; this ineptitude was due, on the one hand, to the political backwardness of both its membership and, more generally, of Iranian society that had just emerged from under the boot of Reza Shah's military dictatorship, and, on the other, to the Stalinists' abuse of Iranians who wished to build a better society but did not know how to.

In addition, a number of adventurist actions were undertaken by the TMO under the encouragement of Kianouri, such as the inept production of hand-grenades during Mosaddeq's premiership, the purpose of which was not clear even to those who produced them. For instance, the explosion of one of them seriously injured a lecturer at the War College, a colonel, forcing him to discontinue his career and disappear inexplicably into a clandestine life and finally to end up in exile in the USSR, leading the Second Bureau of the army to investigate his disappearance. There were other actions, such as an adventurist arson attack on a military airfield after the 1953 putsch[437] and the theft of arms from military depots, all of which reinforced the suspicion of the regime that the party had a military wing.

An equally important factor was a lack of strict security measures to protect the TMO. According to former TMO officer Azarnour, who knew Abbasi, the latter had told him, about a month before his arrest on 12 August 1954, of his fear and anxiety of persecution and surveillance, for he was certainly known to the authorities as a target. Abbasi told Azarnour that he knew all the top cadres of the party and some 150 members of the TMO by name.[438] During his last meeting with Azarnour he was, as usual, carrying a briefcase full of sensitive documents, while eating and talking in a public restaurant. Another TMO officer, Lieutenant-Colonel Ekteshafi of the Air Force, who was also forced to lead an underground life after the arson attack on a military airfield and the manufacture of hand-grenades, recalls the same fear and anxiety expressed by Abbasi before he was caught.[439]

While some Tudeh leaders have accused Abbasi of being a 'traitor' for causing the *débâcle*, because he did not resist to his death the torture to which he was reportedly subjected, others have blamed the TMO leaders and the party's Executive Committee in Tehran for their laxity and inability to react to the menace that had threatened that organisation.

For his part, Lieutenant-Colonel Vakili of the TMO Secretariat in a secret letter smuggled out of prison to his sister states that Abbasi:

> ... who knew everything, had been arrested and resisted torture for *a few days*. Finally, he revealed the names of members of the Secretariat and the

person in charge of his branch. Under torture, he named the six members of the Secretariat (the sixth member Rouzbeh has not been arrested).[440]

In another secret letter, Vakili writes that, according to Colonel Jamshidi, a few days before the latter's arrest, Abbasi had sent a message as follows: "'Soon I will reveal everything." It is not clear why the three members of the Secretariat did not take this report seriously.'[441] Vakili also writes that Rouzbeh of the TMO Secretariat:

... is very self-centred and accepts no one's authority in the party except his own, while he is worth even less than Engineer Mohaqeqzadeh. Abbasi values his [Rouzbeh's] friendship more than party affairs. Before our arrest the news had come that the Office of the [Military] Governor was torturing Abbasi to force him to reveal Rouzbeh's place of residence. Now, it is not clear why he has, instead, exposed the organisation.[442]

On the other hand, almost all Tudeh versions claim that Abbasi resisted, for some 12 days, dreadful torture before divulging his secrets, hoping that in the meantime the safe-houses would be purged of all incriminating evidence.[443] Rouzbeh had claimed Abbasi had been made of 'steel'.[444] Tabari also states that Rouzbeh had confidence in Abbasi and that the story that Abbasi had 'resisted' 15 days torture is something that they had 'rumoured, but I am not certain about its veracity'.[445]

It is, however, difficult to believe that any human being could resist, for 12 long days, the kind of tortures practised in the prisons of the shah. Almost all prisoners broke down, including hundreds of TMO officers. What renders suspect the story of Abbasi's 'heroic' 12-day resistance to torture are the two independent versions that follow.

As for the circumstances of the débâcle, former TPI Central Committee member Dr Keshavarz has stated that, while in exile in Moscow, he and his Central Committee comrades received a report from Tehran, according to which the shah had given Abbasi the choice of either disclosing all the secrets he knew and receive in compensation all he wanted — freedom, money, a passport with a different identity to go to live in a country of his choice and be safe from harm by his former comrades — or to die under torture. According to Keshavarz, Abbasi had accepted the offer.[446] A similar version of this has also been told by a certain Mas'oud Maleki, who had then spent some years in prison.[447] His account, related by a high-ranking Tudeh cadre, is a telling story. Ansari quotes Maleki as follows:

'One day' — Ansari interjects, apparently the tenth day of Abbasi's arrest — 'Abbasi was told he had been summoned by the Military Governor General Bakhtiar in order to talk to him. Abbasi went to Bakhtiar's office. No one ever learned anything about what went on during the encounter and about the content of their conversation.'

What is certain — Maleki goes on — is that, as a result of that encounter, even before the discovery of the TMO, Maleki himself, who then was a military cadet and a TMO member on probation, and his brother Captain Ahmad Maleki were arrested in the same connection.[448] Aside from the day designated as 'apparently the tenth', the version is similar to that related by Dr Keshavarz.

Yet one may easily disbelieve the two accounts above, as many Tudeh leaders and members have, whether they accused Abbasi or not. What, however, renders these accounts credible is a secret report by the US Embassy about what the Military Governor of Tehran General Bakhtiar told the embassy's Second Secretary[449] on 30 August 1954, only some days after Abbasi had divulged all he knew:

> General Bakhtiar stated that these arrests resulted from information obtained from one Captain Abbasi.[450] Abbasi, who had been sought for more than a year in connection with alleged communist activities, was arrested on or shortly before 26 August 1954, and communist documents were found secreted in his clothing and in a suitcase which he carried.
>
> At first Abbasi refused to admit any connection with the [Tudeh] Party or answer leading questions; however, the highest military authority (believed to be HIM the Shah) gave assurances he would not be prosecuted if he would cooperate fully with his interrogators, but would instead be permitted to leave the country or remain in Iran incognito. Thereupon, Abbasi gave full information regarding a Communist ring in the Security Forces. On the basis of this information, [thus far] 50[451] military officers have been arrested in Tehran as well as several in the provinces, and two houses used as headquarters by the ring (one belonging to a Police Lieutenant Madani) were searched.
>
> Three types of documents were found in these headquarters, all in cipher, as follows: (1) personnel lists divided into (a) Tudeh Party members, (b) applicants on probation, (c) sympathisers; (2) Tudeh Party instructions; (3) espionage reports to 'a foreign government', including reports on the activities of United States representatives in Iran. With the personnel lists were statistics showing the number of communist or pro-communist officers in various Iranian towns.[452]

What reinforces further this version as *the* account of what happened is that, according to several reports by former Tudeh cadres who were in prison with Abbasi, the latter received preferential treatment in prison. While other Tudeh prisoners were crammed together, in groups of three to 14, in cells in which it was hardly possible to live, Abbasi, according to one account, was given a studio;[453] he also was treated with 'respect' by his jailers, although the narrator mistakenly relates that the reason was 'his resistance under torture', as if jailers and torturers of the putschist regime shared universalist values! What is more, Abbasi, though not receiving all that the shah had promised him, was not prosecuted or given any formal prison sentence and was released in 1961,[454] despite the fact that, in addition to his 'crime' of having been a member of a communist organisation and the TMO, he had taken part in several murders of individuals, including those of his party comrade Hesam Lankarani and the popular journalist M Mas'oud, in which he was the actual murderer.[455] It is not too far-fetched to assume that, because he knew that the regime was aware of his part in the murders and that he was a candidate for capital punishment, he voluntarily accepted the offer made to him.

It needs to be added that no record of Abbasi's interrogations have been published in the books put out by the authorities of the former regime in Iran or the present one, nor is there any indication that he was ever put on trial and condemned, as other members of the TMO were.[456] Moreover, in prison he spied against his former comrades for the authorities and even wrote a second declaration of loyalty to the shah and his regime.[457] After his release, he never tried to explain his acts or ask for a pardon from his former comrades.

It is also revealing that even after the revolution and the fall of the monarchy Abbasi did not wish to explain to his former comrades — some of whom held him in contempt — how he had been 'forced' to disclose his valuable secrets that had led to the execution of some 30 of his former comrades and to other examples of nefarious and irreparable damage to the country and its future. If the stories that he had been savagely tortured were true, he could show his comrades in prison the traces of the torture to which he had been subjected and explain the circumstances of his arrest, torture and revelations. Paradoxically, his silence is telling about the complicity of a man who was known to have been made of steel. It is interesting that his former TMO comrade Azarnour relates that, after the revolution, he sent Abbasi a message to arrange an appointment with him to discuss the débâcle, but he refused to meet him.[458] This refusal cannot be interpreted but as a sign of his voluntary collaboration with the regime.

Given Abbasi's fear of arrest and his behaviour in prison subsequent to his revelations, one can safely accept the account according to which he consented to the deal offered him by the shah and gave away all his secrets — except the whereabouts of his mentor and close friend Rouzbeh. If this be the case, then one can easily dismiss the myth that became prevalent right after his arrest, and held true thereafter by some, that he was made of 'steel', as his mentor Rouzbeh had claimed. Compared to an honourable man like Lieutenant-Colonel Vakili, who broke down under torture, but neither recanted nor made a deal, and, bidding adieu to his wife and infant child, died for his ideals, Abbasi cannot be remembered but with contempt, for his life was saved at the cost of the lives of many of his comrades and the destruction of their families, the exile of many more, provoking all the evident consequences: the annihilation of the TMO and the TPI, and above all the victory of the dictatorial regime of the shah that, in time, led to the gradual politico-cultural destruction of Iranian society under *dys*-developing capitalism with all the repercussions it entailed, resulting in the establishment of the Islamic State. Of course, one cannot hold Abbasi responsible for all the horrendous repercussions of the débâcle. Above all, one must hold accountable the leaders of the TPI for their political incompetence, irrational leadership and obedience to the 'big brother'.

As a result of this débâcle, one of the points raised in Tudeh circles and beyond was, once again, the infiltration of at least one mole into the upper echelons of the party. Right after the arrest of the TMO's leading officers and the successive confessions, Lieutenant-Colonel Vakili, in a letter smuggled out of prison and addressed to his wife, reports what he had heard from another comrade officer, that Khosrow Rouzbeh, the only Secretariat member whose whereabouts had not been divulged by Abbasi, was said to be 'an agent of the Second Bureau' of the army. In connection with his suspicions about Rouzbeh, Vakili says that 'the probability is not to be excluded', and he does give at least one reason for it:[459] 'circumstantial evidence' showed that the arrests of the TMO officers were due to 'treason'.[460] He further notes that, although he finds this accusation against Rouzbeh 'strange', he thinks it should be treated as 'extraordinarily important, for he [Rouzbeh] is responsible for the [Department of] Intelligence of the party, knows all the top-ranking persons in charge and can destroy the party all by himself'.[461]

The spread of such an accusation against the most important TMO leader throws light on the atmosphere of suspicion reigning in the party at the time. What is more, some TMO officers have, on the basis of exposed secrets known only to a few top Tudeh leaders, thought it probable that a member of the top leadership (possibly a member of the Tehran Provincial Committee) may have been a collaborator of the Second Bureau of the army[462] and had given it the names of some 30 members of the organisation. Withal, Azarnour relates that 'a high-ranking security officer [of the Pahlavi regime[463]] was particularly confident that the army's Second Bureau surely knew that one of the important members of the Tudeh leadership was in contact with the British, but he had no specific knowledge of this person'. He has a confirmation of this point through another officer of the former regime, who had heard the same from Mostafa Fateh, the only Iranian high-ranking employee of the AIOC and a close British collaborator.[464] Withal, the former TPI Executive Committee secretary Shandermani also states that he was nearly certain that someone at the top leadership had been working with the authorities. He remembers that he had reached that conclusion 'long before the 1953 putsch', when he was deputy-chief of the Department of Information. He had raised the question once, asking for an investigation, but had 'faced a strong rebuff by Jowdat, Yazdi and Kianouri'.[465] Baffling also is the fact that at the Fourth Party Plenum in 1957, lasting three weeks, during which many minor quarrels were debated, four important questions were raised but not dealt with: firstly, the role of Kianouri in the 'attempted assassination of the shah' on 4 February 1949 which led to the proscription of the party; secondly, the role played by Kambakhsh in the arrest of Arani's 'Group of Fifty-Three' in 1937; thirdly, the circumstances of the TMO débâcle; and fourthly, the Azerbaijan fiasco.[466]

XI: The TMO's Failure to Confront the Coup

The question that many have asked is whether the TPI could have — in Iran's national interest, rather than that of 'internationalism', which, in the case of Iran, had simply proved to be the interests of Soviet Russia — used the instrument and power it had in the TMO to reverse the situation on 19 August 1953. It is a fact that the party had some 600 well-organised, disciplined members in an army officer corps 8000 strong[467] which was predominantly not pro-monarchy but patriotic, albeit not organised and fearful of Iran falling into the Soviet camp.

As for the possibilities the Tudeh had in the TMO for neutralising the coup on those fateful days as the process unfolded, according to Azarnour,[468] the party had a number officers in key positions who could have attempted to turn the tide on 18 and 19 August. For one thing, the TMO had several of its members in the entourage of both Zahedi and the shah. Lieutenant-Colonel A-S Kheyrkhah, Captain M Homayoni, Captain E Fayyazi,[469] and Lieutenant I Irvani,[470] all these officers in the Royal Guards were members of the TMO. There were others, such as Colonel K Jamshidi,[471] one of many TMO tank commanders; Police Captain M Varqa,[472] chief of the Intelligence Department of the National Police and in charge of the security of ceremonies attended by the shah and the Premier General Zahedi; Lieutenant-Colonel Abdul-Aziz Rostami-Gouran,[473] deputy-commander of the Kermanshah Division under Colonel (later General)

Bakhtiar, the only divisional commander who directly collaborated with the putschists and was thereafter named Military Governor and later the first head of the SAVAK; as well as Captain M Poulad-dezh and Captain H Afkhami-Ardakani,[474] both of the Second Bureau of the army and the office of the Military Governor Bakhtiar.

Former Central Committee member Dr Keshavarz recalls a conversation with an officer of the TMO (a Royal Guard commander) who in Moscow exile had told him that on 19 August, when General Zahedi and others had reached the Tehran Radio station — whence the announcement of Mosaddeq's overthrow was made — he had decided to mow them all down with his machine-gun, but had changed his mind because he thought, since he had received no party instruction, the TPI must have approved of the putsch, because the party had been against Mosaddeq![475] Keshavarz adds that the party had worked 'very systematically' till the evening of 18 August, but it is not clear which party authority, on that evening, had issued the instruction to sever all contact between the party apparatus and its members. He confirms that the 'personal bodyguard of General Zahedi and the chief of the national radio station [guard] were members of the party, but the party paralysed everyone...'.[476] Moreover, Captain Homayouni was with Nasiri's troops who attempted to carry out the 16 August coup; he was arrested with the rest of the putschist officers, but was freed after the second coup and was even awarded for his part in the putsch. He then was put in charge of Tehran airport when the shah returned, who, upon arrival, promoted all the putschist officers, including Homayouni who was made Lieutenant-Colonel.[477]

Surviving TMO member Varqa, whose appraisal of the 1953 coup is similar to, but more clever, than Kianouri's, states that the TMO 'did not have the right to take any initiative on its own and enter the field of action independently, ignoring the state of the revolutionary preparedness of the people, an action whose victory or defeat could not have been known',[478] as if victors always can foresee their triumph in advance. By contrast, Lieutenant-Colonel Rostami-Gouran has stated, in relation to the 'risky' project of starting guerrilla warfare in the north, that, although he had not much hope in its victory, 'the very act would have helped the awakening of the Iranian nation'.[479]

Varqa informs, however, that 'two [TMO] officers of the Royal Guard had the possibilities of preparing the elimination of the shah',[480] just as Gendarmerie Lieutenant A Mohajerani, a TMO officer, was, till his arrest in 1954, General Zahedi's bodyguard, and that neither he nor the TMO ever thought of suppressing the general.[481] Varqa also relates that on the afternoon of 19 August when General Zahedi reached the national radio station, where he made his victory speech, and later at the headquarters of the National Police when Zahedi spoke again to a crowd, he 'and the martyred Captain Shafa were present. Martyred Captain N Madani[482] and Captain Sadeqi-Esfahani[483] (who served a prison term), [both also] TMO members, were accompanying General Zahedi. ... on that day, Madani was chief of the police precinct in which the radio station was situated, and Sadeqi the chief of the Tenth Precinct, the red-light district, in which the putschists recruited roughnecks, whores and their procurers who made up part of the demonstrating royalist crowds.[484]

At the same time, he corroborates that some of the TMO officers were in such appropriate positions that they could have prepared the terrain for the assassination of the shah, Zahedi and others, but, apparently on the basis of the ideological principles dominating the organisation, no officer, whether leader or simple member, found the solution to the country's problems, or thought to attain freedom from the dictatorship and to extinguish internal as well as external exploitation through terrorist acts, for they had faith in the *weltanschauung* of 'scientific socialism'.[485] He does not explain, then, what justified acts of terrorism by the same party when the radical, anti-monarchist journalist M Mas'oud was assassinated by its secret 'hit team', or when its own top-ranking cadre Hesam Lankarani,[486] who had rendered valuable services to the organisation, was murdered in cold blood, or when several other members accused of having spied for the police were eliminated. In his judgement, therefore, a spy in the party was more dangerous than a dictator ruling the country! Were such murders not against the 'principles of scientific socialism'? Might not the failure to assassinate the shah and General Zahedi have been a turning point fatally redirecting the course of Iran's history? More importantly, aside from Lenin's orders to suppress his opponents through his henchmen, such as Kamo,[487] in the light of Stalin's terror against millions of people, Russian and non-Russian Communists and non-Communists, one can hardly believe the sincerity of the arguments presented by Varqa and others in the TPI that the party did not suppress Zahedi on a decisive day, and later the shah — acts which would have turned the tide against the putschists — just on the basis of their contravening the 'principles of scientific socialism'. The reason must lie elsewhere.

On the other hand, one of the prominent leaders of the party at the time, former Central Committee member Keshavarz, asks why that organisation, with 600 officers (in an army with only 15 000 [*sic*: 8000] officers), did not take any 'action in favour of Mosaddeq's government on 19 August' so that it would not, only a year later, fall into the trap, as a result of which 'the best sons of Iran were shot'. He adds that the leadership in exile 'never wanted to analyse such questions in depth, ignored them, and superficially glossed over them.[488]

Also, Varqa knowingly distorts the facts when he affirms that the other problem *to be studied* is the:

> ... submission without resistance, and at times *voluntarily*, of more than 400 TMO officers. Although members witnessed the arrest of their comrades on a daily basis, they found, for various reasons, submission and obedience more correct and less dangerous.[489]

He again consciously ignores the recommendation by Central Committee member Kianouri, as a result of which these officers, blinded by the discipline demanding obedience to the party, could not, at a fatal moment, make their own decision to flee, as Varqa himself did.

Furthermore, to justify his distorted narrative, he asserts that no 'directives' reached TMO members advising what to do, simply because those in charge of the organisation had been arrested, leaving members 'disoriented and in disarray'.[490] Thus, he prefers to forget, just like Kianouri — often imposingly replacing Dr Jowdat as the Central Committee's liaison man with the TMO — who had suggested that TMO officers should voluntarily give themselves up, on the basis that 'in fact, the more [Tudeh] officers are arrested, the better it is. They had better return to their workplaces, for when the number of the arrestees increases, nothing can be done to them.'[491] This was a decision that ran counter to that which Captain Rouzbeh, the only member of the Secretariat at large, had taken.

M Zarbakht, another TMO officer who spent 14 years in prison, is one of many party members who believe that the Tudeh leadership was responsible for the fiasco because of its inaction on 19 August. Thus, there can be little doubt as to the reason why the leadership at the Fourth Plenum in 1957, in spite of the demands of a large number of cadres, decided to postpone the examination of the débâcle to the Third Congress, which was never held. Refuting Kianouri's defeatist argument after the revolution of 1979, Zarbakht states that Kianouri's attempt to reduce the TMO to a group of officers with merely medical and engineering specialties was no more than 'a pretext to rationalise the leadership's inaction in confronting the scandalous putsch of 19 August'. He adds that the party had:

> ... more than 500 militant, patriotic and idealist officers, whom it ordered, on that historically fateful day, to await party orders. In this way, officers who, with their armed units and tanks, were disoriented, awaiting party orders from the 'high party authorities', with tears in their eyes and bleeding hearts watching roughnecks and thugs, assisted by retired army officers, easily take over their tanks, destroy the house of the nation [Mosaddeq's

residence], take [General] Zahedi from his American Embassy hideout, and install him as premier.

Like his comrade Azarnour, Zarbakht then compares this inaction with the undertakings by a few 'patriotic and anti-imperialist officers' in Egypt and Iraq to show the 'depth of the tragedy' in Iran. He attributes this difference to the fact that, while the Iraqi and Egyptian officers were independent of any political party and foreign power, officers in the TPI 'were obedient to unworthy leaders who were obliged to take orders from an authority that probably did not want to oppose the putsch'[492] — that is, the USSR.

What is important in connection with the easy victory of the putschists on 19 August is that neither Kianouri nor the other Tudeh 'analysts' who blame Mosaddeq for the defeat in the coup discuss, as some — such as Azarnour — argue, the grand possibilities of the TPI and its military wing suppressing the putschists during the second coup on 19 August, on the grounds that — unlike Chile — the Iranian army was not entirely backing the putschists. Would it not have been simply sufficient, as some have suggested, to sow the seeds of confusion among the putschists by eliminating a few key figures?

The important question is, therefore: in view of its claim after March 1953 that it had wanted to help the national-democratic movement in the struggle against imperialism, did the Tudeh leadership really want to rescue, or could it have rescued, with the help of its 600 avowedly disciplined TMO officers and junior officers holding strategic positions, especially among the putschists, the Mosaddeq government?

As noted above, some TMO officers, such as Azarnour and Zarbakht, have argued positively, and some others, such as Varqa, along with Central Committee member Kianouri, negatively. But it was not only Kianouri, but the entire Executive Committee, whose brochure *Concerning 19 August* justifies its inaction by stating that, at that stage of the movement, it was the task of the 'national bourgeoisie' to take the lead, to defeat the putschists or to be defeated. The military capabilities that the TPI had at its disposal were such that it is possible to argue convincingly that the party could have turned the tide of events.

The question is why the Tudeh leadership did not act. One might argue that the mole in the leadership made sure that it did not. This explanation is, however, not sufficient to account for the inaction of the whole leadership, unless Kianouri, who was known to be in contact with his KGB liaison officer at the Soviet Embassy, was the mole and acted on behalf of the putschists. It is important that all through the period of Mosaddeq's premiership, Kianouri, whose faction was a minority in the Tehran leadership, managed to sway his colleagues in the name of 'unanimous decisions', the meaning of which the Executive Committee majority understood all too well, in the light of Kianouri's liaison with the Soviets for directives. On every occasion, including and especially on 19 August, the majority of the leadership believed that what Kianouri said was what 'big brother' wanted. As we will see below, on the basis of Comintern instructions — to which we shall refer — and the 1946 Alamouti–Bahrami letter of 'obedience' to the Soviet party, various Tudeh leaders, such as SM Eskandari,[493] Bahrami and Tabari,[494] and, of course, Kianouri and Kambakhsh, had been in touch with Soviet liaison officers.[495] What happened during the long years of exile, particularly at Central Committee plenums where 'representatives' of the Soviet party were always present and intervened at sensitive points, is of course, the most glaring evidence.

Why, then, did Kianouri not act in favour of some action to defend the national-democratic movement on 19 August 1953? On the basis of his contact with the KGB liaison alone, the reason must lie in the fact that the new Soviet leadership did not as yet control the KGB apparatus, run for years by Beria's men, including Kianouri and Kambakhsh, and was thus not able to transmit directives to the TPI to change its line towards Mosaddeq's government. Assuming that the new, post-Stalin Soviet leadership wished to moderate its predecessor's virulently hostile attitude towards Mosaddeq, it is clear that the Tudeh leadership could not have taken any action, especially one as importantly strategic as that of opposing a putsch, without Soviet approval. On that basis, taking the above into consideration, along with the TPI's long-running and profoundly antagonistic stance towards Mosaddeq and the national-democratic movement, and in the light of its inaction when faced with the coup, one may legitimately venture that the Tudeh leaders did not actually wish to defend Mosaddeq's government against the royalist coup, and were in fact indifferent to the possibility of its overthrow, as one TMO officer told Central Committee member Keshavarz. Various justifications, as enumerated above, by the Tudeh leadership about its inaction were, therefore, necessary to 'explain' away to the party membership, and the people of Iran, their immobility on those fateful and fatal days, hence the contradictions which we dissected above.

As for Mosaddeq's own incapacity to defend his government, it is clear that he had never been an organisation man, and he had mobilised and galvanised the people in his support under the relatively democratic conditions and through non-violent methods. In addition, he did not possess a large group of military officers who were convinced to defend the national-democratic movement. Unlike Allende, he did not benefit from the support of the pro-Soviet 'Communist' TPI or the extreme 'left', which crystallised in the Tudeh Youth Organisation under Shermini. Unlike Allende, he did not have his own

Socialist Party. His loyal organised support came from parties of the Patriotic Front, with a small membership: the Iran Party was a minor social-democratic organisation with members from the professional élite; the Third Force Party was a small Marxist party with a membership among the youth and workers; the other small parties were insignificant. Much as in Allende's case, however, the opponent heading the putsch against him was his former Interior Minister, who, initially, had no pro-Anglo-American past; Mosaddeq had dismissed him after the street killings by the police under him on the occasion of Harriman's arrival in Tehran.

Much like the case in Chile, Mosaddeq's most effective and loyal officer, General Afshartous, was kidnapped shortly after his appointment as Chief of the National Police and murdered by a number of officers who were in the putschist camp. Of course, in addition to sharing with Allende the enmity of the CIA and big American corporations, he faced a more formidable foe, British imperialism, that stopped short of nothing to destroy his democratic and anti-imperialist model in the region.[496]

Moreover, Mosaddeq, with his use of non-violent means, was not the kind of statesman to involve the nation in a civil war in which the pro-Western putschists and pro-Soviet forces would tear the country apart. The surprise, rush visit that the American Ambassador Henderson paid him, directly after his return to Iran on the evening of 18 August — after months of absence during which he had been preparing the putsch with the CIA — convinced him of American intentions to go so far as recognising as 'legitimate' the putschist government of Zahedi, based somewhere in the country outside the capital, most probably in oil-rich Khuzistan.

Using anti-American slogans chanted in the streets as a pretext, Henderson said in his telegram that 'if Iranians wanted [the] Americans out, individual attacks' were 'not necessary', the Americans 'would go *en masse*'. Feigning not to know anything about the coup at midnight on 15 August, Henderson expressed the wish to know the position of Mosaddeq on the coup and told him that he 'would be grateful if he [Mosaddeq] would tell me confidentially for [the] use [of] my government just what [had] happened during [the] recent days. [The] US Government [was] interested with respect [to] both events and [the] legal situation.' The 'legal situation' was the key question, implying the recognition of Zahedi's 'legal appointment' by the shah, in response to which Mosaddeq explained that, according to the Iranian Constitution, the shah had no right either to dismiss a prime minister in office or appoint another one in his place. Henderson implied that the shah did have such a right. To insist on his 'legal' question, Henderson also 'said it seemed to me unfortunate for Iran and [it is] no compliment [to the] Iranian people that [the] government of Iran apparently could not be based on a parliament. Iran was in [a] most dangerous international position' — hinting at losing the recognition of its government by the Western powers. Henderson told the premier that he was 'particularly interested in events [of the] recent days. I would like to know more about [the] effort [to] replace him by General Zahedi.' Mosaddeq told him that the shah, prompted by the British, had sent Colonel Nasiri apparently to arrest him, but he was, instead, arrested by his guards. In response to Henderson's question regarding the shah's *firman* 'removing him as Prime Minister and appointing Zahedi in his place', Mosaddeq denied having seen it, but 'if he had, it would have made no difference. His position for some time had been that [the] Shah's powers were only of ceremonial character; that [the] Shah had no right on his personal responsibility [to] issue [a] *firman* calling for change in government.'[497] Thus, Henderson insisted again if 'he should find that [the] Shah had issued such [a] *firman*... in present circumstances, he would consider it to be invalid'. Mosaddeq 'replied "positively"'. Henderson concluded from Mosaddeq's 'unusual reserve' that he was:

> ... suspicious [that the] United States Government, or at least United States officials, [had been] either implicated in effort[s to] oust him or sympathetically aware of such effort[s] in advance. His remarks to me were interspersed with [a] number [of] little jibes... semi-jocular in character... nevertheless barbed. These jibes in general hinted that [the] United States was conniving with [the] British effort [to] remove him as Prime Minister. For instance, he remarked at one point [that the] *national movement was determined [to] remain in power in Iran and it would continue to hold on to* [the] *last man, although all its members would be run over by British and American tanks*.[498]

History proved Mosaddeq right about the American government's direct involvement in the coup.

In spite of his remark to Henderson that *the Iranians would fight to the last man and would have to 'be run over by British and American tanks' to destroy the national-democratic movement*, Mosaddeq seems to have believed that civil war would have to be avoided, given the meagre military forces he had at his disposal. Therefore, when witnessing the second coup unfolding, he decided not to call the people to come on to the streets and support his government, in fear of another massacre like the one on 21 July 1952. Many believe he was wrong in making such a decision and a massive demonstration by the people would have changed the odds.

Preparing himself to be assassinated during the attack on his residence on

19 August, Mosaddeq must have thought that his martyrdom would become a great symbol for the resistance against the putschists, but his colleagues forcefully removed him from his residence, carrying him over the neighbour's wall to safety. True, he became as much a martyr through his arrest a day later, a death sentence demanded by the military prosecutor when court-martialed, and finally his condemnation to three years of solitary confinement, as well as his internal banishment and deprivation of all civil liberties to the end of his life, for another period of 14 years.

Things would have turned differently had the TPI been a genuinely patriotic party on the Left, for Mosaddeq would have trusted it and worked with it, resting assured that its participation in the defence of the national-democratic movement would not have led to a civil war.

XII: The TPI's Department of Information Dismantled

One of the most important organs of the TPI was its Department of Information, that is, the special operations department, for it collected through party members all the information it could put its hands on and then card-indexed them. All party members working in various sectors of society — factories, ministries, schools and university, and particularly the army — were instructed to collect information about everyone and everything of important value to the party. One could name this department an embryonic KGB.

Such information would be used for propagandistic purposes and special operations against the party's foes. In one case, as already noted, the victim was not even a foe of the party. Mas'oud was a brave anti-monarchy journalist who denounced reactionaries in a rowdy style. Because of his denunciations of the ruling class, his newspaper was popular. Nonetheless, the TPI decided to eliminate him and blame the reactionaries for his murder. He was murdered on 11 February 1947. Paradoxically, the Tudeh organ *Mardom* denounced the murder as 'an horrendous political crime'.[499] According to one Tudeh cadre, one branch of the TPI's Department of Information was in charge of the 'persecution' of party enemies. On the basis of official sources, he relates that 'this branch was, in fact, the eye of the Tudeh organisations and carried out the secret, criminal plans of the party'. One of the duties of the department was 'the execution and annihilation of police moles in the party... four of whom were killed'.[500]

This organ was run by former army Captain Khosrow Rouzbeh, who was also one of the TMO leaders. He had a number of permanent close collaborators, some of whom such as A Abbasi, A Shahbzaian, A Nadim, S Stepanian and H Lankarani took part in acts of murder against those considered to be a menace to the party — one of whom, ironically, was, as noted above, Lankarani himself.

Ironically, one of its executioners, Serge Stepanian who, according to his sister was a 'bigoted activist', when arrested and imprisoned, collaborated with the political police — just like some of his victims.[501]

Another possible victim of the TPI was a party thinker named Zakharian, who, according to a rumour in the party, had been tortured to death in prison. This seems difficult to believe, for the repressive apparatus of the former regime never hid its crimes; on the contrary, in the name of security, it even boasted about the elimination of the regime's opponents. Therefore, what Dr Keshavarz relates about Zakharian having been killed by someone, or some group, in the party seems quite reasonable. He recounts that Zakharian had been mandated by the Executive Committee majority faction to go to Moscow and explain to the Central Committee members there the differences prevailing amongst the party leaders in Tehran. Kianouri and his associates, who were firmly opposed to Mosaddeq and believed that Zakharian would not report objectively but would work against their faction, strove to impede his trip; Kianouri then sought the help of the Soviet authorities — that is, the NKVD/KGB — in Iran 'to put a stop to Zakharian's trip to Moscow'. Keshavarz then recounts that, according to the minutes of the Central Committee sessions in Moscow, the Soviets informed Secretary-General Radmanesh that Kianouri was opposed to Zakharian's trip, because he would not report objectively, and that someone from their faction should accompany him. Keshavarz continues:

> A day or two before Zakharian's departure for Moscow, he disappeared. Sometime later, it was rumoured that he had been killed. Later his body was found in a pit in a party safe-house in which 50 000 grenades produced under Kianouri's authority had been stocked...[502]

There is not much more information about the TPI's Department of Information, as the former Soviet regime's archives on this question still remain untouchable. All we know is that under the leadership of Rouzbeh it was the strong arm of the party. Finally, however, with the dismantling of the TMO, the arrest of party leaders who had not escaped abroad, and, at long last, the capture of Rouzbeh himself through the treachery of some of his aides, particularly Ali Mottaqi, a leading member of the Tehran Provincial Committee, the Department of Information also disintegrated in the summer of 1957.[503]

Rouzbeh's arrest occurred on 6 July 1957, and he was executed on 11 May 1958, after long interrogations and a trial, during which he denounced the Tudeh leaders for their ineptitude in leadership, unbounded personal ambitions and personal rivalries leading to nefarious effects on the fate of the organisation. Regarding those Executive Committee members whose orders he carried out, he said, *inter alia*, the following:

> My view of Dr Yazdi, Dr Bahrami and Engineer Ollovi is that these pathetic individuals are cowards who demonstrated their lack of qualification in the leadership. As regards Ahmad Qasemi, I must say that he is an egoist and a position-hunter in the extreme and always strives to push himself within the party and, if possible, to become its number one... Because he formed an anti-party faction, Ahmad Qasemi no longer qualifies for membership of the Central Committee, or even of the party as a simple member.[504]

As regards factionalism in the party, he blamed first and foremost Qasemi and Yazdi, adding that former Executive Committee members Yazdi, Bahrami and Ollovi, 'because of their lack of correct understanding, insufficient knowledge, [lack of] moral character, selfishness, unbounded power-mongering and anti-party factionalism, did not qualify for membership of the Central Committee'. Nor did he spare the others. He added that Eskandari and Rousta were to be criticised for their participation in the Yazdi–Bahrami–Shermini faction. Kianouri was 'extremely aggressive and has a violent streak *vis-à-vis* [party] cadres', and was 'supportive of Qasemi's faction'.[505] Rouzbeh considered the latter responsible for all the wrong slogans adopted by the party during the Mosaddeq era. He adds that, because Yazdi, Bahrami and Ollovi were:

> ... politically commoners, narrow-minded and prone to misjudgement, they capitulated before his views; the damage Ahmad Qasemi has thus done to the party is worse than what any foe has accomplished; the fundamental factor in all this is his extreme selfishness and extraordinary position-hunting.[506]

One could cite a great deal more by Rouzbeh against the Tudeh leaders.[507]

The case of Rouzbeh and the Department of Information is interesting, for it reveals much about the Tudeh leadership. For one thing, he was always in conflict with that leadership and once resigned from the party, but later rejoined it. The conflict was so deep that, despite all the valuable services he performed for the party, he was not made a Central Committee member until he was incarcerated for the last time and it was certain that he would be executed. The Tudeh leadership had to capitalise on his 'heroic' name, just it had done with Arani after his death — their differences in character notwithstanding.

In 1961, Rouzbeh's defence speech at the military tribunal was handed to Tabari by one Pouzdinak of the CPSU's International Department who had received it from Naser Saremi, the former driver of the Executive Committee in Tehran before his escaping abroad, then in Baghdad. He had, in turn, obtained it from 'people devoted' to Rouzbeh,[508] obviously from within the army. The Soviets wanted to use it as a piece of propaganda, obviously for its emotional charge. They then asked to have it translated into Russian and various Western languages. Its Russian translation was published in *Izvestia* in 1962, along with an interview given by First-Secretary Radmanesh to the Novosti news agency.[509] Many in the party held his defence speech at the tribunal to be an 'epic'.[510] Radmanesh and the rest of the party referred to Rouzbeh as not only a Central Committee member, but also as 'the national hero',[511] in spite of the fact that all the leading members of the Central Committee disliked him. In a message to the Seventh Plenum sent just before his arrest he spoke poorly of party leaders, calling at least the most dogmatic among them, Qasemi, a 'traitor, factionalist', etc. Qasemi was known among party cadres as having 'bureaucratic and dictatorial' methods. His message was so devastating that every effort was made to persuade the two individuals to whom he had written not to read his texts, for, according to Eskandari, he had made a negative 'appraisal of Central Committee and Executive Committee members in Iran; this is why they did not want to discuss it there' at the plenum. Yet passages of his letters were read on specific issues. His letter had an impact on the plenum, so much that Qasemi, after three rounds of voting, did not win the necessary number of votes to be elected to the new Executive Committee. His wife, having first fainted — perhaps pretended to have fainted — had to plead with certain cadres such as Azarnour to vote for him.[512]

As we have seen, Rouzbeh was not only harsh on Tudeh leaders in the secret messages he sent to the plenum, but in his interrogations and defence speech he belittled party leaders, above all for their cowardice, leaving the 'battlefield' against the putschist regime. Former First-Secretary Eskandari divulges the fact that 'inexpedient passages' from Rouzbeh's defence speech at the tribunal were 'censored by a committee of four of those who had been in Iran' before the putsch — that is, those most interested in hiding what Rouzbeh had to say. The setting up of this committee also gave the other members of the party leadership the convenient appearance of their not being involved in the censorship of his speech. The four were Qasemi, Foroutan, Kianouri and Jowdat, the first three belonging to the 'extremist minority' of the pre-putsch era.[513] Thus, the short text published by *Izvestia* (and the longer one in Persian) had been purged of its embarrassing passages.[514]

Quoting some passages of his defence speech throws symbolic light on the faith that many TPI members, especially TMO officers, had in their party that had failed them.

Inter alia, Rouzbeh said:

I am standing trial in a court that is undoubtedly hearing one of the most important cases in the history of Iranian courts. If I regard my case as the most important in the history of Iranian court cases, it is not because I seek to pride myself upon it and boast of myself...

The trial proceeds in the prison office, in a room that has left me with the bitterest memories... I regard the organisation of the trial as an attempt to exert pressure on me, and I do not feel I am facing a normal, lawful court...

I bear implacable enmity to the regime that gives all the benefits and rights of life to a thousand privileged families at the cost of the misfortune, penury and hunger of 18 million Iranians. I was raised and educated in a family of medium means and have been left with the most melancholy and harrowing memories from my youth. Woe to the millions of worker and peasant families in Iran whose poverty and penury are ten times worse than those of Khosrow Rouzbeh ever were. This is no idle talk, no story from the *Thousand and One Nights*, nor the figment of an idle tale told by delirium, but reality of life in my country and any country of the capitalist world.

I am sincere in my conviction. I have dedicated my life to the struggle for my beliefs, the service of the people... without personal motives, without fear of death. Among those who claim to serve the people there have been those who turned back half-way, but to turn back halfway and flee from battle is unworthy of a real man...

There is not a shade of doubt that it was my personal deprivations and adversities that prepared the way for my acceptance of the ideas of the [Tudeh] Party, but if I had been thinking only of myself, of my own advantages alone, I would never have dedicated my heart to the storm, never have faced such grave dangers... [As an army captain,] I could have served long enough to rise to the highest ranks in the army and win a topmost post within it. A serene, comfortable and prosperous life lay in store for me...

The fact that I chose the path of the Tudeh Party[515] of Iran against my own interests and despite all the dangers can only be explained in two ways: either by madness or by good intentions. Since I am sound of mind, how else can one explain my participation in politics except by good intentions, humanity, clear and honourable convictions? ...

For that cause I endured great deprivations and difficulties and shall endure yet more. There is the court of history, and that court shall acquit me even if my bones will have mouldered in the ground by then...

Even a superficial study of conditions in modern Iranian society and the comparison of the lives led by the different classes cannot help but provoke horror, compassion and pity. There is an enormous gulf between the propertied classes and the disinherited; and that gulf which has been growing wider and deeper day by day cannot help but overwhelm the imagination of a thinking man and compel him to ponder the matter deeply...

Such expressions as 'lack of honour' and 'had no conception of honour' in the indictment were a great insult to my honour and moral standing, for morals and honour have been great treasures of my life, and I cannot keep silent under such insults...

The adherents of capitalism regard the defence of the pillars of capitalist society as a matter of honour and glory. The supporters of the principles of socialism find honour and glory in defending and strengthening the foundations of the socialist system.

Since the two systems are the direct opposites of each other, one cannot help wondering just how to analyse the 'conception of honour'. In my opinion, a man may be regarded as honest and honourable as long as he is pure of heart, firm and unshakable in his convictions...

Khosrow Rouzbeh and people like him may die, but the Tudeh Party of Iran stays to march along its path to its cherished goal...

The Tudeh Party of Iran, as has been noted by its friends and enemies, is the brightest, the highest, the most highly principled and best-organised party in the 50 years of Constitutional Iran. And the most striking feature of this party is its revolutionary character. This party which was prompted by historical necessity was organised on the basis of scientific principles; it has its own theory and its own scientific world outlook...

I am proud of what I say. If the senators [sic: judges] will use their power to have my death sentence carried out, nothing serious will have actually happened... What really matters is that his views are worth of consideration, and that is why he will live forever...

Esteemed judges! If I have defended my political and social views, I have not done so under the impression that death is a cool, sweet drink. Death is unpleasant under any circumstances, and especially for those whose hearts are filled with hope for the future, a future that is bright and beautiful. But to remain alive by hook and crook is something unworthy of real men... If life is bought at the price of shame and disgrace, loss of honour, the repudiation of one's ideas, of one's cherished hopes and political and social views — death is a hundred times more honest and honourable...

This is perhaps the first time you have ever had to try a prisoner with such ideas and such spirit. Many were sentenced to death in such trials.

These people had their political convictions and were acquitted by public opinion... I am faithful to my duty and obligations. I respect the signature I affixed to the questionnaire of the Tudeh Party of Iran and shall never break my pledge in the face of danger... I do not regard myself as a criminal subject to punishment and deserving of a death sentence. But in view of the fact that my honour is imperilled, I officially demand that the esteemed judges pronounce the death sentence. I demand this in order to share the glory of the [TMO] officers who perished, and to efface the accusations that threaten my honour. Neither I, nor the officers, nor any others who were condemned for political activity, are criminals. On the contrary, we are servants of our dear country; the just and honest Iranian people will regard these sentences as despotic and will acquit their self-sacrificing sons.

You may condemn Khosrow Rouzbeh, but you will never be able to condemn humanity, honesty, patriotism and unselfishness. As soon as the esteemed judges hand down my sentence, I shall thank them with a firm heart and a smile on my lips...[516]

Stripped of its emotional aspects, today not many, even among former Tudeh adherents, who once thought of Rouzbeh as a 'hero', hold him in high esteem, especially because of his involvement in murders of innocent individuals. At the time, his speech encouraged the most prominent poet of contemporary Iran, Ahmad Shamloo — who in his youth had joined the TPI but later left it — to dedicate a poem to him. After the revolution, when it became certain that Rouzbeh had been involved in cold-blooded murders, he publicly withdrew his dedication. As for his praise for the TPI, Rouzbeh did not realise what history had in store for it, both in terms of what was going to happen and how it was to be judged by history, as evidenced, at the very least, by the biggest party gathering after his trial, the Fourth Plenum.

XIII: The 1957 Plenum and its Appraisal of Party Life since its Foundation

The Fourth Party Plenum was held, with the 'encouragement', if not direct initiative, of the USSR under Khrushchev, in a suburb of Moscow from 6 June to 17 July 1957, in which, out of some 350 TPI members in Eastern Europe and the USSR, 55 cadres and 15 leaders took part. In its 'General Report' to the plenum the Central Committee states that, following the arrests, executions, massive recantations and 'apostasy' of members as well as of some leaders, mental disarray and the increasing loss of confidence in the party leadership, in August 1956 the Central Committee members residing in Moscow decided to convene a plenum to probe the party crisis and find solutions to remedy it.

The Tudeh 'theoretician' Tabari recounts that some leaders who did not wish to have party cadres participate in the plenum seriously opposed the idea of an 'enlarged plenum', but 'later accepted its inevitability'.[517] A number of draft resolutions were agreed upon by a majority vote of the Central Committee for presentation to the plenum.[518] The 'General Report', after dealing with a number of generalities, including the 'victories' of the Socialist camp, 'the anti-revolutionary movement' in Hungary, and the 'teachings' of the CPSU's Twentieth Congress, discussed the growing strength of the anti-imperialist movement in Iran after the fall of Reza Shah, the nationalisation of the oil industries, the formation of Mosaddeq's government, the 1953 coup, and the 'astonishing inaction' of the party; it further thrashed out the development of differences within and the weakening of the party leadership. In particular, it mentioned that communication between the Executive Committee inside the country and Central Committee members in Moscow was scant and the former did not keep the latter abreast of party life within the country. The sparse information that the Central Committee members had received indirectly (through personal correspondence) from Tehran about growing differences in the leadership within the country had prompted them to 'invite' a number of Executive Committee members to Moscow, in order to distance them from the field of conflict.

Following the 1953 coup, differences grew within the Executive Committee, especially after the exposure and destruction of the TMO. The development of 'apostasy' among party members and individual or collective recantations published in the press or aired on the radio, as well as letters of supplication addressed to the shah, which, in spite of the heroic acceptance of death by many members, had 'struck a very heavy blow at the prestige and credibility of our party', made the leadership realise the extent of the crisis.

The aim of the plenum was also to exercise 'criticism and self-criticism' of the party's record over the previous 16 years. Almost every important issue in party history was raised and talked about, but they were not necessarily debated in order to clarify complex issues or to determine the responsibility of those who had failed or had taken mistaken decisions: the Soviet demand for an oil concession, the 1948 split, the Mosaddeq 'problem', the TPI's policy towards the nationalisation of oil, the putsch of 19 August 1953, factionalism in the party, the destruction of the TMO, Kambakhsh's treason in 1937, the proscription of the party in 1949, and finally the Azerbaijan crisis and the fall of the Autonomous Government of Azerbaijan. However, the last four issues were shelved for later dates.

Each Central Committee member submitted a 'platform', between 10 and 45 pages long, in which he presented his criticisms and, in some cases, a remedy to improve party life. Each cadre had the right to consult the platforms for two days in a special room and could take written notes in notebooks provided by the organisers. Notebooks provided could be used in the main hall of the plenum, but had to be handed back to the Central Committee at the closure of the plenum — a typically Stalinist method of control even after Khrushchev's denunciation of Stalin. The only participant of the Fourth Party Plenum relating in some detail what went on and giving a summary of what each of the 15 Central Committee members told the long gathering is Lieutenant-Colonel Ekteshafi. The latter managed to keep his notebooks at the end, which he used for his memoirs.[519] The proceedings were recorded in the presence of a Soviet 'representative' named Simiyonov[520] who knew Persian and at times intervened on certain issues of vital interest to the CPSU.

For instance, according to Ekteshafi,[521] Simiyonov, a 'high-ranking party official and certainly of the [Soviet] secret services' — that is, the KGB — played an important role in the plenum. He adds, 'for instance, if a question regarding the Soviet Union came up and there was quarrel, he would intervene, give the Soviet view, and his view would be decisive'.

Such was, for instance, the question regarding Kambakhsh's 'revelations' to the police — or 'treason' — in 1937. In the plenum, a number of people, including Eskandari and Keshavarz, raised the question of Kambakhsh's 'weakness in prison' when the 'Group of Fifty-Three' was arrested under Reza Shah, and whether in fact, 'he committed treason'. Kambakhsh retorted: 'In order that the party [group] would not be [considered] linked with the Soviet Union and the question of espionage would not be raised', he had diverted the question to the issue of the ICP. Later: 'I gave a report to the Comintern, and the Comintern confirmed my view: that I had done the right thing.' At this moment, Simiyonov, who had been listening in the adjacent room where proceedings were being recorded, came into the meeting and said: 'The Comintern confirmed that Kambakhsh's view was correct, and I confirm this.'[522] This is, of course, absolutely untrue, for Kambakhsh's report was first sent to Fitin of the NKVD in December 1941 and arrived at the Comintern in December 1942. Besides, the Comintern never approved Kambakhsh's report.[523] Ekteshafi recalls the 'obedient attitude' of the Tudeh leaders towards Soviet demands during their discussions in the plenum.[524]

On most other issues, according to Ekteshafi, a free atmosphere reigned during the discussions, since there had been an opening up in the USSR after Khrushchev's denunciation of Stalin's crimes. At the plenum, Central Committee members spoke first and then cadres could express themselves on the basis of their notes on the platforms they had read as well as by putting questions to Central Committee members. The unique feature of this Tudeh gathering was the candour with which Central Committee members spoke, pouring out what was in their hearts, as they had never done so previously or would ever do so again, including in their memoirs after the fall of the USSR, except in Ovanesian's aforementioned secret diaries. The reason must reside in the Soviet demand to go completely open, so that the Soviet party would learn what had been going on within the TPI since its foundation. (To be noted is that the people of Iran, or even party members who had lost their loved ones or party members who had suffered a great deal due to the mistaken policies of the leadership, were not to profit from this outspokenness.) It is, thus, a pity that, even half a century after the Fourth Plenum, we have access only to the short notes by Ekteshafi, not to the whole pages of the 'platforms' made available to the cadres, nor to the debates that followed between the cadres and Central Committee members. Nonetheless, even this summary review of the platforms presented by the Central Committee members at the Fourth Plenum[525] throws some light on the internal conflicts of the Tudeh leadership through the accusations and counter-accusations levelled by each of the Central Committee members.

While two Central Committee members pointed to the 'lack of collective leadership', accusing Secretary-General Radmanesh of dominating the party, the party 'theoretician' Tabari criticised the 'absence of democratism' within the party, and Kianouri complained of the 'suffocating atmosphere' within the organisation. While Radmanesh had held fast, with Soviet support, to the position of Secretary-General, Tabari and Eskandari criticised position-hunting and careerism on the part of Shermini, the former leader of the Youth Organisation, as detrimental to the party; two leaders of the minority complained of the unbridled liberty given to Shermini — who had after his arrest recanted and lived a cosy life.[526] Interestingly, Eskandari admitted that he himself had had a tendency towards position-hunting. On the other hand, Kianouri, at first manifesting little willingness to self-criticism, accused the leadership of rejecting any criticism, frightening critics, suppressing critiques and whitewashing past mistakes.

While the party 'theoretician' Tabari decried unfounded accusations against his fellow minority adherents Qasemi and Foroutan, he and Radmanesh criticised the Blanquist and adventurist undertakings by the party leadership in Tehran after the 1953 putsch; the target here was none other than Kianouri, who, by the way, also criticised that tendency! Radmanesh said that Kianouri had 'suggested assassinating torturers at the Office of the Military Governor, such as Colonel Zibayee. Later, it was agreed to kill [Colonel] Mobasser [of the same office], but this was not acted upon'. Radmanesh added that 'as a principle', such acts were 'not correct'.[527] Radmanesh also denounced 'adventurist undertaking', such as the uprising of Tudeh officers in Khorasan in 1945, the murder of an Azerbaijani landlord in the same period which led to repercussions, demonstrations in the north regarding the Soviet oil demand, the instruction for armed resistance in Mazandaran, the formation of 'hit units', extreme leftism on the issue of oil nationalisation, the manufacture of hand-grenades, the arson attack on the military airfield, the destruction of the marine destroyer *Babr*, and the formation of military guards to protect demonstrators.

Most Central Committee members criticised extremist positions held in the leadership. Tabari, in an attempt not to appear 'one-sided' in his criticism, disparaged both 'leftist and rightist sectarianism'. In the same vain, Secretary-General Radmanesh, along with Kambakhsh, denounced 'leftist and rightist deviationism', pointing, in respect of the latter, to the TPI's collaboration in 1941-42 with Mostafa Fateh, the high-ranking AIOC manager, and with the British, in the hopes of obtaining ministerial portfolios.[528]

While Kianouri criticised 'rightist and leftist opportunism', most others disapproved of the 'sectarianism' and 'factionalism' by the Ovanesian faction, the Kianouri faction, the Qasemi–Kianouri minority, and the Kambakhsh–Kianouri–Qasemi trio, as well as their 'secret terrorist group'.

As regards collaboration with Qavam and the ruling class in 1946, which was considered a turn to the right, Noushin and Kianouri criticised the coalition as a compromising step, while others reminded the plenum that the Kianouri–Qasemi faction had, like the other faction, approved of and defended the coalition with Qavam!

Several others disparaged 'right and left opportunism', while Kambakhsh, Tabari and Qasemi accused the majority of 'collusion' against their opponents 'within the party'. Qasemi conveniently attacked Radmanesh and Eskandari for having strengthened Yazdi's hand in the Executive Committee in Tehran, for by then Yazdi had been arrested and had recanted! He added that there had been a putsch within the party, putting power into the hands of Yazdi and Shermini, who had also, by the time of Fourth Plenum, been arrested and had recanted. Their control of the party was 'the background to its defeat', he argued. Qasemi also accused Radmanesh, Jowdat and Mahmoud Boqrati of having conspired to exile him and Foroutan through an invitation to Moscow![529] Others seconded this accusation. For at least two leaders, 'conspiracy' had been part of party life even before the holding of the First Congress. Kambakhsh referred to much factional collusion in between the First Congress and the Azerbaijan crisis.[530] Kianouri and Tabari denounced the resorting to conspiracy by the dominant wing of the Central Committee to the point of threatening the lives of opponents. Tabari also stated that, 'from a point of view of character, members of the majority [in the leadership] are compromisers, unqualified, cowards, indulgent [towards those making mistakes], intriguers [meaning fabricating fraudulent documents to blackmail opponents], power-mongers, dangerous and adventurist'. He held them to be also 'naturally right-opportunists and chasing after ministerial posts'. On the other hand, 'members of the minority in the leadership are adventurous, left-extremists, Blanquists and conspiratorial in party matters'. He also exercised self-criticism by stating that he had kept silent on the Azerbaijan affair; on 'objective issues, I was sometimes on this side and sometimes on the other side'. He admitted his 'lack of militancy' and 'sectarian leftism' in matters exterior to the party. He considered himself 'weak as regards the development of democracy', and 'played no positive role in ridding the party of ideological dogmatism and in the struggle against factionalism'.[531] Tabari also held that 'bureaucratism and dogmatism' dominated the party's organisational and ideological work.

Ekteshafi barely reports the discussion regarding the important question of the nefarious article which Tabari had written under the pseudonym of 'Tudeh' and which had been published by a Cominform review[532] severely attacking Mosaddeq as an 'imperialist agent'. Initially, it was taken to have been written by a Soviet specialist and translated into Persian as proof of the correctness of the TPI's Executive Committee policy against the national-democratic government. By all accounts, that article, because it was thought to be a Soviet view, had a strong impact on the party, with consequently devastating results.[533]

Two members of opposing camps, Kambakhsh and Keshavarz, both considered the leadership to have been 'weak'. Tabari, who maintained that the Central Committee's composition was incongruent and its level of leadership was 'low', also argued that the party's 'subjectivism' was due to its 'petty-bourgeois mentality'. Kianouri who, along with Foroutan, thought that the Central Committee was divided into a dominant wing and its opponents, held it responsible for 'the exposure of the TMO' to the police, which had resulted from its 'inability to lead'. He also asserted that the leadership was partly responsible for the fact that party members were 'terrorised' in prison after the 1953 coup and had subsequently recanted. He conveniently forgot that he had recommended that TMO officers hand themselves over to the authorities instead of going into hiding. Only Saremi, the Executive Committee's driver and the contact with Rouzbeh, and Hakimi, one of the two workers on the Central Committee, dared to tell the plenum that Kianouri had 'ordered members of the TMO to go and give themselves up: "The greater the number, the better it is."'[534] Kianouri denied Saremi's allegation. Tabari, then close to Kianouri, confirms that Saremi made this statement concerning Kianouri's recommendation, but adds that there was no reason for Saremi to have told 'the truth'.[535]

With regard to the 'weakness of the leadership', Babazadeh, the other worker on the Central Committee, pointed out that: 'We are the only two workers on the Central Committee. We are on the Central Committee for demagogic purposes.' That is, window-dressing. He asked: 'Why, at the Second Congress, did they not have seven [workers] elected? ... I was not allowed to remain in Moscow, but Jowdat, Kianouri and Maryam Firouz [all from bourgeois families] were.' He implied that by being left in Baku he would not be able to attend Central Committee meetings. He recommended: 'Bring workers and peasants in [to the Central Committee]!'[536] Rousta, who had headed the Tudeh's workers' unions, defended Babazadeh; he pointed to the 'fear' of the leadership in 'bringing workers into the leadership'.

As regards the attitude of the leadership towards the national-democratic movement and Mosaddeq, almost everyone seems to have criticised the leadership in Iran. Radmanesh, his own similar stand notwithstanding, attacked Kianouri for accusing Mosaddeq of having made compromises and colluded with the imperialists; he also criticised the legal and clandestine newspapers of the party for referring to Mosaddeq upon his resignation on 17 July 1951 with the words 'whoever creates an obstacle on our path will be the target of our indefatigable attacks'; yet he added that 'the Executive Committee of the Central Committee decided to help Mosaddeq'; help which, as he recognised, came too late. Radmanesh argued that the 'lack of the resolution of the national bourgeoisie' on the one hand, and the 'unity of the US and the UK with internal reaction',[537] on the other, were 'factors behind the defeat on 19 August [1953]'; another major factor was that the government and army which the 'national bourgeoisie had in its hand' were not used[538] — the sort of arguments that had been used by the Tehran Executive Committee in the brochure *Concerning 19 August*. Nevertheless, he did acknowledge the Tudeh leadership's inaction on 19 August as *a factor in the defeat*. Interestingly, both Kianouri and Kambakhsh acknowledged the party's failure to recognise the national bourgeoisie as a 'revolutionary force'.[539] Kianouri also confessed that the party had not 'prepared the masses to confront the 1953 putsch'. He acknowledged that the TPI made 'mistakes' on 19 August 1953. To denounce his opponents, he stated that the majority sought to 'impose the brochure *Concerning 19 August* as the ideological document of the EC'.

During the plenum sessions, when cadres severely questioned Central Committee members, some of the latter gave statements that differed from the views that they had presented in their platforms. For instance, Eskandari criticised himself for having scarcely tried to show the 'weaknesses' of other comrades. He further blamed, among others, the Kianouri–Qasemi faction for their 'organisational deviationism' and opposing collective leadership by, *inter alia*, 'threats, intimidation and attacks' against others. He called their 'deviation' 'left-extremist and anarchistic'. As for his own 'weaknesses', he added that he had tried to impose his views on others and wanted to be 'the chief'.[540] He also exposed Kambakhsh's revelations to the police in regard to Arani and his group in 1937. On this issue, as already noted, the Soviet representative Simiyonov put an end to any possible debate. As a result, Ekteshafi writes, the protestations of Eskandari, Rousta, Keshavarz and others came to an end.[541] Keshavarz did not fail to recall Kianouri's role in the 'attempt on the life' of the shah in 1949 which resulted in the proscription of the party. Captain Saghayee of the TMO, at the time an army interrogator, had first-hand information concerning Kianouri's role in that affair. When asked to reveal what he knew, Kianouri's faction tried to persuade him to deny it.[542] Thus Keshavarz's attempt, supported by a couple of others, was to no avail, particularly because it had been previously frustrated in a Central Committee session, where the discussion had been postponed for eternity,[543] as was the case of the TMO fiasco.

The playwright Noushin pointed out that there 'were no ideological differences' between the factions and rival individuals in the Central Committee; it was rather a struggle 'to get hold of the command of the party', that is, position-hunting. He further criticised his Central Committee colleagues on various grounds, including their insufficient political — including Marxist — knowledge. He severely attacked First-Secretary Radmanesh and stated that he was made of the 'same stuff as Bahrami', who had recanted just after his arrest in Tehran, implying that had he been in Iran, he too would have recanted. Withal, he regretted that he had gone to the USSR and not returned to Iran.[544] The reason was obvious, for as a playwright and actor, he had done much to serve the progressive cause in Iran, while in the USSR he merely attended to literary work of no great interest to him.[545]

Kianouri repeated the attacks in his platform against the 'right' wing, further *blaming them for having accused him of being a 'spy'*, naturally of the Western powers. He admitted that he had been wrong in opposing the oil nationalisation question, he also accepted 'one-fifth' of the responsibility for 'the mistake' with regard to the TPI's inaction on 19 August 1953.[546] He also confessed to his 'violent temper, arrogance and [lack of] ability for collective work'.[547]

Keshavarz, while defending himself against the attacks upon him, recalled that he had demanded that the party expel Kianouri for his involvement in the 1949 'attempt on the life of the shah', which went unheeded. He repeated his demand, which was again ignored, no doubt because Kianouri was a close collaborator of the Soviet apparatus.[548]

For his part, Qasemi repeated his previous charges, adding that the dominant group in the leadership proceeded as 'absolute dictators'. Efforts were made to make an 'idol' of Radmanesh; his name was, for instance, repeated '20 times' in a party review. He conceded that the TPI's incorrect 'political slogans' regarding the oil question had 'caused *some* damage'; the only criticism he made of himself was for having written an article in the party organ that called the ancient, popular Persian 'New Year' (*Norouz*) a royal event, not a festivity of the toilers![549]

Dr Jowdat, a European-educated university professor who admitted he had known nothing of political issues and never read anything about Marxism till he entered the party in 1942, nevertheless noted that *the fact that 15 platforms had been presented to the plenum meant that there existed no Central Committee*. He revealed that the establishment of the Democratic Party of Azerbaijan had come as a complete surprise to him, and that he at first felt that it was a 'reactionary affair'. However the TPI was later 'instructed' that it 'must support' the DPA, which was 'here to stay'. He accepted the criticism, among other things, of having taken part in 'all the past [mistaken] decisions'.[550]

Rousta admitted that he, Ovanesian and Eskandari, who were against collaboration with Qavam and participating in his coalition cabinet, went to see the Soviet Ambassador telling him that Qavam was 'a dangerous person'. This was a confession to the fact that had already been related by Kambakhsh to the Soviets, as mentioned above. He told the plenum that regretfully their statement 'had no effect; the mistake was that we did not insist',[551] as if that would have made any difference. This was a curious confession, for in 1962 he wrote a letter to Ponomarev and Walter Ulbricht asking them to dissolve the TPI and appoint him to organise a new party in its place.[552] In this connection, too, it is important to recall that Radmanesh told the plenum that at the Second Congress Ovanesian had not been elected to the Central Committee because 'a piece of information' had been 'received from [Soviet] friends',[553] telling them to exclude him. In other words, the Soviets had a veto on who would be 'elected' to the Central Committee — a trend known to those who are familiar with the Comintern's history.

Radmanesh, after relating his own militant past, asserted that it was not possible to settle any differences with Kianouri; Qasemi together with Kianouri had caused 'the greatest damage' to the party: 'Qasemi was very violent, and all the cadres were dissatisfied with him. Even Kianouri and Shandermani confirmed his violence.' He recalled that in the past Kianouri and Qasemi had been opposed to Tabari, and Tabari to them, but now at the plenum, Tabari bribed them by pouring praise upon them.[554]

Radmanesh claimed that he had 'always wanted to return to Iran',[555] but he did not explain why he did not do so when in the autumn of 1952 the TPI was cleared of all charges of the 'attempt on the life of the shah'. He thought his 'greatest sin' was that he had lived abroad, while his 'greatest honour' was his being the Secretary-General of the party.[556]

Opposed to Radmanesh, Ovanesian called the leadership 'bankrupt' and considered it to be heavily responsible for the crisis. Accordingly, he defended Qasemi, who belonged to his tendency, adding that he 'is not comparable to Beria'![557]

As regards the TPI's policy towards the nationalisation of oil and Mosaddeq, Keshavarz stated that 'we must expressly confess to our mistakes, but we must be careful not to fall into right opportunism'. With regard to 'the major responsibility of the Tudeh Party' in weakening the national-democratic movement, he referred to the article by Tabari, under the pseudonym 'Tudeh', in a Cominform review which had 'misled' the leadership inside the country. 'This article was later criticised in an organ of the CPSU… on the issue of the Tudeh Party's major responsibility.' Now, he said, while the oil sub-committee of the plenum, composed of Radmanesh, Kambakhsh and himself, had unanimously adopted a draft resolution on the party's responsibility, in the plenum certain Central Committee members voted against it — probably meaning Qasemi, Kianouri and Foroutan. For this reason, 'on the whole, I am opposed to the [tabled] resolution', which was 'an attempt to whitewash [past] mistakes'.[558]

On the other hand, Qasemi still insisted that the 'Patriotic Front was created by US imperialism'. Jowdat, while agreeing with Qasemi's position, added that when the Front raised the slogan of nationalisation 'we did not analyse it from a class point of view and within half an hour changed it', that is, to the call for the annulment of the 1933 Agreement. He did not explain what his class analysis would have been. He added:

> [We]… thought some [of its leaders] to be agents of the British, others American agents, and the rest of them deceived… Now reading the analysis of the time, I burst into laughter; the Patriotic Front wanted to profit from our support, and yet not to join in a united front.[559]

In his 'memoirs' written in prison after the revolution he had a different analysis: at the time of the nationalisation campaign:

> … members and leaders of the party, whether in prison or outside, did not appraise this problem in depth and, in lieu of supporting the slogan by the Patriotic Front unconditionally and with all their might, launched a mistaken and divisive slogan and defended it for months long, in spite of the view of a large number of cadres, whence began the first difference of opinion between the leadership and cadres.[560]

As can be seen, the confusion of the Tudeh leadership on policy had continued over the years.

For his part, Kianouri held the view that:

> ... at first US imperialism supported the Patriotic Front in order to be able to obtain a share in British imperialism's oil profits... thus, the Patriotic Front, having class roots, is based on the national bourgeoisie, petty bourgeoisie and the intellectuals. In the second period, the Patriotic Front raised the slogan of reclaiming the rights [of Iran], but our party did not consider this one of its fundamental priorities and kept silent about it for three months... The Americans were always opposed to the slogan of nationalisation; this is characteristic of imperialism. In this period, we did not understand the nationalisation slogan. In the third period, from the nationalisation till the uprising of 21 July 1952, our policy was on the whole wrong, but had correct streaks, like not supporting the national bond [to finance the budget[561]]... We were not prepared for the 21 July uprising and did not believe Mosaddeq had so many supporters. The harsh reality then showed that the popular masses were Mosaddeq's supporters.[562]

With the exception of Qasemi, who refused to admit that either he or the TPI had committed any errors, all the Central Committee members were confessing to nefarious mistakes, mistakes which had cost a nation dearly.

Tabari, for his part, found that the leadership had used 'Machiavellian and demagogic methods'.[563]

Finally, the Central Committee surprised the cadres by raising the hottest issue of party policy: the affair of the Autonomous Government of Azerbaijan. It had not been on the agenda, but it was suddenly tabled during the last few hours of the plenum. It was an issue that was a matter of permanent conflict between TPI members and those of the DPA in exile. According to Ekteshafi, the reason for the belated tabling of the issue was the 'sensibility' of the Soviet government.

On behalf of the Central Committee, Radmanesh informed the cadres that discussions had taken place with 'Soviet friends' in order to get their agreement for the creation of a 'united party of the proletarian class' in Iran. Then, he offered four minutes to each cadre to express his view. There was a storm of protest on the part of two-thirds of the cadres, asking Radmanesh to request the Soviets to extend the plenum time for another week so that the question could be fully discussed. The Central Committee rejected this demand, but the majority of cadres insisted upon more time being given to discuss this controversial issue. At this point, Eskandari and Radmanesh stated that the

Central Committee 'was not morally obliged to accept the views of the cadres; it had made its decision'. According to Ekteshafi, the Central Committee could not break its commitment to the Soviets on this issue; Ekteshafi states that these two leaders gave the Soviets a 'bribe' in order to remain in power.[564] The Central Committee, therefore, did not agree with the proposal to form a commission to investigate the reasons for the creation of the DPA in 1945 and to determine the mistakes, for Radmanesh, Rousta, Jowdat, Boqrati, Kianouri and Kambakhsh severely opposed the idea.[565] Then, a row followed and the plenum ended in chaos. During the row it became clear that the DPA's programme had been drafted by President Bagirov of the Azerbaijan SSR with the aim of separating Azerbaijan from Iran. As we have shown above, some Central Committee members had opposed the DPA, but 'Soviet friends had recommended to them to desist in their opposition'.[566]

At the end came the election of the new leadership in which the cadres were to vote. Naturally, they were lobbied by the candidates and their friends. At long last, seven leaders were elected by open ballots as the new Executive Committee, a method that did not guarantee freedom of expression. They were Radmanesh, Eskandari, Kambakhsh, Tabari, Kianouri, Qasemi and Foroutan.[567] It is strange that, despite all the critical remarks throughout the plenum against the minority responsible for 'left-extremist' policies — from the oil nationalisation question to the débâcle of 19 August 1953 and the disaster annihilating the TMO — the left-extremist faction obtained the majority in the Executive Committee.

At the end of the debates on the platforms, the draft resolutions presented by the Central Committee were discussed by sub-committees and adopted, most probably after some haggling. They concerned:
* An appraisal of the TPI's policy towards the movement for the nationalisation of the oil industry.
* An assessment of the TPI's policy *vis-à-vis* the 1953 *coup d'état*.
* The current stage of the Iranian revolution and the errors of the Executive Committee's brochure *Concerning 19 August* and Kianouri's rejoinder.
* The adventurist mistakes of the party after the coup.
* The exposure and destruction of the TMO.
* The nature of the differences in the party leadership.
* The way out of the crisis.
* The General Report of the TPI Central Committee.

To give a résumé of the first resolution concerning Mosaddeq and the national-democratic movement, let us note that it stated that 'the basis of the left-extremist policy of our party was its failure to recognise the nature of the national bourgeoisie and the anti-imperialist character of this stratum of the bourgeoisie'. It declared that the 'national bourgeoisie', despite its economic weakness, had participated during the past half a century in the anti-imperialist struggle of the Iranian people and played an effective role during the Constitutional Revolution, the struggle during the Great War, the revolution in Gilan, and the insurrections in Azerbaijan and Khorasan in 1918-21. It also stated that the 'national bourgeoisie' was composed of 'various strata', was linked to the 'feudal system', and 'feared the development of the revolutionary movement of toiling masses', which explained its 'inconsistent' policy against imperialism. As for the Patriotic Front, it asserted that the 'national bourgeoisie' had, as of its foundation in 1950:

> ... succeeded in moving on to a new stage on the path to uniting and organising its struggle. In the process of the struggle for the nationalisation of the oil industries across the country, the Patriotic Front managed to draw considerable strata from [various] classes of society behind it; using the general demand of the Iranian people and the contradiction between the British and American imperialists, as well as the conflicts between various groups of the ruling élite; it managed to form the government of Dr Mosaddeq, which represented the wishes of the Iranian national bourgeoisie. Thus, during 1950-53 the Patriotic Front played an effective role in the anti-colonial struggle of the Iranian people.

The resolution also declared that the TPI, by its failure to realise the nature of the Patriotic Front and 'its anti-imperialist role' and having 'lost the political initiative in the anti-imperialist struggle', 'committed important political mistakes'. The resolution pointed out that the party had adopted 'a wrong orientation' on the question of oil nationalisation and a 'mistaken, left-extremist' policy towards Mosaddeq's government; it was the party's 'most important error'. It regretted that the party leadership, in lieu of supporting the Patriotic Front and Mosaddeq's government against imperialism and the most reactionary wing of the ruling élite and encouraging the positive aspects of the policy of national-bourgeois leaders, attacked them for a long period of time, 'till reality refuted this mistaken policy'. Naturally, the resolution could not mention anything about the fact that its mistaken policies had stemmed from its pro-Soviet orientation and its obedience to the CPSU. It added that the 'mistaken policy' of the party prepared the ground for the 'unfair accusations by our enemies which were intended to besmirch our reputation, going so far as alleging that we had made a deal with imperialism'.[568]

This reference to 'unfair accusations' relates to what Mosaddeq had evoked in the military tribunal about the TPI's policy *vis-à-vis* the national-democratic movement, to the effect that there had been pro-British elements in that party

— a point he also raised in his memoirs, that 'a group of Tudeh members had been connected with the policy of the former oil company', that is, the AIOC.[569] What he had meant was that there had been British infiltration into the TPI, with the resulting emergence of two rival wings within the party whose repercussions were reflected in the hysterical policy against the national-democratic movement, a policy that systematically depicted Mosaddeq and his collaborators as hired agents of US imperialism. This suggestion by Mosaddeq has taken root, even among some former Tudeh and TMO militants, particularly in light of revelations, notably by Azarnour, that the British did have agents at the top of the party, with a strong suspicion that one might have been Ali Mottaqi of the Tehran Provincial Committee, or even Kianouri himself.

A second resolution, stating that the 1953 *coup d'état* 'temporarily changed the historical orientation of Iranian society, provoking a regression', attributed its success to 'several factors':

* The 'collusion' between the British and American imperialists.
* The 'shaky and doubtful' attitude of Mosaddeq's government in resorting to effective measures against the putsch and its being caught in a 'surprise attack'.
* 'Disunity among anti-imperialist forces.'
* A 'mistaken policy of our party towards the national bourgeoisie and Dr Mosaddeq's government, which was due to the left-extremist and prolonged sectarian tactics of our party, particularly a series of left-extremist undertakings by us during 16-19 August, which provoked further anxiousness amongst the national bourgeoisie' *vis-à-vis* the TPI.
* A 'lack of preparedness of the party to confront the putsch, in spite of the fact that the leadership had perceived the danger of a coup on the part of imperialist and reactionary circles'.
* A 'lack of attention and confusion resulting from the defeat of the 16 August coup and the flight of the shah'.
* The 'failure to perceive the nature of the 19 August coup at the start, overvaluing Mosaddeq's possibilities and determination, and undervaluing the enemy's possibilities, including the lack of any action whatsoever on the part of the [Tudeh] leadership to confront the 19 August coup; taking no measures to mobilise the people who were prepared for struggle; and our trailing behind the national bourgeoisie'.

The plenum acknowledged that this 'great error' of the leadership had 'caused the credibility of the leadership to suffer among both the people and party members'. The plenum declared that the 'weakness' of the leadership was due to the 'influence of petty-bourgeois thoughts, manifested in leftist and rightist deviations in party tactics and unprincipled and bureaucratic methods'.[570]

A third resolution disputed the analytical accuracy of the Executive Committee's brochure *Concerning 19 August*, which had 'serious theoretical errors', and its rejoinder by Kianouri, stating basically that the stage of the Iranian revolution was one of a 'bourgeois-democratic revolution of a new type' in which, contrary to the assertion of the brochure, the 'hegemony' of leadership belonged to the 'proletarian' party. The resolution reproached the Executive Committee for asserting that the leadership had belonged to the national bourgeoisie, as result of which the national bourgeoisie was held responsible for the 1953 defeat. The Executive Committee was charged with 'opportunistic deviation'. Kianouri, although having 'tried to correct the mistaken statements' of the said brochure, was also 'reproached for not having defined with clarity the stage of the revolution'.[571]

A fourth resolution briefly criticised the Executive Committee for its 'adventurist' policies, such as preparations for partisan warfare.[572]

A fifth resolution declared that the uncovering and destruction of the TMO was 'a heavy blow' to the democratic movement and to the TPI in particular. Apart from the 'savage assault of the reactionary forces' and the police and military espionage agencies, using 'inhuman tortures', upon party members responsible for the débâcle, it also maintained that the centralisation of the TMO, bureaucracy, the concentration of all TMO documents in one place, the unnecessary knowledge of members — read Abbasi — of TMO secrets, the extravagant publication of armed forces' documents in the press, etc, were responsible for the disaster that had struck that organisation.

The resolution criticised not only the Tudeh leadership as a whole for its failure to provide hide-outs and to protect officers who faced the risk of arrest, but in particular Dr Jowdat, who was officially in charge of liaison between the TMO and the TPI Executive Committee, but not Kianouri, who actually advised the officers on the run to surrender to the military authorities.[573]

The next resolution concerned 'the nature of the differences' in the Tudeh leadership. It stated that 'the appraisal of the documents and the proceedings of the Central Committee' demonstrated that 'there was no definite delimitation' within it 'regarding political and ideological problems, and the individuals involved in the conflicts had varying positions and yet, for the most part, reached unanimous decisions'. Withal, concrete cases showed that differences 'within the leadership of our party, generally, were related, one way or another, to the occupation of [party] positions', that is, personal rivalries. The plenum, 'after careful study', did not find 'convincing' the arguments by the two sides of the conflict that the differences had been due to the existence of a dominant group on the one side, and a minority on the other. Yet the resolution stated that both sides within the Central Committee 'used in their struggle unprincipled and unhealthy methods — such as accusations, compiling documents with the aim of blackmailing [*parvandeh-sazi*] their rivals, unwarranted suspicion, careless observation of organisational principles, incompatibility with collective work, overwrought individualism [*takravi*], violence, obstinacy and rancour'. Therefore, said the resolution, 'it condemns strongly and forcefully these improper methods and invites their practitioners to respect [party] principles and exercise clear and indubitable self-criticism'.

The resolution admitted that there had been a faction in the party that had used as a support one or another member of the Central Committee, a faction that had been led by the chief of the Youth Organisation, Shermini, a man who had wanted to dominate the party. Shermini, who had contributed much to the extremism of the party line through his control of the Youth Organisation, was conveniently made the scapegoat for most of the problems that the party had faced during the years preceding the coup, while the young collaborators without whom Shermini could not have carried out his destructive policy were whitewashed, just like the majority faction that had appointed and supported him. The faction led by Shermini was 'severely condemned for the harm it had done to the party'.

The resolution concluded that 'above all, it was the petty-bourgeois, rather than proletarian, ideology that [had] influenced the methods of internal party struggle over differences within the leadership'. It further stated that the leadership organ had suffered from 'a qualitative weakness', that is, a low level of theoretical knowledge; 'its feeble revolutionary character, on the whole, far from resolving its differences, often intensifying them'. It added that the 'lack of democracy' within the party prevented the membership from contributing to the resolution of those differences.[574]

We have no clear indication as to what extent these resolutions reflect the content of the draft resolutions presented by the Central Committee and to what extent the amendments by the cadres. But the categorical and firm language of the resolutions about the past points rather to the amendments. If so, the appraisal of the party cadres demonstrates why the Tudeh leadership had moved from one disaster to another — despite many sacrifices by the party's members, especially those who gave their lives and endured torture in prison — contributing hardly anything to the anti-imperialist movement and the development of the struggle of the toiling masses.

A striking feature of the plenum was that there was hardly any mention of the working class, either in the struggles surveyed, or in the resolutions adopted — a telling aspect of the TPI's endless boasting of its being a proletarian party, while its remnants in exile were drawn from the entire middle stratum, from top to bottom, of Iranian society, a professional élite, however badly educated in history and Marxian theory.

The Tudeh leadership, like most of the cadres and members, considered the plenum to be 'undoubtedly an important step forwards in the history of the development of our party'. Yet the revealing fact about the incorrigible character of the leadership is that it refused to publish the resolutions adopted, thus not informing the Iranian people or even party members of the party's errors, although in its declaration on the plenum resolutions it had stated that the cadres had 'played the role of a fair judge' concerning the 'differences within the leadership organs'.[575] What is more, the very same group of individuals who had been, individually and collectively, responsible for the grave and costly errors were once again elected to the leadership — ironically by the same cadres who had pitilessly criticised them. As we shall see later for the subsequent period, the resolutions served no purpose, for mistakes continued to be made and wrong policies continued to be formulated.

Another incident occurred at the conclusion of the plenum when some Central Committee members close to the old majority considered that the new Executive Committee had been elected in a 'non-Leninist' manner. A meeting of the Central Committee took place where even physical violence erupted. The accusation was also made that the old minority had filled the plenum with its supporters, a remark that was denounced by the cadres. Then, ten of the cadres who had been preselected by the Central Committee, having received the 'approval of the representative of the CPSU', were coopted by the plenum as alternate members of the Central Committee.[576]

It is not surprising that, according to one of the participants, leaders such as Qasemi and Foroutan, active members of the past 'minority' who had now gained a majority as a result of the elections at the conclusion of the plenum, were 'fundamentally' dissatisfied with the resolutions of the plenum, such as the issues regarding Mosaddeq and oil nationalisation, opposed them and prevented their publication. On the other hand, the Executive Committee as a whole did not believe in the resolutions that were critical of the entire Central Committee; and it was for this reason that they were not published.[577]

XIV: A Few Tentative Remarks

Because we still have to bring this short narrative of the history of the TPI up to the demise of the party in the second half of the 1980s and also to compare its performance with those of other leftist organisations that sprang up after the 1953 *coup d'état*, at this stage we defer attempting a conclusion. What, instead, seems useful at this point is to offer a few short critical remarks on two decades of the life of a party which began, admittedly, as a 'united front of progressive forces' in Iran and soon, despite successive setbacks, declared itself to be the 'proletarian party of the new type' pretending to lead the country's 'working class and other toiling masses' successfully towards a 'proletarian revolution'.

There can be no denying that the educated élite, or at least the majority of them, around the founder of the party, SM Eskandari, who helped create and expand the TPI were a group of idealistic and patriotic individuals who wanted to improve the lot of an oppressed people who had been deprived of their political, economic and cultural progress since their attempt at revolution three decades previously, at beginning of the twentieth century. The leading personalities among them, such as Radmanesh, Eskandari and Alamouti, had had been educated either in Europe or had received a European education at modern schools in Iran and had been attracted to socialist goals — though ignorant of the true nature of state capitalism in Russia. A few, like Kambakhsh, Rousta and Ovanesian, had undergone a short Bolshevik training in the Soviet Union as 'professional Bolshevist revolutionaries'. For this reason, their role in the TPI was not surprising. Tudeh leaders were men of their time, a world, on the whole, caught up between a period of recovering capitalism from the great depression and the construction of 'socialism' in Stalinist Russia, one that had been leading astray the international working-class movement by presenting white-Russian state capitalism in a socialist shell.

Thus, the fundamental error these idealistic, patriotic young TPI leaders kept repeating was one of following the Soviet-Russian political line that could lead them nowhere. It is unfortunate that they had not, as young students in Europe, come across Marxists critical of the Soviet line so as to be able, at least, to observe Marx's motto '*de omnibus dubitandum*', so that they could at least look at Russia with critical eyes. By the time they had arrived in Europe, most Marxist schools and trends critical of, or opposed to, Stalinism had been crushed. Taqi Arani was, of course, an exception. If not his Marxist studies, at least some of his personal experiences had made him understand the direction the Soviet Union had taken. Yet those around him failed to understand the reality he had understood and taught, especially about the doubts he had expressed in prison about the relevance of Stalinist attacks upon Trotsky, perhaps because he had been isolated by Kambakhsh's ruse of depicting him as the one who had handed the group over to the police. Soon after they realised their mistake and shook off their mistrust of him, Arani died.[578]

Another reason may have been their Iranian character of unbounded ambition and position-hunting that led them away from political principles that must not be compromised and the need to learn seriously Marxian methods of thinking, if one wishes to serve the oppressed toiling masses.

It was, therefore, not surprising that the Soviet apparatus would decide what kind of organisation these young people, idealistic, inexperienced and — above all — uneducated in Marxian knowledge and methods, should have; what programme they should present to their countrymen and comrades; and, more importantly, what approach they should not apply to confront the complex problems with which Iranian society was faced. As a result, one important question they ignored was that the ready-made formulae the Comintern or its Soviet 'advisers' recommended were not appropriate for Iran, as had already been pointed out by Iranian Communist leaders at the Sixth Comintern Congress. Thus, they had no correct analytical approach, nor the appropriate tools, to examine Iran's socio-economic and politico-cultural problems and appraise them in order to draft a suitable programme of action and decide what political approach to use to put that programme into effect.

Yet another major blunder of the new party in its approach — a natural outcome of their mode of thinking inculcated by Soviet Marxism — was that Iran could, like the Central Asian or Caucasian Soviet republics, once in the Soviet camp, begin to construct 'socialism', thus leaping over the historical bourgeois-democratic hurdle that could not, as the ICP had learned by experience, be skipped. There is no indication that the TPI leaders had been aware of the debates that had taken place on the basis of Marx's letter to Vera Zasulich concerning the possibility for Russia to leap over to socialism, provided some highly industrialised country such as Germany had gone through a socialist revolution. Nor is there any indication that they were aware of the debates amongst Iranian Communists in the 1920s regarding the stage of the revolution; still less of the correspondence between Social-Democrats in Tabriz with Kautsky and Plekhanov regarding the historical necessity of carrying out the struggle for democracy through which the masses can educate themselves, both in democracy and socialism, and construct socialism once having gone through the industrial and cultural prerequisites — a thesis even Lenin had supported then for Russia.[579] They, therefore, opposed the national-democratic movement which was a patriotic movement for the establishment of the independence of the country and also a democratic regime in which both democratic institutions could be strengthened and the economy could be directed towards a healthy development — conditions *sine qua non* for the development of the industrial prerequisites, the working class, the consciousness of their own class interests — what Marx had called consciousness of, not the class in itself, but of the class for itself: *Bewustsein der Klasse fuer sich, nicht an sich* — preparing the grounds for socialism both in Iran and the region.

As a result of these primary errors, the TPI soon suffered a triple defeat: a) its party organisation in the Azerbaijan province dissolved itself without the slightest consultation with the Central Committee and joined the newly-created Democratic Party of Azerbaijan; b) the autonomous 'national' government of

Ja'far Pishevari, the Autonomous Government of Azerbaijan, crumbled under US political pressure and military threat veneered in a compromise offered by the Qavam cabinet to Moscow for an illegal oil concession; c) in a maladroit manoeuvre to accede to power and to help enhance the fortunes of the pro-Soviet forces in Iran, the TPI joined the Qavam cabinet with three ministers, but the party was disgracefully out-manoeuvred by Qavam under American pressure. During this critical period, the party made a great number of political concessions *vis-à-vis* Qavam and the ruling élite of Iran, none of which bore any results.

The Azerbaijan blunder was the point of no return. This stage was important, not only insofar as the party's submissive attitude was concerned, but also insofar as Iranian reaction could, using its Achilles' heel of obedience to the Soviet Union, hatch the 1949 plot to proscribe the party and drive it underground.

Other errors of the party were inadvertent reinforcement of religious inclinations among party members, by paying lip-service to Islam and its sacred Shiite idols through its press, particularly among workers who were first-generation city dwellers; engagement in bank robberies; terrorist acts against friend and foe in a period of relative democratic liberties; inaction during the 1953 putsch, which was again a direct consequence of expecting the Soviet party's 'advice', whose leadership was navigating in the troubled waters of a decisive conflict; and also the TPI's reckless utilisation of its military information and injudicious actions leading to the discovery of its military organisation that could have continued to serve it as its protective shield.

In the next instalment, we shall investigate the efforts that the TPI made to revive itself after the CPSU's Twentieth Congress, when it began a new life, one which nevertheless moved along the old lines, which led to its final demise under the clericratic state led by Khomeini, for whose 'health' the party 'should also look after... lest meetings, interviews and consecutive decision-making sessions wear him out too much'.

Notes
1. As for the Tudeh archives, in 1992 this author was told by the director of the archives of the former CPSU that they were being kept in Siberia, but a copy could be bought — at an exorbitant price.
2. Remnants of the Left linger on mostly abroad, but they are much divided, perhaps into as many as 50 infinitesimal 'organisations', often with only a few members.
3. See C Chaqueri, 'I Eskandari and the Tudeh Party of Iran', *Central Asian Survey*, no 4, 1988; C Chaqueri, 'Moscow and the Tudeh Party: Did the Soviets Play a Role in Founding the Tudeh Party in Iran?', *Cahier du monde russe*, July-September 1999, reprinted in this issue of *Revolutionary History*.
4. 'Note on the Political Parties and Groups now in Existence in Persia', 1942, FO 406/80.

5. For studies of the TPI, which are not devoid of ideological biases from, respectively, pro-Soviet and anti-Soviet positions, see the following works: Ervand Abrahamian, *Iran Between Two Revolutions* (Princeton, 1982); Sepehr Zabih, *The Communist Movement in Iran* (Berkeley, 1966); see also the critique of these works in my article 'The Iranian Left in the Twentieth Century: A Critical Appraisal of its Historiography' in this issue of *Revolutionary History*.
6. Chaqueri, 'Moscow and the Tudeh Party', below.
7. I Eskandari, 'La Constitution du parti Toudeh et l'essor du mouvement démocratique en Iran', *Moyen-Orient*, no 6, December 1949.
8. C Chaqueri (ed), *Historical Documents: The Workers', Social-Democratic and Communist Movement in Iran* (23 volumes, Florence and Tehran, 1969-94), Volume 1.
9. I Eskandari, 'La Constitution du parti Toudeh et l'essor du mouvement démocratique en Iran', *Moyen-Orient*, no 6, December 1949. See also Chaqueri, 'Moscow and the Tudeh Party', below.
10. Contrary to Eskandari's assertion, it was launched on 22 February 1942, not in November 1941 (I Eskandari, 'La Constitution du parti Toudeh et l'essor du mouvement démocratique en Iran', *Moyen-Orient*, no 6, December 1949).
11. For a complete list of the TPI's publications till 1950, see Department of State, Office of Libraries and Intelligence Questions, *Leaders and Members of the Tudeh Party and Other Iranians Engaged in Pro-Soviet Activities* (Washington DC, 1950), pp 158ff. (See Document section for a short list.)
12. For a report of this conference, see FO 371/42187.
13. I Eskandari, 'La Constitution du parti Toudeh et l'essor du mouvement démocratique en Iran', *Moyen-Orient*, no 6, December 1949.
14. Eskandari (ibid) claims that the party had 10 000 members among the workers; as reported to the Comintern the TPI had no more than 2000 members by its first anniversary in the autumn of 1942 (see Chaqueri, 'Moscow and the Tudeh Party', below). Below we shall refer to the varying numbers of members over the years of the party's life.
15. The 1310/1931 Act proscribed the constitution of any group with a membership larger than three, with a 'communistic' goal or anti-monarchic leaning. Those condemned of such a 'crime' would be condemned to three to ten years' imprisonment.
16. A report by the British Oriental Secretary at Tehran reviewed the Tudeh programme in 1943; he did not refer to it as a programme adopted at the Tehran Provincial Conference. This programme refers to reforms in the domains of labour law, employment, agriculture, hygiene, electoral law, legal reform, improvement of the national economy, municipal laws, education and the military. The British Oriental Secretary did not find the programme revolutionary, but feared some provisions might mean 'nationalisation', that is, communism. See FO 371/53705, 1943.
17. The Communist University for the Toilers of the East, established by the Comintern.
18. For the ephemeral life of the Tabriz unions, see C Chaqueri (ed), *The Conditions of the Working Class in Iran* (four volumes, Florence and Tehran, 1969-92), Volume

2, pp 3-14.
19. See Chaqueri (ed), *The Conditions of the Working Class in Iran*, Volume 1, pp 37-41, 52-59, 68-74, 106-07; see also Y Eftekhari, *Khaterat* (edited by K Bayat *et al*, Tehran, 1992).
20. I Eskandari, 'La Constitution du parti Toudeh et l'essor du mouvement démocratique en Iran', *Moyen-Orient*, no 6, December 1949.
21. Eskandari (ibid) provides a Stalinist version of the history of the labour unions of the time. For the documents of the period, see Chaqueri (ed), *The Conditions of the Working Class in Iran*, Volume 1; see also H Ladjevardi, *Labor Unions and Autocracy in Iran* (Syracuse, 1985).
22. Chaqueri (ed), *The Conditions of the Working Class in Iran*, Volume 3.
23. I Eskandari, 'La Constitution du parti Toudeh et l'essor du mouvement démocratique en Iran', *Moyen-Orient*, no 6, December 1949.
24. Abrahamian, *Iran Between Two Revolutions*; Maziar Behrouz, *Rebels with a Cause* (London, 1999).
25. I Eskandari, 'La Constitution du parti Toudeh et l'essor du mouvement démocratique en Iran', *Moyen-Orient*, no 6, December 1949.
26. Similarly, the Tudeh historian Abrahamian makes exaggerated claims of the TPI's membership and its street demonstrators, without taking into account the population of the country and its various cities and towns, as well as the working population (Abrahamian, *Iran Between Two Revolutions*, pp 292-303, 321, etc). His method, as noted in my article 'The Iranian Left in the Twentieth Century', is far from objective.
27. I Eskandari, 'Première phase du gouvernement Qavam. Immense progrès du mouvement démocratique: Essor des syndicats et des unions paysannes', *Moyen-Orient*, no 12, June 1950.
28. TPI, *Salanameh ye Tudeh* (DDR, 1970), p 185.
29. Ibid, p 187.
30. Ibid.
31. Ibid, p 191.
32. Ibid.
33. Ibid, p 200.
34. A Kambakhsh, *Nazari beh jonbesh-e kargari va komonisti dar Iran*, Volume 1 (Leipzig, 1972), p 85.
35. Excerpts from Report R-89-45, USNA/RG 84/Confidential Files, Military Attaché Report (Box 7, 1945).
36. Shandermani's Report, written and handed to Secretary Radmanesh in 1956, p 27. This was a confidential report written by the Secretary of the TPI's Executive Committee, Akbar Shandermani, a copy of which is in the possession of this author.
37. See Shandermani's Report.
38. It should be noted that all these workers were employed by industries; the majority of them worked in menial jobs, construction and road-building.
39. I Eskandari, 'Histoire du Parti Toudeh', *Moyen-Orient*, no 8, February 1950.
40. *Rahbar*, 4 September 1944, puts the total at 154 394.
41. It is not clear why, if, according to Eskandari, the Soviets helped Dr Freydoun

Keshavarz to be elected, they should not have helped others such as Kambakhsh, Artashes Ovanesian and even Eskandari himself! (See I Eskandari, *Khaterat-e siasi* (edited by F Azarnour and B Amirkhosrowi, four volumes, Paris, 1987-89; Tehran edition, 1993, references are to the Paris edition, unless otherwise stated), Volume 4, p 90.) In fact, the Foreign Office archives show that the British made an agreement with the Prime Minister to have the pro-Soviet Tudeh candidate Taqi Fadakar in Isfahan elected (FO 636/147/43; 636/238/43; 248/1428). One British report suggests that the Soviets 'do not, after all, propose to back the Tudeh through thick and thin, but are trying in Azerbaijan to get hold of the propertied classes'! Yet another report in the same minutes states that a Soviet Embassy official named Avalov 'summoned all the deputies [of the Thirteenth Legislature] for Gilan one by one (including [the grandee] Hassan Akbar) and said that they must allow Dr Keshavarz to be elected for [the port city of Anzali] Pahlavi and Dr Radmanesh (editor of *Mardom*) for Lahijan. The fisheries workers would help, and so would Qavam al-Saltaneh.' According to this report, Avalov had received 'Moscow's orders'. As noted elsewhere in this Introduction, Bullard here too jotted down that 'perhaps Avalov had done nothing more than that I had done in Isfahan, where I had advised the wealthy not to sit on the safety valve, but to let Fadakar be elected so as to give the workmen a legitimate outlet for their aspirations'. What is more, the British did not back any candidate in the Russian zone of occupation. See FO 636/92/43; 248/1428. Unfortunately, the Soviet archives remain inaccessible.

42. Qavam's letter dated 22 Ordibehesh 1322/12 May 1943, printed in *Tarikh-e mo'aser-e Iran*, no 12, Winter 1387/1999, p 186. This is confirmed by the number of votes Radmanesh received in the vast rural area of Lahijan (19 734), as opposed by those received (3400) by Keshavarz in the small port city of Pahlavi (Anzali), where the right did not vote for him.
43. Eskandari, *Khaterat*, Volume 4, p 90.
44. FO 371/45448. It should be pointed out that that Bullard, later made Lord, had sympathised with the Labour Party and had a good record of opposing reactionary premiers, although his staff, and later envoys, were not like him.
45. FO 371/35071.
46. See 'Jarayan-e nokhostin kongreh-ye hezbi', *Rahbar*, 4 September 1944.
47. Colonel Ali Zibayee, *Kommonizm dar Iran. Tarikh-e mokhtasar-e fa'liyatha-ye kommonistha dar Iran* (Tehran, 1964), p 530.
48. As opposed to the official vote count, Pishevari's own newspaper, *Azhir* (25 Tir 1323/16 July 1944), stated that the number of votes were 47 for and 50 against; what is more, there was no discussion about any objection anyone might have levelled against Pishevari's credential and a secret ballot was requested so that no one could know who voted for and who against. There is no indication that the Tudeh deputies objected to the secret ballot.
49. As opposed to another allegation by a Tudeh leader, according to which Iraj Eskandari had not voted for him, Keshavarz states that it was the Armenian Tudeh leader Artashes Ovanesian, who was a foe of Pishevari, who did not vote for him (F Keshavarz, *Man Motahamm mikonam komiteh-ye markazi-ye Hezb-e Tudeh ra* (London, 1982), p 66). With the secret ballot, these accusations lose their sense and reflect personal animosity of one leader against another.

50. For independent *ajomans*, see FO 371/31426 (E1646/163/34).
51. Kianouri was the brother-in-law of Kambakhsh, who had been a Soviet collaborator from the early 1920s. He is the man who had betrayed Arani's 'Group of Fifty-Three' to the police, and was impeded from entering the TPI until 1944 when the Soviets imposed his membership upon the party and the Central Committee.
52. See the Persian original of the programme in *Rahbar*, 16 Shahrivar 1323/7 September 1944. For the English translation, see the Documents section.
53. *Rahbar*, 20-24 Mordad 1323/11-15 August 1944; I Eskandari, 'Histoire du Parti Toudeh', *Moyen-Orient*, no 8, February 1950.
54. Unsigned report by a Soviet official in Iran in 1944; RTsKhIDNI, 17/128/818; full text in the Documents section.
55. I Eskandari, 'Histoire du Parti Toudeh', *Moyen-Orient*, no 8, February 1950; Zibayee, *Kommonizm dar Iran*, p 273; see also the TPI organ *Rahbar*, for the period of the congress, 10-20 Mordad 1323/1-10 August 1944.
56. P Eskteshafi, *Khaterat* (*Memoirs*, edited by H Ahmadi, Berlin, 1998), p 163.
57. Report by a Soviet official (Malishef) in Iran in 1944; RTsKhIDNI, 17/128/818; full text in the Documents section. The actual number of Central Committee members was 15.
58. See Chaqueri, 'Moscow and the Tudeh Party', below.
59. A figure might have been given to him by Tudeh leaders with whom he had had talks.
60. Interestingly, Keshavarz was the only Tudeh leader the Comintern appraised as a 'democrat,' that is, 'not a quite a Marxist-Leninist'. See Report by Plyshevskii in RTsKhIDNI 495/74/197.
61. 'Report on Persia, II', *Daily Herald*, 24 April 1946. The Labour MP also notes: 'Twenty years ago... [Zia] assisted Reza Shah in his *coup d'état*. A few months later he was exiled. He returned from exile in 1944 with British assistance...'
62. JAMI, *Gozashteh cheragh-e rah-e ayandeh ast* (Tehran, 1983), p 199.
63. Ibid, p 200.
64. Ibid, p 201.
65. It has thus far been thought that those opposed to the Azerbaijan fiasco were instrumental in the removal of the three in question. Yet it is to be pondered whether the Soviets played a role in their removal for they had been responsible for secretly opposing the Azerbaijan adventure by the Soviets. See further below.
66. I Eskandari, 'Histoire du Parti Toudeh', *Moyen-Orient*, no 8, February 1950.
67. H Kay Ostovan, *Siyasat-e movazeneh-ye manfi dar majles-e chahardahom*, Volume 1 (Tehran, 1327/1948), p 157.
68. K Maleki, 'Sar o tah yek karbas', *Rahbar*, nos 436, 437, 438, Azar 1323/December 1944; reprinted in *Ketab-e jom'eh-ha*, no 6-7, 1986, pp 99-119. Curiously, when these three articles were republished, Maleki's followers put out a brochure attacking the publisher, instead of admitting that Maleki, too, had followed the Soviet line. They behaved in the same Stalinist manner, rejecting any kind of criticism of their mentor. Maleki's supporters have never wanted to speak of their mentor's share in the episode, wish to leave that record buried, and slander those who would speak of it. See Farrokh Sho'a'i, *Khosrow Shakeri, Mosaddeq va Maleki* (publication no 7 of Koushesh baraye pishbord-e nehzat-e melli-ye Iran, Paris,

1986 [?]).
69. *Rahbar*, 19 Azar 1323/10 December 1944; English translation in FO 406/83.
70. I Eskandari, 'Histoire du Parti Toudeh', *Moyen-Orient*, no 9, March 1950.
71. I Eskandari, 'Histoire du Parti Toudeh', *Moyen-Orient*, no 10, April 1950. See also the article 'Ehsasat-e mardom nesbat beh Dr Mosaddeq va tanaffor mellat nesbat be Seyyed Zia' ('The Feelings of the People Towards Dr Mosaddeq and the Nation's Hatred for Seyyed Zia'), *Rahbar*, 7 Esfand 1323/26 February 1944, on Mosaddeq's opposition to the electoral credentials of the putschist leader Seyyed Zia.
72. JAMI, *Gozashteh*, p 224.
73. Radmanesh's statement in the Parliament, cited in ibid, p 216.
74. Eskandari, *Khaterat*, Volume 2, pp 106-12.
75. E Tabari, *Mardom baraye roshanfekran*, 19 Aban 1322/10 November 1943, cited in JAMI, *Gozashteh*, pp 225-27; see also Eskandari, *Khaterat*, Volume 2, p 113. Tabari was no theoretician, for he never produced any theoretical writings regarding Iranian society; he simply gargled the writings of the Soviet party, irrespective of who was in power. This title has been bestowed upon him by pro-Tudeh historiographers such as Ervand Abrahamian, who, in addition, refers to other Soviet *hommes de main* in the TPI, such as Kianouri and Kambakhsh, as 'theoreticians'. It is astonishing that Abrahamian mistakenly refers to him at the age of 26 as a 'leading party theoretician' who 'had studied in Great Britain and Tehran University, where he had met Arani' (Abrahamian, *Iran Between Two Revolution*, pp 296ff). Tabari was a simple high-school student, barely 18 years old, when he joined Arani's circle and thereafter. He himself admits that when he and others joined Arani they knew little about the ICP which had been dissolved by the Soviet apparatus. See E Tabari, *Az didar-e khishtan (Yadnameh-ye zendegi)* (Spånga, Sweden, 1997), pp 49ff. He had never left Iran until he fled to the USSR in 1949.
76. JAMA, *Gozashteh*, pp 222-24. According to this source, Tudeh newspapers tried to minimise the matter by referring to the presence of only a few Russian soldiers!
77. Eskandari, *Khaterat*, Volume 2, pp 84-86; also in the Tehran edition, pp 435-36; Keshavarz's *Man Motahamm mikonam* does not mention the presence of Soviet troops.
78. 'Increased Soviet Reaction to Oil Concession Postponement', US Office of Strategic Studies, 1 November 1944; USNA L48894.
79. Keshavarz, *Man Motahamm mikonam*, p 109; Eskandari in his *Khaterat* does not mention the figure of 100 000.
80. Eskandari, *Khaterat*, Volume 4, p 209.
81. I Eskandari, 'Histoire du Parti Toudeh', *Moyen-Orient*, no 10, April 1950.
82. British Military Attaché's Intelligence Summary, no 42, November 1944; FO 371/40206.
83. Ibid. However exaggerated the British Military Attaché's report may be, there can be no denying that the presence of Russian troops were an encouragement to the party zealots.
84. Eskandari, *Khaterat*, Volume 2, p 86. A former TPI Central Committee member and Minister of Education in the short-lived coalition government, Keshavarz in his book *Man Motahamm mikonam* does not speak of the presence of Soviet

forces on the side of Tudeh demonstrators, while one prominent Tudeh cadre, who in 1948 broke with the party, relates that, while he was at first proud to be part of the group maintaining order in Tudeh demonstrations in support of the Soviet demand for an oil concession, he tore off his armband once he saw that the Soviet army units were present to protect the demonstrators (Jalal Al-e Ahmad, *Dar khedmat va khianat-e roshanfekran* (Tehran, 1376), p 416).
85. Eskandari, *Khaterat* (Tehran edition), p 436.
86. I Eskandari, 'Histoire du Parti Toudeh', *Moyen-Orient*, no 10, April 1950; Eskandari, *Khaterat*, Volume 2, pp 78-80, 106-22.
87. I Eskandari, 'Histoire du Parti Toudeh', *Moyen-Orient*, no 10, April 1950.
88. JAMA, *Gozashteh*, pp 227-28.
89. I Eskandari, 'Histoire du Parti Toudeh', *Moyen-Orient*, no 11, May 1950.
90. For the account of the army Chief of Staff in late 1944 and early 1945, who confirms the attacks upon the TPI, see Hassan Arfa, *Under Five Shahs* (Edinburgh, 1964), pp 326-29, 345-47, 355.
91. The mole attributes another betrayal to Kambakhsh in the 1930s: when he and two air force officers had been arrested, they had been condemned to long prison terms, but he had been freed some months afterwards. No one else had thus far regarded this first incident as a betrayal.
92. Secret Report by STASI Mole Reza, dated 7 September 1984; MfS, XV 4561/64, 14583, Band Nr 7, p 129 (000150). It is interesting that the mole, who previously reported on all Tudeh leaders, made these revelations after Kianouri was in prison and had made his confession on television, thus being no threat to its author.
93. Ibid, pp 000151-60.
94. Ibid, pp 000163-64.
95. *Mardom barayye roshanfekran*, no 44, 3 August 1945, cited in ibid.
96. Eskandari, *Memoirs* (Tehran edition), pp 490-91.
97. Secret Report by STASI Mole Reza, pp 124ff (000164ff). The mole recalls the well-known fact that Kianouri had been a member of the Hitler Youth Organisation in his student days in Nazi Germany.
98. Ibid, p 000170.
99. K Vilkov, 'Spravka', 26 March 1942; Comintern Archives, RTsKhIDNI 495/74/195, pp 15-16.
100. Ibid.
101. Report by Plyshevskii, 11 November 1944; Comintern Archives, RTsKhIDNI 455/74/197.
102. RTsKhIDNI 495/74/195.
103. Emphasis in the original.
104. Louis G Dreyfus to the Department of State, 31 March 1943; USNA, 891.00/2003.
105. M Foot, 'Report on Persia, I', *Daily Herald*, 23 April 1946.
106. M Foot, 'Report on Persia, II', *Daily Herald*, 24 April 1946. This must be qualified for, along with the eight Tudeh deputies, Mosaddeq and a small minority could not be classified as such.
107. Report by American Consul Richard Ford, Tabriz, 31 August 1943, USNA/891.00/2054.
108. 'Criticism of the Land System', report by the American Consul SG Ebling, Tabriz,

July 1944, USNA/RG 84 (Box 5, 1944).
109. Ibid.
110. 'Social Classes in Azerbaijan', report by the American Consulate, Tabriz, USNA/RG 84 (Box 5, 1944).
111. NE Egorova, '"Iranskii krizis" 1945-1946 gg Po Rassekrechennym arkhivnym dokumentam', *Novaia i noveishaia istoriia*, no 3, 1994, pp 7-8.
112. RTsKhIDNI, 17/128/817/1/132, cited in ibid, p 10.
113. RTsKhIDNI, 17/128/817/1/29.
114. For details of this plan, see 'Russo-German Negotiations for a Projected Soviet Sphere of Influence in the Near and Middle East', November 1940. For the full text, see RJ Sontag and JS Beddie (eds), *Nazi-Soviet Relations, 1939-1941: Documents from the Archives of the German Foreign Office* (Department of State, Washington, 1948).
115. At the time, foreign diplomats sent reports on this issue, and this has now been confirmed with the publication of studies: Jamil Hasanli, 'Iranian Azerbaijan: The Epicentre of a Cold War', *The Caucasus and Globalisation*, Volume 2, no 1, 2008, pp 7, 15; Jamil Hasanli, *At the Dawn of the Cold War: The Soviet-American Crisis of Iranian Azerbaijan, 1941-1946* (Lanham MD, 2006), pp 5-15. See also the original Azeri version: Jamil Hasanli, *Guney Azerbaijanda Soviet-Amerika-Ingiltera areshidormasi, 1941-1945* (Baku, 2001).
116. Hasanli, *At the Dawn of the Cold War*, pp 26ff.
117. Ibid, p 57.
118. For a discussion of the rivalry between Beria, Bagirov and other leaders, see G Mamoulia, 'Les Crises turque et iranienne, 1945-1947', *Cahier du monde russe*, Volume 45, no 1-2, 2004; G Mamoulia, 'Les Premières fissures de l'URSS d'après guerre. Le Cas de la Géorgie et du Caucase du Sud, 1946-1956', *Cahier du monde russe*, Volume 46, no 3, 2005.
119. 'Reshenie Politburo CC AUCP (B) O meropriiatiakh po organisatsii separatistskogo dvizhenia v Iuzhnom Azerbaidzhane I grugikh provintsiakh Severnogo Irana', 6 July 1945 g', State Archives of Social-Political History of Russia (SASPHR), rec gr 1, inv 89, f 90, sheet 19, cited in J Hasanli, 'Iranian Azerbaijan: The Epicentre of a Cold War', *The Caucasus and Globalisation*, Volume 2, no 1, 2008, pp 4-5; Hasanli, *At the Dawn of the Cold War*, pp 16ff.
120. J Hasanli, 'New Evidence on the Iran Crisis, 1945-46', *Cold War International History Project Bulletin*, no 12/13, 2001, pp 311-12.
121. Bullard to Eden, 8 December 1944; FO 406/82.
122. Ibid.
123. See Chaqueri, 'Moscow and the Tudeh Party', below.
124. Consul Wall to Bullard, 16 April 1945; FO 406/83.
125. Consul Ebling to American Ambassador, 20 March 1945; USNA, RG 84 (Box 7, 1945).
126. Consul Ebling to American Ambassador, 5 February 1945; USNA, RG 84 (Box 7, 1945). 'Liberal' was the term the American Consul systematically used to describe members of the TPI, because they called themselves 'azadikhahan', literally meaning 'freedom-lovers'.
127. Bullard to Eden, 25 April 1945; FO 406/83.

128. Consul Ebling to American Ambassador, 5 and 19 February 1945; USNA, RG 84 (Box 7, 1945). For reports about the conditions of rug-weavers, see Chaqueri (ed), *The Condition of the Working Class in Iran*, Volume 1, pp 301-02, Volume 4, pp 1-3.
129. Consul Ebling to American Ambassador, 21 March 1945; USNA, RG 84 (Box 7, 1945).
130. Consul Ebling to American Ambassador, 3 August 1945; USNA, RG 84 (Box 7, 1945).
131. Letter by Pishevari, Shabestari, Padegan, Javid and Biriya to Bagirov, 23 December 1945; GAPPOD, AzR, F 1, Op 89, D 110, pp 42-45, cited in Fernande Beatrice Scheid Raine, *Stalin, Bagirov, and Soviet Policies in Iran* (Yale PhD, 2000), p 308.
132. Arfa, *Under Five Shahs*, pp 350-51.
133. Sir Reader Bullard, *The Camels Must Go* (London, 1961), p 284. He was, of course, wrong in thinking that the DPA was the TPI re-clad in Azerbaijan.
134. See H Kay Ostovan, *Siyasat-e movazeneh-ye manfi dar majles-e chahardahom*, Volume 2 (Tehran, 1327/1948), pp 224-27.
135. See M Eslamiyeh, *Foulad-e enqelab* (Tehran, 1381), pp 170-73.
136. Keshavarz, *Man Motahamm mikonam*, pp 61-62.
137. He was correct; see GAPPOD, AzR, F 1, Op 89, D 112, pp 533-56; Report of Pishevari's Meeting with Kambakhsh on 4 April 1946, made on 6 April; GAPPOD, AzR, F 1, Op 89, D 117, pp 60-61; GAPPOD, AzR, F 1, Op 89, D 113, pp 125-27, in Scheid Raine, *Stalin, Bagirov, and Soviet Policies in Iran*, p 338.
138. Eskandari, *Khaterat*, Volume 2, pp 88-89; Keshavarz, *Man Motahamm mikonam*, p 62.
139. Keshavarz, *Man Motahamm mikonam*, p 62.
140. Eskandari, *Khaterat*, Volume 2, p 91.
141. Ibid.
142. Police report, 18 August 1945, in B Tayarani (ed), *Asnad-e ahzab-e siasi*, Volume 2 (Tehran, 2005), pp 704-05.
143. B Tayarani (ed), *Asnad-e ahzab-e siasi*, Volume 1 (Tehran, 2005), pp 228-9.
144. 'Telegram from Prominent Members of the Tudeh Party in Tehran to the President of the Majles', 22 September 1945; FO 248/1452.
145. Eskandari, 'Histoire du Parti Toudeh', *Moyen Orient*, no 11, May 1950.
146. Eskandari, *Khaterat*, Volume 2, pp 88-89.
147. Ibid, p 90; see also Keshavarz, *Man Motahamm mikonam*, pp 62-63.
148. Immigrants were Iranian workers traditionally working in Caucasian and Central Asian parts of the Russian empire and of the Soviet Union who had been expelled from those areas in the second part of the 1930s because they had refused to accept Soviet citizenship. Among the some 60 000 of them, it was believed that many were trained Soviet cadres who had been sent to Iran for the day when the Soviets planned to take over Iran.
149. For the TPI's secret letter (signed by Eskandari), see 'Politicheskaya snachimist' narodnoi partii irana', 20 August 1945, addressed to the Central Committee of the CPSU (RTsKhIDNI, 17/128/818/1.189ff), emphasis added.
150. Eskandari, *Khaterat*, Volume 2, pp 90-96.
151. Ibid, p 89; see also 'Matn-e asli-ye modafe'at-e Aqa-ye Khalil Maleki dar dadgah-e

nezami dabasteh' ['The Original Text of Mr Khalil Maleki's Defence at the Military Tribunal Held in Camera], printed in *Sosyalism* (Paris), second series, no 7, October 1966, pp 46-47.

152. Eskandari remembers having been told by the same Ali Aliev, the NKVD operative at the Soviet Embassy in Tehran, 'not to worry', that Azerbaijan was not a 'problem' for them; it was only a means of helping the revolution in all of Iran! See Eskandari, *Khaterat*, Volume 2, p 104.
153. See the TPI's secret letter to the CPSU, 'Politicheskaya snachimist' narodnoi partii irana', 20 August 1945, addressed to the Central Committee of the CPSU (RTsKhIDNI, 17/128/818/1.189ff).
154. Arfa, *Under Five Shahs*, pp 334-36.
155. I Eskandari, 'Histoire du Parti Toudeh', *Moyen-Orient*, no 9, March 1950.
156. Ibid.
157. Ibid.
158. See Hasanli, *At the Dawn of the Cold War*, pp 63-67.
159. Ibid, p 51; see also 'Beseda A Iakubova s Gavam al-Saltaneh', 10 dekabria 1945 g, Foreign Archives of the Russian Federation (FRA RF), rec gr 094, inv 37, folder 5, f 357, sheets 4-5; in Hasanli, 'Iranian Azerbaijan: The Epicentre of a Cold War', *The Caucasus and Globalisation*, Volume 2, no 1, 2008, p 16.
160. See Cosroe Chaqueri, *The Soviet Socialist Republic of Iran, 1920-1921: Birth of the Trauma* (Pittsburgh, 1995), p 322.
161. 'Personalities of Persia', compiled by Trott, FO 371/40224.
162. Bullard to Foreign Office, FO 371/40180; cited in R Kauz, *Politische Parteien und Bevöklerung in Iran* (Berlin, 1995), p 53; 'Memoirs of General Edward', translated into Persian, Mehdi Nia, *Zendegi-ye siasi-ye Qavam al-Saltaneh* (Tehran, 1986), pp 70-72.
163. I Eskandari, 'Histoire du Parti Toudeh', *Moyen-Orient*, no 9, March 1950, emphasis added.
164. I Eskandari, 'Histoire du Parti Toudeh', *Moyen Orient*, no 11, May 1950.
165. Eskandari, *Khaterat*, Volume 2, pp 122-22.
166. I Eskandari, 'Première phase du gouvernement Qavam. Immense progrès du mouvement démocratique: Essor des syndicats et des unions paysannes', *Moyen-Orient*, no 12, June 1950.
167. Hasanli, *At the Dawn of the Cold War*, p 262. This is what Central Committee member Kambakhsh had told Pishevari, who had protested about the TPI's support for Qavam.
168. I Eskandari, 'Histoire du Parti Toudeh', *Moyen Orient*, no 12, June 1950.
169. Ibid.
170. Qavam was humiliated by Stalin; see Roberts to Bevin, Confidential, 9 March 1946; FO 406/84, pp 21ff.
171. General Walter Bedell Smith, *My Three Years in Moscow* (New York, 1950).
172. Senator Henry Jackson, 'Good Old Days', *Time Magazine*, 28 January 1980.
173. Aldar Ismailov, *Vlasti in narod, godi 1945-1953* (Baku, 2003), p 63; cited from the manuscript in the Archives of the Azerbaijan Republic.
174. Mirzeh Ebrahimov, *Darbareh-ye jonbesh-e demokratik-e melli dar Azerbaijan* (Tehran, 1979 [?]); originally published in *Madaniyat va Enqelab* (Baku), no 4,

1947, pp 61, 63-64.
175. Arfa, *Under Five Shahs*, pp 365ff; Eskandari, 'Histoire du Parti Toudeh', *Moyen-Orient*, no 9, March 1950.
176. I Eskandari, 'Histoire du Parti Toudeh', *Moyen-Orient*, no 7, January 1950.
177. He had already proposed such a dictatorship to the British in 1943; see FO 248/1427.
178. JAMI, *Gozashteh*, pp 423-24; Letter by Regulus to British Embassy at Tehran, FO 248/1474, 1947.
179. Eskandari, *Khaterat*, Volume 2, pp 126-28; see also Keshavarz, *Man Motahamm mikonam*, pp 106-12.
180. *Pravda*, 13 June 1946; English translation in FO 248/1468.
181. For a detailed account of Qavam's life, see Cosroe Chaqueri, *Twilight of 'His Excellency' Qavam's Splendour* [in Persian: *Ghoroub-e shokat Qavam al-Saltaneh 'Hazrat-e Ashraf*], two volumes, forthcoming.
182. Extract from the 'Declaration of the Central Committee of the Tudeh Party of Iran', *Zafar*, volume no 321, 1946.
183. I Eskandari, 'Histoire du Parti Toudeh', *Moyen-Orient*, no 9, March 1950.
184. To save face, they stated that they had resigned of their own will.
185. I Eskandari, 'Histoire du Parti Toudeh', *Moyen-Orient*, no 9, March 1950.
186. I Eskandari, 'Histoire du Parti Toudeh', *Moyen-Orient*, no 13, July 1950.
187. Ibid.
188. I Eskandari, 'Histoire du Parti Toudeh', *Moyen-Orient*, no 14-15, September 1950.
189. Ibid.
190. I Eskandari, 'Histoire du Parti Toudeh', *Moyen-Orient*, no 16-17, October-November 1950.
191. Le Rougetel to Bevin, 16 October 1945; FO 406/84.
192. For the question of rigging the elections see the following: Mosaddeq's two letters to Qavam and another to the shah, in M Turkaman, *Namehha-ye Dr Mosaddeq*, Volume 1 (Tehran, 1995), pp 90-93, and Volume 2 (Tehran, 1995), pp 88-90; Kauz, *Politische Parteien*, pp 251-63; F Azimi, *The Crisis of Democracy, 1941-1953* (New York, 1989), pp 164-68; Yunes Morvarid, *Az mashrouthe ta jomhouri...* (Tehran, 1377 [1998]), p 143; 'Letter by the Coalition Front of Liberty-Loving Parties and Newspapers to Premier Qavam' (in Persian), *Zafar*, 10 Azar 1325/1 December 1946. The Majles dismissed Qavam soon after his accord with Moscow was rejected; see A Aramesh, *Khaterat-e siasi* (Tehran, 1990), p 251.
193. Ambassador Allen, Tehran, to Secretary of State, Washington 'Disintegration of Democrat-e-Iran Party', 30 December 1947, USNA/RG 84 (Box 13, 1946).
194. *Pravda*, 12 June 1946, reported in FO 248/1468.
195. 'The Flunkeys of the Dollar: Ahmad Qavam', *Literaturnaya Gazetta*, no 60, 1947.
196. The article states that the Cossack troops were commanded by the infamous Russian Colonel Liakhov. This may not be correct, as E Browne's *The Persian Revolution* (London, 1910), p 341, notes that he was dismissed sometime after he was confirmed as the Cossack commander after the fall of the shah. It may be that, when Russian troops suppressed the resistance movement of the Constitutionalists in Gilan and Azerbaijan, Colonel Liakhov was the commanding officer.

197. I Eskandari, 'Histoire du Parti Toudeh', *Moyen-Orient*, no 18-19, January 1951.
198. JAMI, *Gozashteh*, p 487.
199. *Mardom*, 15 Day 1325/5 January 1947, cited in ibid, pp 488ff.
200. I Eskandari, 'Histoire du Parti Toudeh', *Moyen-Orient*, no 20, February 1951. It is curious that Eskandari discontinued his series of articles on the TPI. The reason could not have been his expulsion from France in early 1951, for he continued to live in Vienna for several years before settling in Moscow and later in Leipzig. It may have been due to the rise of the national movement for the nationalisation of oil, for there were signs of some dissension within the party. As we will see below, Eskandari has claimed that he did not agree with the party line opposing the national-democratic movement; yet his writings of the 1951-53 period, to which we shall also refer below, do show his opposition to Mosaddeq, albeit not as ferocious as the official line inside the country.
201. I Eskandari, 'Histoire du Parti Toudeh', *Moyen-Orient*, no 18-19, January 1951.
202. He was later accused, in the best tradition of Stalinism, of having been 'a British agent' because he later worked for the UN and taught in England.
203. He wrote one critical pamphlet and reputedly co-authored another criticising the TPI: *Cheh bayad kard?* (*What Is To Be Done?*, a title he obviously borrowed from Lenin, Tehran, Azar 1325/December 1946), reprinted in Chaqueri (ed), *Historical Documents*, Volume 1, pp 275-92; and Alatour (pseudonym reputed to be J Al-e Ahmad and E Eprim), *Hezb-e Tudeh-ye Iran sar-e do rah* (*The Tudeh Party at the Crossroads*, Tehran 1326/1947).
204. I Eskandari, 'Histoire du Parti Toudeh', *Moyen-Orient*, no 18-19, January 1951.
205. Ibid.
206. Ibid.
207. One was Alamouti, one of Eskandari's colleague in the *troika*, who in 1961 became Dr Ali Amini's Minister of Justice; another was Manouchehr Azmon, who was in Sharif-Emami's cabinet of the autumn of 1978 on the eve of the revolution, whose victors executed him.
208. Related by Reza Rousta at the Fourth Plenum, cited by P Ekteshafi, *Khaterat* (Berlin, 1998), p 164.
209. For diplomatic reports on the split and the manifesto of the ITSP, see the following: 'Persia: Formation of New Socialist Tudeh Party', FO 371/68704; Le Rougetel to Attlee, 21 January 1948, FO 416/101; Enclosure 2, Dispatch no 606, 29 January 1948 from US Embassy, 'History of Iran-Tudeh Socialist Party', in USNA, 891.00/1-2248. See also the Documents section.
210. Both printed in the Documents section.
211. J Al-Ahmad, *Dar khedmat va khianat-e roshanfekran* (Tehran, 1997), p 422. On 18 January 1948, *Pravda* in a report from Tehran briefly stated that, according to 'Tehran Circles', the 'leader' of the new 'Socialist People's Society of Iran', breaking from the ranks of the Tudeh, that is, Maleki, was 'connected with the British' and 'is connected with the British and is acting with their consent in striving to disorganise the democratic movement of Persia' (FO 371/68704). See also H Katouzian, 'Introduction' to *Khaterat-e siasi-ye Kh Maleki* (Paris, 1981), pp 54-55. Tabari attributes Maleki's motive for the split to his idea of 'independence' from the Soviet party; this is, of course, meant to accuse him of 'anti-Sovietism' (Ehsan

Tabari, *Kazhraheh* (Tehran, 1987) p 79).
212. Cited in Baqer Momeni, *Rahian khatar* (Paris, 2006), pp 304-05.
213. Le Rougetel to Bevin, 28 January 1948; FO 416/101.
214. Al-Ahmad, *Dar khedmat va khianat-e roshanfekran*, p 422.
215. Ibid, pp 424-25.
216. Ibid, p 425, emphasis added.
217. See the translation of the report on the conversation between Maleki and Bevin, '*Iran*'s version of the Bevin–Maleki conversation, published 11 November 1945', FO 248/1452.
218. It is to be noted that Maleki, when years later he criticised his former party for defending Soviet interests in Iran, never referred to his own share of the blame in defending the Soviet demand for an oil concession in Iran. See his 'Mobarezeh baraye dadan-e emtiaz be Shoravi', reprint in Chaqueri (ed), *Historical Documents*, Volume 3, pp 184-86.
219. For divergent accounts of the split, see Abrahamian, *Iran Between Two Revolutions*, pp 310ff; Zabih, *The Communist Movement in Iran*, pp 125ff; H Katouzian, 'Introduction' to *Khaterat-e siasi-ye Kh Maleki* (Paris, 1981), pp 54-55.
220. USNA, 891.00/1-2248.
221. Al-e Ahmad, *Dar khedmat va khianat-e roshanfekran*, pp 420-22.
222. Ibid, pp 431-32.
223. Peter Avery, *Modern Iran* (London, 1965), p 432. Avery, who had started out as an employee of the AIOC, worked at the Tehran Embassy till diplomatic relations were severed by Mosaddeq's government in November 1952, and ended up as a lecturer at Cambridge University, where he also put his 'make-up' talents at the service of the military dictatorship of the shah — for instance, on the notorious occasion of the '2500-year anniversary of the Persian Empire' in the pages of *The Times*. I had wondered why his name did not appear on the FO or Embassy files in those years until in 1988 the late Professor Richard Cottam, who had, as a young doctoral candidate, worked for the US Embassy in Tehran in those years, told me that Avery had worked for the SIS in Tehran.
224. Maleki, along with Deputy Baqa'i, a member of the Patriotic Front, who later broke with it and joined the royalist camp — if he had not previously had secret dealings with the shah — created the Toilers Party. When Baqa'i openly turned right-wing, Maleki broke with him and created a new democratic-leftist party called the Third Force, more or less on Tito's model. The Tudeh's attacks against the Patriotic Front became even more virulent when directed against the 'renegade Maleki'.
225. See the reprint of three articles in *Hajjar* in a pamphlet named *Seh maqaleh az rouznameh-ye Hajjar* (organ of Jam'iyat-e raha'i-ye Kar va Andisheh, Tehran, 1979), pp 99-128.
226. Ibid, pp 100-01.
227. Ibid, p 112.
228. Ibid, p 122.
229. Ibid, p 125.
230. Ibid, p 128.
231. Ibid, p 149.
232. *Iran Radio*, no 44, 1960, p 10. Khameh'i's evolution was, indeed, different from

Maleki's. After working for the regime's National Radio, he left Iran to study in Friburg, Switzerland, where he received a doctorate with a thesis entitled *Revisionism from Marx to Mao*. Thereafter, he was given a teaching position in Mobuto's Congo. He returned to Iran in the mid-1970s and praised the shah's 'White Revolution' from a 'Marxist' viewpoint (see the 'Interview with the Author of *Revisionism from Marx to Mao*', in the official daily *Kayhan*, 19 March 1977). After the 'Islamic Revolution' and the suppression of the Left, he wrote his three-volume *Memoirs*, distorting the history of the left in terms serving the Clericracy in power. His distortions were severely criticised and denounced (see Keshavarz's critique in *Ketab-e jom'eh-ha*, nos 8-9, pp 156-84). His response was that Keshavarz's interview had been organised by the CIA! A Stalinist statement very pleasing to the IRI! See A Khameh'i, *Pasokh be moda'i* (Tehran, 1989). See also Eskandari's criticism of his distortions in his *Khaterat* (Tehran edition), pp 70-71, 449ff.

233. Testimony related by Shirin Sami'i (Paris, 12 March 2001 and confirmed by e-mail on 13 March 2011).
234. For an hysterical Stalinist example, see Ahmad Qasemi, 'Dar saraship ensh'ab', *Mardom*, no 7, Bahman 1326/January 1948; reprinted in Chaqueri (ed), *Historical Documents*, Volume 3, pp 86-93.
235. Kambakhsh, *Nazari beh jonbesh-e kargari va komonisti dar Iran*, Volume 1, pp 101-13, 121-26.
236. B Alavi, *Kaempfendes Iran* ([East] Berlin, 1955), p 77, emphasis added. This book is written in typically Stalinist style, to the extent that Alavi in his memoirs, written just before his death a few years after the demise of the German Democratic Republic and the USSR, ashamedly dropped it from the bibliography of his publications.
237. See Foroutan's memoirs, *Yadhayee az gozashteh. Hezb-e Tudeh dar sahneh-ye Iran* (two volumes, [Cologne?], 1371/1992), Volume 1, pp 91-105 (hereafter *Hezb-e Tudeh*).
238. FO 371/68704; Letter to FO 28 January 1948; E 1809/25/34 (1948); USNA 891.00/1-2948; 29 January 1948.
239. See 'Ravand va rishehha-ye enshe'ab. Gozaresh beh dovomin kongereh dar mored-e enshe'ab', in TPI, *Asnad va didgah-ha-ye Hezb-e Tudeh-ye Iran az aghaz-e peydayee ta enqelab-e Bahman 1357* (*Documents and Viewpoints...*, Tehran, 1981), pp 96-117.
240. Ibid, pp 125-26.
241. Quoted from 'confessions' related by Central Committee member Hussein Jowdat after his arrest in the Islamic Republic; his 'confessions' are a straightforward account, except where it concerns him, where he rarely accepts responsibility for his role; see *Hezb-e Tudeh az shek-giri ta foroupashi (1320-1368)*, published by the Institute for Political Studies and Research (Tehran, 2008), p 169.
242. I Eskandari, 'Histoire du Parti Toudeh', *Moyen-Orient*, no 20, February 1951.
243. TPI, *Asnad va didgah-ha*, pp 119-42.
244. 'Tahlili az jarayan-e dovvomin kongreh-ye hezbi va karhay'i keh in kongreh anjam dadeh ast', in *Nameh-ye Mahaneh-ye Mardom*, 1 Khordad 1327/22 May 1948; reprinted in Chaqueri (ed), *Historical Documents*, Volume 3, pp 85-88. The most complete account of the Second Congress is, curiously, published in a book

by an officer of the Military Government of the post-*coup d'état* period: Zibayee, *Kommonizm dar Iran*, pp 379ff.
245. Ibid. For 'Krouzhokism', see the article below on SAKA.
246. Kambakhsh, *Nazari beh jonbesh-e kargari va komonisti dar Iran*, Volume 1, pp 127-28.
247. Hasanli, *At the Dawn of the Cold War*, pp 207, 262.
248. See, for instance, the aforementioned article by Qasemi, one of the most dogmatic Tudeh leaders, later to turn Maoist and be expelled from the party in early 1960s, 'Dar saraship-e enshe'ab'; reprint in Chaqueri (ed), *Historical Documents*, Volume 3, pp 93-96.
249. TPI, *Asnad va didgah-ha*, pp 122-25.
250. See the party organ *Rahbar* (Yazd), first year, no 3; facsimile reprint in Chaqueri (ed), *Historical Documents*, Volume 1, pp 168-70.
251. Declaration of the TPI Provincial Committee in Tayarani (ed), *Asnad-e ahzab-e siasi*, Volume 2, pp 706-11, emphasis added.
252. *Rahbar* 10 Mehr 1325/2 October 1946; reprinted in Chaqueri (ed), *Historical Documents*, Volume 1, p 303.
253. 'Declaration of the Central Committee of the Tudeh Party of Iran', 3 Azar 1325/24 December 1946; reprinted in Chaqueri (ed), *Historical Documents*, Volume 1, pp 312-13.
254. 'Economic Policy of the Tudeh Party of Iran', *Razm*, Volume 1, no 65, September 1944, emphasis added.
255. This figure was no doubt based on the Tudeh's propagandistic claims; the British and later the Americans used these figures to paint the horizon red in order to destroy the democratic movement. Internal figures of the TPI were much more modest.
256. FO 371/67705 (13 April 1948). The report was to be made available to 'the Directors of Intelligence, the Petroleum Division, Mr CF Heron, Ministry of Labour, Washington, Moscow [Embassy], British Middle East Office and to Information Research Department, Foreign Office Research Department and Middle East Information Department'.
257. Ibid.
258. Cited in *Hezb-e Tudeh az shek-giri ta foroupashi (1320-1368)*, pp 168-69; 171-72.
259. 'Matne-e kamel-e gozaresh-e Dr Reza Radmanesh, dabir koll-e Hezb-e Tudeh-ye Iran dar sevvomin plenum-e komite-ye markazi hezb...', *Razm*, 29 Mehr 1327/21 October 1948; reprint in Chaqueri, *Historical Documents*, Volume 1, pp 40-326.
260. Kambakhsh also discusses the 12-point memorandum handed to Premier Hazhir (Kambakhsh, *Nazari beh jonbesh-e kargari va komonisti dar Iran*, Volume 1, p 129). For the details, see also 'A Tudeh Memorandum', FO 371/68707, 1948.
261. See Ambassador Wiley to Secretary of State, 1 November 1948, USNA/891.00/11-148.
262. USNA, RG 84, Confidential Files; FO 371/68709 (Box 17, 1948).
263. A book by this author, *The Shah's First Coup d'État: An Inquiry into the 'Perfect Crime' that Changed the Course of Iran's Modern History*, written on the basis of long years of research, has not been published in English, since the stage-managed attempt on the life of the shah has so well impressed Western academia that no

publisher has been interested in publishing it. It is hoped that it will soon be published at least in Persian.

264. Ernest Peron was the shah's playmate from his schooldays in Switzerland. He had been brought by him to Iran and lived in the Palace with the shah until his death a few years before the shah's demise. Peron was the shah's intimate friend and personal confidant with Western embassies. The French Ministry of Foreign Affairs referred to him as 'Conseiller privé du Chah d'Iran' ('Note', 1 June 1946, and 'Suites de l'Attentat contre le Chahinchah', 18 March 1949, in Archives du MAEF, Série Asie, Iran, E 29 (3), and E 30 (1), respectively). In addition to frequent references to Peron in the FO archives, particularly during the 1951-53 crisis, the reader should refer to the new memoirs of the shah's second wife, Soraya Esfandiary Bakhtiary, *Solitude des Palais* (Paris, 1991), Chapter 7, published after the death of her former husband, where she tells of the strange relations the shah had maintained with Peron. Referring to this 'homosexual', 'Machiavellian' and intriguing figure as the 'Devil', Soraya confirms his role as the 'intermediary between the shah and Western Ambassadors', and 'the shah's most intimate adviser' — the two of them 'every morning meeting behind closed doors to discuss the matters of state' (p 124).

265. See 'Projet du coup d'état du Chahinchah', presented by the French Military Attaché, Lieutenant-Colonel Chauvonin, to Monsieur le Président du Conseil, État-Major de la Défense Nationale, 12 February 1949, in Archives du Ministère des Affaires Étrangères, Quai d'Orsay, Série Asie, Iran, E 23 (1).

266. Former Tudeh leader Foroutan, who belonged to the Kambakhsh–Kianouri faction, although admitting that Kianouri had, in advance, been aware of the 'assailant's intention', denies that there was a link between Kianouri's advance knowledge and the pretext for outlawing the TPI. He also refuses to believe that General Razmara, who, as many have asserted, took office with British support, was behind the incident. He naively believes that it was the assailant's hatred of the shah that pushed him along that path (Foroutan, *Hezb-e Tudeh*, Volume 1, pp 113-20).

267. See Keshavarz, *Man Motahamm mikonam*, pp 126-33.

268. *Le Monde*, 27-28 February 1949. The communist daily *l'Humanité* in a piece about Eskandari's press conference wrote: 'Tudeh Secretary-General Dr Radmanesh had managed to escape arrest by the police. Tudeh leaders had gone underground to protect themselves against a government in the hands of Anglo-American imperialists.' (*l'Humanité*, 26 February 1949) Eskandari stated that a 'military dictatorship ruled by terror' had been established in the country.

269. For brief reports of the trials and verdicts, see the British Ambassador's report to the Foreign Office, 16 March, 27 April and 3 May 1949, in FO 371/754641.

270. See Hasan Nazari, *Gomashteh haye bad farjam* (Tehran, 1376/1987).

271. It is curious that Siamak had been known, at least by the British intelligence in Iran, as a communist and a long-time friend of Kambakhsh. In fact, a photograph of these two together in their youth has been published in C Chaqueri, *Taqi Arani dar ayneh-ye tarikh* (Tehran, 2008), p 264.

272. For a study of Tudeh activities in the armed forces, see M-H Khosropanah, *Sazman-e afsaran-e hezb-e Tudeh-ye Iran* (Tehran, 1378/1999). This is the only available study in any language on this subject. In spite of some hearsay statements

he assumes to be fact and errors in judgement, it is useful for its documents in Persian. In several Tudeh leaders' memoirs references are made to the TMO, but they do not really add any more to that which is revealed in this book, except the article by F Azarnour, one of the officials of the TMO: 'What Were the Facts of the Tudeh Military Secrets' (in Persian), *Nimrouz* (London), 27 Bahman 1374/16 February 1996, p 31; and 4 Esfand 1374/23 March 1996, p 31. Below we will refer to US archives in connection with the discovery and dismantling of the TMO.

273. Khosropanah, *Sazman-e afsaran-e hezb-e Tudeh-ye Iran*, p 149.
274. Recall that he had played a nefarious role in revealing to the police the existence of the 'Arani Group' in 1937. Keshavarz reiterates this fact (*Man Motahamm mikonam*, p 71), told also by Eskandari, *Khaterat* (Tehran edition), p 93.
275. Eskandari, *Khaterat* (Tehran edition), pp 490-91.
276. See *Revolutionary History*, Volume 10, no 2, pp 191-96.
277. Cited in Khosropanah, *Sazman-e afsaran-e hezb-e Tudeh-ye Iran*, p 33.
278. For the most serious analytical works on the national-democratic movement and the nationalisation of the oil industry, see the following works: M Elm, *Oil, Power and Principles* (Syracuse, 1992); M Gasiorowski, 'The 1953 Coup d'État in Iran', *International Journal of Middle East Studies*, Volume 19, no 3, August 1987; M Gasiorowski and M Byrne (eds), *Mohammad Mosaddeq and the 1953 Coup in Iran* (Syracuse, 2004); James A Bill and Wm Roger Louis, *Musaddiq, Iranian Nationalism, and Oil* (Austin, Texas, 1988); Enver Kureish [pseudonym], 'Great Britain and Iran', *Civil and Military Gazette*, 19 June 1951; for its diplomatic documentation, see US Government, *Foreign Relations of the United States, 1952-1954*, Volume 10 (Washington DC, 1989).
279. On 22 Tir 1343/13 July 1964, Captain Qobadi, the prison warden who had made possible the escape of the Tudeh leaders from prison and who had fled to the Soviet Union, was handed over to the Iranian authorities on the Soviet-Iranian border and was subsequently executed for 'treason' by the shah's regime. The Tudeh leadership spread the rumour that he had become an alcoholic and wanted to return to Iran. If he had become an alcoholic, he must have become so through depression provoked by his reported disillusionment of what he had discovered in the land of 'really existing socialism'. As an 'alcoholic' who could not command his own mind, he should, and could, have been treated medically instead of being handed over to the Iranian government that, one could be certain, would shoot him for what he had done in 1950.
280. USNA, 788.00 (W)/12-2250; 'Escape of Ten Tudeh Party Leaders from Qasr Prison, Tehran, 16 December 1950', US Embassy to Department of State, 22 December 1950; USNA 788.00/12-2250. For the full text of this report, see the Documents section.
281. Report 27 June 1950; USNA, Confidential Files, Box 34 (file 400.1), USSR.
282. One of the most dogmatic Tudeh leaders, Foroutan, who in mid-1960s turned Maoist and was supported by China and Albania, claims that he, along with two other individuals, was responsible for the 'great escape'. He rejects Dr Keshavarz's version of the events in the latter's *Man Motahamm mikonam*, pp 127-88. Keshavarz, on the basis of what he had heard from some of the escapees in their Moscow exile, relates that originally Hesam Lankarani, of the underground section

of the party, had planned to rescue Kianouri from prison, and when other leaders discovered it by chance, they opposed the idea, suggesting that all the leaders should be rescued. This is what was done. Foroutan accuses Keshavarz, who had left the party earlier than him and lived in the West, of prevarication. Foroutan admits that in the summer of 1948, before the proscription of the party, Kianouri, who was an architect, had taken part in a competition to build a hospital for Princess Ashraf Pahlavi. Keshavarz also mentions Kianouri's construction contract, except that he recalls two versions he had heard in Moscow from Tudeh leaders coming from Iran: firstly, a building for the Finance Ministry; secondly, a palace for Ashraf (Keshavarz, *Man Motahamm mikonam*, pp 130-31). Keshavarz's view, heard from other Tudeh leaders and recorded in Moscow, seems more coherent an account than that by Foroutan. It is to be pondered why the strongest person in the Pahlavi family had granted an important construction contract to a leader of the outlawed TPI! Be that as it may, Foroutan adds that Kianouri had been taken out of prison to oversee and inspect the construction after he had been condemned to 10 years' imprisonment for an attempt to kill the princess' reigning brother. Foroutan explains that Hesam Lankarani had planned to rescue Kianouri during one of his inspection visits outside the prison. He does not explain how Kianouri could have henceforth inspected the construction while at large. He adds that Dr Bahrami, one of the leaders living underground, had opposed the rescue plan for Kianouri alone and proposed that all party leaders jailed be rescued. Foroutan then claims that the rescue operation was organised by him, Captain Qobadi and Colonel Mobasheri of the TMO, denying any involvement of the Premier, General Razmara. See Foroutan, *Hezb-e Tudeh*, Volume 1, pp 148-60. He does not explain either how Kianouri, whose wife Maryam Firouz was from the most prominent ruling family with connections with the shah's Court, finally managed to finish, while still at large, the construction for Princess Ashraf and to hand it over to her. Kianouri's role, in view of his later actions, leaves much room for research and pondering.

283. The title in Persian, 'Jebheh-ye melli', was borrowed from the French model of the anti-Fascist resistance during the Second World War, that is, *le Front national*. Given the connotations of the National Front today in the West, it seems appropriate to translate 'Jebheh-ye melli' as the *Patriotic Front*, especially because 'melli' in Persian has a much vaster meaning than the 'national' of Western languages. It has also a democratic, anti-imperialist connotation, which 'national' in the Western languages does not.

284. See the chapters by M Gasiorowski and F Azimi in Gasiorowski and Byrne (eds), *Mohammad Mosaddeq and the 1953 Coup in Iran*; M Gasiorowski, 'The 1953 Coup d'État in Iran', *International Journal of Middle East Studies*, Volume 19, no 3, August 1987.

285. 'Moda'iyan-e azadikhahi dar darbareh soragh-e azadi miravand' ('The Pretenders of Liberty Seek Freedom at the Royal Court', Broadsheet in Persian), reprinted in Chaqueri (ed), *Historical Documents*, Volume 12, p 17.

286. 'Dr Mosaddeq's Government Does Not Want To Go Beyond Making Fair But Hollow Professions of Friendship' (Broadsheet in Persian), Chaqueri (ed), *Historical Documents*, Volume 12, pp 30-33.

287. 'Relative Strength of Mosaddeq and the Opposition, Taking Into Account Feeling Among Deputies and the Population', not dated, but on the basis of its content probably written at the end of 1951; FO 371/91472.
288. Chaqueri (ed), *Historical Documents*, Volume 12, p 25, emphasis added.
289. It should be pointed out that this term at the very outset in the Comintern referred to the bourgeois elements of the colonial countries whose interests ran against colonial intervention. The term had necessarily no 'patriotic' sense; rather it denoted a bourgeoisie that was local, not foreign.
290. 'Review of Communist Activity in Iran during May 1951', US Embassy to the Department of State, 7 June 1951; USNA 788.001/6-751.
291. On this issue, see Elm, *Oil, Power and Principles*.
292. Tabari, *Kazhraheh*, p 169.
293. F Azarnour, *An Exclusive Interview by Rah-Azadi with F Azarnour: On the Events of 28 Mordad 1332* (Paris, 1993), pp 52-53.
294. Ibid, p 52.
295. A secret internal document called *Darbareh-ye 28 Mordad (Concerning 19 August)*, which will be discussed below.
296. Ambassador Gray to Secretary of State, 17 May 1951; USNA, 788.00/5-1751.
297. 'Review of Communist Activity in Iran during May 1951', US Embassy to the Department of State, 7 June 1951; USNA 788.001/6-751.
298. When it was reported that Tudeh leaders Qasemi, Foroutan and Radmanesh had also been absolved by a judge of the charge of attempting to assassinate the shah, Mosaddeq came under attack for interference in the judiciary. Fatemi denied the accusation of interference. See USNA, 788.00/4-1253 and 788.00/5-553.
299. In fact, the right of female suffrage was one important point of Mosaddeq's programme of reform, but once the bill was prepared and announced, the all-powerful Grand Ayatollah Boroujerdi, who was secretly in league with the shah, sent a message to Mosaddeq telling him that if he tried to legislate that right for women, he would 'instigate sedition'. Mosaddeq shelved the bill till better times, which never arrived. Reported by Boroujerdi's messenger to Mosaddeq, Majles deputy Hussein Makki; see Khosrow Shakeri, 'Nokati chand piramoun-e tariokhnegari-ye jaygah-e zan dar jonbesh-e mashrouteh', *Negah-e no*, vizhehnameh, Mordad 1385/ August 2006.
300. TPI internal document, *Darbareh-ye 28 Mordad*; see also 'Open Letter from the CC of the Tudeh Party to PM Mosaddeq', 7 May 1951; USNA, 788.00/5-951, and 'Review of Communist Activity in Iran during May 1951', US Embassy to the Department of State, 7 June 1951; USNA 788.001/6-751.
301. Other small works were published in Leipzig in the 1970s, in rivalry with non-Soviet Marxist groups such as Edition Mazdak founded in Florence, Italy, in 1969; such were John Reed's *Ten Days that Shook the World* and Marx's *The Eighteenth Brumaire of Louis Bonaparte* translated by M Pourhomozan. Some works of Marx were translated or retranslated after the 1979 revolution by non-Tudeh or non-Marxist translators.
302. Foroutan, *Hezb-e Tudeh*, p 181.
303. Keshavarz, *Man Motahamm mikonam*, p 44. When the young founders of the Tudeh Party Revolutionary Organisation, who themselves had, admittedly, no profound

knowledge of Marxism, met the Tudeh leaders in the early 1960s, they found out that the latter, who had by then gone through Marxist-Leninist schooling in Moscow, had a meagre theoretical knowledge of Marxism. See Kourosh Lashayee, *Negahi az daroun beh jonbesh-e chap-e Iran* (Tehran, 2002), pp 97, 122; M Rezvani, *Negahi az daroun beh jonbesh-e chap-e Iran* (Cologne, 2005), pp 81, 93.

304. The TPI 'theoretician' Tabari in his memoirs of a sort reveals that he and his colleagues, when in prison as 'Marxists', 'did not know anything' about the 'Adalat party (the ICP), nor their policies and experiences. 'We knew the Comintern existed' and had 'heard of' some ICP leaders' names, adding that 'we did not know who they were', let alone 'what they had thought, written and done'. In prison they had learnt some 'facts' from old communist (Stalinist) prisoners, but 'were not able to understand the history of the revolutionary movement in a systematic manner in its historical context'. He admits that he was the 'first person' to try to periodise this history in the Tudeh review *Donya* (second series) published in exile as of 1960! See Tabari, *Az didar-e khishtan*, pp 49ff. In fact, except for some articles by Kambakhsh written in the Stalinist style of distortion, the TPI never carried out any historical research on the socialist or communist movement in Iran. Eskandari's early articles in *Moyen Orient* reveal the poverty of the historical knowledge and the distortions of the Tudeh leaders.

305. For detailed accounts of such efforts, see F Azimi 'Unseating Mosaddeq...', in Gasiorowski, *Mohammad Mosaddeq and the 1953 Coup in Iran*, p 83.

306. Ehsan Tabari, *Barkhi barresiha darbareh-ye jahanbiniha-ye ejtema 'idar Iran* (*Appraisals of Social World Outlooks in Iran*, Tehran 1979; Ehsan Tabari, *Jostarhayee az tarikh* (*Essays on History*, Tehran, 1982). Bozorg Alavi's *Der Kampfaende Iran* is another work of falsification of Iran's history of the first half of the twentieth century. As we have seen, at the end of his life he deleted it from the bibliography in his memoirs!

307. *Besouy-e ayandeh*, no 467, 1951.

308. It is notable that the TPI used the Persian terms for government (*dowlat*) and state (*hokoumat*) interchangeably without knowing the conceptual and practical distinction between the two.

309. *Besouy-e ayandeh*, no 470, 1951.

310. Ibid.

311. *Besouy-e ayandeh*, 15 January 1952. Mosaddeq decided to close down British consulates whose staff were in constant contact with pro-British elements carrying out anti-patriotic actions against the government. He finally even severed diplomatic relations and closed the British Embassy in November 1952, as it directed and financed the opposition.

312. *Besouy-e ayandeh*, no 476, 1952.

313. *Besouy-e ayandeh*, no 479, 1951.

314. *Besouy-e ayandeh*, no 480, 1952.

315. *Jang-qalam*, no 1, 1952.

316. *Farda-ye pirouz*, no 1, 1952.

317. *Besouy-e ayandeh*, no 555, 1952.

318. *Besouy-e ayandeh*, no 522, 1952.

319. *Babak*, no 1, 1952.

320. *Besouy-e ayandeh*, no 717, 1952.
321. *Akharin nabard*, Khordad 1331/1952.
322. *Akharin 'alaj*, 26 Shahrivar 1331/1952. For a discussion of such provocative and nefarious attacks on Mosaddeq's patriotic-democratic government by one of the former cadres and late members of the TPI Central Committee, who broke with Kianouri after the suppression of the party by the Islamic state, see Babak Amirkhosrowi, *Nazari az daroun beh naqsh-e hezb-e Tudeh-ye Iran* (*A View from Within on the Role of the Tudeh Party of Iran*, Tehran, 1996), pp 275-329. He provides a great deal of inside information on this issue which we cannot discuss due to lack of space.
323. 'Communist Activities in Iran, 15 February to 5 March 1952', USNA, 788.001-3-1052.
324. Ibid. The US report accuses the Patriotic Front of either having left the constituency to the shah or, having had a dispute with the shah's forces, 'leaving the district open to the Communists'. This report falls within the kind of ideological falsifications diplomats are fond of when they need to press a point home, for there were three candidates in the district, the Kurdish lawyer S Sadeq-Vaziri for the TPI 'coalition', another Kurdish candidate named Mohammad Mokri for the Patriotic Front, and the Court's candidate, the official Friday Imam of Tehran, a Shiite 'elected' from a Sunni district! In fact, Mosaddeq mocked the election of this 'deputy' as an example of the continued interference of the shah's military in the elections, adding that a good number of the deputies had been elected fraudulently.
325. Ibid.
326. It should be noted that, according to a secret report by the French Embassy in Tehran, when the leaders of the terrorist organisation Fada'iyan Islam — the forefathers of today's Hezbollah— were in prison under Mosaddeq awaiting trial for their terrorist acts, the same chief of police, appointed by the shah, who had Tudeh militants arrested, offered the terrorist leaders special treatment in prison, no doubt on the orders of the Court. See 'De l'organisation et des buts des Fadaïyan-è Islam', 26 February 1952, Archives du Quai d'Orsay, Perse, E 30-1.
327. For an excellent, well documented and analytic study of the Iranian nationalisation issue leading to the 1953 coup against Iran's young democracy, see Elm, *Oil, Power and Principle*.
328. While outwardly, out of fear of alienating the nation, they all professed to be in favour of oil nationalisation, privately in conversation with the British Embassy in Tehran they expressed their disapproval of that law. On this matter there is plenty of evidence in Foreign Office files at the British National Archives. See, for instance, Minutes of Conversation with the Shah, FO 248/1572, 9 October 1950; Sir F Shepherd to Foreign Office, 11 February 1951; FO 371/91522; Lunch with HIM the Shah, 15 March 1951; FO 248/1518. James Bill also refers to the involvement of British agents in these events; see Bill and Louis, *Musaddiq, Iranian Nationalism, and Oil*, p 271.
329. He was absolved by the military court through the shah's influence.
330. K Roosevelt, *The Countercoup*, first edition, p 95, cited in Gasiorowski, 'The 1953 Coup d'État in Iran', *International Journal of Middle East Studies*, Volume 19, no 3, August 1987, p 283, n 44; see also Roosevelt, *The Countercoup* (second edition,

New York, 1979), p 98; for Roosevelt's relations with the Boscoe Brothers, see ibid, pp 16, 79-81, 91-94, 124, 127, 134, 163, 165, 180, 186.
331. TPI brochure, *The Analysis of the Bloody Sunday Incident of 23 Tir 1330* [14 July 1951], in Persian, reprinted in Chaqueri (ed), *Historical Documents*, Volume 12, pp 74-88; that the demonstration was a provocative action against Mosaddeq's government at the outset of the oil negotiations and unjustly blamed on him was later reported in a 60-page secret letter, dated 29 March 1954, by the Secretary of the TPI's Executive Committee, A-A Shandermani (alias 'Zare'), to the Central Committee in Moscow, a copy of which is in possession of this author, and is soon to be published in C Chaqueri, *Shaloudeh-shekani-ye yek afsaneh (Deconstruction of a Myth)*.
332. Shandermani's aforementioned report discusses this matter in detail.
333. Printed in Chaqueri (ed), *Historical Documents*, Volume 12, p 83. Dr Fatemi was the most radical of Mosaddeq's collaborators and was executed by firing squad after the 1953 putsch.
334. Ibid, pp 53, 47, 44.
335. The lawyer of the British government Sir Eric Becket sent a secret note to his government stating that the British Judge Sir Arnold McNair 'has made history by voting against us'. He who had ardently defended the position of the British government, added: 'If I had personally been a judge on the court, my opinion would have been the same as that of Sir Arnold McNair.' Minute by Beckett, 23 July 1952, FO 371/98680; see also Elm, *Oil Power and Principle*, p 214.
336. See, for example, American Ambassador Henderson's report to Secretary of State, 3 August 1953, USNA, 788.00/8-352; 'Probable Development in Iran Through 1953', National Intelligence of the Central Intelligence Agency, dated 13 November 1952; Henderson to Department of State, in *FRUS*, Volume 10, p 514.
337. See 'Message from Mr Eden to Mr Acheson', in *FRUS*, Volume 10, pp 433-34.
338. FO 371/91472.
339. Eskandari, *Khaterat* (Tehran edition), p 263.
340. Iraj Eskandari, 'The Persians Take a Hand — In Persia', *Daily Worker*, 26 June 1951.
341. 'Iranian People Fights British Oil Trust', *World Trade Union Movement*, May 1951, reprinted in Chaqueri (ed), *The Conditions of the Working Class in Iran*, Volume 3, pp 1-13, 55-65, 221-25.
342. Ibid, p 61.
343. Ibid, p 62.
344. See N Kianouri, *Hezb-e Tudeh-ye Iran va Dr Mohammad Mosaddeq. Nokati az tarikh-e Hezb-e Tudeh-ye Iran* (Tehran, 1980), pp 32-33; Foroutan, *Hezb-e Tudeh*, pp 168-82.
345. The source of this information is Dr Keshavarz who informed this author in one of our many meetings in Geneva, Switzerland.
346. One of the very few examples of the latter was the CPGB's Political Committee Statement 'Hands Off Persia!', which considered that 'the mighty mass movement of the Persian people' was illustrated by 'the gigantic demonstration organised by the Tudeh Party'. Tellingly, it made no reference to either Mosaddeq or the national-democratic movement (*Daily Worker*, 25 May 1951).

347. Rajani Palme Dutt, 'Notes of the Month', *Labour Monthly*, November 1951.
348. *Daily Worker*, 2 March 1953. See full text in the Documents section.
349. The author is grateful to Paul Flewers for consulting the *Daily Worker* and *Labour Monthly*.
350. The Iranian case was so desperate in the West that Mosaddeq's government decided to buy a whole page in *The Observer* on 13 November 1952 in order to publish the Prime Minister's open letter addressed to the British people explaining the just cause of the people of Iran.
351. It should be recalled that Russell had taken an active stand against British collaboration with tsarist Russia in suppressing Iran's Constitutional Revolution in the first decade of the twentieth century. He did the same in the 1960s and consistently supported the opposition to the shah, but remained silent in those crucial years.
352. A look at various legal Tudeh front organisation newspapers for the period, such as *Besouy-e ayandeh*, demonstrates this point.
353. JAMI, *Gozashteh*, p 635.
354. Ibid, p 436.
355. *Navid-e ayandeh*, 25 Tir/16 July 1952, cited in ibid, p 437.
356. The revelation is made by Mohammad Turkaman, *Tehran dar atash. Kabineh-ye Qavam va havades-e si om-e tir* (Tehran, nd), p 183. Qavam's long-time assistant and adviser, the notorious Abbas Eskandari, stated that the TPI had sent someone to negotiate the terms of cooperation.
357. 'Appeal of the National Society for Combating Colonialism', in Chaqueri (ed), *Historical Documents*, Volume 1, pp 356-63.
358. *Dezh*, cited in JAMI, *Gozashteh* p 638.
359. Ibid, p 179.
360. Ibid.
361. Foroutan, *Hezb-e Tudeh*, Volume 1, pp 208ff.
362. During the uprising 69 demonstrators were killed and some 750 were injured.
363. Undated letter by Kianouri to the TPI Central Committee in Moscow, printed in Azarnour, *An Exclusive Interview*, p 31. On the basis of its contents, the approximate date of the letter must be March 1954. The figure Kianouri gives is obviously inflated, for the British services that were quite aware of the TPI's strength put its 'effectively organised' membership at the end of 1951 for the Tehran area at 8000; see FO 371/91472, p 6. It could not have tripled in six months.
364. The 'truthfulness' of Foroutan's memoirs is also refuted by his claim that he was one of Mosaddeq's supporters in the Tudeh leadership, for, as shown above, the whole leadership was against Mosaddeq and sabotaged his efforts; moreover, as is well known from all Tudeh sources, Foroutan belonged to the hard-line Stalinist faction led by Kianouri.
365. Ekteshafi, *Khaterat*, p 177.
366. One could look at *FRUS*, Volume 10, as an example, although it does not contain all the correspondence.
367. For the forecasts of economic breakdown in Mosaddeq's Iran and historical analyses, see Embassy to Foreign Office, 4 February and 19 May 1952; FO 371/98625; 'Persia's Economic Situation', 29 October 1951, FO 371/98623, p 4; 'Financial

Difficulties and the Prospects of the Iranian Government', 1951, FO 371/98625; Middleton to Eden, 29 October 1951, FO 371/91483; Bailey, 'Financial Difficulties', Washington to Foreign Office, 26 July 1952, FO 371/98625; 'Economic Report', no 2, June and July 1951, 24 August 1951, FO 371/9148; 'Persia, Economic Report', no 3; 24 October 1951; FO 371/9148; British Embassy to Foreign Office, 30 August 1953, FO 371/98625; 'Estimate of the Possible Inflationary Effects of an Increase in the Persian Note Issue', British Embassy to Foreign Office, 1952, FO 371/98625; Middleton to Eden, 6 October 1952, FO 371/98625; *National Intelligence Estimate, Probable Developments in Iran Through 1953*, Central Intelligence Agency, 13 November 1952, NIE-75, p 4; 'Survey of the Economic and Financial Situation in Iran at the Close of the Iranian Year 1330', FO 371/98623; British Embassy Tehran to Foreign Office, 19 May 1952, FO 371/98625; Foreign Office to Washington Embassy, 7 March 1953, FO 371/104614; Clawson and Sassanpour, 'Adjustment to a Foreign Exchange Shock: Iran, 1951-1953', and H Katouzian, 'Oil Boycott and the Political Economy: Musaddiq and the Strategy of Non-Oil Economics', in Bill and Louis, *Musaddiq, Iranian Nationalism, and Oil*, pp 1-22, 203-22; Ann Heiss, 'International Boycott of Iranian Oil and the Anti-Mosaddeq Coup', in Gasiorowski, *Mohammad Mosaddeq and the 1953 Coup in Iran*, pp 178-200; Elm, *Oil, Power and Principle*, Chapter 18.
368. Azarnour, *An Exclusive Interview*, p 86.
369. Jalal Pezhman, *Khaterat. Foroupashi-ye artesh-e shahanshahi* (Tehran, 2007), pp 258, 260.
370. Such as Makki, Baqa'i and Mullah Kashani.
371. M Mosaddeq, *Khaterat va ta'alomat* (Tehran, 1986), p 187; JAMA, *Gozashteh*, pp 659-62.
372. Report by the US Embassy in Tehran to Washington; copy sent to Foreign Office in London; FO 371/124567.
373. FO 371/104562. The British report to Eden was based on dispatches by the American Embassy that were also sent to the Foreign Office.
374. For details, see M Gasiorowski, 'The 1953 Coup d'État in Iran', *International Journal of Middle East Studies*, Volume 19, no 3, August 1987, pp 270ff.
375. There are now a couple of serious academic studies on the 1953 *coup d'état*. See Mark Gasiorowski, 'The 1953 Coup d'État in Iran', *International Journal of Middle East Studies*, Volume 19, no 3, August 1987; Mark Gasiorowski, *US Foreign Policy and the Shah: Building a Client State in Iran* (Ithaca and London, 1991); Gasiorowski and Byrne (eds), *Mohammad Mosaddeq and the 1953 Coup in Iran*; Bill and Louis, *Musaddiq: Iranian Nationalism and Oil*. In addition to the 'memoirs' of the putsch by CIA and SIS operatives, Kermit Roosevelt and CM Woodhouse respectively, there is the narrative of the coup related by one CIA expert, a Princeton professor, Donald Wilber, *Overthrow of Premier Mosaddeq of Iran: November 1952-August 1953* (Central Intelligence Agency, March 1954, revealed by *The New York Times*) — accounts that have been contested for their lack of precision, or falsifications.
376. For the accounts of the plot to arrest and liquidate Beria (based on Soviet archival sources), see Amy Knight, *Beria: Stalin's Lieutenant* (Princeton, 1993), pp 194ff.
377. Much like in Britain, in the 1906-07 Constitution the shah was a figurehead, had a ceremonial role, and had no right to appoint or dismiss the government, a measure

that was the prerogative of the parliament, which was dissolved in August 1953 through a referendum.
378. For details, see Gasiorowski, 'The 1953 Coup d'État in Iran', *International Journal of Middle East Studies*, Volume 19, no 3, August 1987, p 273.
379. That is: BE DAMN[ED]!
380. Their true identity has not been discovered, but some people have assumed them to be the Rashidian brothers — an idea which seems wrong, for the Rashidians were British agents as of the early 1940s, whereas Nerren and Cilley had worked with the OSS and later the CIA. This author strongly suspects these two to have been the Tafazzoli brothers, of whom one was a lawyer and the other a rather successful journalist who had good relations with the Court, Qavam, the TPI and almost all other politicians, just as a secret agent must have a wide network of contacts.
381. He had been a lecturer in Eastern religions teaching at Oxford. He was sent to Iran on the recommendation of Ann KS Lambton, a prominent British scholar at SOAS. See M Gasiorowski, 'The 1953 Coup d'État in Iran', *International Journal of Middle East Studies*, Volume 19, no 3, August 1987, p 265.
382. It was moved to 15 August (24 Mordad) at midnight instead of 12 or 13 August (21 or 22 Mordad). In his account in his memoirs, Kianouri, who claims that he followed the putschists' plan step by step and informed Mosaddeq accordingly, gives wrong dates (15th and 14th, respectively), a 'mistake' which may reveal his fabrication of the version he gives (Kianouri, *Khaterat*, pp 264-66). This is not a slip, for he gives the same account in a brochure published by the TPI (Kianouri, *Hezb-e Tudeh-ye Iran va Dr Mohammad Mosaddeq*, pp 40-41). Kianouri asserts that he informed Mosaddeq in the afternoon of the same day when the revelation was made by the Tudeh press, as if Mosaddeq would not have been informed through its publication. In this version, he also refers to a short conversation with Mosaddeq which he pretends to have taken place on the afternoon of 12 August, according to which Mosaddeq thanked him after Kianouri gave him information about the planned coup and also revealed to him that the TPI 'have very valuable and selfless friends [comrades?] among army officers who do not have commanding positions. We are ready to introduce these individuals to you. Use them for the defence of your residence and important commanding posts. Only in this way can the danger be avoided.' Such a revelation to Mosaddeq would have been against party secrecy rules, besides revealing the fact that, as is well known now, the TPI had some officers in key positions in the army and the police.
383. Kianouri attributes the delay to the revelation in the Tudeh press, whereas Roosevelt states that the messengers who brought the shah's *firmans* from the Caspian coast to Tehran arrived only late in the evening of 12 August; therefore the delay in the preparation of the 'schedule' (Roosevelt, *Countercoup*, second edition, pp 170-71).
384. Notably Amirkhosrowi, *Nazar az daroun*, pp 512-24; and Azarnour, *An Exclusive Interview*, pp 54ff. In a private letter by one TMO officer to another that has been put in my possession, it is said that, according to Captain Fayyazi and Lieutenant-Colonel Homayouni (both TMO officers in the Royal Guards), it was Lieutenant-Colonel Fouladvand who informed Mosaddeq, for which reason he was dismissed

after the second coup; apparently he died sometime thereafter by poisoning.
385. M Mosaddeq, *Mosaddeq dar mahkameh-ye nezami* (two volumes, Tehran, 1984), Volume 1, pp 105ff.
386. Kianouri pretends that he was that 'unidentified' individual, but that he spoke to the Premier at 10pm, which would not have left enough time for Mosaddeq to prepare the defence of his residence. Besides, Kianouri claims he had previously spoken to Mosaddeq by way of introduction through his wife who was related to Mosaddeq. Since his identity could not have been unknown to Mosaddeq, he could not have been the 'unknown' man. Such prevarications by Kianouri bring to light much about his character.
387. USNA 788.00/8-1853; Roosevelt, *The Countercoup* (second edition), pp 176ff, 183ff.
388. The division was being led by Bakhtiar's deputy Lieutenant-Colonel Rostami-Gouran, a TMO officer, who, once near Tehran at the time of the second putsch, precipitated, in advance of his column, to the capital to ask TPI leaders whether he should join the opposition to the putsch. He was soon arrested by the putschists — an incident that simply proves that a mole at the very top of the party had informed the putschists. See Azarnour, *An Exclusive Interview*, p 48.
389. M Gasiorowski, 'The 1953 Coup d'État in Iran', *International Journal of Middle East Studies*, Volume 19, no 3, August 1987, p 273.
390. In his memoirs, Kianouri admits that not only did the Tudeh launch these slogans, but also the Executive Committee had decided to adopt them. See his *Khaterat* (Tehran, 1993 — a publication of the IRI's Ministry of Information), p 267, as well as the TPI Executive Committee brochure *Darbareh-ye 28 Mordad*.
391. This author was personally present, witnessing all that went on.
392. See Fatemi's second letter from his hideout to Ayatollah Zanjani, 30 Day 1332/20 January 1954, in B Tayarani (ed), *Zendegi-nameh, asnad, va namehha-ye Ayatollah HSR Zanjani* (Tehran, 2009), p 44. The animosity towards him by some Patriotic Front leaders, partly due to personal rivalries, was such that at the time rumours were spread that he had been a 'British *agent provocateur*', a rumour that the TPI had spread before and even repeated after the putsch. Finally, his execution, slightly over a year after the coup by the putschist government, cleared him of such outrageous, baseless charges that are quite common in Iranian politics. Yet a leader of the Tudeh front organisation SSAC claims that only the Patriotic Front leaders accused him of such charges, see Mokri (a pseudonym), *Khaterat-e man az zendeh yad Dr Hussein Fatemi* (Paris, nd,) pp 32ff. He is not frank enough, for such an accusation had been levelled by the Stalinist apparatus against all of Mosaddeq's collaborators. Even decades after the execution of Fatemi at least one Tudeh leader, Kianouri, and a former young Tudeh activist, one of the founders of the guerrilla movement, Bizhan Jazani, levelled the same charges against him. See Kianouri, *Khaterat*, p 212; Kianouri, *Hezb-e Tudeh-ye Iran va Dr Mohammad Mosaddeq*, pp 22ff; *Tarikh-e si saleh-ye siasi fasl-e avval* (*The Thirty-Year Political History: Chapter One*, Tehran, 1979), p 59.
393. See M Gasiorowski, 'The 1953 Coup d'État in Iran', *International Journal of Middle East Studies*, Volume 19, no 3, August 1987, p 274.
394. Azarnour, *An Exclusive Interview*, p 79.

395. See the 'Top Secret' 'Memorandum for the President', by Walter Bedell-Smith from Baghdad to Washington, 17 August 1953, USNA 788.00/8-1853.
396. See N Shifteh, *Zendegi-nameh-ye va mobarezat-e Dr Hussein Fatemi* (Tehran, 1985), p 339.
397. S Dehqan and B Afrasiabi, *Taleqani va tarikh* (second edition, Tehran, 1981, p 282; see also 'NY *Times* Details CIA's Role in 1953 Iranian Coup', (http://fr.news.yahoo.com/000416/2/blnw.html) in which it is, *inter alia*, stated: 'In early August, the CIA stepped up the pressure. Iranian operatives pretending to be Communists threatened Muslim leaders with "savage punishment if they opposed Mossadegh", seeking to stir anti-Communist sentiment in the religious community.'
398. M Gasiorowski, 'The 1953 Coup d'État in Iran', *International Journal of Middle East Studies*, Volume 19, no 3, August 1987, p 274.
399. TPI, *Darbareh-ye 28 Mordad*, pp 19, 22.
400. For a detailed discussion of this issue, see Azarnour, *An Exclusive Interview*, pp 54ff; Amirkhosrowi, *Nazari az daroun*, Chapter 22. Their detailed discussions try to prove that Kianouri was not the 'unknown individual'. Amirkhosrowi argues that it was Colonel Mobasheri, a TMO secretary, who was executed after the coup. Amirkhosrowi belonged, until 1983, to Kianouri's faction in the Central Committee; although right in his assessment of this issue, he has only done so because of Kianouri's attack against him in his aforementioned *Memoirs*.
401. See his letter in Azarnour, *An Exclusive Interview*, pp 23-33.
402. Ollovi told a Tudeh cadre in prison that on 19 August he had proposed a general strike. 'This was the only thing we could do. We could only appeal to workers to go on strike. Perhaps in the process the situation would have turned in our favour, although I do not believe it personally.' See Baqer Momeni, *Rahian khatar* (Paris, 2006), p 25.
403. Ibid, pp 14-15, 55.
404. Bahrami and Yazdi, both friends of Taqi Arani and imprisoned with him as members of the 'Group of Fifty-Three', were broken in prison after their arrests in 1955 and 1956 and recanted. Both died soon after their release. Ollovi was executed.
405. It is to be noted that years later Kianouri spoke of three phone calls.
406. Proceedings of the 'Enlarged Fourth Plenum of the Tudeh Party of Iran', published for the first time in Chaqueri, *Historical Documents*, Volume 1 (third printing, Tehran, 1980), pp 368ff; also cited in JAMI, *Gozashteh*, p 690.
407. That is the scribe, not the Party Secretary, who was Dr Bahrami.
408. He, who was present at the session of the Executive Committee all day on 19 August, and who discusses the issues in detail, in this letter does not mention the claimed phone calls to Mosaddeq.
409. A 46-page hand-written secret report ('Gozaresh') handed to Radmanesh in 1956 in Moscow by A-A Shandermani. Citation from pages 17-18 of a copy of which is in the possession of this author. Curiously, Amirkhosrowi, who disputes Kianouri's claims, relying on the second communication by Shandermani, tends to accept the claim for the first call, adding that the letter by the majority of three of the Tehran Executive Committee also confirms it, whereas they are categorical that the first call to Mosaddeq was not successful (Amirkhosrowi, *Negahi az daroun*, p 676).

410. Gh-H Mosaddeq, *Dar kenar-e pedaram* (Tehran, 1990), p 117.
411. Ibid.
412. Azarnour, *An Exclusive Interview*, p 31. In other words, Mosaddeq had invented the attempt at a coup by the CIA!
413. Ibid, p 32.
414. Ibid.
415. Keshavarz, *Man Motahamm mikonam*, pp 139ff.
416. Zibayee, *Kommonizm dar Iran*, p 595.
417. TPI, *Darbareh-ye 28 Mordad*, p 23. This was circulated internally among cadres of the party by the Executive Committee in Tehran.
418. Mokri, *Khaterat-e man*, p 25. Mokri recalls that he and other leaders of the SSAC had met with Mosaddeq and Fatemi on a few occasions, but not on 19 August (ibid, pp 13-19).
419. In fact, Mokri of the SSAC states no one of that organisation met Mosaddeq on that day (Mokri, *Khaterat-e man*, pp 24-27).
420. Kianouri, *Khaterat*, p 266, quoting daily *Ettela'alt*, 28 Mordad 1358/19 August 1979. Mizani (Javanshir), a KGB member and a Kianouri lackey who was executed by the IRI, repeated this claim frequently. If these two officers were correct in their statement, their memory must by hazy, for no sources confirms it.
421. This is confirmed by two TMO officers, one now living in Canada, who wishes to remain anonymous, and the other is Azarnour, *An Exclusive Interview*, p 46.
422. http://www.setareyehsobh.com/12/MAIN/page%2010.pdf.
423. http://www.irdc.ir/fa/content/6425/default.aspx.
424. Tabari, *Kazhraheh*, pp 171-72.
425. See Tehran Military Governorship, *Ketab-e siah dar bareh-ye sazman-e afsaran Tudeh* (Tehran, 1955), pp 288-89. Every other officer questioned confirms this statement.
426. 'Tudeh Party Central Committee Declaration of 20 August', printed in the Documents section.
427. See the letter by Rostami-Gouran written in 1995, cited in Amirkhosrowi, *Nazari az daroun*, p 761.
428. Tehran Military Governorship, *Ketab-e siah*, pp 259-64; Kianouri, *Khaterat*, p 299.
429. Amirkhosrowi, *Nazari az daroun*, pp 760-62.
430. Azarnour suspects that a high-ranking member of the leadership had informed the authorities about him (Azarnour, *An Exclusive Interview*, p 68).
431. The Military Government of Tehran, *Ketab-siah darbareh-ye sazman afsaran Toudeh* (Tehran, 1955), pp 234-59.
432. For this issue, see Amirkhosrowi, *Nazari az daroun*, pp 772ff; Kianouri, *Khaterat*, pp 300-02; M Naser Qashqai, *Salha-ye bohran. Khaterat-e rouzaneh* (Tehran, 1987), pp 401ff; Azarnour, *An Exclusive Interview*, pp 79-83.
433. Azarnour, *An Exclusive Interview*, pp 83-85.
434. See Zibayee, *Kommonizm dar Iran*, Part 14; Military Government of Tehran, *Ketab-siah darbareh-ye sazman afsaran Toudeh*, passim.
435. For details of names and careers, see *Chap dar Iran beh ravayat-e ansad-e SAVAK. Sazman-e afsaran-e Hezb-e Tudeh*, published by the IRI's Centre for the Study of

Historical Documents (Tehran, 1991).
436. Report by the Chief of the National Police to the Prime Minister, in Tayarani (ed), *Asnad-e ahzab-e siasi-ye Iran (Tudeh Party)* (two volumes, Tehran, 2005), Volume 2, pp 926-27.
437. A Yavari, *Darbareh-ye ba'zi az masa'el-e Hezb-e Tudeh-ye Iran* (Paris, 1969), p 9; JAMA, *Gozashteh*, p 709; Azarnour, *An Exclusive Interview*, p 87.
438. Azarnour, *An Exclusive Interview*, p 90.
439. Ekteshafi, *Khaterat*, pp 95-96.
440. Letter dated 26 October 1954, in B Momeni (ed), *Nameha-ye Sargord Vakili (Lieutenant-Colonel Vakili's Letters from Prison*, Cologne, 2007), p 8, emphasis added.
441. That is, Rouzbeh, Mobasheri and Siamak (ibid, p 15).
442. Ibid, p 15.
443. See, for instance, Ekteshafi, *Khaterat*, pp 92-95; Azarnour, *An Exclusive Interview*, p 91; Khosrow-Panah, *Sazman-e afsaran*, p 213. Naturally, Tudeh cadres and leaders do not believe the veracity of the statement by Lieutenant-Colonel Mobasser (later a five-star general) who supervised the interrogation of Abbasi, according to whom the latter was not tortured and transmitted all he knew to the military authorities rather voluntarily. See M Mobasser, *Pazhouhesh. Naqdi bar khaterat-e arteshbod-e sabeq Fardoust va gozidehhayi az yadmandeh hyae nevisandeh* (London, 1996), pp 321-22. Khosropanah quotes most of these sources and others (Khosropanah, *Sazman-e afsaran-e hezb-e Tudeh-ye Iran*, pp 211-19). Versions of the story spread with approval right after the débâcle, without noting the contradictions and the interestedness of narrators.
444. Khosrow-Panah, *Sazman-e afsaran-e hezb-e Tudeh-ye Iran*, p 210.
445. Tabari, *Kazhraheh*, pp 172-3.
446. Personal conversation with this author on the eve of the 1979 revolution in Iran.
447. See his account as told to S Ansari, *Az zendegani-ye man, pa beh pay-e hezb-e Tudeh* (Los Angeles, 1996), pp 353.
448. Ibid.
449. Second secretaries were usually intelligence officers.
450. Spelt 'Abasi' in the original.
451. Presumably, these names were those given by Abbasi from memory, for the codes had not yet been decoded.
452. 'Arrest of Communist Ring in the Security Forces', report by William Koren, Jr, First Secretary of Embassy, USNA 788.00/9-1354.
453. Ansari, *Az zendegani-ye man*, p 353.
454. His name does not appear on any official lists of the officers, or any of Tudeh cadre, tried and condemned.
455. Zibayee, *Kommonizm dar Iran*, pp 537-54. The editor of the right-wing weekly *Tehran-e Mosavvar* was also assassinated apparently by a Tudeh member, Hasan Ja'fari, who was caught and hanged. It has been rumoured that he did it on behalf of the party, or that he was caught in place of Police Captain Qobadi, who killed the man. Tabari says the leadership had no knowledge of this murder (Tabari, *Kazhraheh*, p 160).
456. The only reference to Abbasi's interrogation is in contradiction with Rouzbeh's

statements regarding murders that he committed as a member of the 'hit team' that he, Rouzbeh, led.
457. *Chap dar Iran*, pp 329, 332-33.
458. Azarnour, *An Exclusive Interview*, p 93.
459. Momeni (ed), *Nameha-ye Sargord Vakili*, p 10.
460. Ibid, p 16.
461. Letter dated 26 October 1954, in ibid, p 10; see also Azarnour, *An Exclusive Interview*, p 79.
462. Momeni (ed), *Nameha-ye Sargord Vakili*, pp 9-10, 16; Azarnour, *An Exclusive Interview*, pp 68-70, 79, 81.
463. In his writings, Azarnour does not mention the name, but I heard from him that it was Colonel Zibayee, from whom he obtained such information through another high-ranking security officer of the regime, General Alavi-Kia, who had been Azarnour's classmate at the War College. I know it was Zibayee because I encouraged Azarnour to find and contact him in Colorado.
464. Azarnour, *An Exclusive Interview*, p 68. This last source was also General Alavi-Kia, who, like Azarnour, lived in Parisian exile. In the same interview, he discusses suspicions about Kianouri, but concludes that he was not the mole. We will discuss this matter below.
465. Amirkhosrowi, *Nazari az daroun*, p 768.
466. Related by Central Committee member Dr Jowdat in his 'confessions' after his arrest in 1983; see *Hezb-e Tudeh az shekl-giri ta foroupashi (1320-1386)*, p 171.
467. Momeni (ed), *Nameha-ye Sargord Vakili*, p 17.
468. Azarnour, *An Exclusive Interview*, p 68.
469. Zibayee, *Kommonizm dar Iran*, pp 827-28.
470. Amirkhosrowi, *Nazari az daroun*, p 516; Zibayee, *Kommonizm dar Iran*, p 831.
471. Zibayee, *Kommonizm dar Iran*, p 826; Mokri, *Khaterat-e man*, p 27.
472. M Varqa, *Dar sayeh-ye bim o omid. Rouydadhayee az sazman-e afsaran-e vabasteh be Hezb-e Tudeh-ye Iran* (Tehran, 2003).
473. Zibayee, *Kommonizm dar Iran*, p 830.
474. Ibid, pp 846, 828.
475. Keshavarz, *Man Motahamm mikonam*, pp 140-41.
476. Ibid, p 141.
477. Khosropanah, *Sazman-e afsaran-e hezb-e Tudeh-ye Iran*, p 259.
478. M Varqa, *Nagofteh-hayee piramoun-e forourizi ye hokoumat-e Mosaddeq va naqsh-e Hezb-e Tudeh* (Tehran, 1995), pp 239-40.
479. Amirkhosrowi, *Nazari az daroun*, p 761.
480. Varqa, *Nagofteh-ha*, p 249.
481. Ibid; Zibayee, *Kommonizm dar Iran*, p 836.
482. Zibayee, *Kommonizm dar Iran*, p 827.
483. Ibid, p 835.
484. Ibid, p 248
485. Ibid, pp 247-48.
486. According to Rouzbeh, the decision to suppress Lankarani had been unanimously made by the Executive Committee; see his confessions cited in Zibayee, *Kommonizm dar Iran*, p 540-41.

487. See J Beynac, *Kamo: Homme de main de Lénine* (Paris, 1972).
488. Keshavarz, *Man Motahamm mikonam*, p 144.
489. Varqa, *Nagofteh-ha*, p 244, emphasis added.
490. Ibid.
491. N Saremi, who had originally heard Kianouri's statement, related it to the East German SED as follows: 'The more officers arrested the better it is.' See STASI archives: MfS-HA II, no 28758 A similar version is also related by Dr Keshavarz, *Man Motahamm mikonam*, pp 145-46, and Artashes Ovanesian in his memoirs, *Khaterat* (Tehran, 1376), pp 432-34, as quoted by Khosropanah, *Sazman-e afsaran-e hezb-e Tudeh-ye Iran*, p 220. Read Saremi's full text in the Documents section.
492. Morteza Zarbakht, 'Kar-e Razmara naboud!', *Adineh*, nos 121-122, 1994; in his memoirs, Zarbakht recalls that at the time he could not swallow the tragedy since he still had 'faith' in the TPI and the USSR as the bastion of socialism; things became clear to him when he read Khrushchev's report on Stalin's crimes (M Zarbakht, *Gozar az toufan* (Berlin, 2001), p 247).
493. See Chaqueri, 'Moscow and the Tudeh Party' below.
494. Bahrami admitted it during interrogations, see Tehran Military Governorship, *Ketab-e siah*, pp 215-16
495. As for these two leaders, everyone in the TPI knows it and talks about it; Tabari is more clear and elaborate about their service to the KGB (Tabari, *Kazhraheh*, pp 277-85).
496. On many occasions the British government stated that, if Mosaddeq should succeed, he would be emulated elsewhere — an argument that more than anything else convinced the American partner. See *FRUS*, Volume 10.
497. Henderson misrepresented the Iranian Constitution and parliamentary tradition, according to which the shah had no right to appoint or dismiss a premier.
498. Extracts from Henderson's telegram to the Secretary of State, sent 18 August 1953, 6:57 pm, see USNA 788.00/8-1853; see also the printed version in *FRUS*, Volume 10, pp 748652, emphasis added.
499. *Mardom*, 15 February 1947, cited in Zibayee, *Kommonizm dar Iran*, pp 427-30. For the confessions of Abbasi (short) and Rouzbeh concerning the murder of Mas'oud, see ibid, pp 430-39.
500. B Momeni, *Rahian khatar* (Paris, 2006), p 125.
501. Ibid, pp 124-27.
502. Keshavarz, *Man Motahamm mikonam*, pp 104-05. This last point about his corpse having been found in a pit was put to a veteran Tudeh cadre who had been in the country at the time. He responded that he *vaguely* remembered such a report; he probably did not wish to commit himself.
503. Keshavarz writes that according to a report reaching the Central Committee in Moscow, the arrest of Rouzbeh was due to Mottaqi's treachery. He had been promoted to the Executive Committee after the departure of Kianouri and Jowdat and the arrest of Yazdi and Bahrami (Keshavarz, *Man Motahamm mikonam*, p 31).
504. Quoted from his interrogation in Zibayee, *Kommonizm dar Iran*, pp 564-65.
505. Ibid.

506. Ibid, p 566.
507. Ovanesian in his secret diaries about party comrades in the leadership devastates them completely — to the point that his diaries have not been published by Tudeh 'historians'. He is, of course, less harsh on Kambakhsh and Kianouri, as they were both, like him, linked directly to the Soviets. His diaries are to be soon published soon in C Chaqueri, *Deconstruction of a Myth...* (in Persian), two volumes.
508. Tabari, *Kazhraheh*, pp 224-27.
509. 'A Soul Dedicated to the Storm...', *Izvestia*, 24 March 1962; English translation in FO 371/164183.
510. Eskandari, *Memoirs* (Tehran edition), p 424.
511. 'A Soul Dedicated to the Storm...', *Izvestia*, 24 March 1962, p 1. Radmanesh praised him as 'a learned mathematician and gifted writer' who had been arrested three times and had escaped three times.
512. Eskandari, *Memoirs* (Tehran edition), pp 279-81.
513. Ibid, p 472.
514. Tabari relates that the Russians had asked to have 'its faulty parts and shortcomings', removed before publication — a 'recommendation' that was observed (Tabari, *Kazhraheh*, p 226).
515. 'People's Party' in the Russian translation.
516. 'A Soul Dedicated to the Storm...', *Izvestia*, 24 March 1962, pp 2-8.
517. Tabari, *Kazhraheh*, p 165.
518. For the Central Committee report to the Fourth Plenum, see Chaqueri, *Historical Documents*, Volume 1 (third printing, Tehran, 1980), pp 374-84. A very short report on this plenum was sent by Radmanesh to the SED: 'Information über das ertwiterte ZK-Plenum der Toudeh-Partei des Iran', Archiv der Parteien und Massenorganisationen der DDR im Bundesarchiv Deutschlands, NL 182/ 1292, pp 131-36.
519. For the resolutions of the Fourth Plenum, see Chaqueri, *Historical Documents*, Volume 1 (third printing, Tehran, 1980), pp 359-74; Ekteshafi, *Khaterat*, pp 153-229.
520. Some have given his name as Simyonenko.
521. Ekteshafi, *Khaterat*, p 178.
522. Ibid, pp 178-89. Dr Keshavarz relates this incident and confirms that when he raised the question and the majority of the plenum was about expel Kambakhsh and Kianouri, the Soviet 'guest', whose party had hosted the plenum, intervened, saying that his party was against a split in the TPI. He adds that the Soviets had been recording the proceedings in an adjacent room (Keshavarz, *Man Motahamm mikonam*, p 72).
523. See the remarks by Plyshevskii of the Comintern on Kambakhsh's Report: Comintern Archives, RTsKhIDNI, 495/4/197.
524. Ekteshafi, *Khaterat*, p 181.
525. Ibid, pp 153-217.
526. Shermini was arrested in 1954 and released a couple of years later after recantation. In 1956 he addressed a short letter to Maleki stating: 'I am today completely convinced that you were right and the Tudeh leaders, who excommunicated you and incited the youth, including me, against you, did something wrong and

unmanly... I bow to you for your scientific judgement and moral courage for having courageously resisted a storm of calumny and slander.' (*Nabard-e zendegi*, no 1, 1956, p 2) He simply preferred to forget that he was one of the leaders who ran the campaign against Maleki. Tabari relates that in an extensive report on Shermini and his doings in the Youth Organisation, Foroutan sought to connect him with the Americans, through such 'facts' that he had studied at the American college in Tehran, his sister had married an American, his father, with the name Karimov, had been executed as a Trotskyist in the Soviet Union, and when the Executive Committee proposed that he go to the Soviet Union, he refused to do so. Tabari says that he defended Shermini in 1952 when he was questioned by a Soviet specialist of Iran called Bashkirov (Tabari, *Kazhraheh*, pp 162-63).

527. Ekteshafi, *Khaterat*, p 167.
528. Radmanesh expediently 'forgot' to mention his meeting with a British Embassy diplomat (initialed ASC) in September 1944, during which in response to the diplomat's question of 'What did he think was the solution?' to Iran's problems, he replied: '... the situation demanded a coalition government of all elements, except perhaps the most extreme reactionary element, that is, S Zia.' (Minutes by ASC, dated 3 September 1944; FO 248/1452) Kambakhsh, too, conveniently forgot his candidacy for the PTT Ministry in 1946.
529. Ekteshafi, *Khaterat*, p 164.
530. Ibid, p 162.
531. Ibid, p 170.
532. It is not clear what the name of the review was; both *For a Lasting Peace, For a People's Democracy* and *World Marxist Review* (*La Nouvelle Revue Internationale*) have been mentioned by Tudeh leaders, although the *WMR* did not start publication until 1958.
533. This question is discussed in the following sources: Eskandari, *Khaterat*, p 261; Kianouri, *Khaterat*, p 225; Amirkhosrowi, *Nazari az daroun*, pp 286-87.
534. Ekteshafi, *Khaterat*, p 168. See also Saremi's letter to the SED in the Documents section.
535. Tabari, *Kazhraheh*, p 167.
536. Ekteshafi, *Khaterat*, p 167.
537. In the Persian text by Ekteshafi there is a *contresens* implying that Radmanesh contended that Mosaddeq was united with the imperialists, whereas at the plenum this was not his position, while as noted above, he had maintained that line even in his interview with *Daily Worker*.
538. Ekteshafi, *Khaterat*, p 164.
539. He must have changed his position under pressure of the atmosphere of the plenum, for two years later at a conference of communist parties, his position was different. After some gymnastics of going over the definition of the 'national bourgeoisie' given by the Comintern's Sixth Congress and 'Comrade Mao Tse Tung', he concludes that 'the national bourgeoisie... because of their dual nature... tend to vacillate and come to terms with imperialism' (N Kianouri, 'The National Bourgeoisie, Their Nature and Policy', *World Marxist Review*, no 8, August 1959).
540. Ekteshafi, *Khaterat*, p 181.
541. Ibid, p 200; see also Keshavarz, *Man Motahamm mikonam*, p 72.

542. Tabari, *Kazhraheh*, p 167.
543. Ibid, p 129.
544. Ekteshafi, *Khaterat*, pp 185-87.
545. He worked with an editorial team on a corrected edition of Ferdowsi's Persian epic, *The Book of Kings*.
546. Ekteshafi, *Khaterat*, pp 187-89.
547. Ibid, p 161. In Ekteshafi's book it is written 'and ability for collective work', which must be a mistake, for Kianouri would not have criticised himself for lacking this ability if he had possessed it; besides, he has been consistently accused of lacking that ability.
548. Ibid, pp 189-91.
549. Ibid, pp 191-92.
550. Ibid, pp 192-94. Qasemi's opposition to the Persian New Year, of pagan origin, may have had its roots in the fact that he came from a clerical family, where such festivities were considered 'un-Islamic', as was the case right after the 1979 revolution when the mullahs wanted to ban such festivities but faced popular resistance. Interestingly, Qasemi's *nom de guerre* inside the party was *akhund*, that is, mullah.
551. Ekteshafi, *Khaterat*, p 196.
552. Letter from Reza Rousta to Walter Ulbricht, 8 February 1962, SED Ausserministerium, in Archiv der Parteien und Massenorganisationen der DDR, J IV 1/202/381.
553. Ekteshafi, *Khaterat*, p 198.
554. Ibid.
555. Ibid, pp 196-98.
556. Ibid, p 199.
557. Ibid, p 200.
558. Ibid, pp 201-02.
559. Ibid, p 203.
560. IPSR, *Hezb-e Tudeh az shekl-giri ta foroupashi (1320-1368)*, p 170.
561. It was a move by Mosaddeq to raise money by borrowing from patriots who could afford to help the government by purchasing national bonds. It was a great success.
562. Ekteshafi, *Khaterat*, pp 203-04.
563. Ibid, p 170.
564. Ibid, p 209.
565. Ibid, pp 206-09.
566. Ibid, p 209.
567. Ibid, pp 211-12.
568. For the full text of the resolution, see Chaqueri (ed), *Historical Documents*, Volume 1, pp 363-65.
569. Mosaddeq, *Khaterat va ta'alomat*, pp 294-95.
570. Chaqueri (ed), *Historical Documents*, Volume 1, pp 366-67.
571. Ibid, pp 368-69.
572. Ibid, p 370.
573. Ibid, pp 371-72.

574. Ibid, pp 372-73.
575. TPI Central Committee 'Declaration', in Chaqueri (ed), *Historical Documents*, Volume 1, p 361.
576. Ekteshafi, *Khaterat*, pp 213-14.
577. Amirkhosrowi in discussion with Eskandari in 1984 (Eskandari, *Khaterat* (Tehran edition), p 284). The 'forbidden' resolutions were put at the disposal of this author by a member of the party and were published for the first time in 1969 in the first volume of *Historical Documents*. After the revolution, First-Secretary Kianouri published the plenum resolutions with long embarrassing passages censored out. See TPI, *Asnad va didgahha*, pp 361-82.
578. See the article on Arani in the previous issue of *Revolutionary History*, Volume 10, no 2, pp 98-114.
579. Paradoxically, even when, in exile, they came across some of this correspondence through the research of Stalinist historians of Iran, they did not take these matters seriously.

Cosroe Chaqueri
Moscow and the Tudeh Party
Did the Soviets Play a Role in
Founding the Tudeh Party in Iran?

Introduction[1]

Various theses have been advanced concerning the founding of the Tudeh Party in the autumn of 1941, after the forced abdication of Reza Shah in consequence of Iran's occupation by the Allies in the late summer of the same year. There are those who, on ideological grounds and without presenting any evidence, claim that the Tudeh was a Soviet creation.[2] The first known source that attributed the founding of the Tudeh to the Soviets was the SAVAK 'historian', Colonel 'Ali Ziba'i, who stated that Rostam Aliev was present among the '27 founding members' of the Tudeh in September 1941. According to this source, most of those present did not know who Aliev was, and those who did kept quiet about his identity. Some of those present wanted to call the party 'Communist', but Aliev opposed the idea as 'not suitable under the present circumstances'. Ultimately, his idea that the party be called 'Tudeh' was accepted.[3] Others, on the other hand, mostly of the Tudeh leadership, have claimed that the Tudeh was created independently of Soviet wishes. Within this latter group, there are those who have advanced the thesis that the Tudeh was 'Communist' from the very start.[4] On the other hand, it has also been affirmed that the Tudeh was not a Communist party in the beginning but was gradually transformed into one. Curiously, Iraj Eskandari, First Secretary of the Tudeh during the Iranian revolution of 1978-79, defended both these theses, albeit at different times in his lifetime.[5] Given the limited space available in this article, it would be impossible to list all these claims and sources; the interested reader is, therefore, referred to most important works among them.[6] It is important, however, to refer to a work published in the West that has now acquired the stature of 'authority' on the history of the Tudeh; it makes the following affirmation on the founding of that organisation:

In launching the organisation, the founders [of the Tudeh] gave the party chairmanship to Sulayman Mirza Eskandari, the highly respected radical prince who had fought in the Constitutional Revolution, helped establish the Democratic Party in the Second Majles,[7] led the Committee of National Resistance during World War I,[8] and presided over the Socialist Party from 1921 until its dissolution in 1926.[9]

The unique, albeit limited, chance of access to consult the Comintern archives in 1992 and 1993 has permitted this author to address this controversial question on the basis of irrefutable documents, particularly in light of the contradictory (seasonal) narratives provided by the Tudeh Party itself. What follows is the account of the founding of the Tudeh Party according to documents found in the archives of the Comintern in Moscow. When necessary, occasional reference will be made to published documents. Because of the controversial nature of the issue, long quotations from the documents will be cited.

The Role of the Soviet Army Intelligence in Establishing and Shaping the Tudeh

In a report to his superior in the Red Army Intelligence Division,[10] Brigade Commissar Il'ichev, Colonel Seliukov writes that 'according to your wish', he met Solayman Mirza Eskandari, the veteran Democrat and Socialist. The meeting took place on 29 September 1941 (7 Mehr 1320),[11] at six o'clock in the evening at his home.[12] The Soviet colonel was introduced to Eskandari by the Soviet embassy counsellor Petrov, and they spoke for 80 minutes in Russian and Persian, through an interpreter.[13]

After an exchange of customary courtesies, the Red Army Colonel Seliukov asked Eskandari what his opinion was regarding 'the current events and the present situation in Iran'. His response was that 'nothing new had happened' in that country:

> We have had nothing similar to the events in Russia [in 1917] when there was a revolution. Here the shah [*sic*, royalty] has remained in place. The Majles and the government are, in fact, the same, and they — for the time being — introduce no improvements for Iran. *Political prisoners have not yet been liberated.*[14]

Eskandari added that Reza Shah 'went away under Russian pressure and the Red Army', and it seems that he departed voluntarily so that his son could 'remain in his place'.[15]

Here Eskandari obviously was patting his Soviet interlocutor, as the historical fact is that Reza Shah had been forced to abdicate under joint Anglo-Soviet pressure and *did not depart voluntarily*, because of the close relations he had continued to maintain with Nazi Germany even after repeated British warnings that German agents had to be expelled from Iran.[16]

In this connection it is indeed noteworthy to mention here a significant piece of information regarding the departure of Reza Shah under duress, which has thus far remained untold. Initially, the British did not intend to force the old shah to abdicate; the Soviets did. In a telegram, dated 17 September 1941, to the Quai d'Orsay, the French Minister at Tehran, Coiffard, reported that:

> The British, who had feared disturbances, would have preferred to keep the shah on the throne. They had to abandon him upon Russian intransigence. They were afraid of their increasing unpopularity by defending a sovereign already discredited, accused in public rumours of having been their own creation. To ensure themselves of the benefits of this gesture, they then took the initiative of exiling him, and carried on, every night, on the English radio [BBC, Radio Baghdad, and Radio Delhi], a most violent campaign in Persian [against him]. All the exactions of the shah were, for the first time, openly related and through a voice [British radio broadcasts] that could no longer be silenced. The considerable effects of these programmes on the Persian people did not escape the attention of the shah, who last Sunday asked the British legation 'What is the aim of all this?' Upon [the receipt of] a British response, the shah, feeling that he had neither the support of the occupying powers nor that of his people, decided to abdicate.[17]

But because Iran was still nominally a sovereign country, the former shah could not be expelled, unless an official warrant permitted the British authorities to arrest and exile him. This unusual warrant was issued by his son and crown prince, Mohammad Reza Pahlavi, who had now taken his place as the new shah of Iran.[18] It was, therefore, after the issuance of this secret warrant by the crown prince, apparently in exchange for the throne, that Reza Shah was escorted out of Iran by British forces. It is, however, true that, as Eskandari stated, the system had remained intact.

Nevertheless, the shah's abdication and expulsion by Anglo-Soviet forces were favourably received by the Iranian political elite[19] that had been deprived of participation in public affairs, although there was still little hope for any change in the political system. As Eskandari put it to the Soviet Army officer:

> Previously, the shah simply named the Majles and the government, and it is now the same situation. The new Majles [Thirteenth Legislature] and government are composed of appointed men — ballots having been

fabricated to suit the young shah.[20]

Eskandari told his Soviet interlocutor:

> We the free-thinking men can write nothing in the newspapers. Many people in Tehran thought that, when the Red Army came, platforms would be erected and they would speak freely about everything to the people, and that all the parasites would be arrested. But this did not occur. The constabulary and the police have remained and the government is ruling as in the past, so that many people have lost hope and are afraid to work [politically].[21]

In response, the Red Army colonel noted — obviously diplomatically — that 'freedom and revolution are not exported and that the Iranian people can and must introduce in their country the order and measures they desire'. Encouraging Eskandari personally, he added:

> You, Mr Solayman Mirza, are an important statesman and political activist of Iran and know better than anyone else what the Iranian people want and what must be done to improve the situation in Iran, and it would be very good if you acted. The presence of the Red Army here certainly produces and will produce effects as regards the people of Iran and their leaders.[22]

Then, Eskandari mentioned that a certain X [H?[23]] had created a party which had already published its call to the people with the promise of improving the situation. He further told the Soviet officer that:

> Of course, we could also create such a party, but both the police and the constabulary will prevent us from working, whereas no one harms them [the other party], and they use the press freely. It is absolutely clear that we the free-thinking people ourselves will not be able to do anything without your [Soviet] help (he is applying to me). We need help. In general, the historical moment that we now live, at the moment the Red Army is in Iran, must be used for the improvement of the situation in Iran.

The Soviet Army officer replied that the situation then was 'most suitable for the creation of the needed party and that help would be granted to him [Eskandari] in his work so long as it was not contrary to our [Soviet] interests'.

In conclusion, Eskandari declared the following:

1. We will deal with the organisation in order to obtain democratic liberties and an easier life for the Iranian people; and:
2. You [the Soviets] must grant us your assistance in this enterprise and help obtain the liberation of, and the restoration of civil rights to, political prisoners.[24]

Colonel Seliukov also reported that he and Eskandari had agreed to meet the following day (8 Mehr 1320/30 September 1941) at noon, while Eskandari would meditate a number of questions, and that he 'agreed to work with our help'.

The second conversation took place at Eskandari's home at the arranged time, and lasted 90 minutes, continuing the previous day's conversation.

The Red Army colonel:

> ... warned Solayman Mirza that no one was to know of our yesterday's conversation. To this the latter replied by an agreement. As an example, he stated that [some] political prisoners had already applied to him, asking him to request help from the Soviet embassy in the matter of their liberation;[25] he had replied that: 'This is our (Iranian) business, and that the Soviet embassy cannot intervene in it.'[26]

Referring to Eskandari's remarks on the previous day regarding the 'actual order in Iran', the Soviet colonel then said that 'it would be well if you [Eskandari] could explain on paper your reasons for dissatisfaction [with the situation] as well as your programme for [its] improvement'. Eskandari was further told that, since on the same day at four in the afternoon he was going to have a conversation with his supporters with whom he intended to group in a party, he should 'state in writing the programme of your [proposed] party and what you are going to discuss at this meeting'.[27]

Eskandari agreed to do all this, saying that until the creation of the party his supporters would be called 'the party group'. He then asked the Red Army colonel for his opinion about the name of the group, to which the latter replied: 'For the time being [and] in principle the appellation does not have much importance, but we might revert to this question in the future.'

Then the Soviet officer stated that, while he was 'sure of his [Eskandari's] statesmanship and political abilities', 'if his work is carried out in a suitable manner and corresponds to our [Soviet] intentions, then it can be trusted that when there is a change of government, he [Eskandari] can hope to participate in it'.

Eskandari noted at this point that he could not participate in the government of the time under Premier M-A Foroughi, because one could not hope for any help from it. It would be 'a different matter if a new government were formed, in which he would have his supporters enter [too].' When asked about his financial situation, he said: 'I have a small income, no more than 250 *tomans* per month. This is sufficient for me. In general, I do not think much about myself; the main thing is the work.' He gave the example that when the former Pahlavi Shah wanted to give him a house as a present, or to sell it to him at a low price, he refused it in favour of the Ministry of Education, of which he was in charge. It is clear here that Eskandari rebuffed Soviet financial assistance to himself. He also 'frequently said' to his Soviet interlocutor that the people 'knew and respected him'.

In the course of this second conversation, the Soviet army officer also learned about the invitation extended to Eskandari to the tenth anniversary of the October Revolution in 1927, his meeting with Stalin and Chicherin then, as well as his past connection with Caucasian revolutionaries some 20 years previously.[28] The Soviet officer 'politely' asked him to write down his autobiography. At the end of the conversation Colonel Seliukov reminded Eskandari that he 'must write down' the following before their next meeting:

1. His attitude towards the prevailing conditions and government in Iran.
2. His views regarding the change of conditions that would satisfy the demands of the Iranian people.
3. The programme of his party and the questions discussed on 30 September during the meeting of his supporters at his home.
4. His autobiography.[29]

The next meeting with Eskandari was to take place on 6 October (14 Mehr), but they met with a five-day delay, on 11 October 1941 (19 Mehr 1320).[30] At this encounter, Eskandari informed the Soviet colonel that the programme he had handed to him through his associates had been sent to newspaper editors for publication, but the press had refused to print it. His intention was to send it to all editorial staffs in the country and if they also refused to publish it, he would go to the speaker of the Majles to ask him what kind of press freedom there existed in Iran when a democratic party had no possibility to publish its programme. He intended to ask him permission to print the party programme, as it was 'time to make public [the existence of] our party, so that the Iranian people might know about it, so that everyone might know about the existence of the national-democratic party of Iran and be acquainted with its programme'.

Then asked by the Soviet officer whether this opinion was personal or shared by the whole group, Eskandari responded that this was 'the opinion of the plenum and presidium of our party' — incidentally, not as yet called the Tudeh — which, made up of 15 individuals, had been 'elected' on 10 October 1941 (18

Mehr 1320).[31]

When questioned in what measure the Iranian people were supporting the party, Eskandari stated that: 'I am sure that the Iranian people will come with us. We can now count on 2000 to 2500 supporters in Tehran.'

The Red Army officer told Eskandari that, having acquainted himself with his party programme, he could tell him that 'essentially, it is in accordance with our opinion and corresponds to the present conditions in Iran'.[32] As to its publication and the legalisation of the party, the officer added, he needed time 'to reflect' upon them before expressing his opinion. These questions were 'unexpected' for him, since at the previous meeting they had spoken of 'the necessity for you and future manifestations, to increase [your] forces, to reinforce and educate the party, as well as to study the strengths and weaknesses of the present government and the Majles'. Clearly, the Soviets did not wish to rock the boat of alliance with the British, etc.

As if the Soviets had manifested dissatisfaction about some points of the programme, Eskandari pointed out:

> We changed the points on our programme regarding the question of the police and the nationalisation [of landed properties], so as not to be accused of desiring disorder and sovietisation. Regarding the police it is changed as follows: 'All those who infringe on liberty will be punished by law.' And the point regarding the nationalisation of land is approximately thus: 'Poor peasants must be supplied with land.'

The programme that Seliukov transmitted to Moscow did not contain the point on the police; it must have been dropped on Soviet advice.

Eskandari added that 'some of my supporters think that I am restraining them too much, but they are mistaken. I understand the present situation quite well.' As if he knew the Soviet Popular Front tactics, he symbolically added: 'I have kept the portraits of Marx and Lenin, but it is not the time to put them out even in this room. When the (suitable) time comes, they will be placed in my room.'

Then the Soviet officer informed Eskandari that he would give him his answers in two days. This delay did not mean, however, that the Soviets 'forbade' him to 'act independently' or he should 'limit' his activity, 'which for the time being coincides with our position'.

Eskandari reminded the Red Army officer that there were 'some hot-blooded, impatient members [of the party] who demand immediate manifestation of Communist and Soviet slogans':

For instance, [Reza] Rousta[33] asks for immediate demonstrations and meetings. He openly says that the Soviet embassy will support us, that we will be supported with money, and that in the near future a new government of Iran will be formed comprising six supporters of the USSR and six of Britain. Rousta presents himself as a Communist and clearly as a person sent by the Soviet embassy. His declarations introduce conflict into our party, and I would ask you to help me preserve unity in our party.

Regarding Rousta, the Soviet Red Army officer replied that 'we [that is, you] are a national party which must win over the majority of the people and then appoint its representative in the government, and we [that is, you] will be able to do this'.[34]

The following meeting between the Soviet officer Seliukov and Eskandari took place on 15 October 1941 (23 Mehr 1320), lasting 30 minutes through an interpreter.

Eskandari informed his Soviet interlocutor that from the Majles he had received the authorisation for the publication of the party's programme, of which 1000 copies would be printed. After its diffusion, he would endeavour to obtain permission to publish his own party organ. He did not elaborate on the composition of the editorial staff of his party organ, but mentioned a number of individuals who, in his opinion, would be able to edit the paper. He also intended to obtain in the near future a place for his party club.

Then the Soviet colonel was also informed that Eskandari had made the acquaintance of the Qashqa'i tribal leader Naser Khan, who resided in Abadeh in the vicinity of Shiraz. Eskandari wished to include him in the party as well.[35]

The Soviet Army officer, Colonel Seliukov, reported to his superiors: 'I approved of his [Eskandari's] line of conduct concerning the publication of his programme and the legalisation of the party, obtaining a press organ, as well as a club for the party.' At the same meeting, the Soviet officer drew Eskandari's attention to the fact 'that at present his party has the task of bringing together all the democratic forces and to struggle against all kinds of leftist attitudes inside the party, such as those of Rousta. As to Rousta, no one in the [Soviet] Embassy had authorised him to establish a connection with the party, much less advise such [radical] conditions.' Colonel Seliukov further advised Eskandari that 'if Solayman Mirza knows Rousta well, [as] he had so stated, and is sure that he is not an adventurer', Eskandari should 'try to persuade him of mistakes in his outlook and proposals'. For 'it is not advisable to push away [individuals with] leftist attitudes, but their mistaken positions must be insistently explained to them'.[36]

As agreed previously, Eskandari and the Soviet Red Army officer Seliukov next met in a week's time, on 22 October 1941 (30 Mehr 1320) at 7.30 in the evening. The conversation, through an interpreter named Ebrahim, lasted 40 minutes.

Eskandari informed his Soviet interlocutor that two days previously he had received a visit from a police colonel who had warned him that he knew some people (that is, the party) were gathering at his, Eskandari's, place, and that because of the war situation such meetings were prohibited. Eskandari added that 'today the military governor published a declaration prohibiting gatherings, a declaration that was aimed at my party'. Eskandari further noted that they had had no time yet to print their programme. Although a permit had been received, no more than 10 copies of it had been printed before the police confiscated them. On the same day a 'congress of the party' had been held. Participants had gathered in a different place, not all arriving at the same time, ostensibly due to police controls. They decided to print the programme in the Arak region (central Iran).[37] In addition, Eskandari 'told his companions what Rousta, who presented himself as the representative of the [Soviet] embassy, [really] was'. Eskandari further informed his Soviet interlocutor that he had received, five days previously, an invitation from Mohammad Reza Shah to attend at the Gulistan Palace the birthday celebration of the new shah. He had turned down the invitation.[38]

Regarding the government ban on meetings, Eskandari intended to send a protest to the premier and wished to know Colonel Seliukov's opinion about it. The Red Army officer responded that 'the situation had taken a wrong turn as regards his party', but this did not mean 'that they had to deplore it... On the contrary, work must be continued with even greater energy, increasing the number of supporters.' As to the protest letter to the premier, the Soviet officer remarked there was 'nothing I could say for the time being as to the form in which it should be done'. In other words, he wanted, as on previous occasions, to obtain instructions from his superiors about it.[39] At this meeting the Soviet officer repeated his request for Eskandari's autobiography.

The Soviet officer met Eskandari again on 11 November 1941 (20 Aban 1320), this time only for 30 minutes. Eskandari told his Red Army interlocutor that 'at the last meeting of his party the question was raised as to the absolute necessity of connection with the Embassy of the USSR'. Eskandari added:

> As they do not know about our connection, I did not tell them about it [either] and declared that we must work on our own. Then, at the same meeting a question was raised about the organisation of groups in the regions occupied by the Red Army.

Eskandari told his Soviet connection:

> *We want to send our representatives to such cities as Ahvaz, Tabriz, Pahlavi [Anzali], Rasht, Gorgan, Mashhad, and other regions occupied by the Red Army in order to organise, on a legal basis, sections of our party.* But I am afraid to hamper your work in these regions. For this reason, I am seeking your advice in this respect. I have already sent two individuals to Tabriz, and they are asking [me] what to do. *I have replied that they must wait.*[40]

Further, responding to the Red Army officer's question, Eskandari remarked that 'in southern Iran he has several men and that he intends to organise his groups there too'. Having had to check this latter point with his superior too, Colonel Seliukov told Eskandari that 'this was a good idea and that I will be able to reply to this question in a few days'.

The Soviet officer concluded his conversation with Eskandari by insisting that 'one of the main problems of Solayman Mirza's party is to increase the number of his supporters and to educate Iranians in the democratic spirit'. The officer also reported that Eskandari could print and distribute no more than '60 to 70' copies of his programme.[41]

In a subsequent conversation with Eskandari, held, as agreed previously, in presence of Soviet interpreter Kommissarov, on 13 November 1941 (22 Aban 1320), the Iranian politician first informed the Soviet officer of the following:

> Two days previously [20 Aban 1320] Solayman Mirza had visited the Iranian Premier, Foroughi,[42] who had asked him his opinion about the new Majles and its composition. Solayman Mirza had rejected this Majles 'as not new' and no elections had taken place. Agreeing to speak to each other, not as politicians, but as 'friends', the Premier had alluded to Reza Shah, who had just abdicated, as 'the cause of Iran's misfortunes'. Concurring with Foroughi, Eskandari had asked him why not remove all the other 'causes', such as the practical ban on a free press. To this Premier Foroughi had replied: 'It is impossible to allow full press freedom, for every [past or present] minister would want to publish a newspaper, and they would be over 200', and given the situation in Iran under Allied occupation and with the presence of a German Fifth Column, the publication of such newspapers 'might inadvertently harm us'.

Then in reply to Eskandari's demand for a newspaper, Premier Foroughi had said that he 'will think it over and will be able to give a reply in 30 days', that is, 'if I remain Prime Minister'.[43]

Further relating his conversation with Premier Foroughi on the type of government Iran should have and the liberty of political parties in democratic countries, Eskandari noted that Foroughi had wanted him to present a 15-point programme within 15 days and, 'if suitable', he would permit it to function. As regards the law proscribing political party activities, Premier Foroughi had assured Eskandari: 'Never mind, we will arrange this somehow.'

Secondly, Eskandari said he had received a letter from A-A Sartipzadeh[44] and A-Q Asadi[45] (his supporters whom he had dispatched to Tabriz) that '*a party had been organised in Azerbaijan, or was being organised, and Asadi did not know what his attitude should be towards that party*'. (See further below.) These two had also asked Eskandari whom he would recommend to stand for the Majles election from Tabriz. Eskandari 'expressed the opinion that this party [in Azerbaijan] must be a democratic one, but he was not so sure' that it was; he wanted his Soviet interlocutor to tell him what kind of party it was and 'whether it was suitable for his men to establish contact with it'.[46] Eskandari added that 'in general, in the northern regions we must work in contact (*v kontakte*) [with the Soviets]; then that will be more advantageous (*togda budet bol'she pol'zy*)'.

The Soviet officer then reported to his superior that 'I approved of his [Eskandari's] visit to the Prime Minister and noted the necessity of closer relations with the government and the Majles in order to study their strengths and weaknesses, to inform me about these points, and to influence them' — a line that was in accord with the Anglo-Soviet wartime collaboration.

Regarding the northern regions under Red Army occupation: 'I recommended [to Eskandari] to abstain from organising his group there so long as I have not studied the question well. With regard to the party that is being organised in Azerbaijan and his [Eskandari's] relations with it, I replied nothing and promised to deal with it in detail at the next meeting', presumably after consultation with Moscow. Colonel Seliukov concluded his conversation by 'recommending to Solayman Mirza to increase his influence in southern and western Iran', which were important British zones of influence and rich in oil.

At the end of this report to his superiors in the Intelligence Division of the Soviet Army, Colonel Seliukov made two recommendations:

1) Through the intermediary of Solayman Mirza it is possible *to organise a party* [*as*] *a single anti-fascist front*.[47] Through this party we could have the possibility of influencing very strongly the government and the Majles. [This was, from the very outset, tantamount to a very conscious instrumentalisation of the Tudeh by Soviet foreign policy.] The party would unite all the parties and groups and would work under the leadership of Solayman Mirza.

Since the government wants to have [that is, allow the existence of] a party, it is possible to organise an anti-fascist party after having overcome certain difficulties.

2) Distinct groups of Solayman Mirza's party in the regions occupied by the Red Army should be submitted to the organisation [in the Soviet Army?] of the Central Committee of [the Communist Party in Soviet] Azerbaijan.[48]

Thus within six weeks, between 29 September and 13 November 1941, the Soviets guided Eskandari and his associates to create an organisation that would not only respond to a desire of a part of Iranian society for political activity on the centre-left, but also — and more importantly — to shape politically-motivated Iranians of the same tendency to establish an 'anti-fascist front' that would serve the Soviets' war needs on the political level in Iran and, eventually, their postwar interests. The recommendations by Colonel Seliukov to his superiors, the programme of the 'party group', which found approval in Dimitrov's letter to Joseph Stalin, VM Molotov, LP Beria, and GM Malenkov (see below), and Stalin's approval as formulated in Dimitrov's instructions to its Iranian agents — Artashes (Ardashir) Avanesian and Reza Rousta — shaped not only the policies of the 'party group', which was to be renamed the 'Hezb-e Tudeh-ye Iran' before Dimitrov's letter was sent to Stalin on 9 December 1941 (18 Azar 1320), but also strongly influenced the destiny of the Iranian left and Iranian national politics for the next four decades.[49]

The Role of Other Soviet Authorities in Founding the Tudeh

In the meantime, an NKVD official, and Stalin's chief of Foreign Intelligence, PM Fitin,[50] wrote to Dimitrov on 5 November 1941 (14 Aban 1320) informing him of the developments concerning the formation of the Tudeh (Popular)[51] Party in Tehran. According to Fitin's account, some 100 members and sympathisers of the Iranian Communist Party had been released from prison or exile. Six Communist activists had constituted 'a guiding kernel' to work 'under the cover of the so-called Popular Party of Solayman Mirza'. This 'kernel' was composed of Artashes Avanesian, Reza Rousta, Iraj Eskandari, Morteza Yazdi, Mohammad Bahrami and Reza Radmanesh, a short biographical notice of each of whom was sent by Fitin to Dimitrov.[52]

Fitin informed Dimitrov that the last five had entered the composition of the 15-member 'unofficial Central Committee' of the Tudeh Party. The programme of the Tudeh was of a 'bourgeois-democratic and anti-fascist content'.

The programme of the 'underground Communist party at present' was:
1. Verification of the composition of the [Tudeh] party, its purging of suspects, provocateurs and Trotskyists.

2. Reinforcement of its [Communist Party's] influence within the Popular Party, so as to carry out under its cover the tasks elaborated in its programme.
3. Creation of party centres in localities, especially in Azerbaijan, organisers having already been sent to Tabriz, Reza'iyeh [Urmia], Sarab, Rasht and Mashhad.

Fitin further informed Dimitrov that the activity of the new Communist leadership proceeded slowly because its members had been 'disconnected' from the life of the country by imprisonment, and that for fear of repression they were acting 'timidly', as it was known that the police was watching the activists of the Communist Party. Fitin also noted that, in order to infiltrate the new Communist group, particularly its leadership, the British attempted, through their men and particularly the leader of the Liberal Party, Mostafa Fateh,[53] to establish contact with various Communist activists, offering them material support, arranging employment for them, etc.[54] Fitin informed Dimitrov that 'our [NKVD] cadres in Iran' had discussed the matter with some leading Communists, given them 'certain advice resulting from the prevailing conditions [in Iran], and granted them important material help'. Dimitrov was further advised that at the last session of the Provincial Bureau of the 'Communist Party' in Tehran, 'an application' for membership in the Comintern had been elaborated 'with the demand for instructions for further work. It was asked to send the reply through our [NKVD] cadres.' Artashes Avanesian had been designated for contact with the Comintern.

Fitin also let Dimitrov know that 'side by side with a highly secret ['conspiratorial' in Russian] relations of our cadres with the representatives of the Communist Party and the Popular [Tudeh] Party, a contact is maintained with the latter through uninvestigated and dubious individuals of the *polpred* [embassy] and the military attaché of the USSR in Iran, which might compromise the party in view of their lack of necessary secretiveness in contact.'[55]

While these discussions were taking place between various Soviet organs themselves, the Iranian Communist playwright Abdol-Hussein Noushin addressed a letter, in mid-November 1941, through the Comintern General-Secretary GM Dimitrov, to the Iranian Communist Morteza Alavi,[56] transmitting the 'greetings of Iranian prisoners', such as Bozorg Alavi and Mohammad Bahrami, 'to those [Iranian comrades] in the USSR'. This was obviously an attempt to encourage the return to Iran of the Iranian Communists who had been resident in the Soviet Union since the late 1920s and the early 1930s, the writer being unaware of what had happened to a large number of them during the purges.

Once the question of the presence of Iranian Communists in the Soviet

Union was raised by Noushin, the Cadres Section of the Comintern provided information on the following Iranian Communists who were still being held by the NKVD: M Akhundzadeh, Hasan Hasanov (Pourafar), A-H Hesabi (Dehzad), Kamran (N Aslani), Ladbon Esfandiari, Mir A-Q Asadi,[57] K Nikbin and H Rezaev (Sharqi).[58] The Director of the Cadres Section of the Comintern, Guliaev,[59] noted in his letter to Dimitrov that 'the majority' of those to whom the greeting from Iranian prisoners were addressed were 'being repressed by the organs of the NKVD'. Guliaev remarked that there was 'nothing astonishing' about the greetings from the Tehran prison, because Alavi or Bahrami 'cannot know what [had] happened to their former party comrades'.

Guliaev, the Director of the Cadres Section of the Comintern, recommended to Dimitrov that it:

> ... would be desirable to put up to the NKVD leadership the question of hastening the re-examination of cases of certain Iranians arrested in 1937 and 1938, and those of Kamran and Hesabi with priority, in whose personal records there are many positive reports as to their work in the conditions of Iranian underground.[60]

In connection with Noushin's 'suggestions about sending members of the ICP from the USSR to Iran' or calling representatives of Iranian Communists to Ashkkabad 'to discuss' the question of the re-establishment of the ICP, the Comintern Cadres Section considered it 'essential to hurry the departure of [other] comrades prepared for work in Iran [see below], supplying them with appropriate instructions'. Independently of the departure of such groups, 'it would be useful *to summon to the IKKI*[61] *comrades Reza Rousta (Farhad) and Artashes Avanesian*,[62] or possibly both, to receive from them detailed information regarding the situation in Iran, especially about the cadres of the CP who are reassembling again after liberation from prison'. Guliaev added that according to the material in the Comintern archives,[63] both '*Avanesian and Rousta* [had] *behaved in prison as the most firm comrades*',[64] that is, had been most faithful to the Soviet line under Stalin.[65] The Cadres Section also pointed out that it was 'essential' to inform Iranian Communists that 'their idea' of joining the leadership of Eskandari's Tudeh Party a legal cover 'deserves approval'.

Guliaev, recalling Eskandari's reputation among the 'radical, democratic and nationalist circles' and his past 'struggle for democratic change in Iran', further emphasised that his party could 'become the centre of attraction for all progressive elements in Iranian society', thereby helping the Communists to:

> ... prepare the basis for the mobilisation of the Iranian masses according to the platform of the struggle against the threat of bloody Hitlerism and

for friendship with the peoples of the USSR, as well as that of a struggle for the democratic rights of the people of Iran and the improvement of material conditions of workers.

As regards the problem of the 'Committee of the Iranian People', formed by Iranian Communists recently released from prison, such as Avanesian and Rousta, as well as the re-establishment of the ICP 'in the present complex situation in Iran, and in such a case, in what organisational form', on 21 November 1941 Guliaev still found it 'very hard' to make a 'definite judgement'. He, therefore, recommended it as 'necessary to receive urgently the fullest possible information about the direction and forms of the movement that was developing under the new regime [*sic*, the shah] in Iran, the newly established parties and social groups, as well their influence among the Iranian masses'.

Furthermore, he found it:

... more useful under the present conditions to direct the energy of Iranian Communists, not towards the re-establishment of the Communist Party, but — primarily — towards the creation and reinforcement of a wider popular party with the participation and active role of Iranian Communists, acting within the framework of this party, and with a single political line agreed upon with the leadership of the IKKI. In such a case, Iranian Communists would act *as a Communist fraction in the framework* of the Popular [Tudeh] Party, but they would have to be covered by some other designation, corresponding to the legal bloc of the left national elements.[66]

Recalling that under Reza Shah even the 'Iranian bourgeoisie' had not enjoyed the right to an organisation of its own, and that the ICP, leading an underground existence until 1936, was supported by no more than 'very limited strata of workers', Guliaev recommended that Iranian Communists, working within the framework of the Tudeh Party and reinforcing their position in it, 'must work, with redoubled energy, at the establishment of labour unions and peasant organisations, thereby laying the basis for the re-establishment of a strong, influential Communist Party'. The Cadres Section of the Comintern considered it 'as absolutely essential to ensure the possibility of discussing these questions before the departure of the Iranian group',[67] namely, the four individuals it had designated to oversee or control Communist activity in Iran (see below).

Comintern's Instructions

Once the programme took shape, on 9 December 1941 (18 Azar 1320)[68] Dimitrov informed Stalin and his closest associates at the time (Molotov,

Beria and Malenkov), asking no doubt for the Soviet leader's approval of the Comintern's united front programme in opposition to the fully Communist initiative of such individuals as Avanesian and Rousta. Because of its historical significance, this letter is quoted in full:

> The group of Iranian Communists, formerly political prisoners, undertook the re-establishment of the Iranian Communist Party. They created a provisional bureau, appointed one comrade, Artashes Avanesian, for contact with the IKKI and are applying to us [the Comintern] for instruction. They also sought our agreement to send their delegate to us. According to the material of the Cadres Section of the IKKI and on the basis of the information provided by NKVD cadres, who are in contact with them locally [in Tehran], it can be considered that these Iranian Communists are absolutely honest revolutionaries and pro-Soviet individuals. At the same time, the Popular Party [Hezb-e Tudeh] has been created in Iran by the militant democrat Solayman Mirza [Eskandari], with a democratic programme. For the last 30 years [Solayman] Mirza has been leading the struggle for the democratic transformation in Iran. A group of Iranian Communists are participating in this Popular Party [Hezb-e Tudeh].
>
> Taking into consideration the special conditions in Iran (occupation together with the British, demagogic and subversive activity by Hitlerites and their agents, as well as the distrustful and hostile attitude of a part of Iran's ruling circles [towards the Soviets], we consider that the re-establishment of the Iranian Communist Party, which always was a small sectarian group,[69] will hardly be useful at the present time and will certainly cause difficulties and complications. This [initiative] will reinforce suspicion and dissatisfaction in the ranks of Iran's ruling circles, enabling German agents to frighten the Iranian bourgeoisie with the possibility of the Sovietisation of Iran, and the British themselves will suspect the Soviet Union more of attempting, in their view, to Sovietise Iran.

For these reasons, Dimitrov went on:

> I consider that in the present circumstances one should not recreate the Communist Party and [Iranian] Communists must work within the Popular [Tudeh] Party, along the following lines:
> 1. To struggle for the democratisation of Iran.
> 2. To defend the interests of workers.
> 3. To reinforce friendly relations between Iran and the Soviet Union.
> 4. To eliminate completely the fascist agency in Iran and to abolish anti-

Soviet propaganda [there].

5. Together with this [agenda], Communists must work for the establishment of professional [labour] unions and peasant organisations. I also consider it useless for Iranian Communists to send a delegate to us [at the Comintern]. Instead, we would dispatch our suitable comrades under an appropriate legal cover. He could help the Iranian comrades to carry out this line [of work]. Unless otherwise instructed by you, I plan to advise the Iranian comrades along this line.[70]

There is little doubt that the response by Stalin,[71] or one of his close associates, was positive, since only a week later Dimitrov addressed a letter to Artashes Avanesian, instructing him how Iranian Communists should conduct themselves, exactly according to his programme submitted to Stalin and within the new circumstances:

> The IKKI considers that in the present situation we should not re-establish the Iranian Communist Party. Communists must work in the Popular Party of Solayman Mirza [Eskandari]. Their task is to pursue a firm, sustained line in: a) struggling for the democratisation of Iran; b) defending the interest of Iranian workers; c) reinforcing friendly relations between Iran and the Soviet Union; d) destroying completely the agency of fascism in Iran and frustrating anti-Soviet propaganda. It must be endeavoured to unite all the democratic and progressive elements in Iran on the basis of this platform. Together with this endeavour, Communists must work for the creation of labour unions and peasant organisations to defend the daily interests and demands of workers and peasants.
>
> At the present stage we must not display socialist and Soviet slogans; we must not abandon the framework of a democratic platform. It is necessary to carry out propaganda, explanatory work in the spirit of Marxism-Leninism, especially among the young generation of Iran, but carefully and prudently. A few active Communists, honest and fully scrutinised [that is, filtered by the NKVD], entering into the Popular [Tudeh] Party must be linked together — but not openly — so as to be able to put into work the policy outlined above. It is absolutely essential to establish the most friendly relations with Solayman Mirza. At present, I do not consider it useful for you to send a representative to the USSR. Such an arrival would be made use of by [our] enemies and would harm your work. Keep us regularly informed of the situation in Iran and of the activity of the Popular Party. Confirm the receipt of this letter.[72]

Plan for a Communist United Front in Iran

At the same time, the Comintern worked out a plan for assistance to Communist activity not only in Iran, to the Tudeh Party as a 'united, anti-fascist front', but also to other Communists in the neighbouring lands.

For the execution of this plan (which is incomplete in the Comintern archives),[73] a group of cadres were designated by the IKKI to go to Iran; their tasks were:

> Organisation of lines of contact with the Communist Parties of:
> 1. Arab countries (Syria, Palestine, Egypt and Iraq).
> 2. India, according to one or two variants as follows.
>   a. Through Basra or Iraqi territory.
>   b. Through the Iranian ports of the Persian Gulf.
>   c. Through Afghanistan.
>   d. Through British Baluchistan [now Pakistan].
> 3. Organisation of direct relations with Iran (establishment of their own radio transmitter).
> 4. Organisational and technical assistance to Iranian Communists for the creation of mass organisations and then in the re-establishment of the Iranian Communist Party.[74]

The plan further stated that:

> In order to put into effect the tasks presented to the group, its members will receive special schooling according to the division of responsibilities between them.

The group was composed of four individuals: K, A, Sh and R. From among these, only two could be identified from the documents available in the Comintern files: A, that is, Fath-Allah Adelov[75] and Sh, that is, Zolaykha Sharif (Asadi).[76] While the detailed description of the tasks of K, A and R were not to be found in the open Comintern archives, Sharif Asadi's were briefly mentioned:

> An Iranian national, she was to go first to Iran. In possession of an Iranian passport, she was to leave towards the end of 1941 through the Turkmeno-Iranian frontier, with the 'legend' that she had completed her medical studies in the Soviet Union, with two years of practical training in hospitals and now was returning to her country. In Tehran she would open a 'private hospital' [clinic]. This enterprise would be financed partly by the funds she would take with her and partly by what her father would provide her with in Tehran.

It was added: 'In reality, we must give her the funds for the organisation of the hospital.'

The Anti-Fascist Programme

A study of the said programme and its related instructions would help us understand the Soviet united front tactics during the anti-fascist war.

On 8 November 1941, Colonel Seliukov, Chief of the Second Section of the Third Department of Intelligence of the Red Army, enclosed SM Eskandari's anti-fascist party programme to the records of conversations he had held with the latter and sent them to his superiors and the Comintern. The programme is as follows:

Introduction

At a time when national independence around the world finds itself threatened by dictatorial regimes and despotism, and when the liberty of the individual, won in the course of centuries at the cost of bloody revolutionary struggle, is being destroyed by dictators and enslavers, when international reaction stamps out and destroys all national liberties, the Iranian people, who were, for the last 20 years, in the clutches of despotism and tyranny, having had to bear the greatest evil and misfortunes, have once more tasted the happiness of freedom.

In order to acquire true freedom and the full destruction of the remnants of the past tyranny and violence, on the one hand, and to deny reaction and despotism the possibility of taking advantage of the situation so as to enslave once more the Iranian people for its own criminal interests, an Iranian group is organised in Tehran. It represents all free Iranians and the working class. It calls upon all the freedom-loving, democratic and enslaved Iranians to unite around it [the group] so as to obtain the satisfaction of their just demands, to establish a democratic regime, and to declare the downfall of reaction and despotism.

The Main Objective of the Group

1. Preserving the independence and integrity of Iran.
2. Establishing a democratic regime and the granting of all personal and social rights to man, such as the freedom of expression (oral and written), of opinion, and of assembly.
3. Combating all kinds of dictatorial and despotic regimes.
4. [Carrying out] the necessary reforms with the objective of making use of land. Organisation of a normal way of life for peasants and workers in Iran.
5. Reforming education and health preservation as well as introducing

generalised, compulsory and free education; providing the popular masses with the benefits of culture and health preservation.
6. Establishing just taxation, taking into consideration the interests of popular masses.
7. Reforming the economy and trade, developing industry, the mines of useful subterranean products, as well as the transport system, such as the building and the preservation of a vast network of roads and the improvement of the railways.
8. Confiscating, in favour of the Iranian people, the properties of the former shah and his supporters who acquired them through criminal and tyrannical abuse of their power.[77]

All the preceding is confirmed by the founders of the party group and will be in force until the party conference is organised. In order to put into effect the above, and taking into consideration the present situation in Iran, the party group sets itself the following tasks:
1. To organise new elections for the Majles; to ensure the election of true representatives of the people and the freedom of elections; and to eliminate all kinds of intrigues.
2. To put an end to the arbitrariness of those in power and to destroy the police state.
3. To raise the standard of living of the popular masses and to modify employment laws so that salaries ensure the vital minimum for civil servants.
4. To struggle in a determined manner against pilferage of state property, bribery and all kinds of illegal use of positions in [government] service.
5. To compensate morally and materially those who under the former shah were subjected to persecution and tyranny. To demand the re-transfer of lands belonging to petty landowners and peasants from whom they had been taken by force.
6. To prosecute according to law and punish the people who harmed the country and freedoms, as well as those who oppressed and suppressed the personal and social rights of man.
7. To provide social security for the people and to facilitate their moral and material life. Special attention must be paid to the creation of larger quantities and cheaper prices of food products. The most intense struggle must be waged against speculation and price increases.
8. To ensure the independence of judges and the real separation of the executive and judicial branches of the state.
9. To abolish all loans and forced orders that existed under the former shah and were meant to harm the popular masses.

10. To change the laws and regulations of military service in the interest of popular masses and to stop the application of violence and disorder in this domain.[78]

New Encounters between Soviet Officials and Eskandari

In a second meeting[79] between SM Eskandari and the Soviet official AA Kuznetsov in late February 1942,[80] the former informed the latter of the imminent arrival of Seyyed Zia Tabataba'i, the notorious pro-British politician who had jointly carried out the coup with Colonel Reza Khan in 1921,[81] and who had been exiled by the latter on account of personal rivalry. Along with a number of other right-wing politicians supporting the 'firm-hand policy', such as M Tadayyon and General Ahmadi, Seyyed Zia was a candidate for the premiership. Further, discussing the growing audacity of the pro-Nazi group distributing handbills declaring 'Long Live Iran and Germany', Eskandari lamented that in the 'absence of a mass party' the reactionaries 'will easily re-establish the military dictatorship'.

As regards the progress of the Tudeh, he added that cells had been organised in Arak, Isfahan, Rasht, Tabriz, Kashan and some other localities.[82] In Tabriz, cell members had gone up to 2500. With regard to the question, put to him by his representative Sartipzadeh, of the attachment of Azerbaijan,[83] from the linguistic viewpoint, to the USSR or Turkey, Eskandari said that he had replied that:

> ... now was not the time to raise this question. It was necessary to uphold the integrity of Iran, because the language was not the most important point; it is required to improve the conditions of the people's living standard and to hold the party in readiness in case of necessity to prevent an attempt to restore the military dictatorship.[84]

Eskandari went on to state that his 'second task was the establishment of a newspaper which he considered essential to publish as the organ of the Popular [Tudeh] Party, adding that he [had] decided to act openly and decisively, otherwise we would be lost as a party.'

Having received a verbal authorisation for the publication of the newspaper, Eskandari thought that even if he managed to publish it, he feared that 'it would be rapidly closed down as in the second issue he would [certainly] publish the programme of the Popular Party'.

Come what may, he was determined to act firmly: 'We must make ourselves known, otherwise we will be strangled one by one.' Then he proceeded to tell his Soviet interlocutor that: 'I am awaiting your advice and help. Statements alone of non-intervention in [Iran's] internal affairs can have regrettable consequences, as happened 20 years ago.'[85] That is when the dictatorship of Reza Khan was installed with British support.

Degradation of the Economic Situation in 1942 and the Tudeh's Success

In a report by the Soviet Naval Intelligence Directorate,[86] Captain Vorontsov provided very interesting accounts of the situation in Iran during 1942: the severe deterioration of economic conditions in Iran; population of entire provinces starving; people dying in the streets in consequence of the scarcity of bread; cities filled with beggars arriving from starving villages; 3000 people in Rasht taking part in pilferage of rice stores: people were killed and injured; fascist propaganda arousing anti-Soviet and anti-British feelings amongst the people; the situation in Iran 'produced different [political] currents in the government circles and among certain influential people'. One of the 'small groups principally working for their own interests and endeavour to reinforce their influence on the government through gaining the support of the people by demagogic manifestations' was the Tudeh Party, which acted legally: 'The leaders of this party have a secret ['conspiratorial' in Russian] centre.' The party published the newspapers *Surat* in Rasht, *Siasat* and *Mardom* in Tehran; and 'the main objective' of the party was 'to improve the situation of the workers of Iran'.

Tudeh's First Self-Image

A report that seems to be an account of the Tudeh's founding and a first annual summary of its activities, sent to the Comintern most probably by Artashes Avanesian, the contact man with the IKKI, notes that the party was organised at the end of 1941, its 'initiators' having been Communists released from prison on the basis of the amnesty granted on the occasion of the accession to the throne of the new shah. Unaware of the secret six-week long discussions between Eskandari and Colonel Seliukov, the report further states:

> After [their] release from Tehran prisons, there formed a group by Communists and intellectuals sympathising with them, who had been condemned to prison terms along with the Communists, that is, Abol-Qasem Asadi, Iraj Eskandari, Dr [Morteza] Yazdi and Reza Rousta. It was decided to create an illegal provisional bureau of the Communist Party, composed of Reza Rousta, Iraj Eskandari, Dr Yazdi, Dr [Reza] Radmanesh and Dr [Mohammad] Bahrami, all of them [except Rousta] were members of the famous group of the 'Fifty-Three'. The bureau decided to establish links with the IKKI. It appointed Artashes Avanesian, who still was in [internal] exile, for this purpose.[87]

The bureau undertook the struggle for the liberation of all Communists, particularly of those condemned in connection with the case of the 'Fifty-Three'. With this task in view, all means were used, including pressure on ministers and parliamentary deputies. Three or four illegal cells were created in Tehran, composed of some 20 men. It was decided to develop all activities on the basis of organisational principles of the Communist Party.

Unaware of the Seliukov–Eskandari secret talks, the author of the annual report notes that the creation of the Tudeh as an 'anti-fascist party' was the idea of the Communist group, which negotiated it successfully with Eskandari, and that a special commission composed of Communists and democrats 'elaborated the party programme'. Subsequently, an organisational assembly of the party was planned, which chose a 'provisional Central Committee'[88] of 15 members. Of the list of the 15 Central Committee members the author provides,[89] except for the first four, the rest had been members of either the ICP or the 'Fifty-Three'.

The report also remarks that when the police threatened Tudeh Central Committee members with banishment from Tehran, the intellectuals among them 'were somewhat afraid'. Thus the Central Committee 'attempted to obtain the support of the Soviet Embassy, with which it entered into contact through Bloshapkin, previously known to Reza Rousta'. At the same time, the Central Committee sought to win the support of the popular masses. The majority of Central Committee members were sent to the provinces, and their trips were 'crowned with success'. Organisations of the Tudeh Party were started 'everywhere'. Yet the report adds that the party was 'not yet numerically large'. Towards September 1942, it counted only 2087 registered members, of whom 1137 were in Tehran and 950 in the provinces.[90] With over 50 per cent working-class membership, this 'sole mass party' in the country 'obliged the government to take it into consideration'.[91]

This incomplete (mutilated) report ends with the comment that the 'weak aspect' of the Tudeh was the non-involvement of the peasantry in party work.

Another report sent, ostensibly on the occasion of the twenty-fifth anniversary of the Bolsheviks' seizure of power in 1917, from Tehran on 7 November 1942, by Artashes Avanesian, informs the Comintern of the composition of the Tudeh Central Committee, with which the author does not seem to have agreed, as 'I did not take part in selecting the existing CC members because I was in prison at Bandar 'Abbas'. Avanesian recommends to the Comintern to study the separate report he had made to the Communist International on the 'characteristics' of the Tudeh Central Committee members — a report that was not to be found in the archives. He also tells the Comintern that upon his release and arrival in Tehran: 'I said that this CC is not wholly suited and is not able to lead the mass movement. ... I also pointed out that the programme of the Tudeh Party is incomplete and promises nothing concrete to the workers and peasants.'[92]

Along with the second report on the Tudeh's first year of existence, the Comintern archives contain a message greetings from Artashes Avanesian to Stalin and the Soviet Central Committee, also dated 7 November 1942, the twenty-fifth anniversary of the October Revolution. Sent to the 'Great Leader and Friend', the message conveys the sentiments of the Communist group within the Tudeh. It indicates that for its author and his companions 'in struggle there is no greater honour than the leadership of the bold battle of the Soviet people against the black armies of reaction and imperialism'. Certain that victory will be Stalin's in this 'sacred war', Avanesian stated that 'workers of the whole world contemplate with admiration the heroic battle of the people of the USSR, the glorious defence of steel fortresses [note the pun with the meaning of Stalin in Russian![93]] of Leningrad, Moscow, Sebastopol and especially Leningrad, realising that the Soviet people are indebted to your [Stalin's] wise leadership for these victories'. Preserving 'the great legacy of Lenin against the attempts of filthy fascist bands', Stalin was 'leading the Soviet Union to victory in this war, the most horrible in the history of mankind'.

Idolisation of Stalin went even further for the Tudeh leader:

> To you befell the greatest honour, to guide the struggle of the proletariat during the period of the underground [work], at the time of the revolution, and finally the construction of the first socialist state. Today, after 25 years of work and victories on the socialist front, we send you, the great leader and friend, [our] warm, revolutionary greetings.

In conclusion, Avanesian expresses the hope that:

> ... for many long years, you will, together with the steel party of Lenin, [continue to] lead the immense armies of workers in the battle for the final liberation of humanity from the yoke of capital. Long live the All-Russian Communist Party (b)! Long live the heroic Red Army! Long live the peoples of the USSR![94]

Conclusion

The evidence we have examined above clearly demonstrates that the Tudeh was a creation of the Soviet state, through the agency of its Red Army, thus demolishing the thesis that this organisation was a genuine party established independently by the progressive elements who had been released from Reza Shah's jails on the morrow of Iran's occupation by the Allies. On the other hand, while there is some 'congruence' between the 'Aliev thesis' and what we have documented in this study, it is important to put an end to the myth disseminated by the SAVAK, which, precisely because it is a myth, would cut both ways, particularly when used by some Communist penitents whose repetition of the myth is denounced along with their repentance by the faithful. In the same breath it must be added, however, that the Tudeh, though established through the agency of the Soviet Army, reflected and yet masterfully used a genuine desire by a number of political prisoners who had wished to lead a progressive political party that would play an important, if not decisive, role in the destiny of their country. The documentation we have perused above also demonstrates that the Soviets instrumentalised the Tudeh from the very outset for their own national interests. From the examination of the very first contact with SM Eskandari down to the detailed approval of its programme by not only the Comintern under Dimitrov, but also Stalin and his closest advisers, we can clearly see that the Tudeh was to be guided by the Soviets in the direction that served their interests. The manner of founding of the Tudeh foretold its expansion, policies in Iran's national politics, and final destiny.

It is thus not surprising that, in spite of the country's great suffering under Reza Shah's dictatorship for nearly 20 years, the strength of the Tudeh remained very limited in its first year of existence (autumn 1941 to autumn 1942), as Hitler's army moved deep into Soviet territory, but began to increase after the Soviet victory over the Reichswehr at Stalingrad in January 1943.[95] No less interesting is the fact that the Soviets, in spite of a clear request put to them by the Communist playwright Noushin and others, refused to return to Iran, and later executed, some Iranian Communists who had survived the great purges and still lived in NKVD detention camps. Apparently, this was due to the fear the Soviets had that a group of 'sectarian' Communists — as Dimitrov put it to Stalin — of the dissolved ICP would carry out policies that would isolate them in Iranian society during a crucial period. But the real reason must be sought elsewhere, that is, in the two decades of the independent line that the ICP had attempted to carry out in spite of Soviet guidance. It is clear that, in view of their alliance with the Western powers in a life-and-death struggle against a ferocious enemy such as Hitler, the Soviets could hardly afford, at a decisive moment, to bring onto Iran's sensitive political field Communists who had been critical of past Soviet policies in Iran. Still less could they afford to turn loose and promote such Communist leaders for the postwar period, as long-term Soviet interests would be threatened by the presence of critical Communists who had, in addition, tasted the fruit of the really existing 'Communist paradise'.

The naiveté of those young Tudeh leaders who, on the one hand, had been collaborators or students of Dr Taqi Arani[96] and had been arrested and jailed with him in 1937, and, on the other, their ignorance of the ICP's history and the Soviet experience partially due to the prevalence of political repression in Iran, prevented them from seeing the light of reality and the trap they were falling into in the hope of realising their ideal of saving Iran from the morass of colonial capitalism and indigenous dictatorship. It is for this reason that when the Tudeh leaders faced their challenge during the Soviet demand for an oil concession in Iran (the Kaftradze mission of the autumn of 1944),[97] they bungled completely and seriously risked losing their increasing popularity, particularly because on that issue they opposed the patrio-democratic leader Dr Mohammad Mosaddeq, not the Iranian reaction. On the occasion of the founding of the Azerbaijan and Kurdish autonomous governments in 1945-46, they also made grave mistakes and were identified in the eyes of the public at large with Soviet expansionism in Iran.[98] Their anti-democratic treatment of their dissidents, leading to the 1948 split, did not improve their public image either.[99] Although officially proscribed in February 1949 under the pretext of participating in a so-called attempt on the life of the shah,[100] the Tudeh remained strong until the advent of the oil nationalisation movement. The biggest challenge that the Tudeh faced was when it opposed Iran's national-democratic movement under Mosaddeq for the nationalisation of the Iranian petroleum industry, which had been in the hands of the British since the beginning of the century. The Tudeh's ferocious opposition to Mosaddeq and its labelling him as an 'American stooge' — no doubt a line recommended by its Soviet mentor — cost the party an enormous price, identifying it increasingly with Soviet interests in Iran. The Tudeh has since been blamed by most Iranians, including a good number of former Tudeh intellectuals, for having largely contributed to the success of the Anglo-American *coup d'état* in 1953.[101] Contrary to what has been generally claimed, the Tudeh, its military organisation included, was not vanquished by the CIA-supported Military Government that issued from the 1953 *coup d'état*, but by the doctrinal and programmatic crisis experienced by its leading cadres and members during the party's opposition to Mosaddeq, depriving them of the necessary confidence in a leadership that partly lived lethargically in Moscow exile and partly in underground at home.[102] The SAVAK only swept up the broken pieces of an organisation already shattered from the inside by Mosaddeq's patriotic and democratic challenge. The revival of the party leadership in 1957 under Khrushchev and the self-criticism made at the fourth party plenum[103] in the same year did not improve the image of the party at home and among its former cadres, nor the new split in 1964 provoked by its pro-Chinese wing. The Tudeh's role in the struggle against the guerrilla groups at home in the 1970s; the party's timid approval of the royal reforms in the same decade under the new General-Secretary Iraj Eskandari, while

Soviet relations with Tehran were steadily improving; the sudden removal of Eskandari and the appointment of Noureddin Kianouri, in January 1979, on the eve of the revolution;[104] support for Khomeini's line under Kianouri;[105] and the unconditional support the party leadership always gave to the Soviet state and party, all appeared to be, not without reason, a reflection of the Tudeh's total subservience to Soviet interests in Iran.

Paradoxically, the life of the Tudeh Party came to an end when the remnants of elements who still hung on to democratic ideals were forced to split from it after the death of Iraj Eskandari on the eve of May Day 1985, and not with the demise of the Soviet state in 1991.

Notes

1. This article was first published in *Cahier du monde russe* (Paris), July-September 1999. The author wishes to express his most sincere thanks to the late Mary Dumont for her assistance with the translation of Russian documents.
2. One of the folkloric theses regarding the establishment of the Tudeh Party is that during its first founding meeting Rostam Aliev, later a Soviet Iranologist at Baku, was present. This myth has been propagated by pro- and anti-Tudeh elements. Such a thoughtless thesis is advanced by Noureddin Kianouri, the Tudeh's last General Secretary in his *Khaterat* (Tehran, 1993), pp 73, 78; and by S Zabih, 'Communism ii', *Encyclopaedia Iranica*, Volume 6 (New York, 1992). According to a 'confession' in 1994 by Ahmad Ashraf, one of the editors of that publication, to this author while he was there too, this information was added by Ashraf with Zabih's consent. Among the 'repentant' pro-Soviet supporters of this inept notion is H Ahmadi, the interviewer and editor of *Memoirs of B Alavi* (Spånga, Sweden), who on page 257 quotes the 'repentant' Stalinist Anvar Khameh'i's claim in *Forsat-e bozorg-e az dastrafteh* (Tehran, 1984), p 21, 'that Rostam Aliev of the Soviet embassy was present' at the founding meeting of the Tudeh at Solayman Mirza Eskandari's residence. Admittedly, Khameh'i was still in prison at that date and based his information on what he had heard from 'those present' at the founding meeting of the Tudeh (ibid, p 22). The said editor who claims to have 'verified' this thesis with two other (unnamed) members of the 'Fifty-Three' puts the same question to Bozorg Alavi. The latter rejects this idea as a 'lie'. Alavi adds that it is not improbable that Reza Rousta, etc, had been in touch with the Russians and had made Eskandari understand that they had the Russians' support. As regards this folkloric thesis, it should be noted that Rostam Aliev was born in 1930, and at the time of Tudeh's founding was no older than 11 years old. He entered Leningrad University in 1949. This author personally met Aliev in September 1993 in Baku. He died of a heart attack a couple of years later. A British report in 1943 suggested that the Tudeh Party was founded either in 'late 1941 or early 1942' (see 'Extracts from the Review of the Foreign Press', no 182, 16 April 1943, FO 371/35061). This means that the British were not at the beginning either aware of or concerned about the founding of a pro-Soviet organisation.
3. Colonel 'Ali Ziba'i, *Komonizm dar Iran, ya tarikh-e mokhtasar-e fa'aliyat-e komonistha dar Iran az avval-e mashroutiyat, ta farvardin 1343* (*Communism*

in Iran, or a Short History of Communist Activity in Iran from the Beginning of Constitutionalism till March 1964, Tehran, 1964), pp 196ff. This was a book published by a former SAVAK officer who had previously taken part in the 1953 coup and helped the post-coup Military Governor of Tehran, General Bakhtiar, to dismantle the opposition to the shah, particularly the Tudeh Party's Military Organisation in 1954. The book is a descriptive mélange of materials collected from various sources, but unfortunately little from the Iranian archives. The book's stated purpose is to show how the workers', Socialist and Communist movement in Iran was an alien body in Iranian society and a tool of a foreign power. The colonel must have been assisted in his task by former Communists as researchers and editors. According to the former Tudeh officer F Azarnour, Ziba'i, who lives in Colorado, has written his memoirs.

4. A publication of the Tudeh, *Programme. Histoire*, Part 1 (Paris, 1977), p 1, claims the party was a '*continuateur*' (successor) of the Iranian Communist Party (ICP); the same claim is made by the Soviet Deputy Foreign Minister and 'adviser' of the Tudeh, NN Semionov ('Trente cinquième anniversaire du Parti Toudeh d'Iran', *Programme. Histoire*, Part 2 (Paris, 1977), p 1). The 'proletarian' nature of the Tudeh is also claimed by Gh-H Foroutan (1911-1998), a leading Stalinist member of the Tudeh Central Committee who turned pro-Chinese in 1965; he denies even the suggestions by such Tudeh leaders as Kianouri that the Soviets had proposed the founding of 'popular' party instead of a purely Communist organisation. See Foroutan's memoirs, *Yadha'i az gozashteh*, Volumes 1 and 2 (np, 1992-93).

5. For his positions in this regard, see C Chaqueri, 'Iraj Eskandary and the Tudeh Party of Iran', *Central Asian Survey*, Volume 7, no 4, 1988, pp 104-05, and his works listed in the bibliography.

6. For a number of contradictory claims, see the bibliography.

7. Historical evidence does not support this claim, although SM Eskandari replaced his murdered brother as the parliamentary leader of the Democratic Party. See C Chaqueri, *The Russo-Caucasian Origins of Iranian Social Democracy in the Iranian Constitutional Revolution, 1905-1911* (London, 2001), Chapter 6.

8. He belonged to the pro-German faction of the so-called National Government; see C Chaqueri, 'Solayman Mirza Eskandari', *Encyclopaedia Iranica*, Volume 8 (New York, 1998).

9. E Abrahamian, *Iran Between Two Revolutions* (Princeton, 1981), pp 281ff.

10. 'Transcription of Conversation with Solayman Mirza', dated 8 November 1941, RTsKhIDNI, 495/74/192; this report was forwarded by Brigade Commissar Il'ichev to the Comintern Secretary-General GM Dimitrov on 8 November 1941.

11. This is the official date of the founding of the Tudeh. Khameh'i, who refers to himself as 'one of known Tudeh leaders' between 1941 and 1948 (*Forsat*, p 10), but admittedly joined the Tudeh only in August 1944 (ibid, p 113), refers both to 29 September and 2 October 1941 (7 and 10 Mehr 1941) as the founding date of the Tudeh (ibid, pp 21 and 44).

12. The Soviet colonel depicts the apartment as having several rooms, 'poorly furnished with old furniture and cheap old carpets'.

13. The conversation was translated by a certain Erkush.

14. Emphasis in the original Russian.

15. 'Transcription of Conversation with Solayman Mirza', dated 8 November 1941, RTsKhIDNI, 495/74/192.
16. Regarding the pro-Nazi propaganda and positions of Reza Shah and his encourage, see IOR/L/PS/12/3513 (London) and Archives du Quai d'Orsay, Asie, Iran, 1930-40, Dossier 98.
17. Archives du Quai d'Orsay, Vichy, 1940-44, Dossier 288. According to information received by the French from the Turkish embassy, it was after the publication of an article in the official daily *Ettela'at* (10 September 1941) 'regretting that the Iranian government was forced to close down the German and Italian legations with which Iran entertained normal economic and political relations', that the British reached the conclusion that the shah must go. See Coiffard's Report dated 22 September 1941, in Archives du Quai d'Orsay, Vichy, 1940-44, Dossier 288.
18. See the German biography, 'Mohammed Resa Pahlawi, Schah in Iran' in 'Intern Biog Archiv', dated 16 October 1941, Iran A2000, Zentrales Staatarchiv (Potsdam). The German biographical notes: 'Um mit allen Mitteln seinen Thron zu erhalten, unterschrieb er am 20 September 1941 sogar einen Arrestbefehl gegen seinen Vater.' It is important to recall that, while the Soviets at this time supported the idea of establishing a republic in Iran, the British wished to return the Qajar dynasty to the throne. It was only after the meeting in London between Sir Anthony Eden and the son of the last Qajar Crown Prince Mohammed Hasan Mirza, the next Qajar prince in line for kingship, Prince Hamid, that the British decided in favour of Mohammed Reza, because the Qajar candidate turned out to be illiterate in Persian. Regarding the British initial attempt to restore the Qajars and the final decision to install Mohammed Reza Pahlavi as the new shah, see C Chaqueri, 'Pishinha-ye jomhouri...', *Ketab-e jom'ehha*, nos 2-3, 1985; FO 371/27205, 371/27212 and 371/27184; and Eshraghi, 'Anglo-Soviet Occupation of Iran', *Middle East Studies*, nos 1-3, 1984.
19. A view that is confirmed by the French legation at Tehran as well: 'Thus the population welcomes his abdication with relief and without regret.' See Coiffard's Report dated 22 September 1941, in Archive du Quai d'Orsay, Vichy, 1940-44, Dossier 288.
20. 'Transcription of Conversation with Solayman Mirza', dated 8 November 1941, RTsKhIDNI, 495/74/192. British Minister Bullard reported (19 September 1941, FO 371/27219) that at this time there was a discussion for fresh elections of the Thirteenth Majles which 'had begun under the [Reza] Shah's control and that [its] members already returned (just a quorum...) might be considered as the Shah's creature'. But Premier Foroughi and apparently Bullard believed that 'to dissolve [the] Majles would involve a departure from the Constitution and be an unfortunate precedent' — a 'precedent' that was finally appended to the Constitution in 1949 after the new shah's 'first *coup d'état*' in February 1949.
21. 'Transcription of Conversation with Solayman Mirza', dated 8 November 1941, RTsKhIDNI, 495/74/192.
22. Ibid.
23. I have not been able to identify Mr 'X' (letter Kh in Russian, which could also be a transliteration of Persian H), unless it refers to the Hamrahan Party created by Mostafa Fateh, the Iranian economist, the highest-ranking Iranian employee of

the Anglo-Iranian Oil Company, who was later put into relations with the Tudeh and helped, within the framework of the Anglo-Soviet entente during the war, to obtain the licence for the publication of *Mardom*, the Tudeh Party's daily. Curiously, 'Hamrahan' in Persian means 'Fellow-travellers'!

24. The majority of them were Communists.
25. According to Khameh'i (*Forsat*, p 24) the amnesty law concerning these prisoners was adopted by the parliament on 16 October 1941.
26. It should be noted that as early as 18 September 1941, the Majles had, in private sessions, discussed, *inter alia*, the 'liberation of innocent prisoners'. See Bullard to FO, dated 18 September 1941, FO 371/27219.
27. Reportedly, the Soviets had also directly presented the Iranian government with a list of 'expected reforms', including the transfer of 'Crown' properties to the people, reduction of taxation, with which the British and Premier Foroughi seemed to be in agreement; there were other demands on the Soviet ambassador's list which 'aroused the anxiety' of the Premier and his Foreign Minister, namely, 'a moderate constitution giving the majority of the population the right to elect [the] Majles' and 'a minimum of local self-government'. See Bullard to FO, dated 19 September 1941, FO 371/27219.
28. Eskandari had been one of the few non-Communist Iranians invited to that event (see C Chaqueri, 'Solayman Mirza Eskandari', *Encyclopaedia Iranica*, Volume 8 (New York, 1998). Some of the others were the journalists 'Ali Dashti and Farrokhi Yazdi, both of whose newspapers had been subsidised, along with Eskandari's Socialist Party, by the Soviets in the early 1920s. In June 1923, the Soviet envoy in Iran Shumiatskii was reported to have paid a number of pro-Soviet newspapers editors: Lesani for *Kar*, 150 *toman*s; 'A Dashti, for *Shafaq-e sorkh*, 160 *toman*s; and Mohammed Vosouq Homayouni, some 100 tomans for *Paykar*; Eskandari's Socialist Party received 2000 *toman*s (see Intelligence Summary, no 23, 19 June 1923, and Intelligence Summary, no 31, 4 August 1923, in FO 416/73). Even as late as 1929, the British ambassador Clive reported from Tehran to Henderson at the Foreign Office (16 July 1929; FO 316/85) that Taymourtash had, in response to his inquiry whether Iranian Communists had any influence in relations with Moscow, stated that Eskandari, though living in Tehran and 'fairly harmless', 'no doubt… still had communication with Moscow'.
29. 'Transcription of conversation with Solayman Mirza', dated 8 November 1941, RTsKhIDNI, 495/74/192.
30. The delay may have been due to the Soviet anticipation that the party executive would be elected on 10 October.
31. Khameh'i (*Forsat*, p 22) says that the programme was adopted on 29 September and not 10 October 1941.
32. The British Embassy report on the first General Conference of the Tudeh Party (held in Tehran during 1-12 August 1944) was that the 'moderation' of the Tudeh programme was 'clearly dictated by the tactical needs of the party in its struggle for power rather than ideological considerations' (British Embassy Report dated 26 August 1944, FO 371/40187).
33. A Communist trained at the Communist University for Workers of the East (KUTV), imprisoned under Reza Shah, and later the leader of the Tudeh-led

labour unions until 1949. He died in exile in the late 1960s.
34. 'Transcription of Conversation with Solayman Mirza', dated 8 November 1941, RTsKhIDNI, 495/74/192.
35. It should be noted that the Qashqa'is, like Eskandari himself, had had pro-German leanings and had collaborated with the Reich during the First World War. See Chaqueri, 'Solayman Mirza Eskandari', *Encyclopaedia Iranica*, Volume 8 (New York, 1998); see also C Chaqueri, *The Soviet Socialist Republic of Iran, 1920-1921: Birth of the Trauma* (Pittsburgh, 1995), pp 53, 86-87.
36. 'Transcription of Conversation with Solayman Mirza', dated 8 November 1941, RTsKhIDNI, 495/74/192.
37. Apparently, the programme of the Tudeh was first published in Arak, as *Siasat*, the organ of the organisation, stated on 24 July 1942 that 'the aims of the Tudeh Party of Arak' were 'the independence of Persia, struggle against reaction and dictatorship, and the strengthening of the fundamental laws of the country'. See 'Extracts from the Review of the Foreign Press', no 182, 16 April 1943, FO 371/35061.
38. This attitude was not to last for long, as Eskandari finally met the shah. For instance, in late August 1943 the shah told a British diplomat that he had just had a 'satisfactory talk' with Eskandari, and that he was about to see Qavam al-Saltaneh, who had also expressed a wish to see him. See 'Minutes' recorded by a British diplomat on 1 September 1943, in FO 248/1427.
39. 'Transcription of Conversation with Solayman Mirza', dated 8 November 1941, RTsKhIDNI, 495/74/192.
40. Emphasis in the Russian original.
41. 'Transcription of Conversation with Solayman Mirza', 8 December 1941, RTsKhIDNI, 495/74/192. When forwarding the above report to GM Dimitrov on 8 December 1941, Brigade Commissar Il'ichev asked him 'to inform him of the possibility of transferring to a more competent person with regard to the work effected by him in Iran' (ibid). This means that a person with more experience in Iranian affairs was now needed to 'guide' Eskandari and his party.
42. Foroughi, a pro-British politician who had previously served Reza Shah, had fallen into disfavour with him. He was invited to take over the reins of power after the abdication of Reza Shah.
43. According to Khameh'i (*Forsat*, pp 25, 36), the first issue of the Tudeh organ *Siasat* was published on 22 February 1942 (3 Esfand 1320) and the 'anti-fascist' daily *Mardom*, on 31 January 1942 (11 Bahman 1320).
44. An old Social Democrat, said to have been a collaborator of the ICP in Tabriz in the 1920s. According to a report by the British consul (dated 9 July 1943, FO 248/1149), Sartipzadeh was, on the eve of the elections for the fourteenth Majles, being supported by the 'pro-German *Sahand* newspaper'. This was unlikely; see further below.
45. A veteran Social Democrat and member of the ICP, who had been excluded from the ICP, but remained pro-Soviet and whose daughter was sent to Iran from Moscow as a Comintern 'agent' in early 1942; see further below.
46. Apparently, this was a party organised by Baqerov, President of the Azerbaijan SSR, with an Azeri chauvinist bent, on the basis of which the Democratic Party of Azerbaijan was created in 1945. See further below.

47. Emphasis in the Russian original.
48. Colonel Seliukov, 'Transcription of Conversation with Solayman Mirza', dated [?] December 1941, RTsKhIDNI, 495/74/192.
49. Although aware of the 'extent to which the Soviet authorities are interested in the fortunes of the party' (British Embassy Report dated 26 August 1944, FO 371/40187), the British did not seem to have the slightest inkling that the Soviets had actually created it. This is a clear refutation of the pervasively held thesis in Iran that the British always knew what happened in Iran.
50. According to information supplied to this author by an old historian of the CPSU archives in Moscow, Fitin had been an NKVD cadre. This is confirmed by Amy Knight, *Beria: Stalin's First Lieutenant* (Princeton, 1993).
51. This is the first time the name 'Tudeh' is mentioned in the Soviet documents.
52. The first two had been members of the ICP and confirmed Stalinists, who had been in Reza Shah's prison in the 1930s; the last four had been arrested in 1937 and tried in 1938 as members of the Communist group called the 'Fifty-Three'.
53. The party was called Hamrahan. Fateh had been educated in the USA and was one of the rare Iranian managers of the Anglo-Iranian Oil Company, which was nationalised by the Iranian Premier Dr Mohammed Mosaddeq in 1951.
54. The two notoriously known cases are those of Bozorg Alavi, the Tudeh novelist (d 1997, Berlin), and Ehsan Tabari (d 1989, Tehran), later its ideologue, who worked for Victory House under the British embassy officer Miss Ann KS Lambton, but were later forced by the Soviets to resign and work for the Irano-Soviet Cultural Society and the TASS agency, respectively. The Comintern man in the Tudeh Party, Artashes (Ardashir) Avanesian, recalls in his unpublished memoirs *Khaterat Darbareh-ye rahbari va rahbaran-e Hezb-e Tudeh* (Yerevan, 1973-75, a copy of which is in this author's possession) his efforts to 'persuade' the two mentioned above to abandon their work in Victoria House and to work for the Russians in Tehran.
55. Fitin to Dimitrov, dated 5 November 1941, RTsKhIDNI, 495/74/192. This last remark about the Soviet military attaché apparently alluded to the complaint by Eskandari about Rousta mentioned above. Fitin's remark also reveals the multiplicity of Soviet contacts with their supporters in Iran, on the one hand, and the rivalry between different Soviet organisations in Iran, on the other.
56. The actual letter by Noushin was not in the relevant Comintern files consulted.
57. He was already back in Iran and working with Eskandari (see above); whether before the occupation of Iran or thereafter, it is not known.
58. Most Iranian Communists had perished in the purges; a few, such as the Communist poet A-Q Lahouti, had been living in exceptional comfort in Moscow or in the Asiatic republics, no doubt due to their collaboration with the Soviet secret police against their compatriots persecuted by the NKVD. For a sympathetic view of Lahouti's life in Moscow, see E Tabari, *Az didar-e khishtan* (Spånga, Sweden, 1997), pp 119ff.
59. Letter dated 21 November 1941, RTsKhIDNI, 495/74/192.
60. Emphasis in the original Russian. It seems that the Communists mentioned on this list were executed within a few months, 'understandably', because they could not have been returned to Iran with the likelihood that they would turn 'Trotskyist' or

'agent-provocateur' of the British!
61. The Executive Committee of the Communist International.
62. Emphasis in the original. This means that Avanesian or Rousta had not, by 21 November 1941, been in contact with the Comintern, but Rousta had been in relation with a member of the Soviet Embassy staff, Bloshapkin, about whose lack of secretiveness Fitin reported on 5 November to Dimitrov (see above).
63. These files were not available to this researcher during the two research visits to the RTsKhIDNI. It would be interesting to know who made these reports too.
64. Almost all accounts by Communists in Reza Shah's prisons relate the active defence of these two of Stalin's line against Trotsky and other rivals of Stalin.
65. This certainly means that the Soviet authorities had informers in prison other than Communists who kept them abreast of the conduct of Communist prisoners.
66. Emphases in the Russian original.
67. Guliaev to Dimitrov, dated 21 November 1941, RTsKhIDNI, 495/74/192.
68. This was more than two months after the date officially declared on which the Tudeh is said to have been founded.
69. The ICP was founded in 1920, and its leaders were, from the outset, always critical of Soviet policy in Iran. Their critique cost the lives of the most knowledgeable and experienced among them during the Stalinist purges. See C Chaqueri, 'Communism, Early Phase, Part 1', *Encyclopaedia Iranica*, Volume 6 (New York, 1992); C Chaqueri, *Victims of Faith: Iranian Communists and Soviet Russia, 1917-1940* (forthcoming).
70. Letter by GM Dimitrov, 'To Stalin, Molotov, Beria and Malenkov', RTsKhIDNI, 495/74/192.
71. Stalin's response was not found in the Comintern archives, because, I was told, all his correspondence is deposited in the Presidential Archives at the Kremlin, to which access by historians has been denied thus far.
72. Letter by GM Dimitrov, dated 15 December 1941, to Artashes Avanesian, RTsKhIDNI, 495/74/192.
73. The Comintern document being incomplete, it is certain that its more political details had been removed from the files before the opening of the archives in the early 1990s.
74. Further parts of this report were not in the Comintern archives.
75. Born in 1902 in the Iranian district of Samarkand, Adelov was an experienced Communist cadre. He had been trained at the KUTV (Communist University of the Toilers of the East) and Workers Faculty (*Rabfak*), knowing Persian, Uzbek, Tajik, Azeri Turkish and Russian. He had been a worker, an employee, a teacher and an educational director in Samarkand, as well as an agitprop director and a party official in Tajikistan. He had never been sanctioned by the All-Russian Communist Party, he had been rewarded by the Tajik SSR for his work, and he was described by Guliaev as having 'valuable qualities': modest, contemplative, prudent and a good observer of underground rules. He could perform his duties in Iran after undergoing 'special training' (Guliaev Report, dated 2 December 1941, RTsKhIDNI, 495/74/192).
76. Born in 1916 in Tehran, she was the daughter of Asadi, the veteran Social Democrat and ICP Central Committee member, who had been excluded from the ICP in

1930, but who had nevertheless remained 'pro-Soviet'. She had pursued medical studies in the USSR, become a physician, and had been member of the Komsomol between 1933 and 1937. She had been excluded from that organisation in 1937 because she had been allowed to join it in 1933 in violation of organisational rules. She had worked for Soviet medical institutions for two years. She was described by Guliaev as 'too trustful of people', for which reason she had to undergo 'special schooling' before being sent to her assignment in Iran as a 'transmission link'. She knew Persian, Russian and some German. See Guliaev's report on her and her father, dated 2 December 1941, in RTsKhIDNI, 495/74/192.

77. The content of this programme, not the exact wording, is provided by Khameh'i (*Forsat*, p 23); he does not indicate his source. A similar version of the 'Fundamental Principles' of the Tudeh and its first 'programme' is given by the Ziba'i SAVAK's handbook, *Komonizm dar Iran*, pp 199ff.
78. Sent by Colonel Seliukov, on 8 November 1941, RTsKhIDNI, 495/74/192.
79. The report of the first meeting with Kuznetsov was not in the Comintern files.
80. The date of the meeting is not mentioned on the document; on the other hand, it is remarked that one copy of the report of conversation was printed on 21 February 1942.
81. For an extensive history of this pro-British *coup d'état*, see Chaqueri, *The Soviet Socialist Republic of Iran, 1920-1921*, chapter 14.
82. According to a British report, by the time the first 'provincial conference' of the party was held on 9 October 1942, the Tudeh had at least provincial committees in Arak, Rasht, Qazvin and Azerbaijan. See 'Extracts from the Review of the Foreign Press', no 182, 16 April 1943, FO 371/35061.
83. Sartipzadeh had put the question to Eskandari because of his differences with pro-Baqerov elements in Tabriz who wanted to enter the Tudeh organisation, raising the question of 'autonomy', the Azeri language, etc, a line that Sartipzadeh strongly opposed. The embryo of the Autonomous Government of Azerbaijan was formed in 1945, this issue, which calls for a separate analysis, is discussed in a two letters in Persian by Asadi to Rousta (RTsKhIDNI, 495/90/218).
84. 'Transcription of Conversation' between SM Eskandari and AA Kuznetsov, 21 February 1942, sent by Lieutenant-Colonel Kalashnikov, RTsKhIDNI, 495/74/192.
85. Ibid.
86. Main Naval Staff of the Marine Fleet, dated 25 September 1942, Moscow, RTsKhIDNI, 495/74/195.
87. 'Popular Party and the Work of Iranian Communists', incomplete text, undated, but no doubt written in late December 1942. See RTsKhIDNI, 495/74/195.
88. Khameh'i (*Forsat*, pp 28-29) provides a different version of these developments and attributes the founding of the Communist group within the Tudeh to Artashes Avanesian. He also states that, after the death of SM Eskandari, Reza Rousta — not Avanesian — became the 'official contact' with the Soviets, not the Comintern, which is informally the same thing — a claim which does not tally with Dimitrov's report at the time.
89. SM Eskandari, 'Abbas Mirza Eskandari, 'Ali-Asghar Sartipzadeh, Abdol-Hussein Noushin, A-H Shafi'i, Mousavi, Bozorg Alavi, Mir Javad Javadzadeh Pishevari,

A-Q Asadi, Reza Rousta, Mohammad Bahrami, Iraj Eskandari, Reza Radmanesh and Morteza Yazdi; Khameh'i (*Forsat*, p 22) also provides a different list of the Central Committee.

90. This does not tally with the number given by SM Eskandari of over 2000 in Tabriz alone.
91. 'Popular Party and the Work of Iranian Communists', incomplete text, undated, but no doubt written in late December 1942. See RTsKhIDNI, 495/74/195.
92. Report by A Avanesian to the Executive of the Comintern, dated 7 November 1942; RTsKhIDNI, 495/74/195; this report was accompanied by a message sent to Dimitrov on the occasion of the twenty-fifth anniversary of the October Revolution.
93. It is widely known in Tudeh history that Avanesian's 'nom de guerre was 'Poulad', that is, Steel — Stalin.
94. Signed 'Artashes [Avanesian] on behalf of Aktiv', dated 7 November 1942, in RTsKhIDNI, 495/74/195. The group 'Aktiv' is not known; it must have been the same as the 'Communist kernel' within the Tudeh Party.
95. Although Semionov's figure of a Tudeh membership of 25 000 at its first congress in 1944 is exaggerated ('Trente cinquième anniversaire du Parti Toudeh d'Iran', *Programme. Histoire*, Part 2, p 2), it nevertheless witnessed a rapid inflation of several fold within the year following the Soviet victory at Stalingrad. The membership of the party seems to have grown very rapidly after the end of the war itself, for according to one delegate to the Tudeh's first congress held in the summer of 1944, 80 per cent of its membership was made up of 'veteran workers of the cause and only 20 per cent of new recruits' (British Embassy Report dated 26 August 1944, FO 371/40187).
96. Taqi Arani (1902-1940) had been educated in Berlin, where he had been introduced to Marxism and had been acquainted with such German Communist leaders as Willi Münzenberg, returned to Iran in 1929 and founded in 1934 the independent Marxist review *Donya*. He was contacted by a Comintern agent in 1935 and his secret intellectual circle was drawn into the 'new ICP' that was being formed by the Comintern after the dissolution of the ICP. The new group was then 'discovered' by the police upon the arrest of two other Comintern agents who confessed to the existence of a new Communist group with Arani at its head. Arani and the others were tried and condemned to various terms of prison. Only Arani died in prison, reportedly under terrible conditions imposed upon him. For a study of Arani's life and activities, see C Chaqueri (ed), *Historical Documents: The Workers', Social-Democratic, and Communist Movement in Iran* (23 volumes, Florence and Tehran, 1969-94), Volumes 14 and 15, 'Introduction'; C Chaqueri, *The Tragedy of Iranian Dissident Communists, 1926-1938* (forthcoming). Assertions or suggestions according to which Arani was the 'founder' of the Tudeh Party are obviously false, since Arani died in prison on 3 February 1940 and the Tudeh was founded in December 1941, nearly two years later; see, for instance, J Droz (ed), *Histoire Générale du Socialisme*, Volume 3 (Paris, 1977), pp 635-38, which implies that Arani founded the Tudeh.
97. For an account of this Soviet demand, see the debate in the fourteenth Majles (1944-46), including Dr Mohammed Mosaddeq's intervention, in H Kay Ostovan

(ed), *Siasat-e Movazeneh-ye Manfi* (two volumes, Tehran, 1948), Volume 1, pp 156-234.
98. On this issue, see L L'Estrange Fawcett, *Iran and the Cold War: The Azerbaijan Crisis of 1946* (Cambridge, 1992); see also its review by this author, *MESA Bulletin*, no 1, July 1993.
99. On the 1948 split, see J Al-e Ahmad, *Dar Khedmat va khianat roshanfekran* (Tehran, 1997), pp 420ff.
100. The Pahlavi regime's claim that in 1949 there was an 'attempt' on the life of the shah — after which the Tudeh was banned, repression was reinforced, and the Constitution was amended under anti-democratic conditions to increase the autocratic power of the shah — has never been questioned. In a detailed study of this issue I have, on the basis of irrefutable archival documents, demonstrated that the 'attempt' was fake and stage-managed by the royal court in order to re-establish Reza Shah's autocracy. See C Chaqueri, *The 'Perfect Crime'* (forthcoming).
101. See B Amirkhosrowi, *Nazari az daroun be Hezb-e Tudeh-ye Iran* (Tehran, 1996).
102. See Anonymous, *Karnameh-ye Mosaddeq va Hezb-e Tudeh* (two volumes, Florence, 1978-80).
103. See Chaqueri (ed), *Historical Documents*, Volume 1.
104. See C Chaqueri, 'Iraj Eskandari and Tudeh Party of Iran', *Central Asian Survey*, Volume 7, no 4, 1988, pp 113-15.
105. I Eskandari, 'U-Turns of Iran's Tudeh Party: What Eskandari told the CPSU in 1981', *Central Asian Survey*, no 1, 1988, reproduced in this issue of *Revolutionary History*.

Cosroe Chaqueri

The Iranian Left in the Twentieth Century
A Critical Appraisal of its Historiography

Foreword

This article was written upon invitation to a conference on the Iranian Left held in June 2000 at the School of Oriental and African Studies (University of London). It was organised by Dr Stephanie Cronin. When it came to its publication in a collection of papers presented at that conference, the organiser of the conference informed me in a letter dated 2 September 2002 that the publisher's readers (contrary to custom, she did not enclose copies of their letters), though 'concerned about [its] length, ... both are extremely complimentary about the scholarship and "immense amount of knowledge" displayed by your piece and consider it, as I do myself, essential to the success of the volume and of inestimable value, particularly to future researchers'. She added that both readers were 'concerned about the language employed in your article. Although they do not object to strong polemic, they feel the language is inappropriately strong, tending even sometimes towards the abusive.' I agreed that the piece was long, but thought that, as a first study ever on the subject, there was little one could do, since the structure of the article would make it very hard to condense. Nevertheless, I agreed that if reasonable short cuts could be proposed in such a way that the demonstrative arguments of the paper would not be damaged, I would consider them. I disagreed with her in regard to the 'strong language'. Next the editor sought my agreement regarding replies by one or two writers whose works are criticised in this historical paper. I agreed, provided that I could add a rejoinder, as is customary in academic journals. She said she did not agree with this customary rule. Next, I asked her at any rate to propose cuts and I would consider them. The cuts she proposed basically boiled down to the removal of frank criticism of Dr Ervand Abrahamian, whose book *Iran Between Two Revolutions* (Princeton, 1981) has become an 'authoritative source'. Precisely because of the serious errors, inexcusable omissions and intentional distortions in that book, I did not agree to the cuts proposed and told the editor that they amounted to censorship of my criticism of a friend of hers — a *démarche* that cannot be considered scholarly. My criticism of other historians such as Ann K Lambton, a scholar held in greater esteem in the academic field, or Shahram Chubin, a scholar of Abrahamian's standing, did not seem to trouble the editor. She wanted to save her historian friend. I, therefore, did not agree to the inclusion in her book of a censored version of my paper, although the chance that I would be able to publish it elsewhere was meagre. The simple reason for me was, and is, that I could not accept at any price the suppression of a value to which my whole life as an historian and human rights militant has been devoted.

Dr Cronin's attitude rather reminds me of that of the Labour Foreign Secretary Herbert Morrison who wanted to dictate his terms in the 'resolution' of the Iranian oil nationalisation dispute. Morrison and his Conservative successor Anthony Eden 'won', but at the price of contempt for the rules of which they pretended to be the standard-bearers.

As for me, I consider myself the spiritual disciple of Ali-Akbar Dehkhoda, as I have also learned much from Western scholars, including a renowned compatriot of Stephanie Cronin.[1] I cannot forget that Arnold Toynbee, the great British historian, held the chair of Byzantine and Modern Greek Language, Literature and History at the University of London, which was financed by a Greek foundation. During a visit to Asia Minor 1921, then under Greek occupation, he chose to express his opinion regarding the conduct of the Greek authorities in that area — an opinion that did not please the Greek foundation. When the latter put pressure on the university authorities, Toynbee, in a letter addressed to *The Times*, announced his resignation from the chair[2] — an example also rare in Western academic circles. What is more, I am quite aware, as others in a similar situation must be, that as an historian one makes more enemies by one's incorruptible exercise of duty, but, in spite of it all, one's attachment to impartiality, objectivity and the truth must remain unshakeable — the *profanum vulgus* never forgiving. By combating manipulative knowledge, our task as historians is to achieve enlightening knowledge.

Since the manuscript's readers for the publisher who had published my most recent book[3] had pointed out that without my contribution the book would be too weak, and not be seriously considered, after my refusal to be censored the editor sought a few additional articles — rehashed from previous published writings, themselves open to serious academic criticism — in order to 'fill the gap'. The result was published in May 2004.[4] The new book edited by Dr Cronin should also be subjected to the same criticism with which the rest of the writings on the Left has been subjected.

It thus becomes clear that from the very start the length of my contribution was no more than a pretext to censor the scrupulous and incontestable criticism made of Cronin's ideological friend and to rescue his reputation. But historians know that criticism is, by nature, dynamic and knows neither friends nor foes, still less frontiers. Modern civilisation rests on this foundation.

It is important to note that while the main body of this long article has remained what was written for the aforementioned conference in 2000, it has been improved upon and amended insofar as other questions have arisen that require criticism, as criticism can never satisfy itself by inertia.

Introduction

One of the many paradoxes of 'modern' Iran is the *dys*-development of the historiography of the Iranian Left. I see this process as paradoxical in relation to the practice of pre-modern historiographers/historians in the Persislamic world. In fact, the historiographers of the Persislamic world, although almost all belonging to the sphere of the ruling dynasties, can be classified into two categories: a) those who wrote court or, at best, dynastic (that is, official) histories; b) those who went beyond the exigencies of the court, and, aware of the concept or the craft of history, did not confine themselves to eulogies of the ruling dynasties; in addition; the latter group were historians in the modern sense of the world, as they possessed well-thought-out methodologies and were analytical. Thus, in various periods of the history of the Iranian world since the Arab conquest of Western and Central Asia, eminent historians and historiographers had produced great histories that Orientalists of the classical period (that is, before the real beginning of the ideological Cold War late in 1917) praised as valuable and serious works of scholarship, some of which have been translated into Latin, French, German and English. This is not to say that such serious historiographers/historians as Jarir Tabari (b 226-310/840-922),[5] Abol-Hasan Mas'oudi (d 344/955 or 346/957),[6] Abolfazl Mohammad Bal'ami (d 310/940), Mohammad b Khavand-Shah Balkhi Mirkhwand (author of *Rozat al-Safa*, d 903/1497 or 904/1498), Qiyas al-Din Khandemir (d ca 941/1534), 'Ata'-Malek 'Ata' al-Din Joveyni (623-681/1226-1283)[7], Hamd-Allah Mostofi (d 750/1349),[8] the well-known Safavid historiographer Eskandar Beg Monshi (934-1038/1527-1628),[9] and particularly the historians Abu 'Ali Ahmad b Miskawayh (d 421/1030; secretary and librarian at the Buyid court) as well as M Bayhaqi (385-470/995-1077),[10] not to speak of the astronomer/mathematician Abu-Rayhan-e Biruni (b 362/973), the author of a serious anthropological history of India,[11] were devoid of any shortcomings or that their works leave nothing to be desired. Indeed, like any other historian coming before or after them, they were subject to personal and professional subjectivities and the ideologies of the eras in which they lived. However, what distinguishes all such eminent historiographers/historians of the pre-modern Persislamic world from their successors is that, even if court chroniclers, they respected certain rules of the craft, most notably the mention of their sources and references — whether folkloric, mythological, documented and even oral — which they had used in order to write their historical accounts, most often viewing them with a critical eye. Some (the historians proper, such as Bayhaqi) were highly analytical and explained their methods as well as the craft or science of history itself (*'elm* or *fan-e tarikh*). They were openly against historical distortion, falsification, outright prevarication, careless and sloppy writing, or personal calumny of the figures they disliked — paradoxically in spite of the limited number of copies their works were reproduced by copyists, as opposed to the vast numbers that their successors score today. They endeavoured, as best they could, to distinguish between historical facts and mythological legends. At any rate, they hardly ever invented 'facts' of their own. Concisely, as Biruni remarked in the Introduction to his work on India: 'The truth does not follow our desires', or, better yet, as he put it, perhaps punningly, in response to the protestation of the imam of Ghazna's great mosque with regard to his construction of the mosque horologe on the basis of the Roman calendar: 'The measure of time is not a religious matter.'

When some of them, such as Mirkhwand, the author of *Rozat al-Safa*,[12] who thought the omission of some historical fact or event was 'expedient', they recommended the mention of such an omission, which implicitly recognised the conditions of political difficulty under which the historian/historiographer found himself. In historical writings, such historians condemned both eulogy and admonition. Formal eulogy of the ruling monarch or dynasty was not always tantamount to blind obedience in historical writings and, *ipso facto*, to falsification of the historical account, especially when it was concerned with events and periods prior to the lifetime of the authors themselves. Seldom were they amateurs, and they respected a code of conduct, even if at the service of a sovereign or a dynasty.

To be sure, the ideological element is always the twin of the historical writing, and it can never be totally eliminated. And in the case of even the most serious historians of this period, we can be sure that they believed in the implicit precepts of Islam, the Iranian monarchic tradition, and the like. But a comparative analysis of such writers among themselves as well as one with those of 'modern' Iran would emphasise the question of the degree of success in the approximate reconstruction of the past that we call history. Implicit historical concepts or the attachment of such writers to a court or dynasty seldom took the form of an ideological crusade against the enemies of the master on whom the historiographer/historian depended financially. There are of course exceptions, such as the *Siasatnameh*[13] of Khwajeh Nezam al-Molk Tousi (d 485/1092), wherein the author historically theorises the elimination of women from the domain of politics solely on account of his personal animosity towards the mother of the Saljuq monarch, who had been the cause of his removal from office, or commits a general ideological distortion of the historical account of the Mazdaki movement during the reign of the Sassanid king Anoushirvan, historically misnamed 'the Just'. There are others to be cited, but the essential trend that demarcates such pre-modern authors from their successors of 'modern' Iran, briefly, is that:

A: They were bound by respect for their sources.
B: As a rule, they seldom distorted intentionally the historical record for the sake of ideological or professional purposes, or rarely did they engage in an ideological crusade; as a result, there existed a plurality of historical views.
C: No less importantly, they were professional historiographers/historians with erudition, and highly skilled writers; above all, their promotion to the position of historian in their own lives, or their recognition posthumously as such, was the product of long years of education, scholarship and even literary refinement.

They could never be pompous claimants to something they did not possess. The secret of their own historical survival and the praise bestowed upon them by the Orientalism of the classical type resides in these qualities of theirs, of which many of their successors are devoid.

I: General Consideration of the Problematic of Sources in the Historiography of the Iranian Left

A striking contrast between, on the one hand, the state and organised groups in Persislamic history, or even in the pre-Islamic history of Persia, and, on the other, the unorganised movements which were totally annihilated by brute force is that the former left behind them histories which were, as remarked above, more often than not tainted with ideological considerations, and although not pluralistic in the modern sense, still not quite monolithic either; but the latter did not, or could not, leave any historical account for posterity at all. If the extinguished movements left no historical accounts of themselves, what we concavely know of them is through the hostile accounts that their official or ideological adversaries wrote about them. Such are, for instance, the history of Smerdis/Geomat (or the false Bardia), who revolted against the Achaeminid dynasty and was overthrown through the conspiracy led by Darius in 20/9/522 BC. The second so-called communistic mass rebellion led by Mazdak was also crushed in blood by King Anoushirvan, with no survivors capable of writing their own ideological version of the history of the movement. By contrast, the Isma'ilis, to name the most notable among them, because they managed to constitute a long-term movement, and even ephemerally a state, have survived and produced, in contrast to those totally liquidated, their own version of history, including a revisionist one crafted ever since a vast adverse propaganda began,[14] in the wake of the 'hostage crisis', in the West against what has been termed as 'Revolutionary Islam'.

In the same manner, the historiographies of the unsuccessful modern Leftist undertakings in Iran, which did not manage to constitute themselves as prolonged movements, or were devoid of official support, remained, at least until recently, almost completely unknown or were ideologically ignored by all sides concerned in the ideological Cold War. Such are, for instance, the histories of the Social Democratic Intellectuals of Tabriz;[15] of the Iranian Communist Party, which, although part of an internationally constituted movement, was treated more or less contemptuously by the official historians of Moscow and their unofficial disciples because it did not subserviently follow the Moscow line, while it was despised and misrepresented by the hostile camp, when it was not ignored; of the Arani circles of 1926-32 in Germany and 1934-35 in Iran (the so-called *Panjaho-se-nafar* — ideological glorification and exploitation notwithstanding); of the various not officially recognised offshoots of the Iranian Left (the dissident Communists such as Yousof Eftekhari and his labour union);[16] of Baqer Imami's *krouzhoks*,[17] a remnant of the ICP which opposed the Tudeh Party and was suppressed by both the Pahlavis and the Tudeh; of SAKA (Sazman-e Enqelabi Komonisti-ye Iran); of the super-secret Mahmoud Tavakkoli Communist Group (known as the Process Group)[18] of the post-*coup d'état* period which was also suppressed both by the Tudeh and the regime's political police. It goes without saying that without the study of these groups one could never understand the history of the Iranian Left in the past century, nor can one explain the relative success of the Tudeh, under Soviet patronage, during the time between the Soviet victory at Stalingrad and the coup against Mosaddeq in 1953.

It should be stated immediately that in addition to negligence and intentional omission of such groups from Iran's historical scene in the twentieth century, or in some cases the distortion of their histories, one of the reasons for our incapacity to offer a narrative on their past is that they hardly left any records for future historians.

To the first category of the Leftist organisations belongs that of the Armenian Social Democrats of Tabriz, which played, *inter alia*, an important, if not a decisive, role in the success of the insurrectionists against the putschist shah Mohammad-'Ali Qajar. As opposed to the movements under Geomat and

Mazdak, these intellectuals were not totally eliminated, although some members were. However, for some unknown reason (on which one can merely speculate), these individuals — by their own self-definition 'Marxists' — never constituted archives of their correspondence, discussions or even newspapers and other publications. It is only thanks to persistent research and at times accidental discoveries[19] that some of their historical records have gradually come to light and have been published and analysed.[20]

To the same category belongs the *Ferqeh-ye Ejtema'iyoun-'Ammiyoun (Mojahed)* (FEAM), which also played an important role in the Constitutionalist resistance to the putsch by the shah, and whose historiography we know, to a minor extent, through Kasravi and some contemporary newspapers, and, to a greater extent, paradoxically, through their persecution by the Tsarist police, whose record-keeping has served us to unravel this past.

Of the same category, of course, are the lesser post-First World War socialist organisations, such as les Socialistes Unifiés (*Socialistha-ye Motahhedeh*) and the *Ejtema'iyoun* (Socialists) formed by 'Ali-Akbar Dehkhoda and Solayman Mirza Eskandari,[21] respectively. The same argument can, and should, be made in the case of the Iranian Communist Party (initially 'Adalat) and the Jangali Movement which was inspired, at least at a later stage, by internationalist ideals. We shall return to the historiography of these organisations.

To the second category belongs exclusively the Tudeh Party, which was, from its very genesis, in spite of the good intentions of some of its leaders who had been Taghi Arani's disciples, an offshoot of the Soviet state in Iran, and whose history has been, more or less, subjected to the iron law of the Stalinist historiography which was established when Stalin wrote his famous article to the editor of the journal *Proletarian Revolution* in 1931.[22]

The third category of organisations embraces, in addition to some of the forgotten ones mentioned above, those that appeared after the 1953 *coup d'état*, exclusively composed of students and recent graduates: the Tudeh's Maoist offshoot, Sazman-e Enqelabi (Revolutionary Organisation) of the Tudeh Party and, in turn, its principal offshoot the Kadrha (the Cadres); Ettehadiyeh-ye Kommonistah (Union of Communists),[23] a rather childish, rowdy student group based in the USA; Gorouh-e Felestin, whose founders came from the ranks of the Mosaddeqist Patriotic Front/ Jebheh-ye Melli; Vahdat-e Kommonisti (Communist Unification), some former members of the left wing of the Mosaddeqist Patriotic Front (Jebheh-ye Melli) in Europe and the USA, based in Europe and the Middle East; Toufan; Gorouh-e Setareh-ye Sorkh, a Maoist student offshoot of the Tudeh; Paykar, which transformed the Mojahedin into a Marxist-Leninist organisation; the People's Fada'is and its numerous splinter groups; Gorouh-e Arman-e Khalq; and, finally, the small but intellectually strong Democratic Front of the Iranian People, founded by the exceptional Leftist thinker Mostafa Sho'a'iyan — the latter three groups having some working-class elements in their membership.

A good example that can bring to light some of the problems an historian can face in the historiography of Leftist organisations is the Confederation of Iranian Students (National Union) (CISNU), of which we now have a general history at hand.[24] It was an organisation in the creation and development of which I personally played a not insignificant role, and which I know first-hand. If CISNU, which was not, *stricto sensu*, a Leftist organisation, but, in the broad Western sense of the word, a democratic, and not clandestine, union of students with progressive demands, presented and still presents enormous problems in its historiography, one can imagine of what order are those of smaller, highly ideological, often sectarian, small, underground and illegal organisations which were modelled on the Leninist line, and which had to watch out for constant police surveillance. It is well known that much of the internal records of the CISNU (of which the leading cadres and secretaries often were members or sympathisers of the above-mentioned postwar Leftist organisations) have disappeared through the repeated splits[25] occurring in the second half of the 1970s, sheer negligence, and, of course, intentional destruction of files; the refusal, on the part of some of the former activists, to grant oral history interviews to interested historians under the pretext of the protracted police persecution of them, has not helped historians either!

Insofar as such post-*coup d'état* Leftist organisations are concerned, one can mention cases where willing authors and autobiographers have been discouraged from historical investigation or publication of their experiences. One former leader of the Ettehadiyeh-ye Kommonistah had prepared for publication a documentary history of his organisation, but he had been dissuaded from publishing it by two brothers who had been leading members of that organisation, for it would, they had argued, 'expose former members to the political police of the present regime' — a false argument, indeed, for most of the activists of that organisation had already been emptied of their organisational information after the end of the 'Mazandaran revolt' in 1981, and some of its participants had been executed while others were already in exile and had become American citizens.[26] The argument was, in my view, more propelled by the self-interest of the former Marxist-Leninists in question who had now turned their coats as 'democrats' and wished no one to remember and know of their past. For such individuals either are ashamed of their doings in the past, or wish to protect their present status as 'successful' professionals integrated into the bourgeois society that they used to curse.

Of the same nature is the threatening response *Rah-e Raha'i* (of the Vahdat-e

Kommonisti) made to a revelation by one of its former leaders in a seminar held in 1983 in Wiesbaden (Germany) according to whom they had been asked by Hamid Ashraf of the Fada'iyan to serve as intermediaries with the Soviets for assistance — a request that had been duly put into effect.[27] The threat in *Rah-e Raha'i*[28] that the revealer would be, in turn, exposed for his 'political misdeeds' in the past 'naturally' put an end to further 'revelations' by him.[29]

This brings us to one of the fundamental problems of the historiography of Leftist movements in Iran, and generally in countries under dictatorial and colonial rule, in which the harsh reality of police persecution is reinforced by the resultant psychology of a particular kind in the militant which, *inter alia*, serves as a convenient pretext to suppress the historical memories or records he possesses. Thus, political persecution is perhaps an important factor which prevented the Iranian Left from its own historical record-keeping, although police records (as well as diplomatic archives) both in Russia and in the West have benefited some historians (such as this author) in the potential reconstruction of the historiography of the Iranian Left. For this reason, all the ills of the historiography of the Iranian Left cannot, and should not, be ascribed to political repression. For, as noted above, in addition to political repression, there is a set of other factors that have prevented historians from reconstructing the history of the Iranian Left. These factors are:

A: A lack of ability, if not willingness, to keep records and diaries, even when political repression did not threaten them.
B: The voluntary suppression of memories and records by the militants and leaders in later periods when their ideas change, or their after defection to the power that they had initially opposed and despised.[30]
C: The ideological Cold War since October 1917, including Stalinist suppression of historical documents.
D: The regime's physical destruction of records.
E: The death or execution of militants and leaders in the course of the struggle who might otherwise have been likely to produce their memoirs and records.[31]
F: The involuntary disappearance of documents of the movement either through negligence or failed plans at conservation.

Two known examples of this last type of loss of historical records are their burying by the Jangali leader Kuchek Khan in the Gilan forests for safe-keeping, which were only known to him and perhaps a few other militants who perished; and by Mostafa Sho'a'iyan, during the late 1960s and early 1970s, in the outlying open terrain around Tehran or in town ruins for the purpose of safe-keeping, the keys to which were also buried with his own death at the hand of the SAVAK.

As a result, of the various Leftist organisations mentioned above, only of the Tudeh Party do we already have general histories, of the official kind, a subject to which I will return below. The first unofficial attempt is the recent short work on the post-1953 coup Leftist movements;[32] it is, alas, an unsuccessful one.

II: Social Democracy

As for the Social Democrats of the Constitutionalist and of the post-First World War periods, one may speculate why such organisations did not leave records, although it is possible that most of their records may have disappeared after their demise. To hypothesise, one may offer the following as possible reasons:

1: Militants in a new movement advanced step by step as if in a dark tunnel (that is, *kourmal kourmal*) unable clearly to see the end until it was too late. Later on, in the cold light of day, having failed in their objective, they realised that it would be best to leave no record of their past, or perhaps at most merely some selections suitable for an official history. In a sense, they might be seen as militants ashamed of their past and the movement to which they had belonged, wishing not to remind anyone of their past association with that movement — a phenomenon that is also not unknown in the West. This is, of course, a very pessimistic interpretation, but has grounds in reality in some known cases.

2: The spiritual disappointment of militants who were left with little faith in political activity and thus saw no use for history in the future, without themselves having become turncoats. There are also known cases of this kind.[33]

3: Nevertheless, the real reason for our poor and distorted historical knowledge of the Leftist organisations active in Iran between the Constitutional Revolution and the demise of the Jangali Movement is the *organised and conscious* attempt by successive generations to produce an official history that suited the ideological aims of the Stalinist state. True, what was written by Communist 'historians' in the early 1920s on the Social Democracy of the Constitutional period was ideologically less tailored for state purposes and was varied, although quite insufficient, perhaps also because the Iranian Leftists at the time were unaware of the social and cultural value and weight of the historical knowledge which their own past could eventually acquire in history.[34]

In short, either they counted on eventually seizing power, in which case they could write official histories; or, defeated and disheartened, they hardly saw the desire or the need to think of their lost efforts — an ahistorical, not Marxian, mode of thought, to be sure. The exceptions were, of course, the articles which, upon an invitation by Karl Kautsky, two of these Social Democrats published *à chaud* in *Neue Zeit*, in addition to a few other articles, mostly of a journalistic type, printed in the progressive press of the Caucasus in the Armenian, Georgian and Russian languages.[35]

In later periods, however, the historiography of the Social Democracy was treated with a strict political prescription to fit the ideological needs of the state, and not necessarily in relation to raising the level of the political consciousness of the movement. It was an holistic policy. Very rare were studies in the Stalinist era that dealt with that history on the basis of available documents on Iran rescued from Tsarist archives.[36] And naturally, the Tudeh could not but follow, and hence no Tudeh historiography of that period, whether of the Social Democracy or the Constitutional Revolution, was ever produced.[37]

Only with the disappearance of Stalin and the advent of the Khrushchevian relative *glasnost* were some people allowed to use archival materials to deal with the historiography of Iran's Constitutional Revolution and its Social-Democratic wing. Even then, only the FEAM was given official recognition, and the Armenian wing was almost totally ignored, or when discussed, belittled and dismissed as impertinent.[38] In this period of openness, we begin to witness a number of studies based on archival research that help us understand this particular past. While the remnants of the hard-line Stalinist historiography of Iran, characterised by the works of MS Ivanov,[39] continue to fight for their own kind of ideological presentation, there gradually appear in the midst of Soviet Iranology subtleties of view and nuanced interpretations which both are based on newer historical documentation and search out fresher evidence of their positions[40] — a process that helps historians banned from the Soviet archives to draw on them profitably.[41] The first Soviet study drawing the line between the hard-line Stalinist historiography and the neo-Stalinist school, under Brezhnev, with fewer party shackles to discuss Iranian history, was undertaken by SL Agaev and published in 1977. A short book, it discussed the opposing views of Communist historiography of Iran in the 1920s with a post-Vyshinsky language, but still siding with those justifying historiography at the service of the state.[42]

Gradual de-Stalinisation in the Soviet Union slowly allowed interested foreign historians to draw on certain archival materials on the Iranian Left for both the pre-Soviet and early Soviet periods. But insofar as the Iranian disciples of the Soviet historiography is concerned, notably in the Tudeh Party,[43] the old Stalinist position,[44] accompanied by a 'modern' lethargic vision of history, is doggedly hung on to. Such are, for instance, the unprofessional, propagandistic articles produced by Abdolsamad Kambakhsh,[45] who was known for his NKVD/KGB connections and his betrayal of the Arani Circle to the police of Reza Shah in the spring of 1937, and also for being a leading member of the Tudeh in its exile years. These writings were accompanied, in the pages of the 'theoretical' journal of the Tudeh in exile (*Donya*[46]), by a few scattered articles written by AH Agahi[47] on the beginnings of the Leftist movement in Iran at the turn of twentieth century, a few memoirs related by some former activists or their survivors but written up by the party's 'theoretical genius', Ehsan Tabari,[48] and a couple of distorted documents based on versions published by such Soviet historiographers of Iran as Bor-Ramenskii.[49]

The basic ignorance of the Tudeh's founders and leaders of the history of the Left was, however, rooted in a rupture caused by the double political repression under Reza Shah and Stalinist historiography, of which the most glaring evidence is the confession of Ehsan Tabari of how little he and his like knew of the history of the Iranian Left in the second half of the 1930s and even some 40 years later on the eve of his arrest by the Islamic Republic — a fatal ignorance that led them straight into total obedience to the Soviet state. It would be useful to quote him briefly:

> Even before [our] imprisonment in the spring of 1937 we had heard some things about those who had taken the road of struggle for scientific socialism: some vague, intermittent information on events; but nothing like 'party history' was clear to us. ... We knew absolutely nothing of the foundation of the 'Adalat [party] before the Communist Party. We knew that there was the Comintern, and the names of Zarreh [Abolqasem Sajjadi], [Dehzad, Abdol-Hosein] Hesabi, Kamran [Nasrollah Aslani], [Karim] Nikbin, and [Avetis Mikailian] Sultanzade had reached our ears, without knowing who they had been.[50]

Tabari, who remained to his last day an admirer of Stalin,[51] adds that they had simply 'heard of' Haidar Khan Amoughli, Asadollah Ghaffarzadeh, Va'ez Kayvani (Qazvini), and Hejazi.[52] What strengthens doubt even about admittedly such little knowledge on the part of Tabari and his colleagues regarding the past of the Leftist movement is that such issues had rarely been discussed even in the publications of the ICP, which had by 1932 come under serious attack from the Stalinist apparatus[53] and had been removed from circulation,[54] let alone reaching a small circle of students around Arani, nor even in the 1940s after the establishment of the Tudeh in the relatively tolerant atmosphere brought about by Iran's occupation by the Allies. Nor did the Tudeh make any serious efforts to reconstruct the history preceding its own establishment even in the post-coup years in exile. Thus some 20 years after the Constitutional Revolution, the third generation of young students attracted to the ideas of the Left had no notion of the Social Democracy's past.[55] What is more, Tabari himself admits that it was only in the 1960s that he periodised (!) the history of the Left (Social Democracy, Communist Party and the Tudeh), which Kambakhsh reflected in his writings, and was later 'enriched' by Taqi Ebrahimov (Shahin)[56] through his 'valuable' (archival) information, throwing light on the Tabriz and Rasht

Social-Democratic organisations, mentioning the ICP briefly, and made brief allusions to the Tudeh, and without 'a friendly tone'.[57] Iraj Eskandari's first of a series of 13 articles on the history of the Tudeh Party in 1949, which deals with the period of the First World War and thereafter,[58] also confirms the poor knowledge of the Tudeh leaders of a past they considered to be theirs.[59] The rupture with the past is thus triply profound: at the real historical level of social action, at the historiographical level of analytical knowledge, and at the level of self-deception, that is, that historical ignorance had not really existed and had been salubriously removed.

Before tackling the ICP's historiography of the ICP in some detail, however, we should briefly refer to a similar kind of handling of Iranian Social Democracy in Iran and the West. In Iran itself, the treatment, to the extent that it existed, was confined to what Kasravi[60] and Malekzadeh[61] have put in their histories of the Constitutional Revolution. While the former's discussion is far from adequate and sparsely documented, it is relatively impartial and not contradictory to later findings. On the other hand, the latter, which seems to appeal to a greater number of Western experts on Iran, is a collection of unverifiable hearsay.[62] Contemporary non-Iranian writers in the West who wrote about this period are, indeed, few. The most important are, of course, EG Browne, M Pavlovich (a Russian left-wing Social Democrat living in Paris at the time, who joined the Bolshevik regime after October 1917), Tria (Vlas Mgladze, a Menshevik Social Democrat from Georgia) and, of course, Marx's grandson, Jean Longuet (1876-1936).[63] Nor should one overlook the contribution of several other Russo-Caucasian writers of the time, such as Sarkis M Moubayadjian (pseudonym, Atrpet),[64] who have left a few valuable works on this period.

By contrast, non-contemporary Western experts of Iran who have dealt with the Iranian Social Democracy are even fewer; and when they have dealt with it, what they have written has had less to do with any desire to contribute to historical understanding of Iran than with the logic and historiographical exigencies of the Cold War. A former military attaché of the British embassy in Tehran, Colonel GE Wheeler, in an academic polemic with Soviet historians of Iran,[65] goes so far as to deny the very existence of the Social Democracy, although he is aware of some of its documents published by Bor-Ramenskii, Belova and others. To disprove the Soviet views, he relies on flimsy evidence in Bahar's *Brief History of Political Parties*.[66] Moreover, his concern is rather how the Stalinist historians treated Taqizadeh, Browne or Shuster in comparison to, say, how Pavlovich appraised them — which has its merits — but not what the role and place of the Social Democracy itself was in Iran's Constitutional Revolution. The confusion he tries to create in respect of the meaning of *Mojahed* and *mojahed* (the former a member of the organisation and the latter any ordinary militant) is as baffling as his denial of the existence of the Social Democracy in Iran.[67]

Ann Lambton, whose academic works cannot be neglected by any serious historian working on pre-modern and modern Iran, also ignores the Social Democracy, although she has published two valuable articles on the issue of *anjomans*.[68] Thus is left in oblivion an important component of the Constitutionalist Movement — in spite of all the references in the published British and Russian diplomatic reports (the *Blue Book* and *Orange Book*, respectively). To comprehend the extent of Cold War influence on this period's historiography, it is worth mentioning, though somewhat amusing, that one internal study of the US Defense Department on the Iranian Left (declassified after the fall of the shah) referred to this first stage of the movement as having been under the influence of the Soviet government![69]

III: Historiography of the Communist Party

This last exaggerated American view of Soviet manipulations in Iran, extrapolated retrospectively to 1905, brings us to the harmful influence of the Cold War on all three senses that the term *history* embraces in Western languages: objective history (that is, what actually took place); historical accounts that various ideological currents produce (that is, ideological historiography); and the various ways in which history reconstructed, on the basis of the widest possible documentation and as far as possible based on value-free methods and concepts, by serious, impartial historians, is understood and made understood, that is, interpretative history. Thus, with the advent of the Soviet regime in the area north of the economically and politically strategic area which Persia has constituted in the modern era, it soon became vital, for both expanding empires, not only to influence events in Iran in a decisive manner, but also to write its historical account according to politico-ideological needs, as well as to interpret and re-interpret that history according to the intensity and exigencies of the continuing ideological crusade; no less important in this ideological warfare was its 'didactic value', not in the propagandistic press, but in the mode of thought, and reproduction of models, categories and concepts with which historians of Iran were to be inculcated.[70] As in the West, where an anti-Communist construction and interpretation of Iran's history was taught to students (including the Iranians ones), the Soviets had their own way of educating young Iranian Communists, beginning with the KUTV (the Communist University for the Workers of the East), of which two notable examples were Reza Rousta and Ardeshir (Artashes) Ovanesian, who were spared by the Stalinist purges by their imprisonment in Iran, but who chose, after their release, to serve the Comintern as secret agents in the Tudeh Party. (Later, when Tudeh leaders and cadres arrived in exile in the Soviet bloc, they had to undergo a Marxist-Leninist schooling.)

The most immediate case in which this kind of multiple historical intervention took place was the Jangali Movement which, in June 1920, culminated in the establishment of the Soviet Socialist Republic of Iran under the leadership of Kuchek Khan and with the participation of the Iranian Communist Party. As I have reconstructed and analysed the history of that short but vital turning point in Iran's history in the twentieth century elsewhere,[71] suffice it to say here that the history of that important episode was being falsified from the *very beginning* of the Cold War — 1918 — during the very existence of the Jangali Movement, particularly from the moment Kuchek Khan entered into relations with Raskolnikov in late May 1920. Articles in the scholarly press with specific missions, such as *Revue du monde musulman*,[72] *Journal of Central Asian Society* and *Yale Review*, were already writing 'the' history of the Jangali Movement, from the Western viewpoint, and on the other side, the Soviet historiography was less subtle and more propagandistic, of course, as in the article by Effendiev entitled 'Enslavement of Persia by the English' in the publication of the Soviet Commissariat for Nationality affairs under Stalin, *Zhizn natsional'nostei*.[73] And since neither side of the Cold War was interested in the history of that movement as it was developing, no serious study of it was ever carried out, and references were continuously made to such reviews as the above, of the kind the French call *histoire actuelle*.

The history of the activities of the Iranian Communist Party was subjected to the same 'law' of the Cold War; it was discussed in the press whenever one of the two sides considered it necessary from the propagandists' viewpoint. At the very early stage, while the Communist movement was still young, that is, until 1925 when M Pavlovich, the chief Bolshevik Orientalist, was still alive, Soviet and Communist differences over Iran revolved around the issue of the socio-economic conditions of the country and its stage of development, which was important to them for the formulation of policy for future political action. By the latter part of the 1920s, however, antagonistic differences emerged also on the place and role of the labour and Communist movements, which also had very close bearings on the fate of political strategy to be adopted in relation to the new Pahlavi regime.[74]

The first serious encounter took place between Avetis Sultanzade[75] and Vladimir Osetrov (who used the pseudonym Irandust, that is, 'Friend of Iran' — a misnomer indeed) over the workers' movement[76] and the role of Iranian Communists during the ephemeral life of the Soviet Socialist Republic of Iran.[77] These differences, expressed within the first years of a relatively tolerant Communist historiography, naturally reflected the different viewpoints, the perspective of an Iranian Communist who did not take orders from his Soviet mentors, and that of a Soviet official who had served in Iran and could not but justify past policies and elaborate a theoretical framework for the future policies of his country, however embellished it may have been through an internationalist parlance.[78]

With the general tendency of the Soviet polity growing increasingly monolithic under the rising absolute power of Stalin, Iranian studies, too, were gradually subjected to the total ideological control of CPSU 'Iran experts' who adapted scientific findings to immediate state and party requirements. As noted above, the totalitarian watershed had been definitely crossed by the time Stalin sent his famous article to the editor of the journal *Proletarian Revolution* in 1931.[79] By then, the battle between the two main lines of interpretation of Iranian history (both in terms of socio-economic structures and immediate political history, including the short life of the ICP) had been fought out and the Iranian Communists had been declared, *ex cathedra*, defeated, and official history (that is, the Soviet viewpoint) had established the 'truth'. From that moment onwards, it was no longer a debate, but articles of denunciation that were being published in order to suppress the ICP. The ferociously hostile articles against Sultanzade by the Soviet official GC Gel'bras,[80] who had served in Iran as a commercial attaché, but was now a leading 'Iran expert', assuming the pseudonym 'Ranjbar' (that is, Toiler — another misnomer), sealed the fate of the ICP and its short history,[81] for which reason future generations of Iranian Leftists, who had been born into and nursed by the Stalinist tradition, could not, and should not, have known the history of the ICP.[82]

Needless to say, Western historians were still less interested in the history of a Communist organisation (as an important social and intellectual movement) that had been buried under library dust by the Stalinist regime in Russia; it could serve them no useful purpose. As a rule, they found it useless to remind future generations of political and cultural challenges to *their* man Reza Shah, often admirably compared to Mussolini, who was carving out a 'new Iran', in the same way that post-Sassanid historians did not need to remind their contemporary generations of the Mazdaki movement and analyse the reasons for its rise and demise. Thus only Mazdak and his movement's history had been exterminated, not the causes of the movement, deeply structured in Iranian society and spirit that gave birth to numerous socio-political movements in Persislamic Iran, in fact, as early as the advent of the Abbasids in Baghdad.

And when the West began to become interested in the history of the Iranian Left, inevitably through a Cold-Warrior who authored a book with a purposeful title,[83] it showed little interest in the ICP, except, paradoxically, for the purpose of demolishing, once again, those who had already been Stalin's victims; the aim now was more than anything else the immediate history of the Tudeh Party.[84] The eradication and effacement of this history were complementary endeavours on both fronts of the Cold War

Thus, the falsification of the history of the ICP and especially the calumnies about its leader and theoretician Sultanzade abound on both fronts of the Cold War. While Soviet historians such as MN Ivanova incessantly blamed all the failures of the ICP on Sultanzade and accused him of having been a 'traitor', the Cold-Warrior George Lenczowski, who stood close to official circles both in the USA and Tehran, referred to Sultanzade as the 'Head of the Soviet Near Eastern Section of the Soviet Commissariat of Foreign Affairs'.[85] Lenczowski went so far as identifying him as Pishevari, who had survived the Stalinist purges through his imprisonment in Iran, thereby negating Sultanzade's liquidation by the Soviets.[86] As if ever incorrigible in their attempt to discredit and demolish Sultanzade, the Iranian students of Stalin's school of falsification have proven no less determined. Witness, for instance, the right track, paved by Gel'bras, Ivanova and Ivanov, of outright distortion of historical records by H Ahmadi, a former trainee and devotee of the Tudeh leader Noureddin Kianouri, turned 'historian'.[87] In one of his sloppy writings, he attributes an unambiguously signed article by Sultanzade in *Paykar*[88] to an imagined rival of his, that is, Abdol-Hosein Hesabi (Dehzad), before going even further by declaring that another signed article by Sultanzade in the following issue of *Paykar*[89] to be a 'reply' to the previous article supposedly 'by Hesabi', that is, in reality, by Sultanzade himself![90] Even the most audacious Stalinist historian had not dared take such a preposterous step.

Ervand Abrahamian, an historian who is normally classified as belonging to the opposite pole to that of Sepehr Zabih, and who prefers to rely heavily on the falsified Tudeh sources for the account, *inter alia*, of the first ICP congress at Anzali instead of using its original text (or its Persian translation), curiously refers his readers to Zabih on the 'general analysis' of ICP programmes.[91] As will be shown below, other historical misrepresentations fill the pages of his work, once again basically because of an over-reliance on Tudeh Party sources, when references are provided, that is. Such are, for instance, the unsubstantiated claims that Asadollah Ghaffarzadeh was a graduate of Dar al-Fonoun;[92] that Ehsanollah Khan Doustdar, one of the Jangali leaders, was an 'Azeri intellectual' educated in 'Paris' and 'influenced by anarchism',[93] although the known facts show that he was from a Baha'i family from Mazandaran, that he had never been abroad, and that the accusation of his anarchism emanated from Stalinist historians;[94] or that Sultanzade's first name was Ahmad[95] instead of Avetis, that the ICP theses opposing Sultanzade's line had been drafted by Haidar Khan (while historical records show them to be drafted by the Soviet Sinologist

Skachko);[96] that these theses had been discussed at the Anzali congress,[97] as opposed to the established records that they had, in fact, been published in January and September 1921, after the death of Haidar Khan; that the Comintern had rejected at the Baku congress the 'ultra-left' proposals by Sultanzade,[98] while just the contrary took place;[99] that a 'plenary meeting of the Iranian Communist Party replaced Sultanzade with Haidar Khan',[100] in lieu of saying that the Stalinists had organised an illegal meeting in Baku to create a counter-Central Committee for the ICP;[101] that most of the workers unionised by the ICP were Azeri and Armenian, even in the printers' union in Tehran,[102] a completely gratuitous affirmation, for the majority of unionised workers were in Tehran; that some of the leaders of the ICP such as Reza Rousta, Karim Nikbin and Ardeshir Ovanesian had been educated at 'Moscow University',[103] not at KUTV (Communist University for the Toilers of the East) where they had undergone, for some two years, a Communist training in Russian, Marxism-Leninism and underground organisational techniques.

The mentality fed by the Stalinist misrepresentation, inherited by the Iranian Left of the post-Reza Shah period, distinguishes itself from such socio-political movements born after the advent of Islam in Iran as Khorram-dinan that continued to feed on the Mazdaki tradition, thus doubly severing them from their past and leaving them historically unschooled. Thus, in addition to having been nursed in the culturally ruptured Iranian society under the Pahlavi regime, with little need for history, they were being nurtured by Soviet Marxism under Stalin, which recognised the 'value of history' solely as an ideological tool.

IV: The Allied Occupation of Iran and the Historiography of the Iranian Left

Paradoxically, the circumstances of the Iranian Leftists' newly-found liberty of action, that is, under Allied occupation of the country, as opposed to the conditions under Reza Shah, determined their future course of action, since they knew almost nothing of the past, neither the history of the Social Democracy nor that of the ICP; still less did they try to learn. The sweet smell of power, at the threshold of which they believed themselves to be standing, intoxicated them beyond cure. 'Brotherly' aid by the Soviet Union and ready-to-chant ideological clichés fabricated in the Stalinist propaganda arsenal seemed to suffice, thereby removing the need for historical knowledge and understanding. And as an increasing number of working people and educated elements rallied around the pro-Soviet party — after the victory at the battle of Stalingrad, let us stress — the bandwagon of success got on its way, so that increasing numbers of former Nazi supporters, such as Khosrow Rouzbeh, 'Ali Mottaqi, Amanollah Qoreyshi and Noureddin Kianouri, could jump on it. With such bewildering success, who would need history as a means of understanding the past? Not until after the advent of the Khrushchevian *glasnost* did they think of history, after several defeats: the Soviet oil episode in 1944; the Azerbaijan debacle, the ephemeral coalition with Qavam; the internal crisis leading to the first split in 1948 by Khalil Maleki and his colleagues; the proscription in 1949 as a result of a stage-managed attempt on the life of the shah; their disastrous sabotage of the patriotic-democratic movement under Mosaddeq; and finally, the destruction of the party organisation, particularly its military wing, in 1954.

The Tudeh leadership's historical obliviousness, on the one hand, and its canonical faith in the big Soviet brother, on the other, were such that even their own bitter experience of the Arani debacle (that is, the exposure of the Circle by Kambakhsh to the police in May 1937, of which they were aware but kept silent about) was thoughtlessly discarded until such time that the appraisal of the past was the order of the day at the Fourth Central Committee Plenum under the auspices of Khrushchev in the summer of 1957.[104] Even then, a simple gesture on the part of the Soviets sufficed to shelf the subject again.[105] Even Arani's defence speech at the tribunal was subjected to *surgical editing*[106] to suit the Soviet wishes of supporting Kambakhsh, who, after his release from prison in December 1941, spent a couple of years under the notorious Bagirov in Baku (during which he prepared his 'Secret Report' for Stalin's counter-espionage Chief Pavel Mikhailovich Fitin) before returning to Iran to be elected deputy (to the Fourteenth Majles in 1944) from Qazvin, a town located in the Soviet occupied zone.

V: The Arani Circles of 1926-32 and 1934-35

The silence of the Tudeh on the morrow of its foundation and under Soviet pressure about what I call the Arani Circles or Iran's National Communist Experience turned out to be fatal both for Iran and the fortunes of the party itself. What were these 'Circles'? It is no wonder that what little is known about them after more than seven decades is restricted to a handful of people, even within the ranks of the Iranian Left; and this obviously tells us more about the Tudeh than about these Circles.

To be brief, it should be recalled that, under the influence of a young Communist named Morteza Alavi, Arani became a Marxist while a student in Berlin. They formed a circle which was called the Revolutionary Republican Party of Persia. The circle was active among young Iranian university students in Germany and France (including those studying at French military academies such as Saint Cyr) as well as a number of students in French high schools preparing for university studies. They stood close to, and were in touch with, the German Communist Reichstag deputy Willi Münzenberg and took part in the International Conference of the Anti-Imperialist League held in 1927 in

Brussels, at which some well-known figures from various countries, including Jawaher Lal Nehru, Henri Barbusse, Fenner Brockway and Willi Münzenberg took part. These young Iranians even contacted the Comintern Executive, sending along their detailed programme, which was no less Communistic. As members of this circle, including Arani himself, gradually returned to Iran, the latter took the initiative for creating study circles among students and publishing a review which, after several refusals by the government authorities, finally took the name *Donya* (*The World*), its first issue being published on 21 January 1934.[107] In the meantime, those who were still in Europe launched the bi-weekly *Paykar* (*Combat*), which was published with the direct involvement of the ICP under the guidance of Avetis Sultanzade. This publication, which ran a very hostile campaign against Reza Shah, was an immediate success both outside and within Iran. It aroused the extreme fury of the shah, who, under the threat of severing profitable economic relations with the German government, demanded and finally, although illegally, obtained the expulsion of Alavi, just as it had succeeded a couple of years earlier in obtaining the deportation of another founder of the RRPP, Ahmad Asadov (Darab). While the latter had returned to Iran, Alavi finally settled in Moscow, whence he was deported to Central Asia after his expulsion, in 1934, from the German and Iranian Communist Parties, under the usual pretext of having had connections with a 'suspicious' German, but in reality for having shown in *Paykar* more hostility towards Reza Shah than the Soviets had wished.[108]

The second circle that Arani formed in Iran[109] was later contacted and infiltrated by Kambakhsh; the attempts by the new Comintern group of Iranians, installed after the removal of independently-minded Communists such as Sultanzade, to bring *Donya* under their control did not succeed, and the journal shut down after 20 months — upon Arani's visit to Moscow with the Comintern officers of Iran, during which he learned of Alavi's deportation to Central Asia. In the meantime, an Iranian underground agent of the Comintern (or rather of the NKVD) who had been assigned to serve as courier between the Comintern and the Second Arani Circle, and had been arrested along with two KUTV students by Iranian border guards but had managed to buy their freedom with bribes, settled in the Abadan-Ahwaz area and began organising provocative theatrical shows, which immediately attracted the attention of the political police, who were already looking for him. Arrested and questioned, he not only led the political police to Kambakhsh, the main Comintern contact in Iran, but also to Arani and his comrade from student days in German, Dr Mohammad Bahrami. Kambakhsh, in turn, not only laid open a whole circle of students around Arani to the police, but (to use Arani's expression) 'authored a whole book on different subjects of organisation, budget... etc'[110] on the activities of the Circle for the police.¹¹¹ What was worse, he arranged with the political police to accuse Arani of having exposed the Circle to the police. As a result, none of the detainees spoke to Arani between the interrogations and the eve of the trial over a year and half later. Arani was completely isolated and boycotted by all as a police collaborator. When the interrogation files were read out on the eve of the trial in the presence of the accused, everyone discovered that Arani was innocent, and that Kambakhsh was the true police collaborator.

During the trial, while Kambakhsh accommodated the police, as he had during the investigations, Arani put up a courageous defence, and condemned not only Kambakhsh, but also Kamran (Aslani), the so-called Iranian representative at the Comintern, whom he called a *hammal* (literally a porter, but figuratively a stupid brute). Arani received the harshest sentence, and was dealt with most brutally in prison until he was killed in captivity in February 1940. When the rest of the Circle were released as a result of the general amnesty granted after the forced abdication of Reza Shah in occupied Iran, Kambakhsh was initially barred from entering the Tudeh Party, for which reason he left for Baku and spent some two years there under the arch-Stalinist Azerbaijani leader Bagirov, Beria's lieutenant. Upon his arrival in Baku, he drafted a long report (dated or *back*dated December 1941) on the question of the Arani Circle for the Soviet counter-intelligence, then under Colonel PM Fitin, who, in December 1942, forwarded it to Georgi Dimitrov. Justifying his misdeed and a making a full character report on each individual member of the Circle, not only did the Kambakhsh show a great deal of hostility towards Dr T Arani, but he also accused Arani of having been a 'bourgeois intellectual' who had uttered, during the trial, 'many anti-Communist remarks, the most important of which is his calling Kamran [Aslani], the Comintern representative, a provocateur and a *hammal* [porter]'.¹¹² Cynically, however, he emphasised how the importance of Arani could be posthumously exploited for the furtherance of the Communist cause.¹¹³ In spite of his hatred for Arani throughout his 'Secret Report' to the Soviet chief of counter-intelligence Fitin, designating Arani as 'careerist', 'anti-Communist', etc, Kambakhsh concluded as follows:

> If I stated here some of his [Arani's] negative features, this is solely to put the record straight. In general, his memory must not be darkened or stained in any way, and we must remember him as the best revolutionary and fighter for Communism who gave his life for the cause of the great Communist Revolution.¹¹⁴

The utterly hypocritical posture adopted by Kambakhsh was put into practice by the Soviet historians of Iran, who kept silent on the history of the Arani

Circles,[115] while the Tudeh did the same thing, glorifying Arani for propagandistic purposes.

The arguments demonstrating the coincidence of the exposure of the Second Arani Circle to and its arrest by the police as a result of collaboration of two Soviet contacts in Iran, Shoureshian and Kambakhsh, with the liquidation of many Iranian Communists in Soviet Russia during the purges of 1936-38 will have to await the publication of the study on this subject in the near future.[116] What should be stressed here, however, is that, while Arani's closest friends, such as Iraj Eskandari, Mohammad Bahrami, and Morteza Alavi, as well as other members of the Circle, who constituted the leadership of the Tudeh, knew of Kambakhsh's treachery, both in exposing the Circle to the police and blaming Arani for it, they did nothing to remedy the situation, that is, to investigate fully the reasons for the exposure of the Circle to the police; the reason for Kambakhsh's treachery; the reason for the Soviet authorities' support for Kambakhsh to enter not only the Tudeh but also the Majles; and above all, the reason why the Communists who had been known to them, such as Morteza Alavi, were not returned to Iran, in spite of the express demand made by the Tudeh leader Abdol-Hussein Noushin in a letter to the Comintern chief Dimitrov. And once Kambakhsh and even Shoureshian were admitted to the Tudeh Party, it became clear that the party leadership could not resist any Soviet demands — a weakness that proved fatal to that organisation. Thus the lack of any historical vision and historical knowledge on the part of the Tudeh leadership was tremendously costly to Iran.

Another indication of the Tudeh's lack of knowledge of the history of the Left in Iran as well as its parroting of the Soviet historiography of Iran, on the one hand, and its adherence to the Stalinist school of falsification and misrepresentation of its own and Iran's history of the Reza Shah and post-Reza Shah eras,[117] on the other, is a series of articles Iraj Eskandari published in the French Communist review *Moyen-Orient*. Here Eskandari could not, of course, tell his readers about the direct hand of the Soviet Union[118] in creating and programmatically shaping the Tudeh from the very first day of its existence.[119] Eskandari's version of the Tudeh's foundation kept changing, of course, according to the historical circumstances in which it was retold.[120] For the same reason, historians who depend on Tudeh sources for the history of the Arani Circles cannot tell us more, nor analyse correctly that historical experience. They cannot utter a word about, or even a hint at, the essential Soviet role in the exposure of the 'Fifty-Three' to the police through the voluntary collaboration of Shoureshian and Kambakhsh with the political police,[121] although it had been discussed at the 1957 Plenum and known outside Tudeh circles.[122] The concern of such historians boils down to a description of the arrest, trial and social composition of the members of the Circle — whatever its worth[123] — without ever bothering to analyse why Arani's Marxism was different from Soviet Marxism, and why he was to be done away with at the time that other Iranian Communists such as Sultanzade were being eliminated in the purges. In addition to an over-dependence on Tudeh sources,[124] the main reason for such neglect is the ideological choices such historians make; it is more important for them to see in Arani's youthful writings a kind of Iranian 'chauvinism' (because of his reference to 'the Great Heroes of Iran' or references to Zoroaster, Ferdowsi, etc) than his passage to Marxism, totally unaware that even the founders of the Iranian Communist Party, such as Ghaffarzadeh, had been 'guilty' of expressing nostalgia for Iran's past glories in their Communist journal *Bayraq-e 'Adalat*[125] — publications that had been hidden away from later generations of Iranian Communists by the Stalinist apparatus.

Their ideological framework apart, it would therefore be naïve to expect Tudeh 'historians' or their disciples to have educated themselves in the history of the ICP, particularly through access to its archives in the Soviet Union, while even the most trusted Soviet specialists of Iran, who had worked for the KGB and its forerunners, could not approach such records until the 1970s; and even when they did have access to them, it was only in dribs and drabs.

Thus, the history of Iran's Left during Reza Shah's monarchy — that is, the experience of the ICP, the formation and activities of the Arani Circles, their suppression at home by Reza Shah as well as in and from Soviet Russia by the Stalinist apparatus, and the collaboration of the Soviet agent Kambakhsh with Reza Shah's police — need to be told with precision[126] in view of the great distortions wrought by Kambakhsh and his faithful students who continue to twist that history in a most flagrant manner.[127]

VI: The Founding of the Tudeh Party

The establishment of the Tudeh Party has also been subject to mystification.[128] The Tudeh Party itself has propagated several myths, especially by Iraj Eskandari. But on the whole the main theme has been that it was founded by Arani's 'disciples', a myth that has been repeated by various writers of the subject, most notably Zabih and Abrahamian, who, although ideologically at odds, repeat, with some minor differences, the same Tudeh tale.

Zabih hits two birds with one stone. He states that the Allies 'as a matter of principle, as well as for tactical reasons... were *eager* [emphasis added] to facilitate the democratisation of Iran'. And the 'desire to win over the people of Iran at a time when Iran's strategic importance was increasing constituted a second factor for the revival of the [Communist] movement, which readily embraced the Allies' anti-Fascist orientation'.[129] According to Zabih, who interprets Eskandari's 1949 account,[130] the Communist movement was revived by the 'hard core' of the 'Arani Circle' as a 'democratic front, dedicated to legally achieving its political goal',[131] which was — one must assume — no other than Communism. A 'number of tactical reasons' are given by Zabih as having guided the Tudeh to disguise its 'Communist affiliations'. These are the 1931 anti-socialist law; 'the best interests of Soviet diplomacy to avoid open identification with its ideological system'; and the need to 'broaden the basis of its support' for which reason it chose Solayman Mohsen [Mirza] Eskandari, a veteran of the old Social Democratic Party, as the chairman of a "provisional committee of 15"'.[132] Although in a subsequent work he introduces Rostam Aliev, at the time only about eight years old, as having been a Soviet 'observer' at the founding session of the Tudeh,[133] Zabih basically reproduces the Tudeh version.

Abrahamian,[134] on the other hand, makes out as if the Tudeh was created painlessly, spontaneously and as an initiative of a handful of Arani's students:

> The Tudeh Party emerged *immediately* after the abdication of Reza Shah and the release of the 'less dangerous' political prisoners... In launching the organisation, the *founders gave the party chairmanship to* Sulayman [Mirza] Iskandari, the highly respected radical prince who had fought in the Constitutional Revolution, helped establish the Democrat Party in the Second Majles,[135] led the Committee of National Resistance during World War I, and presided over the Socialist Party from 1921 until its dissolution in 1926 [my emphasis].[136]

The 'formulation of a broad programme' was such that it '*would not antagonise the 'ulama* [my emphasis], as previous secular programmes had done, but would attract veteran Democrats, Socialists and Communists, as well as young Marxists and even non-Marxist radicals'. Abrahamian repeats his point on the 'ulama:

> To avoid attacks from the 'ulama, the Tudeh kept Marxist demands out of its programme, commemorated Arani's death with a religious service, and organised a mass meeting in memory of Arani, of Mudarres, the leading religious opponent of Reza Shah, and of Farrokhi, the radical but highly devout poet who had been murdered in 1939.

However, the 'founding members of the Tudeh', who according to Abrahamian were 'Marxists (and, as later events showed, staunch supporters of the Soviet Union)..., did not call themselves Communists'. Why? For 'fear of the 'ulama', and also because of 'the 1931 law banning all "collectivist ideologies"'; 25 (sic) years of government propaganda that had 'instilled in segments of the population a hostile attitude toward socialism, Communism, and the Soviet Union'; a desire to attract 'reformers and progressives as well as radicals and revolutionaries'; and a realisation that the industrial working class still constituted 'a small fraction of the total population'.

Before dealing with the above arguments, let us look at Abrahamian's 'unstated and more complex reason' for Tudeh founders to avoid the 'Communist label', namely, to avoid 'subordinating themselves to veteran leaders' of the ICP because of their different political perspectives[137] — an argument that is false, for, contrary to Abrahamian's claim, most of the Tudeh leaders were not educated in Europe,[138] some of the most influential among them were former ICP cadres[139] (the experienced leaders of the ICP having been murdered during Stalin's purges), and the main contact man with the Soviets were former *inféodé* ICP cadres: Ardeshir Ovanesian, Reza Rousta and Abdolsamad Kambakhsh.

Abrahamian, who grounds his arguments in the Tudeh leaders' belated writings between 1966 and 1974, such as those by Eskandari and the Soviet NKVD/KGB agent in the Tudeh, Kambakhsh, glaringly fails to refer to the very first account of the founding of the Tudeh, that is, Eskandari's articles in *Moyen-Orient* in 1949-50. The reason is clear. Firstly, there is nowhere any mention of the *fear* of the 'ulama[140] in any previous writings on the history of the Tudeh Party; in fact, the 'ulama did not constitute as yet an active political force at the time to be feared;[141] secondly, Eskandari had, in 1949, put up the false claims that the Tudeh had, as a 'democratic and progressive party', wished to undertake 'great structural reforms such as the distribution of landed feudal properties, an agrarian reform', that it had, as an 'anti-imperialist organisation', wished to fight 'foreign interference and colonialism', and that it had made its own 'all working-class demands'.[142] Regardless of what has come to light since, mainly from the secret Soviet archives,[143] anyone who had studied the programme of the Tudeh Party of 1941 and followed the efforts for its execution until the end of the war would have known that the Tudeh had never raised the question of the fear of the 'ulama, nor had it ever discussed the question of a general land reform, workers' demands or colonialism. In fact, the Tudeh, in the name of anti-fascism, disregarded legitimate working-class wartime demands not only in northern Iran, but also in the south in the oil industry (a fact clear from Abrahamian's own chart, see page 351);[144] it collaborated with reactionaries who were great landowners, and defended even the 'security' of British economic interests in southern Iran, merely demanding the equivalent for the Soviets in the north.[145] The Tudeh meticulously respected Solayman Mirza's agreement with his Soviet contact from the Red Army Intelligence Division, Colonel Seliukov, who, at the end of a report to his superiors in the Intelligence Division of the Soviet Army, made two recommendations:

1) Through the intermediary of Solayman Mirza it is possible *to organise a party [as] a single anti-fascist front*.[146] Through this party we could have the possibility of influencing very strongly the government and the Majles. [This was, from the very outset, tantamount to a very conscious instrumentalisation of the Tudeh by Soviet foreign policy.] The party would unite all the parties and groups and would work under the leadership of Solayman Mirza.

Since the government wants to have [that is, allow the existence of] a party, it is possible to organise an anti-fascist party after having overcome certain difficulties.

2) Distinct groups of Solayman Mirza's party in the regions occupied by the Red Army should be submitted to the organisation [in the Soviet Army?] of the Central Committee of [the Communist Party in Soviet] Azerbaijan.[147]

However, according to a letter of 5 November 1941 by the NKVD official and Chief of Soviet Foreign Intelligence, PM Fitin, to Georgi Dimitrov, the head of the Comintern, 'a guiding kernel' composed of Ardeshir Ovanesian,[148] Reza Rousta, Iraj Eskandari, Morteza Yazdi, Mohammed Bahrami, and Reza Radmanesh[149] had entered the composition of the 15-member 'unofficial Central Committee' of the Tudeh Party, whose programme was of 'bourgeois-democratic and anti-fascist content', in order to carry out the programme of the 'underground Communist Party at present', that is:

1: Verification of the composition of the [Tudeh] Party, its purge of suspects, provocateurs and Trotskyists.

2: Reinforcement of its [Communist Party's] influence within the Popular [Tudeh] Party, so as to carry out under its cover the tasks elaborated in its programme.

3: Creation of party centres in localities, especially in Azerbaijan, organisers having already been sent to Tabriz, Reza'iyeh [Urmia], Sarab, Rasht and Mashhad.

Fitin further informed Dimitrov that 'our [NKVD] cadres in Iran' had discussed the matter with some leading Communists, given them 'certain advice resulting from the prevailing conditions [in Iran], and granted them important material help'. Moreover, Dimitrov was advised that at the last session of the Provincial Bureau of the 'Communist Party' in Tehran, 'an application' for membership in the Comintern had been elaborated 'with the demand for instructions for further work. It was asked to send the reply through our [NKVD] cadres.' Ardeshir Ovanesian had been designated for contact with the Comintern. Fitin also let Dimitrov know that 'side by side with the highly secret ['conspiratorial' in Russian] relations of our cadres with the representatives of the Communist Party and the Popular [Tudeh] Party, a contact is maintained with the latter through uninvestigated and dubious individuals of the *polpred* [embassy] and the military attaché of the USSR in Iran, which might compromise the party in view of [their] lack of [necessary] secretiveness in contact'.[150]

In fact, as has been made clear elsewhere, the establishment of the Tudeh as well as the limits of its programme of action were decided in minute detail in Moscow, and received Stalin's approval before it was made public.[151] It thus becomes evident that the Tudeh was not really what it has been described by its own 'historians', Ervand Abrahamian, or by Sepehr Zabih, still less by Peter Avery.[152] Different histories of the Tudeh's founding were written to accommodate different ideological needs.

VII: The Azerbaijan Crisis of 1945-46

The Azerbaijan crisis, or the creation and suppression of the 'autonomous government of Azerbaijan' (AGA) under the nominal leadership of Ja'far Pishevari, is perhaps the most complex issue of Iran's modern history for the historian. In spite of piles of documents,[153] a good number of memoirs,[154] and numerous serious and spurious studies by all ideological tendencies,[155] the essential questions of this historical episode — How and when it began, and by whom? How popular was the AGA and why did it collapse so swiftly? And what was the role of the Soviet government in it? — remain unresolved, mainly because of the reasons advanced at the beginning of this study: the elimination of such important figures as Pishevari, the inaccessibility of Soviet, as well as Azerbaijani, archives,[156] and the unwillingness of survivors to write and publish their memoirs.[157]

Nonetheless, it is worth looking at some of the treatments of the issue by those who have made it their task to explore it, in order to assess the degree of their ideological commitment to one side or the other of the Cold War. Zabih offers three factors for the 'insurrections' in Azerbaijan and Kurdistan:

A: 'Outspoken minorities' held 'many anti-government grievances'.

B: They were 'easily infiltrated' by Soviet Azerbaijanis.

C: 'There was a good reason for beginning a fresh revolutionary drive [by whom?] in a place where the Tudeh had not been substantially involved[158] and where the refusal to seat Pishevari in the [Fourteenth] Majlis could be exploited to the full' by him because of his 'contempt' for the Tudeh, 'apparent in the high-handed manner in which he forced the dissolution of its provincial branch and its absorption into his new Democratic Party', as was the case with the United Trade Union Council under Biria.[159]

In spite of a hint,[160] however, Zabih does not go so far as stating the clear-cut intention of Moscow and Baku to bring about the secession of the Iranian provinces of Azerbaijan and Kurdistan, which would have extended direct Soviet influence to the oil-producing regions of Iran (Kermanshah to Khuzistan),[161] and eventually to the Persian Gulf.

Abrahamian's book, published some 16 years after Zabih's, relates, in a few pages,[162] essentially a similar story: popular discontent of the ethnic minorities, the Tudeh Party's 'promptly joining' the Azerbaijan Democratic Party, the 'armed uprising', the 'provincial autonomy' as opposed to secession. He differs from Zabih on one detail, namely, that the Tudeh provincial committee promptly joined the ADP, without speaking of the circumstances. Even an historian without access to archives and participants' memoirs could not fail to see that a large, perhaps the largest, provincial organisation of the Tudeh (with claims to some 60 000 members) could not have 'promptly' joined the ADP if some preparations had not been made in advance.[163] What is more, contrary to Abrahamian's claim,[164] there is no evidence of collaboration by any particular 'survivors' of the Khiabani revolt in creating the ADP, which he himself fails to mention. AGA PTT Minister Kabiri, who came from a well-to-do family, had, in fact, opposed Khiabani.[165] The only 'Communists from the old ICP' who took part in this enterprise were Salam-Allah Javid and Sadeq Padegan, both of whom stood close to the Soviet Azerbaijan Communist Party under Bagirov[166] — two rare Iranian Communists who had not been eliminated in the Stalinist purges.

Moreover, Abrahamian is silent on the manner in which the AGA's ephemeral existence came to an end; the role the Soviets, especially the Azerbaijan SSR under Bagirov, played; indeed, there is hardly any mention of the fact that the whole affair was guided by the Soviets; the Soviets are referred to as an 'ally' of both the FDA and the Tudeh.[167]

The national question acquires such an importance in this historiographical account that the cherished class struggle is replaced by the coalition of all classes; on the other hand, the Jewish identity of Rahim Namvar is glossed over,[168] while the Gilani Reza Rousta acquires an Azeri background;[169] the fact that Pishevari was replaced by Biria and moved to Baku under Soviet *diktat* is reduced to the former 'escaping' to the Soviet Union and the latter 'disappearing'.[170] Indeed, the ideologically tendentious account of the AGA suddenly bottoms out and the FDA loses out because of economic difficulties caused by a 'bad harvest', the 'shah's sabotage' of Qavam's settlement with Stalin, 'disputes' with the Kurdish Republic at Mahabad, and the Soviet's lack of military assistance to the AGA, the reason for which was 'best known to themselves'![171] Pishevari's murder in early 1947, that is, only a few months after his arrival in Baku, is registered under an unidentified Soviet source as having taken place 'two years later', with a dry footnote on the 'claim' by F Keshavarz that he had been murdered by the Azerbaijani leaders.[172] No one else could have managed so conformably to bypass the main issue of the rise and demise of the FDA and AGA, and one of the first factors provoking the Cold War.

The superficial explanations of the rise and demise of the AGA are unfortunately ideological on both sides. What was needed was to release oneself from the ideological binds that close the door to extensive study of the subject. By the time those two authors wrote their versions of history, a great deal of objective documents were available to make possible the writing of a comprehensive and impartial history of that episode in Iran's postwar history: British, French and American archives, UN Security Council proceedings, personal memoirs of some of those involved in the affair, and the publications of the Democratic Party of Azerbaijan as well as those of the Tudeh. The missing link was naturally the documents of the Soviet (Moscow and Baku) archives. Yet no serious impartial effort was undertaken. Since the demise of the USSR, a number of former Soviet historians have had access to some of the forbidden archives, and have written interesting books about the Azerbaijan affair. (Foreign historians have been denied access to those archives.)

A couple of interesting documents that throw light both on the Tudeh's initial position on the issue and its later *volte-face* deserve to be briefly discussed here.

Contrary to all appearances and the hostile propaganda, the initial position that the Tudeh leadership took *vis-à-vis* the DPA and AGA was one of hostility to them. In a letter addressed to the Soviet Central Committee, the Tudeh Central Committee announced its total opposition to that movement as detrimental to Soviet interests in Iran, to the Tudeh Party and its future in the country, and to Iran's interests.[173] This was a wise position. However, it was soon reversed, as the Soviet embassy applied pressure on the Central Committee, two members of which were obliged to address a letter to the Soviet party acknowledging their total accord with what was taking place.[174] This was naturally because of the initial inescapable dependence of the Tudeh on the Soviet party.

VIII: Proscription of the Tudeh or the Shah's First Coup in 1949.

The so-called attempt on the life of the shah in 1949 was unanimously accepted by the community of Iranologists as 'an historical fact'. Of the many experts who wrote on Iran of this period, no one ever questioned the authenticity of the claim by the regime that the Tudeh, hence the Soviets, had planned the attempt in a move for the take-over of Iran, a supposition that was beautifully part and parcel of the Cold War paradigm. On the other hand, the pro-Soviets either clung to their version of the 'truth' that it was an 'imperialist plot' to suppress the Tudeh Party, or joined the 'popular myth' that it was Razmara's attempt to do away with the shah,[175] Thereby the science of history was diminished to the nadir of the worst kind of popular myths. In spite of a large documentation in the American archives and also in those of the British, no one was inquisitive enough to investigate the circumstances of an important turning point in Iran's contemporary history which seriously affected the fate of democracy and sealed, with a time-bomb, the destiny of the Iranian monarchy. No one was interested in what the reality was. What mattered was the Cold War. Relating briefly what apparently led to the proscription of the Tudeh, Abrahamian refers to the affair as 'the mysterious attempt on the shah's life'.[176] Zabih does not even bother to call it 'mysterious'.[177] It was not a paying enterprise for historians through all these years to investigate an 'incident' that was the most decisive turning point in Iran's postwar history: the restoration of the Pahlavi autocracy.[178]

IX: The 1953 Coup and the 1957 Fourth Plenum of the Tudeh

The history of the 1953 *coup d'état* (or what Zabih ignominiously calls 'the crisis' or 'the confused state of affairs'[179]) is well known by now, and all parties involved (except the Pahlavi family) have admitted the direct Anglo-American planning and execution of it.[180] But it was also clear in 1966 that the coup had been prepared by the Anglo-American secret services. Nonetheless, an ideologically-oriented political scientist such as Zabih could not but content himself with the 'obscurity' and 'controversial nature of American involvement' in the that 'affair'.[181] Although he quotes a Tudeh Central Committee declaration (*Mardom*, 18 August 1953) in favour of 'immediately' establishing a 'democratic republic' — a position that, according to Mark Gasiorowski, turns out to have been dictated by the CIA through a mole in the top-level Tudeh leadership in Tehran (could it have been Kianouri?) — Zabih states that 'significantly, the party did not advocate the immediate establishment of a people's democracy or even participation in the now isolated National Front government',[182] leaving the reader to wonder what the exact difference was between a 'people's democracy' and a 'democratic republic' at the time! Repeating the Tudeh's tale about Mosaddeq's alleged refusal to provide the Tudeh with arms, Zabih, on the one hand, justifies that the party's incessant remonstrating of Mosaddeq for that refusal; on the other hand, he claims that the 'victory' over Mosaddeq by the shah 'was not altogether unexpected, inasmuch as past experience had shown that the government could not retain power for long without at least a tacit acquiescence of the shah, to whom the army had largely remained loyal'! Such contradictory positions are, of course, far from being the historical explications needed to clear up the confused history of the coup of 16-19 August 1953. The most amazing thing about Zabih is, of course, his attempt in 1982 (even after revelations by CIA agents such as Kim Roosevelt) to prove that the CIA's role in the *coup d'état* was *not very significant*. To understand Zabih's enterprise after the coup and the occupation of the US embassy by the Students of the Imam Line, one should glance at the 'Foreword' by 'Professor Amos Perlmutter' of the American University to his 1982 book *The Mossadegh Era*,[183] who glorifies his *The Communist Movement in Iran* 'as a well-established classic', and applauds this new book as one that will:

> ... dispel the heavily promulgated myth of the importance of the CIA in the downfall of [*not* 'coup against' — CC] Mossadegh and the return of the shah. In perspective, the CIA's role in these climactic events was not very significant, despite some of the heavily unsubstantiated claims of the old boys such as Kim Roosevelt. If anything, the role of British Intelligence was probably more important than that of the CIA... Zabih's analysis of the struggle [between the Iranians themselves] is masterful, detailed, and fascinating.

On the other hand, Abrahamian, who opens his story of Tudeh–Mosaddeq relations by 'pulling out of a hat' an imaginary 'debate' among the Tudeh leadership in Iran (in *Razm*, 26 June 1950 — some 11 months before Mosaddeq assumed office!), finds the Tudeh 'sharply divided'[184] on Iran's patriotic leader. And to prove his point further, after referring to a few hostile Tudeh articles, he quickly jumps to 'later years', after the Fourth Plenum in 1957 (including some articles in the Communist press by Eskandari and Kianouri),[185] when the Tudeh was finally forced, under pressure from its young remaining cadres, to admit its 'mistaken' policy towards Mosaddeq and the national movement. The astonishing thing, however, is the misrepresentation of the content of the famous and controversial 'analysis' by the Tudeh Executive Committee in Tehran titled *Darbareh-ye bistohasht-e mordad* (*Concerning 19 August*, never published) which, in fact, approved and justified the Tudeh's policy of opposition to Mosaddeq and blamed him for the defeat; but Abrahamian presents it as having 'admitted that the Tudeh had made drastic mistakes in not fully [!] backing Mosaddeq'.[186] (I will refer to Kianouri's own letter to the Central Committee in Moscow that contradicts this claim.) Written by Galoust Zakharian, a member of Tehran Provincial Committee, but on behalf of the majority faction in the Executive Committee of the Central Committee, it was opposed by Kianouri who responded to it in another piece called *Darbareh-ye* '*Darbareh-ye 28 mordad*' (*About 'Concerning 19 August'*) and published in one of the party's 'Instruction Pamphlets' (*Jozveh-ye ta'limati*, no 44),[187] in which he blamed the Tudeh leadership for having 'followed' (!) Mosaddeq and 'not assumed' the 'proletarian leadership' of the anti-imperialist movement. (By the way, it should be emphasised that Kianouri's claim to have telephoned Mosaddeq personally[188] — a claim almost everyone has accepted as a fact — to inform him of the impending coup was not mentioned in his aforementioned Tudeh pamphlet, but only long after Mosaddeq's death when the latter was no longer in a position to contradict him.) As to whom had informed Mosaddeq of the impending coup much speculation has been made, and often without any documentation. It is to be noted that there was a high-ranking Tudeh officer named Poulad-dezh among the Royal Guard officers arrested along with Nasiri who delivered the *firman* of the shah. It is must have been Poulad-dezh who informed Mosaddeq, directly or indirectly, and certainly not through Kianouri, for he did not have good relations with Kianouri, nor could the latter have been, on account of his well-known enmity with Mosaddeq, the best messenger.[189]

Abrahamian's defence of the Tudeh leadership, for years 'advised' by the Soviets, is also reflected in his 'appraisal': 'the discussion of 1951-1953 [among Tudeh leaders] had nonetheless been somewhat academic, since the final decision [the formation of a united front?] rested with Mosaddeq, not with the Tudeh'.[190]

By blaming Mosaddeq for not accepting the Tudeh line lock, stock and barrel, Abrahamian concludes that the 'mutual suspicion between the Tudeh and the National Front eventually helped to destroy Mosaddeq' through the coup. In describing the events of 16-19 August, he distorts their account — including reducing the Tudeh's provocative demand of a 'democratic republic' to a 'republic' and claiming, without presenting any references at all, that 'the organs [sic] of the National Front declared in their early-morning issue [supposedly of 19 August] that the danger from the shah had ended but the danger from the Communists loomed large and would destroy the nation unless promptly stamped out'![191] This claim is based, not on contemporary evidence, but on an article published after the 1979 revolution in *Ettela'at* by Captain Fesharaki to the effect that the 'Tudeh leaders had informed Mosaddeq by phone that their military sympathisers had evidence to prove that the royalist officers had conspired to use the premier's instructions to re-establish law and order as a cover to overthrow the National Front'.[192] This claim has never been confirmed by any Tudeh leader, not even by Kianouri, known among many Tudeh cadres as a master of prevarication.[193]

An historian is duty bound to leave no stone unturned and, at least, search for and use all known and available documents. *One* of the reasons why the second coup succeeded on 19 August is that immediately after the abortive coup, the Tudeh Central Committee published a long declaration on the subject, which the Tudeh propaganda machinery disseminated, containing, among other things, the misinformation that the putschists were not intending to strike from the provinces. The Tudeh's legal organ notably diverted attention from the repetition of the coup in Tehran. It said:

> Now that the coup plot has met with failure in the centre [Tehran], the field of their agents [putschists] who have not been arrested has moved to the provinces. According to information obtained [by the Tudeh Central Committee], one of the important fields of operations is Khuzistan. The Division Commander of Khuzistan Brigadier Maghrouri, who is in touch with the putschists in Tehran, is attempting, on their orders, to create trouble in this sensitive and important province and, by declaring the independence of the province, to embark upon overthrowing the government. Other news relate that General Zahedi, the treacherous shah's so-called premier, having been defeated in Tehran, has also left for Khuzistan; he intends to, along with Brigadier Maghrouri, and all the help he can muster from the areas under British domination (that is, Basra, Kuwait and Bahrain), to continue the treacherous plot... It is planned that the shah, now on the run, will enter Ahwaz in order to take over the government that the colonialists are preparing for him through the suppression of our independence and national sovereignty...[194]

There are three considerations why the government heeded this 'information' and concentrated more energy in the provinces, particularly oil-rich Khuzistan, and neglect the capital. Firstly, Khuzistan was, indeed, the vital province over whose oil the British had mobilised the whole Western world against Iran; secondly, in 1920, when the revolutionaries of the north were seriously threatening Tehran, the British plan was to set up an independent government in Khuzistan in order to protect the oil fields from the 'Bolsheviks'; and thirdly, this 'information' came from the Tudeh, who had been the principal, if not the only, source of information on the first coup for the Prime Minister. Reference to this disinformation is not to absolve Mosaddeq and his colleagues for unpardonable negligence; it is rather to point out that, as one leader of a Tudeh front organisation stated in an open letter to Kianouri's wife after their return to the country,[195] the Tudeh Central Committee's declaration and the subsequent leader in the party organ were, indeed, a diversionary tactic played out by the British mole (or moles) at the Central Committee level.

It is to be emphasised that when the Tudeh said that it had the 'information', it must have meant that the 'information' had reached it through its reliable source, that is, its military officers, just as in the case of the first coup a few days earlier. The same is true about Brigadier Maghrouri. The Tudeh's officers usually knew the political inclinations of division commanders, etc. Now, both these pieces of 'information' turned out to be false, that is, were *disinformation*. Certainly, it cannot be claimed that these two pieces of disinformation emanated from the Tudeh's military organisation. Who was then responsible for this diversionary tactic in the Central Committee? We still do not know, but it can be no other than the British mole(s) in the Tudeh Central Committee.

No less serious, however, is Abrahamian's repetition of *unverified*, propagandistic material about Mosaddeq's alleged acquiescence to 'the urging of the American Ambassador' Henderson (during his short meeting with him on the evening of 18 August) to instruct 'the army to clear the streets of Tudeh demonstrators', and Kianouri repeats the same prevarication, of course, without reference to Abrahamian! This claim is, in fact, a reformulation of what Kim Roosevelt put forth in order to denigrate Mosaddeq.[196] Anyone acquainted with the man who had fought all his life against foreign interference in Iran's affairs would know, even without access to archives, that such a claim could not but be a pure fabrication. Now, the fact is that, according to the long text of the record of his conversation with Mosaddeq, Henderson never made such a request of the Iranian premier. Indeed, the record shows that Mosaddeq spoke firmly and even sarcastically with Henderson, making it known to him that he was not pleased with the American's possible involvement in the coup. Of course, Abrahamian does not provide any source for this preposterous fabrication; but the sources, in addition to Kim Roosevelt's claim,[197] are known: some royalists,[198] and the Tudeh leader Kianouri.[199] Some of the key points in Henderson's telegram of 18 August from Tehran to the Department of State should throw light on this misrepresentation.[200] It should be added that Mosaddeq's attitude *vis-à-vis* Henderson was known long before the declassification of the aforementioned telegram by the US Ambassador. It was already known just three days after the coup. On 22 August 1953, *Khandaniha*,[201] a weekly run by a journalist close to the court, reported the following:

> According to Radio Paris... [Henderson in his meeting with the Iranian premier]... informed Mosaddeq that 'the US government could no longer recognise his government and would not consider him as the lawful Prime Minister. Henderson solemnly told Mosaddeq that the US would, with all its powers, impede him from continuing to rule, and ordered him to resign. But Mosaddeq told Henderson off and threw him out of his house, declaring that he would sever relations with Washington tomorrow.'

Should this not have prompted an historian to be more prudent and impartial? The answer is clear.

As to the historical explanation that tautologically blames the failure of the labour movement on the character of the 'national bourgeoisie', the following observation should suffice. Those who claim that the Tudeh Party had, by mid-1946, unionised 75 per cent of all Iranian workers (350 000 of some 472 500) all over Iran in 186 unions, cannot but offer the following reason for the failure of that movement, in spite of more than two years of unprecedented freedom under Mosaddeq:

> The 1953 coup easily defeated the labour movement, for the armed forces remained loyalist [that is, to the shah]. The ulema, speaking on behalf of the traditional middle class, waged an intense anti-Communist campaign. The Tudeh, for a variety of reasons [which he prefers not to mention!], failed to forge an alliance with the National Front.[202]

This is an explanation that begs the essential question of the defeat of the Tudeh, in addition to being wrong all the way through, because the armed forces, except for a handful, did not really participate in the coup; the 'ulema did not represent the 'traditional middle class'; and that the only reason why the Tudeh refused to forge an alliance with Mosaddeq, or even to support him, was its subservience to the Soviet Union and its policy against truly patriotic and democratic movements which wished to be neutral in the Cold War, for which reason its military organisation under Kianouri did not budge when it should have done so in order to stop the putschists.[203] If not known before, the memoirs that some Tudeh leaders and cadres have published since have made this point amply clear.[204]

X: The Soviet Government and the Iranian National Movement

Another issue on which historians of the period, including Zabih and Abrahamian, have been silent is the policy of the Soviet government towards the Iranian national movement. It is germane, therefore, to make a short observation about the Tudeh's opposition to Mosaddeq in the light of the Soviet attitude. Was the Tudeh's policy of opposition to Mosaddeq adopted on its own, or was it dictated by the Soviet government? Few people can doubt that it was the latter case. Then the question that follows is why the Soviets maintained, until June 1953, a hostile attitude towards the Iranian national movement, and had the Tudeh sabotage it. The answer lies in Stalin's anti-national policy, which was enunciated as late as the Nineteenth Party Congress which he attended some months before his death on 5 March 1953. According to the Central Committee member Gh-H Foroutan, who attended that congress, Stalin's speech at the end of that gathering, where he blasted the national bourgeoisie as having abandoned the banner of independence and democracy, further provided some Tudeh leaders with the pretext 'to justify and continue their policy against the oil question and Mosaddeq in particular, which was a useless venture'.[205] It is, therefore, vital to observe the radical change in Soviet attitude towards Mosaddeq in late June, three months after Stalin's death and on the morrow of the suppression of the East German uprising by Beria's iron fist. This was one of the results of Khrushchev's coup against Beria, who had been preparing to replace Stalin. Beria had joined forces with the weak-minded Malenkov in order to facilitate his own consolidation of power. Frightened by this perspective, Khrushchev, in turn, joined forces with other top leaders, such as Molotov, Bulganin and Gosplan chief M Saburov, finally also managing to win over Malenkov. Having prepared his coup meticulously, during the meeting of party Presidium on 26 June, he and his allies had Beria arrested by a group of trusted military men for 'treason' and 'anti-party activity', and had him shot in December.[206]

It should be recalled that Beria, along with his Azerbaijani ally J Bagirov, had been very close to Stalin, and, what is more, they had played an important role in the creation of the 'Autonomous Government' in Tabriz and the 'Kurdish Republic' in Mahabad. Their plan had been, not only to take over these two Iranian provinces, but also to reach the oil-rich province of Khuzistan and the Persian Gulf both for the oil and access to warm waters — a plan that had already been included in the Germano-Soviet pact of 23 August 1939.[207] Recent studies by three scholars,[208] a Russian, an Azerbaijani and a Georgian, based on declassified documents from the Soviet archives, reveal the plans by these two Caucasian Communist leaders and their chief Stalin to dismember Iran. Moreover, as is well known, the question of Azerbaijan and Kurdistan followed Soviet 'disappointment' over the refusal of the Iranian parliament to grant an oil concession to its powerful neighbour. The refusal was proposed by Dr Mosaddeq in the Fourteenth Legislature, who basically argued that Iran should remain the master of its own resources. The Georgian Kavtradze, the Commissar of Foreign Trade who led the Soviet delegation to Iran, was a close associate of Beria. Thus, in addition to the official thesis about the 'treacherous nature of the national bourgeoisie' whose 'representative' in Iran was considered to be Mosaddeq, Beria and his allies, who controlled the Interior Ministry (MVD) and all the other intelligence services, could have hardly been sympathetic to the Iranian national movement under Mosaddeq. On the other hand, it is now well established that the foreign Communist parties had been controlled since the late 1920s, not by the Comintern, but by the Foreign Intelligence service and their agents in those 'brother' parties.[209] It so happens that the Tudeh was, as of 1943, under the effective control of Kambakhsh, an associate of Soviet Foreign

Intelligence and later under his brother-in-law Kianouri. Thus, there can be little doubt that while the Tudeh's opposition to Mosaddeq was principally dictated by the Caucasian band around Stalin, the change of policy in late June 1953 was a result of their removal through Khrushchev's coup. The policies pursued by Khrushchev in favour of anti-imperialist movements in Egypt, Indonesia and Egypt confirm the thesis that with the demise of Stalin, the policy change towards Iran was led by Khrushchev, under whose auspices, by the way, the Tudeh held its fourth plenum and criticised its own policy towards Mosaddeq's government. Viewed in this light, the silence on the part of such historians about Soviet policy and its later change, as well as their attempt to place the blame for the defeat in August 1953 solely upon Mosaddeq, is very telling about them.

XI: The Leftist Organisations After the *Coup d'État*

The history of the organisations after the coup has also been told according to the logic of the Cold War. Just as the Tudeh Party during its exile years imitated the Soviet writers' Stalinist historiography of the Iranian Left,[210] other Leftist organisations emerging after the 1953 coup wrote their versions of 'history of the Left' for their followers according to the same mode of thought, if not exactly copying the Tudeh line, especially after the publication of the *Historical Documents* began.[211] Without giving themselves the trouble of undertaking independent research, they glorified Haidar Khan, denounced Sultanzade — if they had heard of him at all — they glorified Arani, without looking into the reasons for the arrest of the Arani Circle and its sequels, and so on. Thus, the Stalinist school of the Iranian Left reproduced itself in, for instance, Sazman-e Enqelabi's *The Communist Movement in Iran*[212] and the organisation's own history until the 1979 revolution;[213] the Fada'iyans *Tarikh-e jame' bara-ye nojavanan* by H Mo'meni,[214] and B Jazani's *The Thirty Years' Events of Iran*;[215] as well as Ettehadiyeh-ye Komonistha's *Demokrasi-ye naqes*, dealing with the Tudeh and the Mosaddeq era, as well as a small pamphlet on the labour movement.[216] On the eve of the 1979 revolution, the newly founded Iranian Trotskyist organisation (in the USA) found it useful to write its own short history as well.[217] From among all these writings, the one that has survived and become a revered reference for the Leftists is Jazani's *The Thirty Years' Events of Iran*.

Let us look at some of its details. In spite of the praise that Jazani's work has received, it must be pointed out that this *History* is neither based on serious research nor free from an emotional and hostile outlook shaped by the youthful experiences and disappointments of a man active in the ranks of the Tudeh before and after the 1953 *coup d'état*.[218] In its very beginning, Jazani writes that the ICP was founded 'on the order of the Comintern in 1921... and among its founders were Haidar Amoughli, Pishevari, Ehsan-Allah Khan, Ovanesian, Jowdat, and later Kambakhsh and Dr Javid'.[219] No doubt acquired from scattered information circulating in the Tudeh circles, there are several glaring errors in this very short account. The party was not founded on the order of the Comintern, it was already in existence, as early as 1916, in various parts of the former Russian empire where Iranian labourers had been working; its congress was held in June 1920, not in 1921; only Pishevari was present at the Anzali congress; Ovanesian and Kambakhsh were very young and not even members of the party; nor was Haidar Khan a member of the ICP; he belonged to the radical wing of the Ferqeh-ye Demokrat which was active north of the Iranian frontiers and was, in fact, a rival of the ICP.[220] These errors are not insignificant; they reveal a sense of irresponsibility in the historiography of the Left by the young critical elements of it, thereby reducing one's confidence in other facts that cannot be verified so easily.

Jazani's discussion of the Azerbaijan crisis is incomplete and inaccurate, to say the least, in spite of the fact that it does not take a pro-Soviet position and does recognise the Soviet intervention in Iran and its manipulation of the Tudeh and the popular movement.[221] Suffice it to point out that, contrary to Jazani's assertion,[222] Qavam returned from his trip to Moscow without an agreement, as he pointed out in his report to the Majles.[223] Jazani simplifies the withdrawal of the Soviet forces from Iran,[224] for which much pressure was applied by the West, especially the Americans. No less distorted is his affirmation, oft-repeated, mainly by the Western circles, that Mosaddeq used the Tudeh demonstrations against himself as a scarecrow to warn the USA of the Communist danger in Iran.[225] In spite of his critical position *vis-à-vis* his former leaders in the Tudeh, Jazani cannot understand Mosaddeq's democratism. Nor is his claim true that the Tudeh militants shouted 'Victory to Mosaddeq and Either Death or Mosaddeq' during the 30 Tir demonstrations. Most of the Tudeh's critical writings now have accepted the fact that the Tudeh was absent from the demonstrations of that day. Insofar as the *coup d'état* and the role of the Tudeh is concerned, one can see that his information is based on the kind that the Tudeh leadership disseminated immediately after those critical days,[226] and which was repeated decades later in Kianouri's *Khaterat*, falsely quoting Mosaddeq as having said, during the first alleged contacts, to the Tudeh leadership, notably Khodabandeh: 'There is nothing I can do [against the putschists]; do whatever you can.'[227]

Finally, Jazani also blames Mosaddeq for not having accepted, even to the last day of his government, the hand of collaboration that the Tudeh extended to him[228] — the Tudeh never did that and this is now admitted by former Central Committee member B Amirkhosrowi.[229] There is no lack of miscomprehensions and misrepresentations of those historical events, but the most preposterous falsehood by Jazani is the accusation he throws at the patriotic individuals whom he opposed while in the Tudeh: Dr H Fatemi, Mosaddeq's closest colleague 'had in the past, before joining Mosaddeq, collaborated with the [British] Intelligence Service' — an incredible, unfounded and irresponsible allegation that had never been heard of before, even from a well-known liar such as Kianouri. Regarding the influence of Fatemi on Mosaddeq, suffice it to refer to the book by Mokri, a principled leader of the 'National Association for the Struggle against Colonialism', a satellite of the Tudeh.[230] It is also to be recalled that up until his arrest by the putschists of 1953, Fatemi had been arrested on two other occasions by British agents; once right after the invasion of Iran in September 1941, and the other by General Razmarar. In addition, the CIA propaganda apparatus in its campaign against the national movement published brochures in which it accused Fatemi of sexually immoral conduct and having become a Baha'i.

The most systematic piece on the Left after the 1953 coup, though short, is by T Haqshenas, himself a former Mojahed turned Marxist-Leninist. Based mainly on personal knowledge acquired as a militant as well as on Abrahamian's book from 1982 and Jazani's aforementioned work, though informative, this piece suffers from serious errors and personal partiality and subjectivity.[231]

Another study is Sepehr Zabih's *The Left in Contemporary Iran*, which, in spite of its pretensions as to new research, is exceptionally poor, both in terms of the incorrect as well as misleading information that he provides and the conceptual framework he uses. Notably, it gives too much prominence to certain groups with no influence on the movement as a whole, and too little to those that had a greater impact.[232] Clinging to old clichés that are largely based on rumours and assumptions, if not outright falsifications, gathered from unreliable sources, he disregards hard evidence, such as, for instance, in the case of the first Tudeh split in 1948 and what the Maleki group did thereafter. He fails to give proper references in his discussion of the Mojahedin, leaving his serious reader to wonder where his information had come from; he does not discuss Rah-e Kargar, while referring to the arch-Stalinist Paykar organisation as a Trotskyist party; he fails to give proper references for the material he takes from the London-based pro-Fada'iyan's review *Nouzdah-e bahman-e teorik*; he quotes at length the journal *Jahan* published in the USA by the Minority Fada'iyan and attributes its positions to the Majority faction; he reproduces a Fada'iyan brochure *A Short Analysis*, almost word for word, without the slightest criticism, repeating the false impression that the Fada'is believe themselves to be a group of 'flexible and creative' intellectuals. One is puzzled by the impression Zabih gives that a Leninist organisation such as the Fada'is' was 'democratic'. He is totally silent on the well-known, serious criticism by Mostafa Sho'a'iyan made at the time of the Fada'is, one that was later confirmed when they came into the open. He is also wrong on the 'anti-Soviet' orientation of the Jazani Group. The group's main criticism was directed at the Tudeh leadership that was subservient to Soviet demands, and not at the Soviets themselves. Although he devotes a whole chapter to a very small and inconsequential organisation called 'Enqelabiyoun-e Kommonist', his information on that group is faulty. Indeed, Zabih's second book on Iranian Communism not only fails to provide new facts and information on a vital subject, but it muddles the picture further by giving incomplete and erroneous information and consequently incorrect analysis.[233]

XII: Infiltration of Leftist Organisations and Leaks to the Political Police

In the study of the Left, one cannot overlook an important factor in the serious damage that was done to the new revolutionary organisations in Iran in the late 1960s. That was achieved through the infiltration of these young organisations by the Shahriari group, known as the Tudeh Tehran Organisation (TTO), the official representative of the Tudeh Executive Committee within Iran, under direct orders of First Secretary Radmanesh. 'Abbas Shahriari had been trained, along with P Hekmatjou, A Khavari and a host of other Tudeh cadres, by the KGB in the late 1950s. The date that Shahriari's group, or the TTO, began operations is not clear, but it cannot have been before the Marble Palace Incident in 1965, when a group of Maoists were arrested and tried for an alleged attempt on the life of the shah.[234] The arrests and trial aroused an international campaign against the shah and created a highly favourable atmosphere among the Iranian youth in favour of revolutionary warfare in general, and the Maoist line in particular. At this moment, the TTO began putting out, in the name of the Tehran, Tabriz and Khuzistan 'organisations', a series of pamphlets (including *Zamimeh-ye [Supplement to] Mardom*) that were critical of the Soviet Union, preaching a revolutionary line. Having been known as a top cadre of the Tudeh in the oil region in the pre-coup period, Shahriari soon managed to attract the attention of the new revolutionaries, the Jazani Group, the revolutionary combatants who after their arrest came to known as the Mojahedin-e Khalq, and also the Palestine Group, which needed help in crossing the Iranian border into Iraq and then over to the Palestinian guerrilla training camps. Most members of these groups were arrested by the SAVAK before they realised that the trap had been set up by Shahriari. Once the damage was done, Shahriari was arrested by the SAVAK. He appeared on a SAVAK 'repentance show' as a man with a 'thousand faces'. The revolutionary groups denounced him as a treacherous SAVAK agent. In the meantime, in a struggle to unseat Radmanesh from his position of First Secretary, his opponents Kianouri, Ovanesian and Eskandari united. They told the party plenum in December 1969 that 'Soviet comrades', such as Boris Ponomariev, had informed them of Shahriari's treachery and the need to remove Radmanesh for his gross mistake. Radmanesh resisted and argued that, in fact, Shahriari had been introduced to him by Soviet comrades (alias for KGB operatives), and therefore any fault committed was theirs.[235] Once Radmanesh was removed, Shahriari's picture was published in the Tudeh organ *Mardom*.[236] Soon thereafter, the Fada'is found the well-disguised double agent at his new residence and shot him point-blank, putting out a declaration on the revenge of the people upon the SAVAK agent.[237] Naturally, everyone believed what the Fada'is had said; that is, they tracked down Shahriari. The question that remains to be answered is how a few remaining Fada'is in a big city such as Tehran could have tracked down a man who had changed his home, lived under a different name, and appeared in public only in disguise.

Radmanesh's reminiscences given to Baqer Mo'meni[238] throws serious doubt on the Tudeh and Fada'is versions that the SAVAK was behind the infiltrations by the Shahriari group. In addition to Radmanesh's insistent statement that the Soviets had put Shahriari in his service, there is the serious question as to why the Soviets and the Tudeh First Secretary had never opposed the Shahriari group's critique of Soviet policy towards the shah and did not remove him, allowing him to carry on for nearly four years. The Tudeh tale that the SAVAK had sent an agent to expose Shahriari to Radmanesh and ensure his arrest at the border by the Soviets simply does not make sense and cannot be considered but as an amateurish fabrication.[239]

One must also consider the adamant opposition of the Soviets and the Tudeh to the new revolutionary trends in Iran, all of which were seriously opposed to the Tudeh, and most of them were critical of the Soviet Union and in sympathy with Che Guevara and Mao Zedong. It seems, therefore, useful to explore the idea whether the old Stalinist technique of infiltration of revolutionary groups and organisations and exposing them to the police was not applied here by the Shahriari group, as it had been done in the case of the Arani Circle of 1935-36.

While serious research needs to be undertaken in this direction, one can soberly refute as gratuitous a statement, if not an intentional falsification (or cover-up), the claim according to which the Tudeh Party, although 'opposed [to] the theory of guerrilla warfare', gave 'assistance' to two of the founders of the guerrilla movement, Farahani and Ashtiyani, through its 'First Secretary Radmanesh of the Tudeh and the director of the party's operations in the Middle East'. 'When the Tudeh Central Committee heard of this unauthorised assistance [through the publication of documents by the SAVAK 'proving' this connection between the Fada'is and Radmanesh], it recalled Radmanesh [to Leipzig] and elected Iraj Eskandari as the party's First Secretary.'[240] This account does not tally with that told by Kianouri (which is also unreliable) nor with Ovanesian's, still less with the official Tudeh statement in December 1973,[241] which also published Shahriari's picture. It is to be pondered why the Tudeh denounced Shahriari and published his picture in December 1973 while Radmanesh had been removed in 1970,[242] clearly because of his contact with Shahriari and the latter's 'treachery'. Only if and when the STASI and SED files on the Tudeh and the Tudeh's own archives (formerly kept at the Leipzig headquarters)[243] are made available to historians, can we answer these mysteries which weighed heavily on the destiny of the revolutionary movement in Iran.

In this very connection, it is worth noting another piece written by Shahram Chubin soon after the 1979 revolution, on the eve of the Iraqi invasion of Iran, from the perspective of the Cold War, from the other side of the 'curtain'.[244] In addition to its factual errors — in view of their obviousness, one wonders whether they are intentional[245] — gross contradictions, and sources that 'cannot be identified publicly', Chubin's piece aims at showing the dangers that the Islamic Republic faced from the Left. It exaggerates the strength of the Fada'is: 'Its willingness to resist the government and to field more than 5000 adherents prepared to fight testifies to a new confidence... a reasonable estimate is that the Fada'iyan has between seven and eight million sympathisers throughout the country, perhaps half a million in Tehran...'[246] What is more, it tries to depict a practical collaboration involving the Tudeh, Mojahedin and the Fada'is, which does not conform to the facts known then. His analysis boils down to the following alternatives: either the victory of the Left after the demise of Ayatollah Khomeini or its repression before he dies. Given the prevalence of conspiracy theories in Iran and the importance such 'theorists' attach to Western or Soviet plans and information (particularly published in that kind of journal), the author's intention is obvious. He goes so far as to suggest the need for repression if the Left was not to take over:

> The crowds currently supporting the Imam [Khomeini] have been politically mobilised. They are devoted, but they are suggestible, volatile, and (ultimately) fickle. ... under what conditions could the masses' passion in Iran be harnessed by the Left? ... [Ayatollah Khomeini's]... strength has been one of personality, not dogma. It is dubious that his legitimacy will be transferable or that his allegiance will automatically be extended to his successors. If Khomeini's charisma is not institutionalised (or routinised), the clerical divisions and schisms that fragment the Right would be reflected in the nation at large, and the clerical regime would lose ground to other forces.

To wit, the Left. He then goes on to discuss various scenarios, such as a 'major defeat at the hand of, say, the Kurds, combined with economic problems' or a 'military action by an outside power, such as Iraq', which 'continue to surround the regime. ... The Left stands to benefit from the failures of the present regime. ... If the government falters, therefore, it [the Left] will be there to pick up the pieces.'[247] One wonders what the message is. At any rate, this appreciation of the Left is an exaggerated one, intentional or not.

The latest work published on the Leftist organisations during the period of 1953-83 is *Rebels with a Cause* by Maziar Behrouz.[248] Beginning with a treatment of the Tudeh and other 'classical' Leftist groups,[249] and uncritically using known sources and no archival ones, and without any interviews with the surviving cadres of the Fada'iyan in the West, this study is basically interested in the new organisations born with the currency of the idea of armed struggle in Iran under the influence of the Algerian and Cuban revolutions. Unfortunately, lack of space does not allow a thoroughgoing critique of this superficial account of the Tudeh, which in addition to basically relying on Abrahamian, adds some selective sources which suits his 'thesis',[250] which remains quite unclear as to the relationship of the Tudeh with the Soviet Union and the former's hostile attitude toward the Mosaddeq government. A few gross misrepresentations of his 'facts' do point to the lack of seriousness and lack of deontological care in handling those 'facts'. Firstly, in an academic work he equates Marxists with Communists (p xi), forgetting that the latter refers to members of the Communist parties obedient to Moscow, and later to China; he refers to the Tudeh as a 'Marxist' party,[251] rather than a Marxist-Leninist organisation, at least after 1949. It is not insignificant that he is even unfamiliar with the most basic terms used in the international Communist parlance, thus referring on page 38 to the Leninist 'party of the new type', as 'New Party of the Working Class'. These insignificant examples show that the author is not familiar with the basic literature of the history of the international Communist movement.

Moreover, instead of carrying out serious research into Soviet writings on Mosaddeq both when he was premier and thereafter, Behrouz relies on selective quotations from a book written by pro-Soviet, but anti-leadership, Tudeh cadres[252] who try to portray the Soviets as friendly to Mosaddeq.[253] Another serious error (p 22) picked up from dubious sources is the question of confusing Rostam Aliev, a Soviet specialist in Persian literature, with Haidar Aliev, KGB chief in Azerbaijan and later President (who, by the way, was too young to be an ally of Bagerov and who rose to prominence after the latter's demise), neither of whom were involved in the Tudeh Party in that period.[254] More importantly, contrary to Behrouz's assertion (p 3), until 1957 the Tudeh never claimed to be the 'rightful heir' to the ICP.[255]

A more serious ethical error of the author is the repetition of the unsubstantiated and most unlikely claim by an American CIA operative in Iran, Earnest Oney, to Mark Gasiorowski[256] to the effect that the Lankarani brothers were the British moles who penetrated the Tudeh at a 'high level during the coup period'. It is important to make two brief points in this regard. Firstly, this false claim serves to divert attention from the real mole at the top of the Tudeh, which might be intentional on Oney's part. Secondly, and for deontological reasons, it is vital thoroughly to criticise this prevarication (and irresponsibly repeated) by a CIA operative in Iran who prefers not to name the Iranian collaborators of his organisation, but is generous with the destruction of the honour of the Lankarani Brothers.

Of the five brothers,[257] the eldest, Sheikh Hussein, a liberal clergyman, had a long record of opposition to Reza Khan which earned him a long internal exile at Kalat-e Naderi, and to the British and their supporters, particularly while in the Fourteenth Majles — no doubt with Soviet support. Of the twin brothers Mostafa and Morteza, the former ran a small front organisation of the Tudeh named Jam'iyat-e Azadi-ye Iran (Association for Iran's Freedom),[258] and the latter published a newspaper called *Setareh-ye solh* (*The Star of Peace*), which replaced *Besouy-e ayandeh* when the latter was seized by the censor. Ahmad was one of the leaders of the Jam'iyat-e Irani-ye Havadar-e Solh (Iranian Association Supporting Peace),[259] another Tudeh front organisation with little influence amongst the leadership. The youngest, Hesam, though a professional, underground cadre of the Tudeh and a close friend of Khosrow Rouzbeh, was brutally murdered, in Shahrivar 1331/August-September 1952, under Rouzbeh's direction on the order of the both factions of the Tudeh Central Committee resident in Iran. His 'crime' was 'knowing too much' about the Tudeh, which he might have revealed, so claims Rouzbeh, to the police because he was said to have been 'morally corrupt', that is, an 'alcoholic, an opium addict, and a womaniser'![260] Let us examine this groundless justification.

Firstly, let us see what role Hesam Lankarani played in the Tudeh Party. As far as is known, he had no official position in the party, unless it might have been in the underground organisation collaborating with Rouzbeh. One of the Tudeh leaders in the underground after the proscription of Tudeh, Foroutan, writes in his memoirs:

> Hesam Lankarani, with whom I first became acquainted in the underground in early 1328 [1949], told me that there was the possibility of organising Kianouri's escape from prison. I agreed with the idea. Hesam also discussed the matter with Bahrami [of the Executive Committee], and as far as I can remember, he did not oppose the idea.[261]

Foroutan adds that Hesam and his collaborators 'had once or twice arranged the escape of Rouzbeh and had experience in this matter. ... They had made the plan for Kianouri's escape.' Foroutan adds, after the escape of Tudeh leaders: 'Hesam Lankarani and his collaborators assigned the Tudeh leaders to the three hiding places they had already prepared for them...'[262] According to Oney and those who quote him, the six Tudeh leaders who had escaped from prison and lived in the underground with the help of Hesam Lankarani and his collaborators must have been in greater danger than when in the shah's prison — threatened by their captivity and with death at the hands of a 'British agent'! In the light of this information which could and should have been known by the author who quotes Oney, should not the accusation of against Hesam Lankarani as a 'British agent' be considered irresponsible and unethical?

Secondly, it is not comprehensible why, in an underground, Leninist organisation, somebody should have been privy to so much information and responsibility that this would make his 'murder' necessary. Was Captain Abbasi, who in 1954 immediately betrayed the Tudeh military organisation to the Military Governor, an 'alcoholic, an opium addict, and a womaniser'? Considering that those who were worried about the fate of the Tudeh did not punish Abbasi after he had committed treason, it is not clear why Hesam Lankarani was put to death on the mere suspicion that he might give revelations to the police sometime in the future. Why in the case of the 'probability of such treason' did not both factions of the Tudeh leadership in Tehran vote for the transfer of Hesam Lankarani for treatment in the Soviet Union? It is interesting to note that after his murder, they lied to his family and told them that he had been sent abroad, that is, to the Soviet Union! What is more, contrary to the claim by the CIA operative Oney, none of the other four Lankarani brothers occupied a leadership and decision-making position in the Tudeh, and therefore they were in no position to influence the decisions and the fate of the party. Hesam was the only one in contact with 'high circles' of the party, notably Rouzbeh. *It is most important to emphasise that he was purged, in the Stalinist fashion, in the summer of 1952, a year before the coup d'état; hence the falsity of the claim by Oney, as irresponsibly and unethically publicised by Gasiorowski and Behrouz.* As researchers, they relied on the word of a CIA operative, without taking the trouble to look elsewhere for verification in order to avoid falling into Oney's trap, and would at least consider the pretext offered by Rouzbeh, with whose picture Behrouz has decorated his book, in lieu of Oney's allegation. Historians know that no one man's word is God's! (Since a similar accusation has been levelled by the CIA operative Donald Wilber against Fatemi, calling him a 'British agent',[263] one can ask the question whether the aim of imperialist operatives has not been to portray, in the eyes of future generations, the heroic sons of the nation as traitors?)

It would have been interesting to know the views of the following three Tudeh figures on the allegation pronounced by the former CIA agent Oney: namely, A Qoreyshi and A Mottaqi (both elected in 1949 as alternate members to the Central Committee, and expelled, in the summer of 1958, from the Tudeh for reasons of 'treachery' and 'collaboration with the police'[264]) who had much more influential positions in the Tudeh than any of the Lankarani brothers, and Jahangir Behrouz (who spent time in prison with Mostafa Lankarani after the 1953 coup), with all three of whom the author of the book is personally acquainted.[265] It is not without interest to mention that after Hesam's murder was made public, Ehsan Tabari addressed a letter of regret to Mostafa Lankarani, then resident in Vienna.[266] Finally, it must be said that the accusation against Hesam by Rouzbeh, on the one hand, and the calumny by two CIA operatives, Wilber and Oney, on the other, were intended to tarnish the names of those who were among Mosaddeq's staunchest supporters. The case of Fatemi is sufficiently clear to require any explanation. As for Hesam Lankarani, who had grown up in a patriotic, committed and devout family, it should be said that he had been one of the most audacious and unrelenting opponents of the Tudeh's policy against Mosaddeq, and who deserved, from the viewpoint of the Tudeh and its leaders, nothing but liquidation. And for each political murder a rationale must be invented. The task of the historiographer or historian is not the repetition of statements by irresponsible political actors — be they Rouzbeh or Wilber and Oney; rather it is a critical approach towards them in order to establish the historical fact. Only through this approach can one avoid falling into the trap of the colonial teaching of history.

An historian must never fall for self-serving accounts related by protagonists. Behrouz does just that in the matter of Shahriari, a man who was responsible for handing over to the SAVAK many revolutionary dissidents in the 1960s (p 39); although aware of the arguments by Radmanesh related by Baqer Mo'meni (n 125, p 196), he completely disregards them and accepts the official Tudeh version, which must be pleasing to that reader of his, referred to above, who claims that the Tudeh helped various guerrilla groups. In fact, I can testify that Behrouz had, in a preliminary draft of his book shown to me,[267] made the same arguments I have put forth, which he chose to remove at the time of its publication.

Making an attempt to study these revolutionary organisations on the basis of selective primary sources (and also neglecting important British and American archives), the author succeeds somewhat in disproving the idea that the accounts that had been constructed of Leftist organisations in the post-*coup d'état* decades were in fact correct. However, the author is certainly handicapped by his lack of profound knowledge of the forerunners of these groups, that is, the Social Democracy, the ICP and the Tudeh. What is more, as recent devastating critiques of his book by activists and former activists of the Fada'iyan (both majority and minority factions) show, he surely failed to interview a large number of the important ones among them; should they have refused his call for interviews, he could have blamed them for his limited number of oral sources; instead, he deserves the severe blows from those people about whom he writes.[268]

Thus, the author naturally reproduces the old errors of the faulty historiography of the Left for the earlier periods on which he relies. But there is another factor that impedes the author from grasping the tragedy of the Iranian Left both in this early period and during the post-*coup d'état* years. It is the lack of attention paid to the history of the workers' and Leftist movements in the world that is necessary for reasons of elaborating a comparative study. One of the vital factors in gauging the maturity of a political movement is not how many individuals it mobilises; rather, it is the depth of political, socio-economic and cultural analysis (that is, historical knowledge) which the Tudeh and post-Tudeh organisations might have acquired. It is, thus, useless to repeat that the Tudeh unionised 75 per cent of the workers — if in fact that this is at all true: *according to Olovvi, in the spring of 1953, of 50 000 oil workers only some 300 were Tudeh Party members*[269] — what matters is what it did with the forces it mobilised in the interest of the class of which it considered itself to be the vanguard; as is how successful it might have been in sublating the political consciousness and the degree of resistance of that social force. If analysed from this vantage point, the Tudeh and its splinter groups were not only a failure, but were also detrimental to future healthy developments of the labour movement in Iran. It is time historians rose above the propagandistic eulogies that political parties offer them as source material, concept and historical framework.

It is no longer useful to say that the Left had shortcomings when faced with a coup. One has to analyse the historical reasons for these repeated shortcomings — that is, the ensemble of cultural, political and socio-economic (that is, historical) factors that did not allow the Left, or other progressive forces, in Iran to advance beyond a certain point. To do so, one has to make a clean break with the faulty, incomplete, distorted historiographies which have been produced thus far, whether they have to do with the Social Democracy, the ICP, the Arani Circles, Tudeh–Mosaddeq relations, or the guerrilla movement. It is no longer sufficient to say that the Tudeh did not move on 19 August, but one has to explain why it did not do so, and why its military officers did not take any measures to stop the coup — the gateway to a great disaster that affected the future of Iran for decades, if not for ever — just because of the belief that some wise mentor north of the border knew what was best for Iran. Nothing can be explained by repeating that such and such activist had a 'deep understanding of recent Iranian history... giving him a political insight unmatched by others'.[270] The science of history rejects the deterministic, Nostradamusian school of predictions. No political insight can foresee history months in advance, let alone years or decades. Only followers of astrological predictions can make such claims: *history moves in unchartered waters*. It is worth recalling that Lenin, a master strategist for many, could not foresee in late 1916, when he gave a speech to the young Bolsheviks, his own success in 1917. He said the socialist revolution was the task of future generations. No one could have predicted the eventuality of the revolution of 1979 a decade before, for during the last decade of the regime of the shah there were too many socio-economic and political factors undergoing change in Iran to allow us to take any Nostradamusian predictions seriously.

It is time that those who try their hand at history realised that the chess game of social action is by far more complex than the ancient game of chess, particularly if we take into account the very intricate and unpredictable, multifaceted international factors that intervene in any national situation. Anything less than this realisation draws close to astrology.

The questions that the author of *Rebels with a Cause* raises in the final chapter are worthy of consideration, but one needs to go further if one is not to get bogged down in tautologies. 'Repression' is not good enough an explanation of the failure of the Left in Iran; it is at best tautological. Nor does it help our historical understanding to state that the Marxist-Leninists failed in a 'realistic understanding of the nature of the Islamic state', for the failure was rooted in the mode of thought and analysis of Iranian Marxist-Leninist groups long before Ayatollah Khomeini appeared on Iran's political scene, and these roots also have to be explained. It is still less analytic to say that 'another factor which worked against Marxism[-Leninism] in Iran was social class formation'.[271] It is not clear what Marxism represents in this phrase; if it be an analytical tool and properly applied, then it should have told its applicant something about social class formation in Iran. Nor could one content oneself with repeating, ever since the Constitutional Revolution, that the Iranian peasantry is 'non-revolutionary'. One must explain why it was not, that is, if it was not. One must also explain why a 'revolutionary working class', whether large in size or not, failed to produce the 'desired results' under Tudeh leadership between 1941 and 1953, and under the clearly revolutionary conditions of 1971-79, when it — strikingly — paralysed the imperial regime. Nor does it help our historical understanding to speak of the 'language barrier' of the Left if we do not grasp historically how and why such a language came about and what its nature was, etc. Behrouz would have much improved his understanding of these revolutionary groups had he studied and analysed the critiques by Sho'a'iyan, to whom he refers only as an 'independent Marxist theorist',[272] and whose photography adorns his book.

The more valid point of the author about the factor of 'personal rivalries' which paralysed the Iranian political movements, in the twentieth century at least, must be explained as an aspect of Iran's modern history, or as an historically profound mental structure, reinforced under modern politico-cultural conditions. Obedience to and/or imitation of Moscow, Peking or Tirana must also be explained, not simply stated, just as its corollary, that is, lethargy in intellectual and theoretical training — which, whether home-grown or syncretic (sublating), in pre-modern times had its place in the development of Iranian society — often led to cataclysmic results. In the same manner, the carefree adoption by almost all Leftists and their historians (and Jazani is no exception) of the Stalinist school of falsification should be analysed as a mental process that impaired the movement over the past century. If combating the school of falsification is the order of the day, then every source must be subjected to scrupulous and pitiless examination and scrutiny. If such a method were adopted, then one would have to consider all four 'brilliant' theoreticians of the guerrilla movement[273] with the same eye, and with no favouritism.

On the other hand, one cannot overlook the absence of seriousness on the part of the historical work that lays a 'natural' claim to authority and authenticity on Iranian history in the twentieth century, namely, the seventh volume of *The Cambridge History of Iran*.[274] It treats the important Jangali Movement and the *coup d'état* of 1921, which together constitute a turning point in Iran's contemporary history, in a cursory fashion based on dubious sources; it untruthfully claims that Mosaddeq 'turned to the Left', that is, the Tudeh; it has the history of the Iranian oil nationalisation written by the official historian of British Petroleum (formerly Anglo-Iranian Oil Co), which can hardly been seen as impartial, not to say objective, turning the whole volume into an official history of Pahlavi Iran, although published after the latter's demise.[275]

Finally, one should review, albeit briefly, the Soviet coverage of the Iranian Left of the post-coup period. One must not overlook the fact that, until the 1979 revolution, Soviet Iranologists never discussed any of the non-Tudeh Leftist groups. There were two reasons for this 'indifference': firstly, the Tudeh was *the* Leftist party *par excellence*, with exclusive rights to Marxism-Leninism in Iran; secondly, relations with the shah obliged the Soviets to play down the opposition, especially of a violent form, to his reforms. But after the revolution, with the role that the Soviets considered the non-Tudeh Left had played in the downfall of the shah, there was no choice but to discuss it. The most notable discussion was presented by the prolific neo-Stalinist historian SL Agaev, of which a critical summary follows.[276]

As an historian who had in the past defended the shah, Agaev sees the revolution as a 'spontaneously unified front for the struggle against the monarchy and American imperialism', and the liquidation of their domination in Iran. Contenting himself with the statement that the Leftist movement in Iran was 'formed by the representatives of the educated urban strata, and various categories of workers linked more or less with productive enterprises', Agaev sees the Fada'is and the Mojahedin as having been born in conditions of 'revolutionary struggle', which also led to the formation of small splinter groups without any important social influence. With a brief remark on Pouyan's theory of the 'necessity of armed struggle', and the approximate date of the formation of these two principal guerrilla groups, Agaev accepts the label that was put on the Mojahedin as 'Islamic Marxists' because 'it endeavoured right from the start to unite the dogmas of Islamic religion with Marxist positions, which it claimed as a "guide to activity"'.

Agaev recalls the Tudeh's accusations of 'Infantile Leftism' against the Fada'iyan. He devotes a good number of pages to how the Tudeh 'sincerely upheld all the decisions of the new authority', that is, the Islamic Republic under Khomeini. He states that the Tudeh advanced the slogan for a 'unitary popular front' as a main weapon for the development of the revolution on 'a popular-democratic and anti-imperialist path'. The Tudeh opted for 'an unconditional support of the 'Imam's Line', branding, as of the end of 1979, those who did not follow this line as 'extremist Leftists and sectarians'. He quotes Kianouri's interviews that referred to Ayatollah Khomeini's programme as being 'very much like ours, though we have some ideological differences preventing us from creating a political alliance'. Yet he notes that the Tudeh 'considered it possible to attract Khomeini to its side', as had been the case with Nasser and Gaddafi. Agaev does admit that the Tudeh's position did not meet with the 'understanding' of other Leftist forces. Evoking the refusal of the Fada'i and Mojahedin to give up their arms to the regime, Agaev states that the two groups had 'a certain sympathy for each other', but 'there was no organisational contacts between them'. He sees the hand of the Mojahedin and the Fada'is behind 'the creation of the National-Democratic Front', which soon attracted the 'liberal democratic and Leftist forces'. Agaev recognises that the Tudeh leadership did not share the fears of the NDF, which was soon repressed. Discussing the respective positions of the Leftist groups towards the referenda and elections held in the first two years after the revolution, Agaev provides the comparative weight of the votes obtained by them, the Mojahedin obtaining over half a million, the Fada'iyan over 200 000, and the Tudeh 59 000. (Paradoxically, he attributes much less weight to the Left than Shahram Chubin.) The Soviet historian notes that the Tudeh saw Banisadr as 'the main reason for the dissolution of the popular, anti-imperialist unity' — an incredible weight attributed to such a dubious figure. Observing that the events of 1981 were seen by 'certain circles of the clergy as a "third revolution"', and emphasising the weight of the Hojjattiyeh in those times, Agaev recalls that the Tudeh 'heartily approved the dismissal of Banisadr as a new blow against the "bourgeois liberal circles" and a great victory for the genuinely revolutionary forces'.

Agaev then moves on to the Fada'iyan split, the rapprochement between the Majority and the Tudeh, and the unchanging 'Unitary Front' strategy of the Tudeh. Discussing the new positions of the Mojahedin and the Minority that depicted the regime as 'reactionary', Agaev discusses the failure of the general strike which the Mojahedin had called for. On the other hand, he points to the letter of complaint that the Tudeh addressed in May 1982 to the officials of the Islamic Republic about the repression to which it was being subjected, while still renewing its declaration of 'willingness for close cooperation' with the 'genuine followers of the Imam's Line'. While the Tudeh had, by the end of 1982, modified its theoretical analysis of the situation, recognising a differentiation between the 'traditional, conservative course of Islam' and 'revolutionary Islam', the party still emphasised that Ayatollah Khomeini was moving 'mainly in defence of the workers' interests'. The party considered 'it its duty to remain with the masses, but this was linked to the necessity of achieving the most important objective of all the revolutionary forces in Iran: to reinforce unity and overcome differences'. While it was obvious at this time that the authorities 'were preparing to destroy the Leftist organisations that still continued to survive', Agaves asserts, in October 1982 — that is several months after the defection of Kuzichkin[277] — the Tudeh Central Committee published a declaration in which it once again insisted on the 'unity of the revolutionary Islamic forces, supporting the Line of the Imam along with all other revolutionaries, especially with the supporters of scientific socialism'. Evoking the 'decisive' event in Iran, that is, the arrest on 6 February 1983 by the authorities of 'numerous leaders and activists of the Tudeh under the false accusation of spying and working against state security', the Soviet historian notes that the 'danger' to the party 'appears most clearly in the materials published by the party in March 1983', that is, a month later; he points to 'the conjunction between the two religious trends [within the regime] and the movement of the Islamic Republican Party as a whole to the right on a platform of struggling against the followers of scientific socialism'. Agaev adds that the 'repression' of the Tudeh Party, which its 'leadership did not expect', had no influence on its policy. Party declarations published between February and April 1983 linked 'these repressive measures' to 'provocation'. The party emphasised that it had 'from the outset supported the Islamic Revolution', and still called Ayatollah Khomeini 'the genuine supporter of the genuine anti-imperialist and popular line of the revolution'.

Agaev concludes that the 'very complicated and contradictory political activity of the Islamic revolution necessitated', from the very beginning, 'an adequate political line, free from simplified analysis and one-sided decisions' — by whom he does not specify. He notes that the question of:

> ... winning over the majority of the people dominated by the leadership of the conservatives is best served by the genuine cooperation of all the progressive forces on the basis of sincere criticism of anti-democratic activity. ... There is no doubt, that in the coming political class struggle, the Leftist forces of Iran will take into consideration the tragic lessons of the path they have been forced to take during the past years. In Stolypin's time Lenin wrote: 'We are faced with an original historical period of the birth of a new revolution. We cannot master this original situation nor can we prepare for revolution if we act only on the old basis.'

Agaev does not specify whether or not Lenin had supported Stolypin.

Agaev's piece on the rise and demise of the Leftist forces during the 1978-79 revolution points to several considerations from the Soviet stand.

Firstly, the Leftist forces are worthy of discussion only when they seem to be on the verge of conquering power; thus various other groups, the Minority Fada'iyan, Paykar, the Trotskyists, the Maoists, etc, are discarded from the analysis, particularly if they are hostile to the Soviet Union — an outlook that puts the historian at the service of the state which projects some collaboration in the future with these probable winners of power.

Secondly, the past of these forces are not important, either because the past plays no role in the determination of a political force's chances of victory — a thought that is as far from Marxism as it is from history and correct political analysis — or because power disregards the past so long as a group acquires it, and recognises the present and its future potential — a matter for statesmen not historians.

Thirdly, no discussion is to be entered into regarding the role of those who (as Iraj Eskandari made clear[278]) led or encouraged the Tudeh leadership in its adoption of the line it pursued in the years of 1979-83; nor should the role Kuzichkin played through his revelations in the arrest and subsequent fate of the Tudeh Party be evoked, to believe Agaev, at least at face value; moreover, this Soviet historian does not make it clear whether the Tudeh Party's support of this line only represented the Tudeh leadership's consideration that Islam and Communism are synonymous, and whether its stance towards the Islamic state was genuine or tactical. If it was the former, how can he explain the letter

Kianouri addressed in the summer of 1979 to the Soviet Central Committee demanding delivery of arms, which, as far I know, the Soviets considered serious and worthy of consideration.[279]

Fourthly, it is clear that, despite his diplomatic language, Agaev is unhappy about the line the Tudeh adopted between 1979 and 1983. Was he criticising the KGB, the Foreign Office, the Kremlin, on behalf of one or the other two? Writing the article, was he proposing a new line of unity between the Tudeh, Majority Feda'iyan and the Mojahedin? What is certain, however, was that he was proposing a new line for the potentially pro-Soviet forces, one with the serious intention of seizing power on condition that unity was forged; otherwise, he would have dealt with the ensemble of Leftist forces, discussing their past, present and future all in a more detached and serious analysis. Clearly, he was not writing history, but signalling a new political line; yet the historical events that have taken place in Iran since his article was published disprove his analysis. This raises the question of whether the historiography of the Stalinist or neo-Stalinist schools served any purpose.

Fifthly, it is novel, and refreshing, that a Soviet historian should not open his discussions with quotations from a number of the great theoreticians of Bolshevism, though, as we have seen, Agaev at the end contents himself with some short advice from Lenin.

XIII: Conclusion

It can be briefly stated that the historiography of the Iranian Left has been subjected to many historical ills: the Cold War; *la Raison d'État*; Stalinism; conscious colonial reshaping; but also marketing demands that push writers during 'hot periods' to produce, on order, books that find a wide distribution, and which make their nefarious mediating impact in the long run, because they are pushed by vested interests — in sum, the lack of scruple of those scholars who play the game of the state, the market and ideology.

It is also important to emphasise the theoretical poverty among Iranian Leftists, with a few rare notable exceptions of course — such as Sultanzade, Arani and Sho'a'iyan. The historiography of the Iranian Left, too, has been very poor, insofar as it has almost never occupied itself with the critique of the meagre theoretical discussion that has taken place within the Iranian Left; it has, instead, concentrated either on its Soviet links (if coming from Leftist adversaries of the Soviet Union), or on its own heroic actions, and the 'treachery of the bourgeoisie and its allies', the imperialist powers. Thus the double politico-economic dependency of the former regime was matched by an equivalent double dependency of the majority of Leftists on the Soviet, and later Chinese or Albanian, models, their historical experiences, and their particular kind of historiography. In this light, the harvest of the 1980s should not be astonishing at all.

If we were to classify the history of the Iranian Left in the twentieth century, we might say that four paradoxical stages are discernible:

1: A childhood of intelligence and dexterity — the Social Democracy.
2: A youthful development disproportional to its social base — the Iranian Communist Party and the Arani Circles.
3: A retarded growth (physically growing but intellectually Lilliputian) between 1943 and 1953.
4: A disarrayed, unreflective old age led by younger men, with an intellectual destitution as of the 1960s, matched only by that of the Pahlavi establishment and its other opponents.

One hundred years after its first beginnings, it can be summarily said that the Iranian Left in its youth — that is, in the period beginning with the birth of the Social Democracy on the eve of the Constitutional Revolution, through the Communist Party and Arani's attempt at creating an independent Marxist current — while numerically small, was relatively mature in qualitative terms; in its middle years (between 1943 and 1953) it grew numerous in numbers but remained intellectually a dwarf; and in its old age, it was less numerous in terms of followers and sympathisers, more numerous in the number of organisations that pretended to represent the wage-earning people, but infantile and unsophisticated. The bitter experience of its long life has had the opposite effect on its state of mind, thereby giving rise to the paradoxical labyrinth that has enclosed it mentally.

* * *

One of the problems that historians of twentieth-century Iran overlook is the ethical and intellectual mortification that is the result of political opportunism, unbounded ambition, absence of responsibility, and lack of accountability to Iranian society. Duplicity and intrigues for the sake of personal advancement, which weighed heavily in the defeat of the Constitutional Revolution and its Social Democratic element, are at the root of this state of affairs. The continued absence of self-criticism in the historiography of the Constitutional Revolution deprived the future generation — during the time of the Jangali and similar movements, within the Communist spheres of influence, during the short time of the Mosaddeq era and the subsequent years, from the advent of the Tudeh till its ferocious repression in 1954, and thereafter, worse yet, since the 1979 revolution — has had a devastating effect on an historical comprehension of the long 'transition period' that the twentieth century represented. The failure to analyse notably the economic structures, the old and the newly forming, as well as the mental structures (particularly the reinforced astrological outlook), and, above all, the inability to introduce a self-critical faculty into the society, could not, of course, but damage the course of transition from the so-called traditional society to a dynamically, sublated modern one.[280]

Iranians at all levels have consistently blamed the British for their cunning schemes to deprive them of their liberty. Britain and Soviet Russia, and later the US government, undeniably sought to advance their interests in Iran by all possible means — diplomatic, political, cultural, espionage and military, including *coups d'état*. Yet it is not fruitful — sublating — to assign blame. Moral judgement and lamentations regarding such matters only reflect a failure to understand political realities. A *coup d'état* is a means whereby states advance their national interests — however narrow and short-sighted they may be, as the recent admission by the Clinton administration about the Eisenhower administration clearly shows. As I wrote elsewhere:

> Recrimination also suggests a lack of self-criticism among Iranians, an unwillingness to admit inherent weaknesses in their political culture, the structural flaws and ingrained attitudes that have enabled their enemies to succeed. Iranians should blame neither Curzon nor Ironside [in the 1921 coup], still less the Soviets, for what they did or did not do in Iran; to do so betrays a refusal to overcome their fossilised political culture; it implies that Iranians have not as yet achieved the political maturity required by the exigencies of our time — a sublating historical consciousness.[281]

The history of the Iranian Left, whether during the Constitutional Revolution, the Jangali Movement and the ICP, and after the Second World War, during which the patriotic movement under Mosaddeq flourished and the Tudeh grew numerically, but not organisationally in the true sense of the word, still less intellectually, is portentous still from another perspective: these emotionally strong but intellectually fragile movements draw attention to the weak dynamics of Iranian society, the inability in modern times to develop a coherent social philosophy, and an increasing proclivity to uncritical borrowing and imitation, including outright borrowing from the outside world in the field of the historiography of Iran, the foreign mentors being chosen according to the ideological inclinations of the borrowers.[282]

Given what we have surveyed above and the lessons we draw from past historiographical undertaking, that is, distortions, deletions, falsification through invention of 'facts', plagiarism, etc, it would not be an exaggeration to state that both the historian and the archaeologist work in historical ruins. There are both similarities and dissimilarities between their crafts:

While one delves into past physical remains, the other probes into abstract and intellectual aspects of the past in order to reconstruct it. Archaeologists have two advantages over historians, however. First, their evidence, however incomplete, is concrete, thus verifiable; historians, as a rule, deal with *subjective* remnants of the past. Secondly, although archaeologists may also have to face damaged archaeological data, the harm is usually the work of nature. By contrast, historians must always be mindful that their evidence may have been wilfully tampered with by those who wish to convey a different picture of the past from that revealed by a more dispassionate analysis. In modern times, paradoxically, it may even have been repressively — consciously — meddled with, as the level of political consciousness has risen.[283]

What is more, it is usually victors, at the party level, national level or the international level who write history; those dead or defeated have taken their memoirs to the grave with them; survivors are either afraid of persecution to record their memoirs, or fear that their comrades and parties would denounce them as traitors; or worse yet, as turncoats, that they wish themselves to distort their past, for personal benefit.

Thus in reconstructing the modern history of Iran and its Left, 'the historian must be most meticulous about the negative consciousness that has sought to distort the historical record, thereby victimising not only the history in question and its subjects, but also those who endeavour to capture that particular historical past in all its complexity'.[284]

If the sad history of the 'modernity' of Iranian historiography can be summarised in one point, it is made in an article, recently published in a Tehran daily, by the shah's former religious adviser Seyyed Hussein Nasr, a Harvard graduate teaching since 1979 at one of the most prestigious American universities, as follows: 'Ferdowsi revived the ancient history of Iran.'[285] In the same vein, the historiography of the Iranian Left, whether within or outside the country — it must unfortunately be admitted — follows the historical perception put forth by Nasr, that is, it is in the same state of *dys*-development. To comprehend the history of Iran in the twentieth century, the history of the Iranian Left, just as the rest of Iran's modern history, has to be almost entirely reconstructed.[286]

Postscript

Since this article was finalised for publication and submitted and subsequently withdrawn for reasons explained in the Foreword, a few publications discussing the role of the Left in Iranian politics have been published, including the collection of papers presented at the SOAS conference in 2000, to which the editor added several articles previously published in order to fill the gap created as a result of the withdrawal of this author's paper. The book in question requires, in good time, a thorough critique; but at this moment a few points cannot be omitted here with regard to some of the inadmissible 'mistakes', partly of a deontological nature, in some of the chapters, that might cause further confusion.[287] In addition, there are articles by Ervand Abrahamian,[288] Pezhman Dailami and Maziar Behrouz, and a book by Stephan Kinzer.[289] These, and particularly the last, which has found wide distribution as a popular book, cannot be glossed over because they reproduce some of Abrahamian's 'mistakes' mentioned above — a good demonstration of the point I made in this article about the manipulative historiography of the Left that has, through irresponsible repetitions, led to the creation of historical 'facts'.

Let us first take Kinzer. In spite of his apparent good intentions in denouncing the Anglo-American coup of 1953, he reproduces some of the falsified 'facts' and mistaken judgements based on them. Kinzer's mistaken judgements result from his uncritical reading of poor accounts, often by self-serving agents of the coup days, on all sides.

Contrary to what Kinzer states, it is worth noting, for instance, that the Tudeh did not 'turn' Communist in 1944; it was created and dominated by Communists from the very beginning and began calling itself Marxist-Leninist only after its prohibition in 1949.[290] Nor did the Tudeh have 'tens of thousands' of supporters in Abadan and Tehran (p 65), unsubstantiated figures that even the Tudeh have never claimed. This assertion is as 'exact' as saying that the 'founders' of the Tudeh who had been in jail under Reza Shah, when released, 'constituted themselves as the Group of Fifty-Three' (p 65); or stating that the shah, seizing on 'public sympathy' after the 'assassination attempt of 1949', took 'several other steps to increase his power'. The fact is that the 'attempt' was a fake and the plan for 'amending' the Constitution had been prepared months in advance by the shah and his coterie.[291]

On the events of August 1953, he states:

> The riots that shook Tehran on Monday intensified on Tuesday, thousands of demonstrators, unwittingly under CIA control, surged through the streets, looting shops, destroying pictures of the shah, ransacking the offices of royalist groups. Exuberant nationalists and Communists joined in the mayhem. The police were still under orders from Mosaddegh not to interfere. That allowed the rioters to do the job, which was to give the impression that Iran was sliding toward anarchy. Roosevelt caught the glimpses of them during his furtive trips around the city and said that they 'scared the hell out of me'. (p 175).

There is no evidence that these 'rioters' were under the control of the CIA; even Roosevelt does not claim that, otherwise why would he have been afraid, as Kinzer states. There was no looting of shops and the royalists did not have 'offices' to be ransacked. On the first day after the coup, a huge demonstration took place on the parliament square, at which both the Mosaddeqists and Tudeh forces were present, though in separate columns. The only 'rioting' had to do with destroying the statues of the shah and his father on Monday, 17 August when the Tudeh as well as Mosaddeqists tore down the two shah's statues,[292] and Mosaddeq took responsibility for the action during his trial in the military tribunal. Obviously, Kinzer's account is not precise, to say the least. Is this intended to reinforce the conspiracy theory by inculcating the Iranians with the notion that every action they take is rooted in some imperialist plot?

The self-serving account written by Wilber (the CIA secret report) must be scrutinised, for its author, like the historiographers of all victors, must of necessity make up *ex-post-facto* 'plans' to explain their success caused by socio-political factors that either cannot be explained or have not been subjected to serious historical analysis. As regards the meeting between Mosaddeq and Henderson (ibid), Kinzer basically repeats the account by Roosevelt and Abrahamian, refuted above on the basis of historical evidence.

Moreover, Kinzer states that 'the only group' that could have defended the Mosaddeq government was the Tudeh. He repeats Kianouri's accounts of the telephone calls and attributes another unverified point to the premier: 'If I ever agree to arm a political party, may God sever my arm!' (p 179; note p 241) His source for this unreliable statement is given as Mosaddeq's personal lawyer, N Amini, who was not a political confident of the premier, but who might have heard or read one such rumour over the long years since and believed that he had heard it from the premier himself — as often is the case with oft-repeated invented 'facts'. Kinzer's lack of precision also leads him to consider the Tudeh officers arrested in 1954 as 'loyal to Mosaddeq'. It is thus not clear why such 'loyal officers' did not move on 19 August 1953. Kinzer also states that the Tudeh did not move, but 'spent the day in meetings, unable to decide whether to act'. But a line further below he states that, because like all Communist parties the Tudeh was 'controlled by the Soviet Union, and in time of crisis it followed orders from Moscow', it did not act because 'on this day no orders came'! Why? Because Stalin had died a few months earlier and 'the Kremlin was in turmoil' (p 205). True, as pointed out above, with Stalin's death there was a power struggle that shook the Kremlin and momentarily subsided with the arrest and execution of Beria who controlled the agents in 'brother parties'. If it is correct to state that the Tudeh leaders spent the day in meetings unable to decide whether or not to act, then basically Kianouri is lying when he states that he had asked Mosaddeq to 'arm the shock troops of the party'! If the Tudeh did not move, as explained above, it was because — as we will show below on the basis of the Tudeh's own documents — NKVD chief Beria had just been removed, no longer able to guide his agents in Iran, those who had commanded more than two years of an hysterically anti-Mosaddeq campaign portraying him as an 'imperialist stooge'. Available Tudeh documents can demonstrate that the Tudeh did not act, and Kianouri lies about his contacts with Mosaddeq.[293]

Apparently, even now Kinzer is not aware, unlike the CIA was then, that Beria had been arrested and (as was thought) possibly executed by the end of June 1953, weeks before the coup, otherwise, in order to justify the coup, he would not have made the historically incorrect judgement that a 'reckless brute like Beria might have come to power rather than a relatively moderate Khrushchev, and he might have been ready to launch even the most provocative expansionist adventures. This was a danger the CIA believed it could not ignore.' (p 205) Yet he states that 'an American diplomat who specialised in monitoring Tudeh during the early 1950s, along with two CIA agents who were posted with him at the United States embassy in Tehran', admitted 'that the Tudeh was really not very powerful, and that the higher-level US officials routinely exaggerated its strength and Mosaddegh's reliance on it' (p 206).

Withal, it is wrong to state, as Kinzer does, that 'some of the tens of thousands of people who took over the streets that day had always opposed Mosaddeq for one reason or another. Others were former supporters who had turned against him.' Where do these figures come from?' No source supports this assertion, not even *NY Times* reporter Kenneth Love who stood close to the CIA. Did Tehran have tens of thousands several times over, for the Tudeh, for Mosaddeq, and for his royalist opponents? A review of parliamentary elections of the Seventeenth Legislature would clarify such 'fact-finding' exaggerations. According to a report by the US embassy dated 18 February 1952,[294] the highest number of votes in Tehran elections (112 216) went to Hussein Makki, then a Mosaddeq supporter; the highest number of votes the Tudeh candidates (including Ahmad Lankarani and Ayatollah Boraeh'i) received was about 28 000. Now is it imaginable that everyone who votes also goes to demonstrations in which he is likely to get shot at? Obviously not. This is confirmed by the report on one of the hysterical demonstrations the Tudeh front organisation, the Association for the Struggle against the [British] Oil Company organised against Mosaddeq's oil policy (8 Khordad/29 May 1951). On that day, according to several sources close to the American embassy that had every interest to blow up the figures in order to exaggerate the red scare in Iran, the number of demonstrators, made up of 'workers, unemployed workers, women workers, Iranian mothers, women intellectuals, students, children' chanting anti-Mosaddeq, anti-American and anti-British slogans, was estimated between 5000 and 10 000, which Tudeh insiders themselves estimated no more than 5000.[295]

Kinzer's affirmation that Roosevelt 'had perfectly analysed his adversary's [Mosaddeq's] psyche' (p 176) is as good as his assertion on the 'sharp-mindedness', 'quick wits and perfect English' of Ardeshir Zahedi (pp 169, 198). Anyone who has followed Zahedi's career or has read a few pages of the Foreign Office files from 1965, when Zahedi was the shah's ambassador to London, would know how 'intelligent' he was and how 'perfect' his English was! Truly, Kinzer believes everything he reads. He quotes CM Woodhouse, the SIS agent in charge of the coup, when he 'concedes':

> What we did not foresee was that the shah would gather new strength and use it so tyrannically, nor that the US government and the Foreign Office would fail so abjectly to keep him on a reasonable course. *At the time* we were simply relieved that a threat to British interests [that is, the Mosaddeq government] had been removed. (pp 200-01, my emphasis)

Kinzer would have learned a few things about long-term British policy in Iran and Woodhouse's hypocrisy had he consulted FO reports as to why the British kept supporting the shah until he fell. The following quotation from a Joint Intelligence Committee report for the British Cabinet in 1966 concerning British interests in Iran's geographical position between the Soviet Union and the Indian Ocean, her oilfields, the interconnection between Iranian and British interests in the Persian Gulf, etc, should suffice:

> Britain therefore has a major interest in the type of government in power in Iran and the international policies it pursues. Present British policy towards Iran is based on the judgement that in practical terms the continuance of the shah's regime and the retention by the regime of its present policies suits British interests better than any likely alternative would do.[296]

It is, however, interesting that Kinzer (p 200) informs his readers that SIS operative Woodhouse, knighted as Lord Terrington for his services to British interests, later became director of the Penguin books and wrote extensively on history, as this information emphasises the transit between Western (and of course Soviet) secret services and the academic world, as was the case with Wilber himself and his colleague at Harvard who became a well-known Iran specialist. The nefarious impact of this two-way transit on the impartiality of writing and teaching of history needs no comment.

Interestingly, Kinzer is unaware that American and other historians in the West had long refrained from even mentioning the coup in their writings. If today some have written about it, it is because the interest the West had in the shah no longer exists. Not surprisingly, Western scholars began writing about the coup after agents such as Roosevelt and Woodhouse had published their versions of the coup. Indeed, one owes this pioneering knowledge to Mark Gasiorowski and his mentor Richard Cottam, not to those who used to enjoy the shah's lavish hospitality routinely afforded to Western scholars in order to shut them up. Even today, a historian like Keddie (unlike the SIS agent in Iran Sam Falle who speaks of the 'immorality' of the coup, p 205), still considers that, 'in light of what came later [that is, the revolution], …the triumph [of the coup] seems much *tarnished*' (p 215, my emphasis).

In sum, in spite of an apparent sympathy Kinzer shows for the Iranian national movement, one cannot, and should not, gloss over the lack of precision and the manipulative knowledge the author of this popular book reproduces from sources by interested persons, on both the right and the left wings of the world's political spectrum.

Now we turn to Abrahamian's recent article that, in *some* respects, stands in contrast to his previous writings on Mosaddeq and the coup.[297] The first point that should be made in this regard is the methodological position to the effect that one should not take the CIA 'secret history' written by the CIA operative Wilber as 'an authoritative' account on the coup, but rather as an interested viewpoint that is self-serving (p 183). He rightly states that we cannot write this history (fully) unless we have access to unfiltered sources in the CIA or US National Archives; a statement that is equally true about access to the Soviet archives which we have been denied. He is also right in stating that we have learned from Wilber's self-serving account no more than we had known from previous scattered sources (pp 183-84). Unfortunately, as Abrahamian proceeds his methodology is not so rigorously applied to other aspects of the history of the Iranian national movement. He refuses to be as demanding or as revealing insofar as the Tudeh Party and the Soviet Union are concerned, presenting them as if they had supported the national movement throughout.

He first provides a short description of the oil nationalisation movement, as well as British and American positions towards it, which is not new and has been done far more extensively and effectively by Mostafa Elm.[298] Abrahamian's basic hostility to Mosaddeq is glaring when he once again disapprovingly refers to the 'incorruptible' Mosaddeq and his 'vehement' opposition in 1944 to the Soviet demand for an oil concession in northern Iran (p 185); or when he states that 'the Majlis nationalised the oil industry', without specifying the long and hard struggle under Mosaddeq's leadership that forced the Majles with a right-wing, pro-British majority to bow to the wishes of the people (p 186). Not surprisingly, he is also silent on the Tudeh's hysterical campaign (in a press that was, thanks to Mosaddeq, free, such as *Besouy-e Ayandaeh*) against Mosaddeq before the nationalisation and especially thereafter when he became premier (p 193). An impartial historian cannot but recognise that the Tudeh's press campaign against Mosaddeq was no less destructive than the right-wing press financed by the CIA and the SIS.

When Abrahamian talks about the Tudeh, it is only to give it credit — indeed, there is not a single criticism addressed to the Tudeh's disastrous record in his entire writings. When he speaks about the success of the Si-ye Tir insurrection (21 July 1952), he states that 'large crowds, first from the National Front and then eventually from the Communist Tudeh Party, came into the streets, clashed with the army, and after three days of bloodshed, forced the shah not only to recall Mosaddeq but also to give him the war ministry portfolio' (p 195). Let us see what other sources state in this regard. A young researcher whose work Abrahamian knows and quotes is unambiguous about the Tudeh's role in those three decisive days. Khosropanah clearly states that there is no evidence supporting the claim that the Tudeh had given any instructions for participation in the demonstrations. The only case to which the Tudeh refers is that of Colonel H Parman, who, according to his own account, was not a member of the Tudeh military organisation, but only joined it after those events.[299]

With regard to the participation of the Tudeh in the Si-ye Tir insurrection, Kianouri, in his post-*coup d'état* letter to the Tudeh Central Committee in Moscow, also refutes Abrahamian's claim:

> Perhaps comrades [of the Central Committee in Moscow] know that in the Si-ye Tir events our party forces had, indeed, a small role; first, they took part late in the action; they moved only in Tehran and some other points, and in Tehran, in the height of the struggle on 21 July very few of our forces were in the field, while we had a considerable force directly at our disposal — nearly 25 000 members organised in our Tehran underground organisations. The experience of 30 Tir drew our attention to this shortcoming.[300]

An historian who does research in the British archives should also refer to official publications of the Tudeh when they do not his fit his prefabricated thesis. Clearly, Kianouri's account disproves Abrahamian's.

On the other hand, Abrahamian's lack of familiarity with the Iranian social situation leads to erroneous statements. When he discusses the Rashidian brothers (p 199), he asserts, on the basis of FO files, that they had 'useful contacts in the bazaar: with Sha'ban Jafari... (Brainless), the most dangerous gang leader; with guild leaders among butchers, bakers, confectioners and sugar-loaf makers, and with middle-ranking clerics associated with the conservative Mojahedin-e Islam and the terroristic Fedayyan-Islam'. Jafari had nothing to do with the Bazaris, nor with the various guilds he mentions, although his connection with 'the butchers' sounds credible! In fact, the Bazaar was, at least in its majority, with Mosaddeq, in spite of Kashani's defection, a fact that one can also observe in the early 1960s when the regime met with a crisis and the National Front became active once again. Too much reliance on self-serving British reports can also render historiography worthless.

Another 'analytical' blunder Abrahamian makes in this recent article (pp 201, 204, 208) is repeating the unethical statement by Behrouz: labelling Hesam Lankarani (one of the four Tudeh members assassinated by the Tudeh military leader Rouzbeh), along with Colonel Farzanegan and Boscoe Brothers, as 'local agents' of the putsch. (He is so well informed that he calls Hesam 'Ehsam'!) As I have demonstrated above, this is a preposterous accusation by the CIA Station Chief Oney against a high-ranking Tudeh cadre who had been murdered by Rouzbeh under orders from the Central Committee in Tehran *a year before the coup*. He takes up Rouzbeh's justification for the assassination of Lankarani in cold blood, stating that he had had a 'drug problem'. He calls him 'a perfect *agent provocateur*' who 'bombed the home of a prominent cleric and sent leaflets to others in the name of the Tudeh heralding the imminent dawn of a bright new "atheistic" republic'. By relying on Kianouri's *Memoirs* (p 252), he adds: 'This frightened some, including future leaders of the Islamic Republic', as if in 1953 one knew that Iran would become an Islamic republic and that its leaders were known in advance! His readers then must assume that it is Kianouri, a prominent Tudeh leader at the time, who accuses Hesam Lankarani. Interestingly, however, there is no mention of this in Kianouri's memoirs; instead, his editors at the Islamic Republic' Intelligence Department add a footnote quoting a statement by Ayatollah Taleqani that again has nothing to do with the man who had been murdered a year previously. How can one avoid calling this 'collage' a preposterous prevarication? Difficult, indeed.

Hesam Lankarani was an important figure in the Tudeh's underground organisation. A former Central Committee and Executive Committee member, who became a Maoist in the 1960s, states in his memoirs that he met Hesam Lankarani in 1328/1949 when engaged in underground activity. He told Foroutan that the possibility existed of organising the escape of Kianouri from prison. Foroutan agreed with it. Lankarani discussed the matter also with another Executive Committee member, Bahrami, and apparently he had no objection either. Hesam and his friends had organised Rouzbeh's escape from prison on a couple of occasions. The plan for Kianouri's escape had been prepared by Hesam Lankarani and his aides. Foroutan adds: 'Hesam Lankarani and his aides had already prepared three hiding places for the imprisoned Central Committee members whose escape they had also planned.'

Rouzbeh states that the Tudeh leadership was opposed to his escape from prison in 1950. They only agreed when the planners of the escape, who were from the military organisation, made their escape conditional on the inclusion of Rouzbeh on the list.[301]

That the murder of Lankarani was ordered by the Tehran leadership is clear from the letter of three Executive Committee members (Jowdat, Yazdi and Bahrami) addressed to the Central Committee members in Moscow on the morrow of the 1953 putsch. They write:

> Factionalism on the part of Foroutan, Maryam [Firouz, Kianouri's wife], Qoreyshi and their friends such as Lankarani had reached such a point that they felt confident that they could take over the party and considered Bahrami's presence on the Executive Committee would put their plans in jeopardy. In the summer of 1329/1950, Bahrami officially exposed the gang of Foroutan, Maryam, Qoreyshi and Lankarani and fully denounced their secret plans. Bahrami proved that this gang had secretly created a second centre and intended to take over the whole party and the movement. The aim of this factionalism can be understood from the removal of Borzorg Alavi and his replacement by Lankarani in the sensitive position of an important contact with [Soviet] friends.[302]

The three Tudeh leaders speak of the 'moral corruption' of Kianouri, Qoreyshi and Lankarani, 'about which you have received the documents'.[303] (The accusation of 'honour' was being levelled against Kianouri, and according to Foroutan, by Jodat who 'remained on the side of First Secretary Kianouri until the last moment' when he was arrested in 1983.)[304]

With regard to the Lankarani brothers, it needs to be added that two recent publications in Iran throw light on the degree of involvement of Sheikh Hussein Lankarani and his siblings in Iran's political opposition to the British and the Pahlavi dynasty. A two-part article published in *Tarikh-e mo'aser-n Iran*[305] discusses and documents the relations between the young Ayatollah Khomeini and Hussein Lankarani and the support that the latter gave to the former when he was struggling against the shah and the domination of Iran by foreign powers. On the basis of research in the SAVAK archives (which shows how closely that despised organisation kept track of Lankarani's activities) and personal interviews, the author of the articles brings to light the vast connections Lankarani had with the clerical opposition to the shah, such as Ayatollahs Khomeini, Milani, Taleqani,[306] etc, as well with the National Front and Bazargan's

Freedom Movement. Lankarani kept his contacts with Khomeini even when the latter was in exile in Iraq. Personal letters by Ayatollah Khomeini addressed to Hussein Lankarani also demonstrate the close relationship between the two. The interesting revelation is that Ayatollah Khomeini visited the house of the Lankarani brothers' sister, Banou, and stayed there for the night. But because of their Tudeh connections, Banou's house was also a refuge for Maryam Firouz,[307] Kianouri's wife, for a long time (during 1953-55), and Rouzbeh often visited that house to meet secretly with either the Lankarani brothers or others.

Were all these people dupes of British intelligence and the CIA, while the CIA operative Oney knew the truth? What truth? That the junior among the Lankarani brothers, Hesam, murdered in the summer of 1952, published, *posthumously*, in the summer of 1953, provocative handbills inciting the religious leaders against Mosaddeq? Would 'future leaders of the Islamic Republic' mix with a family that was involved in provocative handbills of the sort Abrahamian talks about? Only ill-intentioned or ignorant individuals can believe and propagate such ridiculous allegations.

It is important to refer to a document that was published long ago concerning the individuals who were responsible for sending out, in the name of Tudeh Party, death threats to the high clergy in order to make them believe that the continuation of the Mosaddeq Government would throw Iran into the arms of the Soviet Union, and therefore incite them to side with the putschists. After the 1979 revolution, the late Ayatollah Taleqani recalled that a mullah connected with reactionary clergy who had worked with the reactionary Ayatollah Behbehani had told him:

> In the house of Ayatollah Behbehani, a mullah connected with the court, a few individuals were sitting and writing, in red ink, flyers in the name of Tudeh Party with following message: 'We shall soon hang you with your own shawls (of your turbans) on the electricity poles. Tudeh Party.' The mullah relating the story had added that they wrote so many of them that their fingers ached for a whole week afterwards.[308]

Should a serious historian not have checked all the possible sources?

A 'masterful' insinuation by Abrahamian to denigrate Mosaddeq and his collaborators is that 'some of them *obtained* refuge in the United States' (p 204). The only Mosaddeq collaborator who *took* refuge in the USA was Dr S Ali Shayegan; but the number of Tudeh or pro-Tudeh and later Fadayee leaders who took not only refuge but citizenship in the USA amounts to thousands. Such 'arguments' do, indeed, lower the historian to the nadir of tabloid journalism.

Abrahamian takes up, once again in this article, the question of Mosaddeq's acquiescence toward Henderson, discussed above. There is little doubt in my mind that when he published his article in 2001 he was already aware of my criticism made of him in 2000. How? A copy had already been sent to the SOAS organiser. Therefore, in lieu of admitting his blunder, Abrahamian, without changing his earlier version, makes an attempt to blame the American ambassador for *false reporting* to the Department of State. This is how he does it (see pages 207-08). He begins his account with a preparatory statement that when Henderson returned to Iran:

> He was greeted by Mosaddeq's son and a contingent of military guards. Mosaddeq's son was there to keep lines open to the United States; guards to protect the ambassador from angry crowds roaming the streets denouncing the shah, calling for a republic, and pulling down royal statues. Although most of these demonstrations were spontaneous reactions against the attempted coup, some were organised by Lankarani [?] and the Rashidian and Boscoe brothers...

What source does he offer for such detailed information? None.

Then he refers to the unusually long telegram by Henderson to the Department of State as a 'short, misleading summary of this interview' with Mosaddeq. 'But a far more detailed one appeared in an uncharacteristically informative piece in *Time* 31 August 1953].' Then he proceeds to relate some of the content of the conversation according to *Time*, adding that Mosaddeq 'telephoned the military government of Tehran and ordered him to use necessary force to clear the street'. Then he approvingly quotes *Time*: 'things began to happen immediately after this interview', and 'Mosaddeq's "fatal mistake" was this unleashing the army.... The National Front, as well as the Tudeh eager to form a united front, asked their supporters to stay off the streets.' (p 209)

Let us examine this claim point by point. Firstly, as stated earlier, Lankarani had been murdered on the orders of the Tudeh leadership *a year earlier*. Secondly, the telegram is not shorter than the *Time* version; it is much longer. (Abrahamian claims the telegram had been passed on to the newspaper; for what reason he does not reveal, as it appeared some 12 days later and had no impact on the events!) Thirdly, there is no evidence that the National Front wanted a united front, although there is no denying that it could have been useful; nor is there any evidence that the Tudeh wanted it, because, as mentioned earlier the Tudeh leadership did not know what to do, and in fact did nothing. Indeed, Kianouri himself stated that they did not expect a second coup, and they even had doubts as to the veracity of the first one claimed by Mosaddeq. Fourthly, there is no evidence that the army officers whom Mosaddeq ordered to 'clear the streets' were the same who took part in the coup. This has to be proven. The whole scenario is one fabricated by Abrahamian with ill intentions, all in order to whitewash the Tudeh's inaction on that day and to blame it on Mosaddeq's 'non-proletarian' character. What a serious historian worthy of the name has to do is to gather all the verified information and analyse the role and the potentialities of each one of the actors in order, not to issue certificates of blame, but to explain why the royalists led by the CIA–SIS won the day so easily.

There is yet another point in Abrahamian's new article. There can be no denying that after Mosaddeq severed diplomatic relations with Britain, the American embassy became the nest of subversion against him. But to insinuate, as Abrahamian does, that the delivery in 1952 of '42 Sherman' tanks to Mosaddeq's government, Mosaddeq having been 'amiable to American advisers', or the training of 300 Iranian officers in the USA, were important reasons for the success of the coup, may serve to put the blame solely on Mosaddeq for the defeat of the movement, but this is not historically credible. Surely, the Irano-American military pact was in the interests of the USA, but Mosaddeq had not signed this pact; as prime minister, he had only prolonged it under duress at a time when he was fighting the British and could not afford (in the absence of Soviet support, nay, in view of its hostility) to open suddenly a new front against the Americans who were already accusing him of being soft on Communism, if not actually being pro-Communist. There is certainly room for criticism of Mosaddeq in this regard, but in the proper context. These 'two reasons' cannot, however, be properly used to put the blame of the failure on Mosaddeq alone. The question is whether the *coup d'état* would have failed had Mosaddeq stopped the American tank deliveries, etc, or would that have accelerated it? One cannot be sure. What is, however, more important — and Abrahamian knowingly does not deal with it — is that many of these officers sent to the USA were Tudeh Party members and the tank commanders belonged to the Tudeh's military organisation. Azarnour, one Tudeh officer in charge of the military organisation states:

> Nearly 70 per cent of young officers of the tank division who commanded the Sherman tanks (bought from the US), having graduated a year or two before the 1953 coup and serving in Tehran, in addition to a few high-ranking commanding officers, were members of the Tudeh military organisation.[309]

We can thus see that the US tanks could have, if the Tudeh had been willing, made a difference to the fortunes of the movement, although there is no evidence to show that any more than just a few of them were actually used in the coup.[310] The mere fact that General McClure, an expert 'on psychological warfare', had recently 'been rushed to Iran from Korea' does not prove, as Abrahamian alleges, that his expertise made the coup successful. Did he know Iranian psychology, if anyone could, at all? Did he know Persian so that he could communicate with Iranian officers on such a delicate subject? How can we measure the impact that he made on army officers within a month or two? There is no way of knowing. Are these seemingly 'reasonable' elements used by Abrahamian not a means of drawing attention away from the fact that the Tudeh had a serious possibility of, at least, forestalling the immediate success of the coup? One can hardly doubt his intentions.

When Abrahamian extensively and approvingly quotes British and American sources to the effect that the coup planners were certain to defeat the Tudeh and National Front parties, if the latter organisations 'came out into the streets' in order to put up resistance, he really intends to justify the Tudeh's inaction (pp 206ff). If the Tudeh is absolved by this argument, so are the rest in the movement. In such a case, what would be the sense of historical analysis? His is a static and deterministic argument, made *a postiori*. The Tudeh and others could not have been sure of the coup's success; even if they had been, they would thereby have been assuming a defeatist position.

Once again, this is demonstrated by the serious arguments put forth by the Tudeh officer Azarnour whose writings, published in Paris, Abrahamian chooses to ignore. Let us consider the detailed arguments of this leader of the Tudeh's military organisation on the Tudeh leadership's failure and its *a postiori* justification. Azarnour, who was in the leadership of the Tudeh's military organisation, gives a totally different account.[311]

After a detailed analysis of Kianouri's falsification of the strength of the organisation, Azarnour, states, as noted above, that 70 per cent of the commanders of the Sherman tanks in Tehran were Tudeh members. One of the officers who defended Mosaddeq's residence was Captain Shoja'iyan, who fought on against the royalists in spite of suffering injuries. He did so without any orders from his party. Another tank commander who *attacked* Mosaddeq's residence as a part of the royalist forces was Captain Irvani, a member of the Tudeh's military organisation. Had he been given an order, Azarnour is certain, he could have turned his gun against the royalists. All Tudeh officers in Tehran, Azarnour states with confidence, were awaiting orders from above, orders that never came. These officers numbered 29 in the air force, seven artillery commanders, 17 in the infantry units, 25 in the engineers' corps, and 23 in the gendarmerie. Withal, the Tudeh had 47 police commanders in the country, of whom 24 were in Tehran, who commanded police stations; their action could have forestalled the second coup, as the police played an important role in Tehran. Moreover, the brigade commander Teymour Bakhtiar, later the founder of the SAVAK, who had moved from Kermanshah towards Tehran to lend support to the putschists, was seconded by Lieutenant-Colonel Rostami-Gouran, who could have, upon orders from the party, eliminated Bakhtiar on his way to Tehran. In the same way, two Tudeh officers were well positioned with the shah and Zahedi. Colonel Javid of the Tudeh military organisation was the shah's personal aide-de-camp, and Zahedi's bodyguard, Gendarmerie Captain Abdollah Mohjerani, was another Tudeh officer. Both officers could have shattered the leadership of the putschists. Had Zahedi been killed on the spot, would the fearful shah have dared to return to Iran? Few people would agree. Azarnour, himself an officer, refutes the claim by Kianouri that the strength of Tudeh military organisation was a myth,[312] adding that the Tudeh officers were by far more numerous than the five in Iraq, 12 in Egypt and 22 in Libya who overthrew the three monarchies. It should be added that Iran had just gone through several years' experience of an anti-imperialist movement of which the aforementioned Arab countries were deprived.

To conclude, we can, in the light of new documents to which Abrahamian could certainly have had access, state that his history of Tudeh relations with Mosaddeq and the course of events during the days of the 1953 putsch are entirely false and disqualify him as an independent historian.

As to the reasons why the Tudeh did not move against the royalist onslaught led by the CIA–SIS operatives in Iran, we need to offer a valid explanation. From what we know from its very foundation in 1941 and its relations with the Soviet Communist Party, sealed by the aforementioned letter by two of its leaders in the autumn of 1945 to the Central Committee of the Soviet Communist Party, we can come to the conclusion that the party did not move, because the new Soviet leadership, having taken over at the end of June through a putsch against Beria[313] and having had begun to improve relations with Mosaddeq's government, did not have the necessary apparatus, previously controlled by Beria, to pass its orders to the Tudeh leadership.[314] But the basic problem remains the poor Marxist education of the Tudeh leaders and their subservience to the USSR.

Another reason is the special character trait historically prevalent in Iranian leadership circles: an *unbounded personal ambition* that leads to the sacrificing of the good of all for one's own ends. Olovvi of the Tudeh Tehran leadership in the letter he addressed, on the morrow of the putsch, to his comrades in Moscow points to this same issue. He states:

> Let us see what is the reason for these internal quarrels? Are they [the result of opposing] political theses? If there are political mistakes, everyone

is to be blamed. The real motivations are unbounded ambition [of individual leaders] and the autonomy sought by some party organs and organisations.³¹⁵

The more basic reason, of course, is that the Tudeh was raised on Soviet thinking and never had a mind of its own, and was therefore deprived both of any independence in analysis and policy-making, and of independence of action in carrying out policy. Accordingly, the historian who, willingly or not, allows himself or herself to fall into the fatal mistake that differences in the party were a result of ideological and policy matters falls victim of his or her own error.

I: The Pahlavi-Stalinist Mental Merger Leading to a New Breed

Now we turn to another piece of writing which, in the name of the Left, aims at destroying the brilliant Iranian Communist theoretician Sultanzade. This piece is a prime example of the mentality discussed above that is, paradoxically, reflected in the writings of Pezhman Dailami, a new 'historian' who did not belong to those officially trained by the Stalinist school, but grew up under the Pahlavi regime, and was apparently opposed to the Tudeh. Thus, as if all the mudslinging by Stalinist historians in the past had not sufficed, this novice has walked on to the scene to throw more mud at Sultanzade, the brilliant but not faultless theoretician and leader of the Iranian Communist Party. Sultanzade is now, whether one believes it not, accused of having been a 'Stalinist before Stalin'.³¹⁶ It is essential to deal with Dailami's falsifications, almost totally based on Soviet Stalinist historians, for they pretend to have been written from an anti-Stalinist viewpoint. This 'anti-Stalinist historian' has written several articles on the association of the ICP with the Jangali Movement in Iran, which led to the rise and demise of the Soviet Socialist Republic of Iran. His doctoral dissertation, apparently defended in 1994 at Manchester University, is also on the subject.³¹⁷ Of course, we cannot deal with all Dailami's falsifications, distortions and omissions. We will confine ourselves to some important issues that reveal his lack of professionalism and his deontological weakness, his plagiarism, and above all his intentional distortion of the history of the ICP.

In his work on the ICP published in 2004,³¹⁸ he admits to his lack of even a rudimentary knowledge of Russian and German (and one should add of French). He also reveals that for the German, French and Russian documents from which he cites, he did not visit the corresponding archives and depended on the people he thanks in his acknowledgement, either by providing them with references taken from previously published works, or simply arbitrary selections by 'archive shoppers' who are not historians of Iran — my appraisal shows that the former is largely the case, as his references to archival sources are hardly original research.³¹⁹ In this regard, it is important to point to his total omission of his knowledge of a book this author published in 1995 on the Soviet Socialist Republic of Iran, lest his readers may discover his indebtedness.³²⁰ Nowhere in his book does he acknowledge his debt to that book, from which he has largely benefited, either by direct information or by references, which must have sent to his 'archive shoppers' in Moscow.³²¹ How do we know his direct, undeniable knowledge of, hence dependence upon, a book, *The Soviet Socialist Republic of Iran*, which is listed in many library catalogues? Soon after the publication of that book, he wrote a scathing 'review' of it in *The Journal of Slavic Military Studies*,³²² in which he accused this author, *inter alia*, of being a 'disillusioned Marxist' who had become a 'nationalist', a term used in a derogatory sense. I beg the indulgence of the reader, for this is not a personal issue, but has to do with the lax manner in which certain universities in the West produce Iranian 'historians' without any deontological underpinning.

A few examples testify to his plagiarism. On pages 89-90 he refers to the publication of the Adalat party (the forerunner of the ICP), *Beyraq-e Adalat*, as if he had the originals of the publication before him, or had studied it in some library. I have toured all the specialist libraries of the West and former Soviet Union and have only seen the original of this journal in a Baku library. I have reproduced the available issues of it in the *Historical Documents* series,³²³ so that other historians can profit from it without having to travel to Baku, that is, if they knew such a journal is available there. Thus, either Dailami has travelled to Baku or he has plagiarised the material. The same is true of his reference to the article by NK Belova in footnote 6 (pp 86-87, 113), a partial translation of which appeared in 1978 and again in 2000.³²⁴ Yet another case of undeniable plagiarism is his reference to *Slovo*, a Russian journal published in Tbilisi dated 4 and 10 August 1920.³²⁵ Now, how does he happen to find the statement in an inaccessible Russian newspaper published in Tbilisi? By going through the paper page by page in some library? No; he must have found it in some book or archives which are not acknowledged. The fact that he does not give the source from which he has taken it makes him a plagiariser.

In another article on the issue,³²⁶ Dailami repeats the same kind of plagiarism. There is hardly any issue or reference that he has not taken from *The Soviet Socialist Republic of Iran*, which he pretends not to know. Let us take a few. In his footnote no 1, he lists a number of books by Sultanzade, Osetrov, Abikh and Ivanova, of which he has no direct knowledge, for he does not have a rudimentary knowledge of Russian. In the same footnote, he lists a number of books in German, a language he does not know either; besides, we must ask how he comes by all these little-known books, some of which are not available in Western libraries, unless one has a 'Crystal Ball', that is, the book of which he wrote a scathing review. Even he does not seem to have any knowledge of the important book by Shoa'i'yan, published by Mazdak in Florence, for he does not comment upon it, as in the case of some other Persian books.

In this article, his whole discussion of the allegations — originally made by Stalinist and official bourgeois historians — that the Jangali leader Kuchek Khan had relations with the Central Powers is almost wholly taken from Chapter 7 of *The Soviet Socialist Republic of Iran*, with the exception that he concedes to the accusers by stating, *inter alia*, that: 'In Gilan itself the Jangalis may have been assisted by the Turkish consul.' As evidence, he quotes an official historian of the Pahlavi regime, saying that the consul gave them 'four rifles'. He is surprised that there was 'little Turkophilia' in the Jangali newspaper published in 1917!'[327] In this connection too, he must have again used the 'Crystal Ball' of *The Soviet Socialist Republic of Iran* to learn of the existence of such documents in the German archives he supposedly obtained from Germany through 'archive shoppers'.

In this article, he also fabricates 'facts'. He states (p 157) that 'as the government of the Baku commune collapsed, the Jangali lost their firmest ally'. As shown in *The Soviet Socialist Republic of Iran* (pp 85-87), the Baku Commune under Shaomian refused to help the Jangalis, apparently under the influence of the Hnchaki Yaqikian and the Bolshevik Chiliapin. He who pretends to know the British archives on this subject overlooks the report by the British political officer Clutterbuck, dated 10 May 1918: 'The Bolsheviks are alarmed by the spread of Pan-Islamism and have officially stated that they consider Kuchek Khan a tool of German–Pan-Islamist coalition.'[328] He goes on to add that: 'We cannot ignore the fact that throughout the story told in this chapter the Jangalis held a firm alliance with the Bolsheviks in Gilan and Baku.' This too initially helped the Jangalis with a police force, their collaboration was limited, and there is no evidence that they sent any help from Baku to the Jangalis, for good reason: the Baku Commune was overthrown under pressure from the Ottoman army, the Bolsheviks went underground and could not afford the luxury of assisting the Jangalis. What is more, on 1 May 1918, in an ultimatum, signed by two members of the Bolshevik 'War-Revolution Committee', the Bolsheviks told the Jangalis: 'Although we once considered you revolutionaries fighting for your country's freedom and a new democratic order and helped you, a series of incidents has shown to us that you are a group of highway bandits.'[329]

As to other substantive points in his article, one can briefly note the following:

* The fact that Kuchek Khan is seen in a photo next to Karim Khan Rashti (p 142) is no proof that he was a Social Democrat at the time, for Karim Khan, though a Constitutionalist, was a medium-size landlord whose

relations with Ordzhonikidze does not make him a socialist either. Nor is the claim by two Stalinist historians, Agaev and Plastun (pp 142, 209), proof of Kuchek Khan being a Social Democrat, for this was, once again, an attempt to prove that Sultanzade was an 'ultra-leftist'. They offer no concrete evidence.

* There is no evidence that Budu Mdivani (p 143) was a member of the Caucasian revolutionary group that assisted the Iranian Constitutionalists.
* The so-called 'Moderate Social Democrats' (p 143) made up of major oppressive landlords, such as Sepahsalar, were not really Social Democrats; they designated themselves as such in order to compete with genuine Social Democrats in a revolutionary atmosphere.
* Pan-Islamism (Ettehad-e Islam) was not a 'passing fancy' (p 144), for several medium-size landlords belonging to that organisation sat on the 'Senate' of the Jangalis and were responsible for not undertaking a seriously needed land reform. It is therefore not true to say that 'no member of the clergy was ever to play a role in the leadership' (p 145) after the establishment of the Soviet Socialist Republic of Iran, the clergy indirectly played an important role in the agitation against collaboration with the ICP and organised meetings to bring pressure to bear on Kuchek Khan.

He also proves himself theoretically unequipped when he interprets Narimanov's statement, that he left out of the Social Democratic Party of Iran's programme the question of the separation of 'church' and state and the separation of schools from the 'church', as 'Social Democrats were populist subordinates of a bourgeois-democratic revolution in Iran' (p 159). True, Narimanov does make this statement, but the facts are that progressive forces and later the Constitutionalists had already, for decades, established schools that escaped the control of the religious authorities. With the advent of the constitutional regime a whole series of state schools were founded. In fact, in the programme of the various socialists, including the one founded by the Hnchaks, which Dailami calls 'right wing' (p 141), a whole series of progressive ideas were put forth for implementation.[330] During the Constitutional period, a long battle was fought to prevent any control by the high clergy over the legislation adopted by the parliament. Eventually, a compromise formula was found as reflected in Article II of the Supplement to the Constitution, stating that all legislation was to be approved by a committee of five religious authorities chosen by the parliament from a list of 20 high clergymen approved by the parliament.[331] This gave the choice of selecting the mullahs who were open to progressive legislation. However, in fact, this article was never put into effect. This shows that not only were the Social Democrats not subordinate to bourgeois democrats, but also that even the bourgeois democrats were in favour of the separation of the parliament and clerical authority. Would such a situation have made Social Democrats 'populists'? He simply does not know what he states.

We can thus see that Dailami's attempt to reconstruct the history of relations of the Jangalis with the Central Powers and the Bolsheviks is no more than a personal construct and has nothing to do with that history that can be — and is — known through available evidence. To sum it up, it is clear that, as he has not even a rudimentary knowledge of Russian, German and French and as he has not visited the corresponding archives, his references, especially to Russian texts, are secondary and often 'borrowed' without acknowledgement, and thus represent plagiarism.

Before we close the treatment of the history of the ICP, we must return to Dailami's chapter published in Cronin's book, although I have treated the question of Adalat/ICP in *The Soviet Socialist Republic of Iran*, albeit only in a summary fashion.[332] In his attempt to demolish Adalat as a 'populist party', he refers to issues of its newspaper with the same name, *Adalat*, for having published, between June and September 1917, the name and photos of the cabinet members of the Russian Provisional Government, that is, some months after the publication of Lenin's 'April Thesis', for having praised Shamil, the celebrated Chechen hero, for having absorbed a couple of socialistically-minded democratic groups (called 'parties/ferqeh', p 89) In this way, he wants to stick the label of 'populist', in his sense, 'opportunistic', on the party. He, then, later accuses the Adalat at its Communist phase of being 'ultra-leftist' just as later Stalinist historians alleged. He overlooks some important facts, namely, that Adalat at this early stage was following the Soviet line, which praised the Islamic faith of the Muslims against Britain and promised to safeguard the mosques. Again, this was the line of the Comintern leadership, including Trotsky, which wanted to have the Muslim masses on its side. I first dealt with this issue in my 1978 article[333] published on the basis of rare, suppressed Soviet publications, as well as British and French archives. There, I show how Islam was made use of by the Comintern, and even in the declarations of the Soviet Commissar for Foreign Affairs, Chicherin, just as I demonstrated the same point in several conferences in Europe and the USA by screening the forbidden rushes of the documentary made by the Comintern of that congress,[334] long before several other researchers who followed suit. Once the sources are known, research naturally becomes easy! This is exactly what Dailami has done, with some distortions beneficial to his thesis, after 26 years, which in historical deontology has a clear name: plagiarism.

As to how Adalat was run, he resorts to 'anything goes'. Taking an incident at the Iranian consulate where the discussion between various parties degenerated because of a gun attack on Adalat's leader, he writes: 'In Baku, the Edalat Party held loosely organised political meetings and was mostly engaged in scuffles with the Iranian consulate.' Someone who cannot even imagine that there may be records of the Adalat in the Soviet archives cannot but transform (without giving the reference) a reported incident by an Adalat leader (Pishevari) into a general statement to denigrate that party. Yet, as an author who praises the Jangali–Bolshevik relations in his other article referred to, he writes about the same 'populist' Adalat whose 'Bolshevik connection was unmistakable' (p 90). When discussing the resistance of Adalat and Himmat vis-à-vis the Bolshevik's integration of their parties into the Russian party, his ignorance of the Adalat party's history, leads him to follow bourgeois historians in using the terminology 'Muslim' for both Adalat and Himmat, stating that: 'In every respect, the Edalat supported the position of Himmat — an indication, perhaps of Muslim solidarity.' Were they Muslims or Communists? The Adalatists, by their socialist thinking, did not consider themselves Muslim. Their national identity was Iranian. Himmatists, an Azeri-speaking people living north of the Arax, had been known, in the absence of a national designation, either as 'Tatars' or 'Muslims'; the Bolsheviks referred to all Communists coming from a Muslim background 'Muslim Communists' until new national identities were coined.[335] What is more, he asserts that 'the Edalat was indeed more Azerbaijani and Russian than Iranian', for 'until 1920, in its three-year history, it had hardly done anything in relation to Iran itself' (p 94). His dislike for Adalat, as a forerunner of the ICP, is so great that he would deprive his uninitiated readers of two important facts: like any other national group in Diaspora, Adalat's feelings in matters political were not geographical; were the Bolsheviks in exile in Europe, to take a good example, more French, German, etc, because they did not attend to home affairs in their everyday activity? Indeed, Adalat was very conscious of its links with the home country and made every effort possible to revive the old Social Democratic cells and groups, or create new groups in Iran; its leader Qafazadeh left for Iran in 1918 and was assassinated by the reactionaries in Gilan. Dailami pretends not to know any other facts and gathers his information from bourgeois historians such as Richard Pipes and Stephen Blank, while he could have known otherwise if he had used fully the book he took for a Crystal Ball.[336]

To build his case against Sultanzade in advance, he introduces his rival Haidar Khan as someone 'who has gone down in history as a hero of the October Revolution. Subsequently, pro-Soviet and Soviet sources always attempted to portray Haidar as an orthodox Bolshevik.' (p 95) What 'history' does he mean? History? Or the 'history of the Stalinist historians' whom he labels 'pro-Soviet and Soviet sources', both Russian and Iranian? Certainly, the latter, as he quotes no one else but such sources.[337] As he admits, Haidar was in contact with Ordzhonikidze because of their participation in the Constitutional Revolution. In fact, there is absolutely no trace of Haidar Khan having even been in Russia at the time the revolution broke out. Indeed, he had joined the Ottoman armies of the Central Powers during the Great War, for a proof of which we have his photography in the Ottoman military uniform.[338] Curiously, Dailami admits that he also asked to collaborate with the Germans (p 96).

Dailami invents history once again. He writes: 'The reorganisation of the left wing of the Demokrat Party occurred in 1919. While in Tehran a Demokrat leader, Solayman Mirza Eskandari, rallied the left-wingers to his side and called them the *Zed-e tashkilis*...' (p 97) It so happens that at this time Eskandari was under arrest by the British in India and was released only in 1921.[339] He also borrows invented history from a Soviet historian to the effect that Haidar translated Soviet literature into Persian (p 97). What literature? No indication is given, and for good reason, for Haidar Kahn hardly knew Persian, at best his familiarity with Persian was rudimentary. Not even a single article in Persian, or any other language,[340] has been attributed to him, even by his most enthusiastic admirers.

Once again he attempts to boost Haidar's place in the events of those days by translating a reference to a letter of *recommendation* from Trotsky to Haidar as a 'mandate' (p 97). He throws in two sentences that have no relation to Haidar Khan, except that they are a clumsy attempt to add some juice to the 'mandate': 'The political commissar of the "Red East"[341] was Georgi Ivanovich Safarov, a personal emissary of Lenin. In Turkestan, heavy recruitment of Muslims, including Iranians, was the priority of the day, and Haidar took up the task.' His reference for the latter claim is still another Stalinist historian, AM Matveev. He also tries to attribute to Haidar Khan the aforementioned article by the Tatar Bolshevik Effendiev[342] in which the author says 'the ideas expressed here are entirely shared by the revolutionary Iranian Haidar Kahn, representative of the Iranian people in the Third International'.[343] The concluding ideas of Effendiev regarding the importance of the Eastern Question and the role the Eastern revolution could play in the world revolution were not only his or those of his friend Haidar Khan, but of almost all Eastern revolutionary thinkers, whose major representative, who has really gone down in History, was Sultan Galiev[344] and not Haidar Khan, as Dailami pretends, simply because he does not know the literature and wishes to make a hero of Haidar Khan. Both the Iranian Sultanzade and the Indian MN Roy contributed to the debate on the Eastern Question; it suffices to read in full the proceedings of the Second Congress. Haidar Khan was not present there.

Having constructed his hero, Dailami then attends to his rival, Avetis Sultanzade (that is, Avetis Sultanovich Mikailian), whose biography he does not discover, but falsifies. He states that Avetis Mikailian Sultanzade,[345] as noted above, 'a Russian Bolshevik', was one of the emissaries Adalat sent in January 1920 to Turkestan. He writes:

> Mikaelian's mentality was that of an inferior foreigner, the likes of whom one frequently encounters in the streets of London, Berlin, Paris. His father, Sultan (as Mikaelian's patronymic, Sultanovich, suggests), was a Muslim; it is not clear where the Christian names of Avetis Mikaelian come from, other than that he had an Armenian mother.[346] Mikaelian, on the whole, and at that stage, was to offer Iran what Lenin had offered to Moscow and Petrograd. He simply tried to copy the Bolshevik revolution, and his hypocritical [?] radicalism (as will be seen) was an integral element of his inferiority [complex?]. He arrived in Turkestan under the name of Mikaelian, and, when he joined the *Sovinterprop* (Soviet of International Propaganda), he changed [his name] to Sultanzade — later Avetis Sultanovich Sultanzade. In Turkestan, where a bunch of chauvinist Russians were carrying out their own revolution, he found the perfect pattern for the Iranian movement. ...
>
> He was a student of the 'Russian' Revolution, and by attempting to copy that revolution in Iran, he was to come into conflict with the old Edalatis, as well as with Haidar Khan. In his struggle with Haidar, Sultanzade was to draw on the Eurocentrist support of the Bolsheviks. In his mind, as it later transpired, the personification of world revolution was the Russian civil war itself, which expanded as the Red Army conquered new territories. His revolution was a proletarian revolution with a military character, as indeed the revolution in Turkestan was. There is no sign of Sultanzade's involvement in Iranian Communist affairs before 1920. He came from the north [?] and he found in Turkestan the perfect pattern for the forthcoming Iranian revolution. He was a Stalinist before Stalin. Indeed, the Iranian upheaval would be just another stage of the Russian civil war, where the Red Army would intervene and establish the dictatorship of the Iranian proletariat that was based in Baku and Turkestan. Sultanzade thus also introduced an element of regional separatism into Iranian Communist politics, which had hitherto been merely a condition of local movements in Iran, particularly of the Jangali movement in the north of the country. Sultanzade did so despite the fact that by copying the Bolshevik's programme for the Iranian Communist Party (Bolshevik)..., he unsuspectingly offered federalism to Iranian society for the first time.

This whole 'indictment' is formulated to demolish this 'half Armenian' revolutionary and to portray the fully Muslim Haidar as a 'skilful diplomat'. Let us go over his points one by one.

* How does Dailami establish that Sultanzade 'was an inferior foreigner, the likes of whom one frequently encounters in the streets of London, Berlin, Paris'? Does he have any facts about Sultanzade permitting him to carry out such a comparison. He does not, for he offers none.
* Does he refer to any sociological study regarding such 'inferior foreigners'? He does not. Are all 'inferior foreigners' in the twentieth century in London, Paris and Berlin alike to offer a model for comparison with an 'inferior foreigner' from Iran in Russia? We do not know, and he does not clarify this either. Such baseless and cheap comparisons can, at best, be found in flyers written by historically and sociologically illiterate individuals.
* Is an author who does not even possess the basic facts about the life of a revolutionary militant equipped to enter into one of the most difficult subjects of modern history, that is, a character analysis of revolutionaries? There is no evidence either.
* Was someone like Sultanzade — the author of many books and articles on the Eastern Question as well as a serious economic study of the world capitalist crisis, published by the Comintern,[347] who debated with and challenged Lenin at the Comintern's Second Congress, a theoretician, with a knowledge of several European languages, who debated the complicated question of Finance Capital with Bukharin at the Sixth Congress, the founder of the first bank in Soviet Russia and the editor of the Soviet banking review[348] — really one of those 'inferior foreigners' walking in the streets of Moscow and Petrograd?
* Should the Armenian, Iranian or Islamic background of a revolutionary militant be important for an historian who aims to establish a factual history, rather than racist categories? According to Dailami, 'yes'. Yet it was no one but Sultanzade himself who, unwittingly, wrote down his family background,[349] which played a role in the development of his character, not knowing that someday someone, just like the anti-Christian Muslim 'Communists' in Baku[350] would hold it against him.
* Did Sultanzade have the right to his choice of social model, even though it might have been a wrong one? According to Dailami, 'no'. In spite of giving his reference to the programme the ICP adopted at the Anzali congress (note 64 on page 116), Dailami seems only to know its content when it suits him, despite the fact that it has been available in Persian since 1976.[351] While he refers to the debates of the Anzali congress,[352] he approvingly cites Obukh (Abukov) one of Stalin's lieutenants who, at the

ICP's Anzali congress, went so far as defending collaboration with the landlords, who were naturally oppressive and opposed any kind of land reform (see *The Soviet Socialist Republic of Iran*, Chapter 8). He claims that Haidar Khan was excluded from the Adalat after the Tashkent conference in April 1920 (p 100), and, for evidence, he refers his readers to one of the most unreliable Iranian students of Stalin, a trainee at KUTV, Reza Rousta, a Gilani like himself, who is widely known to have been an agent of the various Soviet secret services in Iran. By contrast, Haidar Khan was born into a physician's family and had the means to attend university in Tiflis, but never produced any writing really worth mentioning. He was known as Haidar 'bombi', that is, a bomb-maker, to be admired by Dailami as a 'skilful diplomat'.

* Who were this 'bunch of chauvinist Russians' 'carrying out their own revolution' in Turkestan whom Sultanzade is alleged to have emulated? We are not told anything about them. Were they under Safarov, who was 'a personal friend of Lenin'? If not, why did Safarov not stop them? Why would Sultanzade follow such people when he knew and was in contact with the top leaders of the Russian revolution? No answer is available, and no sources are given.

* Dailami accuses Sultanzade of having 'unsuspectingly offered federalism to Iranian society for the first time'. Was this really the first time? No. Dailami is not aware that during the second phase of the Constitutional revolution, two of its prominent leaders, AA Dehkhoda and Y Dolatabadi, published a detailed programme for a type of 'soviet federalism', in Iran[353] that, of course, did not catch fire because of the suffocating compromise by right-wing Constitutionalists with the biggest landlords. The Anzali congress programme attributed to Sultanzade speaks indeed of federalism, but stands against separatism, which constitutes a gross distortion on Dailami's part.[354]

* On what evidence does Dailami base his assertion that Sultanzade was a 'Stalinist before Stalin'? No evidence, except the hateful attitude he holds toward the son of a Muslim worker in a wood-sawing factory and an Armenian washerwoman, who, because of the break-up of the parental marriage, was forced to work for his own education from the age of eight, in Maragha (Iran), Edjmiasin (Armenia), Tbilisi (Georgia), Moscow, etc, and turned out to be a Marxist theoretician who produced some of the best economic studies for the period, not only on Iran, but also on the East — something to be envied by later Iranian pretenders to Marxism. In historiographical works, even those attacking Stalin, I have never read anything worse than what Dailami raises against Sultanzade. How can

one explain this attitude in the mind of a Gilani with a mediocre research record? Difficult to say, if one is not to blunder into the same pitfall as Dailami himself, except that he is profoundly offended by the position Sultanzade took against Kuchek Khan, at times incorrectly.

I would, however, venture to offer a few points for reflection.

Dailami was a fervent Trotskyist in his student days, and must, therefore, have supported the thesis of Permanent Revolution. He should thus have been in favour of Eastern Communists who supported theses close to Trotsky's ideas before he changed his views. Why does he attribute to Sultanzade a thesis that was initially Trotsky's, that is, 'a proletarian revolution with a military character'? On the other hand, I have never seen any reference in Sultanzade's writings which may by far point to a similar idea.

Other misrepresentations of historical facts by Dailami are: (pp 100-03)

* The Jangali Movement was 'the result of the collusion [!] of a whole array of political forces from the Caucasian Bolshevik to anti-Russian *akhund*[s]',
* A profound awareness of Iran's fragmentation also affected the Jangalis' agrarian policy, and then they resolved that a general land reform was impossible until Tehran was captured.
* The Germans and the Ottomans were 'supporters of the Jangalis'.
* Lenin himself wished to come to terms with Iranian bourgeois nationalism, which would weaken Western imperialism and thus would facilitate the advent of world revolution. (Curiously, instead of referring the reader to Lenin's works, he refers him to Dailami's own writing! See note 60 on page 101.)
* The Adalat was no longer under the leadership of old Social Democrats, who had been replaced by individuals such as Sultanzade 'who had no history of involvement in Iranian affairs'.

To respond briefly: the Caucasian Bolsheviks were not part of the Jangali Movement; in fact, they were most of the time opposed to it. The Jangalis' agrarian policy was the result of the economic interests of its leadership elements, not an awareness of anything else. The Jangalis were never supported by the Central Powers. Dailami totally falsifies the discussion of Lenin at the Comintern's Second Congress. The assertion that Lenin wished to come to terms with Iranian bourgeois nationalism is without clear reference, for it is false. Lenin's theoretical position was opposed to this assertion, but his diplomacy is another matter, which was carried out by Chicherin and Rothstein in favour the pro-British putsch leader Reza Khan, who in a way represented bourgeois nationalism. The leadership of Adalat accepted Sultanzade as their own because he knew Iran well, although he had fought in the ranks of the Russian party.

As for the conflict between the ICP Central Committee and Haidar Khan, who was supported by Stalin's men at the Baku congress in September 1920, Dailami leans on the falsifications of Stalinist historians who have told the story for nearly 80 years. And yet he accuses Sultanzade of having been a Stalinist![355] Dailami also asserts that at the Comintern's Second Congress, Sultanzade was 'delirious with his successes' and went on to add his 'wishful thinking in an unprecedented manner' to the resolutions. It thus appears that none of the top brains at the congress, including Lenin, discerned what Dailami noticed some 80 years later!

What does Dailami hides from his readers? This is what Vladimir Geniz, an author he approvingly cites elsewhere, relates on the basis of Comintern documents. In spite of Ordzhonikidze's opposition, Lenin supported Sultanzade's views, saying that in a country like Iran a revolution needs to start with the agrarian revolution; Pavlovich, Radek and Zinoviev supported Lenin's views. Ordzhonikidze and Stalin opposed the idea, and said it was too early to struggle against the landlords![356] In order to prevent Sultanzade from returning to Iran with such support, this is what Stalin's band did. On 2 August in Baku, Sultanzade and Mdivani boarded a ship bound for the Iranian port of Anzali. As the boat was to depart, Mdivani told Sultanzade that the latter should see Ordzhonikidze. Sultanzade took his belongings and got off the boat. He thought it was a serious matter. Then he found out that Ordzhonikidze had already gone to Rostov. Stassova told Sultanzade that the Kavburo wanted to punish him by preventing him from returning to Iran.[357] It can be seen that Dailami's method is far from being deontologically professional.

There is no need here to dwell any more on such baseless assertions, as these subjects have been amply discussed in *The Soviet Socialist Republic of Iran*. Finally, however, we must ask, where do *Dailami's* 'facts' come from? A look at his footnotes shows that, except for a few rare sources in Persian, his references regarding Sultanzade and Haidar Khan are all uncritical borrowings from Soviet Stalinist historians, who cannot be relied upon. Their fiery hatred of the 'left-wing' Sultanzade and his comrades, all of whom paid a heavy price during the purges for their non-observance of the Soviet line, began in 1922 and has continued since, despite the demise of the Soviet Union.

The core of Dailami's opposition to Sultanzade and his blaming him for the ruining of the revolution by means of his 'leftist' policies — a position he has borrowed from Stalinist historians — is his attempt to cover up the treacherous policies of Soviet Russia in Iran and to whitewash Lenin, Trotsky and Stalin. Of course, most regrettable is the fact that the two editors who have published Dailami's two chapters commented on above neither edited his diatribes against Sultanzade nor check the veracity of his 'facts' — a very unprofessional approach indeed.

II: The Tudeh Party and the 1953 Putsch

And finally we must attend to a recent piece of writing, a chapter by Mazia Behrouz in a recent book concerning the coup of 1953[358] which rehashes some of his former writings, commenting upon some of his misleading remarks about the role of the Tudeh Party during the coup.

The first problem with Behrouz is that he seems to accept the assertions by Donald Wilber, the author of the CIA's self-congratulatory 'history' of the coup, to the effect that it was the Soviet threat that led the USA to gang up with the UK to overthrow Mosaddeq (p 103). We know that this was only a pretext for the American oil companies to share the spoils of the Iranian oil.

Reviewing the repercussions of the proscription of the Tudeh as a consequence of the so-called attempt on the life of the shah in 1949, Behrouz affirms that the Tudeh recovered from the assaults upon it; he forgets, however, that this was, to a great extent, the result of the development of the anti-imperialist movement led by Mosaddeq, which seriously weakened the pro-imperialist forces the royal court included. At the same time, he refers to Abrahamian's 'ample evidence that many American and British officials were aware that the Tudeh was not a real danger and that the party was used as a smokescreen' (n 15, p 304). He fails to realise that Abrahamian uses this argument in order to justify the inaction of the Tudeh during the coup, for his whole attempt is directed at blaming the 'national bourgeoisie' and particularly Mosaddeq for the failure of the movement.

In attempting to explain the inaction of the Tudeh during the coup days, Behrouz relies on different explanations that Tudeh or pro-Tudeh individuals such as Jazani, Kianouri, etc, have offered as the 'reason' why it did nothing,. He makes no independent attempt to analyse why the Tudeh remained inactive in those days, except for senselessly indulging in chanting the slogan 'Victory to the democratic republic!', which amounted to a provocation to incite the pro-monarchy elements into action against the Mosaddeq government. One of the weaknesses from which Behrouz suffers is his lack of aptitude for checking the reliability of his sources. For instance, he refers to Ruhollah Abbasi (n 9, pp 303-04) as a reliable source for the history of the Tudeh military organisation, as if the author he mentions is the same Abbasi who was arrested in the late summer of 1954 and betrayed the whole organisation to the military authorities. It so happens that the man to whom he refers is but a namesake of the real Abbasi who has never uttered a word about why, how and when he exactly collaborated with the military governor of Tehran who smashed the Tudeh officers' organisation. He commits the same mistake when he refers to a book attributed to me, which I have never published (n 27, p 304)!

While Behrouz, without studying the officials statistics of the positions of Tudeh officers, asserts that most Tudeh officers were 'in non-combatant positions', he fails to refer to the appraisal of a 'high-ranking officer' of the Tudeh military organisation as a reliable source, although this officer showed the contrary in detail. His selective attitude towards sources demonstrates not only his aptitude for historical appraisal, but also his personal choice for sources convenient for his own thesis. For instance, although he mentions the fact that two of the Tudeh officers were attached to the Imperial Guards (p 105), he fails to emphasise the important fact that some of the Tudeh officers were in key positions whence they could have put an immediate stop to the coup. According to police officer Varqa, who held a key position in the *Shahrbani* (Police Department), when General Zahedi arrived at the Tehran Radio Station, he was accompanied by Tudeh officers, Captains Madani and Sadeqi; what is more, Varqa himself and Captain Shafa were present there.[359] He adds that the two Tudeh officers in the Imperial Guard 'had the possibility of preparing the terrain for eradicating the shah'.[360] Officer M Mohajerani of the Tudeh Party was, until the moment of his own arrest, the personal bodyguard of Zahedi.[361] Varqa states that although these officers were in critical positions, they did not do anything because they received no instructions from the party, because — he adds — according to the 'principles' of socialism, individual terrorism is proscribed! He and his leadership forget that Lenin had a personal henchman who eliminated his enemies by assassination, and that the Tudeh Party used personal assassination to eliminate the journalist Mohammad Mas'oud, and even one of its own leading members, Hesam Lankarani, to whom we referred above.

Thus the argument of 'moral' opposition to assassination does not hold water in their decision not to eliminate Zahedi or the shah; had Zahedi been eliminated right at the radio station, the whole coup would have failed, and the shah would have never returned to the country. The fate of Iran and the destiny of the region would have changed drastically. Therefore, one has to search for the reason why the Tudeh leadership sat there with their arms crossed. Behrouz does not do that. One would have to search for the reason in Stalin's opposition to the patriotic non-Communist movements; in the case of Iran, one should also consider Mosaddeq's opposition to the Russian demand for an oil concession in 1944. Stalin and his right-hand man Beria never forgot nor forgave Mosaddeq for this act. Even after Stalin's death, Beria, who really had the reins of power in his hands, did not instruct the Tudeh to put an end to its hostility to Mosaddeq and to collaborate with him. It was only after the Kremlin coup against Beria by Khrushchev and his Politbureau allies that the Soviet leadership put an end to the policy of hostility to Mosaddeq, when the USSR suddenly made a volte-face. But even then, it was too late to remove all of Beria's men in the Soviet apparatus in order that the Tudeh would change its policy and actively support Mosaddeq, or, better said, actively to oppose the coup. That is why the Tudeh leadership in Tehran remained indifferent to the coup.

It is curious that Behrouz refers to a book that, in spite of its richness for information, has a pro-Soviet position, and which states — incorrectly — that the USSR supported the nationalisation of Iranian oil (n 20, p 304). Had he referred to Soviet sources, he would have reached a quite different conclusion. Even years after the fall of Mosaddeq, Soviet 'Iranologists', such as SM Aliev, S Agayev and MS Ivanov, repeated the same 'criticism of Mosaddeq'. On the other hand, the 'hard-line' faction that Behrouz identifies as the group opposed to Mosaddeq (p 111) were simply those who followed the Stalin–Beria line most faithfully; it had nothing to do with a 'dogmatic understanding of Marxism-Leninism' (p 115) It was simply Marxism-Leninism, and it had nothing to do with a 'theoretical' question that had never existed. Yet he is right (p 114) in pointing out that the differences within the Tudeh leadership was also connected with 'personal differences', mostly related to personal ambitions.

In explaining the Tudeh's inaction during the fateful days of the putsch, Behrouz mistakenly states that 'not wanting to alienate Mosaddeq's government, the Tudeh failed to prepare a contingency plan for coordination with the nationalist government to help it face off the coup'. Interestingly, however, he immediately states: 'The party also failed to plan for a situation where it would have to continue without Mosaddeq.' (p 115) So, inaction had nothing to do with alienating Mosaddeq. In short, the party failed to do anything at all because it had no instructions from Moscow, which, in the first months after Stalin's death, was embroiled in a power struggle — a fierce struggle that encouraged the Anglo-American partnership to press on with their activities and launch the putsch.

The author's claim (pp 116-17) that the Tudeh 'intelligence' warned Mosaddeq of an impending coup is also an unverified repetition of Kianouri's claims. True, a few days before the first coup, a Tudeh publication announced that a coup was in the offing, but there is serious doubt about whether it was the Tudeh, either Kianouri or Mobasheri, who informed Mosaddeq on the eve of the *coup d'état*. Other claims have been made and no one can ever be certain of the identity of Mosaddeq's informer on the telephone. Even Tudeh cadres have seriously questioned Kianouri's version of the informing of Mosaddeq, which Behrouz relates.[362]

Another point by Behrouz to be corrected is his claim that the demonstrators against the coup and the shah on 16 August did not call for a republic: '... even here there was no sign of widespread demand for a republic.' As a participant in that day's demonstration, I can testify that the slogan 'republic' was chanted by many of Mosaddeq's supporters on Baharestan Square; and Tudeh demonstrators called for a 'democratic republic', a personal memory that is verified by reliable sources, including the Tudeh Party Central Committee declaration which, *inter alia*, states: 'Down with the Monarchy! Victory to the Democratic Republic!'[363] This imprecision on the part of the author once again demonstrates his lack of attentiveness to sources.

Finally, in this connection, one must emphasise the author's credulity in believing one of his oral sources, 'a member of the Tehran Provincial Committee', who 'wishes to remain anonymous' (notes 54, 57, pp 306-07). This 'member of the Tehran Provincial Committee', who was 'the person who suggested the "republic"' as the Tudeh demand for the demonstrations of 16 August, and who claims that he was 'surprised to see his proposal turned into an even more radical version', is certainly not telling the truth, for, as his position indicated, he must have read the Central Committee declaration (referred to above) before it was made public. Of course, the reason he wishes to remain anonymous is that he is one of the two high-ranking Tudeh leaders who not only sold out the party to the shah, but began to collaborate with Asadullah 'Alam, the shah's very intimate buddy, court minister and one-time prime minister. These two, pro-Nazi activists before the Second World War, were Ali Mottaqi and Amanollah Qoreyshi, who enrolled in the party after Stalingrad. They rose in the party hierarchy, respectively, to the position of alternate Central Committee member (elected at the second party congress, 1948), and member of the Tehran Provincial Committee. They both were expelled from the party after the coup. Their testimony is suspect, particularly because, at least, one of the two is highly suspected to have been a foreign operative in the Tudeh Party.

This latter part of the historiography of the Left demonstrates, once again, how careless, how ideological and, at times, how intentionally distorting have been those who have tried their hand at writing the history of the Iranian Left — a disastrous result which has, in turn, fed the young Iranians attracted to the cause of the Left, and thus led them astray.

The imprint of Stalinist historiography persists in the minds of those Iranians who think they have liberated themselves from it.

Notes
1. Apparently, when inviting me to that SOAS conference, Dr Cronin had not digested what I had written in the preface of one of my previous works (*The Soviet Socialist Republic of Iran*). It is, therefore, essential to quote a critical passage of that preface so that the reader knows the crucial point she had missed: 'In short, I have always preferred to tell the bitter truth in lieu of preserving my own petty advantages, which would have amounted to maintaining a hypocritical stand and

falsely "harmonious" relationships, both personal and academic.' In short, I prefer the truthfulness of King Lear's fool — or his Iranian counterpart *Bohloul* — to the accommodations of the 'sage' who, in fear of rocking the boat, sacrifices the good of the community on the altar of narrow interests.

2. 'Mr Toynbee's Resignation: To the Editor of *The Times*', *The Times* (London), 3 January 1924.
3. C Chaqueri, *The Russo-Caucasian Origins of the Iranian Left Social Democracy in Modern Iran* (Curzon, London, 2001; also published by the University of Washington Press, Seattle, 2001).
4. S Cronin (ed), *Reformers and Revolutionaries in Modern Iran* (Routledge-Curzon, London, 2004), pp 325, £55.00.
5. Persian translation from Arabic by A Payandeh, Volume 1 (Tehran, 1973); English translation by various translators (Albany NY, 1979-1994).
6. *Morouj al-zahab va ma'aden al-johar* (*Les Preiries d'or...*), Texte et traduction par B de Meynard et P de Courteille (two volumes, Paris, 1861-63).
7. *Tarikh-e jahan gosha*; edited by M Qazvini, English translation by JA Boyle (Manchester, 1958).
8. *Tarikh-e guzida*, in Gibb Memorial Series (1910).
9. *Tarikh-e 'alam ara-ye 'abbasi*, edited by I Afshar (Tehran, 1966; translation by R Savory, Boulder CO, 1978).
10. AM b H Bayhaqi-Dabir, *Tarikh-e Bayhaqi*, edited by AA Fayyaz (Mashhad, 1971).
11. *Le Livre de l'Inde*, translation by Vincent-Mansour Monteil (Paris, 1996).
12. Tehran, 1959.
13. Abu 'Ali H b 'Ali Nezam al-Molk Tousi, *Siasatnameh* (*Seyar al-molouk*) (Tehran, 1985); English translation by H Darke, *The Books of Government or Rules for Kings* (London, 1978).
14. F Daftari, *The Isma'ilis: The History and Doctrine* (Cambridge, 1990).
15. See C Chaqueri, 'The Role and Impact of Armenian Intellectuals in Iranian Politics, 1905-1911' (MESA Convention, November 1987), *The Armenian Review*, Volume 41, nos 2, 4, 1988; idem, 'Armenian-Iranians and the Birth of Iranian Socialism', in *The Armenians of Iran: The Paradoxical Role of a Minority in a Dominant Culture* (Harvard UP, Cambridge, Mass, 1986); idem, *The Russo-Caucasian Origins of the Iranian Left: Social Democracy in Modern Iran* (London, 2001), Chapter 6.
16. The only work on Yousof Eftekhari and his group is that which was published by K Bayat and M Tafreshi, *Khatrat-e doran-e separishodeh* (*Khaterat va asnad-e Yousof Eftekhari*) (Tehran, 1991) — an undertaking which began on the recommendation of this author in 1989 to find Eftekhari and interview him for the sake of historical record. Unfortunately, the interviewers, who did not possess all the professional qualities for the task, or the close acquaintance with the history of the Communist movement necessary for such an undertaking, rushed through the project without seeking further advice.
17. Until recently, the only account we had of this group, apart from the abuse hurled upon it by the Tudeh (repeated by B Jazani, *Tarikh-e si saleh-ye siasi* (Germany, nd), pp 102-04), is a document from the US National Archives; see a Persian translation in *Ketab-e jom'ehha*, no 5, Winter 1985, pp 75ff; the former CIA coup planner Donald Wilber accuses Imami of having been a Soviet 'espionage' agent!

See his *Iran, Past and Present* (London, 1963), p 136. Since this paper was written, an interesting new book has been published in exile by a former member of the Imami *krouzhok*s and a later leader of SAKA. See Albert Sohrabian, *Khaterat, Bargi az jonbesh-e kargari komonisti-ye Iran* (2000).

18. Except for Jazani's biased account (*Tarikh-e si saleh*, pp 104-07) we have, as yet, no study of this group, how it was formed, what it did and to what extent it influenced the new generation of post-coup Leftists, except for the two volumes that it wrote and circulated in limited numbers in the underground, and which were published by this author as Volumes 2 and 5 of the series *Historical Documents: The Workers', Social-Democratic and Communist Movement in Iran* (23 Volumes, Florence and Tehran, 1969-92; Microfilm edition, Joseph Regenstein Library, The University of Chicago, Chicago, USA). Its main thinker was Tavakkoli, and two known collaborators were M Sho'a'iyan and P Baba'i.

19. See Chaqueri, 'The Role and Impact of Armenian Intellectuals in Iranian Politics, 1905-1911'; idem (ed), *Historical Documents*, Volumes 1, 3, 6, 13, 14; idem (ed), *La Social-démocratie en Iran* (second edition, Florence and Tehran, 2001).

20. C Chaqueri, 'The Role and Impact of Armenian Intellectuals'; idem, *The Russo-Caucasian Origins of the Iranian Left*.

21. The Socialist organisation under Solayman Mirza has been cursorily treated, for obvious reasons because of his later role in the Tudeh; see E Abrahamian, *Iran Between Two Revolutions* (Princeton, 1982), pp 127-28.

22. Stalin's ideological instruction regarding how to write history were enunciated in his famous article 'Some Questions Concerning the History of Bolshevism', JV Stalin, *Works*, Volume 13 (Moscow, 1995), pp 87ff, 99, 102. In response to Slutsky's 'anti-party and semi-Trotskyist' article, Stalin established his dogma and 'emphatically' protested against the author as a 'slanderer and falsifier', for the 'question of Lenin's *Bolshevism*, the question whether Lenin did or did not wage an irreconcilable struggle, based on principle, against Centrism as a certain form of opportunism, the question whether Lenin was or was not a real Bolshevik, cannot be made into a subject of discussion'. For Stalin, questions that were 'axioms of Bolshevism' could not be discussed. He went on: 'Who, except archive rats, does not understand that a party and its leaders must be tested primarily by their deeds and not merely by their declarations?' 'The task of the editorial board is, in my opinion, to raise the questions concerning the history of Bolshevism to the proper level, to put the study of the history of our Party on scientific, Bolshevik lines, and to concentrate attention against the Trotskyist and all other falsifiers of the history of our Party, systematically tearing off their masks.'

23. Also known as Sazman-e Enqelabiyoun-e Kommonist.

24. A Matin, *Konfederation. Tarikh-e jonbesh-e daneshjouyan-e irani dar kharej-e az keshvar, 1332-57* (Tehran, 1999); English edition edited by Costa Mesa (California, 2002).

25. My personal experience in this regard confirms A Matin's remarks in *Confederation*, p 13. Unfortunately, Matin, who produced a splendid oral history of the CISNU and used its published materials, could not use the lost or displaced internal records of the organisation.

26. The author of the work told me this personally in 1990 during a visit to Los Angeles.

27. Paper presented by Hasan Massali in *Natayej-e seminar-e Wiesbaden dar bareh-ye bohran jonbesh-e chap-e Iran* (Frankfurt, 1985), pp 52-56.
28. 'Seminar-e Wiesbaden va pasokhi be chand ede'a', *Andisheh-ye raha'i*, no 6, 1987.
29. This is, of course, a tradition that even the self-proclaimed anti-Stalinist organisations such as Vahdat-e Kommonisti had inherited from Soviet practice. Once in the early 1970s one of the leading cadres of the Marxist-Leninist organisation Toufan, disgusted by the methods used by his comrades, left the organisation and published a little pamphlet ('Ozv-i Sabeq-e Hey'at-e Markazi' [Adrom], *Sokhani darbareh-ye Sazman-e M-L Toufan* (Munich [?], 1973 [?]) on his comrades' dirty political methods, which reminded one of Beria. Paradoxically, the organisation that most ferociously attacked the dissident Toufanist was the self-proclaimed anti-Stalinist Vahdat-e Kommonisti in their semi-official organ *Bakhtar-e Emrouz*, fourth series published in the Middle East, asking him to withdraw his pamphlet and apologise for his 'misdeed' of exposing the 'secrets' of his organisation! (I am quoting this from memory since I was not able to locate the particular issue.) It is no less interesting that in 1975 another publication (*'Asr-e 'amal*, no 2) that was jointly published by the same group and the People's Fada'iyan in Lebanon, claimed that the Tudeh's 'political work' was 'in a sense useful and necessary'. This raised a wide protest among Leftists opposed to the Tudeh's subservience to the Soviet Union. See 'Problems of Revolution and Socialism', *Manifestus*, no 5, Winter 1354/1976, pp 53ff.
30. Former Tudeh First Secretary Reza Radmanesh has been quoted as having burnt all his records. His close collaborator and *chef de cabinet* Houshang Garman refused to honour his pre-arranged appointment with this author even after my arrival in his town of residence in Germany.
31. The regime was not alone in this despicable 'exploitation'. After the appearance of my series of *Historical Documents*, members of the Sazman-e Enqelabiyoun-e Kommonisti cut out articles from Tudeh publications that they did not like, or simply 'removed' unbound issues of the Tudeh daily of the Mosaddeq period (*Besou-ye Ayandeh*) from the Hoover Institution Library and the Library of Congress, respectively.
32. M Behrouz, *Rebels with a Cause* (London, 1999).
33. The number of those Leftist militants, including of the Tudeh, continuing decent and humble lives, who are known to have possessed valuable historical information, is not negligible, but they have preferred to keep silent out of mere pessimism.
34. See, for instance, M Pavlovich's writings in M Pavlovich and S Iranskii [Pastukhov], ... *Persiia v bor'be za nezavisimost'* (Moscow, 1925); A Sultanzade, 'The Perspective of Social Revolution in Persia', in *Zhizn natsional'nostei*, no 30, 1920; French and Persian translation in Chaqueri, *Le mouvement communiste en Iran* (Florence, 1979), p 243; idem, *Historical Documents*, Volume 4 (new edition), pp 71-72; idem, *Avetis Sultanzade: The Forgotten Revolutionary Theoretician: Life and Works*,

(Washington DC, 1985), p 23; A Sultanzade, *Sovremennia Persiia* (Moscow, 1922); Persian translation in Chaqueri (ed), *Historical Documents*, Volume 4 (1973, 1986 editions).

35. See Chaqueri, *The Russo-Caucasian Origins of the Iranian Left*, Chapters 5-7.
36. GM Petrov, 'Iranskaia Revoliutsia 1906-1911 Godov', in MC Godesa (ed), *Probyzhdenie Azii. 1905 god Revoliutsii na vostoke* (Leningrad, 1935); G Il'inskii, 'Iranskii Azerbaijan v revoliutsii 1905-1911', *Revoliutsionnyi vostok*, no 4 (38), 1936; E Bor-Ramenskii, 'K voprosu o roli bol'shevikov zakavkaz'ia v iranskoi revoliutsii, 1905-1911', *Istorik Marksist*, no 11, 1940; idem, 'Iranskaia revoliutsia 1905-1911 gg i bol'sheviki zakavkaz'ia', *Krasny arkhiv*, no 105, 1941.
37. True, the Tudeh issued annual declarations on each anniversary of the Constitutional Revolution, but seldom referring to the Social Democracy. After the end of the Second World War it followed the Stalinist interpretation of that revolution. See Tudeh Central Committee's 'Bayaniyeh-ye Hezb-e Tudeh-ye Iran be monasebat-e siohaftomin sal jashn-e mashroutiyat', Tehran, 14 Mordad 1321; and Chaqueri (ed), *Historical Documents*, Volume 10, which contains some of these declarations.
38. MS Ivanov, 'Novye materialy o sotsial-demokraticheskoi grupe v Tebrize v 1908 godu', *Problemi vostokovedeniia*, no 5, 1959; see this author's discussion of the Armenian Social Democrats of Tabriz and their treatment by Ivanov in Chaqueri, *The Russo-Caucasian Origins of the Iranian Left*, Chapter 7.
39. MS Ivanov, 'Vliianie russkoi revoliutsii 1905 g na iranskuiu revoliutsiiu 1905-1911 gg' ('The Influence of the Russian Revolution of 1905 on the Iranian Revolution of 1905-1911'), *Uchenye zapiski*, Seriia Vostokvedcheskikh Nauk, vypuk 1 (Leningrad, 1949); idem, *Ocherk istorii Irana* (Moscow, 1952); idem, 'Convoking the First Iranian Majles and the Struggle for the Establishment of Fundamental Laws', *Uchenye Zapiski Instituta Vostokovedeniia*, no 8, 1953; idem, *Iranskaia rvoliutsia*, Moscow, 1957.
40. For studies, see the following works as well as this author's critique (Chaqueri, *The Russo-Caucasian Origins of the Iranian Left*) GS Arutiunian, *Iranskaia revoliutsia 1905-1911 gg i bol'sheviki zakavkaz'ia* (Erevan, 1956); SM Aliev, 'Nekotorye fakty o znakomstve VI Lenina s iranskimi progresivnymi deiateliami', *Problemy vostoko-vedeniia*, no 2, 1960; idem, 'Neizvestyi dokument ob iranskoi sotsial-demokraticheskoi partii edzhtimaiun-e ammiiun', *Narody Azii i Afriki*, no 2, 1965; idem, 'K voprosu o sviziakh bakinskogo i tifliskogo komitetov RSDRP c iranskimi revoliutsionerami v 1903-1911 gg', in *Slavnnye stranitsy bor'by i pobed* (Baku, 1965); AM Matveev, 'Materialy istorii iranskogo endzhumena v ashkhabade, 1907-1911', *Trudy sagu* NS LXXVII Ist Nauk kn 10, 1956; idem, 'Iranskie revoliutsionnie organisatsii v sredney Azii v nachale XX vek', *Narody Azii i Afriki*, no 2, 1961; MZ Tutaev, 'K voprosu o vliianii pervoi ruskoi revoliutsii 1905-1911 gg', *Uchenye zapiski kazanskogo gasu-darstvennogo universiteta im Ul'ianova-Lenina*, 117/2, 1957; NK Belova and FB Beleliuskii, 'Perviye sviazi sotsialistov c natsional'no osvoboditel'nym dvizheniem', *Narody Azii i Afriki*, no 4, 1970; NK Belova and VN Plastun, 'Proklamatsii i ottiski pechatei iranskikh revoliutsionerov (1906-1908 gg)', *Narody Azii i Afriki*, no 1, 1973; VN Plastun, 'Gruzinskie revoliutsionery v iranskoi revoliutsionii 1905-1911 gg', *Literaturnaia Gruziia*, no 4, 1971; MA Tariverdy and

AI Mageramov, 'Khaidar Khan Amu-Ogli', *Narody Azii i Afriki*, no 5, 1971; IN Kurbatova, 'Pisma sotsial-demokratov Irana i Yaponii GV Plekhanovu', *Vostochnyi sbornik*, vypuk 3 (Moscow, 1972); Sh E Tagieva, 'Neriman Nerimanovun 1905-1911 iler Iran ingilaby ile elagdar fealiyyeti haggynda' ('N Narimanov's Activity in Connection with the 1905-1911 Iranian Revolution'), in *Izvestiia Akademii Nauk Azerbaidzhanskoi SSR*, Seria Istorii, Filosofii i Prava [Baku], no 3, 1973; SL Agaev, 'Iranskaia Revoliutsia 1905-11 gg', *Narody Azii i Afriki*, no 4, 1975; SL Agaev and VN Plastun, 'Spornye voprosy sotsial-Demokraticheskogo dvizheniia v Irane v 1905-1911 gg', *Iran. Istoriia i sovremennost* (Moscow, 1983).

41. Of particular interest are the works by a Georgian historian of Iran published towards the end of the life of the Soviet Union. See GS Chipashvili, *Tavrizkoe vostanie 1908-1909 GG i gruzinskaia pressa* (Tiflis, 1979); idem, 'Iz istorii internatsional'noi dialtel'nosti zakavkazskikh revoliutsionerov v Irane', *Matsne*, Seria Istorii, no 4, 1981; *Sergo Gamdlishvili ('Sergo Gurdzhi') i ego iranskie dnevniki* (in Georgian, Tiflis, 1983); L Bendianishvili, 'The 1905-1911 Iranian Bourgeois-Democratic Revolution and the Georgian Democratic Press' (in Georgian), *Seriia Istorii Arkheologii Etnografii I Istorii Iskysstva*, III, 1989 (Tbilisi), pp 98-110.

42. *Soviet Iranology in the 1920s* (in Russian, Moscow, 1977).

43. For an exemplary view of a Tudeh historian of the Constitutional Revolution who carried over the gross distortion of the Soviet historians, see R Namvar, *Iranskata revoliutsia, podvit'naedin B'lgarin* (*The Iranian Revolution and the Exploits of a Bulgarian*) [Panov] (Sofia, 1970); idem, *Molahezat priamoun-e tarikh-e enqelab-e mashroutiyat* (Tehran, 1979).

44. For the better-known Stalinist views of this period in Iran, see R Rezazadeh-Malek, *Haidar Khan Amoghli, Chakideh-ye enqelab* (Tehran, 1973); idem, *Zaban baray-e engelab, Hop Hop-Nameh* (Tehran, 1978); B Momeni, *Iran dar astaneh-ye enqelab-e Mashroutiyat* (Tehran, 1978) — a book that is a shortened version of the Soviet historiography on the subject; S Sardarinia, *'Ali Monsieur, rahbar-e markaz-e ghaibi* (Tehran, 1980); idem, *Naqsh-e markaz-e ghaibi-ye Tabriz dar er-qelab-e mashroutiyat* (Tehran, 1984); M Ra'isnia, *Haidar Amou-Oghli dar gozar az toufanha* (Tehran, 1981).

45. Republished after his death in a collection by the Tudeh Central Committee under E Tabari's editorship: *Shemmeh'i dar bareh-ye tarikh-e jonbesh-e kargari-ye Iran (Sosial-demokrasi-ye enqelabi, hezb-e kommonist-e Iran, Hezb-e Tudeh-ye Iran)* (Leipzig, 1971). For the opposition of Iraj Eskandari, at the time First Secretary of the party, to their publication as a book, see the latter's memoirs, *Khaterat* (Tehran, 1993), pp 68-69.

46. Published on a quarterly basis between 1960 and 1979 in exile, and in Tehran until 1982.

47. Although still ideologically tainted, these articles were exceptionally informative; see AH Agahi, 'Piramoun-e qadimitarin sanad-e chappi az tarikh-e socializm dar Iran'; idem, 'Nokhostin ashna'iha-ye iranian ba marksizm'; idem, 'Doran avvaliyeh-ye andishehha-ye marksisti dar Iran', reproduced in C Chaqueri (ed), *Historical Documents*, Volume 1 (new edition, Tehran, 1981); see also the reminiscences of 'Ali Kobari and Ebrahim 'Alizadeh, in *Donya*, 12/4, 1971.

48. See the memoirs of A Ovanesian, *Donya*, 3/1, 6/3, 7/3, 8/4 (reproduced in Chaqueri

(ed), *Historical Documents*, Volume 1 (Tehran, 1981), pp 118-45); Mashahdi Kavian, *Donya*, 4/3 (reproduced in Chaqueri (ed), *Historical Documents*, Volume 1, 1981, pp 146ff); Cyrus Bahram (M Akhundzadeh), *Donya*, 9/1; the reprinting of some of Arani's works with a critical introduction, from a Soviet perspective, by Iraj Eskandari, *Donya*, no 4, winter 1348/1970 (after their republication by Edition Mazdak!); and Z Naderi, 'Karim Nikbin, Zartosht. Yeki az rahbaran-e Hezb-e Komonist-e Iran', *Donya*, 11/3, 1970. While Eskandari's memoirs of the student days (*Paykar*, I/1, 2, 1971) were a reaction of the party to the CISNU and were meant to be an encouragement for the newly-founded pro-Tudeh student organisation to oppose the CISNU, other 'historical' works were meant to annul the work of Edition Mazdak founded in 1969 in Florence (Italy).

49. See, for instance, 'Iranskaia revoliutsia 1905-1911 gg i Bol'sheviki zakavkaz'ia', *Krasny arkhiv*, no 105, 1941; for the complete Persian version with the indication of the parts censored by the Tudeh, see the programme of the FEAM in Chaqueri (ed), *Historical Documents*, Volume 1 (third edition, 1981), pp 42-51.
50. E Tabari, *Az didar-e khishtan, yadnameh-ye zendegi*, 1360, edited by F Shiva (Sweden, 1997), pp 49-50.
51. Ibid, pp 143ff.
52. Ibid, p 50. The same lack of knowledge is manifested by A Ovanesian, who claims to have worked closely with the ICP leader Hesabi. He states in *Khaterat darbareh-ye rahbari dar hezb va rahbaran ou* (unpublished, typewritten, from June 1973 to December 1975, Erevan), p 158, that the latter 'definitely' had no children, while we do know that Hesabi (Dehzad) had a son named Sohrab, who had been taken, in September 1936, along with his mother Soghra, from Tehran to the USSR by Shoureshian (Shoureshian's 'Secret Report to Comrade Gromov', RTsKhIDNI, 495/11/146, [received] 26 October 1936); or that Eskandari confuses Hesabi's identity with that of A Zarreh (Sajjadi); *Khaterat*, Volume 1 (Paris, 1987), p 75. There are two editions of the Eskandari *Khaterat*; in the Tehran edition (1993, p 90); the editor added an 'and' between 'the wife of Zarreh, wife of Hesabi', in order to make a distinction between Zarreh and Hesabi, of which obviously Eskandari was not aware.
53. See Randjbar (alias for GC Gel'bras) 'Tov Sultanzade, kok viraztel' melkoburzhuaznovo vliianiia v voprosakh persidsokoye revoliutsii', *Revoliutsionni vostok*, no 1, pp 54-73; no 2, pp 74-90, 1933; as well as the 'Editorial Note' in no 2, 1934, pp 184-85.
54. In the summer of 1992, a former officer of the Tudeh Military Organisation told this author in search of ICP materials in Moscow and Baku: 'By republishing these documents, you will entice young Iranians to become extremists!'
55. The 1942 declaration by the Tudeh Central Committee on the Constitutional Revolution, referred to above, applauds the American war of liberation, the French revolution, etc, as well as the various clerical and lay leaders of the Iranian revolution, such as Asadabadi and Malkam Khan, but is completely silent on Iran's socialist thinkers. The silence is not a tactical manoeuvre, but the result of historical ignorance.
56. TA Ibrahimov (Shahin), *Iran kommonist partiyasynyn yaranmasy* (Baku, 1963); written during the Khrushchevian relative openness, and based on Baku archives,

it still is far from being objective, for three reasons: a) his own Stalinist outlook; b) his incomplete sources; c) his lack of professionalism, which leaves a great deal to be desired. It should also be mentioned that in 1992 and 1993, when I asked to see some of the files to which he gives reference, I was told by a rather helpful archivist, who provided me with other more sensitive materials, that Ibrahimov's references were inexact. What is more, Tabari does not have the courage to say that Ibrahimov was not allowed to see the Social Democratic, ICP and other documents which were available, merely because Stalinist policies in matters historical had not been totally abolished.

57. Tabari, *Az didar-e khishtan*, p 50.
58. For the reprint of these series; see C Chaqueri (ed), *Un Prince iranien, rouge en France* (Florence and Tehran, 2002).
59. 'Histoire du Parti Toudeh', *Moyen Orient*, no 1, November 1949. Eskandari told the story of the Communist students in Europe (the First Arani Circle) only in a couple of propagandistic articles when the Tudeh confronted the Confederation of Iranian Students (National Union). See the Tudeh's publication *Paykar* (Second series), Volume 1, no 2, 1971.
60. A Kasravi, *Tarikh-e Mashrouteh-ye Iran* (Tehran, 1970); *Tarikh-e hijdah saleh-ye Azerbaijan* (fourth edition, Tehran, 1967).
61. M Malekzadeh, *Tarikh-e enqelab-e mashroutiyat-e Iran* (seven volumes, Tehran, nd).
62. See, for instance, F Kazemzadeh, 'Iranian Historiography', in B Lewis and PM Holt (eds), *Historians of the Middle East* (New York, 1962), p 433, who refers to this work as a 'valuable, remarkably reasonable, and unusually well-documented effort'. See also NK Keddie, *Roots of Revolution* (New Haven, 1980), p 282, n 282.
63. EG Browne, *The Persian Revolution of 1905-1909* (London, 1910); idem, *The Reign of Terror at Tabriz: England's Responsibility (With Photographs and a Brief Narrative of the Events of December 1911 and January 1912)* (Manchester, 1912); M Pavlovitch [Weltman], 'Novaia Persiia i eia protivniki', *Sovremennyi mir*, no 2, 1909; idem, 'Die Persische Revolution, ihre Ursachen, ihr Charakter, und ihre Kampfmethoden', *Neue Zeit*, 8 April 1910; Tria, T (Vlas Mgladze), 'Letters from Persia', *Akhali skhivi* (Tiflis), 11 January 1909; idem, 'Le Caucase et la révolution persane', *Revue du Monde Musulman*, XIII, February 1911; J Longuet, *Le Mouvement socialiste international* (Paris, 1913; Geneva, 1976); idem, 'Bombardement du Majles', *Humanité*, 26 June 1908 (Persian translation in Chaqueri (ed), *Historical Documents*, Volume 19); idem, 'Le Mauvais coup russe contre la Perse', *Humanité*, 10 November 1910 (Persian translation in Chaqueri (ed), *Historical Documents*, Volume 19); idem, 'La responsabilité d'Angleterre', *Humanité*, 2 December 1910 (Persian translation in Chaqueri (ed), *Historical Documents*, Volume 19).
64. Atrpet [pseudonym of Sarkis M Moubayadjian], *Mamed 'Ali. Sovremennaia Persiia* (Alexandropol, 1909).
65. GE Wheeler, 'Soviet Writing on Persia from 1906 to 1946', in B Lewis and PM Holt (eds), *Historians of the Middle East*, pp 378-79. It is interesting to note that Cold War sources were used to produce the most obnoxious historiographies of the Left in Iran, such as A Ziba'i, *Komonizm dar Iran ya tarikh-e mokhtasar-e fa'aliyat-e komonistaha dar Iran* (*Communism in Iran, or a Short History of Communist*

Activity in Iran from the Beginning of Constitutionalism till March 1964) (Tehran, 1965), which served as an internal manual of the SAVAK and other security forces whose task was the repression of the opposition forces, notably the Left. This book was officially written by the army colonel who was a deputy to General T Bakhtiar of the Tehran Military Government after the 1953 *coup d'état* and the SAVAK as of 1957; it seems to have been put together by some former members of the Tudeh who knew that party well. Containing a good number of documents and less known sources, the book is ideologically framed to serve Cold War interests.

66. T Bahar, Malek al-Sho'ara, *Tarikh-e mokhtasar-e ahzab-e siasi* (Tehran, 1945).
67. Wheeler, 'Soviet Writing on Persia from 1906 to 1946', pp 376-79.
68. Ann KS Lambton, 'Secret Societies in the Persian Revolution', *St Antony's Papers*, no 4, 1958; idem, 'Persian Political Societies', *St Antony's Papers*, no 16, 1963.
69. 'A History of the Communist Movement in Iran', in *Army Roles, Missions and Doctrine in Low Intensity Conflict* (ARMLIC, Prepared by Carlisle Research Office under Contract No DAAG-25-67-C-0702 for US Army Combat Development Command Institute of Advanced Studies, Carlisle Barracks, Penn, 2 February 1970), p 404: 'The Japanese defeat of the Soviet Union in 1905 encouraged the belief that the great powers were not invincible. In addition, the abortive revolt against the Czar in the Soviet Union caused many rebels to take refuge in Persia, where they found an audience appreciative of their revolutionary ideas. Many of these early associations with revolutionaries were to continue to take broader form after the success of the Bolsheviks.' This study is based mostly on works such as those by Donald Wilber and Walter Laqueur and George Lenczowski.
70. For a good example of uncritical reproduction of Western and Communist sources (Lenczowski as well as Iraj Eskandari) on the history of the Tudeh in a doctoral dissertation, see H Farboud, *L'Evolution politique de l'Iran pendant la second guerre mondiale* (University de Lausanne, 1957), pp 74-75, 168-75.
71. C Chaqueri, *The Soviet Socialist Republic of Iran, 1920-1921: Birth of the Trauma* (Pittsburgh University Press, Pittsburgh, 1995).
72. G Ducrocq (pseudonym), 'La Politique du gouvernement de soviéts en Perse', *Revue du monde musulman*, 39, 1920; AC Edwards, 'German Intrigues in Persia', *Yale Review*, April 1918; LJ Edwards, 'An Autumn Tour in Daylam', *Journal of Central Asian Society*, Volume 11, part 4, 1924.
73. *Zhizn natsional'nostei*, no 39 (47), 12 October, 11 November 1919; for similar writings, see Chaqueri, *The Soviet Socialist Republic of Iran*, Bibliography.
74. The first 'historical' writings on the ICP were those by Sultanzade in his books from 1921 and 1924: *Sovremennia Persiia*, Moscow, 1922; idem, *Persiia* (Moscow, 1924).
75. For relevant issues in Sultanzade's works, see C Chaqueri (ed), *The Forgotten Revolutionary*; see also Sultanzade, 'First Communist Party of the East', *Communist International*, no 13, 1920; idem, *Persiia*; idem, 'On the Congress of the Persian Communist Party Adalat', *Kommunist*, no 49, 1920, in Russian; idem, 'Le Premier congrès des communistes persans du Parti Adalat', *Internationale communiste*, no 14, 1920; idem, 'The Revolutionary Movement in Iran', *Zhizn natsional'nostei*, no 30, 1920; idem, *Sovremennia Persiia*.
76. Irandust [V Osetrov], 'Klassy i Partii Sovremennoi Persii', *Mirovoe khoziaistvo i*

mirovaia politika, no 2, 1926.
77. Irandust [V Osetrov], 'Voprosy gilianskoi revoliutsii' ('Problems of the Gilan Revolution'), *Istorik marksist*, no 5, 1927.
78. The best proof of this independent spirit is reflected, *inter alia*, in the two letters of protestations (in December 1921 and February 1922) that the Iranian Central Committee addressed to Lenin and the Comintern concerning the Tsarist-like policies carried out by Lenin's plenipotentiary minister in Tehran. See Chaqueri, *The Soviet Socialist Republic of Iran*, p 447, and 'Report by the Iranian CP to the Comintern Regarding the Social Conditions in Iran', signed by Hamid Sultanov on behalf of the ICP Central Committee, in RTsKhIDNI, 495/90/59.
79. See note 18.
80. See his articles 'Tov Sultanzade, kok vyraztel' melkobozhuaznogo vliyaniya v voprosakh persidskoy revoliutsii', *Revoliutsionnyi vostok*, nos 1 and 2, 1933; see also the 'Editorial Note' in no 2, 1934.
81. For some of Sultanzade's writings on Iranian situation, which includes pieces on the Left's short life, see A Sultanzade, *Ecrits économiques* (Florence, 1980); idem, *Politische Schriften* (Florence, 1975); Chaqueri (ed), *Le Mouvement communiste en Iran*; idem, *The Condition of the Working Class in Iran* (four volumes, Florence and Tehran, 1978-1991); idem, *Historical Documents*, Volumes 1, 4, 7, 20, 22, 23.
82. The dislike of Sultanzade by historians of this kind was such that even years thereafter, when some of his works were known in Persian, English and French, he was still referred to as 'Ahmad' (a Muslim name) in lieu of 'Avetis' (his real name in Armenian). See Abrahamian, *Iran*, p 113.
83. George Lenczowski, *Russia and the West in Iran, 1918-1948* (Ithaca NY, 1949). Lenczowski, a former Polish junior diplomat in Tehran, had, after the Sovietisation of his country, emigrated to the USA, where he closely worked with powerful American 'political' circles. In 1937, he had obtained a doctorat d'université in Lille (France): *Contribution à l'étude des obligations contractuelles en droit International privé* (Paris, 1938), pp 152.
84. This is Sepehr Zabih's *The Communist Movement in Iran* (Berkeley and Los Angeles, 1966), which deals with the ICP in a cursory manner using secondary sources. There is much to be said about his treatment of the 'expedient nationalist' Haidar Khan Amoghli, Major A Lahouti's supposed presence at the Baku congress in September 1920 (pp 32-33), his misreading of Ivanova 'not blaming' the ICP, his repetition of the Stalinist accusation against Sultanzade as having belonged to the 'extreme left' of the ICP (p 43), and simultaneously repeating the Ducrocq–Lenczowski accusation that he was the head of the Near Eastern Section of the Commissariat of Foreign Affairs in Moscow (p 49), his use of the term 'indoctrination' for the work Arani sought to effect among his students (pp 64ff), his over-reliance on Tudeh sources for Arani (pp 64-72), leading to his unawareness, *inter alia*, of the fact that Arani's works had all been published during his lifetime and in *Donya*, not after the fall of Reza Shah (p 66, n 38). Rouhollah K Ramazani also repeats the accusation by Ducrocq and Lenczowski, seasoning it with a Holmesian adjective: 'A Sultanzadeh, a somewhat mysterious person connected with the Russian People's Commissariat of Foreign Affairs.' (RK Ramazani, *The Foreign Policy of Iran: A Developing Nation in World Affairs, 1500-1941*, Charlottesville, 1966, p 142) The CIA planner of the

1953 coup, Donald Wilber, repeats in the nine editions of his handbook on Iran the latter accusation as well as the belief that Sultanzade was alive under a pseudonym working in the Tudeh and the Azerbaijan Democratic Party (D Wilber, *Iran: Past and Present*, London, 1963, pp 135, 138).

85. Lenczowski, *Russia and the West in Iran*, pp 223-25.
86. For a response to this and other calumnies by the Soviets and Western historians against Sultanzade, see Chaqueri (ed), 'Introduction', to *Historical Documents*, Volume 4; a most recent case is in the following book in Persian: R Ra'isnia, *Akharin sangar-e azadi (Collection of J Pishevari's Articles in Haqiqat*, Tehran, 1998), in the introduction to which the Stalinist author tries to rehabilitate Sultanzade's close colleague Pishevari, who repeatedly took positions against Haidar Khan, and to depict him as an ally of the latter.
87. H Ahmadi, a naval attaché of the Pahlavis in London, joined Kianouri in 1978, helping him to organise a new secret military organisation in the post-revolutionary armed forces of Iran. Having fled the country after the débâcle of the Tudeh in 1983, he was coopted as a Central Committee member in view of the shortage of cadres.
88. A Sultanzade, 'Enqelab-e melli chist va chera ma tarafdar-e an hastim?', *Paykar*, no 8, 1931, reproduced in Chaqueri (ed), *Historical Documents*, Volume 22, pp 253-54.
89. *Paykar*, no 9, 1931, reproduced in Chaqueri (ed), *Historical Documents*, Volume 22, p 261.
90. See H Ahmadi, *Tarikhcheh-ye ferqeh-ye jomhouri-ye enqelabi-ye Iran va 'Grouh-e Arani'* (Berlin, 1993), pp 46-47, 201, 261. In addition, Ahmadi has advanced the incredible thesis that Arani was 'not a Communist'; see ibid (and its critique, C Chaqueri, 'Baznegari dar tarikh bemasabeh-e parcham-e tazeh-ye ideolozhik', *Arash*, nos 31, 32, 36-37, 1993-94), and Ahmadi, 'Arani Kommonist naboud', *Adineh*, no 88, 1993.
91. Abrahamian, *Iran*, p 115, n 32; for an early critique of Abrahamian's book by this author, see *Ketab-e jom'eha*, nos 2-3, Winter 1984-Spring 1985, pp 200-07; English translation in C Chaqueri, *Writing on the Left*, forthcoming.
92. Abrahamian, *Iran*, p 113; Ghaffarzadeh had been killed in 1918, not in 1920!
93. Ibid, p 112.
94. See his biography in Chaqueri, *The Soviet Socialist Republic of Iran*, p 461.
95. The first time 'Ahmad' was said to have been Sultanzade's first name was in the so-called biography of Abol-Qasem Lahouti, *Sharh-e hal-e zendegani-ye man* (np [Karachi?], nd [circa 1952], p 20), said to have been forged by the CIA in its anti-Communist campaign.
96. Abrahamian, *Iran*, p 115; in fact, the claim that Haidar Khan had written these theses had been falsely put forward by Stalinist historian MN Ivanova (see the full translation with indication of Tudeh's censored parts in Chaqueri (ed), *Historical Documents*, Volume 1 (third edition, Tehran, 1981), pp 52-59; Chaqueri, *The Soviet Socialist Republic of Iran*, pp 265-68) and repeated over and over by the Tudeh Party.
97. Abrahamian, *Iran*, pp 115-16.
98. Ibid, p 116.

99. See Chaqueri (ed), 'Introduction', *Historical Documents*, Volume 4; idem, *The Soviet Socialist Republic of Iran*, pp 262-67, 433ff.
100. Abrahamian, *Iran*, p 116.
101. See Chaqueri (ed), 'Introduction', *Historical Documents*, Volume 4.
102. Abrahamian, *Iran*, p 130.
103. Ibid, p 132. Besides, neither Ovanesian nor Rousta were among the party's leaders; Dehgan was born in the Caucasus, not Kashan, etc.
104. For the details of the Fourth Plenum, see F Ekteshafi, *Khaterat* (Berlin, 1998), pp 179, 181, 200.
105. B Amirkhosrowi, a former candidate member of the Central Committee at the time present at that plenum (*Rah-e azadi*, no 60, 1998, pp 14-15), rejects Ekteshafi's version which confirms the presence of the Soviet 'observer' of the Tudeh Simionov at that plenum and naturally his putting an end to the discussion over the Kambakhsh 'affair'. But other Tudeh militants who took part in the party plenum confirm Ekteshafi's version; see M Rouzegar, *Az Anzali to Dushanbeh* (Stockholm, 1994); N Zarbakht, *Gozar az barzakh* (Berlin, 2001). If this should not suffice, it should be added that, during the revolutionary days of early 1979, Kianouri travelled to Baku to meet with Haidar Aliev to win his support in his quest to replace First Secretary Iraj Eskandari. To assure Kianouri the post of first secretary, Aliev's man in the Tudeh Party, Gh Y Daneshian, head of the Azerbaijan Democratic Party, was dispatched to Leipzig for the meeting. (Iran was the fief of Soviet Azerbaijan.) Also present was the Soviet ambassador in East Berlin, to ensure that every member of the Central Committee would loyally vote for the new Soviet candidate for the Tudeh leadership. See Soviet archival material cited by J Hasanli, *At the Dawn of the Cold War: The Soviet-American Crisis over Iranian Azerbaijan, 1941-1946* (Lanham MD, 2006), p 392.
106. According to Iraj Eskandari, the serious attacks Arani had made at the tribunal on Kambakhsh were later removed from his published version by the Tudeh Party because the Soviet 'comrade instructed us to take out the material regarding Kambakhsh'. See Eskandari, *Khaterat* Volume 1, p 36. To see the extent of the distortions, it suffices to compare the Tudeh version (Tehran, 1945; reproduced in *Donya*, 4/1, and Chaqueri (ed), *Historical Documents*, Volume 1 (1981 edition), pp 147ff) with the version published along with Arani's own handwritten notes by H Farzaneh, *Parvandeh-ye panjah o seh nafar* (Tehran, 1994), pp 265-85.
107. This was both the tenth anniversary of Lenin's death and the birthday of Arani's close friend Morteza Alavi!
108. See C Chaqueri, *The Tragedy of Iranian Dissident National Communists*, forthcoming.
109. The following account is based on a long and detailed account of the Second Arani Circle to be published in ibid.
110. See Arani's defence speech in court, in Farzaneh, *Parvandeh*, pp 267-71.
111. All former members of the Circle (Eskandari, Alavi, Jahanshahlou, Khame'i and Maleki) who have written their memoirs have attested to this. In addition, their statements have been independently confirmed by Ovanesian (see *Khaterat*, Paris, 1990, pp 65-66; republished Tehran, 1997, p 132); and also in his secret unpublished memoirs *Khaterat dar bareh-ye Rahbari*, pp 76-78, in both of which he

acknowledges Kambakhsh's guilt but justifies his actions); the Soviet official — of the Comintern or NKVD? — Plyshevskii noted in Kambakhsh's file (RTsKhIDNI, 495/74/194) the following: 'According to information of the former secretary of the Central Committee of the ICP, Mir Ja'far Javadzadeh Pishevari, Kambakhsh committed "treason" in prison, handing all data on party organisation [to the police].'

112. A Kambakhsh, 'Kharakteristika 53-x' ('Characteristics of the "Fifty-Three"'), RTsKhIDNI, 495/74/194, cited in Chaqueri, *The Tragedy of Iranian Dissident National Communists*.
113. Kh Maleki reports that Arani's colleague Mohammad Bahrami made a similar remark after hearing the news of Arani's death: 'Now then we must aggrandise Arani!' (Kh Maleki, *Khaterat siasi* (Tehran, 1981), p 287)
114. Kambakhsh, 'Characteristics of the "Fifty-Three"'.
115. To my knowledge, no Soviet historian ever studied the Arani Circles. The only mentions of Arani in Soviet historical literature are a couple of insignificant reports: a short extract of Arani's defence speech (the Tudeh version) before the tribunal in 1938 ('Iz zashchitnoi rechi Doktora Tagi Erani na syde', in *Khrestomatiia po noveishei istorii*, Volume 1 (Moscow, 1960), pp 828-30; S Khalatai, 'Doktor Taqi Arani sebebiyyat prinsipi va irada asalasi haqqynda', in *Elmi asarlar*, Volume 4, 1964, pp 89-94, and 'A Agahi, 'Erani', in *Sovetskaia istoricheskaia intsiklopedia*, Volume 16 (Moscow, 1976), p 576.
116. See Chaqueri, *The Tragedy of Iranian Dissident National Communists*; for the records of the interrogation of some members of the Circle as well as Arani's last defence in the tribunal, see Farzaneh, *Parvandeh*.
117. See his first article on the Jangalis and other revolts after the Great War, 'Histoire du parti Toudeh', *Moyen Orient*, December 1949.
118. For the role of the Soviets in this regard, see C Chaqueri, 'Did the Soviets Play a Role in Founding the Tudeh Party in Iran?', based on the Comintern archives, *Cahiers du monde russe*, Paris, July-September 1999, reproduced in this journal.
119. See *Moyen Orient*, no 6, December 1949; Eskandari erroneously states that within a few months the Tudeh had some 10 000 members, while a secret report on the first year of Tudeh activities sent to the Comintern put the number of its members at only 2087. See Chaqueri, 'Did the Soviets...', pp 521-22.
120. For an account of Eskandari's life and his changing views on the foundation of the Tudeh, see C Chaqueri, 'I Eskandary and the Tudeh Party of Iran', *Central Asian Survey*, no 4, 1988.
121. Zabih, *The Communist Movement*, pp 64ff; Abrahamian does not breathe a word about Kambakhsh's nefarious role in the arrest of the Circle and his collaboration with the police, although the facts were well known by the time he wrote his book (Abrahamian, *Iran*, pp 154-63).
122. See Chaqueri (ed), 'Introduction', *Historical Documents*, Volumes 14, 15 (Arani's writings in two volumes, Florence, 1973 and 1983).
123. Abrahamian, *Iran*, pp 156ff.
124. One can, for instance, easily tell that such historians have never laid an eye on Arani's journal *Donya*. They simply refer to Tudeh writings on him and his works, which are, of course, self-justifying and far from impartial.

125. See its facsimile reproduction in Chaqueri (ed), *Historical Documents*, Volume 2.
126. See H Ahmadi, *Ferqeh-ye Jopmhouri-e Enqelabi-ye Iran* (Berlin, 1993); see its reviews by C Chaqueri in *Arash* (Paris), nos 31, 32, 36-37, 1993.
127. See C Chaqueri, *Iran's Dissident National Communists: The Arani Circles of 1926-32 and 1934-37*, forthcoming.
128. Next to Lenczowski, the former CIA coup planner Donald Wilber (*Iran*, pp 138ff) was one of the first in the West to write accounts of the Arani Circle ('Fifty Three') and the founding of the Tudeh.
129. Zabih, *The Communist Movement*, p 71.
130. 'Histoire du Parti Tudeh', *Moyen Orient*, no 6, December 1949, p 9.
131. Zabih, *The Communist Movement*, p 73.
132. Ibid.
133. See 'Communism II', *Encyclopaedia Iranica*, Volume 6 (New York, 1992); for a critique, see Chaqueri, 'Did the Soviets...?'.
134. For an earlier critique of Abrahamian's main work on the Iranian Left, see Kh Sh [C Chaqueri], 'Naqd va taqriz-e ketab', *Ketab-e jom'eha*, nos 2-3, Winter 1984-Spring 1985, pp 200-07.
135. Although he was the spokesman for the Democratic Party in the Majles after the departure of Taqizadeh, there is no evidence that he played any role in founding that party; for a history of this party, see Chaqueri, *The Russo-Caucasian Origins*, Chapter 7.
136. Abrahamian, *Iran*, pp 281-83, my emphases. A few inaccuracies should be noted here: there is no evidence that Solayman Mirza had *fought* in the Constitutional Revolution; he had not been among those who had established the Democratic Party; he had replaced his brother Yahya (Iraj's father) who had died as a consequence of the 1908 coup; 'the National Resistance' was nothing but the pro-German party at Kermanshah; and the author fails to mention Eskandari's role in support of Reza Khan's ascending the throne, just as he deletes his Ministry of Culture under Reza Khan; see Chaqueri, 'Solayman Mirza Eskandari', in *Encyclopaedia Iranica*, Volume 8.
137. Abrahamian, *Iran*, p 283.
138. From among the 15 members of the Provisional Central Committee, only five (M Bahrami, M Yazdi, Iraj Eskandari, A-H Noushin and R Radmanesh) had obtained some knowledge of Marxism in Western Europe. F Keshavarz was a French educated physician but had, admittedly, never been political until the founding of the Tudeh; the others, including Pishevari (according to Soviet archives RTsKhIDNI, 495/74/192), had never been to Europe.
139. These were A Ovanesian, A Kobari, R Rousta, A Amirkhizi, N Alamouti; Pishevari; the latter, the only surviving member of the ICP leadership since its first congress at Anzali in 1920, was one of the founding members of the Tudeh, but apparently withdrew from it when Ovanesian joined it, most notably as the contact man with the Soviets, both with the Comintern and the NKVD. Another version has it that he was expelled at the first party congress!
140. One wonders whether Abrahamian would have also used the 'ulama argument before Khomeini's uprising in 1963!

141. See Abrahamian, *Iran*, pp 282ff. The only '*alem*' who might have been feared by the Tudeh was Solayman Mirza himself, who was, after all, a devout Muslim and had made his pilgrimage to Mecca (along with Rouh-Allah Khomeini, later Ayatollah); for which reason, according E Tabari (*Kazhraheh*, Teheran, 1987, p 45), women were not allowed membership in the Tudeh as long as Solayman Mirza was alive!
142. I Eskandari, 'Histoire du Parti Toudeh', *Moyen-orient*, no 6, December 1949, p 9.
143. Regarding the formulation of the Tudeh's programme under direct Soviet dictation, see Chaqueri, 'Did the Soviets...?'.
144. My study of British and American archives on the labour movement amply shows that there was no demand by the Tudeh unions in defence of workers' interests or for the amelioration of their conditions during the war. Tudeh actions began right after the defeat of Japan and the dropping of the atomic bomb by the USA on that country, for which the Tudeh union leader Reza Rousta sent a telegram of congratulation to President Truman; see Chaqueri (ed), *The Conditions of the Working Class in Iran* (four volumes, Florence and Tehran, 1978-1991): Rousta's telegram is in Volume 2, p 22; for the displeasure of the Soviet consul in Tabriz in the matter of workers' demands, see Volume 2, p 4.
145. See the following: E Tabari's article on the need to match the British 'security zone' with one for the Soviets, *Mardom* [as *Mardom baraye roshanfekran*] dated 19 Aban 1323/10 November 1944 in Jebhe-ye Azadi-ye Mardom-e Iran (JAMA), *Gozashteh cheragh-e rah-e ayandeh* (Paris (?), 1978, Tehran, 1979), p 227, also quoted in Katouzian's Introduction to Maleki's *Khaterat*; Kh Maleki's articles 'Sar o tah yek karbas', *Rahbar*, nos 436-438, Azar 1323/December 1944, against Mosaddeq's total prohibition bill on granting oil concessions to foreigners after the Soviets came forward for one. Both Maleki and his editor Katouzian try to justify not only Maleki but also 'the young and active members' of the party as if they 'did not agree' with the Soviet oil concession but 'defended it' for the prestige of the party! See Maleki, *Khaterat-e Siasi*, pp 38-39, 375.
146. Emphasis in the Russian original.
147. Colonel Seliukov, 'Transcription of Conversation with Solayman Mirza', dated [?] December 1941, RTsKhIDNI, 495/74/192; see also Chaqueri, 'Did the Soviets...?', pp 509-10.
148. At the first congress of the Tudeh in 1944, he was elected chairman with 140 out of 168 votes; see *Rahbar*, 11-15 Tir 1323 (1944).
149. A short biographical notice of each of whom was sent by Fitin to Dimitrov. The first two had been members of the Iranian Communist Party and confirmed Stalinists who had been in Reza Shah's prison in the 1930s; the last four had been arrested in 1937 and tried in 1938 as members of the Communist Circle called the 'Fifty-Three'.
150. Fitin to Dimitrov, dated 5 November 1941, RTsKhIDNI, 495/74/192. This last remark about the Soviet military attaché apparently alluded to the complaint by SM Eskandari about Rousta, as mentioned above. Fitin's remark also reveals the multiplicity of Soviet contacts with their supporters in Iran, on the one hand, and the rivalry between different Soviet organisations in Iran, on the other.
151. Chaqueri, 'Did the Soviets...?'.
152. Peter Avery's view, which sees the Tudeh as 'pro-Communist', and paradoxically

'in a sense... the heir of the old secular modernist wing of the Constitutional Movement, the Democrats', is inadvertently correct inasmuch as he does 'discern in the Tudeh Party's nucleus vestiges of the attitudes and aims of the men who trekked away to Kirmanshah in 1915 to join German and Turkish military units; and, more particularly, to discern the programmes and aspirations of the Persian intellectual coterie shut up in Berlin between 1914 and 1918 and which stayed on in the 1920s' (P Avery, *Modern Iran* (London, 1965), pp 380-81).

153. In addition to official documents published by the DPA: FDA, *Sharivarin oun ikisi* (*The Twelve of Shahrivar*, Tabriz 1946; Persian translation as *Davazdahom-e shahrivar*, Rome, 1978), and by the Pahlavi regime: AH Hamzavi, *Persia and the Powers: An Account of Diplomatic Relations, 1941-1946* (London, 1946); A Qavam al-Saltaneh, 'Report to the Majles', in *Azarbaijan va naghmehha-ye tazeh-ye este'mar*, Part 2 (Tehran, 1982), pp 65-94; Khanbaba Bayani, *Gha'eleh-ye Azerbaijan* (Tehran, 1998), see US Government Printing Office, *Foreign Relations of the United States, 1946*, Volume 7 (Washington DC, 1969), and United Nations, *Official Proceedings of the Security Council*, First session (17 January 1946) to 49th session (26 June 1946) (New York, 1949).

154. MR Pahlavi, *Mission for My Country* (London, 1960); H Arfa, *Under Five Shahs* (London, 1964); R Zehtab-Fard, *Khaterat dar Khaterat* (Tehran, 1994); A-H 'Amidi-Nouri, *Ferqeh-ye Demokrat* (Tehran 1979); N Jahanshahlou, *Ma va biganegan, Sargozasht* (two volumes, Düsseldorf, 1982 and 1988); A Khame'i, *Khaterat II: Forsat-e bozorg-e az dast rafteh* (Tehran, 1984); E Tabari, *Kazhraheh, Khaterati az Hezb-e Toudeh* (Tehran, 1987); I Eskandari, *Khaterat siasi* (ed B Amirkhosrowi and F Azarnour, four volumes, Paris, 1988-92); A Ovanesian, *Memoirs (1320-1326)* (Paris, 1990/Tehran, 1997); M-'A Shamideh, *Zendeginameh* (Düsseldorf, 1994); A Zangeneh, *Khaterati az ma'amouriat-e man dar Azarbaijan* (Tehran, 1987); 'AA Darakhshani, *Khaterat* (Washington DC, 1994); Safar Qahremanian, *Khaterat-e Safar Khan* (Tehran, 1999).

155. Najafqoli Pesyan, *Marg boud bazgasht ham boud* (Tehran, 1948), p 22; Iraj Akhgar, *Marg hast va bazgasht nist* (Tehran, 1957); P Homayounpour, *L'Affaire d'Azerbaidjan* (Lausanne, 1967); D Wilber, *Iran, Past and Present* (Princeton, 1958); P Avery, *Modern Iran* (London, 1965); JA Thorpe, 'Truman's Ultimatum to Stalin on the 1946 Azerbaijan Crisis', *The Society for Iranian Studies Newsletter*, Volume 7, no 3, 1972; R Ramazani, 'The Autonomous Republic of Azerbaijan and the Kurdish People's Republic: Their Rise and Fall', in TT Hammond (ed), *The Anatomy of Communist Takeovers* (Princeton, 1975); MS Ivanov in *Noveishaia istoria Irana* (Moscow, 1964); translated (by the Tudeh Party) as *Tarikh-e novin-e Iran* (Stockholm, 1977), Chapter 6; 'A Peripheral View of the Cold War: The Crisis in Iran, 1941-1947', *Diplomatic History*, no 4, Fall 1980; L L'estrange Fawcett, *Iran and the Cold War: The Azerbaijan Crisis of 1946* (Cambridge, 1992); T Atabaki, *Azerbaijan, Ethnicity, and Autonomy in Twentieth-Century Iran* (London, 1993); Mirzeh Ebrahimov, *Dar bareh-ye jonbesh-e demokratik-e melli dar Azarbaijan* (Tehran, 1979 [?]); originally published in *Madaniyat va enqelab* (Baku), no 4, 1947; M Choupanzadeh, *Gousheh'i az mobarezat-e siasi-ye khalq-e Azarbaijan* (Tehran, nd); 'A-R Nabdel, *Azarbaijan va mas'aleh-ye melli* (np, 1977); 'A-H Agahi, 'Owj-e chashmgir az mobarezat mardom-e Iran, *Donya*, no 14, 1979; 'Ali

Tudeh, Pishevari', *Edebiyyat ve injesenet*, 17 June 1988; B Amirkhosrowi, *Nazar az daroun-e be naqsh-e Hezb-e Tudeh-ye Iran* (Tehran, 1996), Chapter 4, pp 97-116; idem, 'Be monasebat-e panjahomin salgard-e majara-ye Azerbaijan', *Rah-e azadi*, no 43, 1996.

156. Requests in 1992, 1993 and 2000 (after the fall of the Soviet Union) in the Baku, Moscow and Tiflis archives to study documents pertaining to the AGA were flatly refused. Since then, however, several studies by Azerbaijani, Georgian and Russian researchers have been published, which have fruitfully used the Soviet sources and, despite the residues of Soviet thinking, do offer a great deal of information on this mysterious subject. They are by NI Egorova, Georgii Mamulia and Jemil Hesenli; see below note 209.

157. During a research trip to Baku in September 1992, that is, after the demise of the USSR, in a meeting with a group of former leading members of the Ferqeh-ye Demokrat-e Azerbaijan, I pleaded with them to write and publish their memoirs. They seemed unwilling or afraid to do so. For some recent revelations regarding the role of Bagirov in the Azerbaijan affair and the 'murder' of Pishevari, see *The Tribunal of Mir Jafar Bagirov* (Baku, 1993); translation of testimonies of witnesses Latif Samadoghlou Salayev and Ayoub Mikailoghlou Gasemov as 'Tazeh-ha'i darbareh-ye qatl-e Ja'far Pishevari, in *Rah-e Azadi*, no 43, December 1995-January 1996. This point is also mentioned in the proceedings of the trial of Biria (AGA leader who replaced Pishevari) in 1948 and his sentencing to 10 years in a forced-labour camp for having attempted to return to Iran while, in his capacity as an AGA and DPA official, he was aware of Soviet intentions and programmes in the Azerbaijan affair (B Amirkhosrowi, *Mohajerat-e sosyalisti va sarnevesht-e iranian* (Tehran, 2003), pp 157-67).

158. A claim that does not tally with the claim of some 60 000 members in Tudeh organisations in Azerbaijan to which Tudeh sources refer; see, for example, Amirkhosrowi, *Nazar az daroun*, p 108.

159. Zabih, *The Communist Movement in Iran*, pp 98-99.

160. In addition to other details, he quotes the NKVD-linked Qazvin deputy and Tudeh Central Committee member Abdolsamad Kambakhsh as having said in the Majles that the Soviet occupation forces 'would not withdraw as long as discrimination against one of Iran's neighbours continued' (ibid, p 105).

161. For the Soviet designs on Iranian territories in accord with Hitler's Germany, see RJ Sontag and JS Beddie (eds), *Nazi-Soviet Relations, 1939-1941: Documents from the Archives of the German Foreign Office* (Department of State, Washington, 1948); also J Kolasky, *Partners in Tyranny: The Nazi-Soviet Pact, August 23, 1939* (Toronto, 1990), pp 133-36; PW Fabry, *Iran, die Sowjetunion und das kriegfuehrende Deutschland im Sommer und Herbst 1940* (Goettingen, 1980).

162. Abrahamian, *Iran*, pp 217, 221, 398-415.

163. Abrahamian's information as to the formation of the FDA by Pishevari, Kaviyan and Javid is inaccurate (Abrahamian, *Iran*, pp 398-99); for the role of Pishevari, Padegan and Shabestari in this matter, see FDA, *Sharivarin*; for further details known thereafter, see B Amirkhosrowi, *Nazar az daroun*, Chapter 4, pp 97-116; idem, 'Be Monasebat-e Panjahomin...', *Rah-e azadi*, no 43, 1996.

164. Abrahamian, *Iran*, p 217.

165. Abrahamian states that Kabiri was a collaborator of Khiabani (Abrahamian, *Iran*, p 401). Jahanshahlou, Pishevari's lieutenant and a member of the Arani Circle (Fifty-Three) states the opposite; *Sargozasht*, p 309; see also *Khaterat-e Safar Khan* (*Memoirs of Safar Qahremanian*, edited by 'A-A Darvishian, Tehran, 1999), p 47. It should be added that Khiabani was against the secession of Azerbaijan; see A Azari, *Qiam-e Sheikh Mohammad Khiabani dar Tabriz* (Tehran, 1967), p 157.
166. Shabestari may have also been in the ICP.
167. Abrahamian, *Iran*, p 408.
168. Ibid, p 405.
169. Ibid, p 404.
170. Ibid, p 413.
171. Ibid, p 411.
172. Ibid, p 413.
173. Letter by the Tudeh Central Committee delivered by a Central Committee member personally in Moscow: 'Narodnnaia partiia Iranazaiaviiaet, chto ona budet podchinaniat'cia vse soiuznoi kommunisticheskoi partii vo vsekhslsluchiakh i vsegda' (RTsKhIDNI, 17/128/818-19).
174. Letter by N Alamouti and A-H Noushin, in ibid.
175. For the most recent expose of the 'Razmara thesis', see 'A Borhan, *Karnameh-ye Hezb-e Tudeh va raz-e soqout-e Mosaddeq*, Volume 2 (Tehran, 1999), Chapter 9.
176. Abrahamian, *Iran*, p 317.
177. Zabih, *The Communist Movement in Iran*, pp 164-65.
178. A study by this author (*The Shah's First Coup d'Etat: 1949: An Inquiry into the 'Perfect Crime' that Changed the Course of Iran's Modern History*) was read at the CNES, University of California, Los Angeles, in 1987. While reading a draft of the study at a UCLA conference, one local but well-known 'Iran expert' interrupted my talk asking me about my precise archival sources; my answer was that she would have to wait until the publication of my study, which has, alas, not yet seen the light of day.
179. Zabih, *The Communist Movement in Iran*, pp 199ff.
180. The American Secretary of State Madeleine Albright admitted it publicly. See *Le Monde*, 20 March 2000.
181. Zabih, *The Communist Movement in Iran*; and note 68 above on the 'alleged' role of the CIA.
182. Ibid, pp 200-01.
183. S Zabih, *The Mossadegh Era* (Lake View Press, Berkeley [?], 1982), pp vii-ix.
184. Abrahamian, *Iran*, pp 319-20.
185. *World Marxist Review*, August and September 1959; Abrahamian, *Iran*, p 323.
186. Abrahamian, *Iran*, p 323, n 90; Abrahamian refers to it as the decision of the 'plenary meeting of the leadership after the 1953 coup', which was, according to him, published in '1963'! To my knowledge, the document was never published, and Abrahamian fails to give the exact page from which he quotes a few words; he refers the reader to pages 1 to 64! A copy of that document shows that it was only 37 mimeographed pages; it has never been published, and in those 37 pages it seeks totally to justify the Tudeh's policy of not supporting Mosaddeq. It in fact goes so far as to claim that the leaders of the National Front and Mosaddeq's government

'did not agree with the neutralisation of the coup in any form or by any means' (p 22)! Such a claim by Abrahamian can only be explained by his devotion to the Stalinist school of falsification of history.
187. Neither of the two pamphlets has been published. Zabih (*The Communist Movement in Iran*, p 220) refers to the first document, but attributes its authorship to the 'exiled Central Committee'! — which is a 'mistake'. Several Tudeh documents and publications discuss these two analyses by the Tudeh leadership of the coup. The most important is the 'resolutions' adopted by the 1957 Fourth Plenum of the party published in full in 1969 in Chaqueri (ed), *Historical Documents*, Volume 1, and reprinted twice (see third edition, Tehran, 1981, pp 358-90); JAMA, *Gozashteh cheragh-e rah-e ayandeh*, pp 619ff. See also N Kianouri (*Khaterat*, Tehran), 1993, pp 302ff.
188. See Kianouri, *Khaterat*, pp 262-63; see also Amirkhosrowi, *Nazar az daroun*, pp 512ff, who reasons that Kianouri's claim is false but persists that it was the Tudeh officer Colonel Mobasheri who called and informed Mosaddeq. Kianouri had already told this story in his brochure *Hezb-e Tudeh-ye Iran va Dr Mohammad Mosaddeq. Nokati az tarikh-e Hezb-e Tudeh-ye Iran* (Tehran, 1359/1980), pp 40-47. It is important to note that the two versions show significant differences; as it has been said, liars have short memory!
189. It is interesting that none of the writings on this affair mentions the name of Colonel Poulad-dezh as the possible person who might have alerted Mosaddeq. He was an important Tudeh officer and closely associated with operations (hence best placed to know all the coup plans). His name, along with those of other putschists, was published in the press after their arrest. For his position and arrest, see USNA, 788.00/8-1753.
190. Abrahamian, *Iran*, pp 323-24.
191. Ibid, p 325.
192. Ibid, p 325; based on Fesharaki's article in *Ettela'at*, 20 August 1979.
193. In fact, Kianouri, most of whose claims are contested by Tudeh writers, does not corroborate what Abrahamian attributes to Fesharaki (*Khaterat*, p 266). For the best refutation of Kianouri's claims about the activities of Tudeh leadership, contacts with Mosaddeq, and his various versions of what he claims to have said to, or heard from, Mosaddeq, see Amirkhosrowi, whose long book *Nazar az daroun* is devoted to this issue; see also Pourpira (pseudonym of Banakonandeh), a former Tudeh cadre who disputes Kianouri's claims, 'Aqa-ye Kianouri dochar-e tavahhom shodeh id', *Kayhan hava'i*, 15 and 22 September 1993.
194. *Shoja'at* (*Besoy-e ayandeh*), no 18, 27/5/1332 (18 August 1953), quoted at length in JAMA, *Gozashteh cheragh-e rah-e ayandeh*, pp 685-56.
195. Ahmad Lankarani, Letter addressed to Maryam Firouz, Central Committee member of the Tudeh Party of Iran and wife of Dr Kianouri, First Secretary of the Tudeh (in Persian), Tehran, 1.3.1360/22 May 1981; published in *Gahnamehha-ye jomhouri* (Paris), no 5, 1983, p 7. It should be added that Brigadier Maghrouri did not cooperate with the putschists and was removed from his post for his allegiance to Mosaddeq.
196. Abrahamian, *Iran*, pp 324-25; Kianouri, *Khaterat*, p 274. See also K Roosevelt, *Countercoup: The Struggle for the Control of Iran* (New York, 1979), p 183 (first

edition withdrawn from circulation).

197. Roosevelt, *Countercoup* (New York, 1981), pp 184-85, claims when Loy Henderson protested to Mosaddeq against Americans being 'harassed most unpleasantly' and he would have his government 'recall all dependents and also all men whose presence here is not required in our own national interest', Mosaddeq 'became confused, almost apologetic', stating 'I would not want you to do that, Mr Ambassador. Let me call my police chief. I'll see [to it] that your citizens are given proper protection.' Before Loy had taken his leave, the police chief had been called and given their instructions. Later Loy and I were to agree that this indeed had been a helpful move, encouraging the pro-shah police force.'

198. Such as the putsch collaborators 'Amid-Nouri and Ardeshir Zahedi; for a detailed discussion of this issue, see Amirkhosrowi, *Nazar az daroun*, pp 595ff.

199. For Kianouri's untruthful claims, based on Zahedi et al, see his *Khaterat*, pp 271ff; the most comprehensive exposition of this false claims are to found in Amirkhosrowi, *Nazar az Daroun*, pp 595-611, which is written in a polemical style and is not devoid of personal motivations on the part of the author who used to be Kianouri's Central Committee collaborator. Another recent book also deals with Kianouri's prevarications. Also written in a highly polemical style, neither free from gross factual errors and speculations nor really introducing any new historical elements, 'A Borhan's work *Karnameh-ye Hezb-e Tudeh* represents the viewpoint of the Malekists and exposes a great deal of animosity, reading like a long political tract.

200. 'He [Mosaddeq] was as usual courteous but I could detect in [his] attitude [a] certain amount of smoldering resentment. [The] usual exchange of amenities [followed], after which I expressed sorrow at [the] chain of events since my departure over two months ago. ... I remarked [that] I [was] particularly concerned [about an] increasing number [of] attacks on American citizens. ... Every hour or two I [was] receiving additional reports [of] attacks on American citizens, not only in Tehran but also [in] other cities. ... [Mosaddeq] said these attacks [were] inevitable. [The] Iranian people thought Americans were disagreeing with them, and therefore, were attacking Americans. I said disagreement [was] no reason for attacks. He replied Iran [was] in throes [of] revolution and in [a] revolutionary stress and strain it would require three times as many police[men] as exist to afford full protection to American citizens. [Mosaddeq went on to say that] I should remember that in American Revolutionary times when Americans wanted [the] British out, many Britishers in [the] US were attacked. I said, if Iranians wanted Americans out, individual attacks [were] not necessary. We would go en masse. He said Iranian Government did not want Americans [to] leave, but individual Iranians did and, therefore, were attacking them. ... I wanted to know what his present attitude was re these American aid missions and also giving adequate protection to members of these missions. ... Prime Minister said he [was] sure [the] law enforcement agencies [were] doing all possible to give protection. I disagreed.' Wishing to know the position of Mosaddeq on the coup, Henderson went on: 'After another lull, I told him I would be grateful if he would tell me confidentially for [the] use [of] my government just what [had] happened during [the] recent days. [The] US Government [was] interested with respect [to] both events and [the] legal situation.

He chose [to] interpret my remarks as reference to President [Eisenhower]'s letter to him last July. ... He maintained [that] American officials either in Washington or in Tehran had directly or indirectly, [and] deliberately leaked [the] information to [the] pro-British Iranian press re this exchange [of letters], and against his will, [the] US had insisted on publishing [the] notes. ... I told him it had been my understanding [that the] leak had occurred in his office, and in view [of] distorted public version of President's letter [which was] unfavorable to US, [the] US Government had thereupon insisted [the] exchange be published. He denied heatedly [that] Iranians had been guilty of leads [sic — leaks]. No Iranian except himself and Saleh, US Embassy, [an] Iranian assistant and interpreter had been aware of [the] existence of these letters. He had kept them among his own private papers, not in [the] office files. I intimated [that] I [was] not sure his private papers were kept in [a] manner which would prevent clever agents [from] having access to them. I also pointed out [that] there were certain modern hearing devices which might result in knowledge [of] this kind falling into possession of agents [and] parties hostile both to Iran and [the] US. He continued [to] insist [that] certain Americans had deliberately leaked [this information] in order that public knowledge of contents of President's letter might weaken his government. ... I said it seemed to me unfortunate for Iran and [it is] no compliment [to the] Iranian people that [the] government of Iran apparently could not be based on a parliament. Iran was in [a] most dangerous international position. ... I told him I [was] particularly interested in events [of the] recent days. I would like to know more about [the] effort [to] replace him by General Zahedi. He said on [the] evening [of August] 15th, Col Nasiri had approached his house apparently to arrest him. Col Nasiri himself, however, had been arrested and [a] number [of] other arrests [had] followed.' With regard to his loyalty to the shah, Mosaddeq said: 'He had taken oath not to try to oust [the] Shah and would have lived up to this oath if [the] Shah had not engaged in [a] venture [of] this kind [that is, *coup d'état*]. Clear[ly,] Nasiri had been sent by [the] Shah [to] arrest him and [the] Shah had been prompted by [the] British.' To Henderson's question regarding the Shah's *firman* [decree] 'removing him as Prime Minister and appointing Zahedi in his place', Mosaddeq 'said he had never seen such [a] decree and if he had, it would have made no difference. His position for some time had been that [the] Shah's powers were only of ceremonial character; that [the] Shah had no right on his personal responsibility [to] issue [a] *firman* calling for change in government. I said... 'Was I to understand (a) he had no official knowledge that Shah had issued [a] *firman* removing him as Prime Minister, and (b) even if he should find that [the] Shah had issued such [a] *firman* in present circumstances, he would consider it to be invalid?' He replied "positively".' Henderson then told Mosaddeq 'point blank' that it was untrue 'that [the] US embassy had been harboring Iranian political refugees [that is, Zahedi]', that his policy was 'if political refugees should endeavor to enter [the] embassy', efforts would be made to stop them, and if they should succeed in entering the compound, 'efforts would be made to persuade them to leave voluntarily', and if they refused to leave voluntarily, 'it [was] my intention to notify Iranian authorities that persons had taken refuge in [the US] Embassy and that I was telegraphing my government for instructions.' Mosaddeq thanked him for his statement and added that 'In case any Iranian political fugitive would take refuge in [the US] Embassy, he would like [the] Embassy to keep them there. I asked if in such event [the] Iranian Government [was] prepared [to] defray [the] expenses for lodging and food, or whether he would expect this to come out of [the] Point IV funds. He said [the] Iranian Government would be glad, despite [its] limited budget, [to] pay expenses [of] these refugees.' Henderson concludes that 'from Mosaddeq's unusual reserve I [was] inclined [to] believe that he [was] suspicious [that the] United States Government, or at least United States Officials, [were] either implicated in effort[s] [to] oust him or sympathetically aware of such effort[s] in advance. His remarks to me were interspersed with number [of] little jibes... semi-jocular in character... nevertheless barbed. These jibes in general hinted that [the] United States was conniving with [the] British effort [to] remove him as Prime Minister. For instance, he remarked at one point [that the] national movement was determined [to] remain in power in Iran and it would continue to hold on to [the] last man, although all its members would be run over by British and American tanks. When I raised my eyebrows at this remark, he laughed heartily.' For the full text of the Henderson telegram to Secretary of State, sent on 18 August 1953, 6:57pm, see USNA 788.00/8-1853; see also the printed version in US Government Printing Office, *Foreign Relations of the United States, 1952-1954, Volume 10, Iran, 1951-1954* (Washington DC, 1989), pp 748652.

201. *Khandaniha*, no 96, 31/5/1332 (22 August 1953), quoted in *Tarikh cheragh-e rah-e ayandeh*, p 681.

202. E Abrahamian, 'The Strengths and Weaknesses of the Labor Movement in Iran, 1941-53', in ME Bonine and N Keddie (ed), *Continuity and Change in Modern Iran* (Albany NY, 1981), pp 217, 230. As is clear from its title, this essay (pp 181-202), like his subsequent work (*Iran*, pp 129ff) hardly deals with the history of the formation of the labour movement, in addition to its being solely based on Tudeh sources. The least incomplete of the works in any Western language on Iran's labour movement is H Ladjevardi, *Labor Unions and Autocracy in Iran* (Syracuse NY, 1985, see this author's review of this work in *Central Asian Survey*, Volume 6, no 3, 1987). Zabih's study *The Communist Movement in Iran*, although devoting two chapters to the ICP period, completely ignores the question of labour unions at that time. W Floor's *Labour Unions, Law and Conditions in Iran (1900-1941)* (Durham, 1985), though drawing on a great deal of published and unpublished material and informative, is flawed by its highly ideological and colonialist perspective (see this author's review in *Middle East Study Association Bulletin*, Volume 23, no 1, 1989). The most complete documentary history of Iran's labour movement is to be found in C Chaqueri (ed), *The Condition of the Working Class in Iran* (hereafter *Working Class*), Volume 1 (Florence, 1978); Volume 2 (Tehran, 1989); Volume 3 (Tehran, 1990); Volume 4 (Tehran, 1991). The most informative and comprehensive studies of the subject by Soviet historians, Abdullaev, Bashkirov and Shamideh, suffer from the usual Stalinist biases and falsifications.

203. For a study of that organisation, see M-H Khosro-Panah, *Sazman-e afsaran-e Hezb-e Tudeh-ye Iran, 1323-1333* (Tehran, 1999); it is regrettable that we know nothing on the internal relations of this organisation, as its prominent leaders were shot and the survivors have said little. See also the memoirs of some of its

members: Gh-H Baqi'i, *Angizeh* (Shiraz, 1979). For a refutation of the idea that the Soviets supported Mosaddeq and that the Tudeh did not follow the 'Big Brother', in addition to the well-known fact that such a thing would have been impossible under Stalin, or even later years, one should read the reasoning by former Central Committee member Amirkhosrowi, *Nazar az daroun*, pp 369ff and 669ff. What Amirkhosrowi leaves open is that if Kianouri or the Executive Committee did not follow the Soviet line, whose line did they follow? It is true that, until the nationalisation of the oil, the Soviets supported Razmara who had signed a commercial treaty with him and shed crocodile tears upon his assassination (see the *Pravda* leader's eulogy, 'Mysterious Doings in Iran', 18 March 1951), while thereafter they supported the Tudeh's line of the 'cancellation' of the D'Arcy concession in opposition to nationalisation, and put the National Front deputies in the Majles next to the 'group of pro-American deputies' (JAMA, *Gozashteh cheragh-e rah-e ayanedeh*, pp 596ff) As a state, the Soviets could hardly assume the preposterous line against Mosaddeq and his followers, and naturally spoke with their tongue firmly in cheek.

204. See memoirs of A Ovanesian, *Khaterat* (Paris, 1990/Tehran, 1997); I Eskandari, *Khaterat-e siasi* (four volumes, Paris, 1987-89); F Kechavarz, *Man mottaham mikonam* (Tehran, 1979); A Khame'i, *Forsat-e Bozorg-e az Dast Rafteh* (Tehran, 1983); N Jahanshahlou, *Sargozasht, ma va biganegan* (np, 1982); E Tabari, *Kazhraheh* (Tehran, 1987); Gh-H Foroutan, *Khaterat* (two volumes Frankfurt [?], 1992-94); M-'A Shamideh, *Zendeginameh* (Düsseldorf, 1994); H Nazari, *Gomashtegha-ye badfarjam* (Düsseldorf, 1992); M Khanbaba Tehrani, *Negahi az daroun be jonbesh-e chap* (Saarbrucken, 1989); A Shafa'i, *Qiam-e afsaran-e Khorasan va 37 sal zendegi dar Showravi* (Tehran, 1986); A-H Tafreshian, *Qiam-e afsaran-e Khorasan* (Tehran, 1982); P Ekteshafi, *Khaterat* (Berlin, 1998); M Rouzegar, *Az Anzali ta Dushanbeh* (Stockholm, 1994); N Zarbakht, *Gozar az barzakh* (Paris, 1994); S Ansari, *Az Zendegi-ye man* (Los Angeles, 1996), as well as the history of the Tudeh by a group of its former members 'Jebhe-ye Azadi-ye Mardom-e Iran' (JAMA), *Gozashteh cheragh-e rah-e ayandeh* (Paris (?), 1978, Tehran, 1979); B Amirkhosrowi, *Nazar az daroun-e be naqsh-e Hezb-e Tudeh-ye Iran* (Tehran, 1996), and the Resolutions of the Tudeh's Fourth Plenum held in 1957 in Chaqueri (ed), *Historical Documents*, Volume 1 (Florence, 1969; third edition, Tehran, 1981).

205. Gh-H Foroutan, *Hezb-e Tudeh dar sahneh-ye Iran*, Volume 1 (Germany, 1992), p 220.

206. For details of Khrushchev's *coup d'état*, see Amy Knight, *Beria: Stalin's First Lieutenant* (Princeton, 1993), Chapter 9.

207. The following extract from the Russo-German secret pact throws light on the later attempt to dismember Iran in Azerbaijan and Kurdistan: 'The Soviet Union declares that its territorial aspirations center south of the national territory of the Soviet Union in the direction of the Indian Ocean. ... The Soviet Government is prepared to accept the draft of the Four Power Pact... regarding political collaboration and reciprocal economic [support] subject to the following conditions: [*inter alia*] Provided that the area south of Batum and Baku in the general direction of the Persian Gulf is recognised as the center of the aspirations of the Soviet Union.' ('Russo-German Negotiations for a Projected Soviet Sphere of Influence in the

Near and Middle East, November 1940', in Sontag and Beddie (eds), *Nazi-Soviet Relations, 1939-1941*, pp 255-59)
208. N Egorova, '"Iranskaia krizis" 1945-1946 gg, po rassekrechennym arkhivniym doumentam', *Novaia i Noveishaia Istoriia* (1994), pp 24-43; Georgii Mamulia, 'Gruziia v pervie khody kholodnoi voiny (neizvestnye stanitsy iranskogo I turetskogo krizisa 1947-1947 gg)', *Vertikali istorii*, no 5, 2003, pp 55-73; Jemil Hesenli, *Ghunej Azerbaijan, Tehran-Baky-Moskva arasynda, 1939-1945* (Baku, 1998); idem, *Suyoq muharebenin bashlandiqi yer-guneu Azerbaijan, 1945-1946* (Baku, 1999); idem, *Ghuneu Azerbijanda Sovet-Amerika-Inkiltera garshydurmasy, 1941-1945* (Baku, 2001).
209. For a detailed study of this issue, see Pierre Broué, *Histoire de l'International Communiste. 1919-1943* (Paris, 1997).
210. The Tudeh has produced the most systematic, influential and numerous, but not the most scholarly, publications, of which two are FM Javanshir, *Safahati az tarikh-e jonbesh-e jahani-e kargari va kommonisti (Darsnamah* [*Manual*]) (Hezb-e Tudeh-e Iran, Stockholm, Sweden, 1976); A Kambakhsh, *Nazari be jonbesh-e kargari va kommonisti dar Iran* (two volumes, Leipzig, 1972).
211. A collection of historical documents researched in various archives around the world and published by this author, it brought to light a great deal of knowledge about the past of the Left, particularly when originals of some documents previously faked and published by the Tudeh were brought to light.
212. Sazman-e Enqelabi, 'Jonbesh-e Kommonisti-e Iran', *Tudeh*, nos 15, 21, 1969, 1971; a German translation of it was published as *Kommunistische Bewegung Irans* (Munich, 1971); one of the former leaders of this organisation has also published his memoirs, I Kashkouli, *Negahi az daroun be jonbesh-e chap-e Iran* (Saarbrucken, 1999).
213. *15 Sal Sazman-e Enqelabi* (Tehran, 1979). B Mortazavi, a former militant of this organisation, has also published, on the Tudeh model, *Yadnameh-ye shahidan* (Leipzig, 1962 [?]); *Yadvareh-ye jan bakhtegan-e Hezb-e Rajbaran-e Iran* (Cologne, 1999 [?]).
214. Reproduced by Sazman-e Daneshjouyan-e Irani dar Amrika, '*Ozv-e Konfedrasiyoun-e Jahani-e Mohassillin va Daneshjouyan-e Irani* (1975).
215. Jazani, *Vaqaye'e si salah*.
216. Sazman-e Enqelabiyoun-e Kommonist, *Jonbesh-e kargari-ye Iran* (1975 [?]).
217. A nad-e jonbesh-e trotskisti-ye Iran (New York, 1978).
218. A Sohrabian, the old Communist militant who met Jazani in prison, criticises him for his lack of objectivity and partiality in his writing about the other Leftist organisations (*Khaterat*, pp 288-89). And the book by Jazani (to whom Maziar Behrouz has dedicated his book) has served the young writer as a reliable source; see Behrouz, *Rebels with a Cause*.
219. Jazani, *Vaqaye'e si salah*, p 17.
220. For the historical material regarding the ICP's first congress, see Chaqueri (ed), *Historical Documents*, Volumes 1, 4, 6, 10, 23.
221. Jazani, *Vaqaye'e si salah*, pp 21ff.
222. Ibid, pp 22-23.
223. See Homayounpour, *L'Affaire d'Azerbaidjan*, pp 101ff; Bayani, *Gha'eleh*, p 442.

224. Jazani, *Vaqaye'e si saleh*, p 25.
225. Ibid, p 38.
226. Ibid, p 43.
227. Ibid, p 44; for a similar but not identical statement attributed to a third contact with Mosaddeq by Kianouri; see Kianouri, *Khaterat*, p 277: 'Sir, everyone has betrayed me; do anything if you are able to; do whatever you can according to your national duty!' It is not without interest to recall that Kianouri's wife, Maryam Firouz, states the very opposite of what Kianouri claims: 'Kianouri also spoke with Mosaddeq in this connection. He said: "Do not do anything."' (*Khaterat* (Tehran, 1994), p 62)
228. Jazani, *Vaqaye'e si saleh*, p 60.
229. Amirkhosrowi, *Nazar az daroun*, pp 498ff.
230. The interviewer refers to this allegation by Jazani and asks the opinion of Kianouri, who goes no further than inventing a 'journalistic collaboration' for Fatemi with the pro-British Seyyed Zia Tabataba'i, Mosaddeq's arch-enemy (*Khaterat*, p 212). With regard to Fatemi–Mosaddeq relations, see Mokri, *Khaterat-e man az zendeh-yad Dr Hussein Fatemi* (Paris, 1985[?]).
231. 'Communism III', *Encyclopaedia Iranica* (New York, 1992); for instance, M Khanbaba Tehrani was not, contrary to his own claim (*Nazari az daroun*, pp 130-31), among the founders of the Tudeh Revolutionary Organisation; Qasemi and Foroutan did not escape from East to West Berlin in December 1963, but after the party's Eleventh Plenum in January 1965; Bahman Qashqa'i had no relations to the Leftist movement either. It is worth mentioning that the Persian original of this entry was sent by *Encyclopaedia Iranica* to this writer for commentary. Although some recommendations were accepted, *Encyclopaedia Iranica*'s editorial board at the time, which included Ahmad Ashraf, who chose not to ask the author of the entry to mention, as recommended, the role and thoughts of Mostafa Sho'a'iyan. The latter was the severe critic of Ashraf's brother — Hamid, the Fad'i leader who was to perish in 1975 — and Ahmad Ashraf personally knew him.
232. S Zabih, *The Left in Contemporary Iran* (London, 1986).
233. For a detailed critique of Zabih's work, see K Shakeri [Chaqueri], 'Iran's Left in its True Colours: A Review Article', *Central Asian Survey*, Volume 6, no 3, 1987, pp 117-28.
234. Tudeh operatives, and at times Radmanesh, remained in Iraq after the overthrow of the monarchy when AK Qasemi entertained friendly relations with Moscow.
235. For various versions of this account, see Eskandari, *Khaterat* (Tehran edition), pp 316-17, 354-57, 364-65; Ovanesian, *Khaterat dar bareh-ye Rahbari*, pp 31ff; Kianouri, *Khaterat*, pp 446ff. Kianouri's account of how he had discovered from the start that Shahriari had been a SAVAK mole contradicts what Ovanesian tells, which is that the Soviets told him that Shahriari was a SAVAK agent.
236. *Mardom*, no 103, December 1973.
237. Sazman-e Cherikha-ye Fada'i-ye Khalq, *E'dam-e enqelabi-ye Abbas-e Shahriari, mard-e hezar chahreh* va *pasokh be payam-e baqaya-ye rahbaran-e Hezb-e Tudeh* (np, 1975).
238. 'Mardi Tanha', *Alefba*, no 5, Winter 1363/1985, pp 164ff; for Kianouri's account of Shahriari, see his *Khaterat*, pp 447ff.

239. See Kianouri, *Khaterat*, pp 455-56.
240. No dates are given for this assertion; Abrahamian, 'The Guerrilla Movement in Iran, 1963-77', in H Afshar (ed), *Iran: A Revolution in Turmoil* (London, 1985), p 172, n 5 reproduced in *MERIP Report*, no 86, 1980); Abrahamian repeats the same story in his 1982 book (*Iran*, p 484). It is curious that Jazani, who writes at length about Shahriari's treachery within the Tudeh's Tehran Organisation (*Vaqay'e si saleh sicsi*, pp 95-97, 165-67), does not mention the fact that his group fell into his trap as well; on the other hand, Behrouz (*Rebels with a Cause*, p 44) confirms that the group did fall into the SAVAK trap through contacts with Shahriari, but Behrouz glosses over the deontological laxity in this regard on the part of Abrahamian, who was one of the readers of his book's manuscript. His loyalty to his publisher's reader overrides his professional obligation not to hide any fact or any distortions from the general readership of his book.
241. *Mardom*, no 103, Azar 1352/December 1973.
242. For Radmanesh's replacement by Eskandari, see C Chaqueri, 'Iradj Eskandari and the Tudeh Party of Iran', *Central Asian Survey*, Volume 7, no 4, 1988, pp 109, 121-22, n 27.
243. While the latter archives have disappeared (perhaps removed to Siberia), the STASI and SED archives are 'sanitised', and repeated visits and correspondence by this author have hardly produced anything of importance.
244. Sh Chubin, 'Leftist Forces in Iran', *Problems of Communism*, July-August 1980, pp 1-25.
245. Chubin calls the Fada'iyan 'an offshoot of the Tudeh' (ibid, p 11).
246. Ibid, p 15. The number of votes the Fada'iyan had in the first parliamentary elections in Tehran and provinces is a good guide that the author of the article was truly exaggerating; there is a clear difference between dangers posed by voting in a secret ballot and by taking up arms against a regime.
247. Ibid, pp 24-25.
248. Behrouz, *Rebels with a Cause*. A number criticisms (or attacks) by cadres of the Fada'iyan have been published in the monthly *Arash* (Paris), no 79, 2001.
249. On the Tudeh, the author is selective in his sources and uses what he feels fits his position.
250. His 'thesis' on the Tudeh is also repeated, almost word for word, in his article 'Tudeh Factionalism and the 1953 Coup d'État', published in the *International Journal of Middle East Studies*, Volume 3, no 33, 2001.
251. One which 'showed a lack of comprehension on the part of... [its] leaders' (*Rebels with a Cause*, p9) towards the most sensitive question in Iran's postwar history!
252. JAMA, *Gozashteh cheragh-e rah-e ayandeh*, pp 668ff.
253. In addition to MS Ivanov's *History of Contemporary Iran* (*Tarikh-e novin-e Iran*, np, 1975), see also SL Aqaev's work on this subject published after the 1979 revolution, *Iran: v proshlom I nastoiashchem* (Moscow 1981), pp 114ff.
254. For clarification of the 'Aliev connection' with the Tudeh, see Chaqueri, 'Did the Soviets ...?'.
255. See the quotation from Tabari and its relevant note no 45.
256. M Gasiorowski, *US Foreign Policy and the Shah: Building a Client State in Iran* (Ithaca and London, 1991), p 70, n 24.

257. Information regarding the Lankarani brothers comes from family circles, as well as the following books: H Key Ostovan (ed), *Siasat-e movazeneh-ye manfi* (two volumes, Tehran, 1948-1950); A Ziba'i, *Komonizm dar Iran*, pp 538ff, quoting Rouzbeh's confessions regarding the murder of Hesam. The following is what British Intelligence wrote about the eldest in the two 'Personality' entries (FO 4306/84 and 416/102, 1946 and 1949, respectively): He 'owed' his election from Ardabil to the Fourteenth Majles 'to Soviet intervention. Without Russian backing [he] would have no influence.' He was depicted as having been known in Tehran as an 'intriguer, mob orator and trouble-maker'. He was also accused of having been in '1943-44 [election for the Fourteenth Majles]... employed by the shah to stir up trouble against Seyyed Zia al-Din', the notoriously known pro-British politician. He was portrayed as 'typical akhund and double-faced'; 'Qavam arrested him in July 1946 but released him in December', and he was 'arrested in March 1948 with his three brothers in connection with the murder of [journalist] Mohammad Mas'oud'.
258. Its organ was *Khalq*.
259. Its organ was *Maslehat*.
260. The accusations against Hesam Lankarani were made public by Rouzbeh after his arrest. Long quotations of his account of the murder and the reasons for it are given in the book by a former SAVAK chief, Colonel 'Ali Ziba'i, *Komonizm dar Iran*, pp 538-48. Rouzbeh admits his close friendship with the four of Lankarani brothers, but does not regret the murder of Hesam. After the 1979 revolution, Ahmad Lankarani addressed an open letter to Maryam Firouz, wife of Kianouri, who had spent a long period of her underground life in the house of Hesam's sister, Banou. In his long and at times sarcastic letter, Lankarani reveals how after the murder of Hesam in the summer of 1952 the Tudeh leadership and Rouzbeh lied to his family, stating that he had gone abroad. He denounces the Tudeh leadership, including Maryam Firouz and her husband Kianouri, at the time First Secretary of the Tudeh, who also voted for the murder of Hesam, comparing them to Stalin's henchmen (Letter by Ahmad Lankarani to Maryam Firouz, Central Committee member of the Tudeh Party of Iran and Wife of Dr Kianouri, First Secretary of the Tudeh, Tehran, 1.3.1360 (22 May 1981); published in *Gahnamehha-ye jomhouri* (Paris), no 5, 1983. It is interesting that in her memoirs (*Khaterat*, Tehran, 1994), Maryam Firouz, Kianouri's wife, does not say even one word about Hesam or her sister who had given her refuge for a long time.
261. Gh-H Foroutan, *Hezb-e Tudeh dar sahneh-ye Iran*, Volume 1 (Germany, 1992), p 141. Rouzbeh states that the Tudeh leadership was opposed to his escape along with the imprisoned Tudeh leaders. They only accepted to include him because those organising the escape would not carry out the plan unless Rouzbeh was included. See MH Khosro-Panah, *Sazman-e afsaran* (np, 1999), p 142.
262. Foroutan, *Hezb-e Tudeh dar sahneh-ye Iran*, p 154.
263. See Donald Wilber's 'Secret Report', revealed by the *New York Times* on the Internet, part 2. One should not gloss over the fact that MA Movvahed, author of the *Khab-e ashoteh-ye naft (The Confused Dream of the Oil)*, has cleverly approved of Wilber's accusation against Fatemi. See his *Gofteh-ha va nagofteh-ha* (Tehran, 2001), pp 38-40.

264. Quoted from the secret Tudeh Party internal bulletin *Masa'el hezbi*, no 6, in *Ketab-e jo n'ehha*, no 4, Autumn 1985, pp 89-90.
265. Personal information obtained from Mostafa Lankarani by telephone in 2003.
266. I have personally seen this letter.
267. When he was my student at UCLA in the spring of 1987.
268. For this critique, see the interviews with former Fada'iyan activists and leaders in *Arash* (Paris), no 79, 2001. It should be pointed out that some of his critics view the author through the prism of their former views, but some of their critique is valid, particularly when it deals with the selectiveness of the interviews.
269. F Azarnour, *Mosahebeh'ye ekhtesasi-ye nashriyeh-ye Rah-e Azadi b F Azarnour* (Paris, 1372/1993), p 22.
270. Behrouz, *Rebels with a Cause*, p 53.
271. Ibid, pp 138-39.
272. Ibid, p 175.
273. Ahmadzadeh, Pouyan, Jazani and Sho'a'iyan.
274. *The Cambridge History of Iran*, Volume 7 (Cambridge and New York, 1991). The 'history' of this seven-volume work is interesting in itself, that is, the 'handsome subsidy' the National Iranian Oil Company provided for the work through the shah's ambassador Nakha'i in London; see 'General Editor's Preface', in Volume 1, p vii.
275. *The Cambridge History of Iran*, Volume 7, pp 208-10, 218, 262 and Chapter 18, respectively.
276. SL Agaev, 'Leftist Forces and the Islamic Regime in Contemporary Iran' (in Russian), *Revoliutsionnaia demokratiia i kommonisty vostoka* (Moscow, 1984), pp 331-70.
277. For Kuzichkin's defection, see *Sunday Times*, 24 October 1982, and *International Herald Tribune*, 25 October 1982.
278. On Eskandari's view, see C Chaqueri, 'Iradj Eskandari and the Tudeh Party of Iran', *Central Asian Survey*, Volume 7, no 4, 1988, pp 109, 121-22, n 27.
279. Soviet Archives: 'Totally secret' letter by N Kianouri to 'Tsentral'nyi Komitet KPSS' (Central Committee of CPSU), 1 August 1979, document no 2107, 89//32/10.
280. Chaqueri, *The Soviet Socialist Republic of Iran*, pp 383-84.
281. Ibid, p 405.
282. Ibid, p 406.
283. Ibid, p 8.
284. Ibid, p 9.
285. Seyyed Hussein Nasr, 'Iran's Cultural and Spiritual Space', *Ettela'at* (Tehran), Part 1, 2 April 2000.
286. This paper was written in the Spring of 2000, and revised in January 2005.
287. S Cronin, *Reformers and Revolutionaries in Modern Iran* (London, 2004).
288. E Abrahamian, 'The 1953 Coup in Iran', *Science and Society*, Volume 65, no 2, 2001. This, too, has been translated into Persian.
289. Stephan Kinzer *All the Shah's Men* (New York, 2003), which has also been translated into Persian.
290. See Chaqueri, 'Did the Soviets…?'.
291. See Chaqueri, *The Shah's First Coup d'État*.

292. See *Bakhtar emrouz*, 27 Mordad/16 August 1953.
293. To make his point credible, Kinzer states that scholars have sought access to Soviets archives, but they have been denied it. Furthermore, Kinzer does not specify who these scholars may have been. They could certainly not have been pro-Soviet or anti-Soviet Western scholars. As far as I know, I am the only person who visited the Soviet archives after the demise of the USSR, and I was denied access to a great deal of documents, including those relating to the question of the coup. Thus Kinzer makes a baseless statement about something he does not know.
294. Tehran dispatch, no 928, USNA, 788.001/2-1852.
295. 'Re Demonstrations [of] 29 May [1951], USNA, RG841/Bx29, Confidential, File 350-Iran.
296. FO 248/1640.
297. E Abrahamian, 'The 1953 Coup d'État en Iran', *Science and Society*, Volume 65, no 2, 2001.
298. M Elm, *Oil, Power, Principle: Iran's Oil Nationalization and its Aftermath* (Syracuse NY, 1992).
299. Khosro-Panah, *Sazman-e afsaran*, p 143.
300. In F Azarnour, *Mosahebeh'ye ekhtesasi-ye nashriyeh-ye Rah-e Azadi b F Azarnour* (Paris, 1372/1993), p 31.
301. Khosro-Panah, *Sazman-e afsaran*, p 142.
302. In Azarnour, *Mosahebeh'ye ekhtesasi-ye nashriyeh-ye Rah-e Azadi b F Azarnour*, p 10.
303. Ibid, p 13.
304. Foroutan, *Hezb-e Tudeh dar sahneh-ye Iran*, p 183.
305. *Tarikh-e mo'aser-n Iran*, Volume 6, nos 21-22 and 23, 1381/2002.
306. See also *Abouzar-e zaman beh ravayat SAVAK* (Tehran, 2003), index.
307. See also M Firouz, *Chehreh-ha-ye darakhshan* published before the revolution in exile, and reprinted in 1979 in Tehran, in which a chapter is devoted to Banou Lankarani.
308. S Dehqan and B Asfrasiabi, *Taleqani va Tarikh* (second edition, Tehran, 1360/1981), p 382.
309. Azarnour, *Mosahebeh'ye ekhtesas-ye nashriyeh-ye Rah-e Azadi b F Azarnour*, pp 45ff.
310. In the same way, it is to be emphasised that all the claims made by Kianouri and those who have followed his line to the effect that the Tudeh Party military organisation was not in reality powerful are completely false.
311. Azarnour, *Mosahebeh'ye ekhtesas-ye nashriyeh-ye Rah-e Azadi b F Azarnour*, pp 40ff.
312. Ibid, p 44.
313. See Knight, *Beria: Stalin's First Lieutenant*.
314. The old ambassador had been recalled home and a new ambassador dispatched to Tehran. On the success of the coup, there were rumours that the new Soviet ambassador in Tehran had committed suicide. He either survived the attempt, or the rumour was false.
315. In Azarnour, *Mosahebeh'ye ekhtesas-ye nashriyeh-ye Rah-e Azadi b F Azarnour*, pp 21-22.

316. P Dailami, 'The First Congress of the Peoples of the East and the Iranian Soviet Republic of Gilan, 1920-1921', in S Cronin, *Reformers and Revolutionaries in Modern Iran* (London, 2004), p 99.
317. P Dailami, *Nationalism and Communism in Iran: The Case of Gilan, 1915-1921*, to which access has been denied by the university library authorities, despite several requests through the Interlibrary Loan at Maison des Sciences de l'Homme, Paris, or later made personally.
318. Dailami, 'The First Congress of the Peoples of the East', p 113.
319. For example, it is legitimate to ask how a person who has not travelled to Moscow nor has even a rudimentary knowledge of Russian can determine to take such and such a page of a Russian document in the archives GARF which deals with such and such an issue, as in footnotes 103, 105-107, p 117 of his article 'The First Congress of the Peoples of the East'.
320. C Chaqueri, *The Soviet Socialist Republic of Iran, 1920-1921: Birth of the Trauma* (Pittsburgh University Press, Pittsburgh, 1995).
321. Dailami, 'The First Congress of the Peoples of the East', p 113.
322. *The Journal of Slavic Military Studies*, Volume 9, no 2, June 1996, pp 458-60, to which I sent a rejoinder, published in *The Journal of Slavic Military Studies*, Volume 10, no 2, June 1997, pp 203-04.
323. Chaqueri (ed), *Historical Documents*, Volume 23, pp 6-84.
324. C Chaqueri, *La Social-Démocratie en Iran. Articles et Documents* (Florence, 1978, 2000), pp 95-103. It so happens that he refers to the same pages, minus one, of the original text, as in the extracts I have published in French, whereas Belova's article is much longer.
325. His footnote 77, p 116.
326. P Dailami, 'The Populists of Rasht: Pan Islamism and the Role of the Central Powers', in T Atabaki, *Iran and the First World War* (London, 2000), pp 207-08.
327. Ibid, pp 141, 145.
328. See WO 95/5043.
329. Vasakouni [Yaqikian], 'Kuchek Khan and his Work', *Zank* [in Armenian] 28 April 1919; cited in *The Soviet Socialist Republic of Iran*, p 89. It is interesting that he overlooks this clear position, but alleges, obviously with no reference, that Sultanzade called Kuchek Khan 'a thieving baron'. I have read all Sultanzade's published writings and have never come across such a statement.
330. See the Programme of Social Democratic Party of Gilan, in Chaqueri (ed), *Historical Documents*, Volume 6; French translation in Chaqueri, *La Social-democratie en Iran* (2000 edition), pp 152-58.
331. For the aforementioned Article II, see EG Browne, *The Persian Revolution of 1905-1909* (London, 1910/1966), pp 372-73; for a sample of the opposition to the mullahs on this matter, see 'Senaye Rohani', *Habl al-Matin*, 17 June 1907.
332. Its exhaustive treatment will be dealt with in the forthcoming work *Victims of Faith*, which has taken many years to be completed.
333. C Chaqueri, 'Le Congrès de Bakou', relation présentée au Colloque International: *Expérience soviétique et la Question Nationale dans le Monde* (Paris, December 1978), CNRS, publiée par l'INALCO (Sorbonne Nouvelle) (Paris, 1980); 'The Baku Congress', *Central Asian Survey* (Oxford), September 1983; Turkish translation:

Ankara University (ODT) Mimarlik Fakultesi, 1984; Persian translation: *Qafqaz dar Tarikh-e Mo'aser* (translated and edited by K Bayat and B Ja'fari, Tehran, 1992), pp 129-52.

334. Such as the American Historical Association, the Middle East Studies Association of North America.
335. See VI Lenin, 'Address to the Second All-Russia Congress of Communist Organisations of the East', *Collected Works*, Volume 30, 1965.
336. I have treated issue these matters in *The Soviet Socialist Republic of Iran*, Chapter 8.
337. See, for instance, his footnote 33 (p 114) for reference to Amirkhizi, a Stalinist member of Tudeh Central Committee, and to Haidar's own brother, Tariverdiev, published in *Narody Azii i Afriki* in 1971. He finds it unprofitable to consult *The Russo-Caucasian Origins of the Iranian Left*, published by this author in 2001, for Stalinist historians would be contradicted.
338. See Chaqueri, *The Russo-Caucasian Origins of the Iranian Left*, Illustrations.
339. Ibid, p 212.
340. Dailami refers to an article by Effendiv in *Zhizn natsional'nostei*, no 59, 11 January 1920, of which a translation appeared in C Chaqueri, *The Revolutionary Movement in Iran versus Great Britain and Soviet Russia* (Florence, 1978), pp 838-41. The only article we have been able to trace to Haidar is one published in *Zhizn natsional'nostei*, no 59, 15 June 1920; translated in Chaqueri, *La Social-démocratie en Iran*, pp 268-71, which is signed GT, possibly for Gaidar Tariverdiev.
341. See Chaqueri (ed), *Historical Documents*, Volume 6, p 79.
342. *Zhizn natsional'nostei*, no 59, 11 January 1920.
343. It should be added that Iran did not have a representative in the Communist International until the Second Congress, where Sultanzade represented the Adalat/ICP. According to records, at the First Congress the Azerbaijani Husseinov, of Iranian origin, represented Iran, without any party label. Haidar was not member of any Communist Party. I have shown this many years ago; Dailami is careful not to repeat Effendiev's 'mistake'.
344. A victim of Stalin's purges.
345. Incidentally, Dailami, when reading his paper to the SOAS conference, referred to Sultanzade's first name as Ahmad. When I pointed out to him this was a mistake, he insisted on his point, naturally without offering any evidence. Fortunately, in the printed version of his contribution, however, he no longer refers to him as Ahmad. What is curious is that he throws in a new name for him, Hormoz, again without offering any source for it. Hormoz, however, is one of several pen-names used by Sultanzade in ICP publications, a fact that I inferred to be Sultanzade's from the contents of those works (see *Central Asian Survey*, Volume 3, no 2, 1984, p 65). It thus becomes clear that Dailami is guilty of both plagiarism and distortion. See more on his 'feats' below.
346. For his source, Dailami refers to V Geniz, *Krasnaia Persiia. Bolsheviki v Gilane, 1920-1921* (Moscow, 2000), while he must have found all this information in the aforementioned 'Crystal Ball', if not in my Introduction to Volume 4 of *Historical Documents*, published in 1973, and in my biography published in both *Iranian Studies*, Volume 17, no 2-3, 1984, pp 215-35, and *Central Asian Studies*, Volume 3,

no 2, 1984, pp 57-73, to which he has himself contributed articles.
347. *Krizis mirovovo khoziastva i noviaia voennaia groza* (Moscow, 1920).
348. I am certain that in addition to the 'Crystal Ball', Dailami knows the biography of Sultanzade published in *Iranian Studies* and *Central Asian Review*, which give ample evidence as to his political and theoretical writings; it would be a serious matter for a researcher on the subject if he did not.
349. See A Sultan-zade, 'Aftobiografia', RTsKhIDNI 495/217/385.
350. See the debate in the Comintern's Eastern Department regarding Haidar Khan's attack on Sultanzade blaming him for being an Armenian (*The Soviet Socialist Republic of Iran*, pp 43ff). It is interesting that in 1909, only a couple of years after his arrival in Iran, this very Haidar Khan collaborated with Armeno-Iranian Social Democrats without raising the smallest objection to their being Christian. Perhaps it was because they were not rivals and the Armenians were more at home in Tabriz than Haidar Khan, who had come from the Caucasus.
351. See Chaqueri (ed), *Historical Documents*, Volume 6, pp 84-95. Here too he commits plagiarism, as this programme was translated from Russian in 1976, after its being obtained with great difficulty from the Soviets. Dailami gives the Russian title, whose facsimile appears in ibid, p 84.
352. See ibid, pp 80-83.
353. See Chaqueri (ed), *Historical Documents*, Volume 13, pp 27-29. Either he has not studied this programme or he merely pretends to know it. The French translation was published in *Revue du Monde Musulman*, Volume 8, June 1909.
354. The following is the translation of the passage regarding federalism: 'In all countries, whenever the ruling classes see the basis of their lives threatened, they artificially whip up national-religious chauvinism, turning one part of the population against another; thus they strengthen their political domination. In Iran, where 15 nationalities and religious sects live, the [national-religious] problem is acute. In order to explain this problem to workers and peasants, whose only enemies are landlords and capitalists who mutually defend one another in the face of social revolution, the party must carry out the most energetic agitation among them, in order to show that the enemy can be overcome by the common efforts of workers of all nationalities. The party struggles for the federal unity of all the nationalities resident in Iran.' (Chaqueri (ed), *Historical Documents*, Volume 6, p 91)
355. For the most revealing account of the removal of Sultanzade and his Central Committee and its replacement by a new one headed by Haidar Khan, see MA Persits, *Zastenchivaia inteventsiia: O sovetskom vtorzhenii v Iran I Bucharu v 1920-1921* (Moscow, 1999), pp 145ff. It is interesting that Dailami is aware of this work by Persits (he uses its English translation), who had spent a whole lifetime defending Stalinist historiography of the East, if he had not been one of its architects. Dailami obtains his ammunition against Sultanzade from the arguments used by Persits (Russian original, pp 102-06, 126-27, 145ff), but does not refer the reader to it but once, for fear that what Persits uses against the whole Bolshevik leadership would also be known; such as, for instance, the decision to liquidate Kuchek Khan in July 1920 emanated from the Kavburo and its subsidiary Iranburo run by the Caucasian Bolsheviks around Stalin, such as Anastas Mikoyan, Budu Mdivani, Sergo Ordzhonikidze, etc, and Stalin himself, and executed by the Caucasian

Prince Abukov, who was later made the scapegoat of the whole policy that was designed to destroy Kuchek Khan (see ibid, pp 144ff). The anti-Sultanzade hysteria that runs through Persits' book is the rehashing of the old charges repeated over and again by Stalinist historians such as Persits himself.

356. Geniz, *Krasnaia Persiia*, pp 190-91.
357. Ibid, p 262
358. Maziar Behrouz, 'The 1953 Coup in Iran and the Legacy of the Tudeh', in M Gasiorowski and M Byrne (eds), *Mohammad Musaddeq and the 1953 Coup in Iran* (Syracuse NY, 2004), pp 102-25.
359. M Varqa, *Na Gofteh hayee piramoun-e Forourizi-ye Hokoumat-e Mosaddeq va Naqsh-e Hezb-e Tudeh* (Tehran, 1384/2005), pp 247-48. It is true that Varqa's book was published after the piece by Behrouz, but these facts were known long before Varqa's book was published.
360. Ibid, p 285.
361. Ibid.
362. See B Amir Khorsowi, *Nazari az daroun beh naqshe-e hezbe-e Tude-ye Iran* (Tehran, 1996), pp 675ff.
363. For the Central Committee's declaration, see JAMA, *Gozashteh cheragh-e rah-e ayandeh*, pp 682-85, a book the author does know, as it is listed in the Bibliography of his book!

Peyman Vahabzadeh

SAKA
Iran's Grassroots Revolutionary Workers' Organisation

Sazman-e Enqelabi-ye Kargaran-e Iran (the Revolutionary Organisation of Iranian Workers), or the SAKA, represents the long-lasting, but largely overlooked, tradition of leftist workers' autonomous movements and independent self-organisation within the Iranian Left. The histories of the analogous groups that precede the SAKA indicate a unique experience in grassroots workers' organisation — an experience that has been distorted and denied by doctrinal self-acclaimed Marxist-Leninist parties in the country. Precisely because the SAKA represents such a unique, long-lasting and relatively successful experience, any history of the twentieth-century Iranian Left is incomplete without it. In what follows, we will review the history of the group, tracing it back to the 1940s, offering a brief account of the group in the 1960s, and revisiting some of the distorted accounts regarding it. Because the history of the SAKA has been adversely affected by such distortions, and since Albert Sohrabian's *Memoirs*[1] constitutes the only insider's, and the only *fairly* reliable, account of the group's history and activities, we rely primarily on this source, while also using other sources.

The *Krouzhoks*[2]

The SAKA was the culmination of a process of building networks of workers' red cells that lasted for almost 30 years from the departure of a number of members of the Tudeh Party of Iran's Youth Organisation[3] in 1942 (1321 Iranian calendar), and continuing through the successive formation of the *Krouzhoks*, the Councils Organisation (*Sazman-e Showraha*), and the Communist Core of Iran (YEKA — *Yadr-e Komonisti-ye Iran*).[4] Several of the first members of the Tudeh Youth Organisation, including Albert Sohrabian and Ovanes[5] Moradian, both Armenian workers, met Baqer Emami (known as Aqa Nuro within leftist circles) around 1946 (1325). Emami had established a workers' network named the *Krouzhoks*. He was an obscure poet and writer, and the younger stepbrother (of the same father, Zeynolabedin, but a different mother) of *Imam Jom'eh*, Tehran's official Friday Prayer Leader appointed by the Shah. He lost his father at the age of two and was raised by his stepbrother.⁶ Sohrabian claims that Emami's earliest political experience was his association with the Social Democratic activists within the so-called 'Blood Committee' during the Constitutional Revolution, but this claim cannot be supported because Emami appears to have been born in 1897, making him 10 years old at the time of the Constitutional Revolution.⁷ The report on Emami by American Embassy, however, attributes his attraction towards the Left to his higher education in the newly-established Soviet Union when he was most probably about 20 years of age. This account also claims that he had 'joined in the activities of [Avetis] Sultanzadeh, a leader of the communist movement in Iran'.⁸ Sohrabian reports that Emami travelled to Moscow where he met Sergei Ordzhonikidze, a prominent figure of the Russian Revolution, who recruited him for the OGPU network in Iran.⁹ Emami worked as a secret agent for the OGPU during the next 10 years until he was arrested in 1927 (1306). When exposed, he first was sentenced to death but his sentence was later commuted to 15 years' imprisonment. He was released upon the fall of Reza Shah in September 1941.¹⁰ The American report, however, holds that he was imprisoned in 1923 for murdering his stepfather but was pardoned on the occasion of Reza Shah's coronation in 1925, only to be imprisoned in 1929 until 1941 'for communist activities'.¹¹

The Tudeh Party was established and based on the new Soviet policy of creating anti-fascist democratic coalitions.¹² As such, while the founders of the Tudeh Party were veteran communists, the party itself was not. Reportedly, this dilemma instigated Emami to create a communist workers' cell named the *Krouzhoks* in 1943-44 (1322-23) after he failed to persuade the Tudeh to announce itself as a communist party.¹³ Another account holds that he had reportedly averred when invited to join the Tudeh Party by Solayman Mirza Eskandari: 'A Communist cannot join a non-communist party.'¹⁴ His aim was to educate the workers through his unsophisticated pamphlets on aspects of Marxism, including his *The Alphabet of Marxism*. According to Sohrabian, Emami succeeded in attracting hundreds within the more or less 10 years of *Krouzhok* activity, but most of them left the group for other leftist organisations, mostly for the Tudeh Party.¹⁵ The group, naturally, was the subject of various accusations by the Tudeh leadership, most of which targeting Emami himself to the extent that the Tudeh and the *Krouzhoks* severed all contact with each other.¹⁶ Noureddin Kianouri, the Tudeh Party First-Secretary on the eve of the 1979 revolution, confirms that, when Emami refused to become a member of the Tudeh, the Tudeh Party 'fiercely fought against this group'.¹⁷

The group's congress was held in the summer of 1947 (1326) in northern Tehran with 52 participating delegates. The congress elected five members of the Central Committee that included Emami, Sohrabian and Ahmad Bastami.¹⁸

The *Krouzhoks* reportedly disintegrated around 1948 because of its waning influence amongst the workers as the Tudeh Party continued its ceaseless attacks against the group. Another factor involved in its disintegration is the aftermath of the Azerbaijan crisis and the split of Khalil Maleki from the Tudeh Party in 1948. Confirming Emami's meeting with the leaders of the Democratic Party of Azerbaijan and the relative, and short-lived, expansion of the *Krouzhoks* in the Autonomous Province of Azerbaijan,[19] the American Embassy report claims that in 1947 Emami was secretly aided by Ardashes Ovanesian, a veteran member of Iranian Communist Party (ICP) and a reluctant member of the Tudeh Party, to re-launch the ICP in January 1948. This angered the Tudeh Party, which in turn, reportedly with the aid of the Soviets, publicly accused Emami, in the Tudeh Party organ, *Mardom* (no 328, 5 May 1948) of being a police agent. The article is said to have been written by a Russian named AN Blov (and published in the Soviet workers' organ *Trud* (no 8263). Emami replied to these accusations in his book *Mard-e Monsef (The Judicious Man)*.[20] That said, it seems that the underlying reason for the disintegration of the *Krouzhoks* must have been his waning influence among the workers, due to the success of the Tudeh Party in leading *Shora-ye Motahedeh-ye Markazi-ye Kargari* (the United Central Council of Workers' Unions).

The Councils' Organisation

A few relentless former members of the *Krouzhoks* who were close to Emami — Sohrabian, Ovanes Moradian, Engineer Hassan Pirouzi, Hojatt Elahi, Ali Akbar Matin-Dezh, Hassan Pirouzju and Khachatour Sohrabian — decided to renew the group.[21] It was named *Sazman-e Showraha*, or the Councils' Organisation. In its short lifespan, the group published *Beh Pish* (*Forward*), licensed to Emami in 1948. However, the third issue of the newspaper, published in red ink to commemorate the anniversary of the Bolshevik Revolution, was seized by the police on 30 December 1949, and the editorial board was arrested. Interestingly, the last issue reportedly contained sharp criticisms of the Soviet government.[22] The remainder of the group, led by Sohrabian, engaged in limited activities until he was arrested in August 1950. Emami was sentenced to five years, while others received three-year terms.[23] In prison, according to Sohrabian, Emami seemed to encourage cooperation with the authorities, alienating Pirouzju and Matin-Dezh. The American intelligence report holds that Emami 'had an ambitious supporter in the army; it is believed that this person was no other than General Razmara who was the Chief of the General Staff at the time'.[24] Soon, Pirouzi also left the group in prison and joined the Tudeh Party after his release. Matin-Dezh was shot and killed by the army during a demonstration in the winter of 1953. Like its predecessor, the Councils' Organisation disintegrated.

The YEKA

The Communist Core of Iran (*Hasteh-ye Komonisti-ye Iran*, or YEKA) was formed when Emami and others from the former group were released from prison around the time when the August 1953 coup had imposed a major setback on Iran's national self-assertion. In an atmosphere dominated by distrust and low morale among activists, the YEKA set itself, yet again, the task of educating workers and organising them in red cells. In a way, the YEKA went against the grain of the leftist activism of the post-1953 period: when activists were trying to hide and erase their traces, the group actually started organising itself. Expectedly, the atmosphere of distrust and low morale was reflected in the painfully slow development of the YEKA. As has been the case with this kind of activism, the workers would hold a job and live their lives, while trying to attract other workers to the group. According to Sohrabian, given the mood of the time, this way of recruitment was not successful.[25] According to the American Embassy intelligence report, written in April 1954, the YEKA had about 100 members (logically, prior to the spring of 1954) but this account cannot be confirmed.

The extensive raiding of all dissident circles in 1957-58 convinced the activists to suspend the YEKA for the time being. A few months later, however, a number of disillusioned former Tudeh Party activists established a group known (for short) as the KDSK (*Kargaran, Dehqanan, Sarbazan, va Karmandan-e Iran*; the Iranian Workers, Peasants, Soldiers and Employees). The KDSK contacted the YEKA, with its prominent members, Alinia (a former Azerbaijan Democrat close to the *Krouzhoks*), Baqer Salimi (also a former *Krouzhok*), and Hamid Sattarzadeh (a former Tudeh activist) negotiating with Emami. Soon, an *ad hoc* unification commission of three (Sohrabian, Moradian, Sattarzadeh) formed the new YEKA organisation, upon the future ratification of the YEKA congress.[26] The prospect of unification renewed the spirit of the group, especially during the relatively relaxed years of 1960-63, when the repressive measures of the post-1953 period were loosened. The congress, held in the spring of 1962, outraged Sattarzadeh, when he was not elected to the Central Committee of the group. Prior to the congress, Emami had warned the participants that Sattarzadeh was 'selfish' and a 'megalomaniac,' while according to Sohrabian, Emami was equally selfish and megalomaniac.[27] In fact, Sohrabian explicitly refers to the presence of a 'personality cult' and 'the blind following of the superior' that dominated the YEKA.[28] In any case, Sattarzadeh levelled accusations against Emami, calling the so-called unification of the group a sham, a trick for the YEKA to absorb the KDSK. Sattarzadeh and his followers split from the group, taking away about 20 per cent of the membership.[29] They established, reportedly in 1965, a group named GAMA (*Gorouh-e Enqelabi-ye Marksisti-ye Iran*).

An interesting feature of the YEKA was the principle, accepted and valued by the membership, that the members should refrain from accumulating any capital 'in order not to sink in a quagmire of greed, one from which there would be no deliverance'.[30]

The SAKA

Emami's suicide, at the age of 64, in the spring of 1967, shocked the group. Reportedly, as a suicide note, he had written these disjointed statements on the wall:

> The more I tried the further I got from my ideals... the Soviet Union has gone towards deviation [*rah-e enheraf dar pish gerefteh*] and is now betraying the proletariat of the world... I am tired and I don't want to live any more... no one is responsible for my death.[31]

Emami had also left a long letter to Moradian, which he read at the group's next Central Committee meeting. The letter contained his disgust of his own inability to make a change and his siding with the Chinese Communist Party against Soviet deviationism. Emami warned members against establishing for-profit enterprises in order to fund the group, an act that would constitute 'treachery' (*khiyanat*). Last but not least, in the letter he referred to his indebtedness to his mother, a woman from a 'very humble and toiling class' to whom Emami, in his own view, owed his humanity. At the same time, however, he attributed his 'treacherous' act (of misplacing the group's funds) to the genes he had inherited from his father, Tehran's Prayer Leader.[32] Given that Emami was well known to the security forces, his suicide caused the YEKA to suspend its activities for a period of time, because the members argued that the police might announce Emami's death as a murder (by implication, an internal purge) and arrest YEKA members for interrogation. The subsequent events showed that the suspicion of members was unfounded. During this time, a 'natural filtering' of half-hearted members of the group took place: those who were not sure about their own motivation for activism left the YEKA.[33] The group decided to re-launch itself in 1969 by holding a plenary meeting. The meeting critically examined the activities and vision of the YEKA in its 15 years of activism and found that the group had been too obsessed with ensuring its security and survival under a police state to effect any meaningful expansion among the working class. The group had enjoyed relative success, the meeting found, in recruiting workers from small shops but had failed to recruit any workers from large factories. Moreover, the undemocratic set-up of the group had left no room for membership feedback. The group decided it had to contact other leftist groups and try to expand its activities.[34]

After Emami's death, the YEKA was contacted by the GAMA.[35] A possible reunification was considered, and Moradian, Ordin and Hunan Asheq from the YEKA negotiated with Sattarzadeh and Hassan Fesharaki from the GAMA. Upon agreement, the two established the *Sazman-e Enqelabi-ye Kargaran-e Iran* or the SAKA (the Organisation of Revolutionary Workers of Iran). It is interesting to see how the word 'Revolutionary' permeated the group's new name when remade in the 1960s. The SAKA organised its publications, structure, finance and nation-wide units, and for the first time in the long history of the group it actually established units outside Tehran, in Mashhad, Isfahan, Arak and Tabriz. The group also published an internal publication. According to Sohrabian, at this time, from 1965 onwards, the group rapidly expanded its network in large-scale factories such as the car assembly plant, Iran-National.[36]

But the time had changed and revolutionary fervour was now in the air. Che Guevara had inspired revolutionary waves throughout the world, and in Iran the idea of an armed movement had found momentum. That is why in the summer of 1970 (1349) a handful of SAKA activists in Isfahan planned and executed a bank hold-up during which three SAKA members (Ahmad Mo'ini Araqi, Mahmoud Navabakhsh and Asghar Fattahi) were arrested while the fourth member of the team (Hadi Pakzad) escaped. This kind of action was obviously contrary to the philosophy of the SAKA. In response, the group decided to feign its dissolution to avoid future security raids. Once again, Sattarzadeh and his comrades split from the group, although Sattarzadeh maintained contacts with the SAKA's veteran activists. The SAKA was left with four veteran members — Asheq, Sohrabian, Fesharaki and Ordin — leading the group.[37]

Finally, the group was raided by the SAVAK in April 1971. First, the three medical personnel and members of the SAKA, Dr Fesharaki (general surgeon), Dr Abtahi (paediatrician) and Sattarzadeh (paramedic/pezeshkyar) were arrested in their small clinic. Available sources concur that Sattarzadeh betrayed the group to the SAVAK, and he was released shortly after all the members of the group were arrested. Sohrabian asserts that those who were not known to Sattarzadeh were not arrested.[38] According to Sohrabian, the SAKA was in touch with a number of activists who were later known as the Palestine Group, and it was through a member of this latter group that the SAKA was exposed to the police.[39] The SAKA was totally eradicated. A total of 130 individuals were tried in the military court in relation to the group, receiving prison terms from six months to six years. Those involved in the Isfahan bank holdup received from 10 years to life.[40] According to the SAVAK, the group had units in Tehran, Isfahan, Mashhad, Qazvin, Arak, Kashan, Shahr-e Kord and Bojnourd.[41] The arrests should be understood in the context of the general crackdown upon opposition as part of the security preparation for the infamously extravagant Persepolis celebration of 2500 years of the Persian Empire in October 1971.

As such, one of the longest-running communist circles in Iran, and arguably the only leftist group to focus on the organisation of the workers, came to an end.

The SAKA and Iran's New Revolutionary Wave

During the late 1960s, around the time when the SAKA was shaping up, the underground networks of the new activist generation and the future People's Fadai Guerrillas felt the need for a decisive turn towards armed, revolutionary movement. The polemical pamphlet, *The Necessity of Armed Struggle and the Refutation of the Survival Theory*, by the future short-lived leader of the Fadai Guerrillas, Amir Parviz Pouyan (1947-1971), played a decisive role. It was written in the spring of 1970 (1349), and while its references to the 'survival theory' implied a critique of the inactivity of the Tudeh Party, the text actually had as its target the kind of red workers' network activism that the SAKA represented. The point of the argument for Pouyan was to disprove the efficacy of SAKA-style 'political' and 'peaceful' activism in such a way that the only possible course available for the Left was armed struggle, and that he would lead the undecided activists of his generation in that direction.

Pouyan argues that under the current conditions of police repression, the revolutionary intellectuals are unable to have any direct and solid relationship with the masses.[42] The unification of the revolutionary Marxist-Leninist intellectuals (*roshanfekran*) is premised upon their acceptance of revolutionary struggle.[43] What he calls the 'theory of survival' implies a critique of the Tudeh Party, but given that the Tudeh did not have any organisation at this point in Iran, the text is directly aimed at the SAKA, which represented an alternative to armed struggle.

> This [survival] theory leans towards confining the struggle to the so parochial resources as the police cannot control. This means to gather elements [activists] without quantitative significance — that in fact hardly ever exceed the number of one's fingers — and have them study Marxist and historical literature in secret. The range of activities of these elements at best is limited to idle and scattered relations with people of all classes and backgrounds. In such [a form of] activity, because every organisational element [cadre] continues with his everyday life, he naturally makes no effort to change [these conditions].[44]

Here is how Pouyan conflates the long-term objectives of the red-workers' organisation with the impatient expectations of his generation: he refers to the 'metaphysical' opportune moment in which the revolution will happen, something that he must have found in SAKA literature of the time — to which this author did not have access. Pouyan asserts that this moment does not exist;[45] hence the necessity of action. Obviously, the SAKA does not wish to bring about this crucial moment; the moment is an historic one and it will materialise when enough workers are ready to instigate a workers' revolution. For a practical and impatient generation, such as that of Pouyan, this moment has to be created. But as Sohrabian reflects, SAKA's activism actually showed that it was quite possible to create red-workers' networks despite the police state. The expansion of SAKA cells within during the years of its activities, and the fact that 130 individuals were tried in relation to the group, attests to the possibility of forms of activism other than armed struggle and urban guerrilla warfare.[46] It must be reiterated that it was because of the militant-style bank hold-up of the Isfahan cell of the SAKA that the group was exposed to the SAVAK.

Pseudo-Historiography of the SAKA

Bizhan Jazani was the founder of the formative group that in 1971 launched the attack on the Siahkal Gendarmerie Post and joined with another group (which included Pouyan) to form the People's Fadai Guerrillas. (See the two articles on this subject in this issue.) He was arrested in 1967 and his *Thirty-Year Political History* was written in prison. In the absence of major research on recent political history, his book soon became an authoritative reference amongst activists. Since it was written secretly in prison, the book relies on memory and the claims of activists whom Jazani could contact. The book, therefore, contains many unfounded claims and distortions mixed with Jazani's personal opinion and sentiments towards other groups.[47] In seeking, like Pouyan, a way historically to convince his readers of the necessity of armed struggle, Jazani calls Emami a police agent, thereby accusing the SAKA and its predecessors of being run by the police. He claims:

> After his release [from the prison in 1952], Emami began his suspicious activities. He contacted the Criminal Investigation Department [*edareh-ye agahi*] and from this point onwards he maintained regular contacts with the police. Some veteran colleagues of Emami were aware of these contacts, but Emami pretended that his contacts were for the purpose of counter-intelligence.[48]

For whom is not known, unless it was for the Soviets as he had earlier been a Communist in the service of OGPU. Other members of the group are naturally viewed as being naïvely manipulated. In the same book, Jazani accuses several other activists of his time of being police collaborators or implicates them as such through guilt by association.[49] Jazani calls Emami a police agent and claims both the YEKA and the KDSK to be his creation, and their unification a sham.[50] Jazani wants to prove that all the non-militant networks end up either serving the police or being manipulated by them; thus, he wishes to argue that the only way to organise dissent in Iran was through underground militant action.

Interestingly, Jazani had spent time in prison with SAKA members such as Ordin and Sohrabian, but, according to Sohrabian, he never consulted with them on the history of the SAKA. Instead, reports Sohrabian, Jazani completely relied on the statements of Abdollah Mehri, who did not possess sufficient information about the SAKA and its predecessors. Sohrabian quotes Hassan Ordin to explain why Jazani chose not to consult SAKA members. According to Ordin:

> To advocate armed struggle and discredit our 'political' activism, Comrade Jazani did not feel that he needed to investigate the matter with us because he wanted in any case to reject our form of politics.[51]

Conclusion

The SAKA and its predecessors represent an overlooked 30-year-old tradition within the Iranian Left of building workers' networks in order to effect social change. From the *Krouzhoks* to the SAKA, these working-class network activists experienced and endured persecution and repressive measures at the hands of the Iranian state, accusations and distortions from the leftist groups from the Tudeh to the predecessors of the Fadai Guerrillas, intra-organisational personality cults and issues, and their own dogmatism. Their success cannot be easily measured, and in fact, overall, they were not successful in creating any weighty workers' movement. Nonetheless, their experience and mode of activism remains unique in the history of Iran after the Constitutional Revolution. While the group's members had a cautious inclination towards the Soviet Union, they asserted their independence from the USSR to avoid the fate of the Tudeh Party as an executor of the Soviet foreign policy in Iran. The Sino-Soviet rift in the 1960s made Emami lean towards the Chinese, while the SAKA still remained an independent group. These groups represent the tendency within Marxism that stresses grassroots workers' organisation and movements, as opposed to the professional party of intellectuals. Aside from a handful of non-workers, the absolute majority of the successive series of groups from the *Krouzhoks* to the SAKA were workers who, as Sohrabian states, were barely literate. In this, the SAKA and its predecessors represent the forgotten political heritage of the ICP, whose rules forbade the recruitment of non-working-class people. While the SAKA and its predecessors did not have such a rule, the nature of their socialisation, activism and networking made them a truly working-class organisation. It seems that, while Emami, with his questionable acts and suspicious background and connections, had been the chief organiser of these groups, it was really due to the constant presence of workers such as Sohrabian, Moradian and Ordin that the group survived and revived itself from time to time. Thus, despite the presence of a small number of non-workers in the series of groups from the *Krouzhoks* to the SAKA, this tradition must be regarded as a genuine Iranian experiment in creating and maintaining a Red workers' network.

Notes

1. Albert Sohrabian, *Khaterat-e Albert Sohrabian: bargi az jonbesh-e kargari komonisti Iran* (*Memoirs of Albert Sohrabian: Pages of Iran's Workers' Communist Movement*, Bidar, Hanover, 2000).
2. '*Krouzhok*' is a Russian word for 'circle'.
3. The Tudeh Party established a Youth Organisation upon its formation. It was led by Dr Reza Radmanesh of the party's Central Committee.
4. '*Yadr*' is a Russian word for 'nucleus'.
5. Different Armenian spellings: Avanes and Hovanes.
6. Sohrabian, *Memoirs*, p 38. See also the report on Emami prepared for the American Ambassador in Tehran by Michael R Gannett, Second Secretary of the Embassy (usually a CIA position), dated 10 April 1954, entitled 'Memorandum Concerning a Splinter Communist Party in Iran', USNA 788.001/4-1054.
7. Sohrabian, *Memoirs*, p 39.
8. USNA 788.001/4-1054. [The US document was, reportedly, written by *Kurish Shahbaz*, a local employee with duties as a political adviser, but Sohrabian (*Memoirs*, pp 1345ff) recalls that Emami had told his comrades that around 1957-58 he had been paid a visit by an American, along with a translator — who probably was Shahbaz — who had introduced himself as a 'researcher' on socio-economic development programmes. He had wanted to know about Emami and his views. Emami had told him that he was a 'loner Communist' and described the socio-economic conditions of the country. Sohrabian states that they had later found out that the American had been a US military adviser — perhaps Michael R Gannett, Second Secretary of the Embassy, who usually a CIA officer — Editor's note.]
9. The Cheka, created in 1917, was the early Soviet security force and predecessor of the KGB; it became the OGPU in 1923 and then the GPU in 1932.
10. Sohrabian, *Memoirs*, pp 38-53.
11. USNA 788.001/4-1054.
12. See Cosroe Chaqueri, 'Did the Soviets Play a Role in Founding the Tudeh Party in Iran?', *Cahiers du monde russe*, Volume 40, no 3 (1999), pp 497-528, reproduced in this issue of *Revolutionary History*. See also Iraj Eskandari, 'Chand nokteh-ye asasi darbareh-ye bonyadgozari-ye Hezb-e Tudeh-ye Iran va tahavvol-e an' ('A Few

Points on the Foundation and Development of the Tudeh Party of Iran'), *Donya*, no 3, August-September 1974, pp 2-7. See also Sohrabian, *Memoirs*, pp 54-55.
13. Bizhan Jazani, *Tarikh-e si sal-e siyasi* (*The Thirty-Year Political History*, Organisation of Iranian People's Fadai Guerrillas, Federal Republic of Germany, nd), p 102. See also USNA 788.001/4-1054. This report confirms Jazani's account, but it holds that Emami sent the *Krouzhoks* to infiltrate the Tudeh and lean it toward Emami's vision of a communist party.
14. USNA 788.001/4-1054.
15. Sohrabian, *Memoirs*, p 65.
16. Ibid, p 69.
17. Noureddin Kianouri, *Khaterat-e Noureddin Kianouri* (*Memoirs of Noureddin Kianouri*, Tehran, 1992), p 468.
18. Sohrabian, *Memoirs*, pp 72-73.
19. Ibid, p 70.
20. USNA 788.001/4-1054. See also Sohrabian, *Memoirs*, pp 77-78.
21. Sohrabian, *Memoirs*, p 82.
22. USNA 788.001/4-1054; Jazani, *The Thirty-Year Political History*, p 103.
23. Jazani, *The Thirty-Year Political History*, p 103.
24. USNA 788.001/4-1054. This document claims that with the help of his secret, insider supporter, the military tribunal exonerated Emami, although Emami served a prison sentence between December 1949 and August 1953 (perhaps 1952). Contrary to Sohrabian's account, the American intelligence document claims that Emami had been in contact with the Soviet Embassy in Tehran, providing them with weekly reports. 'Thus one of Emami's weekly reports to the Soviet Embassy was silently slipped into the hands of the police, whereupon he [Emami] was arrested and Major Fazlollahi, Military Prosecutor, imprisoned him for ten years as a Soviet spy. Emami remained in prison until his release on parole in March 1953.' (Ibid)
25. Sohrabian, *Memoirs*, p 133.
26. Ibid, pp 139-41.
27. Ibid, pp 142, 147.
28. Ibid, p 157.
29. Ibid, pp 147-48.
30. Ibid, pp 148-49.
31. Ibid, p 151. It must be noted that Emami did misplace SAKA funds, for personal use during his failed love affair, hoping to repay the group by means of the income from his mother's estates (ibid, pp 154-55). In his *Memoirs*, Kianouri offers a fabricated explanation of Emami's death. In the SAKA, he states, 'the members learned that Emami had spent the organisation's funds on personal expenditures and had decided to subject him to a tribunal' but before that happened Emami committed suicide (Kianouri, *Memoirs*, p 468). Of course, the attentive reader finds the idea of an internal 'tribunal', normally associated with Stalinist groups, so foreign to a peaceful group like the SAKA that it needs no refutation here!
32. Sohrabian, *Memoirs*, p 152.
33. Ibid, p 157.
34. Ibid, pp 157-59.

35. Ibid, p 161.
36. Ibid, pp 161-64.
37. Ibid, pp 162-67.
38. Ibid, p 169. See also Jazani, *The Thirty-Year Political History*, p 104.
39. Sohrabian, *Memoirs*, pp 169-71.
40. Ibid, p 172.
41. 'Mosahebeh-ye matbu'ati va radio-televizioni-ye maqam-e amniyati-ye Iran' ('The Press Conference of Head of Security Authority of Iran'), *Keyhan*, no 4130 (26 Day 1350/16 January 1972), p 4.
42. Amir Parviz Pouyan, *Zarurat-e mobarezeh-ye mosallahaneh va radd-e teori-ye baqa (The Necessity of Armed Struggle and the Refutation of the Survival Theory*, Gam Publishers, Tehran, 1979), p 2. For further information on Pouyan's text, see Peyman Vahabzadeh, *A Guerrilla Odyssey: Modernisation, Secularism, Democracy and the Fadai Period of National Liberation in Iran, 1971-1979* (Syracuse University Press, Syracuse, NY, 2010), pp 134-38.
43. Pouyan, *The Necessity of Armed Struggle*, p 12.
44. Ibid, p 15.
45. Ibid, p 16.
46. See Sohrabian, *Memoirs*, pp 182-85.
47. In regard to a few of Jazani's distortions in this book, see Cosroe Chaqueri, 'The Iranian Left in the Twentieth Century: A Critical Appraisal of its Historiography', in this issue of *Revolutionary History*. See also Peyman Vahabzadeh, 'Bizhan Jazani and the Problems of Historiography of the Iranian Left', *Iranian Studies*, Volume 38, no 1 (2005), pp 167-78. While Jazani's work deserves reference in relations to the history of the twentieth-century Iranian communism, it cannot be used as a reliable account. The extent of the influence of Jazani's historiography, however, is so great that the sentence-long description of the SAKA under the entry 'Communism' in *Encyclopaedia Iranica* (Volume 6, pp 95-112), written by Torab Haqshenas (p 106), mistakenly relies on Jazani's *Thirty-Year Political History*.
48. Jazani, *The Thirty-Year Political History*, p 103.
49. For example, aside from other accusations that cannot be cited here, Jazani makes an astonishing allegation against Dr Hussein Fatemi, Minister of Foreign Affairs in the patriotico-democratic government of Dr Mohammad Mosaddeq, who was executed by the Shah after the 1953 coup, calling him a collaborator with the British intelligence services prior to his joining Mosaddeq (Jazani, *The Thirty-Year Political History*, p 59).
50. Ibid, p 103.
51. Hassan Ordin as quoted in Sohrabian, *Memoirs*, p 289. In Iran during the 1960s and 1970s, the 'militant' and 'political' approaches were often contrasted.

Peyman Vahabzadeh
Mostafa Shoʻaʻiyan
An Iranian Leftist Political Thinker Unlike His Peers

The Iranian Left has, to a great extent, earned itself the unenviable infamy of being undemocratic, dogmatic and Stalinist. However, during the years of 'steel and blood' of the 1970s, the years dominated by urban guerrilla activity, a maverick militant and theoretician emerged — one who singularly and uncompromisingly challenged the dominant culture of Iran's 'new communist movement' — the designation that the new militant Left chose for itself — both in terms of the Left's ideology and of its prevailing Stalinism.

The 2000 pages of writings of Mostafa Shoʻaʻiyan (1936-1975) contain, among other things, a systematic pathology of the Stalinism that had disfigured the Iranian Left. His writings include studies in history and theory, as well as works of criticism, memoirs, poetry, open letters, reports and policy reviews — all of which were written under severe human conditions, yet enjoying an eccentric lexical system that defies the norm of the leftist jargon of the time. Due to its dexterity, his works remain for the most part unknown and largely unstudied. If during his lifetime he was 'downgraded' by the Stalinists as a 'Trotskyist', he is now gradually being considered as a serious and original thinker,[1] in the light of the collapse of Soviet Marxism and its satellites across the world which has forced much rethinking in respect of the Left and its social project.

In this essay, we shall strive to provide the reader with a succinct, bird's-eye view of Shoʻaʻiyan's short life and the views he elaborated.[2] Of the many dimensions of Shoʻaʻiyan's innovative thoughts, here we probe three aspects we maintain to be his most important. Firstly, we shall look at his strategy to form a wide *front* composed of militant revolutionary groups. Secondly, we will study his tenacious attendance to the Stalinism that defined a period of the Fadaʼiyan's organisational life. Lastly, we will offer an overview of the debate between Shoʻaʻiyan and Hamid Momeni on the role of 'intellectuals' in the 'new communist movement'. The essay will conclude with an outline of the ramifications of Shoʻaʻiyan's pathology of authoritarian tendencies in the Left.

Sho'a'iyan's Life and Times: 'Toward a Ruthless Critique'

Born in 1936 into a lower-class family in southern Tehran, Sho'a'iyan supported himself throughout his secondary school years by working odd evening jobs. He was admitted to the engineering programme at the Tehran Technical Institute (now the Science and Industry University) in 1958, and graduated as the top student of the class of 1962, which qualified him for a state scholarship to the University of Oklahoma, USA — an offer he refused for obvious reasons.[3] He was assigned a position as a secondary school teacher in Kashan, in central Iran. After battling with bureaucracy, he finally transferred himself to Tehran in 1966,[4] where he mostly taught history and social sciences in various secondary schools for two years.[5]

Sho'a'iyan's activism started in 1950 during the Premiership of General Razmara. He joined one of the three splinter groups of the Pan-Iranist party.[6] After the uprising of 21 July 1951 against the Shah which reinstated Dr Mosaddeq as the Premier, he left the Pan-Iranists.[7] Leaning towards Marxism, he joined a small circle of former Tudeh Party members, now critical of the party, in the late 1950s. Informally called *Jaryan* (or *Proseh*, the Persian for 'Process'), the circle was formed around the former officer Mahmoud Tavakkoli,[8] the author of two critical analyses of the Tudeh Party.[9] During his association with Jaryan, Sho'a'iyan wrote an extensive critical essay on Khalil Maleki's Society of Socialists (*Jame'eh-yi Sosialist-ha*).[10]

With the rise of the Patriotic Front (Second Period) (*Jebheh-ye Melli-ye Dovvom*) in 1960, Sho'a'iyan joined the left wing of the Patriotic Front. In this context, between 1962 and 1964, he met Bizhan Jazani, a founding figure of the Fada'i Guerrillas, who later called Jaryan the 'American Marxists'[11] — a label that stuck in the mind of the Stalinist Left and discredited Sho'a'iyan in their eyes.[12] A decade later, the Fada'i theorist Hamid Momeni took Jazani's derogatory label even further, calling Tavakkoli a 'CIA agent' in order to discredit Sho'a'iyan's past.[13]

In the 1950s and 1960s, Sho'a'iyan mingled with the intellectuals around the journal *Andisheh va Honar* (*Thought and Art*), which publicised broader socialist and liberationist ideas. This association gifted Sho'a'iyan with an astute anti-Stalinist inclination. In 1968, he finished his historical-analytical study of Mirza Kuchek Khan's 1920-21 movement in the Caspian region in *A Glance at the Relations between the Soviet Union and the Jangali Revolutionary Movement*.[14] This study led him to his path-breaking *Rebellion* (*Shouresh*), which was renamed, after the author's third revision, *Revolution* (*Enqelâb*).[15] His critical case-study of the betrayal of the *Jangali* movement by Lenin and the Soviets in his first book, led him to trace the ideological roots of the Soviets' betrayal to Leninism itself, and that was the task of his book, *Revolution*.

In 1971, he left his teaching position to create an urban guerrilla cell[16] along with long-time friends Behzad Nabavi, Parviz Sadri and Reza Asgariyeh.[17] Soon they went underground as the group's plan to sabotage the huge Isfahan steel plant — built by the Soviet Union — was exposed to the SAVAK and some members were arrested.[18] The arrestees included Nabavi, a Muslim who became a prominent political figure after the revolution. While underground, however, Sho'a'iyan assisted Reza Reazi, the leader of the Iranian People's Mojahedin, in rebuilding their organisation after the group was nearly eradicated in August 1971.[19] This act should be understood in the context of Sho'a'iyan's advocacy of creating a unified front of revolutionary militants that included the Mojahedin, the Fada'iyan and smaller militant groups. He later became the sole theorist of the national liberation front in the Iranian Left. In the meantime, Sho'a'iyan sent many of his writings abroad.[20] But as he recollected, this led to his exposure to the SAVAK.[21] This coincided with the failure of the Isfahan operation.[22]

After the failure of the Isfahan steel plant operation, in 1972 Sho'a'iyan met Nader Shayegan Shamasbi (hereafter Shayegan). Together they organised a new group, the People's Democratic Front (*Jebheh-ye Demokratik-e Khalq*, or PDF), based on two partitioned teams, each of which being individually commanded.[23] In May 1973, one of the bases of the PDF where the group made its explosives was raided by the SAVAK, and consequently Shayegan, Hassan Rumina and Nader Ata'i were killed in shoot-outs and 10 members arrested. Sho'a'iyan's team remained intact.[24]

Sho'a'iyan and two remaining teams in Tehran and Tabriz subsequently joined the OIPFG. Two women from the PDF, Marzieh Ahmadi Osku'i and Saba Bizhanzadeh, rose significantly in the OIPFG. While Sho'a'iyan joined the Fada'iyan on the condition that his *Revolution* was debated by Fada'i members, the OIPFG under the leadership of Hamid Ashraf merely intended to absorb competent militants of the PDF. Naturally, soon it became clear to Sho'a'iyan that the Fada'iyan would not accept Sho'a'iyan's anti-Leninist treatise. As such, Sho'a'iyan, Shayegan's step-mother Fatemeh Sa'idi and her younger children Nasser and Arzhang Shayegan were sent to Mashhad under the command of Ashraf's lieutenant Ali-Akbar Ja'fari. Due to a risky and mismanaged operation in Mashhad, Sa'idi was arrested. This infuriated Sho'a'iyan, who took the event as evidence of the Fada'iyan's discriminatory treatment against him.

Meanwhile, Jazani was alarmed to hear in prison about the recruitment of Sho'a'iyan. In 1973, Jazani warned Fada'i member Mehdi Fatapour in prison that Sho'a'iyan's recruitment would be 'dangerous' because of his knowledge of theory and his 'radical and Trotskyist ideas'. Upon his release, Fatapour was informed by Anoushirvan Lotfi and Ashraf that Sho'a'iyan was 'cut off' from the OIPFG. It is unknown if Jazani's warning had influenced Ashraf's decision to expel Shoʻaʻiyan,²⁵ although it is probable, since Jazani kept in touch with Ashraf through visitors to prison.²⁶

While still with the OIPFG, Shoʻaʻiyan had detected manifestations of Stalinism and set himself the task of documenting them, and this provides us with an excellent insider's view. Shoʻaʻiyan was accused of 'opportunism, lack of responsibility, and cowardice'. He had lived long enough in leftist circles to understand that the Fada'iyan were in the process of *parvandeh sâzi*, that is, blacklisting for excommunication (*index librorium prohibitorum*) as in the Catholic church. Like Stalin's staged trials of the 1930s, the OIPFG had pressed Oskuʻi to provide reports on his personality,²⁷ as well as on the young Shayegan brothers, now in the custody of the OIPFG after their mother's arrest.²⁸ But Shoʻaʻiyan's isolation, as an observer remarks:

> ... did not simply result from his idiosyncratic language. His style was a symbolic expression of a fighter's dignified distinctiveness who did not wish to succumb to the predominant Stalinism of the Iranian communist movement at the time.²⁹

Shoʻaʻiyan, who had joined the OIPFG in June 1973, was practically 'expelled' from the OIPFG in March 1974.³⁰ He relied on his widespread connections to survive.³¹ A most wanted man and without support, he wrote his open letters in the corners of city parks and buried them in remote areas on the outskirts of Tehran for posterity.³² His last meeting with Ashraf on 8 September 1974 at 14:00,³³ documented in his *Sixth Open Letter to the Fada'i Guerrillas*, reports Ashraf's statement:

> We cannot be together in one organisation. But we are not each other's immediate enemies either. *Of course, if things lead to a confrontation — whose day will inevitably come — then we will stand facing each other.*³⁴

Reciprocating Ashraf's threat, Shoʻaʻiyan adamantly rejects being a Fada'i member.³⁵

After his departure from the Fada'iyan and for almost the next two years, Shoʻaʻiyan mostly stayed in the apartment of his friend Azam Haidarian and her husband Touraj who took some of this writings to Mazdak Publishers in Europe. Most of his time was spent rewriting and editing his works and, above all, *Revolution*.³⁶ He also frequented a certain Fada'i base (of non-militants) in which some of his friends from older times lived.³⁷ But obviously this does not mean that he was once again in contact with the OIPFG. Eventually, however, in the morning of Thursday, 4 February 1976 in Estakhr Street in central Tehran, after firing a single shot at the police officer who had stopped him and finding out that his handgun was jammed, he committed suicide by swallowing a cyanide capsule.[38] His body was taken to the Anti-Terrorist Joint Task Force prison in central Tehran and shown to his imprisoned comrades for identification.

The Thesis of the United Front and the Pathology of Stalinism

Sho'a'iyan's early admiration for, and later bitter relations with, the OIPFG, along with the original importance he attributed to the necessity of creating a liberation front, led him to a systematic investigation into the plague of sectarianism and Stalinism within the Iranian Left.

His admiration for the toppled patriotic Premier Dr Mohammed Mosaddeq, whom Sho'a'iyan calls 'the wise and audacious leader of the Iranian people',[39] shows that he was inspired by the Patriotic Front, but within the Marxist discourse. His unsuccessful attempt, in the early 1960s, to unify the three most influential Ayatollahs — Shari'atmadari, Milani and Khomeini — around the issue of an economic boycott of the state's financial institutions is an early indication of his theory of the front.[40] This effort was admittedly meant to test the potential for 'civic disobedience'.[41] Sho'a'iyan's association with Muslims such as the People's Mojahedin also indicate his attachment to the centrality of the idea of the 'united front' in Iran's liberation. One's sound and critical adherence to Marxism, he held, should not impede the convergence of militants within a *front*.

For Sho'a'iyan, the *raison d'être* of the front arises from the internal plurality of the working class that is the result of the diverse relations of production amongst the various economic sectors. The working class 'enlightener' (*rowshangar*), the vanguard, must educate the class and prepare it for the revolution. The enlightener is therefore the 'educator of the class, an educator who has previously received [his or her own] education in the school of the life of the [working] class'.[42] Given his pluralistic conception of the class, Sho'a'iyan naturally accepts the need for multiple representations of the 'rebellious seeds'.[43] Thus, no single party can totalise the diversity of the working class and each party can only speak for the sector(s) it represents. This constitutes a central feature of the 'rebellious vanguard' (*pishtâz-e shoureshi*): it 'does not have a mono-organisational profile' (*chehreh-ye tak-sâzmani*).[44] The front is the alternative structure, one that weaves together and directs diverse forces within a united front, moving from the few to the many.[45] The formation of the front as a non-ideological and supra-class alliance, in his view, is a task independent from the formation of the working-class party.

Armed struggle and revolutionary consciousness constitute the conditions of the possibility of the liberation front. Here we notice that Sho'a'iyan upholds *the priority of practice over theory*. Thus, armed struggle is deemed to be the nexus of the front, so that militant groups like the OIPFG, the Mojahedin and the People's Ideal would form the front.[46] This front unifies the militant forces that fight against the reactionary-colonial forces. In the conditions of Iran at the time, Shoʻaʻiyan continues, the Fadaʼiyan and the Mojahedin should form the nucleus of the future front by cooperating with each other over their 'unified threads', starting with a special joint bulletin.[47] We must note that for Shoʻaʻiyan the OIPFG is one step ahead of the Mojahedin because the Fadaʼiyan have based their strategy on mobilising the masses.[48]

Shoʻaʻiyan's praxis-centred approach to the front was not well received by the OIPFG leadership. For one thing, Jazani, the imprisoned Fadaʼi theorist, rejected any alliance in which the leadership of militant Marxist-Leninists (read: the Fadaʼiyan) would be in doubt. Likewise, Ashraf reportedly and expectedly rejected the idea of the organisational unity of different ideologies.[49] Shoʻaʻiyan, in fact, accused the Fadaʼiyan of sectarianism, in seeing their group not as an umbrella organisation for militants, but as a party.[50]

In *Revolution* and subsequent works 'rebellion' or '*shouresh*' constitutes Shoʻaʻiyan's central concept. A 'rebellious thought' is based on the principle of the uncompromising revolution of the working masses — an idea resembling Trotsky's 'permanent revolution'. As a form of praxis, armed struggle in the liberation movements of Asia and Africa is the highest manifestation of the rebellious essence of our era. This praxis is therefore the true measure of the 'rebellious essence' (*gowhar-e shoureshi*) of liberation agents. *Shouresh*, strictly speaking, refers to the situation in which the popular resistance against exploitive and suppressive relations is not yet quite in place while the underlying social and productive relations are. Shoʻaʻiyan holds the idea (as did Jazani) that revolutionary conditions did not exist in Iran; therefore, urban guerrilla warfare should not be confused with the revolutionary war of liberation. It is nevertheless *assumed* that guerrilla movements will lead to a popular liberation uprising.[51] The unity of the revolutionary vanguards within a front, therefore, arises from the 'rebellious essence'.[52]

> There are conditions in the life-history of a class in which the vanguard neither has the freedom to deliver its message to the entire class and society nor can it submit to complaint and surrender. And this is an historical condition in which the class intends militantly to shake off its chains, but its organisational solidarity and connections are so shattered that it must start the enlivening battle of armed movement using whatever number of the connecting cords [are available]; and this is precisely the stage of sowing the rebellious seeds.[53]

Sho'a'iyan holds a curious conception of determinacy in that the revolution will happen with or without the Party (read: agency). Fidelity to the essence of revolution supersedes ideological or class belonging — being a communist or a working-class agent. A Marxist-Leninist is not necessarily a revolutionary, just as being a non-communist does not automatically amount to one's being a counter-revolutionary.[54] Through the cultural education of rebellion, the element of consciousness (*âgâhi*) brings together different rebellious classes, leading to a global revolution.[55]

If we take the 'rebellious seed' as the standard-bearer of praxis, then Leninism shows itself as the betrayal of the revolution. Sho'a'iyan's proof for Leninism's counter-revolutionary stance is twofold: Lenin rejected guerrilla warfare, and he proposed the thesis of 'peaceful coexistence' with capitalism, both of which Sho'a'iyan finds 'counter-revolutionary and treason' to the international working-class revolution.[56] Of course, the attentive reader knows that Lenin did not invent 'peaceful coexistence'; it already existed at the time. There is something cunning here for Sho'a'iyan's pathology of Stalinism: theoretically, Lenin accepted Trotsky's 'permanent revolution' (a refutation of the Stalinist thesis of the 'socialist homeland').[57] But in practice he made a concession with the British (who supported the Russian White Guards stationed in Iran) by betraying the *Jangali* movement.

This historic observation leads Sho'a'iyan to investigate further this line of policy back to its Marxian origins — as a limitation of Marxian theory. He boldly entertains this possibility:

> It seems that the criticism made of Lenin's thoughts on the party and the revolution is also pertinent to Marx himself. But for two reasons, I could not start from Comrade Marx. Firstly, I did not have sufficient knowledge in this respect [that is, Marx's thought]. And secondly, the translated works of Comrade [Marx] shows that his political works are few and especially synoptic compared to his philosophical and economic works, as if Marx's political works were only written under certain inevitable urges of responsibility. In any case, the basic reason for which I could not analyse Comrade Marx was my negligible [direct] knowledge of Marx and his ideas.[58]

Sho'a'iyan's approach attests to the practice-oriented spirit of the generation that dominated Iranian politics in the 1970s. Leninism, in Sho'a'iyan's assessment, unleashed further and future opportunism, namely Maoism, within the international communist movement. In Sho'a'iyan's idiosyncratic description, in 1975 the opportunistic abandonment of revolutionary principles, nicknamed '*showravism*' ('Sovietism'), is represented by the Stalinists in the North (the Soviet Union), the new Maoists in the East (China), the Tudehists in the West (the exiled Tudeh party leaders), and the Fada'iyan in the South. Their common denominator is the lack of revolutionary principles, internal purging of dissenting members, and opportunism.[59] Sho'a'iyan astutely observe that only by ascribing Soviet policies to a fictitious working-class politics can one delude oneself about the reactionary nature of the Soviet Union. As such, he holds, the Tudeh Party had never been a working-class party, not even before the 1953 coup,[60] a point the founders of the OIPFG failed to understand.[61] In fact, while Jazani criticised the Soviet Union, he failed to identify the faulty ideological foundations of Soviet policies and thus he implicitly admitted the international hegemony of the USSR. In his pathology of Stalinism within the OIPFG, Sho'a'iyan observes that because the Fada'i leaders did not realise the Tudeh had never been a working-class party, they 'contracted' Sovietism as well. Only an unshakable stance against Sovietism through the 'weapon of critique' can immunise oneself from being transformed into a counter-revolutionary force. As expected, the OIPFG was not interested in a critique of Leninism. For the Fada'i theorists, one could not be a working-class agent without subscribing to Leninism.[62]

For Sho'a'iyan the issues raised above were historical and analytical up to a point, but he gained the unfortunate opportunity to experience it first-hand as a rank-and-file, albeit marginalised, Fada'i member. The OIPFG's Stalinism and sectarianism, Sho'a'iyan observed, had ideological roots. By 1974, the Fada'iyan conceived of themselves as a political party, which led to their sectarianism.[63] The intra-organisational life of the OIPFG, as Sho'a'iyan experienced first-hand, was Stalinist. Sho'a'iyan narrates the excuse for postponing internal democracy within the OIPFG through this dialogue: 'The movement is still very vulnerable', Ali Akbar Ja'fari, the Fada'iyan's second-in-command, reportedly told Sho'a'iyan. 'Let us grow to a certain extent and gain some strength. Then, well, anyone will be free to express any view she or he holds.'[64] Alarmed, Sho'a'iyan replied, making the following uncompromising and insightful statement:

> Dear comrade, an organisation that blocks the opinions which it does not approve at the time of weakness, once formidable will crush any brain that thinks a thought other than that which the organisation dictates.[65]

Revolution and the *Rowshanfekran*

In a rare opportunity in July-August 1973 in Mashhad, Sho'a'iyan had a chance to document his debate with the then OIPFG theorist Hamid Momeni — a published translator who knew Russian and had access to Soviet sources. This debate shows the way the secular-Left-educated and cultural class, commonly referred to as *rowshanfekran* or intellectuals, perceived of its role in the liberation movement. The term *rowshanfekr* caused a conceptual disturbance for Momeni, who deemed the 'intellectuals', following Leninist doctrines, as a parasitic subclass. Sho'a'iyan, *au contraire*, probed the issue in his own critical way, finding himself in an ideological crash course with the school-bookish and superficial notions of intellectuals of the Left of his time.

There is a context to this debate that added to its bitter exchanges:[66] in his writings in general and in the first edition of *Shouresh* in particular, Sho'a'iyan used an élitist style of prose advocated by the secular reformer Ahmad Kasravi (1890-1946). The style of writing added to the convolutions of *Shouresh*, and that angered Momeni, who deemed this issue as symptomatic of the problem caused by the students and educated classes who join a working-class movement. Momeni rejected Sho'a'iyan's distinction between *rowshanfekr* (or intellectual; literally, 'enlightened-minded'), which designates educated classes, and *rowshangar* (literally, 'enlightener'), which denotes revolutionary activists of an educated background. The distinction enabled Sho'a'iyan to undo the conflation of intellectualism with being formally educated.

Momeni criticises the 'flaws' of the concept of the 'enlightener' in another work,[67] calling it a supra-class concept and a deviation from a Marxist class analysis. He charges Sho'a'iyan that the term *rowshangar* entails seven connotations,[68] while under capitalist relations of production there can never be a freestanding layer of people. Momeni submits that all educated classes belong to the (petit-)bourgeoisie, notwithstanding the diverse class origins of educated masses.[69] This is because they all feed off the 'surplus value'. He notes: 'Such and such Harvard professor and Samad Behrangi are both intellectuals. Can one use the stereotypical term "intellectual" to refer to both of them?'[70]

In a different exchange (with the Marxist group *Setareh*) Momeni refers to the danger of intellectuals — these remnants of the abolished bourgeoisie — for socialism.[71] He admits that because of their 'congruity with the masses and their reading revolutionary literature, a small number of intellectuals... may incline towards the masses, especially the working class and its progressive ideology'.[72] These individuals are transformed into proletarian intellectuals. So they take on the responsibility of 'resolving the technical leadership of the proletarian revolution'.[73] While *rowshanfekran* in general remain an economic category, proletarian intellectuals constitute a political category. The revolutionary intellectuals must 'establish organic relations with the masses'.[74]

Sho'a'iyan remains critical of the commonplace term *rowshanfekr*, or intellectual, which has been used in political discourse and has thus gained a political overtone. As such, the term has been over-determined, having lost its other connotations. To remedy this problem, Sho'a'iyan reserves the term *rowshangar* or enlightener for the *political intellectual*.[75] In a fashion resembling the Gramscian 'organic intellectuals',[76] he holds that the enlighteners make up a layer (*lâyeh*) of a class. He states: 'Enlighteners are the products of the class and class conflict.'[77] But diverging from the Gramscian concept, Sho'a'iyan sets the enlighteners apart from the class that they represent because economically they 'do not directly participate in the process of production' and politically they function as the 'mentor [*amuzgar*] of the class'.[78] *Contra* Momeni, for Sho'a'iyan class essence (*seresht-e tabaqâti*) is not determined by class origins. Rather, it is the praxis of a class that allows the 'absorption' of the enlightener by the class. Stated differently: 'Living the life of a class determines one's class essence.'[79] In short, *class position determines class belonging*. Obviously, such a position annuls Momeni's 'arithmetical' conception of class position. In fact, Sho'a'iyan shows the contradiction in Momeni's position: how can the so-called bourgeois militant fight for the proletarian-revolutionary cause?[80]

Momeni's rejoinder entails the key point about encompassing three concepts — the 'conscious layer of the [working] class', the 'revolutionary vanguard', and the 'professional revolutionary' — within the 'enlightener', which simply means the 'revolutionary vanguard'.[81] The educated strata, for the most part, block the cause of proletarian revolution, and only a small segment are transformed into the 'greatest advocates of the masses':[82]

> The proletarian intellectuals make up only a small segment of the large layer of intellectuals. The vast majority of intellectuals simply submit to the socialist revolution without believing it in their hearts.[83]

For Momeni, Trotsky, the former Soviet leaders, Tito and Dubček are among the revolutionaries who lost touch with the masses. Such examples identify to which camp Momeni and his comrades belonged. Momeni's naïve populism can hardly be exaggerated here. In fact, he clearly defends the purging styled after the Chinese Cultural Revolution: 'Moreover, the masses' surveillance over intellectuals and especially the cultural revolution of the masses can prevent bourgeois tendencies in science, arts and politics.'[84] These lines remind us of the OIPFG's Stalinist disciplinary treatment of its members who had doubts about the soundness of armed struggle.

Sho'a'iyan replies by reiterating that the enlightener is the mentor (*âmûzgâr*) of the class, guiding the latter in the revolutionary war: 'The Party is the field of the organic solidarity of [working-]class enlighteners with one another.'[85] Sho'a'iyan maintains the internal plurality of the enlightener theoretically just as in Iran there exist several revolutionary vanguards. In effect, Sho'a'iyan's position implies that Momeni's bookish categories do not reflect or explain the real and existential conditions of Iran's militant revolutionaries. Sho'a'iyan contends that Momeni derives his position from a 'class multiplication table' that utterly ignores the complexity of the issue.[86]

Conclusion

A maverick theorist, Sho'a'iyan boldly stood face-to-face with the Fada'iyan with their rather unsettling record of undemocratic organisation and Stalinist purges. Sho'a'iyan's work, however, is not immune to criticism. His radical conception of the revolution or *shouresh* remains incompatible with the diverse social forces on which his theory of the front is predicated. He remained naïvely unaware of the danger of an alliance with religious forces without the guaranteed leadership of secular forces. The 1979 revolution proved this point to a perilous degree. His theory of 'rebellious essence' has room for further investigation and possibly some important implications for a theory of praxis.

Without a doubt, Sho'a'iyan's in-group experience as a short-term member of the OIPFG who witnessed at first-hand the undemocratic relations within the Fada'iyan made him resolute on exposing the roots of organisational Stalinism and ideological dogmatism, by tracing them theoretically back to Leninism and possibly even Marxism itself, when Marxism was transformed in the hands of inept revolutionaries from a method of critique to a canonical manual and 'religious belief'. Sho'a'iyan therefore moved against the grain of the dominant, formulaic brands of 'Marxism' of Iran. The common denominator of the various strands of the dogmatic Left is that each claim to Marxism can only rise above the others by suppressing the competing claims. Whence arise the roots of sectarianism and Stalinism. There was no forum, within the Iranian Left, for dialogue, critical engagement and mutual action.

Hence the importance of the Momeni–Sho'a'iyan debate on the role of intellectuals in the revolutionary movement. Sho'a'iyan had by experience learned the priority of praxis over theory as manifested through the dedicated action of Iran's young and educated revolutionaries in the 1970s, while his canonical interlocutor simply refused to sanction any action by anyone that did not exactly match the descriptions in his 'holy books' of Marxist-Leninist-Maoist traditions. Momeni's fascination of the formless masses and his suspicion of the intellectuals does, indeed, pave the way for a Cambodian-style labour-camp attitude towards non-conformist activists. Momeni could not see how his approach, if successfully implemented, involved the undoing of the very movement to which he belonged. Sho'a'iyan's concept of the 'enlightener' stresses the revolutionary role of the educated classes — a role that can potentially connect the socially-conscious educated sectors to the uneducated masses while retaining the relative autonomy of the two.

Sho'a'iyan's pluralistic approach — epitomised by the front — in fact captures the two major points mentioned above. The rest is of course history: for his uncanonical, critical and maverick thinking he paid a heavy price: he was ostracised and if it were not for a handful of his dedicated friends he would not have survived for as long as he did.

Let us end this short engagement by acknowledging that while recently Sho'a'iyan's works have been receiving the attention they deserve, his theory of *rebellion* as a unifying and epochal mode of praxis and its implication for the study of social movements, collective action and hegemonic front still remain unstudied.

Notes

1. In regard to new engagements with and reviews of the life and works of Sho'a'iyan, see Anoush Salehi, *Mostafa Sho'a'iyan va romantism enqelabi* (*Mostafa Sho'a'iyan and Revolutionary Romanticism*, Spånga, Sweden, 2010); Peyman Vahabzadeh, *A Guerrilla Odyssey: Modernisation, Secularism, Democracy and the Fadai Period of National Liberation in Iran, 1971-1979* (Syracuse University Press, Syracuse, NY, 2010), Chapter 6; Khosrow Shakeri, 'Sargozasht-e Mostafa Sho'a'iyan' ('The Biography of Mostafa Sho'a'iyan'), in Mostafa Sho'a'iyan, *Hasht nameh beh Cherikha-ye Fadai-ye Khalq: Naqd-e yek manesh-e fekri* (*Eight Open Letters to the People's Fadai Guerrillas: Critique of an Approach*, edited by Khosrow Shakeri Tehran, 2007), pp xxvii-xxxvi; Peyman Vahabzadeh, 'Mostafa Sho'a'iyan: The Maverick Theorist of the Revolution and the Failure of Frontal Politics in Iran', *Iranian Studies*, Volume 40, no 3, June 2007, pp 405-25; Peyman Vahabzadeh, 'Mustafa Sho'a'iyan and Fada'iyan-i Khalq Frontal Politics: Stalinism and the Role of Intellectuals in Iran', *British Journal of Middle Eastern Studies*, Volume 34, no 1, April 2007, pp 43-61; Hushang Mahruyan, *Mostafa Sho'a'iyan: Yeganeh-ye motefaker-e tanha* (*Mostafa Sho'a'iyan: The Singular and Lonely Thinker*, Tehran, 2004).
2. For a longer study of his life and thoughts, see Vahabzadeh, *A Guerrilla Odyssey*, Chapter 6.
3. Salehi, *Mostafa Sho'a'iyan*, p 74.
4. For a detailed description of his efforts to transfer to Tehran, see Salehi, *Mostafa Sho'a'iyan*, pp 76-94.
5. Mostafa Sho'a'iyan, *Shesh nameh-ye sargoshadeh beh Sazman-e Charikha-yi Fada'i-ye Khalq-e Iran* (*Six Open Letters to the Organisation of Iranian People's Fada'i Guerrillas*, Edition Mazdak, Tehran, 1980), pp 11-12.
6. Of the three, one was royalist and the other two were Mosaddeqist and anti-imperialists. He belonged to the Mosaddeqist Parchamdar group [Editor's note].
7. Sho'a'iyan, *Six Open Letters*, p 13.
8. On Tavakkoli, see Salehi, *Mostafa Sho'a'iyan*, pp 47-48.
9. Published abroad as C Chaqueri (ed), *Historical Documents: The Workers', Social-Democratic and Communist Movement in Iran*, Volumes 2, and 5 (Florence, 1972

and 1975). For Tavakkoli's life, see the memoirs of his comrade M Zarbakht, *Gozar az toufan* (*Through the Thunderstorm*, Berlin, 2001). See also 'Benonasebat-e dargozasht-e Mahmoud Tavakkoli'. Faramoush shodeh-ye kou-ye andisheh', *Etemad* (Tehran), Special Issue, Spring 2007.

10. Sho'a'iyan, *Six Open Letters*, p 22, n 2; his work on Maleki's group was published as Volume 10 of Chaqueri (ed), *Historical Documents* (Florence, 1983).
11. Sho'a'iyan recollects that the term 'American Marxists' comes from one of the circle's analyses: Jaryan held that there was a competition in Iran between, on the one hand, American imperialism and the comprador bourgeoisie, and, on the other hand, British imperialism and the 'feudal class'. The latter represented the older imperialism on the evolutionary scale of capitalist social development; therefore the victory of the former would provide the socio-economic structures necessary for the future revolutionary stage (Sho'a'iyan, *Six Open Letters*, p 24, n 3).
12. Bizhan Jazani, *Tarh-e jam'eishenasi va mabani-ye estratezhi-ye jonbesh-e enqelabi-ye khalq-e Iran; bakhsh-e dovvom: tarikh-e si saleh-ye siyasi fasl-e avval* (*A Sketch of the Sociology and Foundations of the Strategy of the Iranian People's Revolutionary Movement; Second Part: The Thirty-Year Political History Chapter One*, Tehran, 1979), p 86. Another group whose name resembled Jaryan was the Process of Marxist-Leninists of Iran; it was created by the SAVAK as an apparently 'underground' group, to serve Iranian intelligence service's sting operation to capture the surviving, dedicated members of the Tudeh after the coup. Jazani intentionally confuses the two groups to discredit the Jaryan. Jazani repeats the charge in 'Gorouh-e Jazani-Zarifi: pishtaz-e mobarezeh-yi mosallahani dar Iran' ('The Jazani-Zarifi Group: The Vanguard of the Armed Movement in Iran', *19 Bahman Teorik*, no 4, April 1976, p 9. Hamid Momeni does the same; see his 'Shoresh na' ('Not Rebellion'), in Mostafa Sho'a'iyan (ed), *Shoresh na, qadamha-yi sanjideh dar rah-e enqelab; Pasokh-ha-ye nasanjideh beh qadamha-yi sanjideh* (*Not Rebellion, Judicious Steps on the Path to the Revolution: Injudicious Replies to Judicious Steps*, Edition Mazdak, Florence, 1975), p 6 (this was cited from a pirate reproduction by the Support Committee for the New Revolutionary Movement of the Iranian People).
13. Hamid Momeni, 'Shoresh na', in Sho'a'iyan, *Not Rebellion*, p 37. For further details regarding Jazani's accusations against Sho'a'iyan, see Peyman Vahabzadeh, 'Bizhan Jazani and the Problems of Historiography of the Iranian Left', *Iranian Studies*, Volume 38, no 1, March 2005, pp 167-78.
14. Seized and destroyed by SAVAK. It was published some years later by Edition Mazdak, Florence. A pirate edition was also published in Tehran after the revolution.
15. The author's third revised edition of the title *Rebellion* was later published abroad as *Revolution*, in a special issue of *Problems of Revolution and Socialism* (Manifestus 4, Florence, 1976).
16. Reportedly, he created the People's Democratic Front (PDF) in 1970, while maintaining contact firstly with the Mojahedin and only later with the Fada'iyan (see Behzad Nabavi, 'Razha-ye Behzad Nabavi' ('The Secrets of Behzad Nabavi'), *Hamshahri*, no 2706, Saturday, 27 April 2002. Sho'a'iyan was much closer to the

Mojahedin, however, to the extent that he had detailed knowledge about their activities (Raf'at, Interview by Peyman Vahabzadeh, 6 November 2001). For detailed information in regard to his activism in 1969-70, see Salehi, *Mostafa Sho'a'iyan*, pp 185-242.

17. Salehi, *Mostafa Sho'a'iyan*, p 187.
18. Sho'a'iyan, *Six Open Letters*, p 14.
19. Ibid, p 23, n 2.
20. Salehi, *Mostafa Sho'a'iyan*, p 227.
21. Mostafa Sho'a'iyan, 'Pardehdari' ('Exposure') in *Chand nevesheh* (*Scattered Writings*, Edition Mazdak, Florence, 1976), p 1; article individually paginated.
22. Mostafa Sho'a'iyan, *Enqelab* (*Revolution*, Edition Mazdak, Florence, 1976), p 13.
23. Salehi, *Mostafa Sho'a'iyan*, p 266.
24. Author's telephone interview with Raf'at (Vancouver, 6 November 2001). See also Salehi, *Mostafa Sho'a'iyan*, pp 269-71.
25. Author's telephone interview with Mehdi Fatapour (Vancouver, 24 November 2001).
26. According to Sho'a'iyan these documents he had lent to Ja'fari upon his joining the OIPFG were never returned to him after his departure from the group (Mostafa Sho'a'iyan, *Sheshomin Nameh-ye Sargoshadeh be Cherikha-ye Fadai* (*The Sixth Open Letter to the Fada'i Guerrillas*, Edition Mazdak, Florence, 1976), pp 35, 38.
27. Osku'i's book, *Memoirs of a Comrade*, was written, according to Sho'a'iyan, on Ashraf's orders. It contained reminiscences of her time in the PDF that never found their way into the published version of her *Memoirs*. Sho'a'iyan was denied a copy of the full version despite Ashraf's promise. See Sho'a'iyan, *The Sixth Open Letter*, pp 5, 20, 23, 34, 42.
28. Sho'a'iyan, *Six Open Letters*, p 133.
29. AK Dastan, 'Seh chehreh-ye Marksism dar Iran' ('Three Marxist Figures of Iran'), *Kankash*, Volume 1, nos 2-3, Spring 1988, p 69.
30. Salehi, *Mostafa Sho'a'iyan*, p 352.
31. Author's interview with Cosroe Chaqueri (Paris, 28 August 2001).
32. Sho'a'iyan, *Six Open Letters*, p 99.
33. Salehi, *Mostafa Sho'a'iyan*, p 367.
34. Sho'a'iyan, *The Sixth Open Letter*, p 5, emphasis added.
35. See Salehi, *Mostafa Sho'a'iyan*, pp 367-69.
36. Ibid, pp 390-91, 403.
37. Ibid, pp 423-24.
38. PSRI (Political Studies and Research Institute), *Sazman-e Mojahedin-e Khalq: az peydai ta farjam (1344-1384)* (*The People's Mojahedin Organisation: From its Origins to its Demise (1965-2005)*, Volume 1 (PSRI, Tehran, 2005), p 566.
39. Mostafa Sho'a'iyan, 'Chehellomin ruz-i dargozasht-i Mosaddeq dar Ahmadabad' ('The Fortieth Day of the Passing Away of Mosaddeq in Ahmadabad'), *Ketab-i Jom'eh*, no 29, 6 February 1980, p 10.
40. See Mostafa Sho'a'iyan, 'Jahad-e Emrooz ya Tezi Baray-i Taharrok' ('Today's Jihad or a Thesis for Mobilisation') in *Scattered Writings*.
41. Mostafa Sho'a'iyan, *Cheh bayad kard?* (*What Is to Be Done?*, unpublished manuscript), p 34.

42. Ibid, p 62. Those familiar with the thought of Antonio Gramsci can clearly see the resemblance between Shoʻaʻiyan's concept of the 'enlightener' and Gramsci's 'organic intellectual'. He must have been acquainted with the Gramscian idea through a draft of Al-e Ahmad's book on the intellectuals (*Dar khedmat and kianat-e rowshanfekran*, Tehran, 1997) which was circulated among friends as early as 1963 and partly published in *Jahan-e No* in 1966. Al-e Ahmad discusses Gramsci's notion of the intellectuals. See *Dar khedmat and kianat-e rowshanfekran*, p 15. Shoʻaʻiyan knew Al-e Ahmad personally.
43. Mostafa Shoʻaʻiyan, 'Cherikha-ye Fada'i-ye Khalq: Naqdi bar "Nimgami dar rah: Jebheh-ye rahaibakhsh-e Khalq"' ('People's Fada'i Guerrillas: A Critique of *Half a Step on the Way: The People's Liberation Front*'), in *Nimgami dar rah: Jebheh-yi rahaibakhsh-i khalq* (*Half a Step on the Way: The People's Liberation Front*, Enqelab Publisher, np, nd), p 7, article individually paginated.
44. Ibid, p 5.
45. See ibid, pp 3-4, 9, 10.
46. Shoʻaʻiyan, *The Sixth Open Letter*, p 39.
47. See Shoʻaʻiyan, 'People's Fada'i Guerrillas: A Critique', *Half a Step on the Way*, pp 4, 14, 27.
48. Shoʻaʻiyan, *The Sixth Open Letter*, pp 39-40.
49. Shoʻaʻiyan, *Six Open Letters*, p 54.
50. See Shoʻaʻiyan, *Six Open Letters*, p 55. It is interesting that after the Leninist splinter from the Muslim Mojahedin, Ashraf and Behrooz Armaghani from the OIPFG, in their newly-released taped debate with the leaders of the Mojahedin (Marxist-Leninist), Taqi Shahram and Javad Qa'edi, rejected the latter's proposal of the united popular front.
51. Shoʻaʻiyan's letter to C Chaqueri, in C Chaqueri's personal archives (unpublished).
52. Shoʻaʻiyan, 'People's Fada'i Guerrillas: A Critique', *Half a Step on the Way*, p 8.
53. Ibid, pp 7-8.
54. Shoʻaʻiyan, 'Chand naqd-i nab' ('Some Pure Criticisms'), in *Scattered Writings*, pp 27-28; article individually paginated.
55. Shoʻaʻiyan, 'An Inquiry Into a Critique', in *Half a Step on the Way*, p 13; article individually paginated.
56. Shoʻaʻiyan, *Revolution*, p 27. According to Shoʻaʻiyan, Lenin became a counter-revolutionary around 1920 (ibid, p 249, n 135), but since the thesis of 'peaceful coexistence' predates Lenin, we infer that this is not accurate.
57. In this respect, see Leon Trotsky, 'Three Conceptions of the Russian Revolution', *Writings of Leon Trotsky (1939-40)* (Pathfinder Press, New York, 1973), pp 55-73.
58. Shoʻaʻiyan, *Revolution*, p 99.
59. Shoʻaʻiyan, *The Sixth Open Letter*, pp 6-7.
60. Ibid, p 13.
61. See, for instance, Hassan Zia Zarifi, *Hezb-e Tudeh va kudeta-ye 28 Mordad 32* (*The Tudeh Party and the 19 August 1953 Coup d'État*, np, Tehran, 1979), p 33.
62. OIPFG, *Jebha-ye mottahed-e zedd-e diktatori va dar o dasteh-ye Hezb-e Tudeh* (*The United Anti-Dictatorship Front and the Tudeh Party Bunch*, OIPFG, np, May 1978), p 20, n 1.

63. Sho'a'iyan, 'People's Fada'i Guerrillas: A Critique', *Half a Step on the Way*, p 7.
64. Ja'fari as quoted in Sho'a'iyan, *Six Open Letters*, p 49.
65. Sho'a'iyan, *Six Open Letters*, p 49.
66. H Momeni and M Sho'a'iyan, *Jouyeshi piramoun-e rowshanfekr ya rowshangar-e tabaqeh-ye kargar* (*An Inquiry into the Intellectual or Enlightener of the Working Class*, Enqelab Publishers, np, nd), p 10.
67. See Momeni, *Not Rebellion*, Chapter 4.
68. Ibid, pp 102-3.
69. Ibid, pp 104-5.
70. Hamid Momeni, *Pasokh beh forsattalaban dar mored-i 'Mobarezeh-yi mosalahaneh, ham stratezhi, ham taktik'* (*A Rejoinder to the Opportunists on 'Armed Struggle: Both Strategy and Tactic'*, M Bidsorkhi Edition, Tehran, 1979), p 28.
71. Momeni, *Not Rebellion*, p 105.
72. Ibid, p 107.
73. Momeni and Sho'a'iyan, *An Inquiry*, p 2.
74. Momeni, *Not Rebellion*, p 119.
75. Momeni and Sho'a'iyan, *An Inquiry*, pp 19-20.
76. Antonio Gramsci, *Selections from the Prison Notebooks* (International Publishers, New York, 1971), pp 5-43.
77. Momeni and Sho'a'iyan, *An Inquiry*, p 6.
78. Ibid, p 5.
79. Ibid, p 7.
80. See ibid, p 16.
81. Ibid, p 23.
82. Ibid, p 26.
83. Ibid, pp 30-31.
84. Ibid, p 33.
85. Ibid, p 36.
86. Ibid, pp 44, 46.

Documents

I: Letter by the Chief of the Information Section of the Tudeh Party Organ (October 1942)[1]

To the American Legation, Tehran
17 October 1942
Sir
We hereby offer our thanks for sending us military plates and would like to mention in passing that the newspaper *Mardom* is the only anti-Nazi paper published in Iran, and, therefore, expects to be encouraged by the Allied governments through the despatch of military plates, statistics, and books and, if possible, anti-Nazi cartoons.
With the assurance of our high consideration.
Editor of *Mardom*
Signature [illegible]

Notes
1. Source: USNA/RG 84/Box 5, 1942. All notes have been added by the Editor except where noted.

+ + +

II: British Ambassador's Directives to British Consular Offices Regarding the Tudeh Party (1943)[1]

Sir
1. Most Persians seem to assume that because the Tudeh Party is pro-Russian and obviously encouraged and supported by the Russians, the British must be anti-Tudeh without qualification.

2. It is true that we are opposed to the Tudeh because it is pro-Russian; or, more precisely, because it is so much under Russian influence as to constitute at least a potential danger to Persia's independence; and there is no harm in letting this be known. But it is not true that we are opposed to the Tudeh on

the grounds of its published programme of far-reaching social reform and it is often assumed by Persians that we, as representatives of the classical example of a capitalist power, must be opposed to the Tudeh on these grounds also.

3. It is essential to correct this impression. You should point out that 'capitalist' Great Britain possesses in fact so advanced a social legislation that there is in fact no reason why the British should sympathise with an extremely backward and socially inadequate régime. There is, on the contrary, every reason, apart from the question of natural affinities, why we should actively disapprove of it. To ensure the integrity and stability of Persia has always been a major British interest, and it is one that cannot be ensured so long as Persian administrations attempt to preserve an antiquated and unjust social order. In short, even if our mutual sympathies were with extreme conservatism, we should be opposed to it in Persia as unstable and hence a menace to our Imperial interests.

4. The published programme of the Tudeh contains nothing very revolutionary. Other political parties have published almost equally advanced programmes; but, although these anti-Tudeh parties have a large majority in the Majles, they have done nothing whatsoever to better the state of the country. The reason is in part their inability to combine with one another, but also a fundamental lack of sincerity with regard to their respective programmes. In these circumstances it is inevitable that the oppressed classes of the population — that is, the great majority — should listen to the Tudeh and believe them more sincere than their opponents in the matter of social reform — as indeed they probably are.

5. In speaking on these lines you should however be particularly careful to avoid giving the impression that the British are swinging over towards support for the Tudeh. Many Persians — perhaps most — are incapable of following a logical exposition of motives, and will therefore tend, unless particular care is exercised by you, to fasten merely on what may seem to them (though wrongly) an indication of a weakening and veering of British policy. We cannot afford to do or say anything which would, by creating doubts as to our political position, have the effect of shaking the present spontaneous and growing opposition to a dangerous party. But neither can we afford to allow the belief to continue that mere unconstructive opposition is enough for us or for Persia herself. You should therefore emphasise that such unconstructive opposition, apart from being intrinsically unjust, is bound to fail in the long run. The advent to power of a party whose real allegiance is to a foreign state would be a disaster for Persia, but that disaster can only be averted by weakening the Tudeh's hold over the oppressed classes; and this in its turn can only be achieved by pressing forward with serious social reforms while the Tudeh is yet in no position to implement its own programme.

6. It follows from the foregoing — and is worth emphasising in your conversations, however obvious it ought to be — that the British disapprove of the resort to violent and illegal methods against the Tudeh. Demonstrations of popular opposition to that party are unobjectionable and indeed welcome provided they remain peaceable and unprovocative.

7. But the avoidance of even the appearance of provocation is none too easy with an opponent who relies ultimately for support upon elements other than the popular will; and extreme caution must therefore always be enjoined. Anything that can be exploited as victimisation of the Tudeh, either by the administrative authorities or by other political parties, is dangerous and at all costs to be avoided.

I am, Sir, Your obedient Servant.
[Sir] RW Bullard[2]

Notes
1. Source: FO 371/45448 (1943).
2. It may be recalled that he was close to the Labour Party.

+ + +

III: UK Foreign Office: Sir Reader Bullard's Instructions to British Consulates (1943)[1]

28 May and 6 June 1943

Tudeh Party is at present the only political party with any established party machinery and regular provincial branches. It has made serious attempts to gain popular support. It is reasonable to expect it to gain a number of seats in the elections and to provide a much needed reforming element in the Majles.

Members of the Tudeh Party and other groups of the left, provided they are not irresponsible, may in many cases be serving the best interests of their country and be far preferable to the present reactionary and obstructive elements in the Majles, and it is not in our interest that such candidates should be prevented from standing at the elections simply because they hold left views. On the contrary, candidates of good character with liberal and progressive ideas who are likely to promote reforms should be encouraged, without too close attention to electoral programmes, which in the country are apt to be vague and unstable.

Notes
1. Source: FO 371/35071.

IV: US State Department: Résumé of Tudeh Party's Programme (November 1943)[1]

Tabriz, November 1943

The following excerpts are quoted from an announcement recently issued by this society:

This party is the standard-bearer of freedom and the fundamental laws:
1. We oppose any kind of colonization policy in Iran.
2. We demand that the officials who were in power at the time of the dictatorship should be brought to trial.
3. We oppose any future dictatorship, as well as the remnants of the former dictatorship of 20 years.
4. This is the only party which aims at destroying reaction.
5. We will try to revive the constitution and execute the fundamental laws.
6. We demand as the right of the nation the revocation of the injurious laws passed during the reign of Reza Khan.
7. We intend to take away the government from the paws of the rotten class of aristocrats and commit it into the hands of the nation.
8. We will try to develop the culture and civilization of the country.
9. We guarantee freedom of speech, writing, and assembly.
10. We will aid the passage of the income tax law during the war.
11. Whatever the results of the elections may be, we will defend the interests of the nation.
12. We will energetically fight against bribery. Those giving and receiving bribes are traitors.
13. We propose the passage of a new civil service law which will give opportunity to the educated youth.
14. We favor political rights being given to young men and we oppose the attempts to prevent young students from interfering in politics.

Notes
1. Source: USNA/RG 84/Box 3/Tehran Confidential Files (1943).

V: UK Foreign Office: Proceedings of the First General Conference of the Tudeh Party (August 1944)[1]

It will be seen that the Resolution on Home Policy confirms the party's hostility to Seyyed Zia-ed-Din Tabatabai and the American Advisers. Its reference to concessions is clearly aimed at the representatives of the British and American oil companies who are now in Tehran.

The declaration of hostility towards separatist tendencies is an admirable sentiment; but few Persians outside the party are likely to believe in it, especially as the Azerbaijani delegates to the conference were allowed to make speeches in Turki.

Resolution no 5 confirms the minimum programme published in February 1944 (reported in Sir Reader Bullard's despatch under reference). The moderation of this programme is clearly dictated by the tactical needs of the party in its struggle for power rather than by ideological conviction.

The proceedings and resolutions reveal considerable dissatisfaction among the delegates at the way the party is being run. It was resolved that a purge should be carried out and an Inspection Committee was appointed to tighten up discipline and keep a watch on the Central Committee. The resolutions on finance and discipline show that the Tudeh Party is not immune from the common faults of Persian organisations, viz, lack of cohesion, inability of section and individuals to cooperate with one another, and confusion in accounts, archives and correspondence. The party appears to have some difficulty in obtaining regular payment of subscriptions by its members.

Resolution 4 calls for the consolidation of labour unions. Some progress has been made by the Tudeh Central Labour Union in bringing a number of unions under its control, and it has recently started a weekly newspaper, the *Zafar*, to urge workers to unite under its protection. The Tudeh Party in Tehran has shown considerable interest in labour troubles; it was represented in negotiations between the Anglo-Iranian Oil Company and certain of their workmen in April 1944, and it is now involved in a dispute between the street-sweepers and the Municipality of Tehran.

The published proceedings of the conference give no information as to the total membership of the party; one delegate complained that 80 per cent of the present membership was composed of veteran workers in the cause and only 20 per cent of new recruits. The nominal total of subscribers would not in any case be a reliable measure of the party's importance, which lies in its capacity to stir up excitement by inflaming any of the numerous workmen's grievances, and in its readiness to use force and intimidation to achieve its aim.

The dominating personalities at the conference appear to have been MM Ovanesian[2] and Radmanesh.[3] M Ovanesian (usually known as Ardeshir), deputy for the Northern Armenians and Assyrians, now seems to be the brains of the party. He was trained at what the local press calls 'the Sociological College' at Moscow (I cannot myself recall any institution with that name), and spent most of Reza Shah's reign in prison for Communist activity. He was one of the founder of the Tudeh Party, and at the conference was elected both to the presidential body of the conference and to the new Central Committee. M Radmanesh, deputy for Lahi Jan, was also one of those imprisoned for Communist activity by Reza Shah; he is regarded even by enemies of the party as sincere and not actuated by the desire for personal gain. He also was elected to the presidential body of the conference and to the new Central Committee of the party.

It was not to be expected that the published proceedings of the conference would throw any direct light on the relations of the party with the Soviet authorities. But the Tudeh Party's terms for the country's friendship with foreign powers (friendship with 'all freedom-loving governments on a basis of mutual respect and complete recognition of the political and economic independence of Iran') can only be interpreted as applying to the USSR alone of the great powers interested in Persia; for the Tudeh press has made it very clear that it regards the attempt by British and American companies to obtain oil concessions as a threat to the economic independence of the country.

The vigour of Russian reaction at Tabriz to the rejection of the credentials of the Tudeh-supported candidate, Pishevari, shows clearly enough the extent to which the Soviet authorities are interested in the fortunes of the party. The great majority of the delegates to the conference came from the Northern zone. It is perhaps not without interest that attempts have been made in the Tudeh press to explain away this significant fact by false accusations of repressive action on the part of the Persian authorities elsewhere. In actual fact, these authorities are everywhere too frightened of the Tudeh phantom to do anything but kowtow to it; but the positive support afforded by the Russians to the party is of course strongest in their own zone.

First General Conference of the Tudeh Party, Tehran, 1-2 August 1944: 164 out of 168 appointed delegates attended.

Of the 168 delegates all but 23 were from the Northern provinces of Gilan, Mazandaran, Azerbaijan, Khorasan, Shahrood, Samnan, Tehran, Qazvin and Zanjan; of the 23 from the rest of Persia three came from Khuzistan, seven from Isfahan and the rest from other places in the centre.

All the Tudeh deputies were delegates to the conference except Khal'atbari (expelled from the party during the conference); except for Fadakar (Isfahan) none of them represented their Majlis districts at the conference. At the first session the following committee was elected to preside over the conference: Ardeshir Ovanesian (deputy for Northern Armenians), Amirkhizi,[4] Dr Bahrami,[5] Jowdat,[6] Noureddin Alamouti.[7] Amirkhizi was selected to translate from Turki for Azerbaijani delegates who did not know Persian.

The conference passed six resolutions; the following is a summary of the resolutions.

Resolution 1: Foreign Policy: approval is given to the retiring Central Committee's policy of opposing Fascist despotism, supporting the struggle of freedom-loving nations and upholding the rightful claims of small nations.

The Tudeh Party desires Persia to have friendly relations with all freedom-loving governments on a basis of mutual respect and complete recognition of the political and economic independence of Persia.

The Tudeh Policy dislikes one-sided policies and any policy which upsets the friendship of Persia with other nations. The Tudeh Party considers that the Persian people have taken a notable part in the final victory over Fascism by enduring great afflictions and making great efforts. Persian representatives at the peace conference should be chosen from men not tainted with reaction.

The Tudeh Party will oppose combinations and arrangements which have an imperialist aspect or involve the exploitation of Persia or other nations.

The economic basis of independence must be strengthened by industrial and agricultural development.

Cultural and economic relations should be maintained with all nations, especially with friendly neighbours.

Resolution 2: Finance: the new Central Committee is to inspect all accounts at once.

The new Finance Committee is to report to the Central Committee every three months, must ensure regular payment of party subscriptions about which members have been very lax, arrange for proper budgeting and proper accounting for central and branch funds and put relations between central and branch finance committees, which have been very bad and irregular, on a firm basis.

Resolution 3: Inspection and Control: the conference found that the former committee of inspection was useless; the new one must do better and meet more frequently.

The new committee of inspection and control is to set up party discipline tribunals, stop slander and disloyal talk in the party and establish an iron discipline. The party must give it the funds and facilities needed for its task.

Resolution 4: Party Organisation: the old organisation is defective and must be reformed.

Various sections of the party organisation have not been cooperating and have been lacking in any proper division of labour; every branch and section has been acting on its own without worrying about one another or the centre.

Relations between the centre and the branches must be improved; the centre must guide the branches.

The party must be purged of doubtful elements, agents of reaction and mischief makers. Greater care in accepting new members must be exercised.

Labour unions must be developed. Officials and peasants must be organised.

The party is in favour of the organisation of women and the grant of women's rights.

Party members must have more contact with the people and reflect their needs. Propaganda has not always taken account of popular psychology and has sometimes produced results the reverse of those intended; this must be put right.

The new committee must see to all these matters.

Resolution 5: Activity of the Tudeh Parliamentary Group: action of the group in fighting Seyyed Zia, the government's illegal actions, the American advisers' illegal actions and in protecting the workers' interests is approved.

The group must make greater use of the Majlis tribune to give publicity to the party's views; it must table bills proposing reform legislation.

The Tudeh deputies must keep in closer touch with their constituencies.

The parliamentary programme published at the beginning of the Fourteenth Majlis must be regarded as a pledge to the nation and the minimum activity expected of the group.

Unnumbered Resolution: Home Policy: the machine of dictatorial government is still in the place of authority; a lawful and democratic government has not been created. Greater efforts must be made to destroy the one and create the other.

The danger of a new dictatorship now threatens the freedom of the Persian people; Seyyed Zia is involved; so are other dictatorial elements; the Tudeh Party will fight this threat. To this end, it is necessary to form a coalition of all freedom-loving individuals, parties and newspapers.

The party must vigorously oppose the grant of any economic concessions which may constrict or weaken the economic independence of the Persian nation.

The party considers the Persian people capable of managing its own affairs and is opposed to all foreign advisers from whatever country they may come.

All governments since the abdication of Reza Shah have represented the corrupt minority; the Tudeh Party will not join such governments; it will only join a genuine popular, democratic government.

The party is utterly opposed to separatist tendencies likely to impair the integrity of Persia and disapproves of propaganda which sows discord between Persian speakers and Turki speakers and between religions.

All tribesmen must be saved from oppression, their grievances must be investigated; they must be given civilisation and education. Their feelings must not be used to the profit of unclean elements.

The conference also took certain disciplinary action; it expelled Rahman Qoli Khal'atbari, deputy for Babol, from the Majlis group and from the party for attending a mourning ceremony for Reza Shah at Shahsavar, knowing such attendance to be contrary to the party's policy.

The Shahsevar committee was temporarily dissolved because two of its members attended the mourning ceremony. A member of the Resht committee, Nikravan, was expelled for weakness in the party line and cooperation with reactionaries.

The following committees were elected.

Central Committee: Noureddin Alamouti (judge; thirty-seventh in Tehran elections for the Fourteenth Majlis); Dr Mohammad Bahrami (one of the 53 imprisoned by Reza Shah for communism in 1938); Parvin-Gonabadi[8] (deputy for Sabzavar, Meshed schoolteacher and journalist, and on the editorial board of *Rahbar*); Ardeshir (Artashes) Ovanesian; deputy for Northern Armenians, founder member of Tudeh Party, frequently imprisoned by Reza Shah for communism); Ehsan Tabari[9] (on the editorial board of *Rahbar*); Iraj Eskandari[10] (deputy for Sari, lawyer, on editorial board of *Rahbar*, imprisoned by Reza Shah; nephew of late Solayman Mirza Eskandari); Ali Amirkhizi (eighty-third in Tehran elections for the Fourteenth Majlis; connected with the Tabriz Tudeh Party; in October 1943 made a speech at Tabriz about Seyyed Zia clearly directed against Great Britain); Dr Reza Radmanesh (deputy for Lahijan; editor of *Mardom*, imprisoned by Reza Shah for Communism); Mahmoud Boqrati[11] (one of the Isfahan leaders); Abdolsamad Kambakhsh[12] (deputy for Qazvin; imprisoned by Reza Shah); Dr Freydoun Keshavarz[13] (deputy for Pahlavi; editor of *Razm*).

Inspection Committee: Dr Morteza Yazdi[14] (became a communist in Germany after the last war, twenty-sixth in Tehran elections for the Fourteenth Majlis; prominent in all party matters; February 1944 on Perso-Soviet Cultural Relations Committee); Dr Jowdat (Ministry of Education employee; with Kuchek Khan; unsuccessful Fourteenth Majlis candidate for Khiav, Azerbaijan); Abdol-Hussein Noushin[15] (playwright; member of the Perso-Soviet Cultural Committee); Khalil Maleki[16] (writes in *Rahbar*); Eng Ali Ollovi[17] (one of the 40 Majlis candidates which the Tudeh Party proposed to put up for the Majlis elections, May 1943); Reza Rousta[18] (owner of the licence for the Tudeh Labour Union paper *Zafar*); Ahmad Qasemi[19] (member of the editorial board of

Rahbar); Dr Kianouri[20] (writes in *Rahbar*); Zia Alamouti[21] (writes in *Rahbar*).[22]

Notes
1. Source: Letter of the British Embassy to Foreign Office, dated 26 August 1944, FO 371/37835. The Conference was held in Tehran during 1-12 August 1944.
2. Ovanesian was 'exiled' by the Soviets after 1946 events and lived in Soviet Armenia. He was not elected to the CC at the second congress in 1948. He died afterwards.
3. Radmanesh left for exile in 1949 after the proscription of the party, lived in Moscow and Leipzig as First Secretary until he was removed in 1970. After the revolution he returned to Iran and spent a few months there before returning to Leipzig where he died on 13 February 1984.
4. Amirkhizi lived in exile in Moscow after the proscription of the party and died there just before the revolution.
5. Bahrami was Arrested in 1955, condemned to death, but recanted and was freed after a while. He died soon thereafter, apparently due to depression.
6. Jowdat was imprisoned after the proscription of the party, he was whisked out of prison and lived in the underground till he went into exile in Moscow, and later to Leipzig. He returned to Iran in 1979 and was arrested in the spring of 1983, recanted, and was then executed by the IRI in 1988.
7. Alamouti left the party after the Azerbaijan crisis and in 1961 became Minister of Justice in Dr Amini's government.
8. Parvin-Gonabadi left the party after its proscription and thereafter led a scholarly life.
9. Tabari left for exile in 1948 for the USSR and remained in Moscow and East Berlin before returning to Iran after the 1979 revolution; he was arrested along with other Tudeh leaders, recanted, and published books and articles against Marxism. He died on 29 May 1987.
10. Eskandari left for exile in 1947 and live in Paris until early 1951 before he was expelled by the French government upon the demand of Premier Ala. He lived in Vienna, Moscow and Leipzig. In 1970 he replaced Dr Radmanesh as First Secretary, but was removed in January 1979 because he refused the Soviets the offer for an Afghan-like policy in Iran. He visited Iran after the revolution, but was forced by the new First Secretary Kianouri to leave for Leipzig, where he died on 31 April 1985.
11. Boqrati was imprisoned after the proscription, but escaped in 1950 to Moscow, where he lived and died on the eve of the revolution.
12. Kambakhsh went underground and was whisked out of Iran by the KGB on Stalin's order. He lived in Moscow and then in Leipzig where he died on 10 November 1971.
13. Keshavarz left for exile after the proscription of the party in 1949. He lived in Moscow until 1958 when, after the republican putsch, he went to Baghdad where he ran a programme on radio in Persian. He resigned from the CC. He left for Algeria after that country's independence where he exercised his medical profession for some years before residing in his old age in Geneva. He died at the age of 100 on 6 October 2006.
14. Yazdi was whisked out of prison in 1950 and lived in the underground until he

was arrested in 1955; he recanted under pressure and torture, and died soon thereafter.
15. Noushin was arrested in 1949 and tried. He was whisked out of prison and went into Moscow exile, where he dedicated himself to scholarly work and died on 2 May 1971.
16. Maleki split from the party in 1948, founded the Toilers Party, from which he also split and founded the Third Force Party in 1952. He was arrested and imprisoned for a while after the putsch. He was arrested in 1960s again, and died shortly after his release in July 1969.
17. Ollovi was arrested in 1949, but was whisked out of prison in December 1950, lived in the underground till his arrest in 1955, and then was shot on 15 June 1959. Not to be mistaken with Bozorg Alavi, also a Tudeh personality, who died in Berlin on 18 February 1997.
18. Rousta went into exile after 1946 strikes and lived in Moscow and Leipzig, where he died in the 1960s.
19. Qasemi was arrested in 1949, but was whisked out of prison in 1950. He lived in the underground till the summer of 1952 when he went into exile. He lived in Moscow and Leipzig, where he was expelled as a Maoist in 1965 and escaped to the West and lived in Paris and West Germany till his death in the 1970s.
20. Kianouri was arrested in 1949, escaped from prison in December 1950, and lived in the underground till his departure for exile in 1954. He was made First Secretary in January 1979. He returned to Iran after the revolution and led the party in support of Khomeini. He was arrested in February 1983, recanted, collaborated with the IRI authorities, handed over his other comrades to them, and died ignominiously on 5 November 1999.
21. Zia Alamouti was arrested in 1949, escaped with other leaders, lived in the underground, and disappeared quietly from the scene after the 1953 putsch.
22. All the Tudeh deputies were elected to the Central Committee except Taqi Fadakar (deputy for Isfahan) and Shahab Ferdows (deputy for Firdows).

+ + +

VI: Soviet Embassy Report on the Tudeh Party's First Congress (October 1944)[1]

TOP SECRET
To:
Molotov, VM
Mikoian, AI
Beria, LP
Malenkov, GM
Shcherbakov, AS
14 October 1944

Report

The People's [Tudeh] Party, formed soon after the arrival of the Allied forces in Iran, now has more than 20 000 members. Like the party's provisional Central Committee, the recently elected one has its headquarters in Teheran. The party has provincial organisations: Teheran, up to 9000 members; Azerbaijan (Tabriz), up to 9500; Khorasan (Mashhad), up to 1800; Isfahan, 950; Mazandaran (Shahi), 1400; Gorgan, 87; Shahrood, 900; Gilan (Resht), 372; Zanjan, 715. In addition, there are committees in certain towns, for example: Qums, 50 members; Qazvin, 300; Duried, 100: Shwar, 15; Andimeshk, 15; etc. The party's organisations are especially small in the southern, south-western and south-eastern provinces of Iran.

The association of trade unions, with up to 50 000 workers,[2] works under the leadership of the People's Party, as does also the League of Youth. The social composition of the party is: workers 75 per cent, intelligentsia 23 per cent, peasants 2 per cent.

Its national composition is: Turkic-speakers 40 per cent, Farsi-speakers 40 per cent, Armenians, Assyrians, Jews, etc, 20 per cent.

The weak spot in the party's work is its insufficient work among the peasantry.

The People's Party has five clubs in provincial towns and one central club in Teheran. In these clubs, lectures and reports are given by the party's leading activists and study circles are carried on. At the central club, a theatrical group has been formed and plays written by party members are performed.

The party's official organ is the newspaper *Rahbar* (*Leader*), edited by a member of the Politbureau and Secretary of the party's Central Committee, Iraj Eskandari.

In order to wage a joint struggle against the reactionary measures of the government and reactionary groups and organisations, a united left bloc of newspapers has been formed, with the title Jabha-ye Azadi (Freedom Front), including 18 newspapers.

The party's CC has organised the translation of certain works by the founders of Marxism-Leninism into the Persian language.[3]

Party schools operate to prepare leading cadres for work with the CC and the provincial organisations.

During the elections to the fourteenth *Majles* (in the summer, autumn and winter of 1943-44), the party carried out much work among the masses and succeeded in getting 10 of its candidates elected.

The basic programmatic theses of the People's Party, as approved by its founding committees, were:

1. To safeguard the independence and territorial integrity of Iran.

2. To establish a democratic regime and protect all individual and social rights by proclaiming freedom of speech, publication, conscience and assembly.

3. To oppose any dictatorial or despotic regime.

4. To introduce necessary reforms in land tenure and farming and to improve the conditions of the agricultural workers and peasants, along with all the working masses of Iran.

5. To introduce radical reforms in public education and health-care, with free and obligatory schooling and the extension of all benefits of public education and health-care to the entire mass of the population.

6. Review of taxation, taking account of the public interest.

7. Reforms in the sphere of the economy and trade, development of manufacturing and mining industry and transport, expansion of the road and rail network and maintenance of this in fit condition.

8. Confiscation of all the property, movable and immovable, of the former Shah and its transfer to the benefit of the Iranian people.

The first conference of the party was held on 9 October 1942, and made some changes in the party's programme:

A: On the Peasants

1. Transfer, free of charge, of all of the Shah's property (the property of Reza Shah) and also of all government lands to the poor peasants.

2. Take over large estates and distribute them among the peasants, while the peasants clear their debts gradually and in part.

B: On the Workers

1. An eight-hour working day.

2. Introduction of a labour law through Parliament.

I: The Congress of the Iranian People's Party

The first congress of the Iranian People's Party opened in Teheran on 1 August 1944. In all, there were present 169 delegates from 49 towns and district organisations. The majority represented organisations in Northern Iran (41 out of 49): the organisations in central and southern Iran were weakly represented. Such Southern organisations of the party as those in Shiraz, Abadan, Bushehr and Kashan failed to send delegates because it had not been possible to hold party conferences there.

The congress had before it the following questions:

1. Report on the work of the provisional CC of the People's Party (by Dr

Radmanesh).
2. Report of the credentials committee.
3. The international and internal situation (by Artashes [Ovanesian]).
4. Programme and tactics of the Party (Iraj Eskandari).
5. The work of the Party's group in the *Majles* (Kambakhsh).
6. Financial report (Dr [Morteza] Yazdi).
7. Election of Central Committee and Control Commission.

The congress was opened by the oldest delegate, and old democrat, Razban, comrade in arms of the late chairman of the organisation committee (of the provisional CC) of the Party, Solayman Mirza [Eskandari].

On the eve of the congress and when it began its work, serious differences emerged among the delegates. A considerable group of delegates, comparatively young members of the Party, including a member of the provisional CC, Artashes [Ovanesian], took up a sharply negative attitude to the provisional CC. This group called the CC opportunist, described its work as politically incorrect and practically insignificant, and demanded a complete renewal of the CC's composition. Especially sharp were the attacks on the CC for its work in the *Majles* elections, of forming a bloc with former Prime Minister Qavam al-Saltaneh and others. This group demanded a change in the party's composition, which would purge it of merchants, landlords and capitalists, regardless of their views, and make it a Party of the working people.

The differences became so acute that there was fear lest the mutual discrediting and calumniating of many leading members of both groups might result in chance elements getting into the party's leadership.

The comrades engaged in work with the People's Party set about intervening in this affair, and, as a result, these differences were eliminated, and the further work of the congress proceeded in a relatively normal fashion.

In view of the particularly sharp differences over the composition of the CC, at a conference of 10 leading members (from both wings) it was agreed to nominate for the CC the following 10 persons:

1. [Dr Reza] Radmanesh
2. [Mohammad] Parvin-Gonabadi
3. Iraj Eskandari
4. [Mahmoud] Boqrati
5. Artashes [Ovanesian]
6. [Reza] Rousta
7. [Dr Mohammad] Bahrami
8. Noureddin Alamouti
9. [Ehsan] Tabari
10. [Ali] Amirkhizi

All the participants in the conference were pledged to work among the delegates for the election of these persons to the CC.

The congress provided evidence that the party had grown substantially and increased its influence on the masses, but it also showed that this influence was insufficiently consolidated organisationally and that questions of organisation needed to basic questions in the work of the new CC. Up to that time, the party's organised consolidation of influence among the peasantry had notably lagged behind.

At the same time, the congress saw the appearance of new active workers for the party such as [Ehsan] Tabari, who was nominated by the CC, and others. Indisputable recognition by the congress as good leaders of the provincial organisations was won by [Mahmoud] Boqrati, [Mohammad] Parvin-Gonabadi, Noureddin Alamouti and others. Many sensible persons emerged, speaking at the congress, who had previously been little known, and this considerably eased the task of deciding on the party's leadership, making possible a better placing of individuals.

The congress greeted warmly the public organisations of the democratic bloc, which had sent delegates (from women's organisations, from large enterprises in Teheran, from journalists, from public organisations of the intelligentsia). The work of the congress was reported in all the newspapers of the 'Freedom Front'.

Most of the reactionary and pro-British papers said nothing about the congress. Only the newspaper called *Rastakhiz*, organ of the Mihan [Fatherland] Party, came out with slanderous articles against the congress. The congress elected leading organs of the party.

Elected to the CC were:
1. [Reza] Radmanesh
2. [Mohammad] Parvin-Gonabadi
3. Iraj Eskandari
4. [Mahmoud] Boqrati
5. Artashes [Ovanesian]
6. Dr [Mohammad] Bahrami
7. Noureddin Alamouti
8. [Ehsan] Tabari
9. [Ali] Amirkhizi
10. [Abdolsamad] Kambakhsh
11. Dr [Freydoun] Keshavarz

Elected to the control commission were:
1. Reza Rousta
2. [Khalil] Maleki

3. [Abdol-Hussein] Noushin
4. Dr [Morteza] Yazdi
5. [Ali] Ollovi
6. [Ahmad] Qasemi
7. [Dr Noureddin] Kianouri
8. Zia Alamouti
9. Dr Hussein Jowdat

The congress discussed the conduct of two prominent members of the People's Party, [Rahman-Qoli] Khal'atbari (deputy of the *Majles* [from Babol]) and [Hussein] Nikravan[4] (editor of the party's provincial paper *Surat*.[5] The congress decided to expel them from the party — Khal'atbari for organising an evening of mourning on the occasion of the death of the former Shah Reza Pahlavi, and Nikravan for accepting money from a governor in the form of aid for the school headed by Nikravan's wife.

The expulsion of these two made a good impression on the party members. Immediately after the congress, the new CC held a meeting at which the CC's leading organs were elected and responsibilities were allocated among the members.

A Politbureau of five members was elected: Iraj Eskandari, Dr Bahrami, Nur Alamouti, Artashes [Ovanesian] and Amirkhizi.

To the Secretariat were appointed Iraj Eskandari, Nur Alamouti and Bahrami.

The following departments were set up:
1. Agitation and Propaganda, led by [Mohammad] Parvin-Gonabadi.
2. Organisation, led by [Abdolsamad] Kambakhsh.
3. Finance, led by Amirkhizi, Rousta and Dr Yazdi.

Boqrati was elected leader of the party's fraction in the trade unions. Radmanesh was elected leader of the youth organisation.

The elections of the CC's leading organs showed that, despite the outward elimination of differences in the party's leadership, these differences survived in concealed forms. Leadership in the Politbureau and Secretariat went to Iraj Eskandari and Bahrami, that is, two men who aspire to various ministerial combinations and wanted to enter the government. This policy was condemned by both the provisional CC and the party congress, but they succeeded in securing positions in the leadership by using their considerable influence. Dr Radmanesh, who headed the party after the death of Solayman Mirza, was relegated to the background.

II: The Position in the *Majles*

The balance of forces in the *Majles* at present is:

1. The Mihan group, headed by Dr Taheri,[6] which has about 30 deputies and is the most influential.

2. The Ettehad Melli group,[7] headed by Seyyed Mohammad-Sadeq Tabataba'i, which also has about 30 deputies.

3. The Azadi group,[8] made up mostly of deputies from Azerbaijan, which also has about 30 deputies.

4. The People's Party group — eight deputies (10 deputies of the People's Party were elected, but [Rahman Qoli] Khal'atbari was expelled from the party, and [S Javad] Pishevari's mandate was not confirmed by the *Majles*[9]).

There are also so-called 'independent' deputies, isolated persons.[10]

In September 1944, the main question before the *Majles* was what attitude to take to Sa'ed's new cabinet. Confidence was voted by 73 deputies with 11 opposing and 14 abstaining. The entire People's Party group voted against the government, along with four other deputies. The People's Party deputy Keshavarz spoke, criticising Sa'ed for weakness and indecisiveness regarding the activity of reactionary circles (the bloodshed in Tabriz, the provocative document in Semnan, etc), and for the government's inactivity in respect of the population's food. This speech made a good impression both in the *Majles* and in the city, as it was published (in an abridged version) in many newspapers.

When the new composition of the cabinet was announced to the *Majles*, the People's Party group left the hall in protest against the violation of tradition, according to which the composition of a new cabinet should be first discussed at a conference of representatives of all the groups. This cabinet's composition has been discussed only by representatives of three groups, without participation by a representative of the People's Party.

The composition of the new cabinet is basically pro-British.

The reactionaries have recently been attacking the Azadi group, which partly supports the People's Party group. It is thought that an appeal against the credentials of some more deputies from Azerbaijan is being prepared, including those of Artashes [Ovanesian].[11]

III: The Labour Movement

In August and September 1944, there were two strikes by Teheran's street-sweepers. On the first occasion, the strike ended with only a partial victory for the strikers as bribery and threats from the police succeeded in making some of the strikers give up.

The second strike proceeded in a more organised fashion. After meetings and conferences in the People's Party club, the strikers organised a march to the building of the *Majles*. All the demonstrators marched through the city, wearing beggar's clothes but in regular ranks of four, with slogans on placards. At a meeting in front of the *Majles* building they called for a representative of the *Majles*, and a delegation of the strikers was received. The following demands were presented: increased wages, provision of protective clothing, and re-engagement of all who had been dismissed for participation in the first strike.

The strike lasted for four days (2-6 September 1944) and ended in complete victory for the strikers.

IV: The 'Freedom Front' Newspapers

The 'Freedom Front' brings together at present 18 Teheran and provincial newspapers: *Azadegan, Farman,*[12] *Damavand, Rahbar, Zafar,* Razm,* Azhir, Hallaj,* Shahbaz,* Haqiqat* [?],* *Maslahat,* No-Bahar,* Rasti* (in Resht [*sic,* Mashhad]),* *Dunya-ye Emrouz,* Ateshgah* (in Isfahan),* *Shaumvr* (in Isfahan),* *Kayfaar** and *Surat.**[13]

V: The Organisation of the Mardom Party

Recently a new party, Mardom (The People), has been organised, bringing together many deputies of the *Majles* and important officials, including ministers. At the head of this party stands the chairman of the *Majles*, Seyyed Mohammad Sadeq Tabataba'i, and one of his associates is the deputy Taheri, whom the British have recently begun to promote in a big way.

Little is known about this party beyond the fact that the British are trying to make use of it, and that it has taken as its aim a struggle against the People's Party.

VI: The Conduct of Seyyed Zia al-Din Tabataba'i[14]

Whereas at first the parliamentary group Mihan and Ettehad Melli supported Seyyed Zia al-Din and there was danger that he would possess overwhelming influence, his situation has now been considerably shaken, both because of a big campaign in the papers of the democratic bloc and because of his exposure in the *Majles*.

Of interest is a small fact which characterises the attitude of Seyyed Zia al-Din. Not long ago (during the Muslim fast, when one is forbidden to eat or drink in daytime), at a session of the *Majles* the deputy Mosaddeq became unwell through fasting and asked for water. Seyyed Zia began to accuse Mosaddeq of forgetting Islam and so on, and indirectly attacked other deputies for 'turning away from religion'.

In response, there rang out from all sides a denunciation of Seyyed Zia as a 'demagogue' and 'hypocrite', and when Mosaddeq apologised for showing human weakness the deputies and visitors applauded him.

Already on 23 June 1944, at the closed session of the *Majles* (present were four deputies from each parliamentary group), the Prime Minister Sa'ed announced that the Americans were proposing that they be given the concession to exploit the northern oilfields, and when they discussed whether the American advisor Millspaugh should be deprived of dictatorial powers in economic matters, but left in control of finance, Seyyed Zia spoke up for Millspaugh. In the corridors, Seyyed Zia observed, cynically, that if Iran was deemed to be a colony, he preferred to have the Americans in charge than any others.

Recently, supporters of Seyyed Zia al-Din have contributed articles to the press in which they write that there is now going on in Iran a struggle between the fox (Britain) and the bear (the USSR), and declare that they must oppose both. One may conclude that the old British agent is showing a tendency to change masters. This could explain the coolness that the British are showing towards Seyyed Zia, who has not lived up to the hopes they placed in him — that he would become chairman of the *Majles*, and would be able to unite a sufficiently influential group of deputies, exert pressure on the government, and at a suitable moment become head of it. The British are now giving only faint support to Seyyed Zia, while strongly promoting Dr Taheri and seeking to base themselves on the new Mardom Party created by him and Seyyed Mohammad Sadeq Tabataba'i.

VII: The Political Situation in the Country

Lately, in connection with the soon expected ending of the war, moods of alarm have appeared, especially among the democratically-inclined intelligentsia. Uncertainty has arisen, fear that reaction will take the offensive when the Allied forces, and particularly the Red Army, leave Iran. The grounds for these moods are as follows:

1. The existence of talk among Iranian officers about preparing a *coup d'état* when the Allied forces go. Some candidates for the principal positions are already being named. Mentioned as head of the movement for a military coup is the chief of the general staff of the Iranian Army, General Razmara, who is hostile to the USSR.

2. Reactionary circles are organising provocative demonstrations. Thus, at the end of August 1944, a group of supporters of Seyyed Zia al-Din attacked the 'House of the Party Workers' belonging to the People's Party. Portraits of Comrade Stalin were torn up and the building was sacked and set on fire. This provocation was exposed, and some of the participants were arrested on the insistence of the Soviet command, but it has found reflection in the moods of some groups of the Iranian intelligentsia.

3. At the end of August, on the initiative of the British, a conference was held, in the South of Iran, of the heads of the southern tribes. At the meeting they

spoke, among other things, about how Bolshevism was advancing, about the danger it represented to Iran in the form of the People's Party, and about the need to fight that party.

VIII: On the Incident in Tabriz[15]

Endeavouring to unite the trade unions in Azerbaijan as they were already united in Teheran, the People's Party accepted a proposal from Khalil Inkilat, one of the leaders of the trade unions that were against unity with the unions led by the People's Party, for a demonstration by him in Tabriz against the head of the unions, Yousef [Eftekhari], who was pursuing a divisive policy, in the expectation that this would facilitate unification. Khalil Enqelab was sent to Tabriz, but, instead of demonstrating for unity, he adopted a line which deepened the split and put forward provocative slogans. When the authorities tried to arrest him, he hid in the trade union building. Members of his trade union organisation tried to defend Enqelab. Among them was the provocateur Brazandeh, who fired on the police. In the skirmish that followed eight workers were killed and 26 wounded. Only one policeman was wounded.

The reactionary press of course blamed the provocation on the People's Party. The party came out against the provocative actions of Khalil Enqelab and also against the behaviour of the police in firing on unarmed workers. All the left-wing papers decided to wage a campaign for a rigorous investigation of the killings in Tabriz and punishment of the police officers who ordered the shooting.

Khalil Enqelab was arrested. His associate Alizade denounced Khalil [Enqelab] and Yousef [Eftekhari] before the members of their trade unions and called for trade union unity. Reactionary circles called for Alizade to be expelled, calling him a provocateur trying to hinder unity. The workers' mood turned in favour of unity, and it is probable that this will be attained in the near future. Yousef [Eftekhari] also tried to hinder unity, but his influence has sharply declined.

IX: What the British are Doing in the South of Iran

In the South of Iran, the British have unceremoniously taken the Iranian administration in hand, and in particular are supervising its business relations with the Soviet representatives.

In Hamedan district (40 kilometres west of Ahwaz)[16] there is an agricultural estate belonging to the state, called Keshavarzi, with a turnover of up to 12 to 15 million touman. This enterprise is working at a loss. In the past year, the shortfall came to nine million toumans. The head of the estate was appointed by the British Colonel Noel, an important [British] Intelligence Officer. The officer in the East has first engaged in agriculture, as he says, only in the sixth decade of his life. Many years ago, he operated in Iran, then in India. He was connected with the Arab tribes of Iraq and Iran. His estate has become a centre of pilgrimage for many local Iranian officials. Coming on the pretext of a hunting trip, they receive instructions from Noel and report to him about their doings. He is also visited by Arabs from Iraq.

In Khuzistan (of which Ahwaz is the chief town), the British Consul, Colonel Fletcher, assembled the local officials and told them that, if they did not carry out his demands, he would send them to such unpleasant places as Bushire [Boushehr] and Bandar Abbas.

After this declaration, even the Governor-General, first calling on the Soviet Consul, went straight to Fletcher and complained of his words. Fletcher himself never goes to see the Governor-General. The head of the town of Ahwaz was removed from office because, without Fletcher's previous agreement, he twice discussed with the Soviet Consul the public services of his town and failed to report to Fletcher on these talks.

In the Tenth Division of the Iranian Army, quartered in Khuzistan, an order was issued forbidding officers (not to mention soldiers) to talk with Russians.

The merchants of Khuzistan have been forbidden to send their goods further north than Qum, lest these goods be used by the Soviet administration.

Against the growing danger from the People's Party, which is striving to strengthen its organisation in the South, the British are creating a party of their own, utilising primarily the clergy. In Khuzistan, the mullahs have organised a 'Strengthening of Islam Party' and are making anti-Soviet propaganda. They have denounced the People's Party as 'Bolshevist'. In some places, the organisations of the People's Party and its trade unions have actually been banned.

Notes

1. Source: Unsigned report by a Soviet official in Iran in 1944; RTsKhIDNI, 17/128/818; translated from Russian by Brian Pearce. I have corrected the misspelling of Persian names and added first names, etc; for cities' names I have used standard spellings.
2. This figure is, of course, an exaggeration, as, for instance, the majority of Iranian industrial workers in the oil industry were not members of Tudeh unions, nor in light industries as in Isfahan and Mazandaran.
3. The number of translations was meagre, most of which had been already translated by the ICP in the previous decades. The pamphlet most read by Tudeh party members as an introduction to 'Marxism-Leninism' had been written by the Franco-Hungarian Communist Georges Politzer, *Principes élémentaires de philosophie* (*Elementary Principles of Philosophy*). The translation of the first volume of *Das Kapital* was published only on the eve of the 1979 revolution.
4. An old-time Communist who had spent time in prison before 1941 and leader of Tudeh branch in Gilan.
5. This was published in the 1940s as a Tudeh paper.
6. An arch-reactionary, pro-British deputy from Yazd.

7. Conservatives.
8. Mostly landlords and conservatives.
9. His credential was rejected by 48 against 48 votes.
10. Curiously, the report makes no mention of Dr Mohammad Mosaddeq, the most influential of the deputies who led the progressive independents, with whom Tudeh deputies at times voted.
11. His was confirmed.
12. Later a right-wing newspaper, close to the Royal Court, whose editor participated in the 1953 putsch.
13. Those marked with an asterisk are not included in a list provided by *Damavand* (2/5/1322, 24 July 1943). Instead the following are listed also as founders of the Front: *Bakhtar, Tajaddod-e Iran, Khorshid-e Iran, Setareh, Seda-ye Iran, Mardom, Nejat-e Iran, Mohit*. See JAMI, *Goashteh cheragh-e rah-e ayandeh* (Tehran, 1983), p 191.
14. Seyyed Zia had originally been a notoriously pro-British journalist before and during the Great War. He advocated the policy of turning Iran into a British protectorate, namely Curzon's 1919 Agreement which the latter signed with the pro-British Premier Vossouq. Seyyed Zia was later promoted by the British Legation in Tehran to the candidacy of directing the 1921 putsch with the help of Cossack Colonel Reza Khan, who in 1925 crowned himself as the shah.
15. Three paragraphs of the report dealing with incidents in Tabriz and not related with the Congress have been deleted.
16. Hamadan is located at a distance of nearly 400 miles north of Ahwas.

+ + +

VII: CPSU: Measures to Organise a Separatist Movement in Southern Azerbaijan and Other Provinces of Northern Iran (July 1945)[1]

Editor's Note: This decree of the Soviet Politbureau is informing the Central Committee of the Communist Party of Azerbaijan and its Secretary Mir Bagirov of the decisions taken regarding the need to organise a separatist movement in Northern Iran. The document sets up a step-by-step plan to ensure that the population in Northern Iran can be manipulated to declare independence and join the Azerbaijan SSR. Handwritten across the upper left-hand corner: 'One copy for Yemel'yanov.'

TOP SECRET
To Cde Bagirov

Measures to Organise a Separatist Movement in Southern Azerbaijan and Other Provinces in Northern Iran

1. Consider it advisable to begin preparatory work to form a national autonomous Azerbaijan district [*oblast'*] with broad powers within the Iranian state. At the same time develop a separatist movement in the provinces of Gilan, Mazandaran, Gorgan and Khorasan.

2. Establish a democratic party in Southern Azerbaijan under the name 'Azerbaijan Democratic Party' with the objective of guiding the separatist movement. The creation of the Democratic Party in Southern Azerbaijan is to be done by a corresponding reorganisation of the Azerbaijani branch of the People's Party of Iran and drawing into it supporters of the separatist movement from all strata of the population.

3. Conduct suitable work among the Kurds of northern Iran to draw them into the separatist movement to form a national autonomous Kurdish district.

4. Establish in Tabriz a group of responsible workers to guide the separatist movement, charging them with coordinating [*kontaktirovat'*] their work with the USSR General Consulate in Tabriz. Overall supervision of this group is entrusted to Bagirov and Yakubov.

5. Entrust the Azerbaijan CP(b) CC (Bagirov and Ibrahimov) with developing preparatory work to hold elections in Southern Azerbaijan to the Fifteenth Convocation of the Iranian Majles, ensuring the election of deputies who are supporters of the separatist movement on the basis of the following slogans:

a) Allotment of land to the peasants from state and large landowning holdings and awarding long-term monetary credit to the peasants.

b) Elimination of unemployment by the restoration and expansion of work at enterprises and also by developing road construction and other public works.

c) Improvement of the organisation of public amenities of cities and the public water supply.

d) Improvement in public health.

e) Use of no less than 50 per cent of state taxes for local needs.

f) Equal rights for national minorities and tribes: opening schools and publication of newspapers and books in the Azerbaijani, Kurdish, Armenian and Assyrian languages; court proceedings and official communications in local institutions in their native language; creating a provincial administration, including the gendarmerie and police, from local national elements; formation of regional, district and city anjomans, and local self-governing bodies.

g) Radical improvement in Soviet-Iranian relations.

6. Combat groups armed with weapons of foreign manufacture are to be created with the objective of self-defence for pro-Soviet people, [and] activists of the separatist movement of democratic and party organisations. Entrust Cde [Nikolai] Bulganin together with Cde Bagirov with carrying out this point.

7. Organise a Society for Cultural Relations Between Iran and the Azerbaijani

SSR to strengthen cultural and propaganda work in Southern Azerbaijan.

8. To draw the broad masses into the separatist movement, [we] consider it necessary to create a 'Society of Friends of Soviet Azerbaijan' in Tabriz with branches in all regions of Southern Azerbaijan and Gilan.

9. Entrust the CC CP(b) of Azerbaijan with organising publication of an illustrated magazine in Baku for distribution in Iran and also three new newspapers in Southern Azerbaijan.

10. Commit the OGIZ [State Publishing House] (Yudin) to allocating three flat-bed printing presses for the use of the CC CP(b) of Azerbaijan to create printing resources [*tipografskaya baza*] for the Democratic Party of Southern Azerbaijan.

11. Commit the *Narkomvneshtorg* [People's Commissariat for Foreign Trade] (Cde [Anastas] Mikoyan) with providing good paper for the publication of the illustrated magazine in Baku and also the three new daily newspapers in Southern Azerbaijan; the total press run is to be no less than 30 000 copies.

12. Permit the NKVD of the Azerbaijan SSR, under the observation of Cde Bagirov, to issue permission for departure to Iran and return from Iran of persons being sent on business connected with putting these measures into effect.

13. To finance the separatist movement in Southern Azerbaijan and also to hold elections to the Fifteenth Convocation of the Iranian Majlis; to create in the CC CP(b) of Azerbaijan a special fund of one million foreign-currency rubles ('for conversion into toumans').

6 July 1945

CC VKP(b) Politbureau

Distribution: 1-2 Cde Molotov; 3-4 Cde Bagirov; 5 Cde Kavtaradze.

Notes
1. Source: GAPPOD AzR, f 1, op 89, d 90, ll 4-5. Obtained by Jamil Hasanli. Translated for CWIHP by Gary Goldberg; http://www.wilsoncenter.org.

+ + +

VIII: Secret Soviet Instructions for a Separatist Movement in Northern Iran (July 1945)[1]

Editor's Note: A Soviet document with instructions on creating the Azerbaijan Democratic Party in provinces in Southern Azerbaijan and Northern Iran, in order to set the basis for a separatist movement.

Strictly Secret
Measures To Carry Out Special Assignments Throughout Southern Azerbaijan and the Northern Provinces of Iran
I: The Question of Creating the Azerbaijani Democratic Party

1. Immediately organise the transport of Pishevari and Kambakhsh to Baku for talks. Depending on the results of the talks keep in mind the transport to Baku of Padegan, the Chairman of the District Committee of the People's Party of Azerbaijan.

2. To create organising committees in the centre (Tabriz) and elsewhere [*na mestakh*], within a month select candidates from authoritative democratic elements from the intelligentsia, middle-class merchants, small and average landowners, and the clergy in various democratic parties, and also from non-party members and bring them into the organising committees of the Azerbaijan Democratic Party. The first priority is to create an organizing committee in Tabriz which, via the existing democratic press *Khavar-e No, Azhir, Jodat* and others, will publish an appeal to organize an Azerbaijani Democratic Party and print leaflets.

3. With the appearance of the appeal, initiative groups elsewhere will speak out in the press in its support and create Azerbaijani Democratic Party committees from the most active organisations of the People's Party and other democratic organisations and elements. Do not permit a mechanical renaming of organisations of the People's Party to committees of the Azerbaijani Democratic Party. Recommend that the Tabriz district committee and its local organisations of the People's Party discuss the appeal of the Azerbaijani Democratic Party, decide to disband the organisations of the People's Party and enter its members in the Azerbaijani Democratic Party.

4. After establishing the organising committee of the Azerbaijani Democratic Party in Tabriz the first priority is to create local committees of the Azerbaijani Democratic Party in the following cities: Ardebil', Reza'iyeh [Urmia], Khoy, Mianeh, Zanjan, Maragheh, Marand, Mahabad, Maku, Qazvin, Rasht, Pahlavi [Anzali], Sari, Shakh, Gorgan and Mashhad. Send representatives of the central organising committee to organise the committees in these cities. Systematically place positive responses and calls to join the Azerbaijani Democratic Party in the democratic press.

5. Create a press agency in the organising committee of the Azerbaijan Democratic Party in Tabriz under the name 'Voice of Azerbaijan'.

6. Organise the drafting of programmes and a charter for the Tabriz organising committee.

II: Ensuring the Election of Deputies to the Fifteenth Convocation of the Majles

1. Begin talks with deputies of the Majles who are supporting them during the elections to the Majles for this convocation with the object of nominating these deputies to the Fifteenth Convocation under the condition that they fight for the implementation of the slogans of the Azerbaijani Democratic Party.

2. Begin work to nominate candidates for deputies to the Majles from democratic elements who would fight for the implementation of the slogans of the Azerbaijani Democratic Party.

3. Review the list of deputies recommended by the Embassy in light of [these] new tasks.

4. Organise a broad popularisation of the selected candidates for election to the Majles in the press and their contacts, [and] meetings with voters.

5. Support meetings, demonstrations, strikes and the disbanding [*razgon*] of electoral commissions unsuitable for us with the objective of ensuring our interests in the elections.

6. In the process of preparing for the elections, compromise and expel from the electoral districts of northern Iran candidates nominated by reactionary circles [who are] actively operating against the candidates of the democratic movement.

7. Demand the replacement of unsuitable reactionary-minded leaders of local bodies [*vlasti*].

III: Creation of the 'Society of Friends of Soviet Azerbaijan'

1. In the matter of organizing the 'Society of Friends of Soviet Azerbaijan', use the delegates participating in the jubilee celebration of the twenty-fifth anniversary of the Azerbaijan SSR.

2. Recruit the workers of our consulates, military commandants, and their active [party] members into the organisation of the Society.

3. The organising group of the 'Society of Friends of Soviet Azerbaijan' in Tabriz is to draw up the charter of the Society.

4. To widely attract the population to the 'Society of Friends of Soviet Azerbaijan', use the press systematically to illustrate the achievements of the economy, culture and art of Soviet Azerbaijan and the historical friendship of the peoples of Southern Azerbaijan and the peoples of Soviet Azerbaijan.

IV: The Organisation of the Separatist Movement

1. Organise work to develop a separatist movement to create an Azerbaijani Autonomous District [and] a Kurdish Autonomous District with broad powers. In Gorgan, Gilan, Mazandaran and Khorasan provinces organise the separatist

movement along local [*korennyye*] questions, in particular: in Gilan Province: the organisation of public services and amenities in the cities of Rasht, [and] Pahlavi, leaving no less than 50 per cent of the tax proceeds collected from the province for this purpose; in Gorgan Province: study in the native Turkmen language in the schools; replacement of the local organisation, gendarmerie and police with Turkomans, leaving no less than 50 per cent of the tax proceeds collected from the province for public services, amenities and health in Gonbad-e-Kavus, Gorgan, and Bandar Shah; in Mazandaran and Khorasan Provinces: return of land to small and average landowners taken by Reza Shah (amlak [*saltanati*] lands).

2. Leaving no less than 50 per cent of tax proceeds collected from the province for public services and amenities of the cities of Sari, Shah, Mashhad and New Quchan. Additionally, bring to light locally such questions so as to organise a separatist movement in the above provinces. Raise the demand to conduct land reform not only in Southern Azerbaijan but in regions of the northern provinces of Iran.

V: Organisation of Anjomans

1. After creating the organising committees of the Azerbaijan Democratic Party at the same time as work is conducted to elect deputies to the Fifteenth Convocation of the Majles, develop a campaign to organise Anjomans, using the electoral enthusiasm of the population for this purpose.

VI: Organisation of Press Organs

1. To organise all the agitation work via the press, establish a publishing house for new magazines in the cities of Rasht, Reza'iyeh [Urmia] and Mahabad in addition to the existing newspapers.

[Illegible signatures]

14 July 1945

Notes

1. Source: GAPPOD AzR, f 1, op 89, d 90, ll 9-15. Obtained by Jamil Hasanli. Translated for CWIHP by Gary Goldberg.

+ + +

IX: US State Department: Report on the Tudeh Party (Extract, August 1945)[1]

16: Numerical Strength and Geographical Distribution

The following estimates of numbers of party members by regions are to be regarded as rough guides only. For even the Tudeh estimates vary greatly among themselves. By way of example, in January 1945, a Tudeh Armenian paper published in Tabriz at the time of the provincial conference there gave the party strength in Azerbaijan as being some 43 000, exclusive of Rezaieh (Urmia). Yet in June of the same year Iraj Eskandari, one of the party secretaries, estimated the strength for all of Azerbaijan at only 11 000. Perhaps he did so in order to play down the predominance of the north-western branches of the party. Another cause of confusion is the question of labor union membership and membership in the party proper. Some sources assert than union membership includes membership in the party. But the party constitution, while making no direct statement, implies the contrary. Whatever their cause, the discrepancies remain. The estimates are:

Tehran and vicinity, 15 000.
Isfahan and vicinity, 2 000.
Azerbaijan, 30 000.
The Caspian Provinces, 9 000.
Khorasan, 6 000.
Kermanshah and vicinity, 1 000.
Yazd and vicinity, 300
Fars, 300.
Khuzistan, 500.
Hamadan and Malayer, 1 200.
Qazvin and vicinity, 2 500.
Arak and vicinity, 1 000.
Qum, 200.

Numbers at other places are negligible. Thus the total is 69 000.[23] Enclosure shows known locations of party activity spotted on a map of Iran. Except for Azerbaijan (material for which was supplied by Mr Thomas Allen, sometime finance director for Western Azerbaijan), the plot is no doubt incomplete, and in particular it is believed that activity in Khorasan is more extensive than would be inferred from the enclosure alone. Nevertheless, the general picture is illuminating. It shows greatest party strength in the north-western quarter of the country, with other centers almost invariably situated on main highways. Activity is by no means confined to the north, however. The plot shows all tribal-controlled areas as completely devoid of party establishments.

In future the party can be expected further to increase its membership and further to extend the area of its activity. But its future strength will be determined largely by whether or not the organization can survive the internal stresses, as yet invisible, which may split it along geographical or ideological lines of cleavage. The party has a considerable reservoir of goodwill and sympathy among those educated young Iranians who are disgusted with prevailing decay and corruption, and who see in the Tudeh Party the only group with a positive social program. The party will lose this goodwill by continuing its present policy of violence, obstruction, and subservience to the Soviets.

Notes
1. Source: Report no R-89-45, USNA/RG 84/Confidential Files, Box 7, Military Attaché Report, 1945.

+ + +

X: US State Department: Tudeh Party Programme[1]

1: Introduction

Largely for purposes of the record, Sections 32 through 40 set forth below the aims and program of the party as contained in the constitution and other official publications. It is hardly necessary to remark that this material, like the published platform of the party, is written for popular consumption, to win friends and influence voters. Hence, its idealistic tenets offend as few interests as possible, and may or may not tell ultimate objectives. Beginning with Section 41 is a more realistic discussion of policy in the light of actual events and accomplishments.

2: Basic Aims of the Tudeh Party

1. It is the party of the oppressed classes, that is, the workers, peasants, the enlightened, the liberty-loving, the trades people and craftsmen.

2. The party stands for the complete independence of Iran and opposes any form of colonial policy (on the part of foreign powers).

3. The party stands for friendly cooperation with all liberty-loving nations toward the attainment of the rights of people and the maintenance of world peace.

4. The party stands for the establishment of government by the people; it stands for a democratic regime.

5. The party opposes such remnants of outworn social systems as pastoral economy and feudalism; it stands for a progressive, centralized economy based on the maintenance of benefits for the majority of the people of Iran. (Note: In contrast to the innocuous statements preceding it, this article is an open declaration of opposition to the pastoral system which supports many of the tribes, and the chiefs who rule them.)

3: Political Program

1. To strive for the establishment of a democratic regime which shall uphold

all individual and social rights: freedom of speech, writing and thought.

2. To oppose dictatorship and despotism.

3. To bring an end to personal grafting on the part of public servants.

4. To set up a high court for trying transgressors against the rights of people.

5. To establish the real independence of the judiciary and to effect the separation of the judicial from the executive branch of the government.

6. To abolish all laws and regulations which operate to the hurt of the masses.

7. To revise the conscription law to the benefit of the masses.

8. To revise the electoral laws.

9. To equalize all social rights; to eliminate discrimination on the basis of race or religion.

10. To establish complete religious and educational freedom for minorities. (Note: In this connection it may be observed that the party does not emphasize minority differences, but it does recognize language and cultural differences to extent of having some exclusively Assyrian or Armenian local branches.)

4: Workers and Peasants

To work for passage by the parliament of a labor law embodying the following provisions:

1. Establishment of the eight-hour work day throughout the country with payment of extra for overtime.

2. Provision of social insurance.

3. Medical treatment for injuries suffered while working.

4. Recognition of the right to organize, to strike, to bargain collectively.

5. Provision of yearly vacations with pay.

6. Prohibition of employment of children under fourteen years of age.

7. Prohibition of discrimination in pay because of sex.

8. Three months leave with pay for women employees who become pregnant.

9. Establishment of a ministry of labor.

10. Promulgation of just rules for settlement of labor disputes.

11. Establishment of a government employment bureau. (Note: Such a law was introduced into the parliament.)

The party favors the following agricultural reforms and measures for bettering the status of peasants:

1. The award of government agricultural lands to landless peasants.

2. The purchase by the government of large estates and their division among tenant farmers.

3. The granting to peasants of financial assistance by the Agricultural Bank.

4. Reform in the methods of dividing the crop with the landowner.
5. Revision of the law regarding the manner of choosing village headmen.
6. Establishment of a school and dispensary in every village.
7. Measures for the preservation of *qanats* (subterranean water channels), the drilling of wells, and the complete utilization of rivers for irrigation purposes.
8. The abolition of exactions on the part of landowners.
9. Attempt passage of a law regulating relationships between landowners and tenant farmers.
10. To secure a just distribution of necessities to villagers.

5: Craftsmen, Tradesmen, and Government Employees

The party favors the setting up of common places of work by craftsmen in order to increase production and to better their economic condition. The party seeks:

1. To revise the civil service system in order to better the living conditions of minor functionaries.
2. To promote the formation of unions of minor governmental employees.
3. To seek to have important governmental work entrusted only to those fitted for it by training and experience.

6: Rights of Women

1. Seek to have women accorded full social rights even to the extent of permitting their election to the parliament or to provincial and municipal councils.
2. To establish the economic independence of women.
3. To assist indigent mothers and small children.
4. To establish equality of rights in marriage, and a revision of the divorce laws.[2]

7: Education and Public Health

1. To work for fundamental reforms in education and hygiene, and for the passage of a law making education free and compulsory and making all educational and medical facilities available to the masses.
2. To reform textbooks and curricula.
3. To inaugurate the teaching of political science in the middle schools and universities.
4. To campaign against the social diseases and against the harmful effects of opium.
5. To oppose strongly censorship of the press.

8: Finance and Economy

1. To revise tax structure with an eye to benefitting the masses; to work for diminution of indirect taxes and complete enforcement of the income tax law.

2. To seek to establish the economic independence of Iran by establishing manufactures, especially heavy industry, to be set up by governmental effort, and by Iranian exploitation of her own natural resources.

3. To set up government guidance in economic affairs.

4. To give tariff protection for domestic products, at the same time keeping the prices of the protected [domestic] products within reason.

5. To prepare long-term agricultural, industrial, and financial plan to prevent the wealthy from fleeing the country.

6. To stabilize the Iranian currency, and to fight inflation.

7. To keep the price level down, [and] the supply abundant; to counter profiteering.

8. To combat corruption and bribery.

9. To lower rents, and to inaugurate a housing program, especially for laborers and for minor government employees.

10. To favor the establishment of cooperatives.

10: The Tribes

1. To redress the wrongs committed against the tribes during the dictatorial regime (that is, the rule of Reza Shah).

2. To change completely the tribal mode of life to an agricultural and industrial one.

Notes

1. Source: Excerpts from Report No R-89-45, USNA, RG 84/Confidential Files, Box 7, Military Attaché Report, 1945.
2. Note by translator: Introduction into parliament of a bill to give women the vote has been noted elsewhere. Women's organizations within the party exist in Tehran and in some of the provinces, their most prominent leader is Maryam Farman-Farma [Firouz], a daughter of the wealthy Qajar prince Farman Farina, now deceased.

+ + +

XI: UK Foreign Office: Tudeh Views Expressed to the British (1945)[1]

Dear Baxter

I enclose a copy of an interesting account by Miss Lambton,[2] Press Attaché, on a conversation in which she served as interpreter between two Labour Members of Parliament, Mr Parker and Mr Fraser[3] and two of the most prominent Tudeh deputies, Dr Radmanesh and an Armenian named Ovanesian. At the same time Lord Faringdon[4] was talking in French to Iraj Eskandari, the leader of the Tudeh Party.

In the morning Miss Lambton had taken these three members of the Parliamentary Delegation to the Majles, at their request. After watching the business of the Majlis for some time and (Lord Faringdon[4] told me) drawing on the incredible store of information about the deputies that Miss Lambton possesses, the Members of Parliament suggested that she should have some Tudeh deputies fetched out to meet them. Miss Lambton wisely discouraged this proposal as likely to create an undesirable sensation and suggested as an alternative that the Members of Parliament should meet a few Tudeh deputies at her house that evening.

Having obtained my approval, which I gave after consulting Colonel Walter Elliot, she organised the party which is described in her minute.

I learned afterwards that the Members of Parliament found the Tudeh deputies very mild. That is true of the Tudeh programme, but the programme is unimportant, what is important is the revolutionary technique by which the Tudeh Party are trying to disrupt the administration.

+ + +

Yesterday evening Dr Radmanesh, Dr Keshavarz, Iraj Eskandari and Mr Ovanesian, Tudeh deputies, came to my house to meet the Labour Members of Parliament. Lord Faringdon spoke in French with Eskandari and Keshavarz. I was unable to catch what they were saying because I was translating for Mr Fraser and Dr Radmanesh and Mr Parker and Ovanesian. The conversation of these two groups centred mainly on the organisation of the Workers' Union, its relations with the employers, the government and any other existing bodies. The Tudeh deputies harped a good deal upon the iniquities of the ruling class, whom they described from time to time as 'fascists'. They exaggerated somewhat, or so it seemed to me, the membership of the union, which they claimed to be 100 000, and also the numbers of industrial workers in the country, which they put at 300 000. They also claimed that the union and its branches were run predominantly by workmen as opposed to intellectuals.

Mr Parker asked Mr Ovanesian what was the number of the Tudeh Party members. He refused to disclose this, saying that conditions were such that they never disclosed the figures. Mr Fraser pointed out that the only way of measuring growth was by declaring the numbers and that workers' movements in England had had to put up with persecution and had had to make sacrifices for their cause. Radmanesh and Ovanesian both agreed that sacrifices were necessary, but that at the present time they could not disclose their numbers. Ovanesian claimed that in the villages in Azerbaijan almost all the peasants were 'sympathisers' of the Tudeh, although not actually members.

Asked what the Tudeh programme for reform was, Dr Radmanesh said of course the Tudeh had a programme, but that with the present Majles and government it had no hope of putting it into practice.

If they were able to obtain representation in the government, they thought they might be able to put a measure of it into effect. They were opposed at every turn at present, and their only possibility of action was to work for the establishment of a block in the Majles. All the Tudeh members brought up, severally, the question of the World Congress of Trades Unions and Citrine's telegram refusing to accept their delegates. They said this action had upset them and asked why it was that delegates from the Persian Workers Union, which had done so much to further Allied war aims, should not have been accepted. Their one expectation from British democracy was that a mission of, say, three or four delegates should be invited to visit England to establish contact and to exchange ideas. In this way they hoped the lot of the Persian worker and peasant might be improved. They also asked that at any future international congress of workers Persian delegates should be invited, emphasising that genuine representatives of the workers should be invited and not nominees of the ruling class. Mr Parker asked why the Persian Workers Union had not sent delegates to the World Congress in spite of Citrine's telegram. The Hungarian delegation's application, for example, had been refused and subsequently accepted.

Radmanesh replied to this that they had been too discouraged by Citrine's reply to take any further steps. Radmanesh, in reply to a question by Mr Fraser, said that the members of any delegation sent abroad by the Workers Union would be predominantly workmen.

Radmanesh claimed that at one moment the Workers Union had had the idea of inviting Russian and British representatives of workers' organisations to visit Persia. They had had to abandon this idea because of lack of funds.

Asked if membership of the Workers Union conferred any benefits other than collective bargaining, Radmanesh said 'No'. This was a great weakness in their position because pressure was put upon the members of the union throughout the country, and the employers were trying to penalise them and also sometimes offered them bribes to leave the union.

Ovanesian emphasised that the movement against Fascism and for freedom in Iran had been begun and continued by the Tudeh Party.

When the Germans were at Stalingrad, it was the Tudeh, and the Tudeh alone among the Persian people, who stood firm in their opposition to the Nazis.

Mr Parker, after describing some of his impressions of Russia, in reply to a question, went on to say that over the entrance of the big tractor works in Moscow was written: 'Discipline is everything; without discipline no plan is possible.' Discipline in Russia was very different from discipline in England. British workers would never put up with the discipline exercised in Russia. Their discipline was a self-imposed discipline. Ovanesian then said, was this not because the means of production belonged to the capitalists and not the state? If the means of production were state-owned, then, no doubt, British workers, too, would submit to discipline similar to Russian discipline. Mr Parker and Mr Fraser both emphatically said 'No'. I think the emphatic nature of their reply surprised Radmanesh and Ovanesian, but did not, I think, altogether convince the latter, who seemed to me to see matters in rather an over-simplified form: everything was either black or white.

Before the Members of Parliament arrived I had a few minutes' conversation with the Tudeh deputies. Radmanesh (who is the editor of *Mardom*) asked whether I had any complaints. So I said, as a matter of fact about international imperialism and international reaction, and I thought, though of course I might be mistaken, that they meant in this way to refer to Great Britain and British policy. Radmanesh denied this and Ovanesian supported him, saying that Great Britain was a socialist country, which they respected. What they were attacking was certain reactionary movements which are to be found throughout the world.

Radmanesh, who talked to me rather as if I was a public meeting, then complained of the venality and lack of principle of the papers which attacked the Tudeh Party. I retaliated by saying that I thought he would admit that certain of the Tudeh papers (notably *Nejat-e Iran*, alias *Hallaj*) belonged to the category of papers which would sell themselves to any buyer. He admitted this, but said that it was not their fault as *Nejat-e Iran* tacked itself on to the Tudeh.

Eskandari then said that there was a need for Anglo-Russian understanding in Iran. Interested persons (that is, fascists, reactionaries, etc) did their best to stir up suspicion and to disturb Anglo-Russian relations in Iran, and it was quite clear who benefited from this.

Meanwhile the arrival of the Members of Parliament prevented this conversation being pursued.

AS Lambton
British Embassy, Teheran

Notes
1. Source: FO 371/45446 (1945).
2. Ann Katharine Swynford Lambton (1912-2008) studied Persian and Arabic at the School of Oriental and African Studies in London, and obtained a PhD for her study of Seljuq institutions in pre-Ottoman Turkey. She was appointed press

attaché at the British Embassy in Tehran at the start of the Second World War. After the war, she lectured in Persian studies at SOAS, and was the author of several major studies on land tenure and land reform, classical Persian theories of the state, and social movements in Persia and Islamic societies. She acted as a contact between the British and Iranian governments during the Azerbaijan crisis in 1946, and advised the British government in its campaign against Mosaddeq and the national-democratic movement.

3. Herbert John Harvey Parker (1906-1987) was Labour MP for Romford during 1935-45, and for Dagenham during 1945-83; he was a junior minister in the Dominions Office during 1945-46. Tom Fraser (1911-1988) was Labour MP for Hamilton during 1943-67.
4. Alexander Gavin Henderson, Second Baron Faringdon (1902–1977) was a Labour hereditary peer.

+ + +

XII: UK Foreign Office: Tudeh's Private Hint to the British (1945)[1]

1. More moderate leaders of Tudeh Party in a recent talk with a member of the Embassy described present situation in this country as intolerable and expressed the view that no reform could be achieved until Persia's foreign policy, that is, her relations with Britain and Russia and Anglo-Russian relations in Persia were clarified. He declared that his extremists desired good relations with both countries but would oppose undue influence by either. While accusing [the British Government?][2] of supporting the present corrupt ruling class and thereby perpetuating the existing situation, he denied that his party wanted a revolution or that the people were ready for a revolution.

2. In his opinion the situation demanded a coalition government of all elements except perhaps the most extreme 'reactionary' elements of Zia and until the standard of education of the people was raised, a kind of 'directed' democracy to take the place of true democracy.

3. In answer to a question about the composition of the Tudeh Party he admitted the existence of corrupt elements who sought to use Russian support for their personal ends but asserted that the party if it came to power would turn them out.

4. Three prominent Tudeh leaders also recently approached the Persian Prime Minister and proposed to him that he should persuade Doctor Taheri, one of the leaders of the pro-government majority in power [...][3] to join forces with Tudeh and bring his followers with him in return for which Tudeh promised Sadr to see that Russia quickly evacuated north Persia altogether.

5. Dr Taheri's reaction to this was that it indicated that Tudeh felt they were losing ground. This may well be so at the moment. Party has recently become

increasingly discredited as a result of its attempt, with open Soviet support, to foment disturbances in the North and many of its members dread the day when Russian troops leave the country and have even openly advocated the retention of Russian troops as necessary.

Notes
1. Source: FO 371/45450 (1945).
2. Text unclear in original document.
3. Text unclear in original document.

+ + +

XIII: Declaration of the CC of the Tudeh Party on the Eve of the Coalition with Premier Qavam (June 1946)[1]

Fellow countrymen, nearly five years have now passed since the foundation of the Tudeh Party of Persia. During this period the Persian nation has encountered many disasters and misfortunes, but our progressive party, with true regard to its historic responsibility and the achievement of real freedom, has never relaxed its activities.

The party, with all its material and moral strength, has invited the peoples of this country to fight the reactionary elements which with corruption and ignorance have made the very foundation of our nationality shaky. The party has always been a pioneer in this struggle.

For this reason, the enemies of Persian freedom and prosperity have risen against our freedom-loving party and have striven to ruin our powerful organisation in order to re-establish despotism and oppression; they flutter like vultures over the ruins of our ancient country and cut to pieces the defenceless peoples of this country with their claws and then leave them to foreigners. To execute this purpose they prepared all their fully corrupt equipment against us and resorted to every shameless means to destroy our progressive party. The flood of calumny and accusation flew in all directions against the Tudeh Party and its leaders. They called us alien worshippers, irreligious and traitors, whereas they, protected by foreigners, sold their religion, country and nation for personal interests.

Today they are known for what they are, their secrets have been uncovered by the Persian nation. Today the Tudeh Party of Persia can, with proudly lifted head, claim that all the inadmissible accusations levelled against the party were unchivalrous and untrue. The facts as repeatedly expressed by the party in connection with the internal and foreign policy of Persia have been proved true to the Persian nation, notwithstanding the mockery and vilification of our antagonists.

If the reactionary governments of Persia had not rejected our reformist views, and if the imposed majority of the Fourteenth Majles had paid a little attention to the suggestions made by our representatives and other freedom-lovers, instead of indulging in childish enmity, the Persian government would surely not have encountered such difficulties and our political and social situation would have been other than what it is today.

Today the Tudeh Party of Persia is proud of its activities because it has resisted all such difficulties and obstacles most courageously and has pursued firmly the path towards the happiness and progress of the Persian nation. The party sent to the Majles representatives who, although small in number and faced with all sorts of difficulties, carried out their national and patriotic duties with absolute truth and courage and left the Majles, in which the 'majority' was known for the theft of cloth and sugar and as hoarders of general foodstuffs both by friend and foreigner, proud and unsullied. It is for the same causes and reasons that innumerable persons of various classes of Persians are continually joining our party and that we are gaining strength every second against the reactionaries.

Foreign troops have now left Persia and the Persian nation holds the opportunity to decide their own internal affairs and destiny without any fear of the agents of imperialism and to save the broken ship from the furious tides of events by adopting a wise policy and by using its national talents.

Changes occurred after the war and the defeat of the Fascist government in international politics, and the innumerable events in our country have once more forced us to declare openly and officially our views and political ideals in this proclamation, so that if our countrymen are still in doubt about our policy because of doubt instilled by our antagonists, then these doubts and errors may be wiped from their minds. One of the unchivalrous accusations always levelled by the enemies of the national Persian movement is that our party is a gathering of people who rely on foreigners and foreign support. Thus they have tried to show that our powerful party organisation derives its strength from a source other than the communal power of the Persian masses. This propaganda was at one time so strong that even the true patriots began to doubt so that some of them, although aware of the aims and ideas of the leaders of the party, were affected by such propaganda and looked upon us with suspicion mixed with precaution, and tried as far as possible to keep away from our party. Obviously such propaganda was not invented merely for our party and we are therefore not the first freedom-loving party to have been the target of such calumny.

The Persian nation knows very well that the imperialists, in order to dominate the countries of the world, are forced to stop any progressive movement in small countries with all their material and moral strength. They not only use their political and military powers to this end but also make use of their propaganda machine to sow the seeds of doubt, difference, suspicion and discord in order to prevent the unity of reformist and progressive elements. In this way they enforce their imperialistic plans through the ignorance and discord of the unfortunate peoples of such countries. It is very clear that if all the freedom-loving Persians unite together in the awakening of the peoples of this country and secure their true freedom by national movement there will be no chance to carry out imperialistic designs. The source of all this extensive propaganda against the Tudeh Party of Persia will easily be discovered by a little study. It is true that the Tudeh Party of Persia in its foreign policy supports friendship with the USSR but is there anyone except the enemies of Persia and those who consider this friendship to be against their personal interest or the imperialistic plans, who would say that opposition and enmity with the powerful northern neighbour are in the interests of Persia? If there is such a person, he is either unaware of political problems or he lacks a healthy mind and logic.

If we side with the elimination of differences with our neighbours it is because we do not wish to see the national talent and powers of Persia used in vain in international struggles, nor do we wish to see our country used for the malicious intentions of the world imperialists.

If we proclaim that all the misunderstandings between Persia and Russia should be eliminated and the policy of cunning and deceit replaced by that of true friendship we do not mean that we support the interests of a foreign country because powerful governments of the world are able to protect their interests without the help of others. They are well aware of the tracks played against them in the international theatres of politics. We mean that our country should not be turned into a theatre where the great nations compete or where their interests clash. Those who accuse us of supporting foreigners are ignorant of the great insult which they level at the Persian nation, because to announce that several hundred thousand workers, peasants, progressive elements and craftsmen of this country support foreigners is in itself the greatest insult to the principles of nationality and patriotism of the peoples of Persia. The Tudeh Party of Persia is not only not a supporter of foreigners, but it will also fight all those who have been paid servants of foreigners for many years and who preferred the interests of the imperialists to the true interests of their own country.

Faithful friendship and establishment of honourable relations in the interest of the Persian nation with all our neighbours are the principles of our foreign policy.

The correctness of our views has today been proved because the Persian nation has observed with its own eyes the difficulties created as a result of wrong and malicious policies of the incapable and treacherous governments in connection with our foreign policy. Others have called us negativitists and seditious, but we analysed the true fact with strong logic and informed the Persian nation with the utmost courage of the proceedings. The best proof is that when Qavam al-Saltaneh came into power, we found that good relations with our neighbours were the first aim of his policy, that he is determined to lay the foundation of Persian foreign policy on a firm and steady basis, and to initiate a number of fundamental reforms in internal affairs in connection with the freedom and prosperity of the peoples of Persia, and as it was ascertained that the Prime Minister was determined to solve the question of Azerbaijan in a logical and correct way, as appropriate to a democratic and progressive government we supported him unconditionally and unreservedly. By the closing down of the Fourteenth Majles which in itself was an obstacle to fundamental reforms in the internal and foreign politics of Persia, our party played a very important role in the creation of a new era in Persian contemporary history.

The Persian nation, in order to protect its national independence, has so far made innumerable sacrifices in the struggle with the imperialists, but these sacrifices are not sufficient for the imperialists. The gods of gold are thirsty and in order to quench that thirst, millions of Arabs, Turks, Persians and Indians, black and yellow, are not sufficient. They must labour and at the price of their dear lives and those of their children, secure continued profits for the gods. Thousands of honourable Persians must work hard and endure the burning heat of the Persian deserts, lie down at nights under the sky without any facilities and by day remain hungry so that the power of these gods of gold may be increased and the chains of Persian captivity and slavery, daily tightened.

Countrymen, in face of such conditions, which threaten our political life and true independence, the duty of each honourable and patriotic Persian and any freedom-loving party or society is that without paying any attention to class problems and party and political contentions he should falter at no sacrifice for the salvation of dear Persia, for securing Persian sovereignty over his country inherited from his honourable ancestors, and thus safeguard Persian territorial and political integrity and prepare the ground for an extensive and powerful unity of all truly patriotic peoples. The Tudeh Party of Persia, whose motto is to fight against any imperialistic activities in Persia, believes that today more than at any other time such unity is needed and has decided to strive with all its material and moral power to create a single national front composed of all freedom-loving parties and groups.

Today all class problems and individual interests should conform to one fundamental purpose and that is a free Persia, an independent, united and progressive Persia. It is of course not meant that all the unfortunate community of Persia should altogether give up their guild interests and rights and sit with hands crossed in expectation of the establishment of such a front. On the, contrary, they should not rest until they have gained their legitimate rights, and in any case they should bring their guild problems and class interests within the sphere of greater and higher aims, that is, the security of Persian national interests and the independence of the country. Of course the mere desires of a group or a union of different parties and groups are not sufficient to secure the independence, freedom and progress of Persia. These desires must be put into practice and they must come into being through a series of fundamental reforms in matters connected with economies, social conditions, education and administrative and political problems.

We fully agree with the opinion expressed by the Prime Minister, that is, until the economic condition of the majority of Persians is correctly and justly improved there is no possibility of reaping the full benefit of all the national forces and talents of the Persians in securing the true independence of Persia; and for this reason, we believe the comment given in his declaration about patriotism to be correct and logical. The true patriot is he who, in addition to endeavouring to protect the soil of his mother country, will also strive to achieve freedom, welfare, education and health for his countrymen.

If the Tudeh Party has proclaimed from the very beginning of its inception that the methods of cultivation should be improved and extensive lands purchased by the government and divided among the peasants, it is not because the party opposes the principles of ownership but it wishes to see the millions of its peasant fellow-countrymen owning land and thus raising their standard of living and improving their economic condition in order to enable them to prepare themselves to defend the independence and freedom of Persia and to train free and patriotic children for our country.

If the Tudeh Party of Persia has made efforts to improve the conditions of the workers it is not due to opposition to the owners of industry who, from the social point of view, have reached a more progressive stage than other capitalists, but because it wishes to see that this young industrial power, the extension of which is vital to our political independence, grows stronger and firmer day by day and Persian industry reaches a stage where at least the essential needs of the country may be met, thus ridding Persia of dependence on foreigners. The toilers of Persia know well that if our young industrial institutions are unable to administer their own affairs their livelihood will be danger. The industrial owners should also remember that their great profits are due to the work and perseverance of the workers who turn the wheels of our factories with able arms, and that, if they cause them to use more energy than they can afford and do nothing to protect their health, not only will the workers be unable within a short time to perform their duties, but serious harm will be done to the future generation of Persia and the young men who should in future keep the wheels of our industries turning. Thus, the great test source of our national wealth which is working power will be destroyed. We wish to see that the workers of Persia do not suffer from unemployment and that their living may be assured so that they may prepare themselves and their children to serve their country with honour. If the Tudeh Party is of the opinion that educational and health facilities should be made general, without any reservation throughout the country, it is because lack of knowledge and weakness are fundamentally responsible for social disorder. In order to increase the population and improve the general health of the future generations of Persia and in order to spread the principles of freedom and strengthen national government, the Tudeh Party regards education and health as essential.

Finally, if the Tudeh Party supports a series of fundamental reforms to improve the condition of the workers, enlightened thinkers and craftsmen, it is because the development of national strength, support of the principles of true democracy, and security of the country's independence will not be possible except by enforcing these reforms but these reforms will not be achieved except by purging the governing class of reactionary agents, the plunderers of the nation's property, thieves and bribe-takers, nor will the these aims be realised except through the combined forces of all parties and progressive individuals and their participation in political and government affairs with the object of strengthening and seriously supporting the government determined to put through these reforms.

In his communiqués, speeches and official statements, Qavam al-Saltaneh has clearly laid down his programme of reforms for the future and since his programme contains points which, when enforced, fit in with our programme, the Tudeh Party of Persia realises it to be its duty to support the progressive ideas of the Prime Minister, and by means of this announcement invites all reformists and freedom-lovers of Persia, all parties and democratic groups, to withhold no assistance or help in achieving the enforcement of the Prime Minister's progressive thoughts and plans, so that with the formation of a progressive and reformist government the important changes which are necessary for a freedom-loving and prosperous Persia may take place, and that, as a result, the Persian nation may truly rule its own destiny.

Therefore this point is now clear that contrary to what our enemies may wish to infer, the Tudeh Party's support of Qavam al-Saltaneh is in no way personal. Since we see him determined to carry out fundamental democratic reforms in Persia, and since his activities during the past few months have confirmed this belief, we realise it to be our patriotic duty to support him with all the forces at our disposal in spite of the enemies of Persia. As long as the Prime Minister remains firm in his decisions and puts into practice this sort of fundamental democratic reform, we assure him of our full support.

May freedom and the independence of Persia be perpetual victory to the struggle of the Persian nation against colonisation!

Honour to the pioneer and progressive Tudeh Party of Persia!

Notes
1. Source: *Rahbar*, 12 June 1946; translation in FO 371/52 705.

+ + +

XIV: *Pravda*: The Tudeh, Premier Qavam and the British (June 1946)[1]

A well-informed person who passed through Tiflis informed me that recently Mr Le Rougetel, the British Ambassador in Tehran, visited Qavam al-Saltaneh and endeavoured to bring pressure to bear on the Prime Minister. Mr Rougetel expressed particular personal dissatisfaction at the fact that the Prime Minister should have come to an understanding with the Tudeh Party and mentioned that it seemed that the officials of the government in Khuzistan were unable to take steps to prevent strikes occurring among the workpeople of the AIOC [Anglo-Iranian Oil Company]. He added that, as it seemed that the government had not taken the necessary steps in regard to these strikes, it was possible that a situation would develop which the Persian government would very much regret. Mr Le Rougetel opposed the inclusion in the Cabinet of representatives of the Tudeh Party, although he was not asked for his views on this matter. The Ambassador threatened the Prime Minister that, if as the result of the elections, a Majles were formed which was not acceptable to Great Britain, and especially if candidates representing the Democrat party of Azerbaijan were elected, the Persian government would have made a great mistake; the British Ambassador insisted that Qavam al-Saltaneh should request the Security Council to send a commission to supervise the elections and to assist in carrying out reforms in Persia. This same well-informed person stated that Qavam al-Saltaneh had repulsed the attacks of the Ambassador and had replied that he desired good relations with Great Britain, but was unable permit that the English should interfere in the internal affairs of Persia. The Prime Minister further reminded the Ambassador that the Persian government in future would vigorously defend the independence of the country.

Notes
1. Source: *Pravda*, 13 June 1946; translated in FO 248/1468 (1947).

XV: US State Department: Foreign Policy of Tudeh Party (August 1947)[1]

Tehran, 25 August 1947
The Honorable Secretary of State
Washington, DC
Sir

I have the honor to give hereunder a translation of a statement of the foreign policy of the Tudeh Party of Iran, as published on 11 August 1944 in the newspaper *Rahbar*, organ of the party:

1. 'The policy of Central Committee is in all its principles to fight against despotism and fascism.'

2. 'The party is in favor of amicable relations with all Allied countries during the war and in peacetime desires the friendship of all countries which fought to protect the rights of small nations, and believes that this friendship should be on equal basis. The party wishes to be friendly with the neighboring countries.'

3. 'The Tudeh Party of Iran opposes any one-sided policy of the government. The party hates the policy which favors only one of the Allied countries. This sort of policy has always been the root of misunderstanding with other countries.'

4. 'The Tudeh Party wishes to have friendly relations with all freedom-loving countries on equal terms which are based on recognition of complete independence of Iran as well as freedom of the people of Iran in their internal affairs. The Tudeh Party of Iran fights any policy which helps the colonization of Iran.'

5. 'The Tudeh Party believes Iran has had a great share in the efforts of the Allies in achieving the victory in this war and Iran should be considered an Allied nation who has fought the evils of Fascism.'

6. 'The party believes that the representatives of Iran to the future Peace Conference should be persons with honesty and love of their country and well experienced in the internal as well as the external policy of Iran.'

7. 'The Tudeh Party will not participate in any activities which will help the imperialist countries to colonize Iran or other countries and the party will fight such activities and will protect the group who fight for the independence of Iran.'

8. 'The Tudeh Party believes one of the mains steps towards the real independence of Iran and its economic development is increase in agricultural and industrial produce of Iran. Economic independence is the basis for political independence.'

9. 'The Tudeh Party of Iran believes that the Iranian nation should have cultural relations with all countries, especially the two great neighboring powers.'

Point 3 of this platform is probably directed at the United States. Tudeh deputies and newspapers of late have become critical of the Iranian government for its failure, as they see it, to put the American advisers in their place and have asserted that the great powers granted to Dr Millspaugh infringes the constitution and sovereignty of Iran. Point 4 doubtless also has the United States in mind, although the British are probably included as well.

Respectfully yours
For the Ambassador
John D Jernegan, Secretary

Notes
1. Source: USNA/RG 84/Box 5, Confidential Files, 1947.

+ + +

XVI: The Tudeh Socialist Party (January-February 1948)

A: US State Department History of the Tudeh Socialist Party[1]

Sir

I have the honor to refer to the Embassy's telegram no 14 of 6 January 1947, and to report that the Iran Tudeh Socialist Society, the dissenting faction of the Communist Tudeh Party, has apparently collapsed after a few brief weeks of controversial existence. The leader of this faction, Mr Khalil Maleki, is recently reported to have expressed his intentions of retiring from the political scene altogether and engaging in education and propaganda work in the cause of 'liberalism'.

The original split in the Tudeh Party occurred in the first week of January and was announced to the public in the form of vociferous manifestoes issued by each side against the other. The original statement of the dissenting group which took the name Iran-Tudeh Socialist Society is given as Enclosure One to this despatch. It will be noted that this statement carefully avoids any specific references to ideological differences with the parent organization but emphasizes tactical and organizational reasons for the split. A résumé of the principal points contained in the full declaration of the Socialist group, which followed the original statement, is given as Enclosure Two. This latter document was published in the newspaper *Iran-e-Ma*, which for a time seemed inclined to act as the official organ of the new group. The principal ideological aims of the Iran Tudeh Socialist Society are thus seen to be identical with those of the Tudeh Party itself. This fact caused considerable speculation among interested observers as to the reasons underlying the dramatic split in what had been hitherto a highly disciplined cohesive organization well adapted to its principal political purpose, namely the furtherance of Communist aims in Iran. In general the explanations fall under three headings as follows:

1. The first theory was that the young members of the Tudeh Party, jealous of the rigid control exercised over party affairs by such men as Dr Radmanesh, Dr Keshavarz, Dr Yazdi, and Reza Rousta, split off from the parent body in order to form an organization of their own which would be controlled by them and which would not be handicapped by the bad odor in which the prominent Tudeh leaders are held. This theory finds some support in the fact that much of the discussion of the incidents leading up to the break was centered around [sic] the election of a new Executive Committee of the Tudeh Party. The dissenting group had apparently called for new elections in which they felt they might win a greater share of control of the party organization. The refusal of the old-line members to permit these elections was apparently the incident directly leading to the schism.

2. Another theory held by many people, including General Saffari, Commander of the Tehran Police, is that the schism was merely a maneuver by which the real leaders of both groups hoped to be able to attract to the new body the liberal opinion which might find the old-line Tudeh Party too patently Soviet-dominated for its taste. In this connection it might be mentioned that the Embassy for some time has been aware of rumors that a movement was on foot to organize a left-wing group ostensibly but not actually divorced from Communist control. The names most frequently put forward in connection with these recommendations have been those of Abbas Eskandari, prominent left-wing Majles deputy, generally considered a Soviet stooge although not directly affiliated with the Tudeh Party, and Engineer Farivar, known principally as the original chief of the Iran Party, once allied with the Tudeh, whose most prominent member, Allahyar Saleh, was included in Qavam's coalition cabinet of the summer of 1946. Engineer Farivar recently returned from Europe, and his return has been linked with the new developments in the Tudeh.

3. The third and most novel explanation of the schism in the Tudeh appeared in the newspaper *Qiam-e-Iran* on 8 January. This theory held that the formation of the Iran Tudeh Socialist Society was inspired by Majles deputy Taqizadeh, acting on British instructions, the purpose of the maneuver being, presumably, to split and thus weaken the progressive movement in Iran. This explanation need hardly be taken seriously, but is an interesting example of the inclination of some groups in Iran to find a sinister British purpose in anything that happens.

The counterblast of the Tudeh Party itself against the publication of the new group's manifesto is to be found in the text of a resolution passed by the Provisional Executive Committee of the Tudeh Party on 7 January 1948. The text of this resolution forms Enclosure Three of this despatch. The Department cannot fail to notice the remarkable similarity of tone shown in this declaration to that of similar Soviet utterances castigating those who, in the Kremlin's opinion, depart from the true path.

One of the principal objectives of the newly-formed Iran Tudeh Socialist Society, if it be granted that this society represented a clean break with the old Tudeh group, appeared to be the winning over of the Iranian labor unions and other liberal organizations in the country. In this the new society was not successful. In a statement published in the newspaper *Mardom*, the organ of the Tudeh Party, the Central United Council of Trade Unions issued a manifesto unequivocally aligning itself with the Tudeh Party and bitterly criticizing the secessionist group as traitors to the common interests of the democratic and laboring elements in Iran.

Similar statements were published in *Mardom* by the 'Youth Organization' and the 'Action Committee' of the Tudeh Party.

For two weeks after the first flurry of manifestoes and mutual denunciations by the two parties there was a lull in the public mention of their affairs, and the Embassy was for a time unable to obtain any precise information which would throw light on the nature of the split or the type of activity contemplated by the newly-formed group. *Mardom* continued to launch occasional editorial blasts against the new organization while *Iran-e Ma*, which had at first shown signs of taking the part of the Iran Tudeh Socialist Society, became less concerned with the affairs. As far as can be ascertained the society established no official headquarters and published no newspapers. During the past week it has become apparent that the ITSS, whatever its original aims or the purpose underlying its creation, has failed to establish itself and is likely to fall to pieces within a very short time. The 22 January issue of *Iran-e Ma* published a statement attributed to Mr Maleki in which he said that continued activities of the ITSS would be to the disadvantage of the liberal movement in Iran, that in order to avoid weakening the Tudeh Party, he considered it wise to refrain from any further political activities.

It would thus appear that the split in the Tudeh Party, if indeed it was a genuine split, has come to an end.

George V Allen
American Ambassador

Notes
1. Source: USNA 891.00/1-2948; 29 January 1948.

+ + +

B: UK Foreign Office: Correspondence on the Tudeh Split[1]

Extract from letter dated 28 January 1948 to the FO from Ambassador Le Rougetel:

> A second proclamation has apparently been issued by the Socialists admitting that, with the cooperation of the Tudeh Party, a left-wing movement is impossible and that the Socialist Group has, therefore, been dissolved. The signatures of this proclamation include: Khalil Maleki, who is reputed to be the leader of the secessionists and who is now being violently attacked in the Tudeh press for engineering the split on behalf of British imperialism.

Burrows at the FO replied on 18 February 1948:

> We have been interested to read the account of the sudden disappearance of the Socialist Tudeh Party... We are most anxious to know as much as possible about the Tudeh Party and it would be very helpful to us if you could let us have any further information you may be able to obtain as to what has really been going on in the Tudeh Party and we are anxious to know if the brief appearance of the Socialist Tudeh Party indicates that there is any substantial body of opinion in the Tudeh Party which favour a break away from the hard Communist core.

Note by LFL Pyman at the FO dated 22 February 1948:

> This will be worth watching. A left-wing party which was not the agent of the Russians would be worth encouraging. Sir J Le Rougetel reserves his opinion as to the significance of the new party.
>
> It is perhaps worth noting that the new party continues to recognise the (Tudeh) Central United Council of Trade Unions as the only workers' organisation in Persia. It may be that they hope to capture the trade union movement from the Tudeh. Alternatively it could be their continuing link with Tudeh.
>
> Of the signatories of the manifesto Khalil Maleki was among the party of Persian journalists who visited this country in the summer of 1945. He was then on the editorial board of *Rahbar*, the principal Tudeh organ.

A note concerning the formation of new political party refers to Tehran despatch no 435 (E10557/40/34) and reports that certain members of the Tudeh Party have formed a new Socialist Tudeh Party. A manifesto has been issued setting out the reason for this and the aims of the new party. The government's reaction is cautious and opinion is reserved until more is known of the party and its activities.

Notes
1. Source: FO E 1809/25/34 (1948); FO 371/68704.

+ + +

C: Statement of Iran Tudeh Socialist Party[1]

The majority of the Provincial Committee of the Tudeh Party in Tehran together with a number of responsible elements of that party have collectively separated themselves from that party and are now carrying on their social activities under the name of Iran Tudeh Socialist Society, aiming at national, progressive and universal objectives. They invite other party comrades who are interested in reforms and other correct party methods to join them.

The reasons for this separation and the particulars of the new course of the Iran Tudeh Socialist Society's activities have been fully discussed in a separate statement for the information of freedom-lovers and in a special publication for the Tudeh Party members.

Notes
1. Source: USNA 891.00/1-1948.

+ + +

D: Moscow's View of the Split[1]

Pravda of 18 January 1948 carried a brief message from Tehran about the formation of the 'New Socialist People's Society of Iran' from among the ranks of the Tudeh Party and alleged that, according to 'Tehran Circles', the 'leader of the new group' was 'connected with the British' and was 'acting with their knowledge and consent in striving to disorganise the democratic movement of Persia'.

Notes
1. Source: FO 371/68704.

+ + +

E: US State Department: Dissension in the Tudeh Party[1]

Early in January a small group of Iran Tudeh Party members disaffiliated themselves, and announced the formation of the Iranian Tudeh Socialist Society (ITSS). In a statement to the press the new organization explained that the Executive Board[2] of the Tudeh Party had committed tactical errors, and had disregarded the majority opinion of the party. The experience of the past year, according to the press statement, has shown that realisation of the reforms supported by the majority of the party was impossible under the present Tudeh leaders; therefore, it had become necessary to break with the party. The new organization stated that it considered itself the champion of the more progressive aspects of the Tudeh Party, and would follow the principles originally laid down by the Tudeh Party. It also stated that it would support the Tudeh [trade] union, which was the only union in Iran it recognized. For its 'logic and philosophy' ITSS revealed that it took 'scientific socialism' as its guide. It held itself as the protector of the working class, especially the peasants, and promised to support Iranian industry against 'foreign monopolistic capitalists'.

ITSS concluded its inaugural statement by expressing the hope that the leaders of the Tudeh Party would remove their defects, and amend their ways so that reunion of the two movements would be possible. The Tudeh Party responded with a resolution signed by the Executive Board condemning the action of the secessionists and granting them a week's period of grace to return to the fold. The resolution scolded that Tudeh members should 'try to show more coolness, refrain from undue expectations and preserve unity in difficulties'. The schism, the Tudeh Executive Board said, was the greatest internal blow that had yet been struck at the 'fighting front of freedom-lovers'. It was also 'the ugliest and most harmful heresy'. The Executive Board as a final word said that their resolution would serve as an ultimatum to those 'who may have gone wrong ignorantly and who may have got upon adventurous road without their own knowledge'.

The reporting officer visited engineer Ismail Zanjani, one of the leaders of ITSS, at his home, and asked for an interview regarding the Iranian Tudeh Socialist Society. Mr Zanjani said he would make no statements about political policies without prior authorization from the organization's central committee. Mr Zanjani displayed a fervid anti-American, anti-British bias and gave evidence of close reading of left-wing publications. The United States, he said, had interfered in Iranian politics. Its influence was responsible for Majles' rejection of the Russian oil proposals. Qavam at the close of his career was an American agent. The United States had its own governments in France, Italy, Greece, and Turkey, and was endeavoring to put its own men in power in every country it could. The real reason for the Indonesian War, he disclosed, was that British capitalists were trying to hold on to their rubber interests in Indonesia. Mr Zanjani was reluctant to speak of the Tudeh Party. He passed over Tudeh with the comment that it had made mistakes, but he added that all parties have and that mistakes are a part of an organization's development. He made the flat statement that the ITSS was satisfied with the Tudeh Party's management of the Tudeh union. ITSS, he said, was purely a political party, and had no present intention of forming workers' unions.

The Iranian Tudeh Socialist Society started off with a whimper and ended with a whimper. A little more than two weeks after its inception, the organization had decided that 'any leftist movement without the cooperation of the Iran Tudeh Party is doomed to failure'. Some of the members of ITSS were apparently intending to retire from political activities; others were ready to reunite unconditionally with the Tudeh Party. Ministry of Labor officials on the whole believe that ITSS harbored real grievances against the leaders of the Tudeh Party. They discountenance the suspicion that the split in the Tudeh Party was engineered by Tudeh itself for the purpose perhaps of setting up a new organization free from discredit to which the Tudeh Party could gradually migrate. They believe that the split constituted a genuine revolt in the Tudeh Party and that ITSS is disbanding simply because it was unable to gather the strength it had calculated upon.

If the Ministry of Labor's interpretation is correct, the significance of the sudden rise and fall of the ITSS lies in the fact that, although there is certain internal disunity within the Tudeh Party, the established leaders retain firm control and command the backing of the great majority of the party members.

Notes
1. Source: USNA/MLR, American Embassy/RG 84/Box 120, 1948.
2. Precisely, the Provisional Executive Committee.

+ + +

F: Résumé of the Principal Points in the Declaration of the Principles of Iran Tudeh Socialist Party[1]

1. Experience has shown during the last year that the realisation of all the reforms supported by the majority of the [Tudeh] party members is impossible under the guidance of the present leaders.

2. The [Provisional] Executive Committee's decision concerning the Party Congress shows clearly that the committee in question is afraid of facing the majority opinion within the party and that it intends to influence the structure of the congress in the course of time and under more suitable conditions.

Taking the above points into consideration the undersigned were forced to separate themselves collectively from the Iran Tudeh Party and organise a new movement under the name of Iran Tudeh Socialist Society, asking their friends who are interested in reforms and in correct party policies, to join them in their endeavour. The particulars of this Society, as far as they can be definitely and precisely stated, are as follows:

1. ITSS considers itself the continuator of the course originally adopted by the Tudeh Party of Iran and will follow the principles and aims originally laid down by that party.

2. ITSS considers itself the continuator of the more progressive aspects of the Iran Tudeh Party. By this we mean that the new Society will refrain from committing the unnecessary and avoidable errors for which the Tudeh leaders are held responsible.

3. ITSS considers itself the real defender of the interests of all the toiling classes against reaction and oppression, and the pioneer in the national struggle against the influence of the imperialists. At the same time it firmly believes that the leadership of the working class is the best guide in the struggle against reaction and imperialism.

4. ITSS takes the logic and philosophy of scientific socialism as its guide, in order to avoid all sorts of hesitation or tactical error. In the meantime it should be noted that according to the very principles of this scientific socialism, our programme cannot be similar to the socialistic programmes of the progressive countries where social, economic and political conditions are more advanced than in our country.

5. We consider ourselves the protectors of the interests of the working classes, especially the peasants, and at the same time we support our national and domestic industries against the foreign monopolistic capitalists. We earnestly fight against Iran's economic enslavement and will cooperate with all anti-imperialistic party elements. In this struggle and in order to safeguard the rights of the toilers and establish the freedom of the Iranian nation, we will act within the limits of the Iranian Constitution, supporting the realisation of its spirit and the execution of its progressive and unfulfilled provisions.

6. We will try to make Iran's progressive industrialists realise the fact that the extension of Iranian industries is in their own interests, and can be achieved through the improvement of the workers' conditions and the struggle against imperialism.

7. In the meantime the signatories of this declaration always hope that in the near future the leaders of the Tudeh Party will make possible the reuniting of the two movements by amending and correcting their policies, so that unity in principles and aims may once more be established. Awaiting that occasion, we

will carry on our struggle to reach these common goals and principles through the new organisation of which the particulars are given above.

8. We promise all freedom-lovers and supporters of social justice to carry on our struggle without any deviations which can be avoided under the conditions existing in our country, which has so far been neglected by the freedom-loving movement.

9. At the same time we assure the enemies of freedom that in the future they will find us in the same groups as we have always been. By this we mean that in our struggle against these enemies we will make a common front with our friends who have remained in the Tudeh Party.

Long live the movement of the Iranian toilers and freedom-lovers.

Notes

1. Source: USNA (NND 83 2934), January 1948.

+ + +

G: Statement by the CC of the Tudeh Party[1]

Comrades: a notice was published last night on behalf of twelve party members revealing the establishment of a society called 'Iranian Tudeh Socialist Society' thus causing a split in the Tudeh Party. The Executive Body of the Tudeh cannot refrain from expressing its surprise and regret at this action which is greatly pleasing to the enemies of the Iranian people. Our party, during six years of struggle against the united forces of imperialism and reaction, has established a precious and sacred tradition. Its glorious banner has always inspired the Iranian toilers to fight for the liberation of the nation and their beloved country.

Our party, during the past six years, has made many sacrifices, and has been a training ground for heroes. It has steadfastly fought in the front lines of our social struggle, and borne the heavy burdens of that struggle. It has emerged victoriously and honorably from difficult crises. Our unity and firmness have been envied by enemies of freedom.

At this hour and under the existing circumstances, when the whole nation looks to this party and wishes to see unity and sincerity among its members, as well as more ardent endeavor in the social struggle, a few of those trained by the party, who owe their reputations and whatever prestige they may enjoy to the existence of the party and to the fact that they were considered as its servants, have indulged in an action — just at a moment when the enemy is spitefully watching us — which is criticised not only by the party members but also by the masses of Iranian nation.

It should be understood that the secession of this group is only a small incident in the history of the Tudeh Party's struggle and if it has any importance it is from the viewpoint of the dissenters who have isolated themselves from the movement of the masses.

Dear Comrades, the Executive Committee of the Tudeh Party has always tried to follow a calm and lenient policy with regard to certain members who sometimes overstepped the limits of the regulations and discipline of the party, and to allow these mistaken persons to realize their mistakes in due course.

Contrary to certain unfounded statements and rumors, the Executive Committee did not intend to take any severe measures even against those who had overlooked repeated reminders concerning their undesirable conduct. The committee has actually shown that it does not fear criticism, in order to save party unity and to observe party principles.

The Executive Committee did not intend and does not now intend to abandon this policy, which it considers to be logical and suitable to the present conditions of our society. In view of this just and wise policy, the undesirability of the conduct of those who have left the party becomes more evident.

Dear Comrades, we will all remain under the sacred banner which has been flown for six years, carrying the symbols of the struggle of Iran's toilers and enlightened elements in securing the rights of the Iranian people, and we shall always be faithful to the party traditions.

Notes

1. Source: USNA (NND 83 2934), January 1948.

+ + +

H: Proclamation of Central United Council of Trade Unions[1]

The Central United Council of the Iranian Workers and Toilers Unions, which is a member of the World Federation of Trade Unions, has always supported progressive and freedom-loving parties and has cooperated with democratic groups in the struggle against Fascism and for the establishment of democracy and world peace.

At this moment, when internal reaction and imperialistic forces are making a joint effort against freedom-loving movements and workers' organizations in Iran and do not stop short of any endeavor to suppress the Iranian democratic efforts, the Central United Council considers any form of party differences, no matter how small they may be, against the interests of the Freedom Front and the Iranian labor movement. The step taken by the signatories of the above-mentioned statement has, therefore, caused great regret to the council, which considers this action to be deplorable and declares its support of the Iran Tudeh Party, which has protected all the legitimate interests of the working classes, thus showing its sincere advocacy of the Iranian workers and toilers during the six years of its glorious struggle.

The Acting Committee of the Central United Council of the Iranian Workers and Toilers Unions

Notes
1. Source: USNA (NND 83 2934), January 1948.

+ + +

XVII: UK Foreign Office: Concern About Tudeh (March-April 1948)

A: Report on the Tudeh after the Second Congress[1]

BAB Burrows, Esq
Foreign Office,
London, SW1
31 March 1948

Dear Burrows

1. You asked in your letter E.1809/2534 of 18 February for further information about the Tudeh Party, and particularly whether there are differences within the party ranks.

2. The policy of the Tudeh organisation during the past twelve months has been to avoid public activities and to concentrate upon consolidating its organisation and recruiting reliable members.

The veil has been so tightly drawn that many opponents of Tudeh in both government and trade union circles have convinced themselves that the organisation is moribund and no longer dangerous. In point of fact, however, there is evidence to show that Tudeh has not wasted its time and that it may have the support, tacit or avowed, of some 35 per cent of the industrial population. To have obtained, and retained, this sympathy whilst the movement has been under a certain amount of pressure from the government and could not arouse enthusiasm by demonstration or positive action is a considerable achievement.

3. The trade union and political branches of the party profess, of course, to be independent but they are in fact indistinguishable, and it is through the unions that the Tudeh movement makes the greatest and most effective appeal. Its professed aims of social reform, higher standards of living and of employment, and improved medical and educational facilities, appear to the Persian worker and peasant to offer the remedy for his starved material needs. He has little faith that the existing order in Persia (the government, employers, other political parties or trade unions) will show equal interest in his wellbeing. Neither the

actual nor the potential strength of the Tudeh movement should, therefore, be underrated.

4. Few of the ordinary members of the Tudeh organisation appear to have any knowledge of Communist theories, practices or policies, and the movement does not, of course, make any public claim to be Communist; in fact, it has at times issued official denials that it is so. This is, no doubt, due in part to legislation of the time of Reza Shah, which makes the formation of Communist or Republican parties a treasonable offence. It is clear, however, that the real control of the Tudeh movement is in the hands of individuals who take guidance and instruction from Russia. This link was demonstrated during the visit to Persia in 1947 of a WFTU[2] delegation, when El Aris and Borisov admitted that their purpose was to protect Reza Rousta and to reorganise the Central United Council of the Federation of Trade Unions. Radio Moscow showed a detailed knowledge of the delegation's day to day activities and strongly supported Rousta and the Central United Council.

Recently, the Tudeh press very definitely took the side of Russia when it was a question of the WFTU's calling a meeting to consider the Marshall Plan. Rousta, Keshavarz and Radmanesh are believed to be the principal recipients of Russia's instructions.

5. Some of Rousta's colleagues in the central organisation are not entirely happy to be instruments of Russian policy. These persons do not, however, present a common front within Tudeh. Either because they are overawed by Rousta, or because they believe that there is no prospect of social progress (or personal advancement) except through Tudeh, they keep their discontent to themselves. Shortly before the WFTU delegation arrived in Persia three members of the Central Executive Committee of the Tudeh organisation (Jowdat, Fadakar and Tabrizi) seemed to be on the point of attempting to form a more moderate and patriotic faction within the Tudeh movement, but they soon had second thoughts. During Rousta's imprisonment there were rumours of dissension within the Tudeh trade union, and there were isolated cases of union leaders resigning from the Tudeh political party. In January 1948 it appeared that the vague discontent of individual leaders might be developing into collective action with the formation of the Socialist group referred to in my despatches no 12 of 14 January and no 29 of 28 January. The speedy collapse of the Socialists suggests that there was little substance in them and that their dissatisfaction with the direction of Tudeh was not sufficiently great to have significance.

Certain of the signatories to the Socialist manifesto have stated that had they found a leader or a sponsor sufficiently strong to oppose Rousta, they would have proceeded with their faction. Such reports as I have received, however, indicate that the formation of the Socialist group was not due to fundamental differences on the question of Russian control, but rather to the expression of personal rivalries or to irritation with the tight control exercised by Rousta. Since their return to the Tudeh fold the Socialists appear to have forgotten their previous dissatisfaction, and as far as is known they are loyal members of the party once more.

6. As regards Rousta himself, in spite of past mistakes made (for example, allowing Tudeh documents to fall into government hands) he is still, as far as can be ascertained, head of the Tudeh movement in Persia.

He has recently dictatorially dismissed from the organisation minor leaders for 'acting against discipline', and he has refused to permit his colleagues on the Central Executive Committee to question his decisions or request explanations. It was Rousta's personal decision to dismiss the Tudeh Provincial Council for Khuzistan and to place the Khuzistan movement under the direct control of the Central Executive Committee in Tehran. Although he has avoided public appearances since his release from prison, he retains his popularity with the working class. There is a recent rumour that, owing to pressure of work, he may delegate control of the trade union side of the movement to Jowdat.

7. The secrecy at present surrounding the movement makes it impossible to prophesy. It is known that in all industrial centres cells have been established and reliable members recruited. Tudeh enthusiasts have been placed in the railway administration, in factories, within rival trade unions, and an attempt to place them within the Ministry of Labour's headquarters and provincial administrations almost succeeded. A campaign has been opened against the Ministry of Labour and against statutory machinery for improving employment conditions and handling disputes or grievances. The time may shortly arrive when the Tudeh movement considers that it has a sufficiently strong nucleus to test the sympathies of the entire industrial population, either by an open recruiting campaign or by strike. There are, indeed, persistent reports that Tudeh will shortly initiate strikes at Abadan and Isfahan.

Ambassador Le Rougetel

Notes
1. Source: FO 371/68705.
2. World Federation of Trade Unions, a pro-Soviet international trade union organisation.

+ + +

B: Report on the Tudeh Party (April 1948)[1]

This is the fullest report on the Tudeh Party which we have received for some time. It should be copied to the Directors of Intelligence, the Petroleum Division,

Mr CF Heron Ministry of Labour, Washington, Moscow, British Middle East Office and to Information Research Department, Foreign Office Research Department and Middle East Information Department.

The picture is a disturbing one. Although the industrial population of Persia, 35 per cent of which is stated to support the Tudeh tacitly or avowedly, is a very small proportion of the whole population (say a couple of hundred thousand in a population of 12 million or 15 million), control of the industrial population would bring rewards out of all proportion to the numbers involved. Altogether apart from the effect of Tudeh control over the labour of the Anglo-Iranian Oil Company (60 000), the Tudeh Party could seriously embarrass the Central Government through control of, for example, the railway workers and printers.

Tehran is now largely dependent upon oil in various forms both for domestic heating and lighting, and for services such as bakeries, public baths and public lighting supplies. The oil is brought to Tehran by rail, and if Tudeh wanted to embarrass the government the surest way they could do it would be to cut off supplies of oil by rail and thus stop the bakeries and the supply of kerosene for domestic consumption; this would soon lead to spontaneous demonstrations by the unfortunate people. If they can control the printers, Tudeh would have the usual Communist hold over the rest of the press.

The report within speaks of possible Tudeh action to initiate strikes at Abadan and Isfahan, no mention being made of Tehran, and the intention would no doubt be, as Sir J Le Rougetel suggests, to test the strength. It is perhaps worth recalling that last time the Tudeh tried to call a strike (a general strike of Tehran workers) in November 1946 to demonstrate their strength it was a dismal failure largely owing to the resolute action of the Persian government of the time.

Perhaps the most disturbing feature of Sir J Le Rougetel's report is the third paragraph. From this it is clear that so far as Persian workers and peasants are aware of any remedy for their needs they look to the Soviet-controlled Tudeh movement for it. I have drawn attention in a draft recently submitted on the papers about constitutional reform in Persia, to the prospect that next summer, when the next Persian elections are due, there will be a situation in which the Tudeh Party will be able to fight the elections as the only party with a genuine programme of reform. The draft suggested that Sir J Le Rougetel be asked if there is nothing that we and the Americans can do to stimulate the formation of a Progressive Party not under Soviet control in order to fill this alarming vacuum. The draft might be linked to this new report from Tehran.

The report within further confirms that we were on the right lines in initiating the joint Anglo-American enquiry now in progress as to what reform measures the Persian government should be urged to take forthwith to produce an immediate return.

A final report on this subject has not yet been received from Tehran but I am preparing an interim report for submission to the Minister of State who is anxious to discuss it. Among the immediate measures which the Persian government should take the establishment of the Persian Ministry of Labour as a separate Ministry should clearly have a high place.

Since the whole of this letter and the last paragraph in particular is of great concern to the Anglo-Iranian Oil Company I think that we ought to ask Mr Gass to come round and that we should inform him of its substance.

Pyman
13 April 1948

Notes
1. Source: FO 371/67705.

+ + +

XVIII: A Tudeh Memorandum (August 1948)[1]

Immediately after departure of Soviet Ambassador from Tehran, on leave on 9 August 1948, two delegates of Tudeh Party visited Persian Prime Minister and presented him with memorandum, setting out conditions which their party considered essential for a restoration of internal political equilibrium and of friendly relations with the Soviet Union. Points enumerated in Tudeh memorandum were as follows:

a. Suppression of Military Government throughout the country.

b. Liberation of thousands of political prisoners.

c. Restoration of complete freedom of association and of the press.

d. Dropping of the Senate Bill, approval of which would only strengthen dictatorship.

e. Approval of Bills for individual and social liberty, notably the Labour Bill for freedom of trades unions.

f. Refusal of all loans which would tighten the chains of the Persian people and increase colonising enterprise in the country.

g. An effective campaign against poverty and a campaign in favour of the right to work of those workers expelled from their employment for political reasons.

h. Establishment by law of relations between the shares of landowners and peasants in agricultural produce.

i. Protection and improvement of home industry and production.

j. Cancellation of the United States Military Mission and Gendarmerie Mission agreements and removal of all United States advisers.

k. Effective measures to lower the cost of living.

l. Abstention from all collaboration, whether overt or secret, direct or indirect, with the war-mongering imperialist countries and the adoption of a logical and pacific foreign policy.

Notes
1. Source: FO 371/68 707, 1948.

+ + +

XIX: US State Department: Memorandum of the US Embassy on the Project to Proscribe the Tudeh Party (November 1948)[1]

Dr Manonchehr Eqbal, the Minister of Public Instruction, came to see me today. He stated in substance that the position of the government was impossible. What with administrative trifles and cabinet meetings his time was taken up from seven o'clock in the morning until midnight. Precisely nothing was being accomplished. Although he had been a cabinet minister now for seven times he had never seen anything comparable to the present situation. The Majles and the press had both become irresponsible and impossible.

The educational system had fallen into a state of complete anarchy. The Tudeh (Communist) Youth Organization had been allowed a free rein and, although representing a small minority, was sweeping everything before it in the universities and in the schools. It had been particularly effective in recruiting students from 15 to 18 years old. The Tudeh Party had likewise been able to recruit a certain number of professors and teachers. Though a relatively small group, through discipline and perfected organisation, they had become most effective. He was doing what he could to remedy the situation. The professors and teachers in question were government functionaries. He was ordering them to other posts in remote and obscure parts of the country. He mentioned Bushire[2] to illustrate what he meant. They were refusing to go, whereupon in each case the professor or teacher was immediately suspended. There was, of course, a great outcry against him. Strong political influences were brought to bear. He had told the government and the Shah that his resignation lay on the table but that he had no intention of weakening in respect of his disciplinary measures.

He, the Minister of Justice, the Minister of War, and Dr Emeni [Ali Amini], Minister of State, have formulated a project for the dissolution and suppression of the Tudeh Party and Communist political activities, in Iran. The project had been approved by the Council of Ministers. He then made it clear that the government does not dare submit the measure to the present Majles. He stated that unfortunately the measure would require parliamentary approval.[3]

My impression from Dr Eqbal's remarks is that the drastic measure against the Tudeh and Communist political activities in Iran is stillborn.

Dr Eqbal is obviously a strong partisan of the school which favors constitutional reform.

I suggested that the moment was such that it might be well for Iranian leaders to concentrate on foreign affairs and national defense.

Wiley [US Ambassador]
3 November 1948

Notes

1. Source: USNA, RG 84, Confidential Files, Box 17. It is curious that the same report is found both in the British and American archives, making it difficult to know whom Eqbal visited and who sent his report to the other embassy in Tehran. I tend to think the report originated in the US embassy.
2. A town on the Persian Gulf with bad climatic conditions.
3. The project was put into effect a few months later, on 4 February 1949, through a fake attempt on the life of the shah by a member of the Second Bureau of the Army pretending to be a Tudeh member. He had been put in contact with Noureddin Kianouri to prepare the pretext for Tudeh involvement.

+ + +

XX: Iranian Government: The Decree Suppressing the Tudeh Party (1949)[1]

For several years disturbing elements have gathered in the Tudeh Party. They consist of naive people who have been deceived by demagogic arguments but who nevertheless create every day troubles and disorder in the country in order to upset the fundamental basis of the Iranian nation. These elements have not hesitated to commit excesses, particularly in Mazanderan, Gilan and Azerbaijan, and they have even gone so far as to plot the secession of a part of our country. The reports we have received show that they not only misguide the guideless and spread the common ownership doctrine among young people and students, but also they are preparing the way for revolution in our country.

As a result of this, and in order to protect the territorial integrity and the independence of our country as well as to prevent troubles and disturbances, the government has come to the conclusion that this party is contrary to the interests of our country, and has given the order that the organisation of this

party must be dissolved all over the country, and that those who are proven traitors should be tried in accordance with the laws of the country, and subsequently punished.
[Signed] **President of the Council: Mohammad Sa'ed**

Notes
1.   Source: FO 371/68707 (1949).

+ + +

XXI: Tudeh CC Against its Proscription and Oppression (July 1949)[1]

Dear Compatriots
Those enemies of freedom who are the rulers of Persia, after establishing political terrorism and creating an atmosphere of political suffocation, have trampled on the most elementary right of the nation to freedom. They are now hastily driving ahead to deprive our people still more of their freedom and pressing upon them more heavily than ever. They are being inspired by their American and English Masters to silence the voice of the Persian Nation. At the conclusion of the ridiculous farce of the Constituent Assembly and after the approval of the reactionary fresh chains on the neck of the nation, Sa'ed's government with a view to trampling openly on the electoral rights of the majority submitted to the Majles the disgraceful new electoral bill. This is nothing but a clear sign of unrestrained enmity of the ruling class towards the Persian workers and peasants. It is clear from the contents of Article 6 and from the explanations poured forth by the government, the Majles and the press subsidised by the army, the Court and the government, that the fundamental intention of the new electoral law is to deprive the great majority of this nation of their established constitutional rights by classing them as illiterates. It is obvious that before the submission of the new bill the majority of the people were not enjoying freedom of elections. As was seen very clearly in the case of the Constituent Assembly elections under the present terror and savagery created by imperialism and its so-called Persian servants practically no free elections existed for individual members of the Persian nation whether literate or illiterate.

Electoral candidates were confined to the list of persons prepared by the Court, the army and the government, no other names could diverge from the 'ballot' box, The point is that those murderers of freedom, the ruling class of Persia, have not been content with depriving the people of this country of their right to free elections in practice, but they want to deprive the great mass of our people officially and 'legally' of their right to vote so that for future terms too great a barrier shall be erected against the expression of the nation's will.

The loudspeakers of the ruling clique and their parasitical newspapers claim that, perhaps as a result of depriving the majority of the people of Persia of their right to vote, freedom of elections will be established. They try with complete shamelessness to shift the responsibility for the disgraceful elections of the past legislative terms from the shoulders of the Court, the army and the government to disregard the open and illegal interference of the imperialistic authorities in the elections and to ignore the influence, the money and the force of the influential elements as well as the effect of the bayonets of the army and the gendarmerie. They seek to blame the people themselves for the dire consequences arising from this very act of trampling on their rights. The fact is that by attributing illiteracy to the people of Iran they cannot be deprived of their human rights. If the majority of the Persian people are unable to read and write, the responsibility rests squarely on the shoulders of the government who, instead of using the wealth accruing from the labour of the people for their training and education, spend it on the purchase of arms and the salaries of military advisers, their object being to collaborate with the imperialists in making war against the interests of the Persian people.

Or they consume it in the entertainment of the slaves of imperialism who, by orders of the foreign imperialist powers, regularly arrive in our country for sinister purposes. On the other hand these same so-called illiterates would, if they were allowed to hold meetings and engage in party activities and liberal organisations, become intelligent individuals able to distinguish the friends and enemies of the people. They would become far more competent in determining the interests of the country than those who have been educated in the school of the present government. Everyone knows that in the last few years, as the result of the inspiring efforts of the Tudeh Party, hundreds of thousands of labourers and peasants in this country have come to know where their interests and those of their country lie. Their increased power has become an embarrassment to imperialism.

Everyone knows how terrified the architects of the Thirteenth and Fourteenth Majleses were of the vigilance of the toiling classes and how they tried by all possible means to stop their activities and deprive them of means to stop their activities and deprive them of their indisputable rights. The present endeavour of the ruling class to deprive the majority of the people of their rights is in fact the consequence of the fear which the imperialists and their servants have of the vigilance of the masses. The imposition of any electoral list is possible if terrorism and brute force on the fascist model are used. If, therefore, the ruling class resort to such a measure as the new electoral bill, it is simply because they fear the newly acquired strength of the nation and seek to shackle the people under the guise of legislation.

The Tudeh Party, representing as it does the Persian people, regards with the utmost hatred and disgust this new reactionary measure taken by the government which is aimed at depriving the majority of the Persian people of their right to vote and making it the monopoly of a limited number of people. The Tudeh Party considers this as an ominous step detrimental to the interests of the people and against their freedom and independence. The Tudeh Party believes that with the existence of the reign of terror in our country no free elections are now possible.

The division of the nation into literates and illiterates is something quite artificial and is in stirred with hypocrisy and demagogy. All of the people, whether literate or illiterate, must unite in a tireless fight to unmask the anti-liberty schemes of the government and to restore the social rights of the people. In this fight ultimate victory will no doubt rest with the people.

Central Committee of the Tudeh Party of Iran

Notes
1. Source: Enclosure to Tehran Dispatch No 271 to the Foreign Office, dated 26 July 1949; FO 248/1486 (1949).

+ + +

XXII: Declaration of the Tudeh Party CC in its Own Defence (1949)[1]

Countrymen, Party Comrades
It is not unknown to you that throughout history the common people's struggle for freedom has been a hard one and has undergone vicissitudes; only those have emerged victorious who with cool-headed perseverance have kept to their faith. In the Tudeh Party's view, the recent incidents in Azerbaijan which ended by averting a fratricidal war, under the present conditions of the world and Persia, are results which are better than they might have been.

It is obvious that the Azerbaijan events were the reaction to the policy which the Cabinets in office had supported against the general trend of the inclination of all classes. From the start we believed that the difficulties created by the reactionaries must be solved with leniency. Past events in the Fourteenth Parliament and the Tudeh Party's support of Qavam's premiership were all efforts to that end [and] to solve the Azerbaijan problem with leniency, and to establish democratic principles and social improvements throughout the whole of Iran.

Lately, foreign and domestic reactionaries, making use of the Azerbaijan question as a pretext, have in the name of Iran's independence aimed at the annihilation of the principles of freedom.

Liberty is In Danger

Now that the Azerbaijan question is finished, it is for history to judge the Tudeh Party's actions. In this respect we have a quieter conscience than we should have. Now the people of Iran are waiting to see whose statue those newly formed democrats, who threw down Sattar Khan's statue and boasted of it in their broadcasts, will put up in its place.

Some people, enemies of freedom, instigated by inside and outside quarters, try to misuse the people's patriotism by taking away the means of propaganda from the hands of the freedom lovers and using it widely themselves to paint freedom as the enemy of independence, patriotism and the worship of God.

Not only the old men, but the young men too have not yet forgotten how, after the establishment of dictatorship, our country's independence became the toy of a one-sided policy. It is not yet forgotten how the clergy were treated, how Moslems in the holiest places were butchered, and how the people's chastity and honour were respected. Of course the landowners and wealthy people have not forgotten how far their principle of ownership was heeded.

All just people agree that after Shahrivar [1320][2] with different excuses, such as the 'high interests of the Allies', they wanted to re-establish the dictatorship. Only in consequence of the Tudeh Party's fight and sacrifices was the freedom of association and opinion more or less maintained. If the clergy are able to deliver their sermons and harangues, if the people have a right to worship their God freely, if freedom of the press and self-expression have been more or less respected, all are due to the liberating efforts of the Tudeh Party and other freedom-loving parties.

It is obvious that the first objective of those inclined to dictatorship must be the strongest fortress of liberty, that is, the Tudeh Party and the Workers Union and soon after, as in the past, one after the other all liberties, political, religious or economic will vanish.

All the people, groups and parties, whether in their political and social views they are in accord with our party or against us, must know that the Tudeh Party's defeat is the defeat of liberty in Persia. But we are confident that in the world where members of UN Organisation sever their political relations with dictatorial Spain, it is not possible to set up 'permanent dictatorship'. No doubt fluctuations will occur in the movement for freedom in Persia, but it will never be extinguished. To maintain the cause of freedom, the efforts of all freedom-loving people and groups are needed.

The Tudeh Party is proud that it has founded the guarantee of the execution and continuation of this movement in the social school of Persia. The great staff of leaders schooled during our five years of social struggle consist of thousands of young, intelligent, seasoned and trained people, who are ready under any circumstances, with the aid of thousands of soldiers of liberty, to realise our aim, which is an independent, free and progressive Iran.

The Tudeh Party school has even become a model for all liberty-loving individuals, groups and parties.

The Historical Necessity of Social Reform

The essential difference between our internal situation after the Second World War and that of the First World War, ending up the establishment of [Pahlavi's] dictatorship, is that now, to say nothing of the world situation, there are thousands of educated and intelligent people who have been in the schools of Europe and known democracy in practice. More than that, there are tens of thousands of young men provided with logic and knowledge of social science, whose liberal ideals cannot be crushed by any kind of force.

The Tudeh movement has penetrated not only in workers' cottages and far off humble dwellings, but has spread in all classes, in the University and in every Persian household. The unusual awareness and knowledge which the Tudeh social school has produced in all minds and opinions is the product and result of the nature of our present society. The indispensability of social improvements and the unavoidable necessity of bettering the material and spiritual position of the common people the middle class and officials in that phase of social revolution is an inevitable event.

The fancies of a statesman or the cupidity of great magnates can retard reforms, but are not able to stop them.

The Tudeh Party of Iran is Not the Cause of Class Struggle

If there are people or groups in accord with these improvements they cannot be hostile to the Tudeh Iran Party, but they must cooperate with us, who have shown ourselves the strongest defenders and propagators of social improvements.

Some people, enemies of liberty and opposed to social reforms, intend to show the Tudeh Party as the cause of class warfare and as against the unity of Persia. We have declared many times that we did not incite class warfare in this country. The cause of the stirring up of class struggle is the past governments, especially that of the period of dictatorship, when Persian people were divided into a majority of workers and workers devoid of everything, and a minority provided with everything. If the Tudeh Party leadership did not exist, the people's wants and unhappiness would be shown by rebellions and revolutions.

The march of the naked and hungry might cause the destruction of both good and bad.

The leadership of the Tudeh Party made considerable efforts to divert this blind force into a beneficial and logical movement. The formation of the great masses of the people into an organisation was not an easy task. What should have taken its natural course over dozens of years was stopped altogether during the period of dictatorship. After Shahrivar the party leadership faced an enormous task: these vast masses, destitute and agitated, many of them demoralised, must be formed in a short time into disciplined party organisations. These burdensome duties, coupled with the lack of material and spiritual means, and the existing obstacles and difficulties, could not be discharged perfectly and ideally.

Tudeh Party Programme the Best Guarantee of National Unity

In spite of everything, the Tudeh Party made great efforts to stop any sort of rebellion and disaffection, and, contrary to the misrepresentations of our enemies, if anything has happened the cause must be sought for in the stubbornness of the ruling class, their obstinacy in stopping all social reforms, and their doggedness in constant opposition to the Tudeh Party.

We declared many times from the start of our party that domestic capital and industries must be upheld, and that Persian merchants and capitalists must not become middlemen to the foreign lords of industries.

Unfair Accusations

Now, those foreign capitalists and magnates, who are the greatest enemies of the people's movement amongst weak nations, do not hesitate to taunt us with everything. All progressive movements in every country, France, Germany, Russia, small nations as well as great ones, have been charged with these unfair accusations. In Britain, too, after the last war, by means of a forged letter they showed the British Labour Party as a servant of foreigners and a spy,[3] but though they postponed the victory of the Labour Party, they could not prevent it. Not only are simple workers of the Tudeh Party devoid of everything but patriotism, but our intelligentsia, who could have had an easy life, because they are amongst the most patriotic and self-denying individuals of our society, have chosen a very ordinary material life. Most of them have not even led a few months of peaceful life, but with great magnanimity allow themselves to be targets for mean people's accusations, and sacrifice an easy life for their great patriotic and national ideals. The Persian people will be grateful for that sacrifice. The clamour of those selling their country cannot sully the most patriotic individuals.

Tudeh Party Deputies and Ministers

In consequence of the Tudeh Party's five years of struggle, the ruling class was forced to grant some advantage for poor people, clerks and freedom lovers. The struggle of the Tudeh Party faction in the Fourteenth Parliament, which was courageous and logical, re-echoed throughout the world. As the speeches of the Tudeh Party deputes were the cries of people, all people of Persia accepted them. The role played by the eight deputies of the Tudeh Party faction in the Fourteenth Parliament will not be forgotten by anybody. Of course the enemies of liberty have every right to fear it in the Fifteenth Parliament.

The 75 days of office of the three Tudeh Ministers was sufficient to show the enemies of reforms that the Tudeh Party's views on social improvements are not a joke, that they would not allow extravagant masters' sons and useless director-generals remain in Europe or sit idle in Iran. That was the reason why pressure from inside and outside was exercised and chieftains armed and incited [trouble], in order to have the Fifteenth Parliament [elected] according to command, and empty of all patriotic and progressive elements, so that the dictatorial organisation be handed over unchanged to the new despot, who will serve the one-sided policy of imperialism.

The Organising Power of the Tudeh Party Frightens the Enemies of the Freedom of Persia

The present government, which came into power with the support of progressive elements, but decided to throw them out of the political arena, in spite of the incessant protests of freedom lovers and even Ministers in office, after the withdrawal of foreign troops, postponed the elections.

The political demonstrations of the Tudeh Party and the Workers Union in which, according to the evidence of foreign and local reporters, sometimes 80 000 and sometimes 100 000 people took part in an organised manner, made all responsible domestic and foreign circles aware of the results of free elections in that they would end in a 100 per cent victory for the Tudeh Party.

More than by Azerbaijan, they were enlightened by the strike of 100 000 oil workers of the south. This number showed all Iranians and the world that free elections would result to the advantage of the Tudeh Party.

The Decision to Destroy the Tudeh Party is the Beginning of the Elimination of Freedom

Therefore to smash the Tudeh Party's power, by executions, occupation of factories and setting up military governments in important centres in the north and south of Persia, they postponed elections in order to find a means to prevent the election of even one single freedom lover to the Parliament. We here point to the documents and evidences given in the declaration of united front of freedom-loving parties concerning the fettered preparations for elections; also we refer to the statement of the committee of the Central Union, which was published in the newspaper *Bidari-ye Ma* and to all the other letters sent to the Prime Minister and other competent authorities by the Tudeh Party Central Committee, relating that with force and armed power all means of canvassing and propaganda have been put out of our reach.

The Tudeh Party, as attested by British, American, Russian, French and other impartial and partial observations, is the greatest organised party of Iran and on the threshold of free elections (!) is under oppression. Many of our active members under different excuses, and even without any, have been detained: all our institutions are occupied, even our clubs in Tehran have been looted under the very eyes of the security forces. Our institutions all over Mazanderan and Gorgan provinces have been ransacked. Some of our candidates have been sent to prison, freedom of speech, press and even location is denied to us by the military government and terrorism.

Tudeh Party and the Elections of the Imposed Parliament

The Tudeh Party, according to its programme and five years of experiences, has chosen the parliamentary method for the achievement of its progressive aims, but now, through the government's pressure, it is deprived of its electoral rights.

Therefore, as long as the present situation exists, and freedom of association is denied, the Tudeh Party cannot participate in the elections. Let the democratic world judge how the possibility of participation in electing is denied in practice to a party which is of an international fame and through long years of struggle has spread its roots deep into the Persian masses, but another party, with the support of the government's might, will obtain an overwhelming majority in the Parliament.

We declare to the democratic world that in Persia, in the name of democracy, nothing is left of that regime, and the people of Persia are denied their legal electoral rights.

Comrades of the Party!

Now we have a heavy and solemn duty to fulfil. We must coordinate our fight with the new conditions, with a strong belief, fortitude and absolute calmness, to discharge our social tasks, and endure all difficulties for the sake of Iran and our high ideals, which are not separate from those of the Homeland. Our way is the right way, and on our road, where we have faith, we will not be diverted! What we have done has been with extreme conviction and sound belief, and has been to the interest of our country and its people. We must take warnings from the past. We must show great sacrifices and self-denial for the sake of National ideals. We must find out how to touch people's hearts more than before, and know their hopes and their distresses. We must show ourselves worthy of the rank people have assigned to us, in order to achieve our high social ideals and make the future of Persia worthy of her glorious past.

Dear Countrymen!

One move in the adventurous history of our beloved country, liberty is in danger. The Tudeh Party, in the face of history and the people of Persia, will fulfil whatever engagement it has undertaken.

We ask all free men to help in our struggle, or at least not to help our enemies. We again shall make the road to freedom smooth. Those who persecute freedom-lovers to please their enemies or to acquit themselves, commit an unpardonable sin. The freedom-loving movement of the Persian masses in its historical course will go sometimes fast and sometimes slow, but will never be stopped or retrace its steps. Without any hesitation we shall go forward to our high goal and our national patriotic and progressive ideal.

Long live the liberty, integrity and independence of Persia!

Long live the Tudeh Iran Party! Long Live the Central United Committee!

Long live the freedom-loving parties of Iran!

The Central Committee of the Tudeh Party of Iran

Notes
1. Source: FO 248/1471 (1949); FO 371/61988.
2. Shahrivar 1320/August-September 1941, when the Allied occupied Iran and dethroned Reza Shah.
3. A reference to the Zinoviev Letter scandal of 1924.

+ + +

XXIII: The Tudeh Party, the Soviet Government and the Pro-Imperialist Government of General Razmara (1950-51)[1]

Editor's Note: On the eve of the revision of the 1933 agreement with the Anglo-Iranian Oil Company (British Petroleum), General Razmara came to power with the support of the Anglo-American governments and the tacit consent of the Soviet Union. Razmara appeased the Soviet government by granting a number of concessions, including an important trade agreement. Razmara was perceived as an agent of Western imperialists and did all he could to prevent the adoption of the nationalisation law proposed by the Patriotic Front led by Dr Mosaddeq, a law that opposed the revision and extension of the old colonial agreement of 1933. In this light, it was hardly difficult for the Tudeh Party not to express its hostility towards the government headed by a military strongman, especially because, after the Tudeh's imprisoned leaders in the Persian Gulf island were transferred to a Tehran prison, whence they escaped and went underground, it was generally believed that Razmara had had a hand in the escape of the Tudeh leaders. (See the US Embassy report in this volume — Document XXVII.) Given the total obedience of the Tudeh to the Soviet Communist Party, and the position of *Pravda* on the assassination of Razmara on the eve of the nationalisation, the Tudeh's declaration against the military government seemed suspect, particularly since, with the advent of that government, the outlawed Tudeh was allowed to publish a couple of front newspapers and distribute its clandestine organ rather freely. The two following documents throw light on the hypocritical position of the Tudeh and the support of its mentor state of a right-wing government tied to colonial powers in the West.

+ + +

A: The Iranian Nation Violently Rejects the Cossack Government

With the advent to power of Razmara, the interference of the Anglo-American imperialists in our country enters upon a new phase; the Razmara cabinet symbolises the influence of the two imperialisms aiming at the total enslavement of our country. The majority in the Majles, by giving their vote of confidence to such a government, have proved their blind obedience to the British and American Embassies. The dignity of the Majles has been degraded.

The Iranian Nation not only expresses its disgust for the law-breaking and abominable Razmara Cabinet and its criminal British and American supporters, but considers the Shah and the two Houses to share the responsibility for having submitted to this imperialist game, even in spite of their personal interests.

The coming of the Razmara Cabinet coincides with the commencement of the activities of Henry Grady, the butcher of Greece, in Iran as the Ambassador of American Imperialism and the flagrant declaration of war of America against the gallant people of Korea. No wonder the Razmara Cabinet is being praised by London and Washington. The British and American Ambassadors see in Razmara a man who is prepared to sacrifice the independence of Iran and stifle any opposition by brute and unrestrained force, to ensure the oil interests of England and plunge our people into bloodshed and ruin, and to turn Iran into an American military base against the USSR. The various childish speeches of Razmara have only increased the hatred of the nation for him. All know that he has come into power to oppose the very things he promises. His criminal record is too well known to deceive anyone.

The Iranian nation considers him a lackey of foreign powers and will continue to fight, under the leadership of the Tudeh Party of Iran, against the police and dictatorial government of Razmara. The Iranian Nation knows that the power of these stupid Cossacks lasts a short time, just as the power of their American and British masters is diminishing before the great storm sweeping across the world in favour of national independence and against imperialism. The Iranian Nation is not afraid of the new tricks of the British and Americans and of the Cossack government of Razmara, and it will show that the will of the Nation will prevail against these adventurous devices.

Notes
1. Source: *Mardom*, no 41, 10 July 1950; FO 248/1494.

+ + +

B: *Pravda*: Mysterious Doings in Iran[1]

On 7 March [1951] the Iranian Prime Minister, General Razmara, was murdered. The murder was committed in broad daylight in the court of a mosque in Tehran, where the Prime Minister was to attend a special religious ceremony. The murderer and his two accomplices, who, according to press reports, tried to commit suicide, were arrested by the police on the spot.

There is no necessity to prove that the assassination of General Razmara, who had been nominated to the post of Prime Minister by the ruling circles of Iran, represents an event right out of the ordinary, an event of the mysterious political significance. And in actual fact the assassination of the Iranian Prime Minister produced a forceful impression both within the country and beyond its borders. For this very reason it is surprising that, although ten days have already passed since the assassination, there have hitherto been no official reports regarding the process and results of the investigation of the murder. Not only is it not perceptible that any steps aimed at getting to the bottom of the crime and its organisation are being taken, but it is not even known whether any investigation is being conducted at all.

Not only has no ado been made about the murder of General Razmara; on the contrary, one forms the impression that someone's guiding hand is trying to hush the matter up, and foster the idea that in actual fact nothing particular happened, that things are going on as usual. It is in this spirit that the official newspaper *Ettela'at* deals with the assassination of the Prime Minister, and the weekly newspaper *Vazifeh*, which is closely connected with court circles, published an item of three lines on the murder of Razmara.

Notes
1. Source: *Pravda*, 8 March 1951.

XXIV: Tudeh: Concerning the Liberal Bourgeois Movement (June 1950)[1]

A new element has, in recent months, made its appearance in Iranian politics. The 'National Front' with its own tactics, newspapers and a group of members of parliament has come into being. The 'National Front' is led by the liberal bourgeoisie and by landlords, while its supporters are drawn from the 'petite bourgeoisie', as was shown on the day of Kashani's return.[2] The leading elements of the National Front are not favourably disposed to the absolute abolition of mediaeval feudalism; and on attaining power, they will endeavour to suppress the masses. The 'National Front' intends to achieve its object by gradual reforms and through parliamentary measures. It prefers cooperation with the worst government to cooperation with the masses. Nevertheless, the working class cannot remain indifferent to the completion of the Bourgeois Democratic Revolution, the main feature of which is the redistribution of land in the interests of the people. It is the vast masses of peasants and workers who constitute the essential forces of revolution. They can and should seize the leadership of the bourgeois democratic movement and seek to detach the Bourgeois Liberals from the masses. The peasants are the natural allies of the workers since their aim is to abolish feudalism and possess property of their own. In contrast to the methods adopted by the bourgeois liberals; that is, gradual reforms and eventual agreement with the ruling class, the working classes should stage meetings, demonstrations and political strikes towards the attainment of their democratic revolution.

Besides the bourgeois liberal principles in the National Front, there are the interests of the American and British imperialists. It is interesting that, in harmony with the 'voice of America', their papers attack the 'thousand families' and cry against British interests. The coming months will show the true colour of the National Front, if no internal disintegration occurs within it.

Notes
1. Source: Clandestine *Razm*, 26 June 1950; translated in FO 248/1494.
2. That is, his return from his exile in Beirut.

XXV: Tudeh: The Martyrdom of [Imam] Ali (July 1950)[1]

The Moslems of the world and particularly our dear compatriots during these days express their homage to the venerable position of Ali on the occasion of his Martyrdom. The trait characterising his life was resistance against cruelty and oppression. He abhorred social and class distinctions as well as the court ceremonies of his day, which he condemned in his discourses. It is befitting that our compatriots, following the glorious example of Ali, should spare no efforts in the fight against cruelty, even at the cost of their lives.

Notes
1. Source: *Mardom*, no 41, 10 July 1950; FO 2481/1494.

+++

XXVI: Tudeh CC Statement Sent to the American, British, and French Embassies (July 1950)[1]

The aggression of South Korea instigated by the Americans, the outbreak of civil war in Korea, and the flagrant armed intervention of the USA has caused apprehension among the Iranian people as regards peace. The Iranian people believe that the ruling class in America are feverishly preparing for a third war. They have started the interference in Viet-Nam and in the Philippines.

While the Stockholm Congress declares its will to maintain peace, Truman shamelessly asks for an even greater war budget to develop Atomic and Hydrogen Bombs. The Iranian nation together with hundreds of millions of people declare 'Korea for the Koreans'! The Iranian people warn UNO and the Security Council not to become sections of the State Department. The representatives of People's China must take their places on the Council and the Korean affair be settled peacefully and in the interests of the Korean people, and American intervention must cease.

Central Committee of the Tudeh Party of Iran
Tehran, 20 July 1950

Notes
1. Source: Tudeh clandestine organ *Mardom*, 22 July 1950; FO 248/1494.

+++

XXVII: US State Department: Escape of Ten Tudeh Party Leaders from Qasr Prison, Tehran (December 1950)[1]

The Embassy reported, in its telegram no 1275 of 6 December 1950, the maneuvers which had occurred in connection with the an apparent endeavor of the Iranian government to find some formula which would, without political embarrassment, allow the release of some of the imprisoned Tudeh Party leaders. The embassy also forwarded in its despatch no 413 of 8 December 1950 a fairly detailed summary of the events referred to in the aforementioned telegram. The culmination of the events mentioned in these communications seems to have been reached on 15 December, when ten important Tudeh leaders 'escaped' from the Qasr prison in Tehran.

Although the Embassy's telegrams nos 1358 and 1367, of 17 and 19 December, respectively, contained all the available information relative to the incident, the following elaboration of these comments may be of interest to the Department.

The incident is basically, though not completely, described in the communiqué issued by General Mohammad Daftari, Chief of Police, on 16 December 1950. A translation of that statement follows:

> At 8:30 in the evening of Friday 15 December 1950, a covered truck with Army signs and a number of people in military uniforms, one of whom was a lieutenant colonel of the Army, the rest being Army sergeants, came to the prison door at Qasr. In conformity with regulations, he referred to the officer in charge of the prison, First Lieutenant Qobadi. After having had a talk with him, they entered the prison compound and went to the door of political prison no 2. The officer in charge of the prison, First Lieutenant Mohammad-zadeh, acting on orders by First Lieutenant Qobadi, brought out ten political prisoners, put them in the truck and took them out of the prison compound. First Lieutenant Qobadi and Mohammad-zadeh, wardens, also accompanied them and instructed their assistants to take charge until they returned. A few hours later, the two assistants, not hearing from the wardens, reported to higher authorities. Investigations were immediately made and it became certain that they had escaped and that the flight of ten prisoners was due to treachery and collusion with these two wardens. Prompt and necessary measures were taken in Tehran and outside to arrest the prisoners and those who committed this act of treachery.

There are several points not entirely brought out in the foregoing communiqué. For example, the 'few hours' mentioned therein as occurring between the escape of the prisoners and the report of the incident to that when the two wardens left with the abductors of the prisoners, they told their assistants remaining behind to keep quiet, which those assistants did throughout the entire night and early morning. Also, it seems that the abductors did have certain official documents in their possession, presumably forged, which were appropriately presented. Finally, according to reports, little time was spent by the abductors at the prison, for it appears that the ten selected prisoners were ready and waiting when the truck arrived.

It might be well to repeat here the names of the Tudeh leaders who escaped. They are: [Dr] Morteza Yazdi, [Dr] Hussein Jowdat, Abdol-Hussein Noushin, Ahmad Qasemi, Nour al-Din Kianouri, Ali-Akbar Shandarmani, Samed Hakimi, Engineer Ali Ollovi,[2] Khosrow Rouzbeh, Mahmoud Boqrati.

The first named six were included in the group seeking a retrial of their cases, as set forth in Embassy despatch no 413. Three of the remaining four, Hakimi, Ollovi and Boqrati, were imprisoned following the attempted assassination of the Shah, while Rouzbeh had been imprisoned prior to the attempt upon the Shah's life. It is interesting to note that a definite selective process was apparently involved in the choice of the prisoners to be released; all of the escapees seem, on their records, to be competent Communist agents.

As already reported, the dominant initial feeling in Tehran was that the 'Government' was involved in the incident. Although perhaps difficult to believe, the Tehran public appeared almost to derive satisfaction from the belief that the escape evidenced the weakness and corruption of the government, while at the same time being more or less apathetic concerning the fact that ten dangerous Tudeh organizers were now at liberty. Some half-heartedly placed the blame for the happening upon the British, charging that the action was designed to divert attention from the oil discussions, which are now starting in the Majles. In general, however, few Iranians making this charge seemed to believe what they were. There was also a rumor circulating to the effect that some means had to be found by the government for releasing the prisoners, so that the Shah could escape the necessity of granting them amnesties on his marriage day. Again, this theory did not seem to be widely believed.

Finally, the rumor which was particularly prevalent at the signing of the Soviet-Iranian Trade Agreement, to the effect that a secret understanding had been arrived at between Prime Minister Razmara and Sadchikov, the Russian Ambassador, concerning the suppression of anti-Soviet propaganda in Iran, the tolerance of greater 'democratic' propaganda activities by the Soviets, and the release of some of the Tudeh leaders, was resurrected and the incident explained as the government's way of carrying out whatever commitment it had made.

While newspapers of all shades of opinion were critical of the government, yet no direct accusations were made against the Prime Minister. A sampling of the press remarks follows:

Bakhtar Emrouz (anti-government):

The Senate was in session in the morning when the news of the release reached the Senators. One of them was delegated to contact the Prime Minister, who gave him a brief account of the flight, adding that the men responsible for the escape were dressed in army uniforms and that it was not certain whether they were really army officers. The impression of the Senators was that the government was trying to shrink from the responsibility which in this way it would have to assume. The investigations by military authorities do not reveal any clue which would indicate military collusion.

Seda-ye Mardom (pro-AIOC):

The truck had ample time to pass the border during the twelve hours between the time of the flight and its discovery. It might have gone to the USSR, though this is no more than a guess. The Police Department should not content itself with issuing a single statement; it must inform the public of the developments.

Darya (anti-government):

The flight of the Tudeh leaders is a disgrace to security officers. Some people would not believe it. Others said the government itself is involved. There are people who said these prisoners have been taken away to be liquidated. A number of people ventured the opinion that this was the outcome of their own cleverness coupled with help by the government. Nobody, however, knows the facts. There seems to be no reason why people should come in the guise of military officers and sergeants, for there are so many people among army officers and sergeants who are opposed to the present regime. It was an easy thing for them to connive with the wardens on duty that night. There seems to be no question in the fact that after the examining magistrate differed with the Supreme Court and the Criminal Court, and, after all the insistence to drag the case of political prisoners to military courts, the plot, if prearranged, was expedited. They left the prison in order not to cause further headaches for the military courts.

Ettelaʿat, in its usual conservative manner, alluded to the fact that prison regulations provide that no prisoner shall be released after six pm, and comments upon the disregard of this regulation. It then adds:

> A well-informed source stated that the fugitives were in Tehran and that they had not left the capital in order to maintain their contact with the members of the Tudeh Central Committee. This source explained that, even when in jail, the Tudeh leaders were being used in the recent political affairs. They may not leave Tehran because they would want to resort to certain activities in the same line.

As so often happens in Iran, it is doubtful whether the truth concerning the occurrence will ever be completely known. One thing, however, does seem certain, and that is that the government knows everything or it knows nothing about the incident. The 'escape' could have been arranged in but two ways: 1) by or with the consent of the government, or 2) by Communist elements acting entirely independently of the government. It might be well to consider the factors which bear upon both of these two possibilities.

It seems reasonably apparent that the government has been trying for some months to find some formula which would allow the legal release of some of the Tudeh leaders, as described in the Embassy's dispatch no 413. It also seems apparent that it was not successful in that maneuver, seemingly not being able to find an official willing to make himself responsible, through signature of the judicial decision, for the release of those leaders. Again reverting to speculation, the 'escape' mechanism bears all the earmarks of a Persian device designed to accomplish the act without assuming the responsibility, especially when one considers that the incident occurred practically on the eve of the opening of parliamentary debates on the oil question, a matter which will consume all the public's emotions for weeks to come. What is not under this premise is the reason for the government's action. There would seem to be only two possibilities. First, that Razmara did enter into some secret understanding with the Soviet Ambassador, and that he has used this means of fulfilling a commitment. Second, that Razmara, seeing his internal position weakening, has decided to court Soviet favor even more than he has during the past several months, believing that the support of the Soviets might eventually be useful to him in a contest of strength with the Shah or other forces seeking to oust him.

There is still another possibility which, while seemingly remote, relates to the foregoing and should be considered. This is that the Shah was behind the incident. Such a supposition could only be made upon the assumption that he thereby intended to embarrass Razmara and encourage his earlier fall. While, as stated, there is a body of opinion which seems to believe that it was politically easier for the Shah to allow the escape of the Tudeh leaders than it would have been to pardon them on his wedding day, yet it is difficult to believe that the Shah would be part of a plan designed to free men pledged to overthrow his regime.

The possibility that Communist elements arranged the escape acting entirely independently poses several interesting questions. First, the bungling of the government in shunting the cases back and forth between the military courts and civil courts had resulted in considerable publicity, and had actually generated quite a feeling among the populace that the Tudeh leaders were innocent and should be released. It is difficult to see what benefits the Soviets hoped to gain through an abrupt disruption of that situation unless, of course, they intend to use these leaders in an operation of fairly immediate interest to them. Also, the presence of the Tudeh leaders in prison under the conditions cited was certainly bringing to the Tudeh cause the political benefits which generally come from political martyrdom. Further, had the Communists planned any jail delivery of this nature, they could more easily have undertaken it at an earlier date or when the prisoners were scattered in the South. Certainly, through the subversion of the wardens and other persons, the Communists could have carried out the operation. However, informed opinion has consistently believed that the Communists were really seeking the legal vindication of some of the Tudeh leaders, which would not only have embarrassed the government as has the escape incident, but in addition would have laid an excellent legal basis for creating a popular demand for the legalization of the Tudeh Party. It would, of course, not be out of keeping with the Iranian character, anticipating the foregoing development, to endeavor to checkmate it in advance through some ruse along the lines of the 'escape' operation. In any event, few local sources believe that the operation was independently carried out by the Tudeh or other Communist organization.

The Embassy is inclined to view the incident seriously. If one assumes that the government's hands were not in it, one cannot but interpret the development as being indicative of the weakness and corruption of the existing security forces of the country, of the inroads which the Communists must have made into those forces and of the strength and organization of the Tudeh Party itself. If, however, one is more inclined to accept the popular view that the government (with the implication that the latter term means Razmara) was involved in the operation, then one becomes worried indeed over the future possible course of events in the country.

Arthur L Richards
Chargé d'Affaires, *ad interim*

Notes

1. Source: USNA 788.00/12-2250.
2. Misreading Persian names without diacritics, the report mentions 'Bozorg Alavi', the Tudeh novelist, who had not been incarcerated. The correct name has been used here.

+ + +

XXVIII: Statement by the CC of the Tudeh Party of Persia on the Anniversary of 4 February 1949 (February 1951)[1]

1. Two years have already elapsed since the *coup d'état* of Bahman 1327 [4 February 1949] was organised by the reactionary imperialists. Gravely apprehensive of the steady progress of the Tudeh Party, notwithstanding the great blow dealt at them in Azar 1325 [December 1946], the reactionary as well as the imperialistic elements in the country considered it necessary to stifle the voice of the people altogether, so as to be able to carry out their sinister plans in connection with such important questions as the oil, the constituent assembly, the Sixteenth Majles, the Imperial Bank and the proposed loan from America, etc. The event of 15 Bahman was used by them as pretext through the traitor Shah of Persia.

2. The Tudeh Party demonstrated however its invincible power in the fight against imperialist and against reactionary plans. The severe measures taken against our party, that is, our party being announced as illegal, the majority of the members of our central organisation imprisoned, etc, created new duties for us, but we did not hesitate to find new means and ways to meet with the emergency.

a) We had to protect our 'cadres' being under pursuance of the police.

b) We had to set up new secret organisations to cope with the new situation.

c) We had to create new means of communication between the 'organs' staffs and the provinces.

d) We had to maintain contact with the members of the party and the non-party masses by the continued publication of our paper, which necessitated the maintenance of a printing house, paper supply, etc.

e) We had to adopt certain methods in our contact with the people and in active participation in our daily campaign.

The events of the last two years have demonstrated our ability to protect ourselves against all attacks and have established the fact that the Tudeh Party is capable of creating new human beings prepared to sacrifice themselves for the sake of their country.

3. During the last two years the British and American imperialists created a number of events; the event of 15 Bahman, the murder of Hazhir,[2] the murder of Dehqan,[3] the constituent assembly, the Sixteenth Majles, the setting in motion of various parties of demagogues and appeasers, and the swaying of the Shah one day towards one imperialism and the other day towards another. The Tudeh Party disclosed to the public the secrets of all these events, as well as the activities of the dishonest Shah and of the appeaser of imperialism.[4]

4. The Tudeh Party not only survived the heavy blows of 15 Bahman, but was also able to achieve remarkable success in its relentless campaign against imperialism and the reactionary elements.

If the Tudeh Party had not been bereft of open activities and was able to have free contact with the masses of worker and peasants it would have made a tremendous progress by now, having regard to the achievements of the last two years and the remarkable victories gained by the World Peace Front led by the USSR. If the *new imperialist agents*[5] have found opportunities to put through their deceitful plans, it is because of the possibilities denied to the Tudeh Party.

5. Our campaign will continue.

Party members, workers and toilers! We must make use of our past experience for achieving greater victories. We must consolidate our organisation and make it more impregnable. We must increase our alertness and watchfulness. We must know the fact that the enemy who is feeling his decline will resort to more barbarous measures. We must prove ourselves a strong deterrent against the activities of the police and of spies trying to penetrate our front. We must do our best to maintain contact with the masses. We must expand our campaign among wider masses of workers and peasants. We must lend a greater support to the Central United Council. We must extend the Tudeh Peasants Organisation in Iran to the obscure corners of our country. We must try and attract to our movement intelligent, freedom-loving and anti-imperialist elements of our country in still greater numbers. We must make it our sacred duty to try and expand the movement for peace, as a national and anti-imperialistic measure.

We must make known more than ever before to the great masses in our country the World Peace [Movement] and Democratic Front and persuade them to join in the campaign against the war front as well as the imperialistic front. We must keep the flame of higher hopes burning in the hearts of the people and stride for the independence and freedom of the country.

Central Committee of the Tudeh Party of Persia

Notes
1.   Source: FO 248/1516 (1951).

2. Court-appointed premier assassinated by the Muslim terrorist group Fada'iyan-e Islam.
3. A journalist who was assassinated on the order of a Tudeh party terrorist cell by a clandestine member named Emami who kept his membership secret and was believed to have acted as a religious fanatic. The party promised to save him at the last minute before hanging. He was hanged at the time he was hoping to be saved and hidden at the last minute.
4. This is a veiled reference to the Patriotic Front led by Premier Mosaddeq.
5. Another veiled reference to the Patriotic Front led by Mosaddeq, emphasis added.

+++

XXIX: Tudeh Party's CC New Year Greeting (March 1951)[1]

Editor's Note: While the whole country lived through its happiest collective New Year, paradoxically the greeting message below to the Iranian nation, issued on the morrow of the nationalisation of the oil industry, makes no reference to the victory of the entire people over British colonialism and internal reaction led by the military and the Court. This confirms the party leadership's systematic opposition to the National Movement as well its animosity toward the Patriotic Front, led by Mosaddeq, which directed the national campaign.

+++

Dear Countrymen

The Central Committee of the Tudeh welcomes the New Year holiday, memorial to freedom and pride of our nation, and trusts the year to come, by endeavor of the nations, will be a year of peace and victory.

You must demand from the government and from parliament the security of freedom-loving groups, and removal of restraints on the Tudeh, the strongest support for peace in our land.

Central Committee of the Tudeh
Mashhad, March 1951

Notes
1. Source: USNA 788.00/3-3151.

+++

XXX: Tudeh: Dr Mosaddeq's Government (May 1951)[1]

Increasing Anglo-American imperialistic rivalry and the unprecedented growth of Iran's national movement made it impossible for Ala's government to survive.

The Washington Conference failed to solve differences which exist between the two imperialistic policies, and the circumstances surrounding their rivalry, together with the determination of the Iranian nation to wrest the southern and Bahrain oilfields from the usurpers, resulted in the decision of the Oil Commission concerning the nationalisation and the dispossessing of the Oil Company of all its institutions.

This decision created great dissatisfaction in British circles and was followed by the impudent declaration of the British Embassy and Sir Francis Shepherd's repeated discussions with Ala with a view to neutralising national efforts by means of political pressure. Ala, who had shown great ruthlessness in slaughtering the brave workers, was unable to resist against Shepherd's threats and had to give up responsibility.

This, however, did not enable the British to find a new way of neutralising the Oil Commission's decision and no sooner Dr Mosaddeq was appointed Prime Minister than the Commission's proposals were approved by both the Houses of Parliament and the Shah and the decision become a law.

Now the country faces new circumstances and, while imperialistic differences still remain unsolved, Dr Mosaddeq's government has come into power with the nationalisation scheme in its hands. Tudeh views concerning all such governments are fairly clear and briefly we can say that so long as imperialist influences try to strangle the Iranian nation and the greatest Iranian party has been outlawed, no government can do much in safeguarding our interests or satisfying the freedom-loving demands of the nation.

As for Dr Mosaddeq, ever since 1322 he has often approved a great deal for the nation. It will nevertheless keep an equitable balance-sheet of the government's deeds and will perform its duties in fighting against any deviation from the path of national freedom and independence.

Item discusses National Front hypocritical activities and states that, promoting AIOC ends, National Front leader had on various occasions created difficulties for the Khuzistan strikers, in order to prevent the prolongation of the strike about which the company was extremely alarmed.

Article discusses recent economic successes in Russia and makes a comparison with conditions in imperialistic countries where economic bankruptcy is apparent. It states that two and a half months ago Joseph Stalin had forecast this situation.

Item gives an account of the May-Day deliberations and considers [them] as a big blow to imperialistic forces.

Article discusses the decision of the Majles concerning the dispossessing of AIOC of its institutions and states that while the decision was a right and sound one, the timid government had, as usual, left certain loopholes in it and had provided for the possibility of considering the company's 'legitimate claims', thus showing signs of weakness. It had also promised to sell oil products to former buyers, while this was against the nation's sovereign will.

Meanwhile, the question of the Bahrain oilfields had been deliberately overlooked, but the nation would not forget its rights and would constantly fight for their establishment.

Notes
1. Source: *Mardom*, 5 May 1951; translated in FO 48/1516.

+ + +

XXXI: An Open Letter by the Tudeh CC to Dr Mosaddeq (May 1951)[1]

Editor's Note: On 7 May 1951 the Tudeh's legal leftist newspaper *Besou-ye Ayandeh* published an Open Letter from the Central Committee of the Tudeh Party to Prime Minister Mosaddeq. The text of the translation from the French version appearing in the *Iran Presse* of 8 May 1951 is transmitted below.

+ + +

His Excellency Prime Minister Mohammad Mosaddeq

The Tudeh Party considers it necessary to draw your attention to the heavy responsibility which you carry on your shoulders. The Iranian people see that you are facing a task of the greatest importance and you will be judged only by your actions. For the past several decades the ruling class has imposed on Iran a criminal regime and has suppressed liberal tendencies. The Iranian people do not wish this to continue and that is why the Tudeh Party turns to you and makes the following demands:

1. Give liberty of action to all parties and all labour unions, particularly to the great Tudeh Party which was banned following the attempted assassination of the Shah on 4 February 1949. This suppression has been contrary to the charter of the United Nations. The events which followed the attempted assassination of the Shah have demonstrated that all efforts to suppress the Tudeh Party are in reality attempts to suppress liberty and democracy. Two and one-half years

have passed and every day the Tudeh Party survives the attacks against it. The party has shown that it is beyond the reach of the different governments who have come to power, and now that you have proclaimed yours in favour of the principles of liberty you must officially authorise the activity of the Tudeh Party. No excuse will be accepted, for the recognition of the great Tudeh Party, the party of the working masses of our country, would be an expression of the will of the Iranian people.

2. Release the hundreds of the best sons of our country who because of their liberalism and their patriotism have been imprisoned.

3. Revoke the judicial and legislative measures passed after the attempted assassination of the Shah on 4 February 1949.

4. End the martial law which has always been used against the people and which caused the death of workers in Khuzistan. In this regard you should submit to parliament legislation to prohibit the establishment of martial law for all times.

5. As regards nationalisation of the oil industry in Iran which is part of your government's programme, do not leave a single trace of the imperialist British oil company, remove all its influence and take measures so that the sovereignty of Iran will be assured over Bahrain and that nationalisation of the oil industry will apply also to the Bahrain oil resources. As regards the financial claims of Iran on the oil resources, propose a new law to parliament.

6. Your government should devote its efforts to maintaining world peace because the Iranian people, like the other people in the world, thirst for peace. Peace is our sacred objective. Avoid alliances with the warmongers. Recognise the People's Government of China which is the base of liberty and peace in Asia. Do not follow the armament policy of previous governments. The Iranian people want bread and not cannons or rifles. The people want to expel from our country foreign military missions. The people want education and sanitation and not war propaganda. The people do not want their country to become a base for military operations directed against the Soviet Union. Our people will not fight against the great Soviet which is the defender of world peace and is against the imperialists. Our people will not permit their children to be victims of the American and English war-mongers.

Notes
1. Source: USNA 788.00/5-951. Reported by Arthur L Richards, Counsellor of Embassy, for the Ambassador, 22 May 1951.
2. The measures referred to are the anti-Communist laws passed in February 1949.

+ + +

XXXII: Tudeh: Dr Mosaddeq and the Oil Problem (May 1951)[1]

The oil problem is becoming more and more critical and Dr Mosaddeq's policy concerning this problem has also become subject to an ever-increasing degree of ambiguity and contrariness. The position is that, while the struggle of the Iranian nation against the usurping Oil Company is increasing in its intensity, the Anglo-American rivalry also, far from being reduced, is getting steadily more acute.

After considerable delay and procrastination, the Iranian Majles and Senate appointed, last week, a mixed commission for taking over the assets of AIOC. But the procedure to be adopted by this commission seems so vague and uncertain that even Reuter's correspondent already talks of their hesitation in this matter and believes that the Iranian government will not take any harsh measures against the company.

All this is due to the above-mentioned cause and the government can do nothing but limit their activities to the scope provided by the fluctuations of this rivalry.

Dr Mosaddeq's interviews and discussions with the British and American authorities and the secrecy which has covered these meetings have duly attracted the attention of the nation. Meanwhile British quarters seem to have become more hopeful, so much so that Shepherd has expressed satisfaction after his second meeting with Dr Mosaddeq, and according to *The Times*: 'The Iranian Prime Minister hopes that a situation will not arise in which existing danger and difficulties may become more severe and complicated.' Moreover, the United Press reports that personally Dr Mosaddeq was respected and trusted by the British government.

With regard to the mixed commission *The Times* says: 'The members of this commission are acting in accordance with the laws of their country and the company also will receive them in a manner suitable to their dignity and position.'

These remarks shows that the Iranian government does not intend to press the matter too far, but wants to reach a compromising settlement According to *Daily Mirror*, Mr Morrison has made some complaints to the American Ambassador in London, stating that the Americans wanted the British to accept the nationalisation of Iran's oil and, at the same time, were encouraging their own oil companies to obtain concessions in Iran.

Dr Mosaddeq and his supporters are, therefore, mainly concerned with the demands of these two rival imperialistic interests and do not acquaint themselves sufficiently with the nation's wishes. For example, the National Front newspaper *Shahed*, criticises the people's peace demonstrations while such activities are essential in any anti-imperialistic struggle.

The mild tone of Dr Mosaddeq's reply to Mr Morrison's note proves clearly that the present government is not bold enough to safeguard Iran's interests.

But the Iranian nation has different views. Thus the Tudeh Party's Central Committee advises Dr Mosaddeq:

> To put a stop further than the limits of complacency, to eradicate the Company's influence completely, to reject all the Company's baseless claims, to establish Iran's sovereignty over Bahrain and apply the principle of nationalisation in that part as well, and to submit a supplemental bill to the Majles, in order to carry out these demands of the Iranian nation.

This is, of course, the right procedure for the nationalisation of oil and the nation will continue its struggle in this connection. Neither Dr Mosaddeq's 'dream', nor his simultaneously modest and ambitious claim to be the main and most effective factor in this struggle, can overshadow the nation's part which is the mainstay of the whole movement. It is fortunate, however, that Dr Mosaddeq's opinion — like his statements — cannot shake the nation's determined and vigilant efforts in connection with this vital issue.

An article entitled 'Mosaddeq's Anti-National Government Intends to End the Oil Affair in Favour of American and British Imperialists' begins by saying that as a result of bold American interference and the traitorous policy of Mosaddeq's government the oil problem is being solved in favour of America and Britain.

The subject of oil is no longer an Iranian problem but a problem between Britain and America because not even the government's opinion has been asked in the matter.

The Shah and his Prime Minister have treacherously given Averell W Harriman full authority on behalf of Iran in the London Conference.

Notes
1. Source: Clandestine Tudeh organ *Mardom*, 19 May 1951; FO 248/1516.

+ + +

XXXIII: The Tudeh Against Mosaddeq (July 1951)[1]

Dr Mosaddeq's anti-national government has set out to kill people, support fascism, tell lies, and serve America's colonial policy.

The roots of the conspiracy that has been designed against the interests of the nation by Dr Mosaddeq's government, inspired by imperialist sources, are becoming visible. The incidence of bloodshed last Sunday could not be disguised. The government, on the one hand, entertains in all humility and servitude Harriman, representative of the independence-shattering US, Harriman the oil broker and warmonger, and, on the other, set up a gory stage against the people to assure Truman's envoy. Dr Mosaddeq has thought it necessary to shed blood in order to prepare the ground for subservient negotiations with the representative of American colonialism

Notes
1. Source: *Shoja'at*, 19 July 1951, a Tudeh front-organisation newspaper published legally under Mosaddeq's government.

+ + +

XXXIV: Declaration of the Tudeh Party CC on the Elections for the Seventeenth Legislature (December 1951)[1]

The elections of the Seventeenth Majles will commence. By its strangling and calamitous domination the ruling class wants to give a legal colouring for a further two years to another imposed Majles. The British and American imperialists who struggle against one another for highway robbery in our country are both plotting new plans to crush the national forces and to overtake their rival.

The struggles by the various sides of the ruling class and their battle arrays for the elections can be seen even now. The changing of the Governors-General who are all of one stock and who differ only as regards their attachment to various imperialistic groups is but the symbol of this contest.

The deceitful maneuvers of detailing electoral inspectors, etc, displayed by Mosaddeq's government nominally for the sake of ensuring freedom of elections and intrinsically for strengthening the illegal influence of the government and for imposing government candidates, were displayed similarly by other anti-national governments. The people have already seen the result, being the formation of anti-national parliaments such as the present one and have already experienced such fraudulent actions of the government.

Mosaddeq's government is trying to finish the elections particularly in the northern districts before its shameful collusion in the oil issues is disclosed. British agents at the same time make every efforts to weaken this American-supported government and bring about its fall so as to be able to secure the interests of their masters in the Seventeenth Majles and make good the failures of the British imperialists in the next Majles.

The Persian people know that in the present circumstances, in the circumstances in which the Persian Tudeh Party and the Democrat Party of Azerbaijan and Kurdistan are living as 'illegal', in which the advocating of peace, freedom and democracy is rewarded by strokes of the whip, by imprisonment, torment and expulsion, in which even girl and boy students are made victims of knives and bayonets, in which the murderers of 23 Tir [1330/July 1951] and 14 Azar [5 December] are members of the government, in which the anti-labour bill of Mosaddeq practically depriving the working class of their right to vote is awaiting the toilers, in which there is no freedom of writing and speech, nor of societies, syndicates and parties, the elections mean nothing but an anti-national plot run by the government.

The Persian people witnessed the fact that Mosaddeq's government at the threshold of the elections for the Seventeenth Majles, when its treacherous collusion on the oil issue was coming to a conclusion with the intervention of the American Bank called International, went so far as to send, on 14 Azar/5 December 1951,[2] vilest roughnecks [*chaqoukeshan*] armed with bayonets among girl and boy students who were killed[3] and injured in the most wicked way known to the fascists.[4]

The Persian people witnessed the fact that the rascals hired by Mosaddeq after having committed so many crimes in front of the Majles and before the eyes of 'Ala's, guided and supported by the police and the army, rushed into the 'House of Peace' and then to all democratic associations and newspaper offices, beating men, destroying houses, pillaging furniture and setting fire to valuable books and places such as the 'Peace Exhibitions'.

The fourteenth of Azar will be recorded as a most shameful fascist stain in the history of Persia.

Mosaddeq's government tries to use these manifest persecutions as means for intimidation of democratic associations and papers and to defeat, it seems to think, the national and anti-imperialistic struggle waged by the people of Persia. The events of 14 Azar show that Mosaddeq's government desires, in the elections plot conceived for the Seventeenth Majles, to suppress in the most barbarous manner any expression of resistance, opposition and national struggle. The shameful election procedure ever conducted by (previous) governments will no doubt be renewed in the present term. But our nation is not living in the circumstances of two years ago for the alert and organised forces that it possesses now.

In the present circumstances our people can and must convert the elections into a wide national and anti-imperialistic campaign.

The goal of the Persian nation in the elections shall not be to secure parliamentary seats alone, for, should the ruling class meet failure from every side, it would resort to the ultimate means of interfering with the ballot boxes, leaving no room for the votes of the nation.[5]

But our people will use the elections as the means to disclose the imperialistic plots, to unveil the machinations and crimes of the ruling class, to demonstrate the nature of the collusions made in connection with the elections and to propagate national and anti-imperialistic slogans. The elections will afford a suitable opportunity and possibility for the equipment of forces and the trial of the national and anti-imperialistic strength on an increased scale.

The Tudeh Party calls on all freedom-lovers and all national and democratic elements as well as on all fellow countrymen to regard indifference in the elections as a failure to carry out a national duty, and actively to take part in the elections and wage their campaign with a view to achieving the above objects.

All freedom-lovers, all democratic elements and all those who are devoted to the preservation and perfection of the constitution, all persons who are fighting imperialism for the sake of independence and freedom of Persia and all democratic groups and societies must enter the elections in a single line.

The masses of the people of Persia must with their common national and anti-imperialistic slogans be called to gather under one and the same banner to fight in the elections.

Those who clamour for being elected can no longer deceive our people by their long speeches and by generalisations. There is no room in the lines of national candidates for those who have left antecedents of enmity with our people.

Although the Tudeh Party and the Democrat Party of Azerbaijan and Kurdistan have been denied the possibility of any sort of open activity and although these real emblems of the will of the masses of Persia cannot put their programmes appropriately into effect yet to those who desire to be national candidates, our democratic slogans must at least be made known and such men must first place before the people their programme of action quite plainly and clearly.

The Persian people will in the elections of the Seventeenth Majles vote for peace and democracy. National candidates will be those who will under no title agree to the conversion of Persia into a war base.

Candidates must undertake before the nation to regard as basis for all their decisions and actions the sovereignty, freedom and independence of our country. Candidates must in pursuing such a policy choose as their target the eradication of all the remnants of the ex-AIOC and similar imperialistic institutions such as the Imperial Bank, etc, as well as waging a campaign against the invading imperialism of America which while having usurped the Bahrain oil is trying hard to capture the positions lost by the defeated imperialism of England. Candidates must condemn with all their might all agreements, undertakings and loans which would weaken the sovereign right of the people.

Candidates must undertake before the nation the task of reviving the progressive tenets of the Constitution, giving reality to democratic freedoms, such as the freedom of opinion, writing and speech and the freedom of societies, parties and syndicates, and fighting every form of military rule of suppressing freedom.

Candidates must undertake to bury Mosaddeq's reactionary bill depriving the workers of their right to vote and to amend the electoral law on such a basis as would ensure the right of electing and of being elected to every individual in the country, whether man or woman, civil or military, soldier or officer.

Candidates must undertake before the nation to pursue a policy of economic independence for Persia on the basis of creating heavy industries, mechanising agriculture, strengthening and expanding home industries through the encouragement of national craftsmen, exploring export markets and transit roads, preventing competition of foreign goods and extending barter transactions.

Candidates must undertake before the nation to take concrete steps to improve the lives of toilers and productive classes, to secure an eight-hour working day, to provide the right for the conclusion of a collective contract, to approve a progressive labour law, to cancel reactionary regulations, to fight against any interference by the government or the police in the affairs of trade unions.

Candidates must undertake before the nation to take active measures in the Majles to improve the conditions of the peasantry by the implementation of the decree setting forth the deduction of 15 per cent from the landowners' share of production, the enactment of more progressive laws, the usage of all the regulations in favour of the peasantry, the eradication of the feudals' inhuman domination, the cancellation of all the unlawful taxes, the impositions and the unpaid labour, the protection of the peasantry and small-holders against the exactions of the feudals and the government and to render technical assistance to them.

Candidates must undertake before the nation to save the Persian artisans and tradesmen from the danger of bankruptcy by preventing the importation of worthless goods and of the goods which can be produced in Persia, by the cancellation of unjust taxes, by stopping the extortion of the municipal and police officials and by government financial help.

Candidates must put on their programme the question of a complete purging in the government departments, the encouragement of the honest and honourable employees and the improvement of the lives of the employees and servants.

Candidates must undertake before the nation to cause the implementation of general education by securing a sufficient budget for the Ministry of Education to provide the means of livelihood for the teachers and the means for the general welfare, etc. The creation of a new and anti-colonisation education must be one of the headlines on the programme of each national candidate.

Candidates must undertake before the nation to secure for the Persian women and youth such rights as are recognised by today's progressive world.

Only those who explicitly and concisely accept such matters in their programmes can be placed in the ranks of national candidates; only those who are interested in these democratic slogans can be proportionately supported by the nation.

Dear Compatriots.

Vote in favour of the national [that is, Tudeh] candidates. Transform the elections into a vast and extensive national anti-imperialistic struggle. Expose the imperialistic plots. Strip the veil from the intrigues, assaults and crimes of the ruling class. Take national and anti-imperialist slogans among the people. Take such measures that electoral propaganda may take the shape of propaganda of peace and of democracy. Involve as much as you can the national and anti-imperialistic forces on the terrain of our struggle.[6]

The Tudeh Party of Persia is sure that our nation will come out of these struggles more fully equipped and that peace and democracy will turn out stronger.

Peace is the holy desire of all nations. May the Persian nation be victorious in its struggles against the dark forces of war, despotism, feudalism and imperialism.

Central Committee of the Tudeh Party

Notes
1. Source: FO 248/1517; declaration dated 25 December 1951.
2. On that day, in spite of a government ban on demonstrations to avoid confrontation with reactionary forces, the leader of the Tudeh Youth Organisation, with the approval of the Tudeh Executive Committee, organised a provocative demonstration on the pretext of the expulsion of a few girl students from their high school; it was directed against Mosaddeq's government, an action that played into the hands of the reactionary forces and their international allies. During scuffles some young people were beaten up by roughnecks in the service of the reactionaries. After the 1953 putsch, Tudeh leaders admitted these 'left-extremist actions' and 'infantile disorders'. See, for instance, Shandermani's 'Secret Letter', dated 28 March 1954, addressed to the Central Committee and also his 1956 'Secret Report' to the Central Committee, both handwritten copies in this author's

possession (Anonymous Tudeh youth leader, *Karnameh-ye Mosaddeq va Hezb-e Tudeh*, Volume 1 (edited by C Chaqueri, Florence, 1978), p 198; B Amirkhosrowi, *Nazar az daroun-e be naqsh-e Hezb-e Tudeh-ye Iran* (Tehran, 1996), pp 290ff). It is interesting that on 7 December 1951 *The Times* carried a piece, 'Fixed Bayonets in Tehran: Boy Demonstrators Dispersed', accusing Mosaddeq's government of 'resuming its activities against school children'! It is a very revealing article lending credibility to accusations of the influence of British agents in the ranks of the Tudeh Party. See also US Department of State, 'Intelligence Report', no 5735, 10 January 1952; USNA 097.3 Z 1092 # 5735. According to this report, Mosaddeq was severely attacked by right-wing senators and deputies for failing to maintain public order.
3. This is a propagandistic prevarication; no deaths were reported.
4. The original translation read: 'to send vilest hireling knife-men under the cover of bayonets among girl and boy students who were made victims of death and injuries in the most wicked manners known to the fascists'.
5. The underlying message is that the party would go beyond electoral means to attain power. The original translation read: 'The goal of the Persian nation in the elections shall not be to secure parliamentary seats alone, inasmuch as the ruling class, even if it should meet failure from every side, would resort to the last means, that is, the changing of the boxes and would leave no room for the votes of the nation.'
6. The original translation read: 'Drag as much as you can the national and anti-imperialistic forces to the struggling grounds.'

+ + +

XXXV: US State Department: The Tudeh Against Mosaddeq (December 1951)[1]

Central Committee of Tudeh Party published and widely distributed proclamation on elections 26 December 1951. Summary of lengthy proclamation follows:

Statement attacks ruling class and Mosaddeq government, ridiculing its claims to free elections:

> Iran people realize that in present circumstances, when Tudeh Party, Azerbaijan Democrat Party, Kurdistan Party have been declared illegal; when those who are partisans of peace, freedom and democracy are persecuted, imprisoned and exiled; when even girls and boys are victims of knife and bayonet; when murderers of 15 July and 16 December are in power; when Mosaddeq's bill depriving workers of right of suffrage is awaiting to be sanctioned; when there is no freedom of speech or assembly elections will mean nothing except conspiracy against nation staged by government.

Proclamation then reviews 'atrocities' of Mosaddeq's government, warns PM attempting to reinstall his type of government:

> Our people, however, can and must turn elections into vast national campaign against imperialism. Goal of Iran people in elections will not be only to gain few seats in Majles; our people will use elections as a means of disgracing imperialistic conspiracies, revealing crimes of the ruling classes, disclosing collusions of elections, and propagating national and anti-imperialistic mottoes. Elections will afford us a suitable opportunity to mobilize our forces and to test the strength of our national and anti-imperialistic forces.
>
> Committee urges all people participate in elections for these aims, terming failure to do so treasonable.

Proclamation continues while Tudeh, Azerbaijan and Kurdistan parties deprived of right to campaign openly, and thus have no opportunity put their program into effect, yet all sympathizers should be familiar with their platform. It is:

1. 'National' candidates should be only those who do not want to 'turn Iran into war base'.
2. Candidates should base all their activities on 'sovereignty, independence and freedom'; and to achieve this end should concentrate on elimination of AIOC and its agents.
3. Candidates should 'fight American aggressive imperialism', which endeavors to take over former British role here.
4. Candidates should 'revive ideals of the Constitution and maintain freedoms of democracy', opposing any form of military government which suppresses freedom.
5. Candidates should undertake to bury reactionary bill of Mosaddeq depriving working class of suffrage and to amend election law in such a way that all individuals have the right to vote and to be elected.
6. Candidates should undertake to base economic policy on the creation of heavy industries, mechanization of agriculture, expansion of home industries, creation of export markets and transit routes; prevention of foreign competition and expansion of barter trade.
7. Candidates should undertake to improve standard of living of workers and producers of wealth, by insisting on eight-hour work day, collective insurance, progressive labor law, and by opposing government and police interference in unions.
8. Candidates should endeavor to improve conditions of farmers by putting into effect resolution regarding deduction of 15 per cent of landowners' profits,

revoking feudalism, abrogating all unlawful taxes, protecting farmers from discrimination by government, extending technical aid.

9. Candidates should undertake to save artisans from danger of bankruptcy by preventing importation of luxury goods and goods which could be produced in Iran, revoking unjust taxes, eliminating oppression of police, and granting financial aid.

10. Candidates should include purge of government departments, encouragement of honest officials, basic improvement of living conditions of government employees.

11. Candidates must ensure public education by providing necessary funds from budget, ensuring good living standards for teachers, and should also install a new anti-imperialist system of education.

12. Candidates should recognize equal rights for men and women.

Proclamation closes with appeal to all voters to select only candidates who will conform to above specifications, to publicize national and anti-imperialistic mottoes, and to turn the election campaign into campaign for peace and independence. Tudeh Party is confident that peace and democracy will emerge victorious out of this campaign — victory to Iran nation in its fight against forces of war, despotism, feudalism and imperialism.

Signed: Central Committee of Tudeh Party.

Notes

1. Source: Report by Ambassador Henderson, Tehran, 28 December 1951; USNA 788.00/12-2851.

+ + +

XXXVI: The Tudeh Party on 'Mosaddeq's Terrorism' (April 1952)[1]

The rotten governing class is trying to suppress the masses who are struggling for their freedom. Every now and again an 'accident' occurs in which a number of our noble sons are murdered.

Under the cover of oil, Mosaddeq and his gang have committed all kinds of atrocities. The oil struggle was only a part of the strategy of the Iranian people in their fight against imperialism. The influence of the Anglo-Americans should be eradicated completely. A superficial operation cannot cure the cancer.

We cannot sit idly by and watch Mosaddeq lead the country to ruin. We have no time for a policy of appeasement.

We can assure Dr Mosaddeq that we shall continue our all-out fight against imperialism. We shall fulfil our mission for peace and for the complete independence and freedom of Iran.

Notes
1.   Source: Tudeh Party's legal organ *Besouy-e Ayandeh*, 4 April 1952.

+ + +

XXXVII: Letter of the National Society Combating Colonialism (August 1952)[1]

To Dr Mosaddeq
Although hardly two months have passed since the people rose against the Anglo-American plot, your policy has caused a great anxiety on the part of the anti-imperialistic people.

Once again we draw your attention to the people's demand and at the same time we will express the views of the Society regarding your policy.

Your appeasement policy toward Washington, the turning of our country into a base of aggression against the Soviets in the interest of the American warmongers, your compromise with the agents of the British and steps adopted by you against democratic organizations prepared the ground for a treacherous Anglo-American plot through the Court.

On many different occasions we reminded you that a plot was brewing. Yet you extended the martial law and made no efforts to expose the diabolic plans of the imperialists.

While the anti-imperialistic people of Tehran were fighting against American tanks with bare hands, the deputies attached to you issued a notorious declaration and asked the people to stay in their houses.

The Society Combating Imperialism, however, asked the people to form a united front against the imperialism, [a united front] which was even favored by the simple people who supported you. The people's rising on 21 July nullified the imperialistic plot and the Court lost its prestige altogether and you came to power.

Following this, even the people demanded the elimination of the Court. They wanted to see that the democratic freedoms are ensured and the American spies who ordered the massacre of the people expelled.

The people wanted all the secret and open treaties imposed on us by the American imperialists cancelled. They wanted the government to take steps to consolidate the relations between Iran, the Soviet Union and other anti-imperialistic countries.

Yet from the very first moment of your resumed leadership you took detrimental steps to the cause of the people.

Your attitude regarding the confiscation of Qavam's property, martial law and US military advisers, has been so incompatible with the people's views that even your closest colleagues could not openly support it.

After your failure to extend martial law the officials of your government with the cooperation of the ruffians of the Court, the American Consulate and the G-2 created chaos and confusion in order to re-establish martial law.

Although some of your closest colleagues were forced to demand the expulsion of US advisers, your government has now and then stated that it does not propose to take such an action.

Far from respecting public opinion, you continued your secret and successive meetings with the US Ambassador and head of the American spies.

The people of Iran demand that:

1. Steps be taken by the government to put an end to the interferences of the imperialists in the Iranian oil question. The government must also do the needful to recover Bahrain. The nation opposes any negotiations on the question of compensation.

2. The interference of the American imperialists must come to an end in our country. US military advisers must be expelled and the espionage centers such as the Point Four, the American Consulates and the Office of Technical Help be closed.

3. Democratic freedoms be ensured throughout the country.

4. The interferences of the Court in the affairs of the country must come to an end.

5. Persons responsible for the recent plot be prosecuted.

6. All the laws which restrict democratic freedoms be cancelled and the budget of the army and gendarmerie be reduced to half.

Failure to comply with these demands entails a historic responsibility for you who are answerable to the people.

Notes
1. Source: *Adineh*, substitute for *Shahbaz*, 29 August 1952, USNA 788.00/9-452.

+ + +

XXXVIII: US State Department: List of Known Tudeh Newspapers in Iran During the Mosaddeq Premiership (October 1952)[1]

1. *Besuy-e Ayandeh* (*Towards the Future*), morning daily; estimated circulation: 6000-8000. Proprietor: Mohamed Zhandi. Board of writers and translators: Davud Novruzi: Leading figure in the Tudeh Youth. Organization: He is an

employee of the Ministry of National Economy. Mahmoud Hormuz: Active in several Tudeh organizations, Hormuz writes primarily for the Peace Partisans' newspaper organ *Maslehat*, as well as for *Besuy-e Ayandeh*. As of late 1951, he was a judge in the Ministry of Justice. Mohammad Hussein Tamaddon:[2] He is known to be an active member of the Tudeh Party. Jahangir Behrouz:[3] He is primarily a news column writer. Reza Azarakhshi: He is an official of the Municipal Government.

The following are only known by name: Mohammad Ja'far Mahjoub;[4] Ali Asghar Soroush; M Fazil; Ali Asghar Morastian; Abbas Baqeri; Aziz Iraj; Shams Zanjani; Ahmad Sadeq.

Presumably, these 'writers and translators' supply part of the required material for the other Tudeh newspapers as well. The above list is not to be considered as exhaustive. In addition, the leading personalities of the 'front' organizations are also contributors to their respective newspapers.

Besuy-e Ayandeh is the leading Tudeh newspaper covering general news.[5] It replaced the newspaper *Rahbar*, which held the same position when the party was legally constituted. The given estimated circulation may have no relation to the number of readers as it is known to be passed from person to person, or read by one literate person to several illiterate ones. Furthermore, if the party finds it necessary to give widespread publicity to an article appearing in a certain issue, that issue may be printed in far larger numbers and simply distributed as a hand-out.

Besuy-e Ayandeh appears in most of the principal cities of Iran.

2. *Shahbaz* (*Falcon*), evening daily; estimated circulation: 3000. Proprietor: Rahim Namvar.[6] This is the organ of the 'Society Combatting Imperialism in Iran'. In effect, it is the evening edition of *Besuy-e Ayandeh*.

3. *Maslahat* (*The Right Way* [*Expediency*]), weekly; estimated circulation: 3000-4000. Proprietor: Ahmad Lankerani. This is the newspaper organ of the 'Partisans of Peace'.

4. *Ayandeh Rowshan* (*Bright Future*), weekly; estimated circulation: 3000, in Assyriac for the Assyrian community. It is the newspaper of the Assyrian branch of the youth organizations.

5. *Bahak* (*Guard*), monthly; estimated circulation: 500; for the Armenian community.

6. *Bani Adam* (*Human* [*Human Being*]) weekly; estimated circulation: 4000. This newspaper is for the Jewish community, but written in Farsi [Persian].

7. *Chalangar* (*Blacksmith*), biweekly; estimated circulation: 2500. Proprietor: Ali Afrashteh. It is suppressed at this time (September 1952). Written entirely in [satiric] verse,[7] *Chalangar* appealed to the poetic nature of Iranians in general. It printed poems from non-Tudeh contributors and was purchased by many

non-Tudeh readers.

8. *Doust-e Mardom* (*Friend of the People*), printed in Shiraz.

9. *Enteqad* (*Criticism*), weekly; newspaper organ of the Society to Aid the Peasants [sic].

10. *Daneshjou* (*Freshman* [*Student*]), weekly; estimated circulation: 3000. This is the newspaper of the [Tudeh-led] University of Tehran Students' Organization.

11. *Danesh Amouz* (*Junior* [*High-School*] *Student*, sporadic; for grammar-school [high-school] children.

12. *Dehqanan-e Iran* (*Peasants of Iran*), weekly; estimated circulation: 2000. Newspaper organ of the 'Society of Aid [to] Peasants'. Previously, it appeared only sporadically, but has recently (September 1952) been more regular. It appears to concentrate on attacks against Point IV.

13. *Arsheh* (*Deck*), published in Bushire. Publication began in September 1952.

14. *Farhangiyan* (*Culturalists* [*Teaching Staff*]), weekly; estimated circulation: 7000. Designed to appeal to teachers and employees of the Ministry of Education. It is read by many persons of non-Tudeh leanings.

15. *Gilan*, sporadic. *Besuy-e Ayandeh* for Gilan Province. Printed in Tehran.

16. *Haji Baba*, weekly. Leftist inclined, humorous, satirical.

17. *Himayateh Koudakan* (*Protection of Children*), sporadic; Organ of the Society for the Protection of Children.

18. *Jahean Zanan* (*Women's World*), weekly; estimated circulation: 5000. Newspaper organ of the Women's Organization.

19. *Javanan-e Democrat* (*Democratic Youth*), weekly; estimated circulation: 2000-3000. It is the newspaper organ of the Society of Democratic Lawyers [sic — Youth].

20. *Kabutar-e Solh* (*Dove of Peace*); estimated circulation: 2000. This newspaper is owned by Reza Lotfi, son of the present Minister of Justice. It used to appear regularly, but now only replaces *Maslahat* when the latter is suppressed.

21. *Khalq* (*People*), weekly; often fortnightly; estimated circulation: 4000. Newspaper organ of the Freedom Society.[8]

22. *Mardom Yazd* (*People of Yazd*). Published at Yazd. It is comparatively new, having begun publication in September 1952.

23. *Mehrgan* [name of autumn festival in ancient Iran], approximately quarterly; estimated circulation: 8000. Designed to appeal to intellectuals.

24. *Naqsh-e Kargar* (*Role of the Worker*), sporadic; estimated circulation: 2500.

25. *Navid Azadi* (*Freedom Herald*), weekly; estimated circulation: 3000-4000. For machinists, electricians, etc.

26. *Payk-e Isfahan* (*Isfahan Courier*), weekly; estimated circulation: 2000. It is the principal Tudeh newspaper of Isfahan, but sometimes printed in Tehran.

27. *Parchamdar-e Solh* (*Standard Bearer of Peace*). It is a relatively new Tudeh newspaper appearing in Shiraz.

28. *Ranj-o-Ganj* (*Toilers and Wealth* [*Toil and Treasure*]), weekly; estimated circulation: 1000.

Clandestine Newspapers

1. *Mardom* (*People*), weekly. *Mardom* is the official newspaper organ of the Tudeh Party; it deals with general questions such as 'Peace', 'Democratic Freedoms', etc. Often its articles serve as models for articles which appear in the legal Tudeh press, particularly *Besuy-e Ayandeh*. The estimated circulation is highly tenuous, but it is known to be distributed throughout the country.

The police have tried to locate the place of publication, but without success.[9] From time to time, the police discover bundles of copies in trains and buses but investigation leads to blind alleys. There is a reward for any information leading to that location. The party obligingly sends copies by open mail to the authorities and foreign embassies, including that of the United States.

2. *Zafar* (*Victory*). It is the official newspaper organ of the Central United Council of Trade Unions. It deals, of course, exclusively with labor affairs, and signals the 'line' to be followed by the other Tudeh newspapers with regard to strikes, labor demands, and labor problems.

3. *Razm* (*Battle*). It is the newspaper organ of the Tudeh Youth Organization. It deals with general issues as well as with matters of particular interest to the youth of the country, and more especially with students. A special feature which appears regularly is a 'Calendar of Important International Events' that describes the Soviet-sponsored international rallies.

Notes

1. Source: Tehran Report, 20 October 1952; USNA 788.00/10-2052. Incorrect translation of newspaper names have been corrected.
2. He was imprisoned after the coup. Upon release he went to London and studied economics at the London School of Economics; then returned to Iran worked professionally and became apolitical.
3. After his release from prison, he worked as a journalist and published *The Echo of Iran*, an annual publication in English on Iranian affairs. Archival reports in the West that he remained in contact with British and American embassies.
4. After the coup he finished his university studies and became a specialist of Iranian literature and folklore. After the 1979 revolution, he collaborated with Shapour Bakhtiar in Paris. After the latter's assassination, he taught in the US for a while before passing away.
5. It did not only deal with very slanted news reporting but also furiously poured dirt

on PM Mosaddeq, abusing him as a stooge of American imperialism.
6. After the coup, he left the country and lived in exile in Bucharest. He worked for the party. After the revolution he returned to Iran, but does not seem to have taken an active part in the renewed Tudeh.
7. It also contained cartoons, many of them abusing PM Mosaddeq.
8. A Tudeh front organisation created by various Tudeh and pro-Tudeh newspapers, also including at one time the pro-British arch-reactionary politician Seyyed Zia Tabataba'i.
9. After the 1953 coup it was discovered on the old road from Tehran to Shemiran on the foot of the Alborz mountain.

+ + +

XXXIX: *Daily Worker*: People's Party Leaders Show Britain the Struggle in Persia (March 1953)[1]

(Here is an interview given to the *Daily Worker* Special Correspondent by Dr [Reza] Radmanesh [General-Secretary], Ehsan Tabari [party 'theoretician'], Mahmoud Boqrati, Ahmad Qasemi and Dr [Gh-H] Foroutan [of the Executive in Teheran until the summer of 1952], Leaders of the Tudeh Party [resident in Moscow], the Party of Persian workers.)

The situation in Persia is dangerous. Both American and British imperialists intrigue and endeavour to extend their grip on the country. We appeal to the British people and especially to the British Labour and trade union movement to support our struggle against these plots. Our struggle for national independence is part of the same struggle of the British people against the financiers of the City of London and of Wall Street. Our party sincerely desires friendship between the Persian and British peoples.

Shah

The most dangerous enemy of the Persian people within Persia is the group of feudal magnates round the shah and those who have commercial connections with the big foreign monopolies.

All the hopes of the Anglo-Iranian Oil company to get back its [sic] oil properties rest on these most corrupt people who form the court of the shah and have their connections with high-ranking officers. The Americans, too, have many friends in these quarters, and the shah's friends have long been preparing a sell-out of their country.

These big landowners, court officials, army generals and merchants are the most reactionary section of the Persian ruling class. The present government of Persia, the Government of Dr Mosaddeq and his National Front, does not belong to these groups who are in many ways opposed to it.

Dr Mosaddeq's Government, however, is grounded in the Persian people, but represents another section of the Persian ruling class.

His government is composed of and supported by the small Persian industrialists who are struggling to free themselves from the grip and restrictions of the big foreign monopolies and also by a section of the landowners. They do not oppose all foreign imperialism. In fact, they are willing to allow the Americans more possibilities of political and economic penetration into Persia. For them the enemy is British imperialism and the Anglo-Iranian Oil Company. They seek to limit the struggle of the Persian people for independence exclusively to the struggle against the British imperialists.

While many groups and parties are organised into the National Front organisation of Dr Mosaddeq, in fact, these groups are chiefly small. They have few members, [and] little organisation. Recently, some divisions have appeared among them, especially the division between Dr Mosaddeq and Seyyed [Abolqasem] Kashani. But they profit especially from the enthusiasm of the Persian people for the struggle against imperialism. They try especially to draw the shopkeepers, peasants and artisans who are numerous in Persia behind the slogans of the National Front.

Tudeh

The National Front, while conducting a limited struggle against British imperialism, in fact helps the penetration of American influence into Persia. And it is hostile to the real national movement which is under the leadership of the Tudeh Party.

The Tudeh party has been illegal since 1949. The Central Council of Trade Unions has also been suppressed. To belong to the Tudeh or to the trade union is officially a crime in Persia. Every organisation defending the rights of the Persian people suffers persecution in some form or another. Government-supported hooligans have twice plundered the Peace Club in Teheran, belonging to the Persian Peace Movement.

Pressure

In Tabriz supporters of the Peace Movement were sentenced to 10 years imprisonment. But in spite all these persecutions the Tudeh Party is still alive and still a force in Persian politics. As crisis follows crisis, more and more the Persian people are looking to the Tudeh to lead them out of the present distress.[2]

Persia is a country of great natural riches, but of pressing poverty for the ordinary peasant, worker and small man. Because of the American and British pressure, the majority of the budget is spent on the army and the police. As a result, social, cultural and health services are pitifully inadequate. The peasants, the majority of the population, are hungry and in many cases literally naked and homeless.

Poverty

Because of their abject poverty, they are forced to abandon their villages and flee to the towns for work. As unemployment in towns is widespread and growing, the peasants starve in the streets. A worker gets on average 30 rials (less than 7s) a day. The handicraftsmen and small shopkeepers and traders, the majority of the town populations, are facing bankruptcy as imports from America more and more flood the markets. What few industrialists Persia has are also feeling the heavy competition of imported foreign goods. Many of them have crashed or are near bankruptcy.[3]

Yet the national movement has not been crushed. It is growing and will win independence for the Persian people from the imperialists, both British and American.

Notes

1. Source: *Daily Worker*, 2 March 1953. The Foreign Office showed great interest in this article; a copy was in the files, see FO 371/104563. It must be noted that this interview was published a few days after the attempt to kill Mosaddeq, during his last visit to the shah's palace on 9 Esfand 1331 (27 February 1953).
2. These false claims were exactly what encouraged the new British government under the Conservatives led by Winston Churchill to argue his case of the imminent 'red peril' threatening Iran in order to convince the newly-elected US Republican administration under General Eisenhower to proceed with the proposed British *coup d'état*. In fact, the Tudeh was losing ground at time as a result of its internal splits over the issue of its wrong appraisal of Mosaddeq as 'pro-American' by its leadership and the need to support him. The crackdown on the Tudeh after the coup was made possible only because many Tudeh militants had lost faith in the wrong policies promoted by a leadership that was half underground and half in Moscow and had little contact with the realities of Iranian society. The criticism of the leadership's mistakes made at the Fourth Plenum of the party held in 1957 in Moscow, particularly with regard to the appraisal of Mosaddeq, and revelations of internal documents by Tudeh militants after the demise of the party, all refute these claims. See C Chaqueri (ed), *Historical Documents: The Workers', Social-Democratic and Communist Movement in Iran* (23 volumes, Florence and Tehran, 1969-94), Volume 1; and the memoirs by F Kechavarz, *Man mottaham mikonam* (Tehran, 1979); I Eskandari, *Khaterat-e siasi* (four volumes, Paris, 1987-89); and F Ekteshafi, *Khaterat* (Berlin, 1998).
3. This statement was also untrue and provocative, helping the British case against Mosaddeq. The country was under severe foreign exchange restraints, and only absolute necessities were being imported, which were in no way in competition with home producers. In fact, exports had picked up and the conditions of artisans and local industries were improving in light of the lack of exchange. Besides, not

even the British or American embassies reported people dying of hunger in the streets. This statement was also to 'prove' that Persia under Mosaddeq was on the precipice, imminently falling into the Soviet camp, hence the need for the coup.

+ + +

XL: Resolution Passed by Pro-Tudeh Demonstrators on the First Anniversary of 1952 Uprising (July 1953)[1]

We, tens of thousands of men and women; workers and enlightened persons; merchants, peasants and artisans of Tehran; who have gathered in Baharestan Square at the invitation of the National Preparatory Committee for Commemorating the anniversary of 21 July, adopt the following resolution:

1. We solemnly take an oath on the blood of the martyrs that we shall always keep hoisted the honorable flag of the national struggle. We solemnly swear that we shall sacrifice ourselves in defense of our national interests and the freedom and independence of our beloved country against the aggressions of the imperialist plunderers. Victory to the Iranian people who are combating for peace, freedom, and national independence.

Long live 21 July, the day of the struggle of the Iranian people against imperialism. Honor and glory to the martyrs of 21 July and to all those who have been assassinated in the struggle for freedom.

2. We demand that:

a) The hirelings of British and American imperialism, who planned the 21 July events in order to break up our national movement, must be tried and punished irrespective of their rank and position.

b) The Court interferences in the internal affairs of the country must be eliminated forever. The Court is the principal center of all intrigue.

c) The Seventeenth Majles be dissolved by holding a referendum.

d) New, free and democratic elections must be held immediately throughout the country.

3. In order to prevent the renewal of intrigues by the imperialist enemies of our country, the interferences of the British and American imperialists, who are the principal masters of anti-national intrigues, must be terminated.

a) The suppression of American imperialist espionage centers, Point Four offices and their other espionage organizations throughout the country. American military advisers must be ejected.

b) The agreements thrust on us by the Americans must be cancelled.

c) The imperialist hirelings who occupy important posts must be tried and punished.

4. We want to reactivate our nationalized oil industry as soon as possible. The

government must rely on the great national forces and establish relations with the countries which respect our freedom and independence by taking advantage of international possibilities for reactivating the oil industry through the sale of oil products to the USSR and other peace-loving countries who are prepared to buy oil from us and extend their economic relations with us with due respect to our independence. In this way the existing economic blockade and deadlock can be broken up.

5. We desire the progress, development and happiness of our country. International peace is an essential requirement to the achievement of our aims. We hate war and aggression and warmongers. We, therefore, demand that the government should use all its influence in international political circles so that peaceful means are adopted for the termination of cold war and the centers of warmongering. They must keep aloof from submitting to force and to aggressive policies which are used by the warmongering imperialists.

6. We reaffirm that so far only the powerful and great national forces have been capable of destroying the plots of the imperialists and to gain great victories for the people. These forces must be given the opportunity to enter the field freely and use their power to get rid of imperialism. For this purpose it is essential that:

a) Martial law be abolished.

b) The freedom-killing and reactionary laws be abrogated.

c) Democratic freedoms and freedom of action must be granted to all democratic parties and organizations throughout Iran.

7. We reaffirm that the principal condition for achieving victory over imperialism is the unification of all anti-imperialist forces. Without the active participation of all anti-imperialist classes and the formation of a united front of all these forces, it will be impossible to achieve a decisive victory over imperialism.

We invite people from all walks of life, from all parties and organizations, great personalities and independents who love freedom, without any regard to their political views and objects, to form a united front, based on the general slogans against the British and American imperialists.

Victory to the unification of all the anti-imperialist forces.

Death to the obstructionists and those who sow the seeds of discord.

Destruction to imperialism. Death to the hirelings of imperialism.

Victory to the united anti-imperialist national front with the participation of workers, peasants and those in favor of nationalization.

Notes
1. Source: Tudeh daily *Jaras*, 22 July 1953; translated in USNA. On this occasion, American Ambassador Henderson reported that, while PF participants numbered 3000, Tudeh supporters numbered 12 000. On other occasions inflated figures were reported. See Embassy despatches dated 24 July 1953 ('Review of 21 July Demonstrations'); 27 August 1953 ('Capacity of Baharestan Square'); and 13 August 1953 ('Round-Up of Communist Activities in Iran'), cited in Despatch by American Embassy First Secretary Roy M Melbourne, copied to Foreign Office: FO 371/104573. On the other hand, a CIA report quoted Tehran Radio that around 100 000 people took part in the PF demonstration. See also 'Current Intelligence Bulletin, CIB', 19 August 1953; 'Current Intelligence Bulletin, CIB', 1 October 1953.

+ + +

XLI: An Open Letter to Dr Mosaddeq by the CC of the Tudeh Party (July 1953)[1]

The events of the past year in Iran which commenced with the imperialist plans of 21 July and perfected by the Court's *coup d'état* plans of August-September, the intrigues of 28 February, the murder of the Chief of Police and finally the recent parliamentary incidents, have all confirmed our views in connection with the enmity of the American imperialists against our National Movement and their complete collaboration with the British imperialists. We have repeatedly informed you that the British and American imperialists are the sworn enemies of our people. Although each one of the two imperialists are competing for increasing their plunders of our natural resources, yet they are completely in accord in their policy of establishing imperialism in Iran.

The American imperialists, both the Democrats and the Republicans, have always supported the British plunderers in all international meetings convened to discuss the oil dispute. During the past two-and-one-half years the British and American imperialists have done their damnedest to nullify the law nationalizing the oil industry and prevent the reactivation of this huge industry.

These governments repeatedly endeavored to carry out a *coup d'état* assisted by the treacherous Shah and his hirelings such as Qavam, Zahedi and the majority of the deputies of the Seventeenth Majles who tried to overthrow the government.

The imperialists (British and American) have created economic difficulties for us and have prevented us from selling our oil. The right thing would have been seriously to combat American imperialism from the very beginning but you have never taken our advice and on the contrary you gave them more scope to establish their espionage system in Iran. You submitted to their servile economic agreements which bar this country from exporting strategic goods, which also includes oil, to Soviet Russia, the People's Government of China, and the democratic countries of Eastern Europe. By signing the agreement regarding the establishment of Point Four in Iran, you handed over the country completely to American spies. During your term of office over 1000 American spies have occupied our country pretending to be military advisers and Point Four technicians. These people have instigated trouble against our peace-loving neighbor and are spying against that country.

The Americans are the center of all intrigues, yet you handed over the army to them and this policy of surrender is contrary to our national aspirations. Eisenhower has written you a vile letter and Dulles has made a statement in the American Senate concerning the necessity of a military coup in Iran. This has even caused comment from neutral papers like *Bakhtar-e Emrouz* and *Jebhehy-e Azadi*.

In addition to the above, you have suppressed the anti-imperialist and freedom-loving combatants and have, therefore, followed the policies of the previous hireling government of Iran. Even Razmara did not dare to put out a law similar to the public security law.

During the election to the Seventeenth Majles you formed a coalition with the Court, the center of all anti-national intrigues, and prevented the real representatives of the people from being elected. You have excited thousands of the anti-imperialist combatants and have so far not punished the culprits of the 21 July and 28 February events.

Dr Mosaddeq: This is a summary of your wrong policies connected with oil and internal problems. Throughout this period the anti-imperialist people sacrificed themselves for you and whenever your government was in danger supported you until the danger was past. But you were more inclined to collaborate with the American imperialists and you did not, therefore, pay attention to this tremendous force.

Without a doubt, the continuation of this policy will nullify all our victories. Today the danger of imperialism is threatening our country more than ever.

The known spies of British and American imperialism, the Shah, Zahedi, the majority of the Majles deputies, the treacherous army leaders, and their other accomplices are openly active. British and American papers are writing about the necessity of a military coup in Iran and the establishment of a military dictatorship.

In such an hour, the grant of freedom of action to the anti-imperialist forces is an element which can save our country from these dangers. Any delay in breaking the chains of captivity tied to the hands and feet of the people such as martial law and the reactionary laws, and the prevention of granting democratic freedom will be considered as service to the cause of imperialism.

On 21 March 1951 you yourself confessed that the vast national demonstrations were the most important weapons for gaining a great victory in nationalizing the oil industry.

If you believe in what you said then, why don't you practice your belief at a time when imperialist intrigues and plots are threatening the country?

Dr Mosaddeq: In this hour of grave crisis we once again ask you to take effective measures to overcome the dangerous intrigues of the imperialists. You have responsibilities to the people and we demand that, in order to break up the imperialist plots, you implement the following immediately:

1. Democratic freedom to be granted to all. Martial law must be terminated, anti-democratic laws must be cancelled. Everybody must be given an opportunity to mobilize their force in a united front.

2. The principal centers of intrigue, that is, the Court and the Majles, must be suppressed. The Majles must be dissolved by holding a referendum. General elections must be held immediately. The Shah must be prevented from interfering in the internal affairs of the country. Anti-national activities by the Court and its elements in the affairs of the army and the police and government departments must be discontinued permanently.

3. American interferences must be terminated. The servile military and economic agreements must be terminated. The Point Four espionage organization and American Consulates must be closed and American spies must be ejected from the country.

4. With regard to the sale of oil, you must depart from the policy of following American policy. You must enter negotiations with Soviet Russia and the democratic countries who are willing to reactivate the huge oil industry and transact business with us despite the imperialist obstacles.

Dr Mosaddeq: The patriotic people of our country are ready to make all kinds of sacrifices for the implementation of their demands and they will fully support the government which implements them.

Dr Mosaddeq: The Tudeh Party which is the center of the most informed and sacrificing combatants of our national anti-imperialist movement has for many years been deprived of being publicly active as the result of the treacherous and direct interferences of the British and American imperialists. Sa'ad's prosecution of the Tudeh Party was the result of direct instructions from the British and American imperialists. You always promised freedom to the people but after taking over the reins of office, you have continued the vile system and policies of the previous governments which you yourself criticized and condemned.

The Tudeh Party, throughout the period of its freedom and during the past four-and-one-half years, when it has been violently suppressed by the police, has always been in the front rank of the anti-imperialist combatants and that is why the British and American imperialists and their hirelings are such deadly enemies of the party.

Today no one can claim that the Tudeh Party in Iran is not a big and effective political power in the political life of Iran. For this reason we demand that you should submit to the will of thousands of the anti-imperialist people and follow the most fundamental principles of internal and international democratic laws of freedom, always bearing in mind the exceptional importance of the open activities of the Iran Tudeh Party in the development of the anti-imperialist movement and the cutting off of the roots of imperialist influence.

You must do away with the illegal and reactionary restrictions which confront our party and which prevent our public activities. Make it possible for our party and its members to benefit from political and social rights.

The Central Committee of the Tudeh Party of Iran

Notes
1. Source: USNA.

+ + +

XLII: Declaration of the Tudeh Party CC on the Morrow of the 1953 Putsch (August 1953)[1]

We must form a united front to combat and destroy the treacherous imperialist plots created by the coalition of Reza Khan's son and the government of hooligans.

In this hour of crisis we once again invite Dr Mosaddeq and his supporters, the National Movement Fraction, the Iran Party, the guilds and merchants' organization, the Third Force Party, the Pan-Iranist and the Liberation of the People of Iran Parties, and all reputable and patriotic people who are not prepared to tolerate the government of the ruffian and the traitor, the government of the American and British hirelings. Everybody must put aside their political beliefs and differences and organize into a single united front.

Compatriots: Anti-imperialist combatants. A great danger is threatening our country. The hirelings of British and American imperialists, who are only supported by the infamous and the ruffians with the pillars of their government based on people like Sha'ban the brainless, Malekeh Etezadi,[2] Shahandeh,[3] Pirasteh,[4] made a military *coup d'état* which was directed from the American Embassy, and treacherous elements like Reza Khan's son, [General] Zahedi, [General] Arfa, etc, were the leaders. They took advantage of the differences existing between national forces and the national government's appeasement policy and occupied government organizations in Tehran and are endeavoring to establish their treacherous government.

These ruffians and treacherous people, who are well aware of their insecure position, are endeavoring to create a reign of terror, like that created by Reza Shah, by threatening people with bayonets and machine-guns, and by putting murderers and hooligans in charge to suppress the people. In this way they wish to establish their black government. These criminals, however, are not aware that international and Iranian conditions are so different from those which existed at the time of Reza Khan and 15 Bahman.[5]

The people of Iran during their struggles of the past twelve years against the plundering imperialists and their hirelings have awakened and have gained considerable and priceless experience, and are not prepared to hand over the freedom and independence of their country freely to the foreigners.

The people of our country have gained much experience during the last four years against imperialism and have also gained glorious victories. They are ready to defend these victories with all their power. The government of the ruffians and the son of Reza Khan is temporary and has no support among the people however much they instil terror. The only government which can remain stable is one which has a place in the hearts of the people and serves the people.

Dear compatriots.

Anti-imperialist combatants.

Workers, peasants, artisans, students, employees, enlightened people, merchants, shopkeepers, people of the bazaar, patriotic employers, you people who do not want your country to become the rambling place for British and American spies; you people who do not want the huge oil resources of your country to fall into the hands of the British and American plunderers once again; you people who do not want the fate of your country to be sold to the British and American imperialists by the Court prostitutes; you people who do not want persons like Sha'ban, the brainless, to endanger and overcome your family chastity and reputation; you people, who love your national honor and independence, must rise and destroy this puppet government with all your power and don't rest until it has been destroyed.

Dear compatriots,

We must learn a lesson from the events of the immediate past. If the forces, which aimed at curtailing the hand of the imperialists from our country, had formed a united front, instead of giving an opportunity to the obstructionists to create differences; such an opportunity would never have been presented to the enemies of the masses. This event, however, must not depress you on any account.

The existing conditions from the point of view of power of the national forces and the favorable international situation, the weakness of the imperialist forces, the increasing international differences, are all far more favorable than the days after 15 Bahman or the period of Razmara's government or at the time of the treacherous Shah–Qavam *coup d'état*.

Today, the pillars of the imperialist rule of British and American have been shaken throughout the world, and is sinking daily in some parts of the world. The imperialists have failed in their endeavor to create a world war and their bogus unity is cracking up daily and these differences are becoming deeper.

The democratic peace front which is the big support behind the national forces in the colonies is strengthening daily and is delivering destructive blows to the ruling imperialists.

Dear compatriots.

It is up to us to acquaint ourselves and understand these suitable conditions and to support the tremendous anti-imperialist forces which are in existence in our country. We must rise and use all our power to destroy the treacherous government of Reza Khan's son without any fear and fully confident of final victory.

The most important factor which will ensure our victory is unity and again unity. Today our national independence, integrity, reputation and honor are threatened. Today the question of political beliefs is not important and is not on our agenda. All the reputable people of Iran must gather under one slogan and this is the safeguarding of our national independence and the termination of the influences of the American and British imperialists, and the overthrow of a tyrant and of the existing puppet government.

We invite all parties and anti-imperialist organizations, all honorable elements to adopt a uniform policy for the creation of a united front for the purpose of all future struggles. We ask all parties and organizations attacked by the ruffians to reorganize their bands without any loss of time, maintain their contacts and communicate immediately with all the other anti-combatants of our party. We ask the members of the national parties and organizations to compel their leaders to take action without any loss of time, and take steps to form a united front. Any obstruction placed in the path of the formation of a united front is in the interest of the enemy.

Anti-imperialist combatants.

You must enlighten the people of all classes and invite them to resist; you must transform localized and small resistance movements into a public resistance based on a united front. If a general resistance is started by the people and becomes a positive resistance, instead of a negative resistance, then the noisy tanks of the enemy will be transformed into little cardboard boxes.

The enemy is endeavoring to separate the army from the people and to suppress the people through the army. They must be contacted and have the situation explained to them of how their commanders committed treason against our national interests.

The seeds of resistance exist in the army. They must be encouraged to disobey the commands of their commanders and to join the ranks of the people. There is no doubt that if the people start the resistance movement considerable numbers of honorable army personnel, officers who respect the national prestige, will join hands with the masses.

Dear compatriots.

Anti-imperialist combatants.

Army elements are available for the victory by the people over the imperialists and their puppet government. We must utilize these elements to our best advantage. Resistance movements must be organized; a united front must be created. Do not fear the preliminary victories of the enemy.

Resist and counter attack.

This is the only way to achieve victory for securing freedom and national independence. This is the road which, without any doubt, will be trodden on by all the real anti-imperialist combatants.

Victory is for the people! The treacherous people will achieve nothing but defeat and dishonor.

Victory to the united national anti-imperialists!

Death to the government of the American and British hirelings!

Death to the government of the ruffians and the son of Reza Khan!

The sacred flag of our struggles for freedom and national independence will remain hoisted!

Death to the imperialists and their hirelings!

The Central Committee of the Tudeh Party of Iran

20 August 1953

Notes
1. Source: USNA.
2. A well-known upper-class call-girl.
3. A reactionary journalist at the service of the Court, who received funding from the US and UK embassies to oppose Mosaddeq.
4. A reactionary politician.
5. That is, 4 February 1949, when a fake attempt was made on the life of the Shah causing the suppression of the Tudeh Party.

XLIII: US State Department: Recent Tudeh Activities and the Zahedi Government (October 1953)[1]

One of the most significant developments of the past month with regard to the Tudeh Party has been the partial resurgence of party activities in spite of the continuance of the government's anti-Communist campaign. Clandestine distribution of Communist leaflets and other propaganda occurs nightly, and Communist sympathizers can be blamed for the sabotage of most of the Iranian Air Force fighters at Qal'ehi-morghi Air Base late in September. During the first few days of October, Tudeh members attempted on several occasions openly to distribute propaganda tracts in honor of the party's twelfth anniversary, but they were effectively suppressed by the security forces.

Communist agitation is probably at least partly responsible for the widespread rumors predicting anti-government disturbances for 8 October and for the unrest in the Tehran University student body over the arrest of a number of suspected pro-Communist professors. Strengthened security forces in the bazaar and at the university apparently discouraged most prospective student demonstrators however, the bazaar shops failed to open in the morning and some remained closed throughout the day. Considered as a move in a sort of war of nerves, the incident undoubtedly served the Communist cause by encouraging anti-government elements and rendering more difficult the maintenance of security.

Tudeh propaganda is being diffused mainly by means of the weekly *Mardom*, by small, crudely-printed leaflets, and by handwritten, stenciled, and micrographed broadsides, all of which are distributed covertly. Except for one issue, most copies of which were confiscated after a raid on a Tudeh cell apparently involved in printing the paper, *Mardom* has been distributed every week during the past month. *Donya-ye Emrouz* appeared as a leftist daily for only five or six days before being suppressed, and despite the freeing of its editor after a brief term in prison, it has not appeared since.

So far as is known, the only incident of Tudeh-inspired sabotage in recent weeks was the occurrence at Qal'ehi-morghi mentioned earlier. On the evening of 22 September [1953], three officers of the guard, all of whom were under suspicion of Communist sympathies, put the electrical and control systems of some 25 fighters out of commission, lighted crude delayed-action fuses designed to set off fires and explosions in two hangars, and drove off the field. A guard detected the fires before any damage could occur, but the saboteurs made good their escape and are still at large. Army authorities declared after the incident that the campaign to locate and uproot Communist elements in the armed forces would be intensified; apart from a number of retirements of suspect Air Force personnel, no concrete action in this regard is known to have been taken to date.

Official recognition of the party's disruptive activities came during the past week, in the form of a government communiqué to the effect that the Tudeh were working to overthrow the government and create disorder.

Activity in support of Tudeh aims has been made punishable by death, however, the government is concurrently encouraging disillusioned ex-Communists to confess their mistake and turn over a new leaf, and is trying to draw a distinction between mere dupes and genuine agitators. Government spokesman Amidi-Nouri made the following comment on the government's position at his 7 October press conference:

> The government, which is bent on serving the people, will prevent provocative activities and it believes that a few hundred lives can readily be sacrificed so that eighteen million people may lead normal lives. Those who have been misled will be duly released, but the guilty will be severely punished.

Purges of pro-Tudeh elements are under way in several ministries and are being carried out with varying amounts of determination and thoroughness. Minister of Health Jahanshah Saleh, who confessed to an Embassy officer recently that he had been amazed at the extent of infiltration in his ministry, is conducting a vigorous campaign, and Minister of Post, Telephones and Telegraph Abbas Farzanegan is following a similar course in his own organization. In the Ministry of Labor, Abdol-Qasem Panahi has unearthed a few known Communists, and he is planning to attack next the problem of infiltration among factory workers. Agriculture Minister Abdol-Hussein Adl, troubled by conflicting evidence in a number of cases, appears uncertain as to how best to deal with Tudeh elements in his department.

In the Ministry of Education, perhaps the most heavily infiltrated of all the government departments, efforts to eradicate pro-Communist elements have resulted in the dismissal of numerous teachers and the revival of a law forbidding any form of political activity on the part of students or instructors. One unfortunate result of the firings of suspect personnel has been the disruption of classes in a number of schools, where there are no longer enough teachers to handle the schedules. Efforts are under way to replace dismiss instructors for the time being with qualified officials from other government agencies.

Little reliable information is available regarding the extent of the purge in the Ministry of Justice, also a favorite target for Communist infiltration. It seems very likely, however, that the Prime Minister [Zahedi] and his aides will keep a close watch over the Ministry which is charged with the treatment of [Tudeh] Communist Party members now under arrest. Possibly significant are the demotions and administrative reprimands recently handed to the two judges who dismissed the case against a number of Tudeh leaders early this year.

Arrests of known or suspected party members are continuing, some three to four thousand having been seized to date in the provinces and approximately 1100 in Tehran. Four to five hundred of the latter have been released for insufficient evidence, and probably a larger number were set free in the provinces. Most of the delegates returning from the Bucharest Youth Congress were arrested shortly after their return to Iran, but the majority of those seized were later released with a warning. In raids on party cell headquarters, many of which have been located and searched, quantities of arms, printing materials, propaganda, and various types of party records have been seized.

The Tudeh have done their best to disrupt the drive against them with quantities of anonymous letters to the security forces securing innocent persons of Communist activities, but this has been more than counterbalanced by the revelations of Tudeh members from within the party's ranks. The Lankarani brothers, as well as some lesser party functionaries and ordinary members, are said to have identified numbers of their former comrades for the government, and most of the Tudeh cells discovered by the police were located as a result of tips from disgruntled or disillusioned party members.

In order to avoid overloading municipal prison facilities and to ensure maximum security, several hundred of the more important prisoners have been incarcerated in the fortress of Falak al-Aflak under guard of units of the Khosrow-Abad garrisons, while other incorrigibles have been deported to the prison island of Khark in the Persian Gulf.

It is expected that those prisoners will be tried at their place of detention and there sentenced to varying terms of imprisonment. No trials have been held as yet, as the government plans to conclude the Mosaddeq trial and the trials of the army officers and government functionaries accused of collaborating and conspiring with him before bringing on the cases of the Tudeh members. In this manner, the authorities hope to avoid congesting the limited court facilities and to supervise more closely the conduct of the trials, thus minimizing the possibilities for accused Communists to escape retribution through bribery or pressure.

The press continues to give some attention to the Tudeh problem, with some papers calling for the severest penalties for recognized Communist leaders. For the rank-and-file members, many of whom are thought to be merely misguided or deceived as to the party aims and activities, the generally favored policy is one of leniency coupled with unequivocal warnings against a fall from grace. Former Tudeh members who repent should, it is felt, be given a chance to redeem themselves in the eyes of society.

Although the government's anti-Communist policy finds favor in the eyes of the press, there is some criticism of the way it has been carried out. Some editorialists say that the security forces were too slow and too lenient in the early days of the new regime, and either let the party's major leaders escape entirely or released them after a few days' detention, and thus gave them an opportunity to go into hiding. So far as is known, no paper has disregard with the government's policy of friendship with Soviet Russia on the international level coupled with relentless pursuit of its subversive agents within Iran.
For the Ambassador
Roy M Melbourne
First Secretary of American Embassy, October 1953

Notes
1. Source: Report by the First Secretary of the US Embassy at Tehran, copy transmitted to the Foreign Office, London; FO 371/104573.

+ + +

XLIV: US State Department: Request for Anti-Communist Material (1954)[1]

Tehran Embassy to Department of State
Copy to Taipei Embassy [China]
A high Iranian official has asked this Embassy's advice regarding certain proposals for a conservative anti-Communist program in Iran. The program is to be directed against Communist influence among laborers on the one hand and intellectuals, particularly teachers and other government employees, on the other. The Embassy would like to respond quickly and helpfully to this request.

It is understood the Republic of China has a program of re-educating prisoners of war from Korea and others who have been indoctrinated by the Communists. If so, the Embassy would appreciate it if the Embassy at Taipei could provide copies of any of its reports regarding this program, particularly those describing specific details and the type of material used in re-education. If copies are not available at the Embassy, it would be appreciated if the Department could be requested to supply them to this Embassy on an urgent basis.

In addition, this Embassy would also be grateful if the Embassy at Taipei would provide any information published by the Chinese Government (in

English) which might be helpful in combating Communist influences among intellectuals.

The Embassy would be pleased to obtain copies of any other material which the Department or the Embassy at Taipei believes might be useful in this connection.

For the Ambassador
William Koren Jr
First Secretary of Embassy

Notes
1. Source: USNA: 788.001/8 (1954).

+ + +

XLV: US State Department: Memorandum Concerning a Splinter Communist Party in Iran (April 1954)[1]

The Embassy encloses for the Department's information a memorandum prepared by Kurish Shahbaz, a local employee with duties as political adviser,[2] relating briefly the history of the Communist Party of Iran.

This party, it should be noted, is distinct from and, indeed, opposed to the Tudeh Party which is generally recognized as the focus of Communist strength and effort in Iran. It may be, however, that the Soviet government finds it expeditious to tolerate the activities of the splinter party, led by a brother of the Imam Jom'eh of Tehran, as a possible alternate political group should the Tudeh Party outlive its usefulness.

It has not thus far been possible to verify the accuracy of this account, but any information relating thereto which may be uncovered in the future will be transmitted to the Department. However, the Embassy attests to the usual dependability of Mr Shahbaz and believes him worthy of commendation for this work and for similar efforts in the past.

For the Ambassador
Michael R Gannett
Second Secretary of Embassy

History of Emami's Communist Party of Iran

Baqer Emami and Dr Seyyed Hasan Emami, the Imam Jom'eh of Tehran, are sons of the same father but of different mothers. Khanum Mardan, by which name Baqer's mother was known, remarried after the death of his father and while he was studying in Russia, and bequeathed to her second husband all of her wealth and property. When Baqer returned to Iran and learned of this situation, he left his mother's home. He joined in the activities of Sultanzadeh, a leader of the Communist movement in Iran. During the chaotic year of 1923 he killed his step-father and was imprisoned. He was freed on the occasion of Reza Shah's coronation in 1925 but in 1929 was imprisoned for Communist activities. He remained in jail until the day in 1941 when the Allies occupied Iran.

In 1941 at the time when the Tudeh Party of Iran was being formed, Solayman Mirza Eskandari invited Emami to join that party but Emami replied: 'A Communist cannot join a non-Communist party.'

In 1944 Emami organized his own group on the Krojok style (the name Krojok refers to a method employed in Russia during the early pre-revolution days, based on Plekhanov's tactics of organizing underground revolutionary cells). In the meantime Emami contacted the Soviet Embassy in Tehran. To his dismay Emami found that the Tudeh Party of Iran and some officials at the Soviet Embassy were not happy about Emami's independent activities and therefore opposed him. To counteract Tudeh pressure, Baqer directed his own party members to infiltrate the Tudeh Party and to grasp the helm of that party from within. He failed to gain control of the Tudeh Party, but won many sympathizers and also managed to manipulate the trade union of Reza Rousta. Intoxicated with this new achievement, he left for Azerbaijan, where he tried to follow similar tactics and met Qolam Yahya, his classmate in Russia. He had some success in gaining a foothold in the Democrat Party which, because of Pishevari and the party's previous knowledge of Emami's ambition, became apprehensive of his activities and politely requested him to leave Azerbaijan. At this time a series of disputes ensued during one of which Emami was shot in the leg. He came to Tehran for medical treatment and remained two months in the Russian Hospital. While in the hospital he expanded his network inside the Tudeh Party. This time he almost succeeded in gaining control of the Central Committee of the Tudeh Party, but was faced with the Azerbaijan debacle. During the fall of the Azerbaijan Republic, the Tudeh Party was crushed and so his [Emami's] own underground movement ceased and was later disbanded.

When things again became lax in late 1947 he gathered his followers but this time his own party assistant, Foulad [that is, Artashes Ovanesian],[3] tried to supplant Emami and take over. Foulad was favored by members from the intellectual class while Emami was favored by the workers. This rift and the subsequent disputes so disrupted his party that Emami formally dissolved it. He informed the Soviet Embassy of the matter. By this time Reza Rousta and other Tudeh and Democrat[ic] leaders [of the Tudeh Party], then fugitives in Moscow, began to question Emami's activities and to suspect him of working for the police. On 17 January 1948, Emami formally reinaugurated his Communist Party of Iran, but the Tudeh, always suspicious of Emami, began attacking him in its local press. Emami ignored the Tudeh, but this time was confronted by Reza Rousta's opposition in Russia. Rousta tried his best to have Emami ousted from the Bolshevik Party of Soviet Russia, but failed in his efforts. However, he managed to incite the trade union newspaper *Trud* to write against Emami. On 7 April 1948 an article published in *Trud* (issue no 8263) by AN Blov, entitled 'Iranian Provokers in the Mask of Democracy', flayed Emami and called him a police agent. This article was broadcast in the Persian service of Radio Moscow and was later published in the paper *Mardom* (issue no 328) on 5 May 1948.

By this time the smoldering fire had burst into open flames and an open fight was going on between the Tudeh and Emami. Emami sought to refute every word of the *Trud* article in his book, *Mard Monsef* (Chapter 2, pages 70-87). He concluded his refutation with an attack on Soviet Russia, by saying: 'What right, if any, has the Soviet Union to meddle in the affairs of the World Communism?'

In early November [1948] Emami began to publish a paper *Bepish* (*Forward*) as the organ of his party. In the third issue, printed in red, on 7 November 1948, he criticized the policy of the Soviet government and maintained that there had been a noticeable drift from the teachings of Frederick Engels and Karl Marx and other Communist leaders. At this time he published a book about an Iranian poet, philosopher and socialist, entitled *Molavi or The Hegel of the East (1770-1831)*.

When the Tudeh realized they could not otherwise surmount Emami's tenacity, they sent some of their men to infiltrate his party. One of these was a man known by the assumed name of Maro who had some success in creating a rift in the party. Nevertheless, Emami held on until February 1949, at which time the abortive attempt was made on the life of the Shah.

After this incident, some of the Tudeh leaders were imprisoned and tried, and others escaped from the country, but Emami and a part of his organization went underground and remained unmolested. The Tudeh leaders in Moscow protested to the Soviets that Emami must be a police agent since he was able even under these circumstances to keep his organization. However, Emami had an ambitious supporter in the army; it is believed that this person was no other than General Razmara who was Chief of the General Staff at the time. Razmara, who was fighting power with power, was keeping an indirect relationship with Emami. However, the Tudeh leaders arranged for Emami to be arrested in July 1949 and tried before a military tribunal, but once again his unknown supporter came to his rescue and exonerated him. When the Tudeh leaders saw that Emami evaded every obstacle, they sent someone by the name of Kamran from

Russia who met with him three times in Shemiran. Apparently, Kamran gave him an ultimatum to stop acting independently and join the Tudeh Party or face death. Emami did not accept the terms and thereafter the Tudeh hounded him to dispose of him. Later the Tudeh openly said to the Soviets that they should support either their organization or Emami's, and the Soviets chose the Tudeh Party. Thus one of Emami's weekly reports to the Soviet Embassy was silently slipped into the hands of the police, whereupon he was arrested and Major Fazlollahi, Military Prosecutor, imprisoned him for ten years as a Soviet spy. Emami remained in prison until his release on parole in March 1953, in accordance with provisions of the Parole Law of 21 February 1953 [under Mosaddeq's law].

On 24 July 1953, Emami once again formed the Communist Party of Iran and announced that it was affiliated with the Cominform. His party constitution is exactly the same as those used by other Communist parties throughout the world. This constitution is known in Iran as the *Yellow Book*. As of the date of this report there are approximately one hundred staunch members, well-seasoned in Communist activities. They work underground and only within the cells, which consist of three persons each, where the members know one another. The party is against the Tudeh Party of Iran (which Emami claims is infiltrated by British and American agents) and any other party in Iran, and is bitterly against the United States and the United Kingdom. It maintains that, although it has no connection with the Soviet government, it recognizes the Communist Party of the Soviet Union as the Headquarters of World Communism. The party cells meet every Thursday; the composition is as follows:

University students and intellectuals — 15

Workers — 70

Others — 15

Kurish Shahbaz

10 April 1954

Notes

1. Source: USNA 788.001/4-1054. See also the article on SAKA in this issue of *Revolutionary History*.
2. He was also one of the Embassy translators.
3. Artashes Ovanesian, an admirer of Stalin, gave himself the pseudonym 'Foulad', which in Persian means 'steel', after which Stalin had named himself. Ovanesian had been trained at KUVT in Moscow, had been active within the ICP, arrested, and imprisoned in 1930. Released in 1931, he joined the Tudeh despite his own wish which was to 'revive' the ICP. He was told by the Comintern to discontinue his collaboration with Emami at an attempt to create Marxist cells.

XLVI: US State Department: Tudeh Party's English-Language Publications Reports of Iran (1954)[1]

Note: This Bulletin, published by the Propaganda branch of the Tudeh Party of Iran, will try to inform foreign readers and interested people about the latest events and developments in Iran and be their guide in passing judgement on the situation in Iran and it will help them recognize and appreciate the heroic anti-imperialist struggle of the Iranian people for peace and national independence. This Bulletin will appear regularly once every month for the time being.

The Oil Question

The 22-man delegation of the so-called Consortium, composed of American, British, French and Dutch companies, arrived in Tehran some time back and they are engaged in deliberations for the purpose of seizing Iran's oil. The questions to be discussed and settled between this mission and the Iranian government are summed up as follows:

1. Settlement of the problem of compensation payable by Iran to the AIOC, as well as the debts of the AIOC owed to Iran.
2. The management of the Iranian oil installations and the problem of foreign experts.
3. The price of the oil.
4. The exchange currency payable to the Iranian government.
5. The financial and military guarantee demanded by the Consortium from Iran.

For the settlement of these problems two commissions — the technical and compensation — and many sub-committees with financial, legal and other experts have been set up. Beside the representatives of eight companies and those of Iran, there are the British and US Ambassadors, Mr Rieber, the German officer who is one of the directors of an American oil company and who is at present oil advisor to the Iranian government and receives 200 dollars for every day he is staying in Iran, is also taking part in the negotiations.

Yet the talks between these teams are by no means known to the Iranian people since complete secrecy is observed. *Ettela'at* of 24 April says in this respect:

> Since according to the statements made by representatives of both sides, the disclosure of any point might compromise the process of the talks, no information as to how much progress has been made has been disclosed to the press and the matter has been confined to issuing vague communiqués on general lines.

Still the information that has been infiltrated as a result of the Anglo-American contradictions is as follows. According to *Mardom*, official organ of the Central Committee of the Tudeh Party of Iran which appears secretly, dated 4 May 1954, the UK claims 180 [million] Pounds Sterling of compensation from Iran and according to the semi-official *Ettela'at* one of the Iranian representatives in the team has declared that the Consortium will not accept the payment of this amount (that is the Iranian government to pay it).

As regards the management of the oil installations, the Consortium representatives believe that since the Consortium has to assume pledges to the purchasers of oil, the installations should be completely under the supervision of the Consortium. Both the British and American imperialists insist that the management of the oil installations should be handed over to their reliable experts.

As to the prices, although the official rates of oil is $7.50 per ton according to the Gulf of Mexico rate list, the Consortium wants to pay $1.50 per ton only and it intends to pocket 50 per cent of it as commission.

As regards the exchange currency payable to the Iranian government, the UK insists on payment of Pounds while the US insists on Dollars. Moreover, the Consortium, apprehensive of the movement of the Iranian people, will ask for the right of maintaining its own police force in the oilfields besides demanding financial guarantees from the Iranian government. The Consortium insists on the conclusion of the secret agreement to ensure for itself the financial and military advantages. Secret talks are in progress in this respect and it is probable that the Iranian government will accept such pledges in a secret agreement.

The greatest obstacle to the settlement of all these disputes is the unanimous stand of the Iranian people against the trampling down of the Law of the Nationalization of the Oil Industries, so much so that there is talk of making slight and insignificant amendments in the Law of the Nationalization of Oil Industries, in course of the secret talks with the representatives of the Consortium.

Mass Arrests in Street Demonstrations

According to reports appearing in the government supported press (*Ettela'at, Dad*, etc) during the recent 10 days, 258 persons have been arrested during the street demonstrations against talks with the Consortium, presentation of flower bouquets to the foreign guests attending the Avicenna millenary celebrations and the street demonstrations on May Day as well as in their own homes.

Students in the National Independence Movement

Upon the appeal of the Tehran University Committee of the Tudeh Party of Iran and the University Committee of the National Resistance Movement, a strike was called at the University on 18 April 1954. This strike, which embraced the entire university, despite the non-cooperation of some sections of the National Resistance Movement, was called on the occasion of the arrival of the Consortium representatives of the imperialist powers and with the following two slogans: 'The Iranian nation condemns all sorts of collusions with the imperialist Oil Consortium'; 'The Iranian nation demands the immediate release of all political prisoners, including Dr Mosaddeq.'

The officers and men who had occupied the faculties made futile efforts to have the lectures resumed by threats and insults and by beating the students and professors. Upon an agreement between the University Committee of the Tudeh Party and that of the National Resistance Movement, common demonstrations were held by the students in the streets of Tehran the same afternoon.

Two Hundred Dollars per Day for American Oil Adviser

The *Tehran-Mossavar* weekly in its issue of 23 April writes that Mr Rieber, the oil adviser employed by the Iranian government, had been a Captain in the German Navy during the First World War and inflicted many losses upon[2] the British forces. After the First World War, he became a naturalized American and at present he plays an important role in the American oil activities. Mr Rieber had come to Iran when Dr Mosaddeq was in power and then the British government protested against his arrival, proclaiming he was an enemy of Britain. The *Donya* in issue no 220 writes that Mr Rieber received $200.00 per day for his activities in favor of the American policy. The *Tehran-Mossavar* reports that Mr Davenport, his assistant, received $150.00 per day from the Iranian government.

Down With the Consortium

As reported by *Mardom*, organ of the Central Committee of the Tudeh Party of Iran, in its issue of 4 May 1954, militant demonstrations were held in the streets and various parts of Tehran on 27 April 1954 coinciding with the third anniversary of the ratification of the nine-articled law of the expropriation of the AIOC against the vile efforts of the imperialists to dominate over the oil resources of Iran. The demonstrators let out slogans such as: 'The formation of the Oil Consortium is against the law of the nationalization of the oil industries'; 'We shall not hand over our oil to the foreigners'; 'Away with the Consortium', etc, etc, and thus they displayed their determination to frustrate the plans of the traitors to the country who intend to surrender our oil to the foreign imperialists.

These demonstrations were held on a very wide scale and their repercussions were so great that they appeared in the government-supported press.

Dr Mosaddeq's Trial

Dr Mosaddeq's trial has entered its final stages in the Military Court of Appeal, and when this bulletin appears, his fate is likely to have already been determined. The readers may be aware that when Dr Mosaddeq was condemned in the Primary Court, his civilian attorneys, on the basis of the law passed by Dr Mosaddeq himself, demanded his case record to be sent to the High Court of Justice so that a court competent to consider his case may take over the trial. However, the ruling classes, fearing the disobedience of the judges of the High Court of Justice, set up the unlawful Military Court of Appeal and rejected the demand on referring the case to the High Court of Justice. The laws were disregarded to such an extent that the Military Prosecutor in the Court of Appeal was appointed the same man who held the office in the Primary Court. After the sentence on Dr Mosaddeq's conviction was passed by the Primary Court, he was kept in solitary confinement until his trial at the Military Court of Appeal. This was against the judicial laws of the country and Dr Mosaddeq protested against it at the hearings of the court.

The *Mardom*, organ of the Tudeh Party of Iran, writes the following on this stage-managed[3] trial under the heading 'The Ignominious Histrionics of Dr Mosaddeq's Trial':

> The signs of freedom could be observed from the very first day of the trial. Even the limited number of seats in the trial hall were left vacant and no one was admitted except the reporters of a few government-supported papers and a handful of open and secret police officials. In the first and second days of the hearing the newspapers were allowed only to publish a distorted résumé of the proceedings, but even this résumé was intolerable to the treacherous ruling class of Iran and was detrimental to the high interests. Although Dr Mosaddeq did not and would not disclose what he could have and ought to have disclosed, even the hints and remarks he made were sufficient to frighten the ruling classes. When Brigadier Azmoudeh claimed yelling that he had broken the charm and brought Mosaddeq down to trial, Dr Mosaddeq replied: 'He does not seem to know that foreign imperialism has thrown[4] me into the prison and that he cannot arrest any single person at will, be it even a moth.'
>
> Addressing this puppet who called himself the prosecutor, Dr Mosaddeq declared: 'What are you? You are but a tool which is dancing according to the tunes of your masters.' In his statements and remarks, Dr Mosaddeq

proclaimed that the sham trial was set up by the order of the imperialists and that it is the British and American imperialists who are, under the guise of the trial, trying him and avenging the chain-tearing Iranian people.

Dr Mosaddeq's statements which were tearing the masks off the criminal faces of foreign imperialists and showing the mean role of the Shah–Zahedi clique, especially at this time, when the representatives of the British-American Oil Consortium are in Tehran, were not tolerable to the usurping ruling classes of Iran. That is why they resorted to the last means in their power. The third day of the hearing they prevented the repercussions of the proceedings of the court in the press. The following days they sent sham circulars under the name 'Résumé of the Court Proceedings to the Press' which appeared in the same form in all the papers without any additions or abridgements. The trial was carried out in secret and the people are not aware of what is going on there and what secrets regarding the crimes of imperialism and its criminal hirelings are being disclosed.

Mosaddeq, basing himself on the French paper *Le Monde*, which in turn had adapted a report from *Mardom*, organ of the Tudeh Party of Iran, announced that the *coup d'état* of August 1953 was financed and brought through with the sum of 32 643 000 rials given as bribe by American circles and through a person named Edward George Donolly by virtue of the cheque no 703352 drawn from the Bank Melli Iran. This court did not allow this question to be studied carefully so that Dr Mosaddeq may not be able to expound his view in this respect.

As announced by the press and the Tehran Radio, the Military Court of Appeal has sentenced Dr Mosaddeq to three years of solitary confinement and General Riahi, the Chief of the General Staff in Mosaddeq's government who was tried at the same court with him, to a sentence of three years of prison with forced labor. Both convicts demanded on the spot the consideration of their cases in the Court of Cassation. In the Primary Court, Dr Mosaddeq was sentenced to three years and General Riahi to two years of solitary confinement.

Plot Against the Irano-Soviet Cultural Society

Mardom, organ of the Central Committee of the Tudeh Party of Iran, in its issue of 4 May 1954, writes:

> The puppet government of Zahedi has started to exert pressure on the Irano-Soviet Cultural Society in the last few weeks. Two weeks ago Mr Karim Keshawarz, the assistant secretary to the said society was kidnapped by the officials of the Martial Law government. The authorities of the

Army G-2 and the Police Administration published a series of false and unfounded news regarding his career and activities. The hired papers of Tehran made use of this arrest to launch all sorts of accusations against the Soviet Union. The Irano-Soviet Cultural Society does not interfere in politics whatsoever and its attempts are solely directed towards the strengthening the cultural and artistic relations between the two countries and introducing the literary and artistic works of the two nations to the peoples of the two countries.

The exertion of pressure on the Iran-Soviet Cultural Society and the arrest of its Assistant Secretary is part of the anti-Soviet plans carried out by the government and military authorities. Pressure on this society which is merely a cultural institution is taking place at a time when the British and American Fifth Column organizations are being extended every day in our country.

250 Million Rials Misappropriation in the Railway Administration

There has been going on a misappropriation of 25 million rials in the purchase of rails transacted by the government authorities with the French companies, according to the Tehran newspapers. Another report states that several million rials have been embezzled in the transaction of the Mercedes Benz buses with the German factories. It is said that as a result of this embezzlement, the transaction is cancelled after the delivery of 150 buses.

Peasants' Struggle Starts Again

The reports published here and there in the papers of the provinces state that as a result of the government and feudals' pressure the peasant movement in some villages are being extended. According to *Donya-ye Emrouz* dated 20 April, the Nahavand peasants have started a mass struggle with the object of receiving their shares of 20 per cent allotted to them according to a decree passed by Dr Mosaddeq. They have also demanded that the labor without pay should be cancelled. In a clash between the peasants and the landowners about 60 persons were wounded and 37 were arrested.

The same paper in its issue no 23, writes that in the Qazvin districts, a landowner has imprisoned a peasant in a dark cell and after 20 days with the help of his followers has cauterized the peasant's body with hot iron bars. The picture of the cauterized body of this peasant has been published in the Tehran newspaper.

Martial Law Extended Thee Months in Tehran

According to the reports published, Martial Law has been extended for another three months in Tehran as per decree passed by the Council of Ministers. It is about 13 years now that the people of Tehran have lived under the Martial Law's bayonet rule and such decrees are not considered to be something new for them. The news published in the papers state that with the object of establishing order in Fars, the Martial Law has been extended in that region for another month, according to a decree passed by the Council of Ministers.

Strikes After 19 August

The newspaper *Zafar*, organ of the CCUS in its issue of 1 May mentions the strikes of the workers of the Pashmineh Tabriz, the Pashmbaf and Reesbaf [textile] factories at Isfahan and the shoe-polish workers at Tehran. All these strikes took place during the month of April as the vanguard of the strike movement of the post-coup of 19 August 1953. This paper suggests that after the February 1949 plot which illegalized all democratic organizations, it took two years until the strikes were started again, but after the coup of 19 August 1953 in spite of the horrible terrors and fascistic pressures imposed on the labor organizations, the mass reaction and struggle of the workers was displayed after one month in the shape of demonstrations in the streets. This situation was intensified during the Senate and Parliamentary elections. This struggle is now being extended not only for the sake of national independence and peace but also for the syndicates' freedoms and corporal demands.

The owners of the Tabriz Pashmineh factory wanted to close down the factory and to invest their capital in trades with the imperialists, but the workers, who were supported by the people of the town, started a mass strike and occupied the factory. The military forces supported by tanks, armored cars and machine guns surrounded the factory but the workers stood firmly and forced the government authorities to submit to their demands. Thus the government decided that the factory should not be closed down.

In the Isfahan factories of Pashmbaf and Reesbaf, the owners intended to refrain from paying the annual compensation under the pretext of the establishment of a cooperative bank. Although the owners of the factories were supported by the spies of Point IV and government authorities, the united struggle of the workers supported by the people of that town led to a mass strike of 24 hours which compelled the owners to pay the annual compensation.

On 15 April, the shoe-polish workers of Tehran went on a 24-hour strike for having one day off in every week and for obtaining the privileges allowed by the incomplete Insurance Law and they consequently succeeded in their aims.

1 May Demonstrations

The Minister of Labor and the Military Governor of Tehran, being aware of the strength of the labor movement in Iran, did all they could to restrict the demonstrations of 1 May as far as possible. A declaration was, therefore, issued by them days before announcing that the celebrations on that day were permitted only in the premises of the factories and inside the workshops. In addition they tried to arrange for certain ridiculous ceremonies in the presence of the heads of the factories and the security officials and called them labor celebrations.

Disregarding the declarations of the military government, the labor unions prepared themselves for extensive demonstrations by distributing leaflets and greeting cards a few days before 1 May in order to show their solidarity with the working class of all the countries of the world. Consequently on this day, meetings in the premises of the factories were so great that they led to extensive demonstrations in the streets. The importance of these demonstrations had been reflected in the press and as it was reported in *Donya-ye Emrouz*, some 60 demonstrators were arrested. The trucks of soldiers stationed in the streets were on guard until late at night.

In view of the fact that 1 May coincided with the tenth anniversary of the formation of the Central Council of the United Syndicates of Iran, all the workers and the toiling classes of this country celebrated this day together with the celebrations of 1 May. On this day all the secret democratic organizations and leading them all, the Tudeh Party of Iran, congratulated the Central Council of the United Syndicates of Iran and sent greetings to its Secretary General Reza Rousta.

Exorbitant Cost of Living

Donya-ye Emrouz in its issue of 29 April writes that owing to the starvation and hunger, the number of suicides has been considerably increased, immigrations to the neighboring countries have increased and the population of Bushire has dropped from 50 000 to 5000. The standard of living of the rural people has dropped to such an extent that 25 farmers of the Shervin village (Shahroud) died in one week from bad nutrition according to the physicians' reports.

Notes
1. Source: USNA.
2. The original states 'losses to'.
3. The original states 'made up'.
4. The original states 'brought'.

XLVII: Isolated Support for Fatemi and Tudeh Officers upon Condemnation to Death (1954-55)

A: Reginald Bridgeman's Letter to Sir Albert Braithwaithe[1]

15 November 1954

Sir Albert Braithwaite, MP
House of Commons
Westminster, SW

Dear Sir Albert

I had the advantage of listening to your address in Pinner at the United Free Church Hall on the United Nations anniversary, and I am now writing to you as one of your constituents in West Harrow to express the earnest hope that you will press Her Majesty's Government to make immediate representations to the Government of Iran with a view to staying the torture and the executions which are taking place in that country.

On Tuesday last 8 November our Prime Minister in his speech at the Lord Mayor's Banquet referred with satisfaction to the agreement recently concluded between the Government of Iran and important British and American interests ensuring the production and marketing of Iranian oil.

Simultaneously with this development a series of executions of Persian democrats and patriotic leaders has taken place in Iran, while more than one thousand army officers are under arrest, many of them faced with the prospect of execution.

Doctor Hussein Fatemi, the Foreign Minister in the Cabinet of Doctor Mosaddeq, which carried through the Parliamentary measure nationalising the Iranian oil industry, has been shot this week, after trial by a military court.

The Labour Government in Britain nationalised the coalmining industry despite bitter opposition; they also nationalised the railways and the road-haulage industry, but when the latter was denationalised there was no thought in any quarter of a vindictive policy against Labour leaders, and anything of the sort would have been sternly condemned.

I myself served as Counsellor of Embassy at the British Legation in Persia at the time of the *coup d'état* in 1921, which overthrew the Government of Vosouq al-Dowleh[2] and established a new Government with Reza Shah [sic — Khan] Pahlavi, the present Shah's father, as Minister of War, but there was no question then of the execution or torture of any of the opponents of the new regime.

It is particularly disquieting that the satisfaction at the new arrangement concerning oil in Iran expressed by Sir Winston Churchill should be followed in Iran with bloodshed and torture of opponents of the policy of denationalisation of Iranian oil. World opinion is deeply stirred by these events, and I hope that you will do all you can to secure the modification of a policy which, although primarily the responsibility of the Government of Iran, nevertheless appears to involve our own country in an indirect responsibility for the violent destruction of democracy.

I am also writing to the Iranian Ambassador on this matter.

Believe me

Yours sincerely

[Signed] **Reginald Bridgeman**[3]

Notes
1. Source: FO 371/109987.
2. Bridgeman's memory must have failed by this time, for Vosouq had been forced to resign in June 1920 and was succeeded by Moshir al-Doleh, and it was the government of the latter's successor Sepahdar that was thrown out of office by the British-led coup.
3. After his resignation or dismissal from the Foreign Service, Bridgeman joined the British anti-colonial movement. He notably worked with the Anti-Imperialist League in the 1920s and was in contact with the Iranian Communist Party and wrote articles for them. See also the tendentious internal note in the Foreign Office, below.

+ + +

B: Internal Foreign Office Note Concerning Bridgeman[1]

7 December 1954

I used to hear a lot about Mr Bridgeman years ago from people who knew him. He has long been — at the least — a 'running dog' of the Communists. He was to have led a delegation, to protest against the same executions, which the Secretary of State is refusing to see.

Parliamentary Undersecretary

Notes
1. Source: FO 371/109987.

C: Foreign Office Memo on Bridgeman's Letter[1]

8 December 1954

1. The Department are asked to suggest a reply to the attached letter from Mr Reginald Bridgeman to Sir Albert Braithwaite, MP, which the latter has forwarded to Mr Turton's Private Secretary.

2. We understand that Mr Bridgeman was virtually dismissed from the then Diplomatic Service in 1923, partly at least as a result of a much publicised adventure with a dancing girl in Tehran. Papers in Personnel Department show that he had also had political differences with the Foreign Office, but it has not yet been possible to determine what these were. He has since engaged in politics and has on several occasions been an unsuccessful candidate for Parliament in the Labour interest. Mr Bridgeman has come to our notice more recently as the leader of a deputation organised by the British Communist Party, and consisting for the most part of known Communists, which has asked to be received by the Secretary of State to protest against the 'terror' in Persia.

3. A draft reply to Sir Albert Braithwaite's Private Secretary is attached.

LAC Fry

Notes

1. Source: FO 371/109987.

+ + +

D: Letter by Albert Camus to *Le Monde*[1]

Reading the letter that the Iranian Ambassador has sent you, I fear that the government of that country does not err as to the real state of French [public] opinion concerning the recent executions in Iran. The representative of that land here in our country seems to believe in fact that only Communists and their allies have felt indignant. That is why he takes pain to reiterate the facts and, above all, to prove the legality of the trials and condemnations.

To tell the truth, there would not have been any reason for many of us to associate ourselves with the protesters, who have never raised their voice, at regular intervals, against executions carried out behind the Iron Curtain [this week two more condemnations to death], and for whom neutrality remains, I dare say, hemiplegic. It is the very weakness of that position, imposing silence upon a certain category of the executed that empties it of all strength for efficient intervention in favour of another category of victims.

But in fact, the Iranian government would be wrong to rest on the comfortable idea that only Communists and their allies are protesting against those executions. Other French men and women do so too.

I would not argue at all with Iranian Ambassador as to the legality of those verdicts. I would concede to him, if it imports to him, that those condemnations were the most legal in the world. For what makes one react towards these condemnations, it is not their illegality, which is difficult to assess from such a distance, but their magnitude. In a word, it is not their quality but their quantity. There is talk of some 60 condemnations. Twenty-three have just been executed. Others are coming up soon.

All the same, even if the government of Iran had all written laws on its side, we could not recognise it the right to massacre on such a scale. Whatever the juridical or national reasons invoked, we cannot be prevented from thinking that such a butchery — for it is one — has no far-fetched link to justice and national dignity, which one pretends to preserve in this affair.

At the same time as many French writers, who are neither partisan nor accomplices [of the Communist Party], I, therefore, beg the Iranian Ambassador to ascertain at its true value the real emotion aroused here in our country by these events, and use all his influence so that an end be put to the executions.

Notes
1. Source: *Le Monde*, 17 November 1954. Translation in FO 371/109987, interpolations by Foreign Office translator.

+ + +

E: Tobacco Workers Union Protest[1]

The Tobacco Workers Union: Incorporating the National Cigar and Tobacco Workers' Union
22-25 Chain Street, Reading
30 November 1954

The Rt Hon Sir Anthony Eden, MP
Foreign Secretary
Foreign Office
London

Dear Sir
On behalf of my National Executive Committee I am writing to ask that you use your good offices to protest to the Government of Iran at the present measures

being taken against many of the inhabitants of that country by means of mass arrests and shootings.

Whilst realising that it is difficult for our Government to interfere in the domestic affairs of another, I think that such happenings warrant a protest as suggested, particularly in view of our recent negotiations with the Government of Iran regarding supplies of oil.

Yours faithfully
General Secretary

Notes
1. Source: FO 371/109987.

+ + +

F: Protest by London Citizen against Repression in Iran[1]

2 December 1954

Sir Anthony Eden MP
Foreign Minister
Foreign Office
Downing Street
Westminster

Dear Sir

The following resolution was passed at a Public Meeting at Denison House, Victoria on 30 November 1954:

> This Meeting of London Citizens protests most strongly at the tortures and murder of thousands of Iranian workers, peasants and intellectuals.
>
> These men and women are being killed because they want Iran to be free and not to be dominated and kept in poverty in order to provide fabulous profits for the Anglo-Iranian and the American Oil Millionaires.
>
> We call upon the British Foreign Office to make the strongest possible protest to the responsible authorities in Iran, to see that the fundamental rights guaranteed by the United Nations Charter are observed.
>
> We demand that the terror against the people of Iran must be stopped and that democratic rights should be restored to the Iranian people immediately.

Yours faithfully
Signed **R Bernard**
Area Organiser

Notes
1. Source: FO 371/109987.

+ + +

G: Protest Against Repression in Iran[1]

22 February 1955

Sir Anthony Eden
Foreign Office
Whitehall, SW

Dear Sir
Since the illegal *coup d'état* made by General Zahedi, with the full support of the Shah, in August 1953, political opponents of the regime have been arrested in thousands. It has been estimated by reliable authorities that there are over 10 000 people in prison for the sole crime of opposing Zahedi and his policy of capitulation to America and Britain. Amongst the many political prisoners, there are followers of the former Iranian Prime Minister, Dr Mosaddeq, of the Tudeh Party, and thousands of sincere patriots not attached to any political party. They have been thrown into gaol and tortured in the most brutal manner. Thousands of the political prisoners have been sent to their death — or to rot on islands round the Persian Gulf, where they are completely cut off from the outside world and are denied medical assistance, proper food and visits from their families.

General Zahedi has kept on 'uncovering' plots and arrested hundreds of army officers who were opposed to the deal he made with the oil companies regarding the extraction of oil. Twenty-six officers and civilians were brought before military tribunals, without proper defence, and sentenced to death. The press noted at the time that Zahedi's way of securing American aim was to convince the Americans that he means to stamp out ruthlessly all opposition to his policies. The Shah, who is now being *fêted* by our Government, is largely responsible for these executions and for the terror now reigning in Iran.

The executions caused a wave of indignation and protest not only in Britain, but [also] all over France. Amongst the illustrious people who protested at these atrocities are François Mauriac, Pierre Cot, George Duhamel, [Pablo] Picasso and hundreds of other writers, professors and intellectuals. Most of the French papers were very indignant at the execution of Hussein Fatemi, the former Foreign Minister of Iran.

On behalf of a large number of British people, we protest to the Foreign Office against these atrocities perpetrated by a so-called ally of Britain and demand that the Foreign Office should do all in its power to bring about the release of the political prisoners in Iran and the restoration of the constitutional and democratic rights of the Iranian people. We particularly urge you to press that there should be no further executions of political prisoners.

Yours faithfully
Reginald Bridgeman
G Hogan
G Pedilos
J Parry
J Sad
L Keely
Jack Grahl
KM Beauchamp

Notes
1. Source: FO 371/114810.

+ + +

XLVIII: UK Foreign Office: Tudeh Party Leaders Arrested (April 1956)[1]

21 93/5/56
Secret, Despatch No S 42
21 April 1956
The Rt Hon Selwyn Lloyd, CBE, MP

Sir

I have the honour to report on the position of the Tudeh Party, which has changed considerably since Mr Titchener wrote his letter 2193/5/55G of 8 November 1955 to Mr Samuel.

2. As a result of the interrogation of the members of the military plot arrested in 1954 and of Dr Yazdi (1955 Personalities, no 159) who was arrested in March of last year, the security authorities obtained a great deal of information about the party's organisation and activities. They were able to increase their penetration of the party at middle and lower levels, and kept close watch on known party members in the hope of getting their hands on the leaders.

Arrests of party members were made from time to time, and the functioning of the party's communications network throughout the country was seriously impeded. These measures added useful pieces to the jigsaw puzzle which the authorities were putting together with growing confidence, and the continuous pressure had an increasingly serious effect on the party's morale. Another important factor in the worsening of morale and the spreading of confusion was that it had become widely known that Dr Yazdi, the most prominent of the party's leaders in Iran, had asked the Shah to pardon him.

3. Unrest in the party found expression in December last when its leaders were presented with a resolution adopted by senior members of the Tehran local committees which demanded radical changes in the direction of the party's affairs, including the expulsion of two members of the Executive Board (the equivalent of the Politbureau) of the Central Committee.

4. Much of the credit for Dr Yazdi's action belongs to Seyyed Zia al-Din Tabataba'i (1955 Personalities, no 150). At the time of the execution in 1954 of some of the officers implicated in the Tudeh military organisation, the Seyyed was known to be strongly opposed to execution and to have interceded with the Shah. Although the Seyyed's main motive in this was his strong opposition to the creation of martyrs, based on his awareness of the powerful emotional appeal which 'martyrdom' *per se* makes the Iranians, his stand attracted considerable sympathy from the officers' families and other elements in the Tudeh Party, in spite of the bitter political enmity which the party nourished against him. In September last year Dr Yazdi's brother approached the Seyyed and showed him a letter which Yazdi had written, asking the Shah for pardon, and which he wanted the Seyyed to hand to the Shah. The Seyyed considered this letter quite unsatisfactory for its purpose and there and then dictated another draft, with the double aim of effectively influencing the Shah and sowing confusion in the Tudeh Party. Yazdi accepted the draft, copied it and signed it. The Seyyed handed this to the Shah and eventually persuaded the latter that his pardoning Yazdi on these terms would strike an effective blow at Tudeh morale. The Seyyed. would have liked the Shah to release Yazdi, arguing that this would create the maximum effect in the Tudeh ranks, but the Shah would not go as far as this.

The Shah delayed action until the turn of the year when he finally commuted Yazdi's death sentence to life imprisonment.

5. In spite of the steadily weakening morale of the party, its leadership kept up for as long as possible a front of unity [...]² need for maintaining cadres intact and propounded the ideas of a 'united front' in collaboration with nationalist elements, whilst the party newspaper *Mardom* maintained its effectively written exploitation of current causes of popular dissatisfaction. The crisis could not, however, be avoided. In the second half of December, before the Shah's act of clemency was announced, Dr Yazdi was unconditionally expelled from the party and Engineer Mohammad Sharmini, who until shortly before his arrest

nearly a year earlier had been the member of the Executive Board responsible for the Tudeh Youth Organisation, was also expelled for having signed a document attacking the party. Sharmini was, however, granted the possibility of readmission, if he confessed his sins and submitted himself to party discipline.

6. A split in the leadership which had been latent for many years was now out in the open. Even if the purely physical obstacles set by the security authorities had not prevented regular meetings of the remaining members of the Executive Board, these decisions, reflecting the views of one wing of the leadership, made it difficult for what was left of the Executive Board any longer to maintain even the appearance of unity. A further blow was the arrest in early February of Dr Mohammad Bahrami, a party veteran and member of the Executive Board, of Engineer Ali Ollovi,[3] another member of the Board, Amanollah Qoreyshi, the 'responsible' of the Tehran provincial committee and an important protagonist in the ideological differences within the party leadership.

Bahrami and Ollovi were the two members of the Executive Board whose expulsion had been demanded in the resolution mentioned in paragraph 3 above. After these arrests, the Military Governor of Tehran, General Taimur Bakhtiar, went so far as to claim that the security authorities could put their hands on the other leaders whenever they wished.

7. As far as is known, the only leaders still at large in Iran are Kianouri, Jowdat and Rouzbeh. There are, of course, a number of important and original party leaders who have been out Iran for the last five or six years. Kianouri, of whom the arrested Qoreyshi was an ally, has been a bitter personal enemy of Yazdi for many years, an enmity probably caused and certainly reflected in ideological differences between these two men. Jowdat's position is less clear, but he seems to have leaned towards Kianouri's side whereas Bahrami collaborated with Yazdi. There is strong evidence that Yazdi and Bahrami are orthodox Communists. Kianouri, Qoreyshi and probably Rouzbeh, the brilliant young officer who organised the Tudeh military organisation, are considered to be 'national' Communists or 'opportunists'. All three are certainly of an 'activist' turn of mind.

8. During the past month or two there has been a series of further arrests of party members, including 'second-grade cadres', who have contributed further to the information about the party's activities and ramifications. The way in which these arrests have been announced at fairly regular intervals suggests that a desire to keep the anti-Communist drive in the public's mind has been an important factor in the government's thinking. It may be only a matter of time before the leaders remaining in Iran are rounded up.

9. The authorities, in addition to normal security action, have aimed at determining party morale by various other measures, using for this purpose

party members, particularly army officers held in prison. In late January a play demonstrating the treacherous activities of the military organisation was given public showings. It was produced and acted by a group of the imprisoned officers, many of them in the parts they had played in real life. These officers are also producing [...][4]

Another move was the amnesty of the 23 Tudeh prisoners of lesser importance on 5 February on the occasion of the anniversary of the attempt against the Shah's life in 1949 and 50 others at the Iranian New Year. It is not known what effect these measures have had on party members, but many members of the general public have greeted them with scepticism.

10. It would not be surprising if the party, as a result of all that has happened, were entirely disrupted. This is not so, but the party is certainly greatly disorganised. There have been obvious tergiversations in the party line; for example, the instructions about tactical denunciations of the party by arrested members have wavered considerably in the last few months. More recent party instructions have, however, managed to keep up a creditable appearance of confidence and resilience, not only stressing the need to maintain cadres, but continuing to push the idea of a 'popular front' with the nationalists. Moreover the newspaper *Mardom* was until recently still being produced in spite of the need for constant changes of printing place and in spite of the discovery by the authorities of the main distribution centre, as a result of which the lower levels of the party did not receive the paper at all regularly.

11. I think it can safely be said that at the moment the party is less of a direct danger than it has ever been since it was firmly established. It cannot, however, be written off, even temporarily. There is still some organisation left, and even if this were to disintegrate, the more disciplined members would no doubt do their best to maintain contact amongst themselves and also probably to participate in other political activities such as the penetration of nationalist and other disaffected groups. The existence abroad of leaders of considerable stature who would be ready to take over at a suitable opportunity can also not be overlooked.

The latter are known to have been in touch with the present leadership and were seriously considering what steps should be taken to remedy the situation, including the possibility at sending one or more of their number to Tehran.

12 Furthermore, the economic, social and political conditions which encouraged, for example, an impressive number of young army officers, a large proportion of whom were of good quality, to join a treacherous conspiracy, still exist. A number of those arrested in the last year or two have not begged for mercy and some of them faced torture and execution in a manner which impressed not only Tudeh Party members and sympathisers. Military

government and military justice, with their concomitants of brutality and arbitrary arrest, produce their own counter-irritants. Fear and dislike of the Military government's methods are common and tend to create sympathy for the victims irrespective of ideological views.

13. The security authorities have done an efficient technical job and have provided a breathing space during which the dangers of Tudeh subversion will be at a minimum. It is now up to the Shah and his government to deal satisfactorily with the much more difficult, but even more essential task of removing at least some of the root causes of genuine popular discontent which have given the Tudeh Party many of its opportunities and which have attracted to it elements who in other circumstances would not have turned to a Communist party in an effort to redress their grievances.

I am copying this despatch to Her Majesty's Representatives at Ankara, Bagdad, Karachi and Washington and to the Head of the Political Office with the Middle East Forces.

I have the honour to be, with the highest respect, Sir, your obedient servant.
Roger Steward

Notes
1. Source: FO 371/120713.
2. Text illegible in the original document, most probably meaning 'insisting upon...'.
3. Mistakenly 'Alavi' in the original.
4. Text illegible in the original.

+ + +

XLIX: UK Foreign Office: Tudeh Military Leader Khosrow Rouzbeh in the Military Tribunal (1958)[1]

Khosrow Rouzbeh described how, at his instigation, eight members of the Tudeh Party, including one woman, had organised the assassinations of Mohammad Mas'oud, the editor of *Mard-e Emrouz*.[2] An interesting point is that one of the assassin [Hesam Lankarani][3] was murdered sometime later [in late summer 1952] by Rouzbeh on the orders of the Central Committee. According to Rouzbeh, the murder of Mohammad Mas'oud had a positive effect from the viewpoint of the party. Firstly, it created fear among the public, and secondly, every group suspected every other group, and this state of affairs was to the advantage of the Tudeh Party.

Rouzbeh then explained how and why five members of the party had been murdered. He said these five persons were considered dangerous elements because they knew too much about the party,[4] and the Central Committee decided, in accordance with Marxist[-Leninist] theories [!], on their liquidation. Rouzbeh and a few others carried out the order.

Rouzbeh said that, as part of a campaign to discredit government departments and organisations, the Tudeh Party leaders started carrying out murders, manufacturing bombs and other weapons, robbing banks and government offices and forging identity cards and checks. The total sum of money stolen by them amounted to 27 800 000 rials.

Rouzbeh says the main object of the Tudeh Party was to create dissatisfaction and pessimism among the masses in order to win them over for the party. General Azmudeh [the military prosecutor] said that, with the fall of the Pishevari and the deliverance of Azerbaijan, the leading cadre of the Tudeh Party, in a bid to promote its Communistic ideas, to arouse animosity toward constitutional monarchy in Iran, and to prejudice Iranian independence, decided to create further disruption among the military organisations and the armed forces of the country. According to his confessions Rouzbeh played an important role in this. Khosrow Rouzbeh disclosed the measures taken by the Executive Committee of the Tudeh military organisation to effect contacts with persons outside the country. [No details were given by Prosecutor Azmudeh.]

The party used every opportunity to gain recruits for the party's military organisation. For example, if an expensive car passed by and splashed the passers-by with mud, any party member who was present would immediately say: 'Why should these people own such luxurious cars and live so comfortably?' Then a general discussion would follow about the living conditions of the farmers and workers and poorer classes. Any of those taking part in the discussion who indicated by their remarks that they were likely party candidates would be introduced to the Tudeh organisation. Such persons would be given instructions on Communism so that they became convinced of the unfavourable conditions of social life and desirous of changing them.

One of the conditions for membership of the Tudeh Party and its military Executive Committee was that persons nominated as officers should not come from wealthy families and should favour a socialist regime or at least hold neutral views. Then the brain-washing would start. One of the principal questions such officers had to answer was: 'What did he think about the events in Azerbaijan in the years 1324-1325 [1945-46] of the Iranian calendar?' The point of this question was to find out how a person felt about the Azerbaijan revolution. If he thought that the Azerbaijani events were advantageous for the integrity and independence of the country, then he would become a member of the party's Military Committee. Such a member had, of course, also to have anti-monarchical views.

Notes

1. Source: FO 371/127075. It should be pointed out that when the voluntary confessions of Rouzbeh in the tribunal were published, which, among other things, severely criticised the Tudeh leadership for their fleeing the country, the latter proclaimed that his statements were fabrications by the regime. The party published a purged copy of his statements in the tribunal. It was only after the revolution of 1979 that it was admitted that the statements were voluntary and genuine. This led Iran's leading poet Ahmad Shamloo, who had composed a poem for Rouzbeh as a hero, to withdraw his dedication of the poem to him.
2. At the time the Tudeh propaganda blamed the assignation on the shah's sister Ashraf Pahlavi in order to reduce the prestige of the Court. People readily accepted the propaganda.
3. He was not actually the assassin. He had been a collaborator who had been part of the teams that had organised the assassination for the party.
4. At least in the case of Hesam Lankarani it is clear that the accusation was that he 'was addicted' and his 'too much knowledge' of the party affairs was 'too dangerous'. In fact, as it became clear after the revolution, he was neither addicted nor was he a danger to the party. His liquidation was due to internal rivalries. See the letter by Hessam's brother Ahmad Lankarani, also a leader of one of Tudeh front organisations, 'An Open Letter to the Wife of Noureddin Kianouri, the First Secretary of the Tudeh Party' (in Persian, Tehran, 1979).

+ + +

Work in Progress

Discussions and Differences in the Fourth International

Our website <http://www.revolutionaryhistory.co.uk/> is publishing documents by many of the leaders of the Fourth International on a variety of topics. We are still working on amassing the documents to show the differences that eventually broke the back of the International. We have published 45 documents on the topic of 'European Perspectives after WWII', well as documents on the Chinese Revolution 1949, the postwar boom, developments in Eastern Europe and the chasing after 'unconscious' Trotskyists in the person of Tito and then Mao. Trotsky felt towards the end of his life that he was 'alone on the planet', which was his way of saying that the leaders were incapable of organising, leading and arming a revolutionary movement. The assassination of the Old Man, by agents of Stalin, was an immense loss to our movement. The publication of these documents, mainly taken from the Marxist Internet Archive, will enable readers to draw their own conclusions on the theories of 'Bonapartism', also known as 'The Strong State', the Permanent Arms Economy, State Capitalism, Stalinism, Proletarian Bonapartism and a whole host of other issues.

Alun Morgan

Letters

Cyril Smith

Dear Comrades

I read with great interest John Plant's obituary of Cyril Smith (*Revolutionary History*, Volume 10, no 2). I had only known Cyril slightly, and it gave a fascinating account of his political evolution. I first encountered Cyril in the 1960s, when I was a member of the International Socialists, and what sticks in my mind was his extremely vituperative manner, a tendency to reinforce political disagreement with personal unpleasantness. So when I encountered him again, 40 years later, on the editorial board of *Revolutionary History*, I was surprised to find a thoroughly charming individual.

It's probably true of a great many of us (myself certainly included) that in our youth we have a certain sectarian style (believing ourselves to be in possession of a unique truth) and that we mellow as we grow older. But in Cyril's case the contrast was particularly shocking; in his younger days he was doubtless acting a role that conflicted with his natural inclinations. Just one more bit of evidence of the terrible harm that the whole Healyite experience did to many good revolutionaries.

May I add a couple of observations.

John is rather dismissive of Brian Behan, described as a 'disruptive ultra-left element'. This is presumably because he opposed Labour Party entry and advocated an open party (a policy to be adopted by Healy, with exquisite mistiming, on the very eve of Labour's 1964 election victory). Behan's closest political ally at the time was Alasdair MacIntyre, who still spoke with great respect of Behan when I met him a couple of years ago. The Will Fancy Papers (now in the Senate House Library) contain a fascinating exchange of letters between Healy and MacIntyre at the time of his departure from the SLL, in which Healy 'explains' idealism to MacIntyre (MS 1171/box 3/4). MacIntyre seems to have continued to agree with Behan. His political break with the International Socialists came, not, as I always supposed, following the 'debate' with Cardan in 1965, but because of IS's refusal to support Richard Gott's anti-Vietnam War candidacy in the 1966 Hull by-election (IS Working Committee minutes, 8 January 1966, Richardson Collection, Senate House, MS 1117/box 209/file 6).

Secondly, John refers to Tony Cliff's attempt to recruit Cyril to the Socialist Review Group (SRG) and his argument that 'differences between his own theory of state capitalism and Trotsky's view in *The Revolution Betrayed* were unimportant'. This story is also told by Jim Higgins in *More Years for the Locust* (London, 1997), pp 17-18, and undoubtedly reflects Cyril's honest recollection of the incident. But is John right to describe this as 'unprincipled inveiglement'?

Firstly, Cliff was arguing in the spirit of the Master. As Trotsky wrote: 'It would therefore be a piece of monstrous nonsense to split with comrades who on the question of the sociological nature of the USSR have an opinion different from ours, insofar as they solidarise with us in regard to the political tasks.' (*In Defense of Marxism* (New York, 1965), p 5)

Secondly, Cliff was apparently in breach of his own organisation's policy. A meeting of the SRG National Committee in December 1950 carried a resolution including the following statement:

> Acceptance of the political attitudes flowing from the State-capitalist position on the Russian question, as and when these are defined by the Party, shall be a condition of membership, but no one shall be excluded from membership because of a different sociological estimate of the Russian society provided that Revolutionary defeatist conclusions are drawn from such an estimate.

Cliff was in attendance and voted for this (Ken Tarbuck papers, Modern Records Centre, Warwick, SRG National Committee minutes book, MSS.75/1/1/1).

This would not be the first or last time that Cliff breached discipline, and his enthusiasm to win a gifted recruit to his tiny organisation must have outweighed the concerns of his more formalistic comrades.

The SRG in the 1950s contained a number of comrades with a considerable capacity for independent critical thought — Ray Challinor, Peter Sedgwick, Mike Kidron, Seymour Papert and others. Would Cyril have lived a happier and more productive life had he succumbed to Cliff's 'inveiglement'? I like to think so.

Ian Birchall

Conrad Noel and the Catholic Crusade

Dear *Revolutionary History*

Ron Heisler's excellent article about Conrad Noel and the Catholic Crusade makes several mistakes ('The Thaxted Tales: Trotskyist Versus Stalinist Pilgrims on the Anglo-Catholic Path', *Revolutionary History*, Volume 10, no 2, 2010).

He confuses the *College* of the Resurrection (where John Groser and Stanley

Evans trained) with the *Community* of the Resurrection, located in the same place, which is a community of celibate monks. Neither Groser nor Evans, both of whom were married with children, were members of the Community.

At one point, Heisler locates Mirfield in Lancashire. It is in Yorkshire, close to Huddersfield. Its best-known member, Trevor Huddleston, who helped to bring apartheid to an end, was not very left-wing and rather patrician, but other members were much more socialist.

I knew Reg Groves and Stewart Purkis very well. It is sometimes claimed that they ceased to be Christians after their links with Trotsky. But Purkis was a daily communicant at St Anne's, Soho, in the 1960s, and Groves was a member of the Jubilee Group of Anglo-Catholic socialists in the 1970s and 1980s. After his death, Daisy, his wife, rang me to ask if Fr Gresham Kirkby could lead his funeral — which he did.

I don't think there is much of the Noel tradition left in Thaxted. When I was there in 1992, the fiftieth anniversary of Noel's death, Kirkby raised his arms and shouted 'Ichabod' — 'The glory has departed.'

Ken Leech

Also available from Socialist Platform and The Merlin Press

The Left in Iran 1905-1940
Revolutionary History Volume 10, Number 2

This first volume on the history of the Left in Iran provides new insights into early Iranian Socialist and radical movements.

The texts probe and consider:

- why the workers' and socialist movements did not make the most of their opportunities
- the role of British imperialism
- how Lenin – and later Theodore Rothstein – influenced the Left in Iran
- whether there were divergent interests between the Iranian working class and the new Russian state

This account does not seek to make such questions easy, nor to tender solace in trying times. It is also filled with admirable, too often tragic, struggles and personal odysseys.

Many of the documents have not previously been published in English and will be invaluable to scholars and activists interested in the roots of the present crisis.

2010, 457 pages, paperback, ISBN. 978-085036-672-3

www.merlinpress.co.uk

www.ingramcontent.com/pod-product-compliance
Lightning Source LLC
Chambersburg PA
CBHW051415290426
44109CB00016B/1302